NEW YORK FIELD CODES SERIES

VOLUME III

NEW YORK FIELD CODES SERIES

Volume I. The Code of Civil Procedure of the State of New-York (1850)

Volume II. The Code of Criminal Procedure of the State of New York (1850)

Volume III. The Civil Code of the State of New York (1865)

Volume IV. The Penal Code of the State of New York (1865)

Volume V. The Political Code of the State of New York (1860)

TO THE LEGISLATURE

OF THE

STATE OF NEW YORK:

The Commissioners of the Code, appointed by the Act of April 6, 1857, having completed their labors, beg leave to make this their NINTH and final

REPORT.

They have already reported, from time to time, the various steps taken by them in the progress of their work. Their duty, it will be remembered, as expressed in the act by which they were appointed, was "to reduce into a written and systematic Code the whole body of the law of this State, or so much and such parts thereof as shall seem to them practicable and expedient, excepting always such portions of the law as have been already reported upon by the Commissioners of Practice and Pleadings, or are embraced within the scope of their reports." This work was to be divided into three portions; one containing the Political Code, another the Civil Code, and a third the Penal Code.

The Codes of Civil and Criminal Procedure, as reported complete by the Commissioners on Practice and Pleadings, were designed to embrace all the law of this State, respecting remedies in the judicial tribunals, civil and criminal, including the law of evidence. There then remained the vast body of substantive law; that is to say, the law of civil rights and obligations affecting all the transactions of men with each other in their private relations, the law of crimes and punishments, and the law of government, including every branch of administrative and political action. This body of substantive law, the Legislature, by the act of 1857, declared should be contained in the three Codes—Political, Civil and Penal, and to them the Commissioners of the Code have ever since devoted themselves.

Their first act was to prepare and report to the Legislature a general analysis of the Codes projected by them. After this their efforts were next directed to the preparation of the Political Code. This was divided into four parts. The first declared what persons composed the people of the State, and the political rights and duties of all persons subject to its jurisdiction; the second defined the territory of the State and its civil divisions; the third related to the general government of the State, the functions of its public officers, its general police and civil polity; and the fourth related to the local government of counties, cities, towns and villages. The draft having been made, was distributed among the judges and other competent persons for examination; and after that the Commissioners re-examined their work and considered such suggestions as had been made to them, and the whole, as finally agreed upon by them, was reprinted and distributed to the judges and other officers before being presented to the Legislature. The Political Code, thus drawn and revised, was presented to the Legislature on the 10th of April, 1860.

A few days afterwards, by an act passed on the 16th of April, 1860, they were requested to prepare a Book of Forms adapted to the Code of Civil Procedure. This duty was performed by them, and the required Forms were submitted to the Legislature on the 30th of March, 1861.

On the 5th of April, 1862, the Commissioners having prepared the draft of the Civil Code, distributed it to the judges and others for examination, and on the 2d of April, 1864, they in like manner distributed the draft of the Penal Code.

Having re-examined these two Codes and considered such suggestions as had been made, they have finally revised and agreed upon them.

The Penal Code is herewith laid upon the tables of the Members of the Senate and Assembly. The Civil Code is in the hands of the printer and will shortly be completed and in like manner furnished to the members of the two houses. But as the term of office of the Commissioners will expire before the close of the present session of the Legislature, it is not possible to make the required distribution among the judges, surrogates and county clerks in time for the more formal presentation of the Civil and Penal Codes to the Legislature for adoption.

The Penal Code, thus prepared, defines all the crimes for which, according to the law of this State, persons can be punished, and the punishment for the same. In preparing it the Commissioners kept the following objects in view: first, to bring within the compass of a single volume the whole body of the law of crimes and punishments; second, to supply deficiencies and correct errors in the present definitions of crimes; third, to make the relative degrees of punishment more nearly equal to the relative degrees of crime; and fourth, to define and punish acts deserving of punishment, but not punishable by the existing law.

The Civil Code was required to embrace the laws of personal rights and relations, of property and of obligations.

It has four general divisions: the first relating to persons, the second to property, the third to obligations, and the fourth containing general provisions relating to these different subjects. In the execution of this vast undertaking, the commissioners have endeavored to bring together and arrange in order, all the general rules known to our law upon the subjects contained within the scope of such a Code, rejecting those which are obsolete or unsuitable to our present condition, and adding such others as appeared necessary or desirable.

The first division, it will be seen, defines the civil condition of different persons in the State, adults, minors, persons of unsound mind and Indians; enumerates their personal rights; declares their personal relations, under the various topics of marriage, divorce, husband, wife, parent, child, guardian, ward, master and servant.

The second division contains the laws respecting property, real and personal, the various interests or estates therein, the modes of acquisition by occupancy, accession, transfer, will or succession; the restrictions on alienation and accumulation, the conditions and qualifications of ownership; uses and powers; the making, interpretation and execution of wills, and various special provisions relating to corporations, copyright, shipping, and the rules of navigation. The third division embraces the whole subject of obligations, whether arising from contract or the operation of law, their definition, interpretation, transfer and extinction, whether by performance, offer of performance, prevention of performance or otherwise; the object and consideration of contracts, the parties thereto and their consent, whether freely given or obtained by duress, menace, fraud, undue influence or mistake; and after these general subjects, the particular subjects are considered of sale, exchange, deposit, loan, hiring, employment, service, carriage, trust, agency, partnership, insurance, indemnity, suretyship, pledge, mortgage, lien and commercial paper. The fourth division specifies the different kinds of relief afforded for the violation of private rights, and the means of securing their observance, whether compensatory, specific, or preventive, and the measure of damages when compensation is the rule. This division contains, also, provisions concerning the special relations of debtor and creditor, and concerning nuisances, and enumerates and explains various maxims of jurisprudence.

In all this immense range of subjects, while it has been the general purpose of the Commissioners to give the law as it now exists, they have kept in mind the injunction of the Constitution to "specify such alterations and amendments therein as they shall deem proper." In obedience to this command of the organic law, they have specified various alterations and amendments which they consider proper to be adopted. These are mentioned in the notes to the different sections, where the reasons for recommending them are generally given.

For all these the Commissioners beg leave to refer to the notes themselves. To detail them here would swell this report to an inconvenient length, and, therefore, three only will be mentioned. In the first division the Commissioners have endeavored to secure the equal rights of married women in respect to their children and their property, abolishing at the same time both dower and curtesy, and they have introduced an article on adoption, by which they have provided that the substituted parent may have all the rights and be subject to all the responsibilities of the real one, who, having once voluntarily renounced his parental rights, should not be permitted to resume them when the affections have grown into the new relation. In the second division the Commissioners have aimed at an assimilation to the utmost extent possible of the laws of real and personal property, by reducing the law of real estate to the simplicity of personal, wherever it could be done without the disturbance of existing rights, establishing for both the same rules of succession.

The Commissioners will not presume to think that in the preparation of the Codes they have foreseen all the cases which can arise in the multifarious affairs of men, or that they have even collected all the general rules which have been announced from the bench in the past history of our law. Some may have been overlooked, some may have been omitted from a mistaken belief that they were obsolete or inapplicable to our present condition, or were contrary to other rules of greater importance that ought to be retained.

All that the Commissioners profess is, that they have endeavored to collect those general rules known to our law which are applicable to our present circumstances, and ought to be continued. They trust that they have arranged these rules in a manner which will be approved by the scientific student, while it will help the lawyer and the citizen to an easier if not a better knowledge of the law. And they flatter themselves that for the unforeseen cases which are certain to arise, there are general principles, rules of interpretation and analogies which will serve as guides for judicial decision.

The question whether a Code is desirable is simply a question between written and unwritten law.

That this was ever debatable is one of the most remarkable facts in the history of jurisprudence. If the law is a thing to be obeyed, it is a thing to be known, and if it is to be known, there can be no better, not to say no other, method of making it known than of writing and publishing it. If a written constitution is desirable, so are written laws. The same reasons which affect the one, affect also the other. There may be countries where the conflicts between the different orders in a state render a written definition of their relative rights a difficult or an impossible task, and there, of course, a written constitution is not likely to be attempted; and because a written constitution is not thought desirable, written laws are supposed to be undesirable. These reasons have no application to this country. We have no orders in the state; no classes of society clashing with each other. The will of the people is the supreme law; that will is fitly expressed by their written constitution and their written laws. It should seem indeed to have no other fit expression.

There are those who argue that an unwritten law is more favorable to liberty than a written one. The contrary should seem to be more consonant with reason. It can scarcely be thought favorable to the liberty of the citizen that he should be governed by laws of which he is ignorant, and it can as little be thought that his knowledge of the laws is promoted by their being kept from print or from authentic statement in a written form.

Whatever is known to the judge or to the lawyer can be written, and whatever has been written in the treatises of lawyers or the opinions of judges, can be written in a systematic Code.

It is no answer to say that nothing can be written which will not be susceptible of different interpretations. That may be true. But it is no more susceptible of different interpretations when written in a code than when written in the reports. On the contrary, when expressed with care, for the very purpose of stating a rule which is to govern all cases alike, there is more likelihood of precision in language than when expressed with reference to a particular case.

For these eight years the Commissioners have been engaged in the preparation of the Codes with which they were charged by the Legislature of 1857. The task which they undertook was untried and difficult. No code of the common law of America or of England had ever before been attempted. How they have acquitted themselves it is not for them to say. Their work is before the Legislature and the people. If it shall effect half the good which the Commissioners have ventured to hope from it, and the thought of which has cheered them through their long task, they will be rewarded.

The Codes which the Commissioners have thus prepared, together with the Codes of Civil and Criminal Procedure heretofore submitted by the Commissioners on Practice and Pleadings, complete that work of codification which was contemplated by the Constitution of 1846; and, when the same shall have been considered and sanctioned by the Legislature, the people of New York will have the whole body of their laws in a written and systematic form, as full, at least, the Commissioners venture to think, as the code of any other people.

In the last months of their service, when their task was well nigh ended, and while the sheets of the Civil Code were passing through the press, one of the members of the Commission was taken away by death. On the 25th of December, 1864, after an illness of two days, Mr. Noyes died, to the inexpressible grief of his associates; having been suddenly struck down in the fullness of life, leaving to the surviving Commissioners the mournful duty of signing their names, without his, to this last report of their common labors.

All which is respectfully submitted.

DAVID DUDLEY FIELD.
ALEX. W. BRADFORD.

New York, February 13th, 1865.

INTRODUCTION.

The Civil Code mentioned in the preceding report, is contained in this volume. Its history is as follows: The Constitution of the State of New York, as revised and adopted in 1846, has two provisions looking to a codification of the laws. One is in the 17th section of the first article, in these words:

"The Legislature at its first session after the adoption of "this Constitution, shall appoint three Commissioners whose "duty it shall be to reduce into a written and systematic "Code, the whole body of the law of this State, or so "much and such parts thereof as to the said Commissioners "shall seem practicable and expedient; and the said Com-"missioners shall specify such alterations and amendments "therein as they shall deem proper, and they shall at all "times make reports of their proceedings to the Legisla-"ture when called upon to do so; and the Legislature shall "pass laws regulating the tenure of office, the filling of "vacancies therein, and the compensation of said Com-"missioners, and shall also provide for the publication of "the said Code, prior to its being presented to the Legis-"lature for adoption."

The other is the 24th section of the 6th article. "The "Legislature at its first session after the adoption of this

"Constitution, shall provide for the appointment of three "Commissioners, whose duty it shall be to revise, reform, "simplify and abridge the rules and practice, pleadings, "forms and proceedings of the courts of record of this "State, and to report thereon to the Legislature, subject to "their adoption and modification from time to time."

Both Commissions were filled by an act passed on the 8th of April, 1847; that under the 1st article by the appointment of REUBEN H. WALWORTH, ALVAH WORDEN and JOHN A. COLLIER, as "Commissioners of the Code," to hold office for two years; and that under the 6th article, by the appointment of ARPHAXED LOOMIS, NICHOLAS HILL, Jr., and DAVID GRAHAM, as "Commissioners on Practice and Pleadings," to hold office till the 1st of February, 1849. Changes, however, were afterwards made in both Commissions.

In the *Practice Commission*, Mr. HILL having resigned, DAVID DUDLEY FIELD was, on the 29th of September, 1847, appointed in his place. The Commission thus reorganized was, by an act passed on the 31st of January, 1849, continued till April, and in April was further continued till the 31st of December of that year. On that day it completed its labors, submitting to the Legislature as complete, two Codes, one of criminal, and the other of civil procedure, including the law of evidence. These Commissioners had previously made four partial reports, the first, on the 29th of February, 1848, containing the Code of Civil Procedure as subsequently enacted, and embracing the substance of the reforms proposed in the practice of the courts in civil cases; the second, on the 29th of January,

1849, containing additions and amendments to the Code as enacted; the third, on the 30th of January, 1849, containing still further provisions; and the fourth, on the same day, containing the draft of a Code of Criminal Procedure. When the completed Codes of Civil and Criminal Procedure were submitted, the Commissioners reported, at the same time, a special act enumerating and repealing the various statutes covered by those Reports.

In the *Code Commission*, Mr. WALWORTH having declined the appointment, ANTHONY L. ROBERTSON was, on the 13th of May, 1847, named in his stead. In January, 1848, Mr. COLLIER resigned, and SETH C. HAWLEY succeeded him. In April, 1849, a new act was passed, appointing Mr. WORDEN and Mr. HAWLEY, with JOHN C. SPENCER, Commissioners of the Code, till the 8th of April, 1851. Mr. SPENCER declined to serve on this Commission, and the Commission itself was abolished by an act passed on the 10th of April, 1850. The Commission, however, was revived in 1857, by an act passed on the 6th of April of that year, by which Mr. FIELD, Mr. WILLIAM CURTIS NOYES, and Mr. ALEXANDER W. BRADFORD were appointed Commissioners, to continue in office five years, and to prepare Codes of all the law not considered by the Practice Commission. In April, 1862, the term of office of these Commissioners was extended to April, 1865.

The labor of this Commission is sufficiently detailed in the Report prefixed to this volume. The works, in their completed forms, of both Commissions, that is, of the Practice Commission as it was reorganized in October, 1847, and of the Code Commission as it was reorganized in April,

1857, are now comprised in six volumes, containing the Code of Civil Procedure (including the Law of Evidence), the Book of Forms, the Code of Criminal Procedure, the Political Code, the Penal Code, and the Civil Code.

Whether the task which these two Commissions had before them was impossible or useless; in other words, whether it was possible, and, if possible, expedient to reduce into a Code "the whole body of the law," had been much debated, both in this country and in England. One view of the subject has been given in the preceding Report. Others may be given here. The question, as was there said, is between written and unwritten law; that is to say, between law written by the lawgiver, and law not thus written; between law promulgated by that department of the government which alone has the prerogative of making and promulgating the laws, and law not so promulgated.

Whether a general Code of the law be *possible*, should seem, from the nature of the subject, hardly to be doubtful. The common law of New York, like the common law of England, from which it is in great part derived, consists of a vast number of rules of property and of conduct, which have been applied by the judicial tribunals, and which had their origin either in legislative enactments, now forgotten, or in traditions from ancient times, or in the consciences of the judges, as the cases came before them. The decisions of the tribunals have been for ages preserved in writing. If there was ever a time when they were held in the memory alone, that time has long passed. All that we now know of the law, we know from written records. To make a Code of the known law is therefore but to make a complete, analytical, and authoritative compilation from these records. The records of the common law are in the reports of the decisions of the tribunals; the records of the statute law are in the volumes of legislative acts. That these records are susceptible of collation, analysis, and arrangement, might have been assumed beforehand, even if we had not the proof in our libraries, in digest upon digest, more or less perfect, to which we daily resort for convenience and instruction. The more perfect a digest becomes, the more nearly it approaches the Code contemplated by the Constitution. In other words, a complete digest of our existing law, common and statute, dissected and analyzed, avoiding repetitions and rejecting contradictions, moulded into distinct propositions, and arranged in scientific order, with proper amendments, and in this form sanctioned by the Legislature, is the Code which the organic law commanded to be made for the people of this State. That this was possible, was all but proven by what had been already done among ourselves.

It was fully proven by what had been done in respect to the law of other countries. The law of Rome in the time of JUSTINIAN was, to say the least, as difficult of reduction into a Code as is our own law at the present day. Yet it was thus reduced, though, no doubt, to the disgust and dismay of many a lawyer of that period. The concurring judgment of thirteen centuries since, has, however, pronounced the Code of JUSTINIAN one of the noblest benefactions to the human race, as it was one of the greatest achievements of human genius.

France, at the beginning of her revolution, was governed partly by Roman and partly by customary law. The French Codes made one uniform system for the whole country, supplanting the former laws, and forming a model by which half of Europe has since fashioned its legislation. It should seem, therefore, to be quite beyond dispute, that a general Code of the law is *possible.*

Whether it is also *expedient,* is a different question. One of the objections made is, that it is not possible to provide for all future cases. You may, it is said, stretch your foresight to its utmost limit; you may exhaust all the sagacity and ingenuity of the human mind; the future, nevertheless, is a sealed book: you cannot look into its unopened leaves; and, therefore, attempting to provide for what they contain, is spending your strength in a vain and fruitless effort. This does not appear to be an objection of any weight whatever. Because we cannot provide for all cases, should be thought a poor reason for not providing for as many as possible. To render the existing law as accessible, and as intelligible as we can, is a rational object, though we cannot foresee what ought to be the law in cases yet unknown. To cast aside known rules which are obsolete, to correct those which are burdensome, or unsuitable to present circumstances, to reject anomalous or ill-considered cases, to bring the different branches into a more perfect order and agreement, may be of immense value, though we cannot look beyond the present, to make provision for what has never yet appeared.

The objection, however, assumes more than should be granted without qualification. There are certain departments of the law, of which we may affirm with perfect confidence, either that we have provided for every possible case, or that when a new case arises, it is better that it should be provided for by new legislation, than by judicial decision. Thus, in respect to the Penal Code it may be affirmed, that every act for which punishment may be inflicted, ought to be designated beforehand; that no man ought to be punished for an act not thus designated, and that if any act should be committed, for which society has prescribed no punishment, it may go for once unpunished, and a new law be made against other like acts in the future. As to the Political Code, it must by its very nature cover the whole subject. And for the Code of Civil Procedure, it is enough to say, that when the first report was before the Legislature, some of the members were troubled with similar fears about the want of provision for future cases, and, to satisfy them, this provision was introduced: "If a case shall arise in which an action for the enforcement or protection of a right, or the redress or prevention of a wrong, cannot be had under this act, the practice heretofore in use may be adopted so far as may be necessary, to prevent a failure of justice;" but no such case has ever yet arisen.

If a case unprovided for could not arise under the Code of Civil Procedure, much less could it arise under the Code of Criminal Procedure. It may, therefore, be safely affirmed, that there is but one of the five Codes, that is to say, the Civil Code, to which, with any semblance of justice, it may be made an objection that it cannot provide for all future cases. This Code is, undoubtedly, the most important and difficult of all; and of this it is true, that it cannot provide for all possible cases which the future may disclose. It does not profess to provide for them. All that it professes is, to give the general rules upon the subjects to which it relates, which are now known and recognized, so far as they ought to be retained, with such amendments as seemed best to be made, and saving always such of the rules as may have been overlooked. In cases where the law is not declared by the Code, it is to be hoped that analogies may nevertheless be discovered which will enable the courts to decide. If, in any such case, an analogy cannot be found, nor any rule which has been overlooked and omitted, then the courts will have either to decide, as at present, without reference to any settled rule of law, or to leave the case undecided, as was done by Lord MANSFIELD, in King *v.* Hay, 1 *W. Bl.*, 640, trusting to future legislation for future cases.

The language of the Code in this respect should seem to be sufficiently guarded, thus:

"§ 2. Law is a rule of property and of conduct, prescribed by the sovereign power of the State.

§ 3. The will of the sovereign power is expressed:

1. By the Constitution, which is the organic act of the people;

2. By statutes, which are the acts of the Legislature, or by the ordinances of other and subordinate legislative bodies;

3. By the judgments of the tribunals enforcing those rules, which, though not enacted, form what is known as customary or common law.

§ 4. The common law is divided into:

1. Public law, or the law of nations;

2. Domestic, or municipal law.

§ 5. The evidence of the common law is found in the decisions of the tribunals.

§ 6. In this State there is no common law, in any case, where the law is declared by the five Codes.

§ 2032. The rule that statutes in derogation of the common law are to be strictly construed, has no application to this Code.

§ 2033. All statutes, laws and rules heretofore in force in this State, inconsistent with the provisions of this Code, are hereby repealed or abrogated; but such repeal or abrogation does not revive any former law heretofore repealed, nor does it affect any right already existing or accrued, or any proceeding already taken, except as in this Code provided."

Therefore, if there be an existing rule of law omitted from this Code, and not inconsistent with it, that rule will continue to exist in the same form in which it now exists; while if any new rule, now for the first time introduced, should not answer the good ends for which it is intended, which can be known only from experience, it can be amended or abrogated by the same lawgiving department which made it; and if new cases arise, as they will, which have not been foreseen, they may be decided, if decided at all, precisely as they would now be decided, that is to say, by analogy to some rule in the Code, or to some rule omitted from the Code and therefore still existing, or by the dictates of natural justice.

Another objection to the expediency of a Code, is its supposed uncertainty. The argument is this: In the attempt to be systematic and concise, you must of necessity leave the language open to different interpretations. Now, it is quite true that, as a word has often various meanings and a change in the structure of a sentence may suggest different ideas, it is difficult to frame a section that may not be tortured into a meaning unlike that which its framers attached to it. But it is a great mistake to consider this true only of the concise propositions of a Code. Diffuseness is not a help to clearness. The longest judicial opinions are generally the least precise and the least comprehended. As a long document is usually more obscure than a short one; as a statute of many sections is commonly less understood than one of a few; as many words tend to confusion rather than enlightenment, so a single proposition, carefully expressed and made as concise as possible, is more likely to be precise and susceptible of one meaning only, than if the same idea were put into a different form and a greater number of words.

If it be urged, that reported decisions have this advantage in point of certainty, that, being made in each case with reference to a given state of facts, those facts are illustrations of the rule announced, and tend to explain it. the answer is, that the facts of a case reported serve for limitation, as well as illustration, and just in that proportion the rule announced is partial and not general, and if acted upon as general tends to mislead; so that, after all, we are brought back to the same point, which is, that the rule of the decision, whatever it may be, partial or general, can be more precisely and accurately stated in a few short sentences, than in the opinion more or less diffuse in which it is stated or from which it may be evolved.

So far as reported cases serve for illustration, the present Code makes use of them; for the references to adjudged cases, which in most instances follow the sections, are intended as much to answer the purpose of illustration as to justify the text. It is a favorite idea with many that, for promoting certainty, the propositions of a Code should be accompanied by illustrative examples. Whatever advantage there may be in this method, these references, it is supposed, will afford the best kind of illustration.

A still further objection to the expediency of a Code is its supposed inflexibility. Expressed in formal propositions, and couched in positive terms, it is not as flexible, say the objectors, as the common law. This is the objection most insisted upon by those who oppose a Code, and it should, therefore, receive the most careful consideration. It may be first observed, that flexibility, in its ordinary sense, is one of the worst qualities which a law can have, or rather that it is inconsistent with the idea of law. As the law is a rule of property and of conduct, it should be fixed. If it be meant that a rule, made for a certain state of facts, may not be applicable to a different state of facts, that will not be disputed; if it be meant that such a rule ought not to be applied to the same state of facts under all circumstances, the objection amounts only to this, that the rule is too broadly stated; if it be meant that a rule ought to be subject to the discretion of the Judges, the proposition is unsound, for the Judges should not have dispensing power.

Another way of stating the objection, is to say that while the common law is expansive, a Code does not expand or adapt itself to the expanding exigencies of society. A different phrase for the same idea is, that the common law is elastic and accommodating, and that a Code will be the opposite. Now, to say that a law is expansive, elastic or accommodating, is as much as to say that it is no law at all. The real significance of the objection, if it has any significance, is, that it is better to let the Judges make the law as they go along, than to have the lawgiver make it beforehand. For, if the Judges are to decide according to known rules, those rules can be written by the lawgiver as easily as they can be spoken from the Bench, or taken down by the Reporters. And even though, in particular cases, the Judges should fail to find such rules, and should have to make rules as the cases occur, that, too, can be done as easily when the known rules are placed in a Code, as when they repose in the breasts of Judges, or in the leaves of Reports. So long as a Code is confined to the rules of law as they now exist, it is neither more nor less expansive than the common law. When the inquiry concerns new cases, it is divisible into two parts, one relating to those cases which are foreseen, and the other to those which are not foreseen. Those which are foreseen, the lawgiver can provide for, and it is his duty to provide for them. Those which are not foreseen, cannot be provided for, except by directing the courts to decide according to the analogy of existing rules, when there is such an analogy, and when there is none, then to decide according to the dictates of natural justice. In this last respect, the Judges will be in the same predicament under a Code as under the common law; so that really, the only point of difference respects those new cases which can be foreseen or reasonably anticipated, and if there be persons who think that for such cases, it is better that the Judges should make the law, after the cases arise, than for the Legislature to make it as a guide beforehand, then they think that government ought not to be divided, according to the fundamental American maxim, into three separate legislative, executive and judicial departments.

If we look, for example, at any of the leading cases reported, we see the facts given, the conclusion of the Judges and the reasoning by which the conclusion was reached. Whatever legal proposition is necessarily involved in this conclusion is to be deemed an established rule of law. This rule may be written in a Code, or it may be left in the Reports. Is it any more flexible in the one form than in the other? Certainly not, unless the Judges feel themselves at liberty to depart from it, so long as it remains in the Reports alone. But that would be to declare that the decision is not law.

It is possible that the idea of flexibility in one form, and inflexibility in the other, has arisen from not sufficiently attending to the distinction between general and partial rules. It may be perfectly safe to lay down a certain general rule, but not at all safe to undertake the enumeration of all the particulars to which the rule may be applied. A code which should attempt to do the latter would fail, not because it would be inflexible, but because it would be defective. Take, for example, the rule that implies a promise to pay over money which the party ought not to retain, as announced by Lord MANSFIELD in Moses *v.* McFarlane (2 *Burr.*, 1005), in this language: "In one word, the gist of this kind of action is, that the defendant, upon the circumstances of the case, is *obliged by the ties of natural justice and equity to refund the money.*" This, as a general rule, could be introduced into a code with perfect safety, while it would be certain and inflexible. But if there should be an effort to go into details, and to enumerate all the particular cases to which the rule has been or could be applied, the enumeration would be defective, inasmuch as it would be impossible for human foresight to discern all the occurrences to which it might be applicable. It might be possible to collect and enumerate all the instances in which the rule has been applied, and to state the circumstances; it might also be possible to mention many cases likely to arise in the future to which it would also be applicable; but it would never be safe to pronounce absolutely that it should only be applied to the cases enumerated, for the obvious reason that others may occur, just as urgent, which human foresight has failed to discover. The objection to a code which should attempt this would be, not that the rules given were inflexible, or that the code itself was inflexible, in any other sense than that it attempted too much, and was fashioned upon a false principle.

Even in the case supposed, a code and the common law would stand upon the same footing, unless something was put into the former which was not in the latter; for neither in one form or the other are either the general or the particular rules flexible; the general rule is comprehensive, the particular rules are not comprehensive; the latter would be of little value except as pointing to the former, and if that is once given it covers as many cases when inserted in a code as when left in the common law at large.

There is, for instance, a rule of the common law, that a contract is void which is against public policy. What is or is not against it is left for the courts to decide, since the policy changes from generation to generation, and almost from year to year. The judges are not thereby invested with power to change the law, but to apply established law to the circumstances of each case as it arises, and is then compared with the policy of the State for the time being, or with the general policy of nations. The power to decide the question of compatibility in such a case, between the act and the policy, is not a legislative but a judicial power, as much as to decide whether a by-law of a corporation is or is not reasonable, or whether, in considering the effect of an act performed, the time of performance was reasonable or unreasonable. It may indeed be affirmed, that certain acts are against public policy, and so far the present Code has attempted to go, but it has not attempted, and could not safely attempt, to define all the acts by which men might hereafter seek to countervail that policy, or to foresee what the policy itself should be in ages to come.

If by flexibility be meant susceptibility of progression, then it may be affirmed with confidence, that a code, upon the theory on which this is framed, not only adapts itself to the present wants of society better than the existing common law, but that it contains within itself, in a greater degree, the elements of future progress; not because its rules are any more or less flexible than those of the common law, but for the reasons which will now be stated.

The first of these reasons is, that while the judicial department has been unable, or if able, unwilling, to make necessary amendments of the law, the legislative department, to which the power of amendment of right belongs, has been embarrassed, first, by the disjointed and comparatively inaccessible form in which the great body of the law has lain, and secondly, by that maxim of the common law by which the judges were taught that every statute in derogation of it was to be strictly construed. The first cause of embarrassment is removed so soon as the Legislature and the people have before them the whole body of the laws in an accessible and compact form, by which the relation of the several parts to each other and to the whole can be better seen, a defect in any part sooner discovered, and the particular amendment indicated which ought to be made. The second cause is removed by the declaration, that the maxim of strict construction has no application to a general code.

Nothing is more conspicuous in the history of jurisprudence than the tenacity with which the Judges of America and England, unlike those of continental Europe, have adhered to precedents, even though the reason for them has ceased, and their mischiefs have become palpable.

Take for example the practice of the courts as it existed before the Code of Civil Procedure. If any part of the common law should have been flexible, that should have been, for it was made almost entirely by the Judges. And yet both here and in England, while they expressed their regret at the state of things, they were compelled to declare that the evils of the system were too deeply rooted to be removed by any power short of the Legislature. Whenever the Legislature did interpose, the courts refused to go beyond the strict letter of the statute. No fact of early English history is more certain than that the existence of equity, as a separate system, was owing to the rigid adherence of the common law judges to form, in other words, to the iron inflexibility of the common law. Equity itself soon fell into the same predicament. It would not at any time have been thought proper or safe for the courts to disregard an established precedent at law or in equity, upon the idea that the circumstances of the community had so changed as to make the precedent oppressive. Decisions have been frequently overruled, it is true, but upon some such excuse, as that they were made by a divided court or an inferior one, or with reference to particular circumstances or without sufficient consideration.

In almost every instance where an improvement has been made in the laws, it has come from the Legislature. Had society been left to the discipline of the common law, whether it be called flexible or inflexible, the most cruel and bloody of criminal systems would still have shamed us; feudal tenures with all their burdensome incidents would have remained; land would have been inalienable without livery of seizin, and wives would have had only the rights which a barbarous age conceded them.

Even in the matter of contracts, that portion of the common law where the attribute of flexibility would have been, if ever, desirable, what do we still see? While it cannot be denied, that in nine instances out of ten, tenants hire houses in the belief that landlords must repair them if necessary; that tenants who agree to repair, have no suspicion that if the house is burnt they are bound to rebuild; that when a creditor accepts part payment in full satisfaction, the bargain is supposed to be binding; that an instrument under seal, signed by an agent in his own name, but expressly declaring that he signs for his principal, is considered by both parties to be obligatory upon the principal;

yet upon each of these points the common law holds otherwise, and has obstinately refused for hundreds of years to accommodate itself to the undoubted intentions of the parties whose rights it determines.

Either the common law had within itself the flexible, elastic, and accommodating elements, which would have enabled the courts to adapt it in these respects to the expanding exigencies of society, or it has been greatly misunderstood or misrepresented by the opponents of a Code.

The second of the reasons for considering a Code more favorable to progress than the common law, is, that in all those particulars in which the common law does take hold of the business and usages of society, and make use of them in its jurisprudence, it does so not so much by way of incorporating those usages into the law, or indeed making any change in the substance of the law itself, as by way of interpreting the acts and intentions of parties, and applying fixed principles to the ever changing concerns of human life; in all which respects, a Code may and should be more liberal than the common law. Thus it is, that by the present Code, not only are the particular anomalies rectified, which have just been mentioned, but by sections 801, 802, 809, 811 and 1829, the details of the law of contracts are made subordinate to the intentions of the parties, ascertained not by inexorable rules of legal construction, but by all the light which can be thrown upon them by law, usage and surrounding circumstances, except in those few cases, where for reasons of public policy an absolute rule has been established.

Section 1829, it will be seen, is in these words:

"Except where it is otherwise declared, the provisions of the foregoing fifteen Titles of this Part, in respect to the rights and obligations of parties to contracts, are subordinate to the intention of the parties, where ascertained in the manner prescribed by the chapter on the INTERPRETATION OF CONTRACTS, and the benefit thereof may be waived by any party entitled thereto, unless such waiver would be against public policy."

The usages of society vary with its wants and its pursuits. The law refers to those usages because the parties contract with reference to them, and they must be taken into account when it considers what these parties ought to do and what they ought not to do. In this way, and in this alone, has the common law adapted itself to the exigencies of society, and in this respect the present Code goes not only as far but farther than the common law.

Having thus considered the principal objections to the codification of the law, it should next be considered whether there are advantages in it. Assuming that it is possible to have a body of written law in a convenient form, and in scientific order, containing the materials and framed in the manner already described, what benefits will it confer? In the first place, it will enable the lawyer to dispense with a great number of the books which now incumber the shelves of his library. In the next place, it will thus save a vast amount of labor, now forced upon lawyers and judges, in searching through the reports, examining and collecting cases, and drawing inferences from the decisions, and so far facilitate the dispatch of business in the courts. In the third place, it will afford an opportunity for settling, by legislative enactment, many disputed questions, which the courts have never been able to settle. In the fourth place, it will enable the Legislature to effect reforms in different branches of the law, which can only be effected by simultaneous and comprehensive legislation. Thus, for example, the closer assimilation of the law of real and personal property, and the changes in the relation of husband and wife, as to property, cannot be effected by any other means so wisely and safely, as by a General Code. The making of a Code involves a general revision of the law. It is indeed in this way alone that such a revision seems practicable. The occasion is thereby afforded to look at the law of the land, as a whole, to lop off its excrescences, reconcile its contradictions, and make it uniform and harmonious. In the fifth place, the publication of a Code will diffuse among the people a more general and accurate knowledge of their rights and duties, than can be obtained in any other manner. This is an object of great importance in all countries, but more especially in ours. If every person can have before him, in an authentic form, the laws which are to affect his property, and govern his conduct, he can have an additional guaranty of his rights, and a better acquaintance with his duties. Here, more than anywhere else, all classes of citizens interfere in all the affairs of the State. They elect, directly, nearly all the officers who make, administer, or execute the laws. If in Holland, or in Germany, or France, a Civil Code has been found beneficial, much more is it likely to be beneficial to us.

So far as the choice lies between law, to be made by the legislature, and law to be made by the judiciary, there cannot be a doubt that whatever may be the determination elsewhere, the people of this State prefer that theirs shall be made by those whom they elect as legislators, rather than by those whose function it is, according to the theory of the Constitution, to administer the laws as they find them. Hence, the idea of a Code has taken such hold of our people that they have made provision for it by their organic law.

Besides the changes to which attention was particularly directed in the preceding report, relating to the rights of married women, the adoption of children, and the assimilation of the laws of real and personal property, there are others, of less importance, which ought not to be overlooked. They will be found, with few exceptions, in the following sections:

30, 32, 89, 90, 97, 135, 136, 139, 151, 170, 176, 182, 243, 331, 390, 392, 394, 395, 396, 397, 398, 399, 422, 486, 621, 623, 625, 626, 627, 628, 629, 647, 673, 705, 709, 713, 717, 720, 723, 735, 741, 743, 755, 781, 785, 830, 831, 832, 833, 836, 862, 864, 886, 887, 924, 941, 943, 977, 990, 991, 992, 998, 1013, 1065, 1071, 1109, 1140, 1141, 1162, 1166, 1198, 1213, 1263, 1296, 1301, 1302, 1315, 1352, 1353, 1376, 1401, 1406, 1416, 1422, 1439, 1608, 1620, 1623, 1632, 1641, 1643, 1646, 1648, 1651, 1652, 1660, 1729, 1737, 1750, 1751, 1752, 1759, 1762, 1768, 1779, 1781, 1783, 1789, 1791, 1793, 1817, 1847, 1852, 1893, 1901, 1928, 1931, 1936, 1939, 1940.

It remains to take notice of what there is novel in the classification of the subjects treated in this Code. The reasons for the changes in this respect are generally set forth in the notes. It will be observed that there has been some departure from the ordinary arrangement, resulting principally from the desire of the Commissioners to confine each title to a single branch of a general subject, and not to permit the repetition of a principle once stated. In the first part of the third division, that which treats of obligations in general, many provisions are placed, particularly in respect to the extinction of obligations, which have generally been referred to contracts alone. The subject of bailments is not treated by itself, but under different titles, as deposit, loan, hiring, service, carriage, trust, agency and pledge. The matters usually treated under the title of principal and agent, are here treated under service, trust and agency. The principles governing all confidential relations are brought together under the head of trust. In the title upon insurance, the general rules are collected into one chapter. Suretyship is treated under the title of guaranty. Mortgage, equally with pledge, is treated under the head of lien, an effort having been made to clear the law of mortgage from the confusions and contradictions which have been produced by the counter action of law and equity for so many years. And in treating of relief, compensatory, specific and preventive, the general principles which determine the measure of damages, and which fix the limits of specific and preventive remedies, are so arranged as to reflect upon and explain each other.

The Commissioners take this occasion to express their sense of the invaluable services rendered to them by THOMAS G. SHEARMAN, Esq., of the New York Bar, who has been engaged on the Civil Code from its commencement, and whose industry, accuracy and intelligence they cannot praise too highly.

ANALYSIS OF THE CONTENTS.

GENERAL DEFINITIONS AND DIVISIONS.

DIVISION FIRST.

PERSONS.

PART I.

PERSONS.

PART II.

PERSONAL RIGHTS.

PART III.

PERSONAL RELATIONS.

TITLE I.

MARRIAGE.

CHAPTER I.

THE CONTRACT OF MARRIAGE.

ARTICLE I.

VALIDITY.

ARTICLE II.

AUTHENTICATION.

CHAPTER II.

DIVORCE.

ARTICLE I.

NULLITY.

ARTICLE II.

DISSOLUTION.

ARTICLE III.

SEPARATION.

ARTICLE IV.

GENERAL PROVISIONS.

CHAPTER III.

HUSBAND AND WIFE.

TITLE II.

PARENT AND CHILD.

CHAPTER I.

CHILDREN BY BIRTH.

CHAPTER II.

ADOPTION.

TITLE III.

GUARDIAN AND WARD.

TITLE IV.

MASTER AND SERVANT.

DIVISION SECOND.

PROPERTY.

PART I.

PROPERTY IN GENERAL.

TITLE I.

NATURE OF PROPERTY.

TITLE II.

OWNERSHIP.

CHAPTER I.

OWNERS.

CHAPTER II.

MODIFICATIONS OF OWNERSHIP.

ARTICLE I.

INTERESTS IN PROPERTY.

ARTICLE II.

CONDITIONS OF OWNERSHIP.

ARTICLE III.

RESTRAINTS UPON ALIENATION.

ARTICLE IV.

ACCUMULATIONS.

CHAPTER III.

RIGHTS OF OWNERS.

CHAPTER IV.

TERMINATION OF OWNERSHIP.

TITLE III.

GENERAL DEFINITIONS.

PART II.

REAL OR IMMOVABLE PROPERTY.

TITLE I.

GENERAL PROVISIONS.

TITLE II.

ESTATES IN REAL PROPERTY.

CHAPTER I.

ESTATES IN GENERAL.

CHAPTER II.

TERMINATION OF ESTATES.

CHAPTER III.

SERVITUDES.

TITLE III.

RIGHTS AND OBLIGATIONS OF OWNERS.

CHAPTER I.

RIGHTS OF OWNERS.

ARTICLE I.

INCIDENTS OF OWNERSHIP.

ARTICLE II.

BOUNDARIES.

CHAPTER II.

OBLIGATIONS OF OWNERS.

TITLE IV.

USES AND TRUSTS.

TITLE V.

POWERS.

PART III.

PERSONAL OR MOVABLE PROPERTY.

TITLE I.

PERSONAL PROPERTY IN GENERAL.

TITLE II.

PARTICULAR KINDS OF PERSONAL PROPERTY.

CHAPTER I.

THINGS IN ACTION.

CHAPTER II.

SHIPPING.

ARTICLE I.

GENERAL PROVISIONS.

ARTICLE II.

RULES OF NAVIGATION.

CHAPTER III.

CORPORATIONS.

ARTICLE I.

THE CREATION OF CORPORATIONS.

ARTICLE II.

CORPORATE STOCK.

ARTICLE III.

CORPORATE POWERS.

ARTICLE IV.

DISSOLUTION OF CORPORATIONS.

CHAPTER IV.

PRODUCTS OF THE MIND.

CHAPTER V.

OTHER KINDS OF PERSONAL PROPERTY.

PART IV.

ACQUISITION OF PROPERTY.*

TITLE I.

MODES IN WHICH PROPERTY MAY BE ACQUIRED.

TITLE II.

OCCUPANCY.

TITLE III.

ACCESSION.

CHAPTER I.

ACCESSION TO REAL PROPERTY.

CHAPTER II.

ACCESSION TO PERSONAL PROPERTY.

TITLE IV.

TRANSFER.

CHAPTER I.

TRANSFER IN GENERAL.

ARTICLE I.

DEFINITION OF TRANSFER.

ARTICLE II.

WHAT MAY BE TRANSFERRED.

ARTICLE III.

MODE OF TRANSFER.

ARTICLE IV.

INTERPRETATION OF GRANTS.

ARTICLE V.

EFFECT OF TRANSFER.

CHAPTER II.

TRANSFER OF REAL PROPERTY.

ARTICLE I.

MODE OF TRANSFER.

ARTICLE II.

EFFECT OF TRANSFER.

CHAPTER III.

TRANSFERS OF PERSONAL PROPERTY.

ARTICLE I.

MODE OF TRANSFER.

ARTICLE II.

WHAT OPERATES AS A TRANSFER.

ARTICLE III.

GIFTS.

CHAPTER IV.

RECORDING TRANSFERS.

ARTICLE I.

WHAT MAY BE RECORDED.

ARTICLE II.

MODE OF RECORDING.

ARTICLE III.

PROOF AND ACKNOWLEDGMENT OF INSTRUMENTS.

ARTICLE IV.

EFFECT OF RECORDING, OR THE WANT THEREOF.

CHAPTER V.

UNLAWFUL TRANSFERS. Page.

TITLE V.

WILL.

CHAPTER I.

EXECUTION AND REVOCATION OF WILLS.

CHAPTER II.

INTERPRETATION OF WILLS, AND EFFECT OF VARIOUS PROVISIONS.

CHAPTER III.

GENERAL PROVISIONS.

TITLE VI.

SUCCESSION.

DIVISION THIRD.

OBLIGATIONS.

PART I.

OBLIGATIONS IN GENERAL.

TITLE I.

DEFINITION OF OBLIGATIONS.

TITLE II.

INTERPRETATION OF OBLIGATIONS.

CHAPTER I.

GENERAL RULES OF INTERPRETATION.

CHAPTER II.

JOINT OR SEVERAL OBLIGATIONS.

CHAPTER III.

CONDITIONAL OBLIGATIONS.

CHAPTER IV.

ALTERNATIVE OBLIGATIONS.

TITLE III.

TRANSFER OF OBLIGATIONS.

TITLE IV.

EXTINCTION OF OBLIGATIONS.

CHAPTER I.

PERFORMANCE.

CHAPTER II.

OFFER OF PERFORMANCE.

TITLE I.

NATURE OF A CONTRACT.

CHAPTER I.

DEFINITION.

CHAPTER II.

PARTIES.

CHAPTER III.

CONSENT.

CHAPTER IV.

OBJECT OF A CONTRACT.

CHAPTER V.

CONSIDERATION.

TITLE II.

MANNER OF CREATING CONTRACTS.

TITLE III.

INTERPRETATION OF CONTRACTS.

TITLE IV.

UNLAWFUL CONTRACTS.

TITLE V.

EXTINCTION OF CONTRACTS.

CHAPTER I.

CONTRACTS, HOW EXTINGUISHED.

CHAPTER II.

RESCISSION.

CHAPTER III.

ALTERATION AND CANCELLATION.

PART III.

OBLIGATIONS IMPOSED BY LAW.

PART IV.

OBLIGATIONS ARISING FROM PARTICULAR TRANSACTIONS.

TITLE I.

SALE.

CHAPTER I.

GENERAL PROVISIONS.

ARTICLE I.

SALE.

ARTICLE II.

AGREEMENTS FOR SALE.

ARTICLE III.

FORM OF THE CONTRACT.

CHAPTER II.

RIGHTS AND OBLIGATIONS OF THE SELLER.

ARTICLE I.

RIGHTS AND DUTIES BEFORE DELIVERY.

ARTICLE II.

DELIVERY.

ARTICLE III.

WARRANTY.

CHAPTER III.

RIGHTS AND OBLIGATIONS OF THE BUYER.

CHAPTER IV.

SALE BY AUCTION.

TITLE II.

EXCHANGE.

TITLE III.

DEPOSIT.

CHAPTER I.

DEPOSIT IN GENERAL.

ARTICLE I.

NATURE AND CREATION OF DEPOSIT.

ARTICLE II.

OBLIGATIONS OF THE DEPOSITARY.

CHAPTER II.

DEPOSIT FOR KEEPING.

ARTICLE I.

GENERAL PROVISIONS.

ARTICLE II.

GRATUITOUS DEPOSIT.

ARTICLE III.

STORAGE.

ARTICLE IV.

INNKEEPERS.

ARTICLE V.

FINDING.

CHAPTER III.

DEPOSIT FOR EXCHANGE.

TITLE IV.

LOAN.

CHAPTER I.

LOAN FOR USE.

CHAPTER II.

LOAN FOR EXCHANGE.

CHAPTER III.

LOAN OF MONEY.

TITLE V.

HIRING.

CHAPTER I.

HIRING IN GENERAL.

CHAPTER II.

HIRING OF REAL PROPERTY.

CHAPTER III.

HIRING OF PERSONAL PROPERTY.

TITLE VI.

SERVICE.

CHAPTER I.

SERVICE WITH EMPLOYMENT.

ARTICLE I.

DEFINITION OF EMPLOYMENT.

ARTICLE II.

OBLIGATIONS OF THE EMPLOYER.

ARTICLE III.

OBLIGATIONS OF THE EMPLOYEE.

ARTICLE IV.

TERMINATION OF EMPLOYMENT.

CHAPTER II.

PARTICULAR EMPLOYMENTS.

ARTICLE I.

MASTER AND SERVANT.

ARTICLE II.

AGENTS.

ARTICLE III.

FACTORS.

ARTICLE IV.

SHIPMASTERS.

ARTICLE V.

MATES AND SEAMEN.

ARTICLE VI.

SHIP'S MANAGERS.

CHAPTER III.

SERVICE WITHOUT EMPLOYMENT.

TITLE VII.

CARRIAGE.

CHAPTER I.

CARRIAGE IN GENERAL.

CHAPTER II.

CARRIAGE OF PERSONS.

ARTICLE I.

GRATUITOUS CARRIAGE OF PERSONS.

ARTICLE II.

CARRIAGE FOR REWARD.

CHAPTER III.

CARRIAGE OF PROPERTY.

ARTICLE I.

GENERAL DEFINITIONS.

ARTICLE II.

OBLIGATIONS OF THE CARRIER.

ARTICLE III.

BILL OF LADING.

ARTICLE IV.

FREIGHTAGE.

ARTICLE V.

GENERAL AVERAGE.

CHAPTER IV.

CARRIAGE OF MESSAGES.

CHAPTER V.

COMMON CARRIERS.

ARTICLE I.

COMMON CARRIERS IN GENERAL.

ARTICLE II.

COMMON CARRIERS OF PERSONS.

ARTICLE III.

COMMON CARRIERS OF PROPERTY.

ARTICLE IV.

COMMON CARRIERS OF MESSAGES.

TITLE VIII.

TRUST.

CHAPTER I.

TRUSTS IN GENERAL.

ARTICLE I.

NATURE AND CREATION OF A TRUST.

ARTICLE II.

OBLIGATIONS OF TRUSTEES.

ARTICLE III.

OBLIGATIONS OF THIRD PERSONS.

CHAPTER II.

TRUSTS FOR THE BENEFIT OF THIRD PERSONS.

ARTICLE I.

NATURE AND CREATION OF THE TRUST.

ARTICLE II.

OBLIGATIONS OF TRUSTEES.

ARTICLE III.

POWERS OF TRUSTEES.

ARTICLE IV.

RIGHTS OF TRUSTEES.

ARTICLE V.

TERMINATION OF THE TRUST.

ARTICLE VI.

SUCCESSION OR APPOINTMENT OF NEW TRUSTEES.

TITLE IX.

AGENCY.

CHAPTER I.

AGENCY IN GENERAL.

ARTICLE I.

DEFINITION OF AGENCY.

ARTICLE II.

AUTHORITY OF AGENTS.

ARTICLE III.

MUTUAL OBLIGATIONS OF PRINCIPALS AND THIRD PERSONS.

ARTICLE IV.

OBLIGATIONS OF AGENTS TO THIRD PERSONS.

ARTICLE V.

DELEGATION OF AGENCY.

ARTICLE VI.

TERMINATION OF AGENCY.

CHAPTER II.

PARTICULAR AGENCIES.

ARTICLE I.

AUCTIONEERS.

ARTICLE II.

FACTORS.

ARTICLE III.

SHIPMASTERS AND PILOTS.

ARTICLE IV.

SHIPS' MANAGERS.

TITLE X.

PARTNERSHIP.

CHAPTER I.

PARTNERSHIP IN GENERAL.

ARTICLE I.

ARTICLE II.

ARTICLE III.

ARTICLE IV.

CHAPTER II.

ARTICLE I.

ARTICLE II.

POWERS AND AUTHORITY OF PARTNERS.

ARTICLE III.

MUTUAL OBLIGATIONS OF PARTNERS.

ARTICLE IV.

LIABILITY OF PARTNERS.

ARTICLE V.

TERMINATION OF PARTNERSHIP.

ARTICLE VI.

LIQUIDATION.

ARTICLE VII.

OF THE USE OF FICTITIOUS NAMES.

CHAPTER III.

SPECIAL PARTNERSHIP.

ARTICLE I.

FORMATION OF THE PARTNERSHIP.

ARTICLE II.

POWERS, RIGHTS AND DUTIES OF THE PARTNERS.

ARTICLE III.

LIABILITY OF PARTNERS.

ARTICLE IV.

ALTERATION AND DISSOLUTION.

TITLE XI.

INSURANCE.

CHAPTER I.

INSURANCE IN GENERAL.

ARTICLE I.

DEFINITION OF INSURANCE.

ARTICLE II.

WHAT MAY BE INSURED.

ARTICLE III.

PARTIES TO THE CONTRACT.

ARTICLE IV.

INSURABLE INTEREST.

ARTICLE V.

CONCEALMENT AND REPRESENTATIONS.

ARTICLE VI.

THE POLICY.

ARTICLE VII.

WARRANTIES.

ARTICLE VIII.

PREMIUM.

ARTICLE IX.

LOSS.

ARTICLE X.

NOTICE OF LOSS.

ARTICLE XI.

DOUBLE INSURANCE.

ARTICLE XII.

RE-INSURANCE.

CHAPTER II.

MARINE INSURANCE.

ARTICLE I.

DEFINITION OF MARINE INSURANCE.

ARTICLE II.

INSURABLE INTEREST.

ARTICLE III.

CONCEALMENT.

ARTICLE IV.

REPRESENTATIONS.

ARTICLE V.

IMPLIED WARRANTIES.

ARTICLE VI.

THE VOYAGE AND DEVIATION.

ARTICLE VII.

LOSS.

ARTICLE VIII.

ABANDONMENT.

ARTICLE IX.

MEASURE OF INDEMNITY.

CHAPTER III.

FIRE INSURANCE.

CHAPTER IV.

LIFE AND HEALTH INSURANCE.

TITLE XII.

INDEMNITY.

TITLE XIII.

GUARANTY.

CHAPTER I.

GUARANTY IN GENERAL.

ARTICLE I.

DEFINITION OF GUARANTY. Page.

ARTICLE II.

CREATION OF GUARANTY.

ARTICLE III.

INTERPRETATION OF GUARANTY.

ARTICLE IV.

LIABILITY OF GUARANTORS.

ARTICLE V.

CONTINUING GUARANTY.

ARTICLE VI.

EXONERATION OF GUARANTORS.

CHAPTER II.

SURETYSHIP.

ARTICLE I.

WHO ARE SURETIES.

ARTICLE II.

LIABILITY OF SURETIES.

ARTICLE III.

RIGHTS OF SURETIES.

ARTICLE IV.

RIGHTS OF CREDITORS.

ARTICLE V.

LETTER OF CREDIT.

TITLE XIV.

LIEN.

CHAPTER I.

LIENS IN GENERAL.

ARTICLE I.

DEFINITION OF LIENS.

ARTICLE II.

CREATION OF LIENS.

ARTICLE III.

EFFECT OF LIENS.

ARTICLE IV.

PRIORITY OF LIENS.

ARTICLE V.

REDEMPTION FROM LIEN.

ARTICLE VI.

EXTINCTION OF LIENS.

CHAPTER II.

MORTGAGE.

ARTICLE I.

MORTGAGES IN GENERAL.

ARTICLE II.

MORTGAGE OF REAL PROPERTY.

ARTICLE III.

MORTGAGE OF PERSONAL PROPERTY.

CHAPTER III.

PLEDGE.

CHAPTER IV.

BOTTOMRY.

CHAPTER V.

RESPONDENTIA.

CHAPTER VI.

OTHER LIENS.

CHAPTER VII.

STOPPAGE IN TRANSIT.

TITLE XV.

NEGOTIABLE INSTRUMENTS.

CHAPTER I.

NEGOTIABLE INSTRUMENTS IN GENERAL.

ARTICLE I.

GENERAL DEFINITIONS.

ARTICLE II.

INTERPRETATION OF NEGOTIABLE INSTRUMENTS.

ARTICLE III.

INDORSEMENT.

ARTICLE IV.

PRESENTMENT FOR PAYMENT.

ARTICLE V.

DISHONOR OF NEGOTIABLE INSTRUMENTS.

ARTICLE VI.

EXCUSE OF PRESENTMENT AND NOTICE.

ARTICLE VII.

EXTINCTION OF NEGOTIABLE INSTRUMENTS.

CHAPTER II.

BILLS OF EXCHANGE.

ARTICLE I.

FORM AND INTERPRETATION OF A BILL.

ARTICLE II.

DAYS OF GRACE.

ARTICLE III.

PRESENTMENT FOR ACCEPTANCE.

ARTICLE IV.

ACCEPTANCE.

ARTICLE V.

ACCEPTANCE OR PAYMENT FOR HONOR.

ARTICLE VI.

PRESENTMENT FOR PAYMENT.

ARTICLE VII.

EXCUSE OF PRESENTMENT AND NOTICE.

ARTICLE VIII.

FOREIGN BILLS.

CHAPTER III.

PROMISSORY NOTES.

CHAPTER IV.

CHEQUES.

CHAPTER V.

BONDS, BANK NOTES AND CERTIFICATES OF DEPOSIT.

TITLE XVI.

GENERAL PROVISIONS.

DIVISION FOURTH.

GENERAL PROVISIONS

APPLICABLE TO PERSONS, PROPERTY, AND OBLIGATIONS, OR TO TWO OF THOSE SUBJECTS.

PART I.

RELIEF.

TITLE I.

RELIEF IN GENERAL.

TITLE II.

COMPENSATORY RELIEF.

CHAPTER I.

DAMAGES IN GENERAL.

ARTICLE I.

GENERAL PRINCIPLES.

ARTICLE II.

INTEREST AS DAMAGES.

ARTICLE III.

EXEMPLARY DAMAGES.

CHAPTER II.

MEASURE OF DAMAGES.

ARTICLE I.

DAMAGES FOR BREACH OF CONTRACT.

ARTICLE II.

DAMAGES FOR WRONGS.

ARTICLE III.

PENAL DAMAGES.

ARTICLE IV.

GENERAL PROVISIONS.

TITLE III.

SPECIFIC AND PREVENTIVE RELIEF.

CHAPTER I.

GENERAL PRINCIPLES.

CHAPTER II.

SPECIAL RELIEF.

ARTICLE I.

POSSESSION OF REAL PROPERTY.

ARTICLE II.

POSSESSION OF PERSONAL PROPERTY.

ARTICLE III.

SPECIFIC PERFORMANCE OF OBLIGATIONS.

ARTICLE IV.

REVISION OF CONTRACTS.

ARTICLE V.

RESCISSION OF CONTRACTS.

ARTICLE VI.

CANCELLATION OF INSTRUMENTS.

CHAPTER III.

PREVENTIVE RELIEF.

PART II.

SPECIAL RELATIONS OF DEBTOR AND CREDITOR.

TITLE I.

GENERAL PRINCIPLES.

TITLE II.

FRAUDULENT INSTRUMENTS AND TRANSFERS.

TITLE III.

ASSIGNMENTS FOR THE BENEFIT OF CREDITORS.

PART III.

NUISANCE.

TITLE I.

GENERAL PRINCIPLES.

TITLE II.

PUBLIC NUISANCES.

TITLE III.

PRIVATE NUISANCES.

PART IV.

MAXIMS OF JURISPRUDENCE.

PART V.

DEFINITIONS AND GENERAL PROVISIONS.

THE

CIVIL CODE

OF THE

STATE OF NEW YORK.

AN ACT TO ESTABLISH A CIVIL CODE.

The People of the State of New York, represented in Senate and Assembly, do enact as follows:

GENERAL DEFINITIONS AND DIVISIONS.

SECTION 1. This act shall be known as the CIVIL CODE OF THE STATE OF NEW YORK. Title of Code.

§ 2. Law is a rule of property and of conduct prescribed by the sovereign power of the state. Definition of law.

§ 3. The will of the sovereign power is expressed: Action of sovereign power.

1. By the constitution, which is the organic act of the people;

2. By statutes, which are the acts of the Legislature, or by the ordinances of other and subordinate legislative bodies;

3. By the judgments of the tribunals enforcing those rules which, though not enacted, form what is known as customary or common law.

Two kinds of law.

§ 4. The common law is divided into:

1. Public law, or the law of nations;

2. Domestic, or municipal law.

Common law.

§ 5. The evidence of the common law is found in the decisions of the tribunals.

Id.

§ 6. In this state there is no common law in any case where the law is declared by the five CODES.

Two kinds of civil rights.

§ 7. All original civil rights are either:

1. Rights of person; or,

2. Rights of property.

Rights, how modified.

§ 8. Rights of property and of person may be waived,[1] surrendered or lost by neglect, in the cases provided by law.

[1] Conkling *v.* King, 10 *N. Y.*, 440.

Divisions of the Civil Code.

§ 9. This CODE has four general divisions:

1. The first relates to Persons;

2. The second to Property;

3. The third to Obligations;

4. The fourth contains General Provisions relating to Persons, Property and Obligations.

DIVISION FIRST.

PERSONS.

PART I.

PERSONS.

§ 10. A minor is a person under the age of twenty-one years. Definition of a minor.

§ 11. All other persons are adults. Definition of an adult.

Unborn child.

§ 12. A child conceived, but not yet born, is to be deemed an existing person, so far as may be necessary for its interests in the event of its subsequent birth.

Marsellis *v.* Thalheimer, 2 *Paige*, 35; Jenkins *v.* Freyer, 4 *id.*, 47; Hone *v.* Van Schaick, 3 *Barb. Ch.*, 488.

Persons of unsound mind.

§ 13. Persons of unsound mind, within the meaning of this CODE, are idiots, lunatics, imbeciles and habitual drunkards.

Custody of minors, &c.

§ 14. The custody of minors and persons of unsound mind is regulated by Part III of this Division.

Powers of minors.

§ 15. A minor cannot give a delegation of power.

Bennet *v.* Davis, 6 *Cow.*, 393. Such a delegation is not merely voidable, but absolutely void (See Bool *v.* Mix, 17 *Wend.*, 119). The propriety of this rule has, however, been seriously doubted (Whitney *v.* Dutch, 14 *Mass.*, 462).

Contracts of minors.

§ 16. A minor may make a conveyance or other contract in the same manner as any other person, subject only to his power of disaffirmance[1] under the provisions of this Title, and to the provisions of the Title on MARRIAGE.

[1] Palmer *v.* Miller, 25 *Barb.*, 399; Slocum *v.* Hooker, 13 *Barb.*, 536; Bool *v.* Mix, 17 *Wend.*, 119; Gillett *v.* Stanley, 1 *Hill*, 121; Van Nostrand *v.* Wright, *Hill & D. Supp.*, 260; Clark *v.* Levi, 10 *N. Y. Leg. Obs.*, 184. It has been doubted whether a minor who has a guardian, can make a contract (Stafford *v.* Roof, 9 *Cow.*, 626, 630; Kline *v.* L'Amoureux, 2 *Paige*, 419); but it seems now to be settled that he can (Bartholemew *v.* Finnemore, 17 *Barb.*, 428).

When minor may disaffirm.

§ 17. In all cases[1] other than those specified by sections 18 and 19, the contract of a minor may, upon restoring the consideration[2] to the party from whom it was received, be disaffirmed by the minor himself, either before his majority,[3] or within a reasonable time afterwards,[4] or, in case of his death within that period, by his heirs or personal representatives.[5]

[1] Conroe *v.* Birdsall, 1 *Johns. Cas.*, 127; Brown *v.* M'Cune, 5 *Sandf.*, 224; Merriam *v.* Cunningham, 11 *Cushing*, 40.

[2] Bartholomew *v.* Finnemore, 17 *Barb.*, 428.

[3] By the existing law he cannot in all cases conclusively disaffirm his conveyance of real property before he comes of age (Bool *v.* Mix, 17 *Wend.*, 119, 132, 134).

[4] Tafft *v.* Sergeant, 18 *Barb.*, 320.

[5] *Bac. Abr.*, Infant, I, 6; 8 *Co.*, 42 *b*.

Cannot disaffirm contract for necessaries.

§ 18. A minor, or a person of unsound mind of whatever degree,[1] cannot disaffirm a contract, otherwise valid, to pay the reasonable value of things necessary for his support,[2] or for that of his family,[3] entered into by him when not under the care of a parent[4] or guardian[5] able to provide for him.

[1] Ingraham *v.* Baldwin, 9 *N. Y.*, 45.

[2] Smith *v.* Oliphant, 2 *Sandf.*, 306; Randall *v.* Sweet, 1 *Den.*, 460.

[3] Turner *v.* Frisby, *Strange*, 168.

[4] Wailing *v.* Toll, 9 *Johns.*, 141.

[5] Kline *v.* L'Amoureux, 2 *Paige*, 419.

Nor certain obligations.

§ 19. A minor cannot disaffirm an obligation, otherwise valid, entered into by him under the express authority or direction of a statute.

This is intended to provide for such cases as the execution of a bond in bastardy proceedings, or a voluntary assignment under the statute relating to the imprisonment of insolvent debtors, or an enlistment, or articles of apprenticeship.

Contracts of persons without understanding.

§ 20. A person entirely without understanding has no power to contract, except in the case mentioned in section 18, unless expressly authorized by statute.

See Jackson *v.* King, 4 *Cow.*, 207.

Contracts of other insane persons.

§ 21. A person of unsound mind, but not entirely without understanding, may make a conveyance or other contract, before his incapacity has been judicially determined, subject to rescission, as provided in the chapter on Rescission.

Jackson *v.* King, 4 *Cow.*, 207; Person *v.* Warren, 14 *Barb.*, 488; Odell *v.* Buck, 21 *Wend.*, 142. Thus a mortgage by a lunatic is at most voidable (Ingraham *v.* Baldwin, 9 *N. Y.*, 45; 12 *Barb.*, 9). The mere existence of lunacy does not revoke a power (Wallis *v.* Manhattan Co., 2 *Hall*, 495). Compare, however, the proposed change in the law of Agency. As to the cases in which such a contract should be set aside, see Sprague *v.* Duel (11 *Paige*, 480); Loomis *v.* Spencer (2 *id.*, 153).

Powers of persons whose incapacity has been adjudged.

§ 22. After his incapacity has been judicially determined, a person of unsound mind can make no conveyance or other contract, nor delegate any power, nor waive any right, until his restoration to capacity is judicially determined. But if actually restored to capacity, he may make a will, though his restoration is not thus determined.

See 1 *R. S.*, 719, § 10; Fitzhugh *v.* Wilcox, 12 *Barb.* 235.

Wrongs.

§ 23. A minor,[1] or a person of unsound mind, of whatever degree,[2] is liable for a wrong done by him, in like manner with any other person.

[1] Fish *v.* Ferris, 5 *Duer*, 49; Campbell *v.* Stakes, 2 *Wend.*, 139; Hartfield *v.* Roper, 21 *id.*, 615; Green *v.* Burke, 23 *id.*, 490; Bullock *v.* Babcock, 3 *id.*, 391; Wallace *v.* Morss, 5 *Hill*, 391; Conklin *v.* Thompson, 29 *Barb.*, 218; Burnard *v.* Haggis, 14 *C. B.* [*N. S.*], 45.

Krom *v.* Schoonmaker, 3 *Barb.*, 647; see Williams *v.* Cameron, 26 *id.*, 172.

Id.

§ 24. A minor, or person of unsound mind, cannot be subjected to exemplary damages, unless at the time of the act he was capable of knowing that it was wrongful.

Krom *v.* Schoonmaker, 3 *Barb.* 647.

Minors may enforce their rights.

§ 25. A minor may enforce his rights by civil action, or other legal proceedings, in the same manner as a person of full age, except that a guardian must be appointed to conduct the same.

2 *R. S.*, 445, § 1.

§ 26. Indians resident within this state have the same rights and duties as other persons;[1] except that: Indians.

1. They cannot vote or hold office; and that,

2. They cannot grant, lease, or incumber Indian lands, except in the cases provided by special laws.[2]

[1] The course of legislation and of decision, following the modifications which time has made in the actual condition of the Indians, is such that, by the act of 1843, Indians are authorized to purchase, hold and convey lands; and such as become freeholders to the value of $100, are liable on contracts and to taxation and the jurisdiction of the courts, as if citizens. There seems to be no sufficient reason why a simple general provision like that here proposed, should not now be adopted.

[2] Lee *v.* Glover, 8 *Cow.*, 189; St. Regis Indians *v.* Drum, 19 *Johns.*, 127; Jackson *v.* Wood, 7 *id.*, 290; Chandler *v.* Edson, 9 *id.*, 362.

PART II.

PERSONAL RIGHTS.

§ 27. Besides the personal rights mentioned or recognized in the POLITICAL CODE, every person has, subject to the qualifications and restrictions provided by law, the right of protection from bodily restraint or harm, from personal insult, from defamation, and from injury to his personal relations. General personal rights.

There is no doubt that persistent public insults, *e. g.*, continually shouting at a person in the street, or even silently dogging him, are personal injuries, against which he ought to be protected. Why is not an act which the law admits *almost* to justify, certainly to mitigate, the crime of assault and battery, sufficient foundation for a civil action? Compare Adams *v.* Rivers, 11 *Barb.*, 390, where an action for use of insulting words, by one standing in the highway in front of plaintiff's land, was sustained on the ground of the trespass involved in standing in the highway after being ordered to depart, for the malicious purpose evinced.

§ 28. Defamation is effected by: Defamation, what.

1. Libel; or,

2. Slander.

In all definitions of libel or slander at common law, malice is treated as a necessary ingredient. But in the absence of a proper notice for the publication, malice is conclusively presumed, and the publisher of a libel is responsible, although clearly free ,from actual malice

(Hunt *v.* Bennett, 19 *N. Y.*, 173; Lewis *v.* Chapman, 16 *id.*, 369.) In the definitions of both classes of defamation, therefore, the commissioners omit the ingredient of malice, and consequently the rules concerning presumption of malice.

Libel, what.

§ 29. Libel is a false and unprivileged publication by writing, printing, picture, effigy or other fixed representation to the eye, which exposes any person to hatred, contempt, ridicule or obloquy, or which causes him to be shunned or avoided, or which has a tendency to injure him in his occupation.

2 *Kent Com.*, 17; Stone *v.* Cooper, 2 *Den.*, 293; Cooper *v.* Greeley, 1 *id.*, 347; Steele *v.* Southwick, 9 *Johns.*, 214.

The law of libel has passed in the last hundred years from one extreme to another; from excessive severity to excessive laxity. The abuse of the freedom of the press, not only in the wantonness of its attacks upon public men, but in its assaults upon private citizens, has become so great, that a remedy for the evil must be sought, or violence will take the place of law. The license into which this freedom has degenerated leads, not only to the frequent invasion of private rights, but to the corruption of public morals. If the Commissioners had been certain of the true remedy, they would have proposed it in the text of the Code. They will venture only to suggest that a more certain punishment for wanton or careless defamation being needed, a remedy may perhaps be found in affixing to it a penalty, to be recovered in every civil action for libel, in addition to the damages which the jury may find. This would, at least, render it unsafe for libellers to rely upon the caprice or prejudice of juries as the means of escape with nominal damages. Requiring the name of the writer to be signed to every personal article, might also have a salutary effect. If the Legislature should think these provisions desirable, two sections like the following would auswer the purpose:

§ . Any article published in a newspaper containing matter which would be libellous if it were false, must be signed by the writer, and his name must be published at the foot of the article. A violation of this section is a misdemeanor.

§ . In every civil action for libel, if the plaintiff recovers a verdict, he shall be entitled to judgment against the defendant for dollars, as a penalty, in addition to the damages found by the jury, and the costs of the action.

§ 30. Slander is a false and unprivileged publication, other than libel, which: Slander, what.

1. Charges any person with crime, or with having been indicted, convicted or punished for crime;[1]

2. Imputes in him the present existence of an infectious, contagious or loathsome disease;[2]

3. Tends directly to injure him in respect to his office, profession, trade or business, either by imputing to him general disqualification in those respects which the office or other occupation peculiarly requires, or by imputing something with reference to his office, profession, trade or business that has a natural tendency to lessen its profit;

4. Imputes to him impotence or a want of chastity;[3] or,

5. Which, by natural consequence, causes actual damage.

[1] This definition is possibly a little broader than the language of the decisions (see Young *v.* Miller, 3 *Hill*, 21; Smith *v.* Stewart, 5 *Penn. St.*, 372). But the definition of a "crime" in the Penal Code removes all the grounds of distinction in the decisions.

[2] Williams *v.* Holdredge, 22 *Barb.*, 376.

[3] This provision is new. The House of Lords, in a recent case, condemned the common law in this respect as "barbarous" (Lynch *v.* Knight, 9 *H. L. Cas.*, 577).

§ 31. A privileged publication is one made: What communications are privileged.

1. In the proper discharge of an official duty;

2. In testifying as a witness, in any proceeding authorized by law, to a matter pertinent and material,[1] or in reply to a question allowed by the tribunal;

3. In a communication, without malice, to a person interested therein, by one who was also interested, or who stood in such a relation to the former as to afford a reasonable ground for supposing his motive

innocent, or who was requested by him to give the information;[2] or,

4. By a fair and true report in a newspaper, without malice, of a judicial, legislative or other public official proceeding, or of anything said in the course thereof.[3]

[1] Perkins *v.* Mitchell, 31 *Barb.*, 461; see 4 *H. & N.*, 569.

[2] Lewis *v.* Chapman, 16 *N. Y.*, 369.

[3] *Laws* 1854, *ch.* 130.

Protection to personal relations.

§ 32. The rights of personal relation forbid:

1. The abduction of a husband from his wife, or of a parent from his child;[1]

2. The abduction or enticement of a wife from her husband,[2] of a child from a parent, or from a guardian entitled to its custody,[3] or of a servant from his master;[4]

3. The seduction of a wife, daughter, orphan sister, or servant;[5] and,

4. Any injury to a servant, which affects his ability to serve his master.[6]

[1] Perhaps this provision is new, and doubtless as a matter of fact it would rarely be taken advantage of. Nevertheless, the injury is a very great one, and one, unhappily, not entirely unknown.

[2] Bennett *v.* Smith, 21 *Barb.*, 439; Scherpf *v.* Sczadeczky, 4 *E. D. Smith*, 110.

[3] See People *v.* Olmstead, 27 *Barb.*, 9.

[4] Lumley *v.* Gye, 2 *Ell. & Bl.*, 216.

[5] This provision is new, as to the sister and daughter (Dain *v.* Wyckoff, 7 *N. Y.*, 191). 'The legal fiction, by which the action of seduction has long been sustained, has always been considered too narrow for the purposes of justice.

[6] Woodward *v.* Washburn, 3 *Den.*, 369; Martinez *v.* Gerber, 3 *M. & G.*, 88.

Right to use force.

§ 33. Any necessary force may be used to protect from wrongful injury the person[1] or property[2] of oneself, or of a wife, husband, child, parent or other relative to the third degree, a ward, servant or master.

[1] *Rol. Abr.*, Trespass, D.; Leeward *v.* Basilee, 1 *Salk.*, 407; Seaman *v.* Cuppledick, *Owen*, 150.

[2] Blades *v.* Higgs, 10 *C. B.* (*N. S.*), 713.

PART III.

PERSONAL RELATIONS.

TITLE I.

MARRIAGE.

CHAPTER I.

THE CONTRACT OF MARRIAGE.

ARTICLE I.

VALIDITY.

Definition of marriage.

§ 34. Marriage is a personal relation, arising out of a civil contract, to which the consent of parties capable of making it is alone necessary.

By 2 R. S., 138, § 1, marriage is declared to be a civil contract to which consent is necessary; but whether anything more than consent is necessary has been mooted; some authorities deeming that either consummation or solemnization is also requisite (Jaques *v.* Public Administrator, 1 *Bradf.*, 499; and see 2 *Parsons on Contracts, 5th ed.*, 74). This provision makes consent alone sufficient, and is in accordance with the views declared in Starr *v.* Peck, 1 *Hill*, 270; Jackson *v.* Winne, 7 *Wend.*, 47; Caujolle *v.* Ferrie, 23 *N. Y.*, 106; Hayes *v.* People, 25 *N. Y.*, 390.

Consent, how proved.

§ 35. Consent to a marriage may be manifested in any form, and may be proved like any other fact.

Starr *v.* Peck, 1 *Hill*, 270; Clayton *v.* Wardell, 4 *N. Y.*, 230.

Persons capable of marriage.

§ 36. Any unmarried male of the age of fourteen years or upwards, and any unmarried female of the age of twelve years or upwards, and not otherwise disqualified, is capable of consenting to marriage; subject, however, to the provisions of section 54 of this Code.

Bennett *v.* Smith, 21 *Barb.*, 439. The reference is to the provision below, allowing a divorce where a female is married under fourteen against consent of parent or guardian.

Consent must be given to a present marriage.

§ 37. The consent to a marriage must be to one commencing instantly, and not to an agreement to marry afterwards.

Cheney *v.* Arnold, 15 *N. Y.*, 345.

Certain marriages incestuous.

§ 38. Marriages between parents and children, ancestors and descendants of every degree, and between brothers and sisters of the half as well as of the whole blood, are incestuous, and void from the beginning; whether the relationship is legitimate or illegitimate.

2 *R. S.*, 139, § 3.

Certain marriages when to be deemed void.

§ 39. If either party to a marriage is incapable of consent for want of age or understanding, or is incapable, from physical causes, of entering into the marriage state, or if the consent of either is obtained by fraud or force, the marriage is void from the time its nullity is adjudged by a competent tribunal.

§ 40. A subsequent marriage contracted by any person during the life of a former husband or wife of such person, with any person other than such former husband or wife,[1] is illegal and void from the beginning, unless: Polygamy forbidden.

1. The former marriage had been annulled or dissolved for some cause other than the adultery of such person; or,

2. Unless such former husband or wife had been finally sentenced to imprisonment for life; or,

3. Unless such former husband or wife was absent, and not known to such person to be living, for the space of five successive years immediately preceding such subsequent marriage; in which case the subsequent marriage is void only from the time its nullity is adjudged by a competent tribunal.[2]

[1] This exception is new.

[2] 2 *R. S.*, 139, §§ 5, 6. The language of subdivision 3 has been modified to make it appropriate to the retrospective effect given to section 6, by the construction adopted by the Court of Appeals in Bowers *v.* Brower, 9 *N. Y. Leg. Obs.*, 196.

§ 41. No pardon granted after the twelfth day of April, one thousand eight hundred and twenty-two, to any person sentenced to imprisonment for life in this state, restores such person to the rights of any previous marriage, or to the guardianship of any issue of such marriage. Conjugal rights, &c., not restored by pardon.

2 *R. S.*, 139, § 7.

§ 42. Indians contracting marriage according to the Indian custom, and cohabiting as husband and wife, are lawfully married. Marriages of Indians.

Laws 1849, *ch.* 420, § 4.

Certain parts of Code not applicable.

§ 43. The provisions of other portions of this Code in relation to contracts and the capacity of persons to enter into them, have no application to the contract of marriage.

Promise of marriage.

§ 44. A promise of marriage is subject to the same rules as contracts in general, except that neither party is bound by a promise made in ignorance of the other's want of personal chastity,[1] and that either is released therefrom by unchaste conduct on the part of the other.[2]

[1] See Beachey *v.* Brown, *El. Bl. & E.*, 976; Baker *v.* Cartwright, 10 *C. B.* [*N. S.*], 124.

[2] Palmer *v.* Andrews, 7 *Wend.*, 142.

ARTICLE II.

AUTHENTICATION.

Mode of authenticating marriages.

§ 45. For the purpose of authentication, according to the provisions of this article, a marriage must be solemnized in this state, in the manner herein prescribed, by one or more of the following persons, namely: Ministers of the gospel or priests of any denomination; mayors, recorders or aldermen of cities; judges of the county courts or justices of the peace; and, in case of Indians, also the peacemakers acting within their respective jurisdictions.

2 *R. S.*, 139, § 8; applied to Indians by *Laws of* 1849, *ch.* 420, § 4.

In 2 *Kent's Com.*, 89, note, it is said that these provisions of the Revised Statutes are not law, because by the act of 1830, which declared that marriages contracted without this form of solemnization should be valid, they no longer are required to be obeyed. They are here embodied, however, for the obvious reason that, though solemnization is not compulsory, it is optional, and the form prescribed may be and constantly is resorted to, for the sake of the convenient authentication of the contract which it affords.

§ 46. No particular form is required upon a marriage, but the parties must solemnly declare, in the presence of the person solemnizing the marriage, and of at least one witness, that they take each other as husband and wife. *Form of marriage.*

2 *R. S.*, 139, § 9.

§ 47. The person solemnizing a marriage must ascertain, to his satisfaction: *Duties of the officer before whom a marriage is solemnized.*

1. The identity of the parties;

2. Their real and full names, and places of residence;

3. That they are of sufficient age to be capable of contracting marriage; and,

4. The name and place of residence of the witness, or of two witnesses, if more than one is present.

2 *R. S.*, 140, § 10.

§ 48. The person solemnizing a marriage must enter the facts ascertained by him pursuant to the last section, and the date of the solemnization, in a book to be kept by him for that purpose. *Id.*

2 *R. S.*, 140, § 11.

§ 49. The person solemnizing a marriage must furnish to either party, on request, a certificate thereof, signed by him, specifying: *Certificate to be given to either contracting party, if desired*

1. The names and places of residence of the parties married:

2. That they were known to him, or were satisfactorily proved, by the oath of a person known to him, to be the persons described in such certificate:

3. That he had ascertained that they were of sufficient age to contract marriage;

4. The name and place of residence of the attesting witness or of two witnesses;

5. The time and place of such marriage; and,

6. That, after due inquiry made, there appeared to be no lawful impediment to such marriage.

2 *R. S.*, 140, § 13.

The certificate. § 50. The certificate mentioned in the last section may, within six months after the marriage, be filed with the clerk of the city or town where the marriage was solemnized, or where either of the parties reside, and when thus filed, must be entered in a book to be provided by the clerk, in the alphabetical order of the name of each party, and in the order of time in which it is filed.

The entry thereof. § 51. The entry required by the last section must specify:

1. The name and place of residence of each party;

2. The time and place of marriage;

3. The name and official station of the person signing the certificate; and,

4. The time when the certificate was filed.

Authentication of the certificate. § 52. If a certificate of marriage is signed by a minister or priest, there must be indorsed or annexed, before filing, a certificate of a magistrate residing in the same county with the clerk, that the person by whom it is signed is personally known to such magistrate, and has acknowledged the execution of the certificate in his presence; or, that the execution of the certificate, by a minister or priest of some religious denomination, has been proved to the magistrate, by the oath of a person known to him, and who saw the certificate executed.

2 *R. S.*, 141, §§ 14–16.

Certificate, entry, &c., evidence. § 53. A certificate of marriage, or the entry thereof, made as above directed, or a copy of the certificate or entry, duly certified, is presumptive evidence of the fact of the marriage.

2 *R. S.*, 141, § 17.

CHAPTER II.

DIVORCE.

The provisions of this chapter have been modified from those of the Revised Statutes, with a view to produce conformity with the present procedure, and to establish the rule that in one action between husband and wife, in which a judgment of nullity or a dissolution of marriage or separation is sought, the whole controversy may be passed on and settled; and for this purpose to allow a defendant to interpose a demand for affirmative relief, asking a divorce or separation against the plaintiff, instead of requiring cross actions.

ARTICLE I.

NULLITY.

§ 54. A marriage may be annulled for any of the following causes, existing at the time of the marriage:[1] Cases where marriages may be annulled.

1. That the party seeking to have the marriage annulled was under the age of legal consent;[2] unless, after attaining the age of consent, such party for any time freely cohabited with the other as husband or wife;[3]

2. That the former husband or wife of either party was living, and the marriage with such former husband or wife was then in force;[4]

3. That the wife was under the age of fourteen years, and that the marriage was without the con-

sent of the person having the legal charge of her person, and was a punishable offense on the part of the husband, and has not been followed by cohabitation, nor ratified by any mutual assent of the parties since the wife attained the age of fourteen years;[5]

4. That either party was of unsound mind;[6] unless such party, after coming to reason, freely cohabited with the other as husband or wife;[7]

5. That the consent of either party was obtained by fraud, unless such party afterwards, with full knowledge of the facts constituting the fraud, freely cohabited with the other as husband or wife;[8]

6. That the consent of either party was obtained by force,[9] unless such party afterwards freely cohabited with the other as husband or wife;[10] or,

7. That either party was, at the time of marriage, physically incapable of entering into the married state;[11] and such incapacity continues, and appears to be incurable.[12]

[1] 2 *R. S.*, 142, § 20.
[2] *Id.*
[3] *Id.*, § 21.
[4] *Id.*, § 20.
[5] *Laws of* 1841, *ch.* 257; 3 *R. S.* (*5th ed.*), 233, § 34.
[6] 2 *R. S.*, 142, § 20.
[7] *Id.*, 143, § 27.
[8] *Laws of* 1862, *ch.* 246.
[9] 2 *R. S.*, 142, § 20.
[10] *Id.*, 143, § 31.
[11] 2 *R. S.*, 142, § 20.
[12] New, but in accordance with the decisions in Devanbagh v. Devanbagh, 5 *Paige*, 554; 6 *id.*, 175.

Application for a decision of nullity.

§ 55. Within the time limited by law for the commencement of actions, application to annul a marriage may be made:

1. If for the cause that a former husband or wife was living; by either party during the life of the other, or by such former husband or wife;

2. If for the cause of idiocy; by any relative of

the idiot, interested to avoid the marriage, during the life of either party;

3. If for the cause of insanity other than idiocy; by any relative of the insane party interested to avoid the marriage, and at any time during such insanity, or after the death of the insane party in that condition, and during the life of the other party; or by the insane party after the restoration of reason;

4. If for the cause of fraud or force; by the injured party, or the parent or guardian of such party, or a relative of such party interested to avoid the marriage, during the life of either party;

5. If no application has been made by the party or a relative, application may be made in any of the foregoing cases, at any time during the life of both parties, by a guardian of the insane or injured party, appointed by the court for the purpose;

6. If for the cause of physical incapacity; application can only be made by the injured party against the incapacitated party, and in all cases must be made within two years from the time of contracting the marriage;

7. If for the cause specified in subdivision 3 of section 54, by the wife only.

2 *R. S.*, 142, §§ 22, 24, 27, 30, 33.

2 *R. S.*, 144, § 36, should be inserted in the Code of Civil Procedure.

The words "within the time limited by law" have been inserted in accordance with the construction put upon a similar provision (§ 30), in Montgomery *v.* Montgomery, 3 *Barb. Ch.*, 132, where it was held that the intent of the reference to the lifetime of the parties, was to prohibit the annulling of the marriage after the death of the parties, but not to extend the limitation to any period within the lifetime of the other.

§ 56. Where a marriage is annulled on the ground that a former husband or wife was living, and it is adjudged that the subsequent marriage was contracted in good faith, and with the full belief of the parties

Children of annulled marriage.

that the former husband or wife was dead, or where a marriage is annulled on the ground of insanity, children begotten before the judgment must be specified in the judgment, and are entitled to succeed in the same manner as legitimate children to the estate of the parent, who, at the time of the marriage, was competent to contract.

2 *R. S.*, 142, §§ 23, 28.

Custody of children.

§ 57. The court must award the custody of the children of a marriage annulled on the ground of fraud or force, to the innocent parent, and may also provide for their education and maintenance out of the property of the guilty party.

2 *R. S.*, 142, § 32.

Effect of judgment of nullity.

§ 58. A judgment of nullity of marriage rendered during the life of the parties, is conclusive evidence of nullity; but if rendered after the death of either party to the marriage, it is conclusive only as against the parties to the action, and those claiming under them.

2 *R. S.*, 144, § 37.

ARTICLE II.

DISSOLUTION.

Marriage, how dissolved.

§ 59. Marriage is dissolved:

1. By the death or sentence to imprisonment for life of either of the parties; or

2. By the judgment of a competent tribunal.

Divorce for adultery.

§ 60. The dissolution of a marriage may be adjudged, whenever adultery has been committed by husband or wife, in any of the following cases:

1. Where both husband and wife were actual inhabitants of this state at the time of the commission of the adultery;

2. Where the marriage took place within this state;[1]

3. Where the injured party, at the time of the commission of the adultery, and at the commencement of the action, was an actual inhabitant of this state;[2]

4. Where the adultery was committed in this state, and the injured party, at the commencement of the action, was an actual inhabitant of this state.[1]

[1] 2 *R. S.*, 144, § 38; modified by substituting "took place" for "was contracted or solemnized," and the word "inhabitant" for "resident," wherever the latter occurs.

[2] *Laws of* 1862, 446, *ch.* 246.

§ 61. Although the fact of adultery is established, a judgment of divorce may be denied: Cases in which divorce for adultery is denied.

1. Where the application for divorce was not made within five years after the discovery by the applicant of the adultery charged;

2. Where the adultery appears to have been committed by the procurement, or with the connivance of the party asking the divorce;[1]

3. Where the injured party has expressly forgiven the adultery charged, or has voluntarily cohabited with the guilty party as husband or wife, with full knowledge of the fact; and has ever since been treated by the latter party with conjugal kindness;[2] or,

4. Where it appears that the applicant has also been guilty of adultery,[3] without the procurement or connivance of the other party.[4]

[1] 2 *R. S.*, 145, § 42, subds. 1, 2.

[2] Modified from 2 *R. S.*, 142. See *Bish. Mar. and Div.*, § 57; Johnson *v.* Johnson, 14 *Wend.*, 637; 4 *Paige*, 640; Hoffmire *v.* Hoffmire, 7 *Paige*, 660.

[3] 2 *R. S.*, 145, § 42, subd. 4.

[4] These words are substituted for "under such circumstances as would have entitled the other party, if innocent, to a divorce," in accordance with the opinion in Leseuer *v.* Leseuer, 31 *Barb.*, 330; see Morrell *v.* Morrell, 3 *id.*, 236, 241; doubting S. C., 1 *id.*, 318.

Legitimacy of issue.

§ 62. When a divorce is granted for the adultery of the husband, the legitimacy of children of the marriage, begotten of the wife before the commencement of the action, is not affected.

Id.

§ 63. When a divorce is granted for the adultery of the wife, the legitimacy of children begotten of her before the commission of the adultery is not affected; but the legitimacy of other children of the wife may be determined by the court, upon the evidence in the case. In every such case all children, begotten before the commencement of the action, are to be presumed legitimate until the contrary is shown.

2 *R. S.*, 145, §§ 43, 44.

When re-marriage is forbidden.

§ 64. When a divorce is granted for adultery, the innocent party may marry again during the life of the other; but the guilty party cannot marry any person except the innocent party, until the death of the other.

2 *R. S.*, 146, § 49, modified by the exception. Several other provisions of the Revised Statutes, in respect to the effect of the judgment on the rights of property of the parties, are omitted as being superseded by other provisions of this Code.

Should the last clause be retained? After much discussion, it was abandoned in England. Its operation in this state is much less a punishment of the guilty than a trap for the innocent (See Cropsey *v.* Sweeney, 27 *Barb.*, 310; 7 *Abb. Pr.*, 129).

ARTICLE III.

SEPARATION.

When separation may be adjudged

§ 65. A separation of husband and wife from bed and board, for life or for a limited time, may be adjudged for the causes mentioned in the next section[1]:

1. When the husband and wife are both actual inhabitants of this state;

2. When the marriage took place[2] within this state, and the applicant is an actual inhabitant[3] at the time of the application; or,

3. When the marriage did not take place within this state,[3] but the parties have since been[4] actual inhabitants of this state for at least one year, and the applicant is an actual inhabitant at the time of the application.

[1] 2 *R. S.*, 146, § 50. The restriction of this provision to applications by the wife for relief against the husband has been omitted. This is doubtless the just rule, and probably it does not change the existing law (*Laws of* 1824, *ch.* 205, § 12; Perry *v.* Perry, 2 *Paige*, 501; 2 *Barb. Ch.*, 311).

[2] The words "took place" are substituted for "contracted or solemnized," for the reason that the latter words might be construed as including a marriage contracted and consummated out of the state, but celebrated publicly for the first time in this state.

[3] The statute uses the word "resident" here, for which the commissioners substitute "inhabitant" for the sake of uniformity.

[3] The present statute is a little ambiguous on this point. The commissioners have expressed more clearly what they suppose to be its actual meaning, as it stands. "Since been" substituted for "become and remained," as more accurately expressing the meaning of the statute.

§ 66. A separation of husband and wife may be adjudged for any of the following causes: Causes for separation.

1. Cruel treatment of one party by the other;

2. Conduct on the part of one towards the other, rendering cohabitation unsafe or improper; or,

3. Abandonment, accompanied by[1] refusal to fulfill the obligations of husband or wife, as they are prescribed by the chapter on HUSBAND and WIFE.[2]

[1] Ahrenfeldt *v.* Ahrenfeldt, *Hoffm.*, 47.

[2] 2 *R. S.*, 147, § 51; see notes to the last section.

When denied.

§ 67. Notwithstanding the existence of a cause for separation as declared in section 66, a judgment of separation may be denied, when it appears that the applicant has been guilty of a cause of divorce.

2 *R. S.*, 147, § 53.

Relief may be adjudged in some cases where separation is denied.

§ 68. Though judgment of separation be denied, the court may, in an action for divorce, provide for the maintenance of the wife and her children, or any of them by the husband, or out of his property.

2 *R. S.*, 147, § 55; P—— *v.* P.——, 24 *How. Pr.*, 197.

Judgment of separation, when revoked.

§ 69. A judgment for separation, whether for life, or for a limited period, may be at any time revoked, under such regulations as the court may impose, upon the joint application of the parties, with satisfactory evidence of their reconciliation.

2 *R. S.*, 147, § 56.

ARTICLE IV.

GENERAL PROVISIONS.

Residence of wife.

§ 70. A wife who resides in this state at the time of applying for a divorce, under article II or III, is to be deemed an actual inhabitant, though her husband resides elsewhere.

2 *R. S.*, 147, § 57.

Expense of action.

§ 71. While an action for divorce is pending, the court may, in its discretion, require the husband to pay any money necessary to enable the wife to support herself or her children, or to prosecute or defend the action.

2 *R. S.*, 148, § 58. This provision is extended to the cases of actions to annul a marriage, in accordance with the decision in North *v.* North, 1 *Barb. Ch.*, 241; and amended by inserting the words "or her children."

§ 72. In an action for divorce, the court may, before or after judgment, give such direction for the custody, care and education of the children of the marriage, as may seem necessary or proper, and may at any time vacate or modify the same.

Orders respecting custody of children.

2 *R. S.*, 148, § 59.

§ 73. Where a divorce is granted for an offense of the husband, the court may compel him to provide for the maintenance of the children of the marriage, and to make such suitable allowance to the wife, for her support, during her life, or for a shorter period, as the court may deem just, having regard to the circumstances of the parties respectively; and the court may from time to time modify its orders in these respects.

Support of wife and children on divorce or separation granted to wife.

2 *R. S.*, 145, § 45; 147, § 54.

It has been questioned whether alimony can be granted to continue beyond the life of the husband. It was held in Burr *v.* Burr, 10 *Paige*, 20, 37, that it may.

§ 74. The court may require the husband to give reasonable security for providing maintenance, or making any payments required under the provisions of this chapter, and may enforce the same by the appointment of a receiver, or by any other remedy applicable to the case.

Security for maintenance and alimony.

2 *R. S.*, 148, § 60. Modified to conform to the practice under the Code of Procedure.

CHAPTER III.

HUSBAND AND WIFE.

The provisions of this chapter are intended to complete, so far as seems just and desirable, the removal of the disabilities of married women, and thus to simplify the law of this vexed subject.

Mutual obligations of husband and wife.

§ 75. Husband and wife contract towards each other obligations of mutual respect, fidelity and support.

Rights of husband as head of the family.

§ 76. The husband is the head of the family. He may choose any reasonable place or mode of living, and the wife must conform thereto.

Duties of husband to wife as to support.

§ 77. The husband must support himself and his wife out of his property or by his labor. If he is unable to do so, she must assist him so far as she is able.

In other respects their interests separate.

§ 78. Except as mentioned in section 77, neither husband nor wife has any interest in the property of the other, but neither can be excluded from the other's dwelling.

Husband and wife may make contracts.

§ 79. Either husband or wife may enter into any engagement or transaction with the other, or with any other person, respecting property, which either might if unmarried;[1] subject, in transactions between themselves, to the general rules which control the actions of persons occupying confidential relations with each other, as defined by the Title on TRUSTS.[2]

[1] This provision is new.

[2] See Jaques *v.* Methodist Ch., 17 *Johns.*, 548; Fry *v.* Fry, 7 *Paige*, 461.

§ 80. A husband and wife cannot by any contract with each other alter their legal relation, except that they may agree to an immediate separation, and may make provision for the support of either of them and of their children during such separation. How far may impair their legal relation.

Beach *v.* Beach, 2 *Hill*, 260; 1 *Sharsw. Black.*, 441, and note.

§ 81. The mutual consent of the parties is a sufficient consideration for such an agreement as is mentioned in the last section. Consideration.

A special consideration is now necessary to support such an agreement (Cropsey *v.* M'Kinney, 30 *Barb.*, 47).

§ 82. A husband and wife may hold real or personal property together, jointly or in common. May be joint-tenants, etc.

The contrary was held under the Acts of 1848 and 1849 in Goelet *v.* Gori, 31 *Barb.*, 314.

§ 83. Neither husband nor wife, as such, is answerable for the acts of the other. Neither answerable for the acts of the other.

This provision is new, but manifestly just, under the present state of the law.

§ 84. If the husband neglects[1] to make adequate provision for the support of his wife, any other person may, in good faith, supply her with articles necessary for her support, and recover the reasonable value thereof from the husband.[2] Support of wife.

[1] If the husband and wife separate by consent, and the husband, by agreement, secures to her a separate maintenance, suitable to their circumstances, he is not liable for anything furnished to her, so long as he performs such agreement (Calkins *v.* Long, 22 *Barb.*, 97, and cases there cited).

[2] Cromwell *v.* Benjamin, 41 *Barb.*, 558. This obligation is not founded merely upon a supposed agency of the wife (Read *v.* Legard, 6 *Exch.*, 636; see Sykes *v.* Halstead, 1 *Sandf.*, 483).

Abandonment of husband by the wife.

§ 85. If the wife abandons the husband, he is not liable for her support[1] until she offers to return,[2] unless she was justified, by his misconduct, in abandoning him.

[1] Blowers *v.* Sturtevant, 4 *Denio*, 46, and cases there cited.

[2] McGahay *v.* Williams, 12 *Johns.*, 293.

TITLE II.

PARENT AND CHILD.

CHAPTER I.

CHILDREN BY BIRTH.

§ 86. All children born in wedlock are presumed to be legitimate. *Legitimacy of children born in wedlock.*

Caujolle *v.* Ferrie, 23 *N. Y.*, 139.

§ 87. All children of a woman who has been married, born within ten months after the dissolution of the marriage, are presumed to be legitimate. But if during such period she marries again, and afterwards has a child, it is presumed to be her legitimate offspring by the second husband. *Legitimacy of children born out of wedlock*

§ 88. The presumption of legitimacy can be disputed only by the husband or wife, or the descendant of one or both of them. Illegitimacy, in such case, may be proved like any other fact. *Who may dispute the legitimacy of a child.*

§ 89. The parent entitled to the custody of a child must give him support and education suitable to his circumstances.[1] If the support and education which the father of a legitimate child is able to give are inadequate, the mother must assist him to the extent of her ability. *Obligation of parents for the support and education of their children.*

[1] At present the mother is released from this obligation, if indeed it exists at common law (see Raymond *v.* Loyl, 10 *Barb.*, 483; Pray *v.* Gorham, 31 *Me.*, 241; Tilton *v.* Russell, 11 *Ala.*, 497; Com. *v.* Murray, 4 *Binn.*, 487), by marrying again (Williams *v.* Hutchinson, 5 *Barb.*, 122; Wilkes *v.* Rogers, 6 *Johns.*, 576, 578, 593). This exception is inconsistent with the control now given to the wife over her own property.

§ 90. The father[1] of a legitimate unmarried minor is entitled to its custody, services and earnings;[2] but he cannot transfer such custody or services to any other person, except the mother, without her written consent, if she is living and capable of consent.[3] If the father is dead,[4] or is unable, or refuses to take the *Custody of legitimate child.*

same, or has abandoned his family, the mother is entitled thereto.[5]

[1] Cartlidge v. Cartlidge, 2 *Swabey & Tristram*, 567; People v. Humphrey, 24 *Barb.*, 521.

[2] Emery v. Kempton, 2 *Groy*, 257.

[3] *Laws of* 1862, 345, *ch.* 172, § 6.

[4] Regina v. Clarke, 7 *Ell. & Bl.*, 186; People v. Boice, 39 *Barb.*, 307.

[5] At present the mother's right of guardianship is terminated by her re-marriage, or by the child's attaining the age of fourteen (Williams v. Hutchinson, 5 *Barb.*, 122; 3 *N. Y.*, 321; Freto v. Brown, 4 *Mass.*, 675; Worcester v. Marchant, 14 *Pick.*, 512). This distinction is incompatible with the spirit of the statutes of 1848, 1860, and 1862, which have to a great extent released married women from the control of their husbands.

Custody of an illegitimate child.

§ 91. The mother of an illegitimate unmarried minor is entitled to its custody, services and earnings.

Allowance to parent.

§ 92. The supreme court may direct an allowance to be made to the parent of a child, out of its property, for its past[1] or future[2] support and education, on such conditions as may be proper,[3] whenever such direction is for its benefit.[4]

[1] Matter of Bostwick, 4 *Johns. Ch.*, 100; Matter of Kane, 2 *Barb. Ch.*, 375.

[2] Maberly v. Turton, 14 *Ves.*, 499; Simon v. Barber, 1 *Taml.*, 22.

[3] Wilkes v. Rogers, 6 *Johns.*, 577, 578.

[4] Matter of Burke, 4 *Sandf. Ch.*, 617.

Parent cannot control the property of child.

§ 93. The parent, as such, has no control over the property of the child.

Combs v. Jackson, 2 *Wend.*, 153; 7 *Cow.*, 36; Fonda v. Van Horne, 15 *Wend.*, 631; Hyde v. Stone, 7 *id.*, 354.

Remedy for parental abuse.

§ 94. The abuse of parental authority is the subject of judicial cognizance in a civil action brought by the child, or by its relative within the third degree, or by the supervisor of the town where the child resides; and when the abuse is established, the child may be freed from the dominion of the parent, the parent punished, and the duty of support and education enforced.

This provision is in part new.

§ 95. The authority of a parent ceases: When parental authority ceases.

1. Upon the appointment by a court of a guardian of the person of the child;

2. Upon the marriage of the child; or,

3. Upon its attaining majority.

§ 96. If a parent chargeable with the support of a child dies, leaving it chargeable to the town, and leaving an estate sufficient for its support, the supervisor of the town may claim provision for its support from the parent's estate by civil action, and for this purpose may have the same remedies as any creditor against that estate, and against the heirs, devisees and next of kin of the parent. Remedy when a parent dies without providing for the support of his child.

§ 97. It is the duty of the father, the mother, and the children, of any poor person who is unable to maintain himself by work, to maintain such person to the extent of their ability. The promise of an adult child to pay for necessaries previously furnished to such parent is binding. Reciprocal duties of parents and children in maintaining each other.

The provisions of the Poor Laws declare the duty of parents and children to support each other (1 *R. S.*, 614, § 1); but it is held that the obligation on the part of children is purely statutory, and no other remedy exists except that provided by proceedings under those laws (Edwards *v.* Davis, 16 *Johns.*, 281). It is the object of this section to recognize the obligation as a ground of legal liability independent of those provisions. On the part of parents, the obligation is not now merely statutory (Cromwell *v.* Benjamin, 41 *Barb.*, 558). But in England it has been so held (Shelton *v.* Springett, 11 *C. B.*, 452; Mortimore *v.* Wright, 6 *M.* & *W.*, 488).

§ 98. If a parent neglects to provide articles necessary for his child who is under his charge, according to his circumstances. a third person may in good faith When a parent is liable for necessaries supplied to a child.

supply such necessaries, and recover the reasonable value thereof from the parent.

Van Valkenburgh *v.* Watson, 13 *Johns.*, 480; Chilcott *v.* Trimble, 13 *Barb.*, 502; Clinton *v.* Rowland, 24 *id.*, 634; Henry *v.* Betts, 1 *Hilt.*, 156; and see Raymond *v.* Loyl, 10 *Barb.*, 483. The age of the child is immaterial (Cromwell *v.* Benjamin, 41 *Barb.*, 558).

When a parent is not liable for support furnished his child.

§ 99. A parent is not bound to compensate the other parent[1] or a relative[2] for the voluntary support of his child without an agreement for compensation, nor to compensate a stranger[3] for the support of a child who has abandoned the parent without just cause.

[1] Burritt *v.* Burritt, 29 *Barb.*, 124; Finch *v.* Finch, 22 *Conn.*, 411. Compare Stanton *v.* Willson, 3 *Day*, 37.

[2] Chilcott *v.* Trimble, 13 *Barb.*, 502.

[3] Raymond *v.* Loyl, 10 *id.*, 483; Clark *v.* Fitch, 2 *Wend.*, 459; Johnson *v.* Gibson, 4 *E. D. Smith*, 231.

Husband not bound for the support of his wife's children by a former marriage.

§ 100. A husband is not bound to maintain his wife's children by a former husband;[1] but if he receives them into his family and supports them, it is presumed that he does so as a parent, and where such is the case, they are not liable to him for their support, nor he to them for their services.[2]

[1] Gay *v.* Ballou, 4 *Wend.*, 403; Williams *v.* Hutchinson, 5 *Barb.*, 122; Bartley *v.* Richtmeyer, 4 *N. Y.* (4 *Comst.*), 38; Elliott *v.* Lewis, 3 *Edw.*, 40.

[2] Sharp *v.* Cropsey, 11 *Barb.*, 224; Williams *v.* Hutchinson, 3 *N. Y.* (3 *Comst.*), 312.

Compensation and support of adult child.

§ 101. Where a child, after attaining majority, continues to serve and to be supported by the parent, neither party is entitled to compensation, in the absence of an agreement therefor.

Dye *v.* Kerr, 15 *Barb.*, 444; Andrus *v.* Foster, 17 *Verm.*, 556; Resor *v.* Johnson, 1 *Carter* [*Ind.*], 100; Rex *v.* Sow, 1 *B. & Ald.*, 179; and see Cropsey *v.* Sweeney, 27 *Barb.*, 310; S. C., 7 *Abbotts' Pr.*, 129; Moore *v.* Moore, 21 *How. Pr.*, 211.

Parent may relinquish services and custody of child.

§ 102. The parent, whether solvent or insolvent,[1] may relinquish to the child the right of controlling him and receiving his earnings.[2] Abandonment by the parent is presumptive evidence of such relinquishment.[3]

[1] McCloskey *v.* Cyphert, 27 *Penn. St.*, 220.

[2] McCoy *v.* Huffman, 8 *Cow.*, 84; Burlingame *v.* Burlingame, 7 *id.*, 92; Whiting *v.* Earle, 3 *Pick.*, 201; Morse *v.* Welton, 6 *Conn.*, 547; Varney *v.* Young, 11 *Verm.*, 258.

[3] Canovar *v.* Cooper, 3 *Barb.*, 115; Stiles *v.* Granville, 6 *Cush.*, 458; Clinton *v.* York, 26 *Me.*, 167; Wodell *v.* Coggeshall, 2 *Metc.* [*Mass.*], 91; Cloud *v.* Hamilton, 11 *Humph.*, 104.

Wages of minors.

§ 103. The wages of a minor employed in service may be paid to him, unless, within thirty days after the commencement of the service, the parent or guardian entitled thereto gives the employer notice that he claims such wages.

Laws 1850, *ch.* 266, § 1. Same stat., 3 *R. S.*, 5*th ed.*, 242, § 8.

Right of parent to determine the residence of child.

§ 104. A parent entitled to the custody of a child has a right to change his residence, subject to the power of the supreme court to restrain a removal which would prejudice the rights or welfare of the child.

Wood *v.* Wood, 5 *Paige*, 596.

Parent not liable for acts of child.

§ 105. Neither parent nor child is answerable, as such, for the acts of the other.

Tifft *v.* Tifft, 4 *Den.*, 175.

Wife in certain cases may obtain custody of minor children.

§ 106. When a husband and wife live in a state of separation, without being divorced, any court or officer of competent jurisdiction, upon application of the wife, if she is an inhabitant of this state, may grant the proper writ to inquire into the custody of any minor unmarried child of the marriage, and may award the custody of the child to either party for such time, and under such regulations, as the case may require. The decision of the tribunal is to be guided by the rules prescribed in section 127.

2 *R. S.*, 149, §§ 1–6.

CHAPTER II.

ADOPTION.

The provisions of this chapter are new.

Child may be adopted. § 107. Any minor child may be adopted by any adult person, in the cases, and subject to the rules, prescribed in this chapter.

The total absence of any provision for the adoption of children is one of the most remarkable defects of our law. Thousands of children are actually, though not legally, adopted every year; yet there is no method by which the adopting parents can secure the children to themselves, except by a fictitious apprenticeship, a form which, when applied to children in the cradle, becomes absurd and repulsive. It is, indeed, so inappropriate in every case, that it is rarely resorted to. The consequence is, almost invariably, that if the real parents of the child live to see it grow to an age of usefulness and intelligence, they are certain to attempt to reclaim it, sometimes through the mere selfishness of natural affection, but more commonly from base and sordid motives. The chances of an adopting parent for the retention of the child upon which, perhaps, his whole heart is centered, are therefore in the inverse ratio to the degree of his benevolence in its selection, and of his care and affection in its training. Benevolence dictates a choice from among children whose parents are least able or willing to take care of them. To relieve a child from a cruel and heartless parent is a greater mercy than to take even an orphan. Yet these are the parents who are, of all others, most likely to reclaim the child as soon as any money can be made out of it. Affection will give the child such a training as will develop its beauty and intelligence to the highest degree. Yet every grace of the child is but a premium upon the extortion of its heartless parents, This is not mere theory. Facts within the knowledge of almost every one justify these statements. There are very many childless parents who would gladly adopt children, but for their well founded fears that they could never hold them securely.

§ 108. The person adopting a child must be at least twenty years older than the person adopted, and must have been married, and if a woman, must be a widow, or be lawfully divorced from her husband, without her fault. Who may adopt.

§ 109. A married man, not lawfully separated from his wife, cannot adopt a child without the consent of his wife. Consent of wife necessary.

§ 110. A legitimate child cannot be adopted without the consent of its parents, if living, nor an illegitimate child without the consent of its mother, if living, except that consent is not necessary from a father or mother deprived of civil rights, or adjudged guilty of adultery, or of cruelty, and for either cause divorced, or adjudged to be an habitual drunkard, or who has been judicially deprived of the custody of the child, on account of cruelty or neglect. Consent of child's parents.

§ 111. The consent of a child, if over the age of twelve years, is necessary to its adoption. Consent of child.

The age of twelve is fixed upon, as being the period at which the marriage of a female child is allowed.

§ 112. The person adopting a child, and the child adopted, and the other persons whose consent is necessary, must appear before the county judge of the county where the person adopting resides, and the necessary consent must thereupon be signed, and an agreement be executed by the person adopting, to the effect that the child shall be adopted, and treated in all respects as his own lawful child should be treated. Proceedings on adoption.

§ 113. The judge must examine all persons appearing before him pursuant to the last section, each Judge's order.

separately, and if satisfied that the interests of the child will be promoted by the adoption, he must make an order declaring that the child shall thenceforth be regarded and treated in all respects as the child of the person adopting.

Effect of adoption.

§ 114. A child, when adopted, takes the name of the person adopting, and the two thenceforth sustain towards each other the legal relation of parent and child, and have all the rights, and are subject to all the duties, of that relation.

Effect on former relations of child.

§ 115. The parents of an adopted child are, from the time of the adoption, relieved of all parental duties towards and of all responsibility for the child so adopted, and have no right over it.

Adoption of illegitimate child.

§ 116. The father of an illegitimate child, by publicly acknowledging it as his own, receiving it as such, with the consent of his wife, if he is married, into his family, and otherwise treating it as if it were a legitimate child, thereby adopts it as such; and such child is thereupon deemed for all purposes legitimate from the time of its birth. The foregoing provisions of this chapter do not apply to such an adoption.

This provision, like the rest, is new, but is so manifestly just, and the present state of the law is so unmerciful to innocent children, that it is presumed that no objection will be made to the change. The seducer can make reparation to the mother of his child, though she is more or less culpable, but can at present make absolutely none to the child, though perfectly innocent. By the law of France, and of almost every European nation, and in this country, by the law of Maine, Vermont, Massachusetts, Connecticut, Ohio, Illinois, Indiana, Maryland, Virginia, Georgia, Alabama, Mississippi, Louisiana, Kentucky and Missouri, a child is legitimatized by the marriage of its parents after its birth.

Privacy is an indispensable element of such an adoption. To compel the father to appear before a judge, or in any way to place the matter upon record, would brand the child with the very stigma from which a repentant father would desire to save it.

TITLE III.

GUARDIAN AND WARD.

Under this head are placed not only the provisions of law relating to the guardianship of minors, but also those relating to the custody and care of persons of unsound mind. The "committee" of a lunatic is here termed a "guardian."

§ 117. A guardian is a person appointed to take care of the person or property of another. Guardian, what.

§ 118. The person over whom, or over whose property, a guardian is appointed, is called his ward. Ward, what

§ 119. Guardians are either: Kinds of guardians.

1. General; or,

2. Special.

§ 120. A general guardian is a guardian of the person, or of all the property of the ward within this state, or of both. General guardian, what.

Special guardian, what.

§ 121. Every other is a special guardian.

Appointment by parent.

§ 122. A guardian of the person of a child born, or likely to be born, may be appointed, by will, or by deed, to take effect upon the death of the parent appointing:

1. If the child is legitimate, by the father, with the written consent of the mother; or by either parent, if the other is dead, or incapable of consent;

2. If the child is illegitimate, by the mother.

No person guardian of estate without appointment.

§ 123. No person, whether a parent or otherwise, has any power as guardian of property, except by appointment as hereinafter provided.

By the existing law (1 *R. S.*, 718, § 5), if any infant has real property, the father or mother, or if he has none, the nearest and eldest relative, males being preferred to females of the same degree, is declared the guardian of the child, and of the real property. When a parent dies in possession of real property leaving an infant heir thereof, and his guardian by nature enters thereon, the entry is presumed to be as guardian, unless accompanied by acts or declarations inconsistent with such character (Byrne *v.* Van Hoesen, 5 *Johns.*, 66; Jackson *v.* DeWalts, 7 *id.*, 157; Putnam *v.* Ritchie, 6 *Paige*, 390; Beecher *v.* Crouse, 19 *Wend.*, 306).

Appointment by court.

§ 124. A guardian of the person or property, or both, of a person residing in this state, who is a minor, or of unsound mind, may be appointed in all cases by the supreme court, when there is no such guardian, and by a surrogate in the cases provided in the CODE OF CIVIL PROCEDURE.

Id.

§ 125. A guardian of the property within this state of a person not residing therein, who is a minor, or of unsound mind, may be appointed by the supreme court.

Jurisdiction.

§ 126. In all cases, the court first making the appointment of a guardian has exclusive jurisdiction to appoint and control him, except in case of a removal pursuant to section 134.

§ 127. In awarding the custody of a minor, or in appointing a general guardian, the court or officer is to be guided by the following considerations: Rules for awarding custody of minor.

1. By what appears to be for the best interest of the child, in respect to its temporal and its mental and moral welfare; and if the child is of a sufficient age to form an intelligent preference, the court may consider that preference in determining the question;[1]

2. As between parents adversely claiming the custody or guardianship, neither parent is entitled to it as of right, but, other things being equal, if the child is of tender years, it should be given to the mother; if it is of an age to require education and preparation for labor or business, then to the father;

3. Of two persons equally eligible in other respects, preference is to be given, as follows:

(1.) To a relative;[2]

(2.) To one who was indicated by the wishes of a deceased parent;[3]

(3.) To one who already stands in the position of a trustee of a fund to be applied to the child's support.[4]

[1] Foster *v.* Mott, 3 *Bradf.*, 409; Stuart *v.* Bute, 9 *H. of L. Cas.*, 440.

[2] Morehouse *v.* Cooke, *Hopk.*, 226.

[3] Underhill *v.* Dennis, 9 *Paige*, 202; Re Pierce, 12 *How. Pr.*, 532. But such wishes are not conclusively binding (Foster *v.* Mott, *supra*; Cozine *v.* Horn, 1 *Bradf.*, 143).

[4] Bennett *v.* Byrne, 2 *Barb. Ch.*, 216.

§ 128. A guardian appointed by a court has power over the person and property of the ward, unless otherwise ordered. Powers of guardian appointed by court.

§ 129. A guardian of the person is charged with the custody of the ward, and must look to his support, health and education.[1] He may fix the residence Duties of guardian of the person.

of the ward at any place within the state, but not elsewhere, without permission of the court.

Ex parte Bartlett, 4 *Bradf.*, 221; Clarke *v.* Montgomery, 23 *Barb.*, 464.

Duties of guardian of estate.

§ 130. A guardian of the property must keep safely the property of his ward. He must not suffer any sale, waste or destruction of the real property, but must maintain the inheritance, its buildings and appurtenances, out of the moneys of the estate, and deliver the same to the ward at the close of his guardianship, in as good condition as he received them, inevitable decay and injury only excepted.

2 *R. S.*, 153, § 20.

Relation confidential.

§ 131. The relation of guardian and ward is confidential, and is subject to the provisions of the Title on TRUST.

Guardian under direction of court.

§ 132. In the management and disposition of the person or property committed to him, a guardian may be regulated and controlled by the court.

This section is new. It is intended to qualify the common law rules which empower him to dispose of personalty in his discretion, and of the realty during the term of his guardianship.

Death of a joint guardian.

§ 133. On the death of one of two or more joint guardians, the power continues to the survivor, until a further appointment is made by the court.

People *v.* Byron, 3 *Johns. Cas.*, 53.

Removal of guardian.

§ 134. A guardian may be removed by the supreme court for any of the following causes:

1. For abuse of his trust;

2. For continued failure to perform its duties;

3. For incapacity to perform its duties;

4. For gross immorality;

5. For having an interest adverse to the faithful performance of his duties;

6. For removal from the state;

7. In the case of a guardian of the property, for insolvency; or,

8. When it is no longer proper that the ward should be under guardianship.

§ 135. The power of a guardian appointed by a parent is superseded:

Guardian appointed by parent; how superseded.

1. By his removal, as provided by section 134;

2. In the case of a female ward, by her marriage;[1] or,

3. By the ward's attaining majority.

[1] By the existing law, this rule extends only to the case in which the ward is a female (Brick's estate, 15 *Abb. Pr.*, 12; People *v.* Kearney, 31 *Barb.*, 430). At present, the powers of a female guardian cease with her marriage (Corrigan *v.* Kiernan, 1 *Bradf.*, 208); but the provisions of the Code in relation to husband and wife remove the reason of the rule.

§ 136. The power of a guardian appointed by a court is superseded only:

Guardian appointed by court, how superseded.

1. By the order of the court;[1] or,

2. If the appointment was made solely because of the ward's minority, by his attaining majority.[2]

[1] It has been held that a guardian of the children of a convict, appointed during his civil death, is superseded by his pardon (Matter of Deming, 10 *Johns.*, 232, 483), and that a guardian improvidently appointed by the court, is superseded by the production of an appointment by the father (People *v.* Kearney, 31 *Barb.*, 430), but it seems proper that the guardian should be superseded only by order of the court.

[2] See 2 *R. S.*, 151, § 10.

§ 137. After a ward has come to his majority, he may settle accounts with his guardian, and give him a release,[1] which is valid if obtained fairly and without undue influence.[2]

Release by ward.

[1] Kirby *v.* Taylor, 6 *Johns. Ch.*, 242; Kirby *v.* Turner, *Hopk.*, 309.

[2] Fish *v.* Miller, *Hoffm.*, 267.

Guardian's discharge.

§ 138. A guardian appointed by a court is not entitled to his discharge until one year after the ward's majority.

Matter of Van Horne, 7 *Paige*, 46.

Insane persons.

§ 139. A person of unsound mind may be placed in an asylum for such persons, upon the order of the county judge of the county in which he resides, as follows:

1. The judge must be satisfied, by the oath of two reputable physicians, that such person is of unsound mind, and unfit to be at large;

2. Before granting the order, the judge must examine the person himself, or if that is impracticable, cause him to be examined by an impartial person;

3. After the order is granted, the person alleged to be of unsound mind, his or her husband or wife, or relative to the third degree, may demand an investigation before a jury, which must be conducted in all respects as under an inquisition of lunacy.

This section, which is new, is designed to remedy the present loose and dangerous state of the law which allows a commitment for lunacy without judicial intervention.

TITLE IV.

MASTER AND SERVANT.

§ 140. Male minors, and unmarried females under the age of eighteen years, with the consent of the persons or officers hereinafter mentioned, may bind themselves, by a writing called an indenture, as fully as if they were of age, to serve as clerks, apprentices or servants in a particular calling, until majority (except in the case of females, who cannot bind themselves further than until the age of eighteen), or for any shorter time. Who may bind themselves as apprentices.

2 *R. S.*, 154, § 1.

§ 141. Consent to an indenture of apprenticeship must be given by a certificate at the end thereof, or indorsed thereon, signed: Who to consent to such binding.

1. By the father and mother of the apprentice;

2. If the father lacks capacity to consent, or has abandoned or neglected to provide for the family, or is dead, and no testamentary guardian or executor has been appointed by him, with power under the will to bring up the child to a calling, and a certificate of such fact is indorsed on the indenture by a justice of the peace of the town, then by the mother;

3. If the father is dead, and such guardian or executor has been appointed by him, then by such guardian or executor;

4. If the mother is dead, or lacks capacity to consent, then by the father;

5. If there is no parent of capacity to consent, and no such executor, then by the guardian; or,

6. If there is no such parent, executor or guardian, then by the officers of the poor of the town or county,

or by any two justices of the peace of the town, or by the county judge.

2 *R. S.*, 154, §§ 2, 3, 4. Modified in accordance with *Laws* 1862, 345, *ch.* 172, § 6.

Parent or guardian, when liable for breach of indenture.

§ 142. A parent, executor or guardian, consenting to an indenture, is not liable for a breach thereof by the apprentice, unless the indenture or consent expresses an intention to bind him therefor.

Ackley *v.* Hoskins, 14 *Johns.*, 374; Blunt *v.* Melcher, 2 *Mass.*, 228; Bull *v.* Follett, 5 *Cow.*, 170.

Pauper children may be bound to service.

§ 143. Any child who is chargeable, or whose parents are chargeable, to a county, town, or city poor house, or who is in such poor house, may be bound to service until attaining twenty-one years, or if a female, until attaining eighteen years, by the officers of the poor of such county, town or city, as effectually as by the child himself with the parents' consent; but such binding, by the officers of a town or city, must be with the consent, in writing, of two justices of the peace of the town, or of the mayor, recorder and aldermen of the city, or any two of them.

2 *R. S.*, 155, § 6.

Special provision as to Indian children.

§ 144. No child of an Indian woman can be bound, under this Title, except in the presence, and with the consent of a justice of the peace; and his certificate of consent must be filed with the clerk of the town where the indenture is executed.

2 *R. S.*, 155, § 7.

Age of infants to be inserted in indentures.

§ 145. In every indenture of apprenticeship the age of the apprentice must be stated, and such statement is presumptive evidence thereof; and before an officer executes an indenture, or consents thereto, he must inform himself of the age of the apprentice.

2 *R. S.*, 155, § 8. The statement of the age in the indenture may be contradicted by proof (Drew *v.* Peckwell, 1 *E. D. Smith*, 408; Banks *v.* Metcalfe, 1 *Wheel. Cr. Cas.*, 381; Matter of Brennan, 1 *Sandf.*, 711).

§ 146. If there is any pecuniary consideration for an indenture of apprenticeship on either part, it must be stated therein. Pecuniary consideration to be inserted.

2 *R. S.*, 155, § 9.

§ 147. The indenture of an apprentice, executed by officers of the poor, must bind the master to cause him to be taught reading, writing, and the general rules of arithmetic, and to give him a new bible at the expiration of his term of service. Special agreement to be inserted in certain cases.

2 *R. S.*, 155, § 10; slightly modified.

§ 148. Every officer executing an indenture of apprenticeship must file a counterpart thereof with the clerk of the county, town or city of which he is an officer. Certain indentures, where to be deposited.

2 *R. S.*, 155, § 11.

§ 149. An immigrant minor may bind himself to service, until he attains majority, or for a shorter term, in such manner as may be prescribed by the law of the country in which the contract is made. If the indenture is made for the purpose of enabling him to pay his passage to this country, it may be for the term of one year, although such term extends beyond his majority; but in no case for a longer term. Indentures by foreigners, being minors.

§ 150. Every indenture under section 149 must be acknowledged by the minor on a private examination before a mayor, recorder, or alderman of a city, or a justice of the peace, and a certificate of the acknowledgment must be indorsed upon the indenture. Id.

2 *R. S.*, 156, §§ 12, 13.

§ 151. The master, under an indenture specified in section 149, may assign it, by writing indorsed thereon, and with the approval, also indorsed, of a magistrate mentioned in section 150. How assigned.

2 *R. S.*, 156, § 14. The requirement of two witnesses to this assignment has been omitted. The commissioners regard such provisions as founded upon a state of society and of the law, which no longer exists.

Indentures, when invalid.

§ 152. No indenture or contract for the service of an apprentice is binding upon him, unless made as hereinbefore prescribed.

2 *R. S.*, 158, § 26.

County superintendents and overseers to be guardians of servants.

§ 153. The county superintendents of the poor, and the overseers of the poor of cities and towns, must see that every apprentice or other servant in their respective counties, cities or towns, is properly treated, and that the terms of the contract are fulfilled in his favor; and it is their duty to redress any grievance of such persons in the manner prescribed by law.

2 *R. S.*, 158, § 27.

Penalty on apprentices absenting themselves from service.

§ 154. If an apprentice, for whose instruction the master receives no pecuniary compensation, willfully absents himself from service without leave, he may be compelled to serve double the time of such absence, unless he makes satisfaction for the injury; but such additional term of service cannot extend more than three years beyond the original term.

2 *R. S.*, 158, § 28.

No servant or apprentice bound by any restriction as to time and place where he shall work when free.

§ 155. No person may accept from an apprentice or servant, an agreement, oath or promise not to exercise his vocation in any particular place; nor may any person exact from an apprentice or servant, any consideration for exercising his vocation in any place after his term of service has expired.

Penalty.

§ 156. Any consideration exacted contrary to the last section, may be recovered back with interest, and every person accepting such agreement or exacting such consideration, is liable to the apprentice or servant in a penalty of one hundred dollars.

2 *R. S.*, 160, §§ 39, 40.

When the executor or administrator of a deceased mas-

§ 157. The executors or administrators of the master of any apprentice bound by officers of the poor, may assign the indenture, with the written consent of the apprentice, acknowledged before a justice of the peace. ter may assign a contract of service.

2 *R. S.*, 160, § 41.

§ 158. If an apprentice refuses consent to an assignment under the last section, the court of sessions may authorize such assignment without his consent, upon application after fourteen days' notice to the apprentice, or to his parents or guardian, if he has any in the county. Assignment by court.

2 *R. S.*, 160, § 42.

7

DIVISION SECOND.

PROPERTY.

The following memorandum will show where the provisions of the Revised Statutes relating to property are inserted in this Division.

Sections 1, 3, and 4 of article I of Part II of the Revised Statutes, have been, in substance, embodied in the Constitution, and are therefore omitted here. Section 2 is embodied in the title on Succession. Sections 5–7 are superseded by Title IV of Part III of Division I.

The provisions of article II of the same statute, entitled "Of the persons capable of holding and conveying land," are thus disposed of; —section 8 is extended to the case of *all* persons, and the provisions of the subsequent sections, and other statutes, extending the right of aliens, are omitted. This is in accordance with the recommendation of the governor, in his message of January, 1862.

The capacity of Indians is fixed by section 26 of Part I of Division I, on Persons, and reference to them is omitted in this part of the Code. Section 9 (like other saving clauses elsewhere) is omitted as being sufficiently provided for by the general clause of the provision at the end of the Code, saving vested rights; and section 10 is omitted as provided for in Part I on Persons.

Article I of title II of the same part of the Revised Statutes, entitled "Of the Creation and Division of Estates," is embodied partly in Title II of Part I of this division, and partly in Title II of Part II.

Article II of that title, entitled "Of Uses and Trusts," is embodied in Title IV of Part II.

Article III, entitled "Of Powers," is embodied in Title V of the same.

Article IV, "Of Alienation by Deed," is embodied in the Title on Transfers.

Title III (p. 740) "Of Dower," is omitted, it being proposed to abolish Dower and Curtesy.

The provisions of Title IV (p. 744) are inserted in title III of part II, except sections 1, 2 and 3, which are in the chapter on The Hiring of Real Property, and sections 4–6, and 26, which are to be inserted in the Code of Civil Procedure.

The provisions of title V (p. 748) are disposed as follows:

Section 1 is inserted in the chapter on Transfers, and on Wills.

Section 2 is stated in the Division relating to Obligations, as a general principle of interpretation.

Section 3, with important modifications, is embodied in the Title on Succession.

Sections 4 and 5 are inserted in the Title on Mortgage.

Section 6 is embodied in the Code of Civil Procedure, as reported complete, p. 750.

Sections 7–9, are embodied in title III of part II.

Chapter II (p. 751), of Descent, is superseded by the chapter on Succession.

Chapter III (p. 756) is embodied in the article on Recording Transfers.

PART I.

PROPERTY IN GENERAL.

TITLE I.

NATURE OF PROPERTY.

§ 159. The ownership of a thing is the right of one or more persons to possess and use it to the exclusion of others. In this Code, the thing, of which there may be ownership, is called property. **Property, what.**

§ 160. There may be ownership of all inanimate things which are capable of appropriation, or of manual delivery; of all domestic animals; of all obligations; of such products of labor or skill, as the composition of an author, the good will of a business, trade-marks and signs, and of rights created or granted by statute. **In what property may exist.**

§ 161. Animals wild by nature are the subjects of ownership while living, only when on the land of the **Wild animals.**

person claiming them, or when tamed, or taken and held in possession, or disabled and immediately pursued.

Real and personal.

§ 162. Property is either:

1. Real or immovable; or,

2. Personal or movable;

Real property.

§ 163. Real or immovable property consists of:

1. Land;

2. That which is affixed to land; and,

3. That which is incidental or appurtenant to land.

Land.

§ 164. Land is the solid material of the earth, whatever may be the ingredients of which it is composed, whether soil, rock, or other substance.

Fixtures.

§ 165. A thing is deemed to be affixed to land when it is attached to it by roots, as in the case of trees, vines or shrubs; or imbedded in it, as in the case of walls; or permanently resting upon it, as in the case of buildings; or permanently attached to what is thus permanent, as by means of nails, bolts or screws.

Appurtenances.

§ 166. A thing is deemed to be incidental[1] or appurtenant[2] to land, when it is by right used with the land for its benefit;[3] as in the case of a way, or watercourse, or of a passage for light, air or heat from or across the land of another.

[1] Smyles *v.* Hastings, 22 *N. Y.*, 217, 222.
[2] Lampman *v.* Milks, 21 *N. Y.*, 505, 511.
[3] Ackroyd *v.* Smith, 10 *C. B.*, 164, 187.

Personal property.

§ 167. Every kind of property that is not real is personal.

TITLE II.

OWNERSHIP.

CHAPTER I.

OWNERS.

§ 168. All property has an owner, whether that owner is the state, and the property public, or the owner an individual, and the property private. The state may also hold property as a private proprietor. Owners.

§ 169. The state is the owner of all land, below high water mark, bordering upon tide water; of all land below the water of a lake or stream which constitutes an exterior boundary of the state; of all property lawfully appropriated by it to its own use; of all property dedicated to the state, and of all property of which there is no other owner. Property of the state.

The ultimate right of the state to all other property is declared by chapter II of title II of part III of the POLITICAL CODE (§§ 249, 250).

§ 170. Any person, whether citizen or alien, may take and hold property, real or personal. Who may own property.

Substituted for 2 *R. S.*, 57, § 4. See note on page 51.

CHAPTER II.

MODIFICATIONS OF OWNERSHIP.

ARTICLE I.

INTERESTS IN PROPERTY.

Ownership, absolute or qualified.

§ 171. The ownership of property is either:

1. Absolute; or,

2. Qualified.

When absolute.

§ 172. The ownership of property is absolute, when a single person has the absolute dominion over it, and may use it or dispose of it according to his pleasure, subject only to general laws.

Thus the use of gunpowder is restricted by general laws, but its ownership may nevertheless be justly called absolute.

§ 173. The ownership of property is qualified: When qualified

1. When it is shared with one or more persons;

2. When the time of enjoyment is deferred or limited; or,

3. When the use is restricted.

§ 174. The ownership of property by a single person is designated as a sole or several ownership. Several ownership, what.

§ 175. The ownership of property by several persons is either: Ownership of several persons.

1. Of joint interests;

2. Of partnership interests; or,

3. Of interests in common.

§ 176. A joint interest is one owned by several persons in equal shares, by a title created by a single will or transfer which confers a right of survivorship. Joint interest, what.

This provision is intended to confine the right of survivorship to cases in which its creation was clearly intended.

§ 177. A partnership interest is one owned by several persons, in partnership, for partnership purposes. Partnership interest, what.

Collumb *v.* Read, 24 *N. Y.*, 505; Buchan *v.* Sumner, 2 *Barb. Ch.*, 165; extending the doctrine of Phillips *v.* Phillips, 1 *Myl. & K.*, 649; Broom *v.* Broom, 3 *id.*, 443.

§ 178. An interest in common is one owned by several persons, not in joint ownership or partnership. Interest in common, what.

These last five sections are substituted for 1 *R. S.*, 726, § 43.

§ 179. Every interest created in favor of several persons in their own right, including husband and wife,[1] is an interest in common,[2] unless acquired by What interests are in common.

them in partnership, for partnership purposes,[3] or unless declared in its creation, expressly or by necessary implication,[4] to be a joint interest, with a right of survivorship.[2]

[1] This is contrary to the present law (Wright *v.* Saddler, 20 *N. Y.*, 320, 323; Torrey *v.* Torrey, 14 *id.*, 430), but seems necessary to make the rule consistent with the provisions of the Code relative to married women.

[2] 1 *R. S.*, 727, § 44.

[3] See § 177, *supra.*

[4] Downing *v.* Marshall, 23 *N. Y.*, 366, 388; Coster *v.* Lorillard, 14 *Wend.*, 343.

Interests as to time.

§ 180. In respect to the time of enjoyment, an interest in property is either:

1. Present or future; and,
2. Perpetual or limited.

See 1 *R. S.*, 722, § 7. These distinctions exist in regard to personal property as well as real (Westcott *v.* Cady, 5 *Johns. Ch.*, 334; Gillespie *v.* Miller, *id.*, 21; Randall *v.* Russell, 3 *Meriv.*, 190; Hyde *v.* Parrat, 1 *P. Wms.*, 1; 2 *Vern.*, 331; Smith *v.* Clever, *id.*, 59; Upwell *v.* Halsey, 1 *P. Wms.*, 651; see Phelps *v.* Pond, 23 *N. Y.*, 69; 28 *Barb.*, 121; Kane *v.* Astor, 5 *Sandf.*, 467; Beeckman *v.* Schermerhorn, 3 *Sandf. Ch.*, 181; Mason *v.* Jones, 2 *Barb.*, 229).

Present interest, what

§ 181. A present interest entitles the owner to the immediate possession of the property.

1 *R. S.*, 723, § 8.

Future interest, what

§ 182. A future interest entitles the owner to the possession of the property only at a future period.

This definition corresponds to that of "expectant estates" in 1 *R. S.*, 723, § 9. A future interest is there distinguished from a reversion. This distinction is not, however, logical. A reversion is as truly a future estate as a remainder.

Perpetual interest, what.

§ 183. A perpetual interest has a duration equal to that of the property.

Limited interest, what.

§ 184. A limited interest has a duration less than that of the property.

§ 185. A future interest is either: **Kinds of future interests.**

1. Vested; or,

2. Contingent.

From 1 *R. S.*, 723, § 13, as to real property. The same language is used in regard to personal property (Phelps' ex'r *v.* Pond, 23 *N. Y.*, 69).

§ 186. A future interest is vested, when there is a person in being, who would have a right, defeasible[1] or indefeasible, to the immediate possession of the property, upon the ceasing of the intermediate or precedent interest. **Vested interest, what.**

1 *R. S.*, 723, § 13.

[1] The words "defeasible or indefeasible" are inserted to answer the objection that a future interest might be vested, and also contingent, within the meaning of these definitions of the Revised Statutes (Coster *v.* Lorillard, 14 *Wend.*, 302); *e. g.*, a remainder to descendants in being subject to open and let in after-born descendants. Such remainders have always been held to be vested (Powers *v.* Bergen, 6 *N. Y.*, 360; Root *v.* Stuyvesant, 18 *Wend.*, 268; Dubois *v.* Ray, 7 *Bosw.*, 287; Williamson *v.* Field, 2 *Sandf. Ch.*, 533).

§ 187. A future interest is contingent, whilst the person in whom, or the event upon which, it is limited to take effect, remains uncertain. **Contingent interest, what.**

1 *R. S.*, 723, § 13.

§ 188. Two or more future interests may be created to take effect in the alternative, so that if the first in order fails to vest, the next in succession shall be substituted for it, and take effect accordingly. **Two or more future interests.**

1 *R. S.*, 724, § 25; Loddington *v.* Kime, 1 *Ld. Raym.*, 203; 2 *Smith's Fearne*, 43.

§ 189. A future interest is not void merely because of the improbability of the contingency on which it is limited to take effect. **Certain future interests not to be void.**

1 *R. S.*, 724, § 26.

§ 190. When a future interest is limited to successors, heirs, issue or children, posthumous children are **Posthumous children.**

entitled to take, in the same manner as if living at the death of their parent.

1 *R. S.*, 725, § 30. Mason *v.* Jones, 2 *Barb.*, 234, 252.

Qualities of future interests.

§ 191. Future interests pass by succession,[1] will[2] and transfer,[3] in the same manner as present interests.

1 *R. S.*, 725, § 35.

[1] Wood *v.* Keyes, 8 *Paige*, 365, 368; Wendell *v.* Crandall, 1 *N. Y.*, 491.

[2] Pond *v.* Bergh, 10 *Paige*, 140, 154.

[3] Lawrence *v.* Bayard, 7 *Paige*, 70, 76; Grout *v.* Townsend, 2 *Hill*, 554, 557.

Mere possibility.

§ 192. A mere possibility, such as the expectancy of an heir-apparent, is not to be deemed an interest of any kind.

Jackson *v.* Bradford, 4 *Wend.*, 619; Tooley *v.* Dibble, 2 *Hill*, 641; see Conderman *v.* Smith, 41 *Barb.*, 404; Miller *v.* Emans, 19 *N. Y.*, 384.

Interests in real property.

§ 193. In respect to real or immovable property, the interests mentioned in this chapter are denominated estates, and are specially named and classified in Part II of this Division.

It has been deemed unadvisable to apply the technical names of estates in real property to interests in personal property, although precedents for such a course are not wanting.

Id.

§ 194. The names and classification of interests in real property have only such application to interests in personal property as is in this Division of the Code expressly provided.

What future interests are recognized.

§ 195. No future interest in property is recognized by the law, except such as is defined in this Division of the Code.

Substantially the same as 1 *R. S.*, 726, § 42.

ARTICLE II.

CONDITIONS OF OWNERSHIP.

§ 196. The time when the enjoyment of property is to begin or end may be determined by computation, or be made to depend on events. In the latter case, the enjoyment is said to be upon condition. *Fixing the time of enjoyment.*

§ 197. Conditions are precedent or subsequent. The former fix the beginning, the latter the ending of the right. *Conditions.*

§ 198. If a condition precedent requires the performance of an act wrong of itself, the instrument containing it is so far void, and the right cannot exist. If it requires the performance of an act not wrong of itself, but otherwise unlawful, the instrument takes effect, and the condition is void. *Certain conditions precedent, void.*

§ 199. Conditions imposing restraints upon marriage, except upon the marriage of a minor, or of the widow of the person by whom the condition is imposed, are void; but this does not affect limitations where the intent was, not to forbid marriage, but only to give the use until marriage. *Conditions restraining marriage, void.*

§ 200. Conditions restraining alienation, when repugnant to the interest created, are void. *Conditions restraining alienation, void.*

De Peyster *v.* Michael, 6 *N. Y.*, 496.

ARTICLE III.

RESTRAINTS UPON ALIENATION.

How long it may be suspended.

§ 201. The absolute power of alienation cannot be suspended by any limitation or condition whatever,[1] for a longer period than during the continuance of not more than two[2] lives[3] in being at the creation of the limitation or condition,[4] except in the single case mentioned in section 229.

1 *R. S.*, 723, § 15; *id.*, 773, § 1.

[1] This includes a trust of real property (Coster *v.* Lorillard, 14 *Wend.*, 265, 313; Hawley *v.* James, 16 *id.*, 121, 173, 174, 208; Kane *v.* Gott, 24 *id.*, 641, 662, 667).

[2] Amory *v.* Lord, 9 *N. Y.*, 410; Phelps' ex'r *v.* Pond, 23 *id.*, 79.

[3] Hone *v.* Van Schaick, 20 *Wend.*, 564, 566; Boynton *v.* Hoyt, 1 *Den.*, 53, 58; Beekman *v.* Bonsor, 23 *N. Y.*, 298, 316.

[4] The words "limitation or condition" are substituted for "estate," so as to include powers (See Hawley *v.* James, 16 *Wend.*, 135, 178, 208; Coster *v.* Lorillard, 14 *id.*, 324, 325; Hone *v.* Van Schaick, 20 *id.*, 566, 567, 569).

Future interests void, which suspend power of alienation.

§ 202. Every future interest is void in its creation which, by any possibility,[1] may suspend the absolute power of alienation for a longer period than is prescribed in this chapter. Such power of alienation is suspended when there are no persons in being by whom an absolute interest in possession can be conveyed.

1 *R. S.*, 723, § 14; 1 *R. S.*, 773, §§ 1, 2.

[1] The words "by any possibility may" are new, but in accordance with Hawley *v.* James, 16 *Wend.*, 120, 126, 171, 178, 227; Everitt *v.* Everitt, 29 *Barb.*, 112; Jennings *v.* Jennings, 7 *N. Y.*, 547, 549; Amory *v.* Lord, 9 *id.*, 415; Thompson *v.* Carmichael's Exec'rs, 1 *Sandf. Ch.*, 395; Arnold *v.* Gilbert, 3 *id.*, 558.

§ 203. Restrictions upon the power to affix qualifications to the right of enjoyment are contained in sections 14 and 15 of article I of the Constitution of the state. Restriction on qualification of enjoyment.

ARTICLE IV.

ACCUMULATIONS.

§ 204. Dispositions of the income of property to accrue and to be received at any time subsequent to the execution of the instrument creating such disposition, are governed by the rules prescribed in this Title in relation to future interests. Dispositions of income.

1 *R. S.*, 725, § 36.

§ 205. All directions for the accumulation[1] of the income of property, except such as are allowed by this Title, are void.[2] Accumulations, when void.

1 *R. S.*, 726, § 38.

[1] Titus *v.* Weeks, 37 *Barb.*, 136, 146.

[2] Vail *v.* Vail, 4 *Paige*, 317; Levy *v.* Levy, 40 *Barb.*, 590, 618.

§ 206. An accumulation of the income of property, for the benefit of one or more persons, may be directed by any will or transfer in writing, sufficient to pass the property out of which the fund is to arise, as follows: Accumulation of income.

1. If such accumulation is directed to commence on the creation of the interest out of which the income is to arise, it must be made for the benefit of one or more minors[1] then in being,[2] and terminate at the expiration of their minority; or,

2. If such accumulation is directed to commence at any time subsequent to the creation of the interest

out of which the income is to arise, it must commence within the time in this title permitted for the vesting of future interests, and during the minority of the beneficiaries, and terminate at the expiration of such minority.[3]

1 *R. S.*, 726, § 37.

[1] Boynton *v.* Hoyt, 1 *Den.*, 53, 58; Hawley *v.* James, 16 *Wend.*, 117.

[2] Gilman *v.* Reddington, 24 *N. Y.*, 19; Kilpatrick *v.* Johnson, 15 *N. Y.*, 322.

[3] Mason *v.* Jones, 2 *Barb.*, 250, 253.

Other directions, when void in part.

§ 207. If, in either of the cases mentioned in the last section, the direction for an accumulation is for a longer term than during the minority of the beneficiaries, the direction only, whether separable or not from other provisions of the instrument, is void as respects the time beyond such minority.

1 *R. S.*, 726, § 38. The clause from "only" to "instrument" is new, but sustained by Williams *v.* Williams, 8 *N. Y.*, 425; Kilpatrick *v.* Johnson, 15 *N. Y.*, 322; See, however, King *v.* Rundle, 15 *Barb.*, 139, 145.

Application of income to support, &c., of minor.

§ 208. When a minor, for whose benefit an accumulation has been directed, is destitute of other sufficient means of support and education, the supreme court, upon application, may direct a suitable sum to be applied thereto, out of the fund.

1 *R. S.*, 726, § 39; 773, § 5.

CHAPTER III.

RIGHTS OF OWNERS.

Increase of property.

§ 209. The owner of a thing owns also all its products and accessions.

In certain cases who entitled to income of property.

§ 210. When, in consequence of a valid limitation of a future interest, there is a suspension of the power of alienation or of the ownership, during the continuation of which the income is undisposed of, and no valid direction for its accumulation is given, such income belongs to the persons presumptively entitled to the next eventual interest.

1 *R. S.*, 726, § 40. Held to apply to personal property (Gilman *v.* Reddington, 24 *N. Y.*, 19; Kilpatrick *v.* Johnson, 15 *id.*, 322; but see Phelps' ex'r *v.* Pond, 23 *N. Y.*, 83).

CHAPTER IV.

TERMINATION OF OWNERSHIP.

§ 211. A future interest, depending on the contingency of the death of any person without successors, heirs, issue, or children, is defeated by the birth of a posthumous child of such person, capable of taking by succession. Future interest, when defeated.

1 *R. S.*, 725, § 31.

§ 212. A future interest may be defeated in any manner, or by any act or means, which the party creating such interest provided for or authorized in the creation thereof; nor is a future interest, thus liable to be defeated, to be on that ground adjudged void in its creation. Id.

1 *R. S.*, 725, § 33.

§ 213. No future interest can be defeated or barred by any alienation or other act of the owner of the intermediate or precedent interest, nor by any destruction of such precedent interest by forfeiture, surrender, merger or otherwise, except as provided by the next section, or where a forfeiture is imposed by statute as a penalty for the violation thereof. Future interests, when not defeated.

1 *R. S.*, 725, § 32.

§ 214. No future interest, valid in its creation, is defeated by the determination of the precedent in- Id.

terest before the happening of the contingency on which the future interest is limited to take effect; but should such contingency afterwards happen, the future interest takes effect in the same manner and to the same extent as if the precedent interest had continued to the same period.

1 *R. S.*, 725, § 34; modified by substituting the words "future interest" for "remainder."

TITLE III.

GENERAL DEFINITIONS.

Income, what.

§ 215. The income of property, as the term is used in this Part of the Code, includes the rents and profits of real property, the interest of money, dividends upon stock, and other produce of personal property.

Time of creation, what.

§ 216. The delivery of the grant, where a limitation, condition, or future interest is created by grant, and the death of the testator, where it is created by will, is to be deemed the time of the creation of the limitation, condition, or interest, within the meaning of this Part of the Code.

Modified from 1 *R. S.*, 726, § 41; see Lang *v.* Ropke, 5 *Sandf.*, 369, 370.

PART II.

REAL OR IMMOVABLE PROPERTY.

TITLE I.

GENERAL PROVISIONS.

§ 217. Real property within this state is governed by the law of this state.

TITLE II.

ESTATES IN REAL PROPERTY.

CHAPTER I.

ESTATES IN GENERAL.

Enumeration of estates.

§ 218. Estates in real property, in respect to the duration of their enjoyment, are either:

1. Estates of inheritance, or perpetual estates;
2. Estates for life;
3. Estates for years; or,
4. Estates at will.

1 *R. S.*, 722, § 1. The term "estates by sufferance" has been omitted, as it is proposed to designate all such as estates at will. The words "in respect to the duration of their enjoyment," are new.

What estate a fee simple.

§ 219. Every estate of inheritance, notwithstanding the abolition of tenures, continues to be called a fee simple, or fee; and every such estate, when not defeasible or conditional, is called a fee simple absolute, or an absolute fee.

1 *R. S.*, 722, § 2.

Estates tail abolished; their nature declared.

§ 220. Estates tail are abolished; and every estate which would be adjudged a fee tail, according to the law of this state, as it existed previous to the twelfth day of July, one thousand seven hundred and eighty-two, is a fee simple; and if no valid remainder is limited thereon, is a fee simple absolute.

1 *R. S.*, 722, § 3.

§ 221. Where a remainder in fee is limited upon any estate, which would by the law mentioned in the last section be adjudged a fee tail, such remainder is valid as a contingent limitation upon a fee, and vests in possession, on the death of the first taker, without issue living at the time of his death. Certain remainders valid.

1 *R. S.*, 722, § 4.

§ 222. Estates of inheritance and for life, are called estates of freehold; estates for years are chattels real;[1] and estates at will are chattel interests, but are not liable as such to sale on execution.[2] Freeholds; chattels real; chattel interests.

1 *R. S.*, 722, § 5.

[1] Pugsley *v.* Aikin, 11 *N. Y.*, 498; Averill *v.* Taylor, 8 *N. Y.*, 52; Bigelow *v.* Finch, 17 *Barb.*, 396.

[2] Dickinson *v.* Smith, 25 *Barb.*, 108; Bigelow *v.* Finch, 11 *Barb.*, 498.

§ 223. An estate during the life of a third person, whether limited to heirs or otherwise, is a freehold only during the life of the grantee or devisee. After his death it is a chattel real. Estates for life of a third person, when a freehold, &c.

1 *R. S.*, 722, § 6. Mosher *v.* Yost, 33 *Barb.*, 277.

§ 224. A future estate may be limited[1] by the act of the party to commence in possession at a future day, either without the intervention of a precedent estate,[2] or on the termination, by lapse of time, or otherwise,[3] of a precedent estate, created at the same time. Future estates, what.

1 *R. S.*, 723, § 10.

[1] Nicoll *v.* N. Y. & Erie R. R., 12 *N. Y.*, 121, 139. "The definition in this section is so framed as to comprehend every species of expectant estates created by the act of the party, remainders strictly so called, future uses and executory devises." (*Rev. Notes*, 5 *Edmonds' Stat., App.*, 305).

[2] "Introduced to embrace estates *in futuro*, as they are technically called." *Ib.*

[3] "The words 'by lapse of time or otherwise' are necessary to provide for contingent limitations operating to abridge or defeat the prior estate." *Ib.*

Reversions. § 225. A reversion is the residue of an estate left, by operation of law, in the grantor, or his successors, or in the successors of a testator, commencing in possession on the determination of a particular estate granted or devised.

1 *R. S.*, 723, § 12. The words "by operation of law" are new, and "successors" substituted for "heirs."

Remainders. § 226. When a future estate, other than a reversion, is dependent on a precedent estate, it may be called a remainder, and may be created and transferred by that name.

1 *R. S.*, 723, § 11. Modified by inserting the words "other than a reversion."

Limitations of chattels real. § 227. The provisions of Title II of Part I of this Division, relative to future estates, apply to limitations of chattels real, as well as of freehold estates, so that the absolute ownership of a term of years cannot be suspended for a longer period than the absolute power of alienation can be suspended in respect to a fee.

1 *R. S.*, 724, § 23.

Suspension by trust. § 228. The suspension of all power to alienate the subject of a trust, other than a power to exchange it for other property to be held upon the same trust, or to sell it and reinvest the proceeds to be held upon the same trust, is a suspension of the power of alienation, within the meaning of section 201.

This section, though not in the Revised Statutes, is simply declaratory of the existing law (Hawley *v.* James, 16 *Wend.*, 163; Belmont *v.* O'Brien, 12 *N. Y.*, 402; Williams *v.* Williams, 8 *id.*, 531.)

Contingent remainder in fee. § 229. A contingent remainder in fee may be created on a prior remainder in fee, to take effect in the event that the persons to whom the first remainder[1] is limited die under the age of twenty-one years, or upon any other contingency by which the estate of such persons may be determined, before they attain majority.

1 *R. S.*, 723, § 16.

[1] Temple *v.* Hawley, 1 *Sandf. Ch.*, 153.

Remainders, future and contingent estates, how created. § 230. Subject to the rules of this Title, and of Part I of this Division, a freehold estate, as well as a chattel real, may be created to commence at a future day; an estate for life may be created in a term of years, and a remainder limited thereon; a remainder of a freehold or chattel real, either contingent or vested, may be created, expectant on the determination of a term of years; and a fee may be limited on a fee, upon a contingency, which, if it should occur, must happen within the period prescribed in this Title.

1 *R. S.*, 724, § 24. Maurice *v.* Graham, 8 *Paige*, 483, 486; Sherman *v.* Sherman, 3 *Barb.*, 385.

Limitations of successive estates for life. § 231. Successive estates for life cannot be limited, except to persons in being at the creation thereof; and where a remainder is limited on more than two successive estates for life, all the life estates subsequent to those of the two persons first entitled thereto are void, and upon the death of those persons the remainder, if valid in its creation,[1] takes effect in the same manner as if no other life estates had been created.

1 *R. S.*, 723, § 17.

[1] The words "if valid in its creation" are new. See Amory *v.* Lord, 9 *N. Y.*, 419; Vail *v.* Vail, 7 *Barb.*, 241.

Remainder upon estates for life of third person. § 232. No remainder can be created upon an estate for the life of any other person than the grantee or devisee of such estate, unless such remainder is in fee; nor can a remainder be created upon such an estate in a term for years, unless it is for the whole residue of such term.

1 *R. S.*, 734, § 18.

Id. § 233. When a remainder is created upon an estate for the life of any other person than the grantee or devisee thereof, and more than two persons are named as the persons during whose lives the life estate shall continue, the remainder, if valid in its creation, takes effect upon the death of the two persons first named, in the same manner as if no other lives had been introduced.

The words "if valid in its creation" are new. Otherwise, the section is the same as 1 *R. S.*, 724, § 19.

Contingent remainder on a term of years.

§ 234. A contingent remainder cannot be created on a term of years, unless the nature of the contingency on which it is limited is such, that the remainder must vest in interest during the continuance of not more than two lives[1] in being at the creation of such remainder, or upon the termination thereof.

1 *R. S.*, 724, § 20.

[1] Butler *v.* Butler, 3 *Barb. Ch.*, 304.

Remainder of estates for life.

§ 235. No estate for life can be limited as a remainder on a term of years, except to a person in being at the creation of such estate.

1 *R. S.*, 724, § 21. Hawley *v.* James, 16 *Wend.*, 248.

Remainder upon a contingency.

§ 236. A remainder may be limited on a contingency which, in case it should happen, will operate to abridge or determine the precedent estate; and every such remainder is to be deemed a conditional limitation.

1 *R. S.*, 725, § 27; Tyson *v.* Blake, 22 *N. Y.*, 563.

Heirs of a tenant for life, when to take as purchasers.

§ 237. When a remainder is limited to the heirs, or heirs of the body, of a person to whom a life estate in the same property is given, the persons who, on the termination of the life estate, are the successors or heirs of the body of the owner for life, are entitled to take by virtue of the remainder so limited to them, and not as mere successors of the owner for life.

1 *R. S.*, 725, § 28, modified so as to avoid the use of the technical phrase "take as purchasers."

Construction of certain remainders.

§ 238. When a remainder, on an estate for life or for years, is not limited on a contingency defeating or avoiding such precedent estate, it is to be deemed intended to take effect only on the death of the first taker, or the expiration, by lapse of time, of such term of years.

1 *R. S.*, 725, § 29.

§ 239. A general or special power of appointment does not prevent the vesting of a future estate limited to take effect in case such power is not executed. Effect of power of appointment.

Root *v.* Stuyvesant, 18 *Wend.*, 268, per NELSON, Ch. J.; 2 *Smith's Fearne*, 193. This section is new.

CHAPTER II.

TERMINATION OF ESTATES.

§ 240. A tenancy or other estate at will, however created, may be terminated by the landlord's giving notice to the tenant, in the manner prescribed by the next section, to remove from the premises within a period specified in the notice, of not less than one month. Tenancy at will may be terminated by notice.

1 *R. S.*, 745, § 7.

§ 241. The notice prescribed by the last section must be in writing, and must be served by delivering the same to the tenant, or to some person of discretion residing on the premises; or if neither can, with reasonable diligence, be found, the notice may be served by affixing it on a conspicuous part of the premises, where it may be conveniently read. Form and service of notice.

1 *R. S.*, 745, § 8.

§ 242. After the notice prescribed by sections 240 and 241 has been served in the manner therein directed, and the period specified by such notice has Effect of notice.

10

expired, but not before,[1] the landlord may re-enter, or proceed according to law to recover possession.[2]

[1] Livingston *v.* Tanner, 14 *N. Y.*, 67.
[2] Substantially from 1 *R. S.*, 745, § 9.

Re-entry, when and how to be made.

§ 243. Whenever the right of re-entry is given to a grantor or lessor in any grant or lease, or otherwise, such re-entry may be made at any time after the right has accrued, upon fifteen days' previous written notice of intention to re-enter, served in the mode prescribed by section 241.

Laws of 1846, *ch.* 274, § 3; same stat. 3 *R. S.*, 5 *ed.*, 36, § 12; modified as to mode of service, and extended to all cases in which a right of re-entry is given for the non-performance of any of the terms of the agreement.

Notice not necessary before action.

§ 244. An action for the possession of real property leased or granted, with a right of re-entry, may be maintained at any time after the right to re-enter has accrued, without the notice prescribed in section 243.

CHAPTER III.

SERVITUDES.

Servitudes attached to land.

§ 245. The following land burdens, or servitudes upon land, may be attached to other land as incidents or appurtenances, and are then called easements:[1]

1. The right of pasture;
2. The right of fishing;
3. The right of taking game;
4. The right of way;[2]

5. The right of taking water,[3] wood, minerals and other things;

6. The right of transacting business upon land;[4]

7. The right of conducting lawful sports upon land;[5]

8. The right of receiving air, light or heat from or over, or discharging the same upon or over, land;

9. The right of receiving water from or discharging the same upon land;

10. The right of flooding land;[6]

11. The right of having water flow without diminution or disturbance of any kind;[7]

12. The right of using a wall as a party wall;[8]

13. The right of receiving more than natural support from adjacent land[9] or things affixed thereto;[10]

14. The right of having the whole of a division fence maintained by a co-terminous owner;[11]

15. The right of having public conveyances stopped,[12] or of stopping the same, on land;

16. The right of a seat in church;[13]

17. The right of burial.

[1] These rights are generally called easements (Wolfe *v.* Frost, 4 *Sandf. Ch.*, 72), although a distinction is drawn, for some purposes, between a mere easement, and a right to take the produce of the land (Wickham *v.* Hawker, 7 *M. & W.*, 63; Race *v.* Ward, 4 *El. & Bl.*, 702).

[2] Huttemeier *v.* Albro, 18 *N. Y.*, 48; 7 *Bosw.*, 546; see Hamilton *v.* White, 5 *N. Y.*, 9; Holmes *v.* Seely, 19 *Wend.*, 507; Boyce *v.* Brown, 7 *Barb.*, 80; James *v.* Plant, 4 *Ad. & El.*, 749; Durham Railway Co. *v.* Walker, 2 *Q. B.*, 940; Hinchcliffe *v.* Kinnoul, 5 *Bing. N. C.*, 1.

[3] Race *v.* Ward, 4 *El. & Bl.*, 702; Manning *v.* Wasdale, 5 *Ad. & El.*, 758; Weekly *v.* Wildman, 1 *Ld. Raym.*, 407.

[4] Tyson *v.* Smith, 9 *Ad. & El.*, 406; 6 *id.*, 745.

[5] Abbott *v.* Weekly, 1 *Levinz*, 176.

[6] Tabor *v.* Bradley, 18 *N. Y.*, 109.

[7] Northam *v.* Hurley, 1 *El. & Bl.*, 665.

[8] Giles *v.* Dugro, 1 *Duer*, 331.

[9] Lasala *v.* Holbrook, 4 *Paige*, 173.

[10] Partridge *v.* Gilbert, 15 *N. Y.*, 601; Eno *v.* Del Vecchio, 3 *Duer*, 53; Keteltas *v.* Penfold, 4 *E. D. Smith*, 122.

[11] Adams *v.* Van Alstyne, 25 *N. Y.*, 235.

[12] Pitkin *v.* Long Island R. R., 2 *Barb. Ch.*, 221; Day *v.* N. Y. Central R. R., 31 *Barb.*, 548.

[13] Lousley *v.* Hayward, 1 *You. & J.*, 583; Mainwaring *v.* Giles, 5 *B. & Ald.*, 356. In this state, pews are not, as a matter of fact, held as easements (Shaw *v.* Beveridge, 3 *Hill*, 26), but they *might* be.

Servitudes not attached to land.

§ 246. The following land burdens, or servitudes upon land, may be granted, and held, though not attached to land:

1. The right of fishing and taking game;
2. The right of a seat in church;[1]
3. The right of burial;[2]
4. The right of taking rents and tolls;
5. The right of way.[3]

[1] McNabb *v.* Pond, 4 *Bradf.*, 7; Voorhees *v.* Presb. Ch., 17 *Barb.*, 103; Matter of Ref. Dutch Ch., 16 *id.*, 237; see First Bap. Ch. *v.* Witherell, 3 *Paige*, 296.

[2] Richards *v.* Northwest Dutch Ch., 11 *Abb. Pr.*, 30.

[3] It has been held that a right of way is not assignable, except in connection with land (Ackroyd *v.* Smith, 10 *C. B.*, 164).

Designation of estates.

§ 247. The land to which an easement is attached is called the dominant tenement; the land upon which a burden or servitude is laid is called the servient tenement.

Wolfe *v.* Frost, 4 *Sandf. Ch.*, 72.

By whom grantable.

§ 248. A servitude can be created only by one who has a vested estate in the servient tenement.

Earl of Portmore *v.* Bunn, 3 *Dowl. & Ryl.*, 145, 151.

By whom held.

§ 249. A servitude thereon cannot be held by the owner of the servient tenement.

Huttemeier *v.* Albro, 2 *Bosw.*, 556; 18 *N. Y.*, 48; Tabor *v.* Bradley, 18 *N. Y.*, 109; James *v.* Plant, 4 *Ad. & El.*, 749.

§ 250. The extent of a servitude is determined by the terms of the grant,[1] or the nature of the enjoyment[2] by which it was acquired. *Extent of servitudes.*

[1] Dixon *v.* Clow, 24 *Wend.*, 188.
[2] Corning *v.* Gould, 16 *Wend.*, 531.

§ 251. In case of partition of the dominant tenement, the burden must be apportioned, according to the division of the dominant tenement, but not in such a way as to increase the burden upon the servient tenement. *Apportioning easements.*

The latter clause is added to meet the objection that common of estovers cannot be apportioned because so doing would multiply the burden (See Livingston *v.* Ketcham, 1 *Barb.*, 592).

§ 252. The owner of a future estate in a dominant tenement may use easements attached thereto, for the purpose of viewing waste, demanding rent, or removing an obstruction to the enjoyment of such easements, although such tenement is occupied by a tenant. *Rights of owner of future estate.*

Proud *v.* Hollis, 1 *Barn. & Cr.*, 8.

§ 253. The owner of any estate in a dominant tenement, or the occupant of such tenement, may maintain an action for the enforcement of an easement attached thereto. *Actions by owner and occupant of dominant tenement.*

Brouwer *v.* Jones, 23 *Barb.*, 153.

§ 254. The owner in fee of a servient tenement, may maintain an action for the possession of the land, against any one unlawfully possessed thereof, though a servitude exists thereon in favor of the public. *Actions by owner of servient tenement.*

Carpenter *v.* Oswego & Syr. R. R., 24 *N. Y.*, 655; Wager *v.* Troy Union R. R., 25 *N. Y.*, 526, 534. To the contrary was Redfield *v.* Utica & Syracuse R. R. Co., 25 *Barb.*, 54; approved, Wilklow *v.* Lane, 37 *Barb.*, 244.

Extinction of servitudes.

§ 255. A servitude is extinguished:

1. By the vesting of the right to the servitude and the right to the servient tenement in the same person;[1]

2. By the destruction of the servient tenement;[2]

3. By the performance of any act upon either tenement, by the owner of the servitude, or with his assent, which is incompatible with its nature or exercise;[3] or,

4. When the servitude was acquired by enjoyment,[4] by disuse thereof by the owner of the servitude for the period prescribed for acquiring title by enjoyment.[5]

[1] Huttemeier *v.* Albro, 18 *N. Y.*, 48; 2 *Bosw.*, 546; James *v.* Plant, 4 *Ad. & El.*, 749.

[2] Voorhees *v.* Presbyterian Church, 17 *Barb.*, 109; Regina *v.* Bamber, 5 *Q. B.*, 279; Regina *v.* Chorley, 12 *id.*, 515.

[3] Corning *v.* Gould, 16 *Wend.*, 539; 3 *Kent*, 449; see Crain *v.* Fox, 16 *Barb.*, 184.

[4] A servitude created by deed is not extinguished by mere non-user for any period (Smyles *v.* Hastings, 22 *N. Y.*, 217; 24 *Barb.*, 44; Jewett *v.* Jewett, 16 *id.*, 157).

[5] Robie *v.* Sedgwick, 35 *Barb.*, 329.

TITLE III.

RIGHTS AND OBLIGATIONS OF OWNERS.

CHAPTER I.

RIGHTS OF OWNERS.

ARTICLE I.

INCIDENTS OF OWNERSHIP.

§ 256. The owner of land owns water standing thereon, or flowing over[1] or under[2] its surface, but not forming a definite stream.[3] Water running in a definite stream, formed by nature[4] over[5] or under[6] the surface, may be used[7] by him as long as it remains there; but he may not prevent the natural[8] flow of the stream, or of the natural spring[9] from which it commences its definite course, nor pursue, nor pollute[10] the same. Water.

[1] Broadbent *v.* Ramsbotham, 11 *Exch.*, 602; better reported, 25 *L. J.* [*Exch.*], 122; Rawstron *v.* Taylor, 11 *Exch.*, 369, 382.

[2] Ellis *v.* Duncan, 21 *Barb.*, 230; Acton *v.* Blundell, 12 *M. & W.*, 324; Chasemore *v.* Richards, 7 *H. of L. Cas.*, 349.

[3] Chasemore *v.* Richards, *supra;* see Dickinson *v.* Grand Junction Canal Co., 7 *Exch.*, 282, 301.

[4] Wood *v.* Waud, 3 *Exch.*, 748; Greatrex *v.* Hayward, 8 *id.*, 291. But compare Belknap *v.* Trimble, 3 *Paige*, 577.

[5] Gardner *v.* Newburgh, 2 *Johns. Ch.*, 162; Reid *v.* Gifford, *Hopk.*, 416; Crooker *v.* Bragg, 10 *Wend.*, 260; Arnold *v.* Foot, 12 *Wend.*, 330.

[6] See Chasemore *v.* Richards, 7 *H. of L. Cas.*, 384; Smith *v.* Adams, 6 *Paige*, 435.

[7] Mason *v.* Hill, 5 *B. & Ad.*, 1; Embrey *v.* Owen, 6 *Exch.*, 353. There is no right of ownership, only a right of use (Van Hoesen *v.* Coventry, 10 *Barb.*, 518; Arnold *v.* Foot, 12 *Wend.*, 330).

[8] Bellinger *v.* N. Y. Central R. R., 23 *N. Y.*, 42; Corning *v.* Troy Factory, 34 *Barb.*, 485.

[9] Dudden *v.* Clutton Union, 1 *Hurlst. & N.*, 627.

[10] Honsee *v.* Hammond, 39 *Barb.*, 89; Thomas *v.* Brackney, 17 *id.*, 654; see Carhart *v.* Auburn Gaslight Co., 22 *id.*, 297.

Rights of tenant for life.

§ 257. The owner of a life estate may use the land in the same manner as the owner of a fee simple, except that he must do no act to the injury of the inheritance.

Jackson *v.* Brownson, 7 *Johns.*, 227, 234; Bradstreet *v.* Pratt, 17 *Wend.*, 44; Livingston *v.* Reynolds, 2 *Hill*, 157; 26 *Wend.*, 115.

Rights of tenant for years, &c.

§ 258. A tenant for years or at will, unless he is a wrongdoer by holding over, may occupy the buildings, take the annual products of the soil, work mines and quarries open at the commencement of his tenancy,[1] and cultivate and harvest the crops growing at the end of his tenancy.

[1] Freer *v.* Stotenbur, 36 *Barb.*, 641.

Id.

§ 259. A tenant for years or at will has no other rights to the property than such as are given to him by the agreement or instrument by which his tenancy is acquired, or by the last section.

Rights of grantees of rents and reversion.

§ 260. A person to whom any real property[1] is transferred or devised,[2] upon which rent has been reserved,[3] or to whom any such rent[4] is transferred, is entitled to the same remedies for recovery of rent, for non-performance of any of the terms of the lease, or for any waste or cause of forfeiture, as his grantor or devisor might have had.[5]

[1] Childs *v.* Clark, 3 *Barb. Ch.*, 58.
[2] Van Rensselaer *v.* Hays, 19 *N. Y.*, 68, 85, 86.
[3] The words "whether upon a lease in fee or otherwise," omitted.
[4] Willard *v.* Tillman, 2 *Hill*, 274; Moffat *v.* Smith, 4 *N. Y.*, 126.
[5] 1 *R. S.*, 747, § 23.

§ 261. Whatever remedies the lessee of any real property[1] may have against his immediate lessor, for the breach of any agreement in the lease, he may have against the assigns[2] of the lessor, and the assigns of the lessee may have against the lessor and his assigns, except upon covenants against incumbrances or relating to the title or possession of the premises. Rights of lessees and their assignees, &c.

1 *R. S.*, 747, § 24.
[1] The words "whether in fee or otherwise" omitted.
[2] Day *v.* Swackhamer, 2 *Hilton*, 4.

§ 262. The provisions of the last two sections apply to all grants reserving rent,[1] except grants in fee executed before the ninth day of April, 1805, or after the fourteenth day of April, 1860,[2] the rents reserved by which have been transferred since the latter date. Application of last two sections.

[1] 1 *R. S.*, 748, § 25; Van Rensselaer *v.* Hays, 19 *N. Y.* 68; Van Rensselaer *v.* Ball, *id.*, 100.
[2] The exception is intended to enact the amendment to this section contained in *Laws of* 1860, *ch.* 396; as construed in Main *v.* Green, 32 *Barb.*, 448, 457; 33 *id.*, 136.

§ 263. Rent due upon a lease for life may be recovered in the same manner as upon a lease for years. Remedy on leases for life.

1 *R. S.*, 747, § 19.

§ 264. Rent dependent on the life of a person may be recovered after, as well as before, his death. Rent dependent on life.

1 *R. S.*, 747, § 20.

Remedies of reversioners, &c.

§ 265. A person having an estate in fee,[1] in remainder or reversion, may maintain an action for any injury done to the inheritance, notwithstanding an intervening estate for life or years,[2] and although, after its commission, his estate is transferred, and he has no interest in the property at the commencement of the action.[3]

[1] The words "in fee" are new. No one but the owner in fee could have a right to maintain the action.

[2] 1 *R. S.*, 750, § 8; see Van Deusen *v.* Young, 29 *Barb.*, 9, 15. The rest of the section is new, though in accordance with existing law.

[3] Robinson *v.* Wheeler, 25 *N. Y.*, 252.

ARTICLE II.

BOUNDARIES.

Rights of owner.

§ 266. The owner of land in fee has the right to the surface, and to everything permanently situated beneath or above it.

Boundaries by water.

§ 267. When land borders upon tide-water,[1] or upon water which constitutes an exterior boundary of the state,[2] the owner of the upland takes to high-water mark; when it borders upon a navigable lake where there is no tide, the owner takes to the edge of the lake at low-water mark;[3] when it borders upon any other water,[4] the owner takes to the middle of the lake or stream.

[1] Gould *v.* Hudson River R. R., 6 *N. Y.*, 522.

[2] See Kingman *v.* Sparrow, 12 *Barb.*, 206; Canal Appraisers *v.* People, 17 *Wend.*, 570.

[3] Champlain R. R. *v.* Valentine, 19 *Barb.*, 484, 492.

[4] Ledyard *v.* Ten Eyck, 36 *Barb.*, 102; Hooker *v.* Cummings, 20 *Johns.*, 90, 99, 101; Canal Commissioners *v.* Kempshall, 26 *Wend.*, 404.

§ 268. An owner of land, bounded by a road or street, is presumed to own to the centre of the way, but the contrary may be shown. **Boundaries by ways.**

Mott *v.* Mayor of N. Y., 2 *Hilton*, 358, 363; Bissell *v.* N. Y. Central R. R., 23 *N. Y.*, 61; Wager *v.* Troy Union R. R., 25 *N. Y.*, 529. In the city of New York the fee in many of the streets is in the corporation, as trustees for the public; still, it is held that the above rule applies even to streets in that city.

§ 269. Each coterminous owner is entitled to the lateral[1] and subjacent[2] support which his land by nature receives from the land of the other. **Lateral and subjacent support.**

[1] Farrand *v.* Marshall, 21 *Barb.*, 409, 421; but see Radcliff *v.* Brooklyn, 4 *N. Y.*, 195; Panton *v.* Holland, 17 *Johns.*, 92. See also Lasala *v.* Holbrook, 4 *Paige*, 169.

[2] Rowbotham *v.* Wilson, 8 *El. & Bl.*, 123; 8 *House of Lords Cas.*, 348; Bonomi *v.* Backhouse, *El.*, *B. & El.*, 622; 7 *Jurist* (*N. S.*), 809, aff'd, 9 *H. L. Cas.* 503.

§ 270. Trees whose trunks stand wholly upon the land of one owner, belong exclusively to him, although their roots grow into the land of another. **Trees whose trunks are wholly on land of one.**

See Dubois *v.* Beaver, 25 *N. Y.*, 123, 126.

§ 271. Trees whose trunks stand partly on the land of two or more coterminous owners, belong to them in common. **Line trees.**

See Dubois *v.* Beaver, 25 *N. Y.*, 126, 127.

CHAPTER II.

OBLIGATIONS OF OWNERS.

§ 272. The owner of a life estate must keep the buildings and fences in repair from ordinary waste,[1] and must pay the taxes[2] and other annual charges,[3] **Duties of tenant for life.**

and a just proportion of extraordinary assessments benefiting the whole inheritance.[4]

[1] Sarles *v.* Sarles, 3 *Sandf. Ch.*, 601, 607.

[2] Fleet *v.* Dorland, 11 *How. Pr.*, 489; Graham *v.* Dunigan, 2 *Bosw.*, 516.

[3] Moseley *v.* Marshall, 22 *N. Y.*, 200, 202.

[4] Stilwell *v.* Doughty, 2 *Bradf.*, 311.

Monuments and fences.

§ 273. Coterminous owners are mutually[1] bound equally to maintain:

1. The boundaries and monuments between them;

2. The fences between them; unless one of them chooses to let his land lie open as a public common, in which case, if he afterwards incloses it, he must refund to the other a just proportion of the value, at that time, of any division fence made by the latter.[2]

[1] They owe this duty only to each other, and not to the public generally (Ryan *v.* Rochester & Syracuse R. R., 9 *How. Pr.*, 453).

[2] 1 *R. S.*, 353, §§ 30, 31, as amended; *Laws* 1860, *ch.* 267. The mode of determining controversies as to fences is prescribed by the POLITICAL CODE.

TITLE IV.

USES AND TRUSTS.

The provisions of this title are from 1 *R. S.*, 727; modified only as to the form of expression, except where otherwise noted. Sections 66, 69, 70, 71 and 72 are inserted in the title on TRUSTS in the Third Division of this Code. Section 67 is transferred to the title on SUCCESSION.

§ 274. Uses and trusts, in relation to real property, are those only which are specified in this Title. What uses and trusts may exist.

1 *R. S.*, 727, § 45. The commissioners have not considered it advisable to propose an amendment to this section in respect to charitable uses.

§ 275. Every estate which is now held as a use, executed under any former statute of this state, is confirmed as a legal estate. Executed uses existing.

1 *R. S.* 727, § 46.

§ 276. Every person who, by virtue of any transfer or devise, is entitled to the actual possession of real property, and the receipt of the rents and profits thereof, is to be deemed to have a legal estate therein,[1] of the same quality and duration, and subject to the same conditions,[2] as his beneficial interest. Right to possession of land creates legal ownership.

1 *R. S.*, 727, § 47.

[1] Post *v.* Hover, 30 *Barb.*, 312, 320; Leggett *v.* Hunter, 19 *N. Y.*, 454.

[2] Rawson v. Lampman, 5 *N. Y.*, 456, 461.

§ 277. The last section does not divest the estate of any trustees in a trust existing on the first day of January, one thousand eight hundred and thirty, where the title of such trustee is not merely nominal,[1] but is connected with some power of actual dis- Certain trusts unaffected.

position or management in relation to the real property which is the subject of the trust.

1 *R. S.*, 727, § 48.

[1] Frazer *v.* Western, 1 *Barb. Ch.*, 238, 239.

Trustees of estate for use of another take no interest.

§ 278. Every disposition of real property, whether by transfer or will, must be made directly to the person in whom the right to the possession and profits[1] is intended to be vested, and not to any other, to the use of or in trust for such person; and if made to any person, to the use of or in trust for another, no estate or interest[2] vests in the trustee; but he must execute a release of the property to the beneficiary on demand, the latter paying the expense thereof.[3]

1 *R. S.*, 728, § 49.

[1] Hotchkiss *v.* Elting, 36 *Barb.*, 44.

[2] Ring *v.* McCoun, 10 *N. Y.*, 268; Rawson *v.* Lampman, 5 *N. Y.*, 456, 462; Wright *v.* Douglass, 7 *N. Y.*, 564.

[3] This provision is new, and contrary to the existing law (Ring *v.* McCoun, 10 *N. Y.*, 268); but seems desirable to avoid difficulties in titles (see South Baptist Church *v.* Yates, *Hoffm.*, 142).

Preceding sections qualified.

§ 279. The preceding sections of this Title do not extend to trusts arising or resulting by implication of law, nor prevent or affect the creation of such express trusts as are hereinafter authorized and defined.

1 *R. S.*, 728, § 50.

Trust to be in writing.

§ 280. No trust in relation to real property is valid, unless created or declared:

1. By a written instrument, subscribed by the trustee, or by his agent thereto authorized by writing;

2. By the instrument under which the trustee claims the estate affected; or,

3. By operation of law.

Enlarged from 2 *R. S.*, 134, § 6.

Transfer to one for money paid by another.

§ 281. Where a transfer of real property is made to one person, and the consideration therefor is paid by or for[1] another, no use or trust results in favor of the person by or for[1] whom such payment is made;

but the title vests in the grantee, subject only to the provisions of the next two sections.[2]

[1] The words "or for" are intended to supersede the doctrine of Sieman *v.* Austin, 33 *Barb.*, 17; a decision which leaves much room for the frauds which this section was meant to avoid.

[2] 1 *R. S.*, 728, § 51; Davis *v.* Graves, 29 *Barb.*, 480.

Rights of creditors.

§ 282. Every such transfer as is described in the last section is presumed[1] to be fraudulent as against the creditors, at that time,[2] of the person paying the consideration; and where a fraudulent intent is not disproved, a trust results in favor of such creditors,[3] to the extent necessary to satisfy their just demands.

1 *R. S.*, 728, § 52.

[1] Wood *v.* Robinson, 22 *N. Y.*, 564, 566.

[2] Brewster *v.* Power, 10 *Paige*, 568, 570.

[3] Garfield *v.* Hatmaker, 15 *N. Y.*, 475; Wood *v.* Robinson, 22 *N. Y.*, 564; McCartney *v.* Bostwick, 31 *Barb.*, 390.

Section 281 qualified.

§ 283. Section 281 does not apply:

1. To cases where the grantee took the grant as an absolute[1] transfer in his own name, without the consent[2] or knowledge of the person paying the consideration; nor,

2. To cases where the grantee, in violation of a trust, purchased the real property so transferred, with property belonging to another person.[3]

1 *R. S.*, 728, § 53.

[1] Lounsbury *v.* Purdy, 18 *N. Y.*, 517.

[2] *Id.*, 518, 519.

[3] Reid *v.* Fitch, 11 *Barb.*, 399.

Purchasers protected.

§ 284. No implied or resulting trust can prejudice the rights of a purchaser or incumbrancer of real property, for value[1] and without notice[2] of the trust.

1 *R. S.*, 728, § 54.

[1] Wood *v.* Robinson, 22 *N. Y.*, 564, 567.

[2] Sieman *v.* Austin, 33 *Barb.*, 14.

For what purposes express trusts may be created.

§ 285. Express trusts may be created for any of the following purposes:

1. To sell[1] real property for the benefit of creditors;

2. To sell, mortgage or lease real property, for the benefit of annuitants[2] or other legatees, or for the purpose of satisfying any charge thereon;

3. To receive the rents and profits of real property, and pay them to[3] or apply them to the use of any person, whether ascertained at the time of the creation of the trust or not,[4] for himself or for his family[5] during the life[6] of such[7] person, or for any shorter term,[8] subject to the rules of Title II of this Part;[9] or,

4. To receive the rents and profits of real property, and to accumulate the same for the purposes and within the limits prescribed by the same Title.

1 *R. S.*, 728, § 55.

[1] Rogers *v.* Tilley, 20 *Barb.*, 641, 642; Darling *v.* Rogers, 22 *Wend.*, 483; Van Nest *v.* Yoe, 1 *Sandf. Ch.*, 4, Planck *v.* Schermerhorn, 3 *Barb. Ch.*, 644.

[2] The words "annuitants or other" are new, but supported by Lang *v.* Ropke, 5 *Sandf.*, 371; Hawley *v.* James, 16 *Wend.*, 61, 117.

[3] The words "pay them to, or" are new, but supported by Leggett *v.* Perkins, 2 *N. Y.*, 297, 306, 309; Leggett *v.* Hunter, 19 *N. Y.*, 454; Noyes *v.* Blakeman, 6 *N. Y.*, 581.

[4] The words "whether ascertained at the time of the trust or not" are new, but conform to Gilman *v.* Reddington, 24 *N. Y.*, 13, 14.

[5] The words "for himself or for his family" are new, but are sustained by Rogers *v.* Tilley, 20 *Barb.*, 639, 641.

[6] Though a trust for the minority of the beneficiary is valid (Lang *v.* Ropke, 5 *Sandf.*, 369), it is so upon the ground that it terminates at his death, even while yet a minor (*id.*; Hawley *v.* James, 16 *Wend.*, 61; 5 *Paige*, 463).

[7] Downing *v.* Marshall, 23 *N. Y.*, 377.

[8] Gilman *v.* Reddington, 24 *N. Y.*, 12; 1 *Hilt.*, 492.

[9] Coster *v.* Lorillard, 14 *Wend.*, 318; Hawley *v.* James, 16 *id.*, 174, 265.

Certain devises in trust to be deemed powers.

§ 286. A devise[1] of real property to executors or other trustees, to be sold or mortgaged, where the trustees are not also empowered to receive the rents and profits, vests no estate in them;[2] but the trust is valid as a power in trust.

1 *R. S.*, 729, § 56.

[1] Hawley *v.* James, 16 *Wend.*, 114, 115; Darling *v.* Rogers, 22 *id.*, 492.

[2] Germond *v.* Jones, 2 *Hill*, 573; Campbell *v.* Johnston, 1 *Sandf. Ch.*, 148.

§ 287. Where a trust is created to receive the rents and profits of real property, and no valid direction for accumulation is given, the surplus of such rents and profits, beyond the sum that may be necessary[1] for the education and support of the person for whose benefit the trust is created, is liable to the claims of the creditors[2] of such person, in the same manner as personal property which cannot be reached by execution.

Profits of land liable to creditors in certain cases.

1 *R. S.*, 729, § 57.

[1] Sillick *v.* Mason, 2 *Barb. Ch.*, 79; Clute *v.* Bool, 8 *Paige*, 83.

[2] L'Amoreux *v.* Van Rensselaer, 1 *Barb. Ch.*, 34; Noyes *v.* Blakeman, 6 *N. Y.*, 567.

§ 288. Where an express trust in relation to real property is created for any purpose not enumerated in the preceding sections, such trust vests[1] no estate in the trustees; but the trust, if directing or authorizing the performance of any act which may be lawfully performed under a power,[2] is valid as a power in trust, subject to the provisions in relation to such powers, contained in Title V of this Part.

Other express trusts to be powers in trust.

1 *R. S.*, 729, § 58.

[1] This expression is substituted for "no estate shall vest in," conformably to the decision in Darling *v.* Rogers, 22 *Wend.*, 494.

[2] Hotchkiss *v.* Elting, 36 *Barb.*, 45.

§ 289. Nothing in this Title prevents the creation of a power in trust, for any of the purposes for which an express trust may be created.

Creation of certain powers not prohibited.

This section is new. The contrary was assumed by BRONSON, J., in Hawley *v.* James, 16 *Wend.*, 174, 175, followed in Arnold *v.* Gilbert, 3 *Sandf. Ch.*, 563; the amendment enacts the construction adopted expressly by DUER, J., in Lang *v.* Ropke, 5 *Sandf.*, 367, 372, 373, and by implication in Tucker *v.* Tucker, 5 *N. Y.*, 408, and Downing *v.* Marshall, 23 *N. Y.*, 380.

And land, &c., to descend to persons entitled.

§ 290. In every case where a trust is valid as a power in trust, the real property to which the trust relates, remains in, or passes by succession to, the persons otherwise entitled, subject to the execution of the trust as a power in trust.

1 *R. S.*, 729, § 59. The words "in trust" are new.

Trustees of express trusts to have whole estate.

§ 291. Except as hereinafter[1] otherwise provided, every express trust in real property, valid as such, in its creation, vests the whole[2] estate in the trustees, subject only to the execution of the trust. The beneficiaries take no estate or interest in the property, but may enforce the performance of the trust.

1 *R. S.*, 729, § 60.

[1] "Hereinafter" is substituted for "herein." It was said in Darling *v.* Rogers, 22 *Wend.*, 492, 493, and Hawley *v.* James, 16 *Wend.*, 148, that this exception referred to § 282. But the express trusts mentioned in that section are not express trusts valid as *such*, but valid as *powers in trust*. The amendment enacts the construction adopted in Briggs *v.* Davis, 21 *N. Y.*, 576, without referring to the cases above cited.

[2] Savage *v.* Burnham, 17 *N. Y.*, 569; Noyes *v.* Blakeman, 6 *N. Y.*, 578, 581; Coster *v.* Lorillard, 14 *Wend.*, 304.

Author of trust may devise, &c.

§ 292. Notwithstanding anything contained in the last section, the author of a trust may, in its creation, prescribe to whom the real property to which the trust relates shall belong, in the event of the failure or termination of the trust, and may transfer or devise such property, subject to the execution of the trust.

1 *R. S.*, 729, § 61. See Corse *v.* Leggett, 25 *Barb.*, 395.

Title of grantor of trust property.

§ 293. The grantee or devisee of real property subject to a trust acquires a legal estate in the property, as against all persons except the trustees and those lawfully claiming under them.

1 *R. S.* 729, § 61.

§ 294. Where an express trust is created in relation to real property, every estate not embraced in the trust, and not otherwise disposed of, is left in[1] the author of the trust, or his successors.

Interests remaining in grantor of express trust.

1 *R. S.*, 729, § 62.

[1] Substituted for "remains in or reverts to," so as to conform to the definition of a reversion, § 225. The whole section, indeed, seems to be superfluous, but it is thought best not to omit it.

§ 295. The beneficiary of a trust for the receipt of the rents and profits of real property cannot transfer, or in any manner dispose of, his interest in such trust.

Powers over trust of party interested.

1 *R. S.*, 730, § 63; Belmont *v.* O'Brien, 12 *N. Y.*, 402.

§ 296. The beneficiary of a trust for the payment of an annuity out of the rents and profits[1] of real property, or of a sum in gross, can dispose of his interest in such trust.

Id.

1 *R. S.*, 730, § 63.

[1] Modified so as to adopt the construction given to this section of the Revised Statutes in Hawley *v.* James, 16 *Wend.*, 61, 275 (*decree*, section 4), and followed in Lang *v.* Ropke, 5 *Sandf.*, 371; Griffen *v.* Ford, 1 *Bosw.*, 143. To the contrary, see McSorley *v.* Wilson, 4 *Sandf. Ch.*, 524; Clute *v.* Bool, 8 *Paige*, 86.

§ 297. Where an express trust is created in relation to real property, but is not contained or declared in the grant to the trustee, such grant must be deemed absolute, in favor of the subsequent creditors of the trustees, not having notice of the trust, and in favor of purchasers from such trustees, without notice, and for a valuable consideration.

Effect of omitting trust in conveyance.

1 *R. S.*, 730, § 64. Davis *v.* Graves, 29 *Barb.*, 480.

§ 298. Where a trust in relation to real property is expressed in the instrument creating the estate, every transfer or other act of the trustees, in contravention of the trust, is absolutely void.

Certain sales, &c., by trustees void.

1 *R. S.*, 730, § 65. Belmont *v.* O'Brien, 12 *N. Y.*, 394, 405; Briggs *v.* Davis, 20 *N. Y.*, 21; 21 *N. Y.*, 577. This rule applies to purchasers in good faith, as well as to any others.

When estate of trustee to cease. § 299. When the purpose for which an express trust was created ceases, the estate of the trustee also ceases.

1 *R. S.*, 730, § 67.

TITLE V.

POWERS.

The provisions of this title are from 1 *R. S.*, 732; omitting § 127, which is embodied in the title on Succession, and § 126, which is inserted in the chapter on Interpretation of Wills.

§ 300. Powers, in relation to real property, are those only which are specified in this Title. *What powers exist.*

1 *R. S.*, 732, § 73. The phraseology of this section has been altered, in the same manner, and for the same reasons, as in the case of sections 195 and 274.

§ 301. The provisions of this Title do not extend to a simple power of attorney to convey real property in the name of the owner and for his benefit. *Application of this title.*

1 *R. S.*, 738, § 134.

§ 302. A power, as the term is used in this Title, is an authority to do some act in relation to real property, or to the creation or revocation[1] of an estate therein, or a charge thereon, which the owner[2] grant- *Definition of a power.*

ing or reserving such power might himself perform for any purpose.[3]

1 *R. S.*, 732, § 74.

[1] The words "or revocation" are new, but declaratory of existing law.

[2] Selden *v.* Vermilya, 3 *N. Y.*, 536.

[3] The words "for any purpose" are new, but do not alter the law (see §§ 288, 289; Downing *v.* Marshall, 23 *N. Y.*, 377–380; Belmont *v.* O'Brien, 12 *N. Y.*, 404).

Terms "author of a power" and "holder of a power" defined.

§ 303. The author of a power, as the term is used in this Title, is the person by whom a power is created, whether by grant or devise; and the holder of a power[1] is the person in whom a power is vested, whether by grant, devise or reservation.

1 *R. S.*, 738, § 135.

[1] Barber *v.* Cary, 11 *N. Y.*, 401, 403.

Division of powers.

§ 304. Powers are general or special, and beneficial or in trust.

1 *R. S.*, 732, § 76.

Definition of general powers.

§ 305. A power is general, when it authorizes the alienation or incumbrance of a fee in the property embraced therein, by grant, will or charge, or any of them,[1] in favor of any person whatever.

Ib., § 77.

[1] See Tallmadge *v.* Sill, 21 *Barb.*, 51, 52, 53.

Definition of special powers.

§ 306. A power is special:

1. When a person or class of persons is designated, to whom the disposition of property under the power is to be made;[1] or,

2. When it authorizes the alienation or incumbrance, by means of a grant, will, or charge, of only an estate less than a fee.

Ib., § 78.

[1] Wright *v.* Tallmadge, 15 *N. Y.*, 313, 314.

Beneficial powers.

§ 307. A power is beneficial, when no person other[1] than its holder has, by the terms of its creation, any interest in its execution.

Ib., § 79.

[1] Coster *v.* Lorillard, 14 *Wend.*, 325, 329, 361, 362; Barber *v.* Cary, 11 *N. Y.*, 402.

§ 308. A power is in trust, when any person or class of persons, other than its holder, has, by the terms of its creation, an interest in its execution. Powers in trust.

This section is new; but merely states the general principle upon which the two following sections are founded (see Coster *v.* Lorillard, 14 *Wend.*, 329, 362).

§ 309. A general power is in trust, when any person or class of persons, other than its holder, is designated as entitled to the proceeds of the disposition or charge authorized by the power, or to any portion of the proceeds or other benefits to result from its execution. General powers, when in trust.

1 *R. S.*, 734, § 94.

§ 310. A special power is in trust: Special powers, when in trust.

1. When the disposition or charge which it authorizes is limited to be made to any person or class of persons,[1] other[2] than the holder of the power; or,

2. When any person or class of persons, other[2] than the holder, is designated as entitled to any benefit from the disposition or charge authorized by the power.

Ib., § 95.

[1] Wright *v.* Tallmadge, 15 *N. Y.*, 314.

[2] Coster *v.* Lorillard, 14 *Wend.*, 325, 329, 361, 362.

§ 311. No person is capable of creating a power, who is not at the same time capable of granting some estate in the property to which the power relates. Who may create power.

1 *R. S.*, 732, § 75; Dempsey *v.* Tylee, 3 *Duer*, 97.

§ 312. A power may be vested in any person. To whom power may be given.

1 *R. S.*, 735, § 109; omitting all the restrictions of the statute, in accordance with § 170.

§ 313. A power may be created only: How to be created.

1. By a suitable clause, contained in a grant of some estate in the real property to which the power relates, or in an agreement to execute such a grant;[2] or,

2. By a devise contained in a will.[3]

1 *R. S.*, 735, § 106.

[1] Selden *v.* Vermilya, 3 *N. Y.*, 536; overruling S. C., 2 *Sandf.*, 580.

[2] The last clause is new, but is founded upon the equitable doctrine that a thing agreed to be done is to be considered as done (see Wadhams *v.* Missionary Society, 12 *N. Y.*, 422, *per* DENIO, J.)

[3] Dorland *v.* Dorland, 2 *Barb.*, 80.

Reservation of powers in conveyance.

§ 314. The grantor in any conveyance may reserve to himself any power, beneficial or in trust, which he might lawfully grant to another; and every power thus reserved is subject to the provisions of this Title, in the same manner as if granted to another.

Ib., § 105.

When powers irrevocable.

§ 315. Every power, beneficial or in trust, is irrevocable, unless an authority to revoke it is given or reserved in the instrument creating the power.

Ib., § 108; Wright *v.* Delafield, 23 *Barb.*, 517.

When power a lien.

§ 316. A power is a lien upon the real property which it embraces, from the time the instrument in which it is contained takes effect; except that against creditors, purchasers and incumbrancers, in good faith and without notice, from any person having an estate in such real property, the power is a lien only from the time the instrument in which it is contained is duly recorded.

Ib., § 107.

Power of sale in mortgage.

§ 317. Where a power to sell real property is given to a mortgagee or other incumbrancer, in an instrument intended to secure the payment of money, the power is to be deemed a part of the security, and vests in and may be executed by any person, who, by assignment or otherwise, becomes entitled to the money so secured to be paid.

1 *R. S.*, 737, § 133.

Beneficial powers, &c., transferred by insolvent assignments, &c.

§ 318. Every beneficial power, and the interest of every person entitled to compel the execution of a trust power, passes to the assignees, pursuant to statute, of the estate of a non-resident, absconding, insolvent or imprisoned debtor, or of a person of unsound mind, in whom such a power or interest is vested.

1 *R. S.*, 735, § 104.

§ 319. A power cannot be executed by any person not capable of disposing of real property. **Who to execute powers.**

Ib., § 109, omitting the reference to the next section, as being no exception, under the present state of the law.

§ 320. A married woman may execute a power during her marriage, without the concurrence of her husband, unless otherwise prescribed by the terms of the power. **Married women.**

Ib., § 110.

By this section "the disability of coverture is completely taken away, and a married woman may execute during coverture any power which may be lawfully conferred upon any person" (Denio, J., Wright *v.* Tallmadge, 15 *N. Y.*, 313; S. P., Leavitt *v.* Pell, 27 *Barb.*, 322, 332). Section 117 is in part to the same effect.

§ 321. No power can be executed by a married woman before she attains her majority,[1] nor without being acknowledged by her in the manner prescribed by the chapter on Recording Transfers.[2] **Id.**

[1] 1 *R. S.*, 735, § 111.
[2] 1 *R. S.*, 736, § 117. See page 152.

§ 322. A power can be executed only by a written instrument which would be sufficient to pass the estate or interest intended to pass under the power, if the person executing the power was the actual owner. **How executed.**

1 *R. S.*, 735, § 113.

§ 323. Where a power is vested in several persons, all must unite in its execution; but in case any one or more of them is dead, the power may be executed by the survivor or survivors, unless otherwise prescribed by the terms of the power. **Execution by survivors, &c.**

Ib., § 112. The exception is new, though probably in accordance with existing law.

Execution of power to dispose by devise.

§ 324. Where a power to dispose of real property is confined to a disposition by devise or will, the instrument of execution must be a will duly executed according to the provisions of the Title on WILLS.

1 *R. S.*, 736, § 115.

Execution of power to dispose by grant.

§ 325. Where a power is confined to a disposition by grant, it cannot be executed by will, even though the disposition is not intended to take effect until after the death of the person executing the power.

Ib., § 116.

Directions by author, when disregarded.

§ 326. Where the author of a power has directed or authorized it to be executed by an instrument which would not be sufficient in law to pass the estate, the power is not void, but its execution is to be governed by the rules before prescribed in this Title.

Ib., § 118.

Id.

§ 327. Where the author of a power has directed any formalities to be observed in its execution, in addition to those which would be sufficient to pass the estate, the observance of such additional formalities is not necessary to a valid execution of the power.

Ib., § 119.

Nominal conditions.

§ 328. Where the conditions annexed to a power are merely nominal, and evince no intention of actual benefit to the party to whom, or in whose favor, they are to be performed, they may be wholly disregarded in the execution of the power.

Ib., § 120.

When directions of author to be observed.

§ 329. With the exceptions contained in the preceding sections, the intentions of the author of a power as to the mode,[1] time[2] and conditions[3] of its execution must be observed, subject to the power of the supreme court to supply a defective execution in the cases provided in sections 338 and 362.

Ib., § 121.
[1] Demarest *v.* Ray, 29 *Barb.*, 563.
[2] Richardson *v.* Sharpe, 29 *Barb.*, 222; Allen *v.* De Witt, 3 *N. Y.*, 278, 279.
[3] Hotchkiss *v.* Elting, 36 *Barb.*, 46.

§ 330. When the consent of a third person[1] to the execution of a power is requisite, such consent must be expressed in the instrument by which the power is executed, or be certified in writing thereon. In the first case the instrument of execution, in the second, the certificate, must be subscribed by the party whose consent is required; and to entitle the instrument to be recorded, such signature must be duly proved or acknowledged, according to the chapter on RECORDING TRANSFERS. Consent of third person to execution of power.

Ib., § 122.
[1] Barber *v.* Cary, 11 *N. Y.*, 398.

§ 331. Where the consent of several persons to the execution of a power is requisite, all must consent thereto; but, in case any one or more of them is dead, the consent of the survivors is sufficient, unless otherwise prescribed by the terms of the power. Id.

This section is new. Compare § 323.
It was held in Barber *v.* Cary, 11 *N. Y.*, 397, on a strict construction of section 323, that the consent of the survivors would not suffice. There is no reason why survivors should not be allowed to consent, if survivors are allowed to execute.

§ 332. Every instrument executed by the holder of a power, conveying an estate or creating a charge which such holder would have no right to convey or create except by virtue of his power, is to be deemed a valid execution of the power, even though not recited or referred to therein. Omission to recite power.

1 *R. S.*, 737, § 124.

Instruments deemed conveyances.

§ 333. Every instrument except a will, in execution of a power, even though the power is one of revocation only, is to be deemed a conveyance within the meaning of the chapter on RECORDING TRANSFERS.

1 *R. S.*, 736, § 114.

Certain dispositions not void.

§ 334. A disposition or charge, by virtue of a power, more extensive than was authorized thereby, is not therefore void; but every estate or interest so created, so far as it is embraced by the terms of the power, is valid.

1 *R. S.*, 737, § 123. The words "or charge" are new.

Computation of term of suspensions.

§ 335. The period during which the absolute right of alienation may be suspended by an instrument in execution of a power, must be computed, not from the date of the instrument, but from the time of the creation of the power.

Ib., § 128.

What estate may be given.

§ 336. No estate or interest can be given or limited to any person, by an instrument in execution of a power, which could not have been given or limited at the time of the creation of the power.

1 *R. S.*, 737, § 129, modified by substituting the words "which could not," &c., for the words "which such person would not have been capable of taking under the instrument by which the power was granted," so as to remove the difficulty of construction suggested in Dempsey *v.* Tylee, 3 *Duer*, 73, 98, 101, 102. Compare Hoey *v.* Kenny, 25 *Barb.*, 396.

Married women, their authority.

§ 337. When a married woman, entitled to an estate in fee, is authorized by a power to dispose of such estate during her marriage, she may, by virtue of such power, create any estate which she might create if unmarried.

1 *R. S.*, 737, § 130.

Defective execution.

§ 338. Purchasers for a valuable consideration, claiming under a defective execution of a power, are entitled to the same relief as similar purchasers claiming under a defective conveyance from an actual owner.

Ib., § 132; Barber *v.* Cary, 11 *N. Y.*, 400.

§ 339. Instruments in execution of a power are affected by fraud in the same manner as like instruments executed by owners or trustees. Fraud.

Ib., § 125.

§ 340. A general and beneficial power is valid, which gives to a married woman power to dispose, during her marriage, and without the concurrence of her husband, of a present or future estate in real property conveyed or devised to her in fee. General and beneficial powers to married women.

1 *R. S.*, 732, § 80, changed in phraseology, so as to render it consistent with the present law concerning the rights of married women. A married woman may now dispose of property as if she were unmarried, and for all women married since 1848, this provision is unnecessary. But there may be powers heretofore created, the validity of which it is proper to recognize.

The words "a present or future estate in" are added, in conformity to the construction of WALWORTH, Ch., in Jackson *v.* Edwards, 7 *Paige*, 386, 401.

§ 341. Where an absolute power of disposition, not accompanied by any trust, is given to the owner of a particular estate for life or years, such estate is changed into a fee, absolute in favor of creditors, purchasers, and incumbrancers, but subject to any future estates limited thereon, in case the power should not be executed, or the property should not be sold[1] for the satisfaction of debts. Estate of owner for life, &c., when changed into a fee.

Ib., § 81.

[1] Jackson *v.* Edwards, 22 *Wend.*, 509.

§ 342. Where an absolute power of disposition, not accompanied by any trust, is given to any person to whom no particular estate is limited, such person also takes a fee, subject to any future estate that may be limited thereon, but absolute in favor of creditors, purchasers, and incumbrancers. Certain powers create a fee.

Ib., § 82.

Id.

§ 343. In all cases where an absolute power of disposition is given, not accompanied by any trust, and no remainder is limited on the estate of the holder of the power, he is entitled to an absolute fee.

1 *R. S.*, 733, § 83.

Effect of power to devise inheritance in certain cases.

§ 344. Where a general and beneficial power to devise the inheritance is given to the owner of an estate for life or for years, he is deemed to possess an absolute power of disposition, within the meaning of the last three sections.

1 *R. S.*, 733, § 84. See Tallmadge *v.* Sill, 21 *Barb.*, 52, 53.

Power to dispose of fee.

§ 345. Every power of disposition is deemed absolute, by means of which the holder is enabled in his lifetime to dispose of the entire fee, in possession or in expectancy, for his own benefit.

Ib., § 85.

The words "in possession or in expectancy" are added, in conformity to the construction of WALWORTH, Ch., in Jackson *v.* Edwards, 7 *Paige*, 401.

Power to revoke.

§ 346. Where the grantor in any conveyance reserves to himself, for his own benefit, an absolute power of revocation, such grantor is still to be deemed the absolute owner of the estate conveyed, so far as the rights of creditors and purchasers are concerned.

Ib., § 86.

Special and beneficial powers, who may take.

§ 347. A special and beneficial power is valid, which is granted:

1. To a married woman, to dispose, during the marriage, of any estate less than a fee, belonging to her, in the property to which the power relates; or,

2. To the owner of a life estate in the property embraced in the power, to make leases for not more than twenty-one years, commencing in possession during his life.

Ib., § 87. See note to § 340.

§ 348. A special and beneficial power to make leases for more than twenty-one years given to the owner of a life estate, is void only as to the time beyond twenty-one years, and authorizes leases for that term or less.

Construction of leasing powers.

This section is new.

The contrary was held in Root *v.* Stuyvesant, 18 *Wend.*, 257, "by a divided vote against the opinion of all the judges" (Williams *v.* Williams, 8 *N. Y.*, 539). It is "an anomalous case, to be rejected and shunned, not to be followed; as an authority it ought never to be quoted" (DUER, J., Lang *v.* Ropke, 5 *Sandf.*, 372), "an adjudication between the amicable parties then before the court, and not a precedent which can affect the rights of third persons" (BRONSON, J., Hone *v.* Van Schaick, 20 *Wend.*, 569; and see Darling *v.* Rogers, 22 *Wend.*, 496).

§ 349. The power of the owner of a life estate to make leases is not transferable as a separate interest, but is annexed to his estate, and will pass, unless specially excepted, by any grant of such estate. If specially excepted in any such grant, it is extinguished.

Power to make leases by owner for life.

1 *R. S.*, 733, § 88.

§ 350. The power of the owner of a life estate to make leases may be released by him to any person entitled to a future estate in the property, and is thereupon extinguished.

Release of such power.

Ib., § 89.

§ 351. A mortgage, executed by the owner of a life estate having a power to make leases, or by a married woman, by virtue of any beneficial power, does not extinguish or suspend the power; but the power is bound by the mortgage in the same manner as the real property embraced therein.

Mortgages by party having power to lease, &c.

Ib., § 90.

§ 352. The effects on the power, of a lien by mortgage such as is mentioned in the last section, are:

Effect thereof.

1. That the mortgagee is entitled to an execution of the power, so far as the satisfaction of his lien may require it; and,

2. That any subsequent estate created by the owner, in execution of the power, becomes subject to the mortgage in the same manner as if in terms embraced therein.

1 *R. S.*, 733, § 91.

Special and beneficial powers liable to creditors.

§ 353. Every special and beneficial power is liable to the claims of creditors, in the same manner as other interests that cannot be reached by execution, and the execution of the power may be adjudged for the benefit of the creditors entitled.

Ib., § 93.

Future beneficial powers.

§ 354. No beneficial power, general or special, not already specified and defined in this Title, can hereafter be created.

Ib., § 92.

It has been thought that the omission of this section would not affect the authority to create such powers (Nelson, Ch. J., Root *v.* Stuyvesant, 18 *Wend.*, 271; Cowen, J., *ib.*, 292). But the Revisers say: "We have deemed it very important to limit the authority of owners in the creation of beneficial powers. * * We have not been able to discover that any practical good can result from their permission, except in the cases that we have *specified*" (5 *Edmonds' Stat. at Large, Rev. Note*, 328). And see Jackson *v.* Edwards, 7 *Paige*, 400.

Trust powers imperative.

§ 355. Every trust power, unless its execution is made expressly to depend on the will of the trustee,[1] is imperative, and imposes a duty on the trustee, the performance of which may be compelled for the benefit of the parties interested.

1 *R. S.*, 734, § 96.

[1] Arnold *v.* Gilbert, 5 *Barb.*, 195, 198.

Effect of right of selection.

§ 356. A trust power does not cease to be imperative, where the trustee has the right to select any, and exclude others, of the persons designated as the beneficiaries of the trust.

Ib., § 97.
Hoey *v.* Kenny, 25 *Barb.*, 396.

§ 357. Where a disposition under a power is directed to be made to, among, or between several persons, without any specification of the share or sum to be allotted to each, all the persons designated are entitled in equal proportion. Construction of certain powers

Ib., § 98.

§ 358. Where the terms of a power import that the estate or fund is to be distributed among several persons designated, in such manner or proportions as the trustee of the power may think proper, the trustee may allot the whole to any one or more of such persons in exclusion of the others. Id.

Ib., § 99.

§ 359. If the trustee of a power, with the right of selection, dies leaving the power unexecuted, its execution must be adjudged for the benefit, equally, of all the persons designated as objects of the trust. When court to execute power.

Ib., § 100.
Hoey *v.* Kenny, 25 *Barb.*, 396.

§ 360. Where a power in trust is created by will, and the testator has omitted to designate, expressly or by necessary implication, by whom the power is to be executed, its execution devolves on the supreme court. Id.

Ib., § 101.
The words "expressly or by necessary implication" are added, upon the authority of Meakings *v.* Cromwell, 5 *N. Y.*, 139.

§ 361. The execution, in whole or in part, of any trust power, may be adjudged for the benefit of the creditors or assignees of any person entitled, as one of the beneficiaries of the trust, to compel its execution, when his interest is transferable. Execution of trust power, when compelled by creditors, &c.

1 *R. S.*, 735, § 103.

Defective execution.

§ 362. Where the execution of a power in trust is defective, in whole or in part, under the provisions of this Title, its proper execution may be adjudged in favor of the persons designated as the objects of the trust.

1 *R. S.*, 737, § 131.

Application of certain sections.

§ 363. The provisions of the Title on TRUST, saving the rights of other persons from prejudice by the misconduct of trustees, and authorizing the court to remove and appoint trustees; the provisions of the Title on SUCCESSION, devolving express trusts upon the court,[1] on the death of the trustee; and the provisions of section 299, in the Title on USES AND TRUSTS,[2] apply equally to powers in trust, and the trustees of such powers.

1 *R. S.*, 734, § 102.
Hoey *v.* Kenny, 25 *Barb.*, 396.
Hutchings *v.* Baldwin, 7 *Bosw.*, 236, 241.

PART III.

PERSONAL OR MOVABLE PROPERTY.

TITLE I.

PERSONAL PROPERTY IN GENERAL.

§ 364. If there is no law to the contrary in the place where personal property is situated, it is deemed to follow the person of its owner, and is governed by the law of his domicile. By what law governed.

§ 365. Where one has the present and another the future interest in a thing personal, and the thing is perishable, the latter may require it to be sold, and the proceeds invested, for the benefit of both parties, according to their respective interests; except in case of a thing specially appropriated to a particular use. Future interests in perishable property, how protected.

This provision is new.

TITLE II.

PARTICULAR KINDS OF PERSONAL PROPERTY.

CHAPTER I.

THINGS IN ACTION.

Things in action defined.

§ 366. A thing in action is a right to recover something by a judicial proceeding.

Transfer and survivorship.

§ 367. A thing in action, arising out of the violation of a right of property, or out of an obligation, may be transferred by the owner. Upon the death of the owner it passes to his personal representatives, except where, in the cases provided in the CODE OF CIVIL PROCEDURE, it passes to his devisees or successor in office.

This section is proposed to establish one rule for the assignability and the survivorship of things in action. Though the cases on this subject are conflicting, this view is generally received (See McKee *v.* Judd, 12 *N. Y.*, 622; Meech *v.* Stoner, 19 *id.*, 26).

CHAPTER II.

SHIPPING.

ARTICLE I.

GENERAL PROVISIONS.

§ 368. A ship is any structure fitted for navigation. Every kind of ship is included in the term "shipping." Definition of a ship.

§ 369. All things, belonging to the owners, which are on board a ship, and are connected with its proper use, for the objects of the voyage and adventure in which the ship is engaged, are deemed its appurtenances. Appurtenances and equipments.

See the cases on this subject in 1 *Pars. Mar. L.*, 71.

§ 370. Ships are engaged either in foreign or domestic navigation, or in the fisheries. Ships are engaged in foreign navigation, when passing to or from a foreign country; and in domestic navigation, when passing from place to place within the United States. Foreign and domestic navigation.

§ 371. A ship in a port of the state to which it belongs is called a domestic ship; in another port it is called a foreign ship. Foreign and domestic ships distinguished.

§ 372. If a ship belongs to several persons, not partners, and they differ as to its use or repair, the Several owners.

controversy may be determined by any court of competent jurisdiction.

This provision, which is new, is intended to establish a rule for all cases of difference, whether a majority concur in one opinion or not (See 2 *Pars. Mar. Law*, 555).

Owner for the voyage.

§ 373. If the owner of a ship commits its possession and navigation to another, that other, and not the owner, is responsible for its repairs and supplies.

Registry, enrollment and license.

§ 374. The registry, enrollment, and license of ships, are regulated by acts of Congress.

3 *Kent*, 133; Hesketh *v.* Stevens, 7 *Barb.*, 488.

ARTICLE II.

RULES OF NAVIGATION.*

Collisions.

§ 375. In the case of ships meeting, the following rules must be observed in addition to those prescribed by that part of the POLITICAL CODE, which relates to Navigation:

Rules as to ships meeting each other.

1. Whenever any ship, whether a steamer or sailing ship, proceeding in one direction, meets another ship, whether a steamer or sailing ship, proceeding in another direction, so that if both ships were to continue their respective courses they would pass so near as to involve the risk of a collision, the helms of both ships must be put to port so as to pass on the port

* The subjects of Pilotage and Wrecks are regulated by the POLITICAL CODE.

side of each other; and this rule applies to all steamers and all sailing ships, whether on the port or starboard tack, and whether close-hauled or not, except where the circumstances of the case are such as to render a departure from the rule necessary in order to avoid immediate danger, and subject also to a due regard to the dangers of navigation, and, as regards sailing ships on the starboard tack close-hauled, to the keeping such ships under command.[1]

2. In the case of sailing vessels, those having the wind fair must give way to those on a wind. When both are going by the wind, the vessel on the starboard tack must keep her wind, and the one on the larboard tack bear up strongly, passing each other on the larboard hand. When both vessels have the wind large or abeam, and meet, they must pass each other in the same way on the larboard hand, to effect which two last mentioned objects the helm must be put to port. Steam vessels must be regarded as vessels navigating with a fair wind, and should give way to sailing vessels on a wind of either tack.[2] The rule for sailing vessels.

3. A steamer navigating a narrow channel must, whenever it is safe and practicable, keep to that side of the fair way or mid-channel which lies on the starboard side of the steamer.[3] Rules for steamers in narrow channels.

4. A steamer when passing another steamer in such channel, must always leave the other upon the larboard side.[4]

5. When steamers must inevitably or necessarily cross so near that, by continuing their respective courses, there would be a risk of collision, each vessel must put her helm to port, so as always to pass on the larboard side of each other.[5] Rule for steam vessels on different courses.

6. The rules of this section do not apply to any case for which a different rule is provided by the regulations for the government of pilots of steamers approaching each other within sound of the steam whistle, or by the regulations concerning lights upon Meeting of steamers.

steamers, prescribed under authority of the acts of Congress, approved August 30, 1852, and April 29, 1864.*

[1] This rule is from the English Mercantile Shipping Act of 1854. 17 and 18 *Vic.*, *c.* 104.

[2] This rule is from the Rules of Navigation of Trinity House, 1840.

[3] 17 and 18 *Vic.*, *c.* 104.

[4] Rules of Trinity House.

[5] Rules of Trinity House.

---

* The regulations prescribed by the Board of Inspectors, under authority of the act of 1852, are as follows:

All pilots of steamers navigating seas, gulfs, lakes, bays, or rivers (except rivers emptying into the Gulf of Mexico, and their tributaries), when meeting or approaching each other, whether by day or by night, and as soon as within sight and fully within sound of the steam whistle, shall observe and comply with the following

REGULATIONS:

RULE 1. When steamers meet "head and head," it shall be the duty of each to pass to the right or larboard side of the other. And either pilot, upon determining to pursue this course, shall give, as a signal of his intention, *one* short and distinct blast of his steam whistle, which the other shall answer promptly by a similar blast of the whistle. But if the course of each steamer is so far on the starboard of the other as not to be considered by the rules as meeting "head and head," or if the vessels are approaching in such a manner, that passing to the right (as above directed) is deemed unsafe, or contrary to rule, by the pilot of either vessel, the pilot so deciding shall immediately give *two* short and distinct blasts of his steam whistle, which the other pilot shall answer promptly by *two* similar blasts of his whistle, and they shall pass to the left or on the starboard side of each other. NOTE.—*In the night*, steamers will be considered meeting "head and head," so long as both the colored lights of each are in view of the other. *In the day*, a similar position will also be considered "head and head."

RULE 2. When steamers are approaching each other in an oblique direction (as shown in diagram of fifth situation), they will pass to the right, as if meeting "head and head," and the signal, by whistle, shall be given and answered promptly, as in that case specified.

RULE 3. If, when steamers are approaching each other, the pilot of either vessel fails to understand the course or intention of the other, whether from the signals being given and answered erroneously, or from other cause, the pilot, so in doubt, shall immediately signify the same by giving several short and rapid blasts of the steam whistle, and if the vessels shall have approached within half a mile of each other, both shall be immediately slowed to a speed barely sufficient for steerage way, until the proper signals are given, answered and understood, or until the vessels shall have passed each other.

RULE 4. When steamers are running in a fog, or thick weather, it shall be the duty of the pilot to cause a *long* blast of the steam whistle to be sounded at intervals not exceeding two minutes. And no steamer shall, in any case, be justified in coming into collision with another vessel if it be possible to avoid it.

RULE 5. Whenever a steamer is nearing a short bend or curve in the channel, where, from the height of the banks or other cause, a steamer approaching from the opposite direction cannot be seen for a distance of half a mile, the pilot of such steamer, when he shall have arrived within half a mile of such curve or bend, shall give a signal by *one* long blast of the steam whistle, which signal shall be answered by a similar blast given by the pilot of any approaching steamer that may be within hearing. Should such signal be so answered by a steamer upon the further side of such bend, then the usual signals for meeting and passing shall immediately be given and answered. But if the *first* alarm signal of such pilot be not answered, he is to consider the channel clear, and govern himself accordingly.

RULE 6. The signals by blowing of the steam whistle shall be given and answered by pilots in compliance with these rules, not only when meeting "head and head," or nearly so, but at all times, when passing or meeting, at a distance within half a mile of each other, and whether passing to the starboard or larboard.

N. B.—The foregoing rules are to be complied with in all cases, except when steamers are navigating in a crowded channel or in the vicinity of wharves,—under these circumstances steamers must be run and managed with great caution, sounding the whistle as may be necessary to guard against collision or other accidents.

STEAMERS' LIGHTS, TO PREVENT COLLISION AT NIGHT.

RULE 7. *When under weigh.* All steamers rigged for carrying sail must carry a bright white light at the foremast head, and all other steamers must carry a bright white light on the *stem* or near the bow, and another on a mast near the stern, or on the flag-staff at the *stern*, the last named being at an elevation of at least twenty feet above all other lights upon the steamer. All steamers must carry a green light upon the starboard side, and a red light on the port side.

§ 376. If it appears that a collision was occasioned by failure to observe any rule of the foregoing section, the owner of the ship by which such rule is infringed cannot recover compensation for damages sustained by the ship in such collision, unless it appears that the circumstances of the case made a departure from the rule necessary.

If collision ensues from breach of the above rules, owner not to be entitled to recover.

NOTE.—Steamers, although rigged for carrying sail, instead of the foremast head light, may adopt the forward and stern lights provided for steamers *not* rigged for carrying sail, provided such lights are so arranged and placed on the vessel as to secure the contemplated objects.

When at anchor. A bright, white light at least twenty feet above the surface of the water. The lantern so constructed and placed as to show a good light all around the horizon.

FIRST. The masthead light of steamers rigged for carrying sail to be visible at a distance of at least five miles in a clear dark night, and the lantern to be so constructed as to show a uniform and unbroken light over an arc of the horizon of twenty points of the compass, namely, from right ahead to two points abaft the beam on either side of the ship.

SECOND. The stem and stern lights of steamers not rigged for carrying sail to be visible at a distance of at least five miles in a clear dark night, and the respective lanterns to be so constructed that the stem light shall show a uniform and unbroken light over an arc of the horizon of twenty points of the compass, namely, from right ahead to two points abaft the beam on either side of the ship, and that the stern light shall show a uniform light all around the horizon.

THIRD. The colored side lights to be visible at a distance of at least two miles in a clear dark night; and the lanterns to be so constructed as to show a uniform and unbroken light over an arc of the horizon of ten points of the compass, namely, from right ahead to two points abaft the beam on their respective sides.

FOURTH. The side lights are to be fitted with inboard screens of at least *six feet* in length (clear of the lantern), to prevent them from being seen across the bow. The screens are to be placed in a fore and aft line with the inner edge of the side lights, and in contact therewith.

NOTE FIRST. The object of carrying the bright white light at the foremast head of steamers rigged for carrying sail is merely to intimate to other vessels the approach or presence of such steamer.

NOTE SECOND. The object of the colored lights required to be carried on *all* steamers, is to indicate to other vessels the course or direction such steamer may be steering.

NOTE THIRD. The object of requiring steamers not rigged for carrying sail to carry a white stern light in connection with a white light on the stem or near the bow, is to provide (when the vessel's rig will admit of it) a method of determining, by a central range of lights, more correctly the course that such vessel is running.

The regulations of the act of April 29, 1864, which apply to all "mercantile marine," are as follows:

REGULATIONS FOR PREVENTING COLLISIONS ON WATER.

PRELIMINARY.

ARTICLE 1. *What to be considered sailing-ships and what ships under steam.* In the following rules every steamship which is under sail, and not under steam, is to be considered a sailing-ship; and every steamship which is under steam, whether under sail or not, is to be considered a ship under steam.

RULES CONCERNING LIGHTS.

LIGHTS.

ART. 2. The lights mentioned in the following articles, and no others, shall be carried in all weathers between sunset and sunrise.

LIGHTS FOR STEAMSHIPS.

ART. 3. All steam vessels when under way shall carry—(*a*.) At the foremast head, a bright white light, so fixed as to show an uniform and unbroken light over an arc of the horizon of twenty points of the compass, so fixed as to throw the light ten points on each side of the ship, viz.: from right ahead to two points abaft the beam on either side, and of such a character as to be visible on a dark night, with a clear atmosphere, at a distance of at least five miles. (*b*.) On the starboard side, a green light, so constructed as to throw an uniform and unbroken light over an arc of the horizon of ten points of the compass, so fixed as to throw the light from

Breaches of such rules to imply willful default.

§ 377. Damage to person or property arising from the failure of a ship to observe any rule of section 375, must be deemed to have been occasioned by the willful default of the person in charge of the deck of such ship at the time, unless it appears that the circumstances of the case made a departure from the rule necessary.

---

right ahead to two points abaft the beam on the starboard side, and of such a character as to be visible on a dark night, with a clear atmosphere, at a distance of at least two miles. (*c.*) On the port side, a red light, so constructed as to show an uniform and unbroken light over an arc of the horizon of ten points of the compass, so fixed as to throw the light from right ahead to two points abaft the beam on the port side, and of such a character as to be visible on a dark night, with a clear atmosphere, at a distance of at least two miles. (*d.*) The said green and red side lights shall be fitted with inboard screens, projecting at least three feet forward from the light, so as to prevent these lights from being seen across the bow.

LIGHTS FOR STEAM-TUGS.

ART. 4. Steamships, when towing other ships, shall carry two bright white masthead lights vertically, in addition to their side lights, so as to distinguish them from other steamships. Each of these masthead lights shall be of the same construction and character as the masthead lights which other steamships are required to carry.

LIGHTS FOR SAILING-SHIPS.

ART. 5. Sailing-ships under way or being towed, shall carry the same lights as steamships under way, with the exception of the white masthead lights, which they shall never carry.

EXCEPTIONAL LIGHTS FOR SMALL SAILING-VESSELS.

ART. 6. Whenever, as in the case of small vessels during bad weather, the green and red lights cannot be fixed, these lights shall be kept on deck, on their respective sides of the vessel, ready for instant exhibition, and shall, on the approach of or to other vessels, be exhibited on their respective sides in sufficient time to prevent collision, in such manner as to make them most visible, and so that the green light shall not be seen on the port side, nor the red light on the starboard side.

To make the use of these portable lights more certain and easy, they shall each be painted outside with the color of the light they respectively contain, and shall be provided with suitable screens.

LIGHTS FOR SHIPS AT ANCHOR.

ART. 7. Ships, whether steamships or sailing-ships, when at anchor in roadsteads or fairways, shall, between sunset and sunrise, exhibit where it can best be seen, but at a height not exceeding twenty feet above the hull, a white light in a globular lantern of eight inches in diameter, and so constructed as to show a clear, uniform and unbroken light, visible all around the horizon, and at a distance of at least one mile.

LIGHTS FOR PILOT-VESSELS.

ART. 8. Sailing pilot-vessels shall not carry the lights required for other sailing-vessels, but shall carry a white light at the masthead, visible all around the horizon, and shall also exhibit a flare-up light every fifteen minutes.

LIGHTS FOR FISHING-VESSELS AND BOATS.

ART. 9. Open fishing-boats and other open boats shall not be required to carry side lights required for other vessels, but shall, if they do not carry such lights, carry a lantern having a green slide on the one side and a red slide on the other side, and on the approach of or to other vessels, such lantern shall be exhibited in sufficient time to prevent collision, so that the green light shall not be seen on the port side, nor the red light on the starboard side. Fishing-vessels and open boats when at anchor, or attached to their nets and stationary, shall exhibit a bright white light. Fishing-vessels and open boats shall, however, not be prevented from using a flare-up in addition, if considered expedient.

RULES GOVERNING FOG-SIGNALS.

FOG-SIGNALS.

ART. 10. Whenever there is a fog, whether by day or night, the fog-signals described below shall be carried and used, and shall be sounded at least every five minutes, viz.:

(*a.*) Steamships under way shall use a steam whistle placed before the funnel, not less than eight feet from the deck.

(*b.*) Sailing-ships under way shall use a fog-horn.

(*c.*) Steamships and sailing ships when not under way shall use a bell.

§ 378. Losses caused by collision are to be borne as follows: Loss, how apportioned.

1. If either party was exclusively in fault he must bear his own loss, and compensate the other for any loss he has sustained;[1]

2. If neither was in fault, the loss must be borne by him on whom it falls;[2]

3. If both were in fault the loss is to be equally divided,[3] unless it appears that there was a great disparity in fault, in which case the loss must be equitably apportioned; or,

---

STEERING AND SAILING RULES.

TWO SAILING-SHIPS MEETING.

ART. 11. If two sailing-ships are meeting end on, or nearly end on, so as to involve risk of collision, the helms of both shall be put to port, so that each may pass on the port side of the other.

TWO SAILING-SHIPS CROSSING.

ART. 12. When two sailing-ships are crossing so as to involve risk of collision, then, if they have the wind on different sides, the ship with wind on the port side shall keep out of the way of the ship with the wind on the starboard side, except in the case in which the ship with the wind on the port side is close hauled, and the other ship free, in which case the latter ship shall keep out of the way. But if they have the wind on the same side, or if one of them has the wind aft, the ship which is to windward, shall keep out of the way of the ship which is to leeward.

TWO SHIPS UNDER STEAM MEETING.

ART. 13. If two ships under steam are meeting on, or nearly end on, so as to involve risk of collision, the helms of both shall be put to port so that each may pass on the port side of the other.

TWO SHIPS UNDER STEAM CROSSING.

ART. 14. If two ships under steam are crossing so as to involve risk of collision, the ship which has the other on her own starboard side, shall keep out of the way of the other.

SAILING SHIP AND SHIP UNDER STEAM.

ART. 15. If two ships, one of which is a sailing-ship and the other a steamship, are proceeding in such directions as to involve risk of collision, the steamship shall keep out of the way of the sailing-ship.

SHIPS UNDER STEAM TO SLACKEN SPEED.

ART. 16. Every steamship, when approaching another ship, so as to involve risk of collision, shall slacken her speed, or, if necessary, stop and reverse; and every steamship shall, when in a fog, go at a moderate speed.

VESSELS OVERTAKING OTHER VESSELS.

ART. 17. Every vessel overtaking any other vessel, shall keep out of way of the said last mentioned vessel.

CONSTRUCTION OF ARTICLES 12, 14, 15 AND 17.

ART. 18. Where, by the above rules, one of two ships is to keep out of the way, the other shall keep her course subject to the qualifications contained in the following article:

PROVISO TO SAVE SPECIAL CASES.

ART. 19. In obeying and construing these rules, due regard must be had to all dangers of navigation, and due regard must also be had to any special circumstances which may exist in any particular case, rendering a departure from the above rules necessary in order to avoid immediate danger.

NO SHIP UNDER ANY CIRCUMSTANCES TO NEGLECT PROPER PRECAUTIONS

ART. 20. Nothing in these rules shall exonerate any ship, or the owner, or master, or crew thereof, from the consequences of any neglect to carry lights or signals, or of any neglect to keep a proper lookout, or of the neglect of any precaution which may be required by the ordinary practice of seamen, or by the special circumstances of the case. *Approved, April* 29, 1864.

4. If it cannot be ascertained where the fault lies, the loss must be equally divided.[4]

[1] The Scioto, *Daveis*, 359; The Woodrop-Sims, 2 *Dods.*, 83; The Sappho, 9 *Jur.*, 560; Reeves *v.* The Constitution, *Gilpin*, 579.

[2] The Woodrop-Sims, *supra;* Stainback *v.* Rae, 14 *How.* [*U. S.*], 532; The Itinerant, 2 *W. Rob.*, 236.

[3] This is the rule in admiralty courts (Cushing *v.* The Fraser, 21 *How.* [*U. S.*], 184; Rogers *v.* The St. Charles, 19 *id.*, 108; The Catharine *v.* Dickinson, 17 *id.*, 177; Vaux *v.* Sheffer, 8 *Moore P. C.*, 75). It is otherwise at common law (Dowell *v.* Gen. St. N. Co. 5 *El. & Bl.*, 195; Gen. St. N. Co. *v.* Mann, 14 *C. B.*, 127; see Barnes *v.* Cole, 21 *Wend.*, 188).

[4] The Scioto, *Daveis*, 359; The Catharine of Dover, 2 *Hagg. Adm.*, 145; Lucas *v.* The Swann, 6 *M'Lean*, 282; The Nautilus, *Ware*, 529.

CHAPTER III.

CORPORATIONS.

ARTICLE I.

THE CREATION OF CORPORATIONS.

§ 379. A corporation is a creature of the law, having certain powers and duties of a natural person. Being created by the law it may continue for any length of time which the law prescribes. Corporations defined.

§ 380. A corporation can only be created by authority of a statute. But the statute may be special for a particular corporation, or general for a number of corporations. How created.

§ 381. Every grant of corporate power is subject to alteration, suspension or repeal, in the discretion of the legislature. Reservation of power to repeal.

1 *R. S.*, 600, § 7.

§ 382. One who assumes an obligation to an ostensible corporation, as such, cannot resist the obligation on the ground that there was in fact no such corporation, until that fact has been adjudged in a direct proceeding for the purpose. Dealers with a corporation cannot question its corporate existence.

§ 383. Every corporation must have a corporate name, which it has no power to change unless expressly authorized by law; but the name is to be deemed so far matter of description, that a mistake in the name, in any instrument, may be disregarded, if a sufficient description remains by which to ascertain the corporation intended. Name.

Ang. & Ames on C., 93, 94.

§ 384. Corporations are either: Distinction of corporations.

1. Public; or,

2. Private.

§ 385. A public corporation is one that has for its object the government of a portion of the state. Such Public corporations defined.

corporations are regulated by the POLITICAL CODE, and by local statutes.

Private corporations.

§ 386. Private corporations are of three kinds:

1. Corporations for religion;
2. Corporations for benevolence;
3. Corporations for profit.

Charters.

§ 387. The instrument by which a corporation is constituted is called its charter, whether that be a statute, as in case of a special charter, or the document prescribed by a general statute, for the constitution of the corporation.

Acceptance of charter.

§ 388. In order to constitute a private corporation, there must not only be a statutory grant of corporate authority, but an acceptance of that grant by a majority of the corporators, or their agents.[1] The acceptance cannot be conditional or qualified.[2]

[1] *Ang. & Ames on Corp.*, 75–77.
[2] *Id.*, 80, 81; 3 *Edw.*, 353.

Id.

§ 389. Except when otherwise expressly provided, the acceptance of a grant of corporate authority may be proved like any other fact.

Number of corporators

§ 390. Private corporations may be formed by the voluntary association of three or more persons, for the purposes and in the manner mentioned in the following sections of this article.

This section, which is new, is intended to provide a uniform rule as to the number of persons who may form a corporation. Under the existing statutes there are great differences in this respect.

Purposes for which corporations may be formed.

§ 391. The purposes for which the private corporations mentioned in the last section may be formed are:

1. The support of public worship;[1]

2. The support of any benevolent, charitable, educational or missionary undertaking;[2]

3. The support of any literary or scientific undertaking;[3] the maintenance of a library;[4] or the promotion of painting, music or other fine arts;[5]

4. The encouragement of agriculture and horticulture;[6]

5. The maintenance of public parks, and of facilities for skating and other innocent sports;[7]

6. The maintenance of a club for social enjoyment;[8]

7. The maintenance of a public[9] or private[10] cemetery;

8. The prevention and punishment of theft or willful injuries to property, and insurance against such risks;[11]

9. The insurance of human life, and dealing in annuities;[12]

10. The insurance of human beings against sickness[13] or personal injury;[14]

11. The insurance of the lives of domestic animals;[15]

12. The insurance of property against marine risks;[16]

13. The insurance of property against loss or injury by fire, or by any risk of inland transportation;[17]

14. The transaction of a banking business;[18]

15. The construction and maintenance of a railway[19] and of a telegraph line[20] in connection therewith;

16. The construction and maintenance of any other species of roads,[21] and of bridges in connection therewith;[22]

17. The construction and maintenance of a bridge;[23]

18. The construction and maintenance of a telegraph line;[24]

19. The establishment and maintenance of a line of stages;[25]

20. The establishment and maintenance of a ferry;[26]

21. The building and navigation of ships, and carriage of persons and property thereon;[27]

22. The supply of water to the public;[28]

23. The manufacture and supply of gas,[29] or the supply of light or heat to the public by any other means;[30]

24. The transaction of any manufacturing, mining, mechanical or chemical business;[31]

25. The transaction of a printing and publishing business;[32]

26. The establishment and maintenance of an hotel;[33]

27. The erection of buildings,[34] and the accumulation and loan of funds for the purchase of real property;[35] or,

28. The improvement of the breed of domestic animals, by importation, sale or otherwise.[36]

[1] 2 *R. S.* (*5th ed.*) 604, 606, 612; *Laws* 1854, *ch.* 218.

[2] *Laws* 1848, *ch.* 319; *Laws* 1857, *ch.* 302; *Laws* 1861, *ch.* 239.

[3] *Id.*

[4] *Laws* 1853, *ch.* 395.

[5] *Laws* 1860, *ch.* 242; extended to musical societies.

[6] *Laws* 1855, *ch.* 425.

[7] *Laws* 1861, *ch.* 149.

[8] New. See special charters, *Laws* 1860, *ch.* 49, 473, 474; *Laws* 1861, *ch.* 46, 304; *Laws* 1862, *ch.* 342; *Laws* 1864, *ch.* 31, 184, 244, 294, 382, 459.

[9] *Laws* 1847, *ch.* 133; *Laws* 1854, *ch.* 112.

[10] *Laws* 1854, *ch.* 112.

[11] *Laws* 1859, *ch.* 168.

[12] *Laws* 1853, *ch.* 463.

[13] *Id.*

[14] New. A special charter was, however, granted for this purpose in 1863.

[15] *Laws* 1853, *ch.* 463.

[16] *Laws* 1849, *ch.* 308; *Laws* 1853, *ch.* 463.

[17] *Laws* 1853, *ch.* 466.

[18] *Laws* 1838, *ch.* 260; *Laws* 1847, *ch.* 160.

[19] *Laws* 1850, *ch.* 140.

[20] *Laws* 1848, *ch.* 265.

[21] *Laws* 1847, *ch.* 210.

[22] *Laws* 1848, *ch.* 259.

[23] *Id.*

[24] *Laws* 1848, *ch.* 265.

[25] *Laws* 1854, *ch.* 142, as to New York city.
[26] *Laws* 1853, *ch.* 135.
[27] *Laws* 1852, *ch.* 228; *Laws* 1854, *ch.* 3, 232.
[28] New. See special charters, *Laws* 1859, *ch.* 336, 512; *Laws* 1863, *ch.* 397, 447; *Laws* 1864, *ch.* 451, 452.
[29] *Laws* 1848, *ch.* 37.
[30] New.
[31] *Laws* 1848, *ch.* 40.
[32] *Laws* 1857, *ch.* 262.
[33] New. See special charters, *Laws* 1863, *ch.* 74; *Laws* 1864, *ch.* 136, 137, 463.
[34] *Laws* 1853, *ch.* 117.
[35] *Laws* 1851, *ch.* 122.
[36] *Laws* 1857, *ch.* 776; *Laws* 1854, *ch.* 269.

§ 392. A charter must be prepared, setting forth: **Charter to be prepared**

1. The name of the corporation;

2. The purpose for which it is formed;

3. The place or places where its business is to be transacted;

4. The term for which it is to exist;

5. The number of its directors or trustees, and the names and residences of those who are appointed for the first year; and,

6. The amount of its capital stock, if any; and the number of shares into which it is divided.

§ 393. The charter of a road company must also state: **Charter of road company.**

1. The kind of road intended to be constructed;

2. The places from and to which the road is intended to be run;

3. The counties through which it is intended to be run; and,

4. The estimated length of the road.

Laws 1850, *ch.* 140; *Laws* 1847, *ch.* 210; made uniform with each other.

§ 394. The charter of an intended corporation must be subscribed by three or more persons, two of whom at least must be citizens of this state, and must be **Subscription and acknowledgment.**

acknowledged by them before a commissioner of deeds.

Banking and insurance companies.

§ 395. The charter of a corporation designed to carry on the business of banking or insurance must be presented to the superintendent of the banking or insurance department, as the case may be, who must indorse his approval thereon, but may, as a condition thereof, require the name of the corporation to be changed, if it is, in his judgment, likely to mislead the public.

This provision is at present applicable only to insurance companies (*Laws* 1853, *ch.* 466).

Petition.

§ 396. A petition must be presented with the charter of an intended corporation, to the county court of the county in which its principal place of business is to be situated, asking that the charter be examined, approved and filed, and an order of incorporation granted.

This, and the next three sections, are new.

Id.

§ 397. A petition for incorporation must declare the truth of the statements of the charter, and must be subscribed by all the persons who subscribed the charter, and verified by their oaths.

Proceedings on petition.

§ 398. Upon the presentation of a petition for incorporation, the court must inquire into the facts; and if satisfied that the matters stated in the petition are true, and that the proceedings have been had in conformity with the law, an order must be made by the court declaring that the charter is approved, and that upon the filing of the order, charter and petition, the subscribers of the charter shall be a corporation, for the purposes, and upon the terms therein stated.

Corporation, when formed.

§ 399. Upon the filing of the order, charter and petition, mentioned in the last section, with the clerk of the county in which the order was made, and of a duplicate thereof with the secretary of state, the subscribers of the charter are a corporation for the purposes and upon the terms therein stated.

§ 400. Except when otherwise provided, a person becomes a corporator in a private corporation, upon the issue of stock to him and his acceptance thereof. Who are corporators.

ARTICLE II.

CORPORATE STOCK.

§ 401. A subscription to the stock of a corporation about to be formed, is to be held for the benefit of the corporation, when it is formed, and may be enforced by it. Subscriptions for stock.

Hamilton & Dansville Plankroad Co. *v.* Rice, 7 *Barb.*, 157; Schenectady & Saratoga Plankroad Co. *v.* Thatcher, 11 *N. Y.*, 102; Lake Ontario, &c., R. R. Co. *v.* Mason, 16 *N. Y.*, 451; Rensselaer & Washington Plankroad Co. *v.* Barton, *Id.*, 457, *note;* but see Poughkeepsie & Salt Point Plankroad Co. *v.* Griffin, 24 *N. Y.*, 150.

§ 402. When a corporation is authorized by its charter, or by the terms of subscription, to forfeit stock for non-payment, it may either forfeit the stock, or recover the amount of the subscription,[1] but cannot do both.[2] Remedies for non-payment of subscription.

[1] Harlem Canal Co. *v.* Seixas, 2 *Hall*, 504; The Same *v.* Spear, *id.*, 510; Palmer *v.* Lawrence, 3 *Sandf.*, 161; Union Turnpike Co. *v.* Jenkins, 1 *Cai.*, 381; Goshen Turnpike Co. *v.* Hurtin, 9 *Johns.*, 217; Dutchess Cotton Manufactory *v.* Davis, 14 *id.*, 238.

[2] Small *v.* Herkimer Manufacturing Co., 2 *N. Y.*, 330.

§ 403. Stock is issued by placing it in the name of the stockholder upon the books of the corporation;[1] unless the issue of a certificate is required by the charter or by-laws, in which case the stock is issued by the execution and delivery of the certificate.[2] Issue of stock.

[1] Thorp *v.* Woodhull, 1 *Sandf. Ch.*, 411.

[2] Jones *v.* Terre Haute R. R. Co., 17 *How. Pr.*, 529.

Transfers of stock.

§ 404. A certificate of stock may be transferred like any other personal property; and a transfer on the books of the corporation is not necessary between the parties to the transfer;[1] but a certificate is not a negotiable instrument,[2] and a transfer does not confer greater rights against the corporation than the former holder of the stock possessed.

[1] Bank of Utica *v.* Smalley, 2 *Cow.* 770; Commercial Bank *v.* Kortright, 22 *Wend.*, 348; Gilbert *v.* Manchester Iron Co., 11 *Wend.*, 627.

[2] Dunn *v.* Commercial Bank, 11 *Barb.*, 580; Stebbins *v.* Phœnix Fire Ins. Co., 3 *Paige*, 350; Mechanics' Bank *v.* N. Y. & New Haven R. R. Co., 13 *N. Y.*, 599; McCready *v.* Rumsey, 6 *Duer*, 574.

Overissue of stock.

§ 405. A corporation whose capital is limited by its charter, either in amount or in number of shares, cannot issue valid certificates in excess of the limit thus prescribed.

Mechanics' Bank *v.* N. Y. & New Haven R. R. Co., 13 *N. Y.*, 599.

Purchase of stock by the corporation.

§ 406. Unless otherwise provided, a corporation may purchase, hold and transfer shares of its own stock.

City Bank of Columbus *v.* Bruce, 17 *N. Y.*, 507. But to the contrary was Barton *v.* Port Jackson Plankroad Co., 17 *Barb.*, 397.

Dividend.

§ 407. A dividend belongs to the person in whose name the stock stands upon the books of the corporation on the day when it becomes payable.

ARTICLE III.

CORPORATE POWERS.

§ 408. Every corporation, by virtue of its existence as such, has the following powers, unless otherwise specially provided:[1] General powers.

1. To have succession by its corporate name, for the period limited by its charter; and when no period is limited, perpetually; subject to the power of the legislature as hereinbefore declared;

2. To maintain and defend judicial proceedings;

3. To make and use a common seal, and alter the same at pleasure;

4. To hold, purchase and transfer such real and personal property as the purposes of the corporation require, not exceeding the amount limited by its charter;

5. To appoint and remove[2] such subordinate officers and agents, as the business of the corporation requires, and to allow them a suitable compensation;

6. To make by-laws, not inconsistent with the law of the land, for the management of its property, the regulation of its affairs, and the transfer of its stock;

7. To admit and remove members;[3] and,

8. To enter into any obligation essential to the transaction of its ordinary affairs.[4]

[1] The first six subdivisions are in substance the same as 1 *R. S.*, 599, § 1.

[2] Fawcett *v.* Charles, 13 *Wend.*, 473.

[3] 2 *Kent's Com.*, 224. See Fawcett *v.* Charles, 13 *Wend.*, 473.

[4] Beers *v.* Phœnix Glass Co., 14 *Barb.*, 358; Partridge *v.* Badger, 25 *id.*, 146; Mead *v.* Keeler, 24 *id.*, 20; Curtis *v.* Leavitt, 15 *N. Y.*, 9.

By-laws and other powers.

§ 409. The by-laws of a corporation are the regulations subordinate to the charter, prescribed for the government of its officers. They must be made by the corporators in general meeting, unless the charter prescribes another body or a different mode.

This and the four sections following are new.

Id.

§ 410. The powers and duties of corporations, the time, place and manner of exercising the corporate powers, the means by which persons may become members or lose membership, the kind and number of officers, and the manner of their appointment or removal, are prescribed by this Code, or by the statutes relating to the corporations respectively, or the by-laws made in pursuance of law.

Mode of acting.

§ 411. A corporation may act:

1. By writing, under the corporate seal;

2. By writing, signed by an authorized agent;

3. By resolution of the corporators, directors, or other managing body; or,

4. By an authorized agent.

B'k of Columbia *v.* Paterson, 7 *Cranch*, 297; Dunn *v.* St. Andrews, 14 *Johns.*, 118; Danforth *v.* Schoharie Turnp. Co., 12 *id.*, 227. See East London W. Wks. *v.* Bailey, 4 *Bing.*, 283; Beverly *v.* Lincoln Gas Co., 6 *Ad. & El.*, 829; Henderson *v.* Royal Mail Nav. Co., 5 *El. & Bl.*, 409.

Meetings and agencies.

§ 412. Unless otherwise expressly authorized by its charter, the meetings of the corporators, directors or other managing body of a corporation, must be held within the jurisdiction of the state by whose authority the corporation was created. It may, however, also have agencies elsewhere.

Meetings of public corporations.

§ 413. The meetings of a public corporation, or of its officers, must be held within the limits of its own jurisdiction.

§ 414. Where the law expressly confers power upon a corporation to do an act in a certain mode, its power is confined to the mode prescribed. Mode of exercising power.

McSpedon *v.* Mayor of N. Y., 7 *Bosw.*, 601; McCullough *v.* Moss, 5 *Denio*, 567; Farmers' Loan and Trust Company *v.* Carroll, 5 *Barb.*, 613; Brady *v.* Mayor, &c., of New York, 2 *Bosw.*, 173.

§ 415. Besides the powers and duties specified in this chapter, and such others as are expressly conferred by statute, or may be necessary to the exercise of the powers so conferred, a corporation has no other power. General restriction.

1 *R. S.*, 600, § 3.

§ 416. No corporation, unless it is expressly incorporated for banking purposes, possesses the power of discounting bills, notes or other evidences of debt, of receiving deposits, of buying gold and silver bullion or foreign coins, of buying and selling bills of exchange, or of issuing bills, notes or other evidences of debt, upon loan or for circulation as money. Exercise of banking powers prohibited.

1 *R. S.*, 600, § 4.

§ 417. When the whole capital of a corporation is not paid in, and the capital paid is insufficient to satisfy the claims of its creditors, each stockholder is bound to pay, on each share held by him, the sum necessary to complete the amount of such share as fixed by the charter, or such proportion of that sum as is required to satisfy the debts of the corporation. Liability of stockholders.

1 *R. S.*, 600, § 5.

§ 418. When the corporate powers of a corporation are directed by its charter to be exercised by any particular body, or number of persons, a majority of such body, or persons, if not otherwise provided by the charter, is a sufficient number to form a board for the transaction of business. Such board must be convened in the mode prescribed by the charter or by-laws, or by notice to all the members thereof Quorum.

within the state; and every decision of a majority of the persons thus duly assembled as a board, is as valid as if made by all.

1 *R. S.*, 600, § 6.

Powers of foreign corporations.

§ 419. A foreign corporation can perform no act in this state, which is forbidden by the laws or is contrary to the policy of the state.

Their liabilities.

§ 420. Every act of a foreign corporation done in this state is subject to its laws, and the corporation itself may be sued in the manner prescribed by the CODE OF CIVIL PROCEDURE.

Power of colleges, &c., to take property.

§ 421. Any corporation, being a college or other literary institution of this state, may take and hold property, both real and personal, subject to such conditions and visitations as may be prescribed by the donor, and agreed to by the corporation, in trust for any of the following purposes:

1. To establish and maintain an observatory;

2. To found and maintain professorships and scholarships;

3. To provide and keep in repair a place for the burial of the dead; or,

4. For any other specific purpose comprehended in the general objects authorized by its charter.

Laws of 1840, *ch.* 318.

Power of cities to take property.

§ 422. The corporation of any city or village of this state may take and hold property, both real and personal, subject to such conditions as may be prescribed by the donor, and agreed to by the corporation, in trust for any purpose of education, or for the diffusion of knowledge, or for the relief of distress, or for fire-engine houses, reservoirs, or public docks, or for parks, gardens, or other grounds for health and recreation, or for ornament or military exercise and parade, within or near such incorporated city or village.

Ib., with some additions.

§ 423. The school commissioners of any town, and the trustees of any school district, may take and hold property, both real and personal, in trust for the benefit of the schools of the town or district, and for such purposes are to be deemed corporations. Power of school officers to take property.

Ib.

ARTICLE IV.

DISSOLUTION OF CORPORATIONS.

§ 424. A corporation is dissolved:

1. By the expiration of the time limited by its charter; or, How dissolved.

2. By a judgment of dissolution, in the manner provided by the CODE OF CIVIL PROCEDURE.

The reference is to the Code of Civil Procedure, as reported complete.

§ 425. If any corporation hereafter created is not organized, and engaged in the transaction of business, within one year from the date of its incorporation, its dissolution may be adjudged;[1] unless a different time within which its business must be commenced, is fixed by law.[2] Forfeiture for non-user.

[1] 1 *R. S.*, 600, § 7, omitting the words "by the legislature," after "created;" and modified by making the delay cause for a *judgment* of dissolution only.

[2] This qualification which, by *Laws of* 1846, *ch.* 155, was applied to railroad corporations, is here made applicable to all kinds.

§ 426. Upon the dissolution of any corporation, unless other persons are appointed by the legislature, or by some court of competent authority, its directors, trustees or managers, at the time of its dissolution, become the trustees of the creditors and stockholders Trustees in case of dissolution.

of the corporation dissolved, and have power to settle its affairs, collect and pay debts, and divide among the stockholders the property that remains after the payment of debts and necessary expenses; and for this purpose may maintain or defend any judicial proceeding.

1 *R. S.*, 600, § 9.

Their powers. § 427. The trustees mentioned in the last section are jointly and severally responsible to the creditors and stockholders of the corporation, to the extent of its property in their hands.

1 *R. S.*, 601, § 10.

Revival. § 428. A corporation once dissolved can be revived only by the same power by which it could be created.

CHAPTER IV.

PRODUCTS OF THE MIND.

How far the subject of ownership. § 429. The author of any product of the mind, whether it is an invention, or a composition in letters or art, or a design, with or without delineation, or other graphical representation, has an exclusive ownership therein, and in the representation or expression thereof, which continues so long as the product, and the representations or expressions thereof made by him, remain in his possession.

Joint authorship. § 430. Unless otherwise agreed, a product of the mind, in the production of which several persons are jointly concerned, is owned by them as follows:

1. If the product is single, in equal proportions; or,

2. If it is not single, in proportion to the contribution of each.

§ 431. The owner of any product of the mind, or of any representation or expression thereof, may transfer his property in the same. Transfer.

§ 432. If the owner of a product of the mind intentionally makes it public, a copy or reproduction may be made public by any person, without responsibility to the owner, so far as the law of this state is concerned. Effect of publication.

The protection afforded by act of Congress is a matter of federal legislation, with which the state cannot interfere.

§ 433. If the owner of a product of the mind does not make it public, any other person subsequently and originally producing the same thing, has the same right therein as the prior author, which is exclusive to the same extent, against all persons except the prior author, or those claiming under him. Subsequent inventor, author, &c.

§ 434. Letters, and other private communications in writing, belong to the person to whom they are addressed and delivered; but they cannot be published against the will of the writer, except by authority of law. Private writings.

See Woolsey *v.* Judd, 4 *Duer*, 389, and cases there cited; Eyre *v.* Higbee, 22 *How. Pr.*, 198.

CHAPTER V.

OTHER KINDS OF PERSONAL PROPERTY.

§ 435. One who produces or deals in[1] a particular thing, or conducts a particular business,[2] may appropriate to his exclusive use, as a trade-mark, any form, Trade-marks and signs.

symbol or name, which has not been so appropriated by another, to designate the origin or ownership thereof; but he cannot exclusively appropriate any designation or part of a designation, which relates only to the name, quality or description of the thing or business.[3]

[1] Taylor *v.* Carpenter, 2 *Sandf. Ch.*, 603.
[2] Howard *v.* Henriques, 3 *Sandf.*, 725.
[3] Amoskeag Manufacturing Co. *v.* Spear, 2 *Sandf.*, 599; Fetridge *v.* Wells, 4 *Abb. Pr.*, 144.

Good-will of business. § 436. The good-will of a business is the expectation of continued public patronage, but it does not include a right to use the name of any person from whom it was acquired.

Howe *v.* Searing, 6 *Bosw.*, 354; 10 *Abb. Pr.*, 264.

Id. § 437. The good-will of a business is property, transferable like any other.

Title deeds. § 438. Instruments essential to the title of real property, and which are not kept in a public office as a record pursuant to law, belong to the person in whom, for the time being, such title may be vested, and pass with the title.

PART IV.

ACQUISITION OF PROPERTY.

TITLE I.

MODES IN WHICH PROPERTY MAY BE ACQUIRED.

§ 439. Property is acquired by
1. Occupancy;
2. Accession;
3. Transfer;
4. Will; or,
5. Succession.

TITLE II.

OCCUPANCY.

§ 440. Occupancy for any period confers a title sufficient against all except the state and those who Simple occupancy.

have title by prescription, accession, transfer, will or succession.

Jackson *v.* Hazen, 2 *Johns.*, 22; Smith *v.* Lorillard, 10 *id.*, 338; Jackson *v.* Denn, 5 *Cow.*, 200; see Spencer *v.* Tobey, 22 *Barb.*, 260; Clute *v.* Voris, 31 *id.*, 511.

Prescription. § 441. Occupancy for the period prescribed by the CODE OF CIVIL PROCEDURE as sufficient to bar an action for the recovery of the property, confers a title thereto, denominated a title by prescription, which is sufficient against all.

TITLE III.

ACCESSION.

CHAPTER I.

ACCESSION TO REAL PROPERTY.

Fixtures. § 442. When a person affixes his property to the land of another, without an agreement permitting him to remove it, the thing affixed belongs to the owner of the land, unless he chooses to require the former to remove it.

Alluvion. § 443. Where, from natural causes, land forms by imperceptible degrees[1] upon the bank of a river or stream, navigable or not navigable, either by accumulation of material,[2] or by the recession of the stream,[3] such land belongs to the owner of the bank, subject to any existing right of way over the bank.

[1] Halsey *v.* McCormick, 13 *N. Y.*, 147; Emans *v.* Turnbull, 2 *Johns.*, 313. If the formation is sudden, it belongs to the state (*Ib*).

[2] Emans *v.* Turnbull, 2 *Johns.*, 313.

[3] *Code Napoleon, Art.* 556, 557.

§ 444. If a river or stream, navigable or not navigable, carries away, by sudden violence, a considerable and distinguishable part of a bank, and bears it to the opposite bank, or to another part of the same bank, the owner of the part carried away may reclaim it, within a year after the owner of the land to which it has been united takes possession thereof. Sudden removal of bank.

This and the four sections following are similar to those of the *Code Napoleon*, Art. 559–563.

§ 445. Islands, and accumulations of land, formed in the beds of streams which are navigable, belong to the state, if there is no title or prescription to the contrary. Islands in navigable streams.

§ 446. An island, or an accumulation of land, formed in a stream which is not navigable, belongs to the owner of the shore on that side where the island or accumulation is formed, or, if not formed on one side only, to the owners of the shore on the two sides, divided by an imaginary line drawn through the middle of the river. Islands in streams not navigable.

§ 447. If a stream, navigable or not navigable, in forming itself a new arm, divides itself and surrounds land belonging to the owner of the shore, and thereby forms an island, the island belongs to such owner. Islands formed by division of streams.

§ 448. If a stream, navigable or not navigable, forms a new course, abandoning its ancient bed, the Abandoned bed of stream.

owners of the land newly occupied take, by way of indemnity, the ancient bed abandoned, each in proportion to the land of which he has been deprived.

CHAPTER II.

ACCESSION TO PERSONAL PROPERTY.

The provisions of this chapter, except § 455, are similar to those of the Code Napoleon and the Code of Louisiana.

Accession by uniting several things.

§ 449. When things belonging to different owners have been united so as to form a single thing, and cannot be separated without injury, the whole belongs to the owner of the thing which forms the principal part, who must, however, reimburse the value of the residue to the other owner, or surrender the whole to him.

Principal part, what.

§ 450. That part is to be deemed the principal, to which the other has been united only for the use, ornament or completion of the former, unless the latter is the more valuable, and has been united without the knowledge of its owner, who may, in the latter case, require it to be separated and returned to him, although some injury should result to the thing to which it has been united.

Id.

§ 451. If neither part can be considered the principal, within the rule prescribed by the last section, the more valuable, or, if the values are nearly equal, the more considerable in bulk, is to be deemed the principal part.

§ 452. If one makes a thing from materials belonging to another, the latter may claim the thing on reimbursing the value of the workmanship, unless the value of the workmanship exceeds the value of the materials, in which case the thing belongs to the maker, on reimbursing the value of the materials. Uniting materials and workmanship.

§ 453. Where one has made use of materials which in part belong to him and in part to another, in order to form a thing of a new description, without having destroyed any of the materials, but in such a way that they cannot be separated without inconvenience, the thing formed is common to both proprietors; in proportion, as respects the one, of the materials belonging to him, and as respects the other, of the materials belonging to him and the price of his workmanship. Inseparable materials.

§ 454. When a thing has been formed by the admixture of several materials of different owners, and neither can be considered the principal substance, an owner, without whose consent the admixture was made, may require a separation, if the materials can be separated without inconvenience. If they cannot be thus separated, the owners acquire the thing in common, in proportion to the quantity, quality, and value of their materials; but if the materials of one were far superior to those of the others, both in quantity and value, he may claim the thing on reimbursing to the others the value of their materials. Materials of several owners.

§ 455. The foregoing sections of this article are not applicable to cases in which one willfully uses the materials of another without his consent; but, in such cases, the product belongs to the owner of the material, if its identity can be traced. Willful trespassers.

Silsbury *v.* McCoon, 3 *N. Y.*, 379.

§ 456. In all cases where one, whose material has been used without his knowledge, in order to form a product of a different description, can Owner may elect between the thing and its value.

claim an interest in such product, he has an option to demand either restitution of his material, in kind, in the same quantity, weight, measure, and quality, or the value thereof; or where he is entitled to the product, the value thereof in place of the product.

Wrongdoer liable in damages.

§ 457. One who wrongfully employs materials belonging to another, is liable to him in damages, as well as under the foregoing provisions of this chapter.

TITLE IV.

TRANSFER.

The obligations of the parties to a transfer for consideration, or to a contract of hiring, are regulated by the titles on Sales, on Exchange, and on Hiring. Transfers in trust for the benefit of creditors are regulated by the Part on Debtor and Creditor.

CHAPTER I.

TRANSFER IN GENERAL.

ARTICLE I.

DEFINITION OF TRANSFER.

§ 458. Transfer is an act of the parties, or of the law, by which the title to property is conveyed from one living person to another. Transfer, what.

§ 459. A voluntary transfer is an executed contract, subject to all rules of law concerning contracts in general;[1] except that a consideration is not necessary to its validity.[2] Transfer a contract.

[1] Fletcher *v.* Peck, 6 *Cranch*, 136; People *v.* Platt, 17 *Johns.*, 195; Varick *v.* Briggs, 22 *Wend.*, 543; see Van Rensselaer *v.* Ball, 19 *N. Y.*, 100, 105.

[2] This clause was proposed for enactment, in regard to grants of real property, by the Revisers in 1828 (see 3 *R. S.* [2*d ed.*], 593), but was not enacted. It is, however, undoubted law, both as to real and personal property (Bunn *v.* Winthrop, 1 *Johns. Ch.*, 329; Irons *v.* Smallpiece, 2 *B. & Ald.*, 551, 554; Jackson *v.* Garnsey, 16 *Johns.*, 189).

ARTICLE II.

WHAT MAY BE TRANSFERRED.

SECTION 460. What may be transferred.
461. Possibility.
462. Right of entry.

§ 460. Property of any kind may be transferred, except as otherwise provided by this article. What may be transferred.

See Conderman *v.* Smith, 41 *Barb.*, 404; Lintner *v.* Snyder, 15 *id.*, 621.

§ 461. A mere possibility, not coupled with an interest, cannot be transferred. Possibility.

Jackson *v.* Bradford, 4 *Wend.*, 619; Tooley *v.* Dibble, 2 *Hill*, 641; Otis *v.* Sill, 8 *Barb.*, 111; Edwards *v.* Varick, 5 *Den.*, 664; see 41 *Barb.*, 404; 19 *N. Y.*, 384.

§ 462. A mere right of re-entry, or of repossession for breach of a condition subsequent, cannot be transferred to any one except the owner of the property affected thereby. Right of entry.

Nicoll *v.* N. Y. & Erie R. R., 12 *N. Y.*, 121; Underhill *v.* Saratoga & W. R. R., 20 *Barb.*, 455, 464; Van Rensselaer *v.* Ball, 19 *N. Y.*, 103.

ARTICLE III.

MODE OF TRANSFER.

When oral. § 463. A transfer may be made without writing, in every case in which a writing is not expressly required by statute.

4 *N. Y.*, 497; 7 *Exch.*, 581.

Grant, what. § 464. A transfer in writing is called a grant.

Delivery necessary. § 465. A grant takes effect, so as to vest the interest intended to be transferred, only upon its delivery by the grantor.

1 *R. S.*, 738, § 138. A delivery after the grantor's death is of no effect (Roosevelt *v.* Carow, 6 *Barb.*, 190; Jackson *v.* Leek, 12 *Wend.*, 107).

Date. § 466. A grant duly executed is presumed to have been delivered at its date.

Harris *v.* Norton, 16 *Barb.*, 264.

Delivery to grantee is necessarily absolute. § 467. A grant cannot be delivered to the grantee conditionally. Delivery to him[1] or to his agent as such[2] is necessarily absolute, and the instrument takes effect thereupon, discharged of any condition on which the delivery was made.

[1] Braman *v.* Bingham, 26 *N. Y.*, 483; Worrall *v.* Munn, 5 *N. Y.*, 229.

[2] Where one person is the agent of both parties, delivery to him is not necessarily absolute (Iliff *v.* Cincinnati, &c., R. R., 13 *Ohio St.*, 235).

Delivery in escrow. § 468. A grant may be deposited by the grantor with a third person, to be delivered on performance of a condition, and, on delivery by the depositary, it will take effect.

Clark *v.* Gifford, 10 *Wend.*, 310.

§ 469. Redelivering a grant of real property to the grantor, or canceling it, does not operate to retransfer the title. Surrendering or canceling grant.

Jackson *v.* Anderson, 4 *Wend.*, 474; Jackson *v.* Chase, 2 *Johns.*, 84; Raynor *v.* Wilson, 6 *Hill*, 469; Nicholson *v.* Halsey, 1 *Johns. Ch.*, 417.

§ 470. Though a grant be not actually delivered into the possession of the grantee, it is yet to be deemed constructively delivered in the following cases: Constructive delivery.

1. Where the instrument is, by the agreement of the parties at the time of execution, understood to be delivered, and under such circumstances that the grantee is entitled to immediate delivery;[1] or,

2. Where it is delivered to a stranger for the benefit of the grantee, and his assent is shown or may be presumed.[2]

[1] Scrugham *v.* Wood, 15 *Wend.*, 545; see Roosevelt *v.* Carow, 6 *Barb.*, 190.

[2] Church *v.* Gilman, 15 *Wend.*, 656.

§ 471. A grant made as a mere gratuity takes effect upon its execution, even though the grantor retains its possession, unless a contrary intention appears. When voluntary settlement takes effect.

Souverbye *v.* Arden, 1 *Johns. Ch.*, 240; Bunn *v.* Winthrop, 1 *id.*, 329; see Roosevelt *v.* Carow, 6 *Barb.*, 190.

ARTICLE IV.

INTERPRETATION OF GRANTS.

Grants, how interpreted.

§ 472. Grants are to be interpreted in like manner with contracts in general, except so far as is otherwise provided by this article.

Limitations, how controlled.

§ 473. A clear and distinct limitation in a grant is not controlled by other words less clear and distinct.

Nicoll *v.* N. Y. & Erie R. R. Co., 12 *N. Y.*, 129; Jewett *v.* Jewett, 16 *Barb.*, 150; see Thornhill *v.* Hall, 2 *Clark & Fin.*, 22, 36.

Recitals, when resorted to.

§ 474. If the operative words of a grant are doubtful, recourse may be had to its recitals to assist the construction.

Ringer *v.* M'Cann, 3 *M. & W.*, 343; Bailey *v.* Lloyd, 5 *Russ.*, 330; Doe *d.* Rogers *v.* Brooks, 3 *Ad. & El.*, 513; Walsh *v.* Trevanion, 15 *Q. B.*, 733.

Interpretation against grantor.

§ 475. A grant is to be interpreted in favor of the grantee,[1] except that a reservation in any grant,[2] and every grant by a public officer or body, as such, to a private party,[3] is to be interpreted in favor of the grantor.

[1] Vincent *v.* Spicer, 22 *Beav.*, 383; Jackson *v.* Gardner, 8 *Johns.*, 394; Jackson *v.* Blodget, 16 *id.*, 172.

[2] Bowes *v.* Ravensworth, 15 *C. B.*, 512.

[3] See note 4 to section 819.

Irreconcilable provisions.

§ 476. If several parts of a grant are absolutely irreconcilable, the former part prevails.

Jewett *v.* Jewett, 16 *Barb.*, 157.

Meaning of "heirs" and "issue" in certain remainders.

§ 477. Where a future interest is limited by a grant to take effect on the death of any person without heirs,[1] or heirs of his body, or without issue,[2] or in equivalent words; such words must be taken to mean successors or issue living at the death of the person named as ancestor.[3]

[1] Norris *v.* Beyea, 13 *N. Y.*, 273.

[2] Tyson *v.* Blake, 22 *N. Y.*, 558.

[3] 1 *R. S.*, 724, § 22.

Words of inheritance unnecessary.

§ 478. Words of inheritance or succession are not requisite to transfer a fee in real property.

1 *R. S.*, 748, § 1.

ARTICLE V.

EFFECT OF TRANSFER.

§ 479. A transfer vests in the transferee all the actual title to the thing transferred which the transferrer then has, unless a different intention is expressed or is necessarily implied,[1] and no more,[2] except in the cases specified in sections 480, 499, 1745 and 1773.

What title passes.

[1] This provision is already enacted with respect to real property (1 *R. S.*, 748, § 1; see Nicoll *v.* N. Y. & Erie R. R. Co., 12 *N. Y.*, 121, 129), and is undoubted law as to personal property.

[2] Wooster *v.* Sherwood, 25 *N. Y.*, 278; Wheelwright *v.* De Peyster, 1 *Johns.*, 471; 1 *R. S.*, 739, § 143; Sage *v.* Cartwright, 9 *N. Y.*, 49; Warren *v.* Leland, 2 *Barb.*, 624.

§ 480. A transfer cannot affect any interest of the transferrer which he does not own when it is made; but, if it is made with a covenant, neither the transferrer nor any person claiming under him can be permitted to take in contravention of the covenant.

What interests affected.

Jackson *v.* Winslow, 9 *Cow.*, 13; Jackson *v.* Wright, 14 *Johns.*, 194; see Jackson *v.* Bradford, 4 *Wend.*, 619, 622.

§ 481. The transfer of a thing transfers also all its incidents[1] unless expressly excepted; but the transfer of an incident to a thing does not transfer the thing itself.[2]

Incidents.

[1] Battle *v.* Coit, 26 *N. Y.*, 404; Lampman *v.* Milks, 21 *id.*, 505; Huttemeier *v.* Albro, 18 *id.*, 48; Leroy *v.* Platt, 4 *Paige*, 77; Bowdoin *v.* Coleman, 6 *Duer*, 182; 3 *Abb. Pr.*, 431; Langdon *v.* Buel, 9 *Wend.*, 80; Jackson *v.* Blodgett, 5 *Cow.*, 202; Green *v.* Hart, 1 *Johns.*, 580; see Rose *v.* Baker, 13 *Barb.*, 230.

[2] Battle *v.* Coit, 26 *N. Y.*, 404; Kellogg *v.* Smith, 26 *N. Y.*, 18; see Nostrand *v.* Durland, 21 *Barb.*, 478.

Grant may inure to benefit of stranger.

§ 482. A present interest, and the benefit of a condition or covenant respecting property, may be taken by any natural person under a grant, although not named a party thereto.

This provision is contrary to the common law (Craig *v.* Wells, 11 *N. Y.*, 315; Hornbeck *v.* Westbrook, 9 *Johns.*, 73). But a similar provision has been enacted in England (8 & 9 *Vict.*, c. 106, § 5).

CHAPTER II.

TRANSFER OF REAL PROPERTY.

ARTICLE I.

MODE OF TRANSFER.

Requisites to convey certain estates.

§ 483. An estate in real property, other than an estate at will or for a term not exceeding one year, can be transferred only by operation of law, or by an instrument in writing, subscribed by the party disposing of the same, or by his agent, thereunto authorized by writing.

2 *R. S.*, 134, § 6.

Grants in fee, or of freeholds how executed; when to take effect.

§ 484. A grant of an estate in real property, other than an estate for years or at will, must be sealed by the grantor or his agent; and if not duly acknowledged, previous to its delivery, according to the provisions of chapter IV of this Title, its subscription and seal must be attested by at least one witness; or if not so attested, it has no effect as against a subsequent purchaser or incumbrancer, or those claiming under him, until so acknowledged.

1 *R. S.*, 738, § 137. The word "subsequent" is inserted on the authority of Wood *v.* Chapin, 13 *N. Y.*, 509, 524. A grant is not absolutely void for want of attestation (*Ib.*). The words "subscription and seal" are substituted for "execution and delivery."

A grant of an estate in land in fee (Jackson *v.* Wendell, 12 *Johns.*, 73), or for life (People *v.* Gillis, 24 *Wend.*, 201), and a grant of an estate in an incorporeal hereditament in fee (Wickham *v.* Hawker, 7 *M. & W.*, 76; Brown *v.* Woodworth, 5 *Barb.*, 555), for life (see Hewlins *v.* Shippam, 5 *B. & C.*, 221; Wood *v.* Leadbitter, 13 *M. & W.*, 838), for years (Somerset *v.* Fogwell, 5 *B. & C.*, 875; Wallis *v.* Harrison, 2 *M. & W.*, 538; Mayfield *v.* Robinson, 7 *Q. B.*, 487; Thomas *v.* Fredericks, 10 *id.*, 775; Bird *v.* Higginson, 2 *Ad. & El.*, 696; but see to the contrary, Warren *v.* Leland, 2 *Barb.*, 618), at will (see Wood *v.* Leadbitter, 13 *M. & W.*, 838), or of uncertain duration (Roffey *v.* Henderson, 17 *Q. B.*, 574), must at common law be under seal. The only exception was the grant of an original chattel of a thing properly lying in grant (see Hewlins *v.* Shippam, 5 *Barn. & Cr.*, 230; Somerset *v.* Fogwell, *id.*, 882).

§ 485. A grant of an estate in real property may be made, in substance, as follows: Form of grant.

"This grant, made the .. day of ...., in the year ......, between A. B., of ...., of the first part, and C. D., of ...., of the second part, witnesseth:

"That the party of the first part hereby grants to the party of the second part, in consideration of .... dollars, now received, all the real property situated in ...., and bounded ....

"Witness the hand and seal of the party of the first part.

"A. B. [SEAL.]"

In England, the following form is prescribed by 8 & 9 *Vic.*, c. 119:

"This indenture, made, &c., in pursuance of an act to facilitate the conveyance of real property, between A. B. and C. D.: witnesseth: that in consideration of ...., now paid by the said C. D. to the said A. B. (the receipt whereof is hereby by him acknowledged), he, the said A. B., doth grant unto the said C. D., his heirs and assigns forever, all that ....

In witness whereof, the said parties hereto have hereunto set their hands and seals."

Chancellor Kent (4 *Com.*, 461), recommends the following:

"I, A. B., in consideration of one dollar to me paid by C. D., grant to him the lot of land [describing it.]

Witness my hand and seal," &c.

A form briefer still was held sufficient in Kentucky (Chiles *v.* Conley, 2 *Dana*, 23).

Grant by married woman must be acknowledged.

§ 486. No estate in the real property of a married woman passes by any grant purporting to be executed or acknowledged by her within this state, unless the grant is acknowledged by her in the manner prescribed by section 521.

1 *R. S.*, 758, § 10. Modified by making the requirement apply to grants executed, and acknowledgments taken within the state, instead of to acknowledgments, wherever taken, of a married woman residing in the state. The fact of residence is often difficult to ascertain, and the validity of the acknowledgment should not be made to turn upon it.

Livery of Seizin.

§ 487. The mode formerly in use, of conveying lands by feoffment, with livery of seizin, is abolished.

1 *R. S.*, 738, § 136.

ARTICLE II.

EFFECT OF TRANSFER.

What easements pass with property.

§ 488. A transfer of real property passes all easements attached thereto,[1] and creates in favor thereof an easement to use other real property of the person whose estate is transferred, in the same manner and to the same extent, as such property was obviously and permanently used by the person whose estate is transferred, for the benefit thereof,[2] at the time when the transfer was agreed upon or completed.[3]

[1] Eno *v.* Del Vecchio, 4 *Duer*, 53; United States *v.* Appleton, 1 *Sumn.*, 492; see Huttemeier *v.* Albro, 18 *N. Y.*, 48.

[2] Lampman *v.* Milks, 21 *N. Y.*, 505; Huttemeier *v.* Albro, 18 *id.*, 48; Thayer *v.* Payne, 2 *Cush.*, 327; Nicholas *v.* Chamberlain, *Cro. Jac.*, 121; Robbins *v.* Barnes, *Hobart*, 131.

[3] Although the question does not seem to have been decided, there can be little doubt that the grantee is entitled to the benefit of these quasi easements whether existing at the time a grant is bargained for, or at the time when it is actually delivered.

§ 489. No covenant is implied in any grant of an estate in real property, whether it contains special covenants or not, except as provided by the Title on HIRING. **No implied covenants in grants.**

1 *R. S.*, 738, § 140. A demise of an estate for years in an incorporeal hereditament (Mayor of N. Y. *v.* Mabie, 13 *N. Y.*, 151), or in land (Tone *v.* Brace, 11 *Paige*, 566), has been held not to be "a conveyance of real estate;" but a transfer of an existing lease (see Tone *v.* Brace, 11 *Paige*, 569), or an original lease in fee (Carter *v.* Burr, 39 *Barb.*, 59, 65) is such a conveyance. The words "grant of an estate in real property," are inserted in place of the words above quoted, in order to avoid these distinctions.

§ 490. Every grant of an estate in real property is conclusive against the grantor and every one subsequently claiming under him, except a purchaser or incumbrancer who, in good faith, and for a valuable consideration, acquires a superior title or lien by an instrument that is first duly recorded. **How far conclusive on purchasers.**

1 *R. S.*, 739, §§ 143, 144.

§ 491. A grant, made by the owner of an estate for life or years, purporting to transfer a greater estate than he could lawfully transfer, does not work a forfeiture of his estate, but passes to the grantee all the estate which the grantor could lawfully transfer. **Conveyances by owner for life or for years.**

1 *R. S.*, 739, § 145.

Title to highway.

§ 492. A transfer of land, bounded by a highway, passes the title of the person whose estate is transferred to the soil of the highway in front thereof.

Bissell *v.* N. Y. Central R. R., 23 *N. Y.*, 61.

Attornment by tenant, when unnecessary.

§ 493. When real property is occupied by a tenant, a grant of any estate therein, by his landlord, is valid without an attornment of the tenant to the grantee;

Liabilities of tenant.

but the payment of rent to such grantor, by his tenant, before notice of the grant, is binding upon the grantee; and the tenant is not liable to the grantee for any breach of the condition of the lease, until he has had notice of the grant.

1 *R. S.*, 739, § 146.

Lineal and collateral warranties.

§ 494. Lineal and collateral warranties, with all their incidents, and all the incidents of feudal tenures, not expressly retained by this Code, are abolished. The liability of those who acquire the real property of a decedent, by will or succession, is regulated by the CODE OF CIVIL PROCEDURE.

1 *R. S.*, 739, § 141. See Appendix D. in the original draft of this Code.

CHAPTER III.

TRANSFERS OF PERSONAL PROPERTY.

ARTICLE I.

MODE OF TRANSFER.

When must be in writing.

§ 495. An interest in a ship,[1] or in an existing trust,[2] can be transferred only by operation of law, or by a written instrument, subscribed by the person making the transfer, or by his agent.

[1] This provision is intended to settle a doubtful question. The uniform language of the authorities is that a bill of sale is the customary and proper mode of transfer. Agreements for sale are regulated by the Title on Sale.

[2] 2 *R. S.*, 137, § 2.

§ 496. The mode of transferring other personal property by sale, is regulated by the Title on that subject in the Third Division of this Code. Transfer by sale, &c.

ARTICLE II.

WHAT OPERATES AS A TRANSFER.

§ 497. The title to personal property, sold or exchanged, passes to the buyer whenever the parties agree upon a present transfer, and the thing itself is identified,[1] whether it is separated from other things or not.[2] Transfer of title under sale.

[1] This is essential (McCandlish *v.* Newman, 22 *Penn. St.*, 460).

[2] Kimberly *v.* Patchin, 19 *N. Y.*, 330; see contra, Aldridge *v.* Johnson, 7 *E. & B.*, 885. Delivery is not essential (Wooster *v.* Sherwood, 25 *N. Y.*, 278).

§ 498. Title is transferred by an executory agreement for the sale or exchange of personal property, only when the buyer has accepted the thing, or when the seller has completed it, prepared it for delivery, and offered it to the buyer, with intent to transfer the title thereto, in the manner prescribed by the chapter upon OFFER OF PERFORMANCE. Transfer of title under executory agreement for sale.

Andrews *v.* Durant, 11 *N. Y.*, 35; Tompkins *v.* Dudley, 25 *N. Y.*, 272; Johnson *v.* Hunt, 11 *Wend.*, 138; see Rohde *v.* Thwaites, 6 *B. & C.*, 388; Wood *v.* Bell, 5 *E. & B.*, 772; Reid *v.* Fairbanks, 13 *C. B.*, 692.

§ 499. Where the possession of personal property, together with a power to dispose thereof, is transferred by its owner to another person, an executed When buyer acquires better title than seller has.

sale by the latter, while in possession, to a buyer in good faith and in the ordinary course of business, for value, transfers to such buyer the title of the former owner, though he may be entitled to rescind, and does rescind the transfer made by him.

Fassett *v.* Smith, 23 *N. Y.*, 252: Brower *v.* Peabody, 13 *id.*, 121; Smith *v.* Lynes, 5 *id.*, 41; Beavers *v.* Lane, 6 *Duer*, 236; Saltus *v.* Everett, 20 *Wend.*, 267.

ARTICLE III.

GIFTS.

Gifts defined. § 500. A gift is a transfer of personal property, made voluntarily and without consideration.

Gift, how made. § 501. A verbal gift is not valid, unless the means of obtaining possession and control of the thing are given, nor, if it is capable of delivery, unless there is an actual or symbolical delivery of the thing to the donee.

This doctrine is too well settled in this state to be questioned (Woodruff *v.* Cook, 25 *Barb.*, 505; Hunter *v.* Hunter, 19 *id.*, 631; Huntingdon *v.* Gilmore, 14 *id.*, 243; Noble *v.* Smith, 2 *Johns.*, 52; Grangiac *v.* Arden, 10 *id.*, 293; Cook *v.* Husted, 12 *id.*, 188); but the cases from which the strictness of the rule has been derived (Irons *v.* Smallpiece, 2 *B. & Ald.*, 551, and others) are not recognized as good authority in England in respect to gifts not in view of death (Winter *v.* Winter, 4 *Law Times* [*N. S.*], 639; 101 *Eng. C. L.*, 997; Lunn *v.* Thornton, 1 *C. B.*, 381; Ward *v.* Audland, 16 *M. & W.*, 870, per PARKE, B.).

Gift not revocable. § 502. A gift, other than a gift in view of death, cannot be revoked by the giver.

§ 503. A gift in view of death is one which is made in contemplation, fear, or peril of death, and with intent that it shall take effect only in case of the death of the giver. Gift in view of death, what.

It has not been thought necessary to declare what may be the subject of a gift in view of death, as in this state there is no difference in this respect between such a gift and any other transfer of personal property. (See Coutant *v.* Schuyler, 1 *Paige*, 316; Harris *v.* Clark, 3 *N. Y.*, 93.)

§ 504. A gift made during the last illness of the giver, or under circumstances which would naturally impress him with an expectation of speedy death, is presumed to be a gift in view of death. When gift presumed to be in view of death.

Merchant *v.* Merchant, 2 *Bradf.*, 432.

§ 505. A gift in view of death may be revoked by the giver at any time,[1] and is revoked by his recovery from the illness, or escape from the peril, under the presence of which it was made,[2] or by the occurrence of any event which would operate as a revocation of a will made at the same time.[3] Revocation of gift in view of death.

[1] Merchant *v.* Merchant, 2 *Bradf.*, 432.
[2] Staniland *v.* Willott, 3 *Macn. & G.*, 664.
[3] Bloomer *v.* Bloomer, 2 *Bradf.*, 339.

§ 506. A gift in view of death is not affected by a previous will; nor by a subsequent will, unless it expresses an intention to revoke the gift. Effect of will upon gift.

§ 507. A gift in view of death must be treated as a legacy, so far as relates only to the creditors of the giver. When treated as a legacy.

CHAPTER IV.

RECORDING TRANSFERS.

Substantially from 1 *R. S.*, 755.

ARTICLE I.

WHAT MAY BE RECORDED.

Instruments affecting real property.

§ 508. Any instrument or judgment, affecting the title to real property, may be recorded under this chapter.

The present statutes authorize deeds, powers of attorney, wills, letters patent of the state, judgments in partition &c., to be recorded.

Instrument must be acknowledged.

§ 509. Before an instrument may be recorded, its execution must be acknowledged by the person executing it, or proved by a subscribing witness, and the acknowledgment or proof certified in the manner prescribed by article III of this chapter.

When deed to be recorded.

§ 510. An instrument, proved and certified pursuant to sections 524 and 525, may be recorded in the proper office, if the original is at the same time deposited therein to remain for public inspection, but not otherwise.

1 *R. S.*, 761, § 32.

Transfers of personal property, &c.

§ 511. Transfers of property in trust for the benefit of creditors, and transfers of or liens on property, by way of mortgage, are required to be recorded in the cases specified in the Title on special relations of DEBTOR and CREDITOR, and the chapter on MORTGAGES, respectively.

ARTICLE II.

MODE OF RECORDING.

§ 512. Instruments recorded under this chapter, must be recorded with the register of deeds, or, if there is none, with the clerk, of the county in which the real property affected thereby is situated. In what office.

§ 513. Grants, absolute in terms, and not intended as mortgages, or as securities in the nature of mortgages, are to be recorded in one set of books, and mortgages and securities in another. Books of record.

1 *R. S.*, 756, § 7.

§ 514. The duties of clerks and registers of deeds, in respect to recording instruments, are prescribed by the POLITICAL CODE. Duties of clerk, &c.

§ 515. The mode of recording transfers of ships, registered under the laws of the United States, is regulated by acts of Congress. Transfers of vessels.

ARTICLE III.

PROOF AND ACKNOWLEDGMENT OF INSTRUMENTS.

By whom acknowledgments may be taken in this state.

§ 516. The proof or acknowledgment of an instrument may be made at any place within this state, before a judge of the court of appeals,[1] or of the supreme court.[2]

[1] New.

[2] 1 *R. S.*, 756, § 4.

Id.

§ 517. The proof or acknowledgment of an instrument may be made, in this state, within the city or county for which the officer was appointed,[1] before:

1. A judge of a court of record;[2]
2. A mayor or recorder of a city;[2]
3. A justice of the peace;[3]
4. A commissioner of deeds;[2] or,
5. A notary public.[4]

[1] The statute (1 *R. S.*, 756, § 4,) seems to make this limitation only with respect to county judges, justices of the peace, and commissioners of deeds. But other statutes in effect limit the powers of all judges of local courts in the same manner.

[2] 1 *R. S.*, 756, § 4.

[3] *Laws of* 1840, 187, *ch.* 238.

[4] *Laws of* 1859, 869, *ch.* 360.

By whom taken, without the state.

§ 518. The proof or acknowledgment of an instrument may be made without the state, but within the United States, and within the jurisdiction of the officer,[1] before:

1. A judge of the supreme court, or of a district court, of the United States;[1]

2. A judge of the supreme, superior or circuit court of any state or territory;[1]

3. The mayor of any city;[2]

4. Any other officer of the state or territory where the acknowledgment is made, authorized by its laws to take the proof or acknowledgment;[3] or,

5. A commissioner appointed for the purpose by the government of this state, pursuant to special statutes of this state.[4]

[1] 1 *R. S.*, 757, § 4.
[2] *Laws* 1845, ch. 109.
[3] *Laws* 1848, ch. 195.
[4] *Laws* 1850, ch. 270.

§ 519. The proof or acknowledgment of an instrument may be made without the United States, before: By whom taken without the United States.

1. A minister plenipotentiary, or minister extraordinary, or *chargé d'affaires*, of the United States, resident and accredited in the country where the proof or acknowledgment is made;

2. A consul of the United States resident in that country;

3. A judge of the highest court of any of the British American provinces, acting in his own jurisdiction; or,

4. The mayor or chief magistrate of any city in the British islands, acting in his own jurisdiction.

From 1 *R. S.*, 759, § 6; *Laws of* 1829, 348, ch. 222; *Laws* 1845, ch. 109.

§ 520. The acknowledgment of an instrument cannot be taken, unless the officer taking it knows, or has satisfactory evidence, that the person making such acknowledgment is the individual who is described in and who executed the instrument. Requisites for acknowledgments.

1 *R. S.*, 758, § 9.

§ 521. The acknowledgment of a married woman to an instrument, purporting to be executed by her, cannot be taken within this state, unless she acknowledges to the officer, on a private examination, apart from her husband, that she executed such instrument freely, and without any compulsion or fear of her husband. Acknowledgments by married women.

1 *R. S.*, 758, § 10.

Id.

§ 522. A conveyance by a married woman has the same effect as if she were unmarried,[1] and may be acknowledged in the same manner, except as mentioned in the last section.[2]

[1] This provision is in accordance with the present law concerning married women.

[2] See 1 *R. S.*, 758, § 11.

Proof by subscribing witness.

§ 523. The proof of the execution of an instrument must be made by a subscribing witness thereto, who must state his own place of residence, and that he knew the person who is described in and who executed the instrument; and such proof must not be taken, unless the officer is personally acquainted with such subscribing witness, or has satisfactory evidence that he is the subscribing witness to the instrument.

1 *R. S.*, 758, § 12.

Proof of deed when witnesses are dead.

§ 524. When all the witnesses to an instrument which might be recorded are dead, it may be proved before any officer mentioned in sections 517, 518 or 519, other than commissioners of deeds, justices of the peace and notaries public.

1 *R. S.*, 761, § 30.

What proof to be made and certified.

§ 525. The proof of the execution of an instrument, in the case mentioned in the last section, must be made by satisfactory evidence of the death of all the witnesses thereto, and of the handwriting of such witnesses, or of one of them, and of the grantor; all which evidence must be set forth by the officer taking the same, in his certificate of the proof.

1 *R. S.*, 761, § 31.

Certificate of acknowledgment.

§ 526. An officer taking the acknowledgment or proof of any instrument must indorse upon the instrument a certificate thereof, signed by himself personally, setting forth all the matters required by law to be done or known by him, or proved before him, on the proceeding, together with the names of all the witnesses examined before him, their places of residence respectively, and the substance of their evidence.

1 *R. S.*, 759, § 15.

§ 527. A certificate of proof or acknowledgment before any officer in this state other than a judge of a court of record, when used in any county other than that in which he resides, must be accompanied by a certificate, under the hand and seal of the clerk of the county in which the officer resides, setting forth that such officer, at the time of taking such proof or acknowledgment, was duly authorized to take the same, and that the clerk is acquainted with his handwriting and believes that the signature to the original certificate is genuine. **Certificate of officer's authority.**

1 *R. S.*, 759, § 18, slightly modified so as to conform to the present judicial system.

§ 528. When an instrument is proved or acknowledged before one of the officers mentioned in subdivision 4 of section 518, the certificate of such officer must be accompanied by a certificate under the name and official seal of the clerk, register, recorder, or prothonotary, of the county in which such officer resides, or of the county or district court or court of common pleas thereof, specifying that such officer was, at the time of taking the proof or acknowledgment, duly authorized to take the same, and that such clerk, register, recorder or prothonotary, is acquainted with the handwriting of the officer, and believes his signature to be genuine. **Id.**

Laws of 1848, *ch.* 195, as amended by *Laws of* 1856, *ch.* 61, § 2.

§ 529. When an instrument is proved or acknowledged before one of the commissioners mentioned in subdivision 5 of section 518, the certificate of such commissioner must be accompanied by the certificate of the secretary of state of this state, attesting the existence of the officer, and the genuineness of his signature; and such commissioner can only act within the city or county in which he resided at the time of his appointment. **Id.**

1 *R. S.*, 757, § 4, *subd.* 2; *Laws of* 1845, 89, *ch.* 109; *Laws of* 1850, 582, *ch.* 270, amended by *Laws of* 1857, 756, *ch.* 788.

ARTICLE IV.

EFFECT OF RECORDING, OR THE WANT THEREOF.

The provisions of sections 16 and 17, 26 and 27, and of part of sections 22, 33 and 39 of chapter 3 of Part II, of the Revised Statutes, have been omitted as part of the law of evidence, contained in the Code of Civil Procedure.

Conveyances to be recorded. § 530. Every conveyance of real property, other than a lease for a term not exceeding three years, is void as against any subsequent purchaser or incumbrancer (including an assignee of a mortgage, lease, or other conditional estate) of the same property, or any part thereof, in good faith and for a valuable consideration, whose conveyance is first duly recorded.

1 *R. S.*, 756, § 1.

Conveyance, what. § 531. The term "conveyance," as used in the last section, embraces every instrument in writing by which any estate or interest in real property is created, aliened, mortgaged or incumbered, or by which the title to any real property may be affected; except wills, executory contracts for the sale or purchase of real property, and powers of attorney.

1 *R. S.*, 762, §§ 36–38.

Letter recorded, how revoked. § 532. No instrument containing a power to convey real property, which has been recorded, is to be deemed revoked by any act of the party by whom it was executed, unless the instrument containing such revocation is also recorded in the same office in which the instrument containing the power was recorded.

1 *R. S.*, 763, §§ 39, 40.

§ 533. The recording and deposit of an instrument proved and certified according to the provisions of sections 510, 524 and 525 are constructive notice of the execution of such instrument to all purchasers and incumbrancers subsequent to the recording; but the proof, recording and deposit do not entitle the instrument or the record thereof, or the transcript of the record, to be read in evidence. Effect of recording and deposit.

1 *R. S.*, 761, § 33.

§ 534. The provisions of this chapter do not extend to leases for life, or for years, in the counties of Albany, Ulster, Sullivan, Herkimer, Dutchess, Columbia, Delaware and Schenectady. Certain leases in counties named not affected.

1 *R. S.*, 763, § 42.

CHAPTER V.

UNLAWFUL TRANSFERS.

§ 535. Every instrument, other than a will, affecting an estate in real property, including every charge upon real property, or upon its rents or profits, made with intent to defraud prior or subsequent purchasers thereof, or incumbrancers thereon, is void as against every purchaser or incumbrancer, for value, of the same property, rents or profits. Certain instruments void against purchasers, &c.

2 *R. S.*, 134, § 1, made more definite by the introduction of the word "incumbrancer" instead of using the word "purchaser" only, and afterwards explaining that incumbrancers are purchasers, which would be inconsistent with the provisions of the Code relative to mortgages. See § 1923.

Not void against purchaser having notice, unless fraud is mutual.

§ 536. No instrument is to be avoided under the last section, in favor of a subsequent purchaser or incumbrancer having notice thereof at the time his purchase was made or his lien acquired, unless the person in whose favor the instrument was made, was privy to the fraud intended.

2 *R. S.*, 134, § 2, modified by omitting "actual or legal" before "notice," inasmuch as "notice" is elsewhere defined as meaning constructive as well as actual notice.

Power to revoke, when deemed executed.

§ 537. Where a power to revoke or modify an instrument affecting the title to, or the enjoyment of, an estate in real property is reserved to the grantor, or given to any other person, a subsequent grant of or charge upon the estate, by the person having the power of revocation, in favor of a purchaser or incumbrancer for value, operates as a revocation of the original instrument, to the extent of the power, in favor of such purchaser or incumbrancer.

This provision is intended to embody the substance of sections 3 and 4 of 2 *R. S.*, 134. It is thought that there is no necessity for the distinction made by those sections between a power reserved to the grantor, and a power created in favor of a third person.

The provision is also expressly extended to *all* instruments affecting real property, as was no doubt the intention of the statute, and probably is its effect.

Id.

§ 538. Where a person having a power of revocation, within the provisions of the last section, is not entitled to execute it until after the time at which he makes such a grant or charge as is described in that section, the power is deemed to be executed as soon as he is entitled to execute it.

Substantially the same as 2 *R. S.*, 134, § 5.

Purchaser in good faith not affected.

§ 539. The rights of a purchaser or incumbrancer in good faith and for value are not to be impaired by any of the foregoing provisions of this chapter.

2 *R. S.*, 137, § 5, modified by adding the words "or incumbrancer," and by a slight change of phraseology.

§ 540. Every grant of real property, other than one made by the state,[1] or under a judicial sale, is void, if at the time of the delivery thereof, such real property is in the actual possession of a person claiming under a title adverse to that of the grantor.[2] Conveyance of land adversely possessed.

[1] Brady *v.* Begun, 36 *Barb.*, 533; Candee *v.* Haywood, 34 *id.*, 349; People *v.* Mayor, &c., of N. Y., 8 *Abb. Pr.*, 724; Jackson *v.* Gumaer, 2 *Cow.*, 552.

[2] 1 *R. S.*, 739, § 147. This provision does not apply to mortgages, which are not recognized in this Code as grants in any sense.

§ 541. Other provisions concerning unlawful transfers are contained in Part II of the Fourth Division of this Code, concerning the special relations of DEBTOR and CREDITOR. Other provisions.

TITLE V.

WILL.

In this Title, taken, for the most part, from the existing law, are inserted many new provisions relating to nuncupative wills; mutual and conditional wills; partial and total revocation; revocation of wills executed in duplicate; effect of alteration or obliteration; wills procured by undue influence; republication by codicil; placing power to devise real property on the same footing as personal estate; the execution of wills in foreign countries; the law of domicil; the interpretation of wills; the payment and abatement of legacies.

CHAPTER I.

EXECUTION AND REVOCATION OF WILLS.

Who may make will.

§ 542. Every male person of the age of eighteen years or upwards, and every female of the age of sixteen years or upwards, of sound mind, and no others, may dispose of real and personal property, by a will duly executed, according to the provisions of this Code.

2 *R. S.*, 56, § 1; 60, § 21; modified by enabling minors to dispose of real as well as personal property by will, and by omitting the exception as to married women.

Monomaniac incompetent.

§ 543. A person having any insane delusion is incompetent to make a will.

This provision is new (see Stanton *v.* Wetherwax, 16 *Barb.*, 259; Waring *v.* Waring, 12 *Jurist*, 947; 6 *Moore P. C. C.*, 341).

§ 544. A will or part of a will procured to be made by duress, menace, fraud or undue influence, may be denied probate; and a revocation, procured by the same means, may be declared void. Will procured by fraud, &c.

This section is new.

§ 545. Every estate and interest in real or personal property, to which heirs, husband, widow or next of kin might succeed, may be disposed of by will. What may pass by will.

From 2 *R. S.*, 57, § 2.

§ 546. A testamentary disposition may be made to any person capable by law of taking the property so disposed of, except that no corporation can take under a will, unless expressly authorized by its charter or by statute so to take. Who may take by will.

2 *R. S.*, 57, § 3.

§ 547. A nuncupative will of real or personal property, or both, is valid, when made in contemplation, fear or peril of death: Nuncupative will.

1. By a soldier, while in actual military service, whether he is an officer or private, or a surgeon, or a servant of the army; or,

2. By a sailor (whether he is an officer or surgeon, a marine or mariner, or a servant of the vessel), after he finally goes on board the vessel for the voyage, and before he comes on shore, in port, after the voyage is over.

Modified from 2 *R. S.*, 60, § 22. By this section the nuncupative will may pass real as well as personal property; but it can be made only in contemplation, fear or peril of death (See Prince *v.* Hazleton, 20 *Johns.*, 502). A nuncupative will may be made by a ship's cook or other servant (*Exp.* Thompson, 4 *Bradf.*, 154), and while the ship is at anchor, as well as on the open sea (Hubbard *v.* Hubbard, 8 *N. Y.*, 196).

§ 548. A conjoint or mutual will is valid, but it may be revoked by any of the testators, in like manner with any other will. Mutual will.

Ex parte Day, 1 *Bradf.*, 476.

Conditional will.

§ 549. A will, the validity of which is made by its own terms conditional, may be denied probate, according to the event, with reference to the condition.

This section is new.

Written will, how to be executed.

§ 550. Every will, other than a nuncupative will authorized by section 547, must be executed and attested as follows:

1. It must be subscribed at the end thereof, by the testator himself, or by some person in his presence and by his direction;

2. The subscription must be made in the presence of each of the attesting witnesses, or be acknowledged by the testator to each of them, to have been made by him or by his authority;

3. The testator must, at the time of subscribing or acknowledging the same, declare to the attesting witnesses that the instrument is his will; and,

4. There must be two attesting witnesses, each of whom must sign his name as a witness at the end of the will, at the testator's request.

From 2 *R. S.*, 63, § 40.

Nuncupative will, how to be executed.

§ 551. A nuncupative will is not required to be in writing, nor to be declared or attested with any formalities.

Hubbard *v.* Hubbard, 8 *N. Y.*, 196.

Witness to add residence.

§ 552. A witness to a written will must write, with his name, his place of residence; and a person who subscribes the testator's name, by his direction, must write his own name as a witness to the will. But a violation of this section does not affect the validity of the will.

From 2 *R. S.*, 64, § 41.

Republication by codicil.

§ 553. The execution of a codicil, referring to a previous will, has the effect to republish the will, as modified by the codicil.

Will made out of this state.

§ 554. A will of real or personal property, or both, or a revocation thereof, made out of this state by a person not having his domicil in this state, is as valid, when executed according to the law of the place in which the same was made, or in which the testator was at the time domiciled, as if it were made in this state, and according to the provisions of this chapter.

§ 555. No will or revocation is valid unless executed either according to the provisions of this chapter, or according to the law of the place in which it was made, or in which the testator was at the time domiciled. Will not duly executed, void.

The last two sections are modified from 2 *R. S.*, 67, § 68, 69.

§ 556. Whenever a will, or a revocation thereof, is duly executed according to the law of the place in which the same was made, or in which the testator was at the time domiciled, the same is regulated, as to the validity of its execution, by the law of such place, notwithstanding that the testator subsequently changed his domicil to a place, by the law of which such will would be void. Subsequent change of domicil.

This section is new. Compare Moultrie *v.* Hunt, 23 *N. Y.*, 394, and Parsons *v.* Lyman, 20 *N. Y.*, 103.

§ 557. Every surrogate, county clerk or register of deeds must deposit, in his office, any will delivered to him for that purpose, and give a written receipt to the depositor; and must inclose such will in a sealed wrapper, so that it cannot be read, and indorse thereon the name of the testator, his residence, and the date of the deposit; and such wrapper must not be opened until its delivery under the provisions of the next section. Wills may be deposited for safe keeping.

2 *R. S.*, 405, § 68.

§ 558. A will deposited under the provisions of the last section must be delivered only: To whom to be delivered.

1. To the testator in person;

2. Upon his written order, duly proved by the oath of a subscribing witness;

3. After his death, to the person, if any, named in the indorsement on the wrapper of the will; or,

4. If there is no such indorsement, and if the will was not deposited with the surrogate having jurisdiction of its probate, then to the surrogate who has jurisdiction.

2 *R. S.*, 405, § 69.

Will, when to be opened by surrogate.

§ 559. The surrogate with whom a will is deposited, or to whom it is delivered, must, after the death of the testator, publicly open and examine the will and file it in his office, there to remain until duly proved, or deliver it to the surrogate having jurisdiction of its probate.

2 *R. S.*, 405, § 70.

Lost or destroyed will.

§ 560. A lost or destroyed will of real or personal property, or both, may be established in the cases provided in the CODE OF CIVIL PROCEDURE.

The reference is to section 12 of Appendix D, in the original draft of this Code.

Written will, how revoked.

§ 561. Except in the cases in this chapter mentioned, no written will, nor any part thereof, can be revoked or altered, otherwise than:

1. By a written will, or other writing of the testator, declaring such revocation or alteration, and executed with the same formalities with which a will should be executed by such testator; or,

2. By being burnt, torn, canceled, obliterated or destroyed, with the intent and for the purpose of revoking the same, by the testator himself, or by some person in his presence and by his direction.

2 *R. S.*, 64, § 42.

Evidence of revocation.

§ 562. When a will is canceled or destroyed by any other person than the testator, the direction of the testator, and the fact of such injury or destruction, must be proved by two witnesses.

Ib.

§ 563. A revocation by obliteration on the face of the will may be partial or total, and is complete if the material part is so obliterated as to show an intention to revoke; but where, in order to effect a new disposition, the testator attempts to revoke a provision of the will, by altering or obliterating it on the face thereof, such revocation is not valid unless the new disposition is legally effected. **Revocation by obliteration on face of will.**

McPherson *v.* Clark, 3 *Bradf.*, 92.

§ 564. The revocation of a will, executed in duplicate, may be made by revoking one of the duplicates. **Revocation of duplicate.**

§ 565. A prior will is not revoked by a subsequent will, unless the latter contains an express revocation, or provisions wholly inconsistent with the terms of the former will; but in other cases the prior will remains effectual so far as consistent with the provisions of the subsequent will. **Revocation by subsequent will.**

Conover *v.* Hoffman, 15 *Abb. Pr.*, 100; Robinson *v.* Smith, 13 *Abb. Pr.*, 359; McLoskey *v.* Reid, 4 *Bradf.*, 334; Nelson *v.* McGiffert, 3 *Barb. Ch.*, 158; Brant *v.* Willson, 8 *Cow.*, 56.

§ 566. If, after making a will, the testator duly makes and executes a subsequent will, the destruction, canceling or revocation of the latter does not revive the former, unless it appears by the terms of such revocation that it was his intention to revive the prior will, or unless after such destruction, canceling or revocation, he duly republishes the prior will. **Revocation of subsequent will does not revive the first.**

2 *R. S.*, 65, § 53.

§ 567. If, after having made a will, the testator marries, and has issue of such marriage, born either in his lifetime or after his death, and the wife or issue survives him, the will is to be deemed revoked, **Revocation by marriage and birth of issue.**

unless provision has been made for such issue by some settlement, or unless such issue are provided for in the will, or in such way mentioned therein as to show an intention not to make such provision; and no other evidence to rebut the presumption of such revocation can be received.

2 *R. S.*, 64, § 43.

Revocation of woman's will by marriage.

§ 568. A will executed by an unmarried woman is revoked by her subsequent marriage.

2 *R. S.*, 64, § 44.

Contract of sale not a revocation.

§ 569. An agreement made by a testator, for the sale or transfer of property disposed of by a will previously made, does not revoke such disposal; but the property passes by the will, subject to the same remedies on the testator's agreement, for a specific performance or otherwise, against the devisees or legatees, as might be had against the testator's successors, if the same had passed by succession.

2 *R. S.*, 64, § 45.

Charge or incumbrance not a revocation.

§ 570. A charge or incumbrance upon any real or personal property, for the purpose of securing the payment of money, or the performance of any other obligation, is not a revocation of a will relating to the same property, previously executed; but the dispositions made by the will take effect subject thereto.

2 *R. S.*, 64, § 46.

Conveyance, when not a revocation.

§ 571. A conveyance, settlement, or other act of a testator, by which his interest in a thing previously disposed of by his will is altered, but not wholly divested, is not a revocation; but the will passes the property which would otherwise devolve by succession.

2 *R. S.*, 65, § 47.

When it is a revocation.

§ 572. If the instrument, by which an alteration is made in the testator's interest in a thing previously disposed of by his will, expresses his intent that it shall be a revocation, or if it contains provisions wholly inconsistent with the terms and nature of the testamentary disposition, it operates as a revocation thereof, unless such inconsistent provisions depend on a condition or contingency, by reason of which they do not take effect.

2 *R. S.*, 65, §§ 47, 48.

§ 573. The revocation of a will revokes all its codicils. Revocation of codicils.

§ 574. Whenever a testator has a child born after the making of his will, either in his lifetime or after his death, and dies leaving such child unprovided for by any settlement, and neither provided for nor in any way mentioned in his will, the child succeeds to the same portion of the testator's real and personal property, that he would have succeeded to if the testator had died intestate. After-born child, unprovided for, to succeed.

2 *R. S.*, 65, § 49.

§ 575. Whenever any real or personal property is disposed of by will to a descendant or a brother or sister of the testator, and such legatee or devisee dies during the lifetime of the testator, leaving a successor who survives the testator, such disposition does not lapse, but the thing so disposed of vests in the surviving successors of the legatee or devisee, as if such legatee or devisee had survived the testator and had died intestate. Devises and bequests, in certain cases not to lapse.

2 *R. S.*, 66, § 52; substituting "successors" for "descendants."

§ 576. If a person is an attesting witness to the execution of a will wherein any beneficial devise, legacy, interest or power of appointment of any real or personal property, is made to such witness, and the will cannot be proved without his testimony, the devise, legacy, interest or power is void so far only as concerns such witness, or any one claiming under him, and the witness is competent to prove the execution of the will. Witness to will cannot take under will.

Modified from 2 *R. S.*, 65, § 50; omitting the disqualification of husband or wife of witness.

When witness may succeed.

§ 577. An attesting witness to a will, without whose testimony it cannot be proved, and who would have been entitled to a share of the testator's estate in case the will had not been established, succeeds to the same portion of the testator's estate that he would have succeeded to if the testator had died intestate, not exceeding the value of the devise or bequest to him in the will.

2 *R. S.*, 65, § 51.

Creditor a competent witness.

§ 578. A creditor, whose debt is by a will charged upon property, is not thereby disqualified as a witness to prove the execution of the will.

2 *R. S.*, 57, § 6. These three sections are retained because they seem to correspond to the exceptions made by the present Code of Procedure to the admission of parties in interest as witnesses.

CHAPTER II.

INTERPRETATION OF WILLS, AND EFFECT OF VARIOUS PROVISIONS.

§ 579. A will is to be construed according to the intention of the testator.[1] Where his intention cannot have effect to its full extent, it must have effect as far as possible.[2] Testator's intention to be carried out.

[1] 1 *R. S.*, 748, § 2; Brown *v.* Lyon, 6 *N. Y.*, 420; see Chrystie *v.* Phyfe, 19 *id.*, 348.

[2] Kane *v.* Gott, 24 *Wend.*, 665; Savage *v.* Burnham, 17 *N. Y.*, 577; Doe *v.* Gallini, 5 *B. & Ad.*, 621.

§ 580. In case of uncertainty, arising upon the face of a will, as to the application of any of its provisions, the testator's intention is to be ascertained from the words of the will, taking into view the circumstances under which it was made; exclusive of his oral declarations. Intention to be ascertained from the will.

See Bullock *v.* Evans, 9 *H. of L. Cas.*, 24; Maddison *v.* Chapman, 5 *Jur.* [*N. S.*], 277.

§ 581. In interpreting a will, subject to the law of this state, the rules prescribed by the following sections of this chapter are to be observed, unless an intention to the contrary clearly appears. Rules of interpretation.

§ 582. Several testamentary instruments, executed by the same testator, are to be taken and construed together as one instrument. Several instruments to be taken together.

Howland *v.* Union Theo. Sem., 5 *N. Y.*, 193, 214; Haven *v.* Haven, 1 *Redf. Surr.*, 374; Jauncey *v.* Att'y-Gen., 3 *Giff.*, 308; Stone *v.* Evans, 2 *Atk.*, 86.

§ 583. All the parts of a will are to be construed in relation to each other,[1] and so as if possible to form one consistent whole,[2] but where several parts[3] are absolutely[4] irreconcilable, the latter[5] must prevail. Harmonizing various parts.

[1] Arcularius *v.* Geisenhainer, 3 *Bradf.*, 64; affirmed 25 *Barb.*, 403; Egerton *v.* Conklin, 25 *Wend.*, 224, 238;

Covenhoven *v.* Shuler, 2 *Paige*, 130; Ford *v.* Ford, 6 *Hare*, 492; Stewart *v.* Jones, 3 *De Gex & J.*, 532.

[2] Carter *v.* Hunt, 40 *Barb.*, 391; Morrall *v.* Sutton, 1 *Phillips*, 533; Mutter's estate, 38 *Penn. St.*, 314; Jennings *v.* Newman, 10 *Sim.*, 223.

[3] Whether in the same sentence or in different sentences, Morrall *v.* Sutton, 1 *Phillips*, 537, 547.

[4] Barclay *v.* Maskelyne, *H. R. V. Johns.*, 131; Sweet *v.* Chase, 2 *N. Y.*, 79; Covenhoven *v.* Shuler, 2 *Paige*, 123.

[5] Trustees of Theolog. Seminary *v.* Kellogg, 16 *N. Y.*, 88; Norris *v.* Beyea, 13 *N. Y.*, 284; Campbell *v.* Rawdon, 18 *N. Y.*, 414; Griffen *v.* Ford, 1 *Bosw.*, 123; Bradstreet *v.* Clarke, 12 *Wend.*, 602.

Id.

§ 584. A clear and distinct devise or bequest cannot be affected by any reasons assigned therefor,[1] or by any other words not equally clear and distinct,[2] or by inference or argument from other parts of the will,[3] or by an inaccurate recital of or reference to its contents in another part of the will.[4]

[1] Cole *v.* Wade, 16 *Ves.*, 46; see Thompson *v.* Whitlock, 5 *Jur.* [*N. S.*], 991.

[2] Thornhill *v.* Hall, 2 *Cl. & F.*, 22; Barclay *v.* Maskelyne, *H. R. V. Johns.*, 126. This rule applies equally to prior (Greenwood *v.* Sutcliffe, 14 *C. B.*, 226) and to subsequent words (Arcularius *v.* Geisenhainer, 3 *Bradf.*, 75; affirmed 25 *Barb.*, 403; Kiven *v.* Oldfield, 4 *De Gex & J.*, 30; Borrell *v.* Haigh, 2 *Jur.*, 229).

[3] Campbell *v.* Harding, 2 *Russ. & M.*, 409; Jennings *v.* Newman, 10 *Sim.*, 223.

[4] Hillersdon *v.* Lowe, 2 *Hare*, 355, 372; Mortimer *v.* Hartley, 3 *De Gex & Sm.*, 332.

Id.

§ 585. Where the meaning of any part of a will is ambiguous or doubtful, it may be explained by any reference thereto, or recital thereof, in another part of the will.

See Hyatt *v.* Pugsley, 23 *Barb.*, 285; Marsh *v.* Hague 1 *Edw.*, 174.

Words taken in ordinary sense.

§ 586. The words of a will are to be taken in their ordinary and grammatical sense, unless a clear intention to use them in another sense[1] can be collected, and that other can be ascertained.[2]

[1] Hone *v.* Van Schaick, 3 *N. Y.*, 538; Cromer *v.* Pinckney, 3 *Barb. Ch.*, 466; Bullock *v.* Downes, 9 *H. of L. Cas.*, 24.

[2] De Nottebeck *v.* Astor, 13 *N. Y.*, 98; affirming S. C., 16 *Barb.*, 412; Bradhurst *v.* Bradhurst, 1 *Paige*, 331; Covenhoven *v.* Shuler, 2 *id.*, 122; Rathbone *v.* Dyckman, 3 *id.*, 9; Crosby *v.* Wendell, 6 *id.*, 548.

§ 587. The words of a will are to receive an interpretation which will give to every expression some effect, rather than one which will render any of the expressions inoperative.

Words to receive an operative construction.

Griffen *v.* Ford, 1 *Bosw.*, 123, 140; Mason *v.* Jones, 2 *Barb.*, 229; Butler *v.* Butler, 3 *Barb. Ch.*, 304; Pond *v.* Bergh, 10 *Paige*, 140; Doe *v.* Gallini, 5 *B. & Ad.*, 621; 3 *Ad. & El.*, 340; see Chrystie *v.* Phyfe, 19 *N. Y.*, 348.

§ 588. Of two modes of interpreting a will, that is to be preferred which will prevent a total intestacy.

Intestacy to be avoided.

Booth *v.* Booth, 4 *Ves.*, 407.

§ 589. Technical words in a will are to be taken in their technical sense,[1] unless the context clearly[2] indicates a contrary intention.[3]

Effect of technical words.

[1] Moore *v.* Lyons, 25 *Wend.*, 154, 155; Campbell *v.* Rawdon, 18 *N. Y.*, 417; Brown *v.* Lyon, 6 *N. Y.*, 419; Jackson *v.* Luquere, 5 *Cow.*, 228; Jenkins *v.* Hughes, 8 *H. of L. Cas.*, 571; Doe *v.* Perratt, 6 *Man. & Gr.*, 335, 342, 350.

[2] Doe *v.* Gallini, 5 *B. & Ad.*, 621; 3 *Ad. & El.*, 340; Jesson *v.* Wright, 2 *Bligh.*, 57.

[3] Corrigan *v.* Kiernan, 1 *Bradf.*, 208; Sherwood *v.* Sherwood, 3 *id.*, 230; De Kay *v.* Irving, 5 *Den.*, 646; Parks *v.* Parks, 9 *Paige*, 107.

§ 590. Technical words are not necessary to give effect to any species of disposition by a will.

Technical words not necessary.

Jackson *v.* Luquere, 5 *Cow.*, 228; Parks *v.* Parks, 9 *Paige*, 117.

§ 591. The term "heirs," or other words of inheritance, are not requisite to devise a fee, and a devise of real property passes all the estate of the testator, unless otherwise limited.

Certain words not necessary to pass a fee.

1 *R. S.*, 748, § 1; to similar effect, 1 *Vict.*, c. 26, § 26, 28.

§ 592. Real[1] or personal[2] property embraced in a power to devise, passes by a will purporting to devise all the real or personal property of the testator.

Power to devise, how executed by terms of will.

[1] 1 *R. S.*, 737, § 126.

[2] Van Wert *v.* Benedict, 1 *Bradf.*, 123; Amory *v.* Meredith, 7 *Allen*, 397. See a similar provision, 1 *Vict.*, c. 26, § 27, as regards a general and beneficial power.

Devise or bequest of all real or all personal property or both.

§ 593. A devise or bequest of all the testator's real[1] or personal[2] property, in express terms, or in any other terms denoting his intent to dispose of all his real or personal property, passes all the real or personal property which he was entitled to dispose of by will at the time of his death.

[1] 2 *R. S.*, 57, § 5.

[2] McNaughton *v.* McNaughton, 41 *Barb.*, 50.

Residuary clause.

§ 594. A devise of the residue of the testator's estate, property, or real property, passes all the real property which he was entitled to devise at the time of his death, not otherwise effectually devised by his will.

It has been doubted (Van Cortlandt *v.* Kip, 1 *Hill*, 596; 7 *id.*, 352; see Prescott *v.* Prescott, 7 *Metc.*, 141, 146) whether this is the effect of a residuary devise, except where the beneficial taker under the prior devise is the same person as the residuary devisee (see Tucker *v.* Tucker, 5 *N. Y.*, 421), where the prior devise has been revoked by the testator (Kip *v.* Van Cortlandt, 7 *Hill*, 346), or where the prior devise is only a charge upon, and not an exception from the residuary devise (Cook *v.* Stationers' Co., 3 *Myl. & K.*, 262).

Id.

§ 595. A bequest of the residue of the testator's estate, property or personal property, passes all the personal property which he was entitled to bequeath at the time of his death, not otherwise effectually bequeathed by his will.

"Heirs," "relatives," "issue," "descendants," &c.

§ 596. A testamentary disposition to "heirs," "relations," "nearest relations," "representatives," "legal representatives" or "personal representatives," or "family," "issue," "descendants," "nearest" or "next of kin" of any person, without other words of qualification, and when the terms are used as words of donation and not of limitation, vests the property*

---

* If the provisions of Appendix A to the draft of this Code are adopted, the following words should be substituted for the words following the asterisk: "If real, in those who would be entitled to succeed to the property of such person according to the chapter on Succession to Real Property; if personal, then in those who would be entitled according to the chapter on Succession to Personal Property."

in those who would be entitled to succeed to the property of such person, according to sections 642 and 643 of this Code.

§ 597. The terms mentioned in the last section are used as words of donation, and not of limitation, when the property is given to the person so designated, directly, and not as a qualification of an estate given to the ancestor of such person. Words of donation and of limitation.

§ 598. Words in a will referring to death[1] or survivorship,[2] simply, relate to the time of the testator's death, unless possession is actually postponed, when they must be referred to the time of possession. To what time words refer.

[1] Adams *v.* Beekman, 1 *Paige*, 631; Ive *v.* King, 16 *Beav.*, 41; Howard *v.* Howard, 21 *Beav.*, 550; Schenck *v.* Agnew, 4 *Kay & J.*, 405.

[2] Young *v.* Robertson, 4 *Macq.*, 319, 330; Young *v.* Davies, 9 *Jur.* (*N. S.*), 399. The contrary was held as to real property in Moore *v.* Lyons, 25 *Wend.*, 119, on the supposed English rule; but that rule does not exist (Taaffe *v.* Conner, 10 *H. of L. Cas.*, 77; 22 *Beav.*, 271).

It makes no difference that there is a postponement without any preceding life interest (Hodgson *v.* Micklethwaite, 2 *Drewry*, 294). This rule is not now law when the life tenant dies before the testator (Spurrell *v.* Spurrell, 11 *Hare*, 154).

§ 599. A testamentary disposition to a class includes every person answering the description at the testator's death;[1] but when the possession is postponed to a future period, it includes also all persons coming within the description, before the time to which possession is postponed.[2] Devise or bequest to a class.

[1] Tucker *v.* Bishop, 16 *N. Y.*, 402; Campbell *v.* Rawdon, 18 *N. Y.*, 415. Persons who die before the testator are not included (Stires *v.* Van Rensselaer, 2 *Bradf.*, 172; Campbell *v.* Rawdon, 18 *N. Y.*, 414, 415).

[2] Tucker *v.* Bishop, 16 *N. Y.*, 402; Johnson *v.* Valentine, 4 *Sandf.*, 36. To the contrary, Doubleday *v.* Newton, 27 *Barb.*, 444.

§ 600. When a will directs[1] the conversion of real property into money, such property and all its pro- When conversion takes effect.

ceeds must be deemed personal property,[2] from the time of the testator's death.[3]

Forsyth *v.* Rathbone, 34 *Barb.*, 405; Fowler *v.* Depau, 26 *Barb.*, 239; Harris *v.* Clark, 7 *N. Y.*, 260; Phelps *v.* Pond, 23 *N. Y.*, 76.

[2] Meakings *v.* Cromwell, 5 *N. Y.*, 136; King *v.* Woodhull, 3 *Edw.*, 79; Bramhall *v.* Ferris, 14 *N. Y.*, 46; Johnson *v.* Bennett, 39 *Barb.*, 252.

[3] Kane *v.* Gott, 24 *Wend.*, 669.

When child born after testator's death, takes under will.

§ 601. A child conceived before, but not born until after a testator's death, or any other period when a disposition to a class vests in right or in possession, takes, if answering to the description of the class.

Rawlins *v.* Rawlins, 2 *Cox*, 425; Trower *v.* Butts, 1 *Sim. & Stu.*, 181; Jenkins *v.* Freyer, 4 *Paige*, 53.

Mistakes and omissions.

§ 602. When, applying a will, it is found that there is an imperfect description,[1] or that no person[2] or property[3] exactly answers the description, mistakes[4] and omissions must be corrected, if the error appears from the context of the will or from extrinsic evidence;[5] but evidence of the declarations of the testator as to his intention[6] cannot be received.[7]

[1] Fleming *v.* Fleming, 8 *Jur.* (*N. S.*), 1042.

[2] Conolly *v.* Pardon, 1 *Paige*, 291; Smith *v.* Smith, 4 *id.*, 271; Wightman *v.* Stoddard, 3 *Bradf.*, 405; Hart *v.* Marks, 4 *id.*, 161; Lee *v.* Pain, 4 *Hare*, 249.

[3] Roman Cath. Asylum *v.* Emmons, 3 *Bradf.*, 144; Smith *v.* Wyckoff, 3 *Sandf. Ch.*, 82, 88.

[4] Hart *v.* Tulk, 2 *De Gex, M. & G.*, 300.

[5] Stanley *v.* Stanley, 2 *Johns. & Hem.*, 513; see Blundell *v.* Gladstone, 1 *Phillips*, 279.

[6] See Blundell *v.* Gladstone, 1 *Phil.*, 282.

[7] Doe *v.* Hiscocks, 5 *Mees. & W.*, 563. To the contrary, *Ex parte* Hornby, 2 *Bradf.*, 420. Otherwise if the words are equally descriptive of several persons (Doe *v.* Allen, 12 *Ad. & El.*, 451; Fleming *v.* Fleming, 8 *Jur.* [*N. S.*], 1042) or subjects of ownership (See Douglass *v.* Fellows, 1 *Kay*, 114, 120).

When devises and bequests vest.

§ 603. Testamentary dispositions, including devises[1] and bequests[2] to a person on attaining majority, are presumed to vest at the testator's death.

[1] Post *v.* Hover, 30 *Barb.*, 312, 319.

[2] Dupre *v.* Thompson, 8 *Barb.*, 537.

§ 604. A testamentary disposition, when vested, cannot be divested unless upon the occurrence of the precise contingency prescribed by the testator for that purpose. **When cannot be divested.**

Williams *v.* Jones, 1 *Russ.*, 517; Humberston *v.* Stanton, 1 *Ves. & B.*, 485.

§ 605. If a devisee or legatee dies during the lifetime of the testator, the testamentary disposition to him fails, unless an intention appears to substitute some other in his place. **Death of devisee or legatee.**

Savage *v.* Burnham, 17 *N. Y.*, 575.

§ 606. The death of a devisee[1] or legatee[2] of a limited interest, before the testator's death, does not defeat the interests of persons in remainder, who survive the testator. **Interests in remainder are not affected.**

[1] Downing *v.* Marshall, 23 *N. Y.*, 370; 23 *How. Pr.*, 7; Campbell *v.* Rawdon, 18 *N. Y.*, 421.
[2] Downing *v.* Marshall, 23 *N. Y.*, 370.

§ 607. A conditional disposition is one which depends upon the occurrence of some uncertain event, by which it is either to take effect or be defeated. **Conditional devises and bequests.**

§ 608. A condition precedent in a will is one which is required to be fulfilled before a particular disposition takes effect. **Condition precedent, what.**

§ 609. Where a testamentary disposition is made upon a condition precedent, nothing vests until the condition is fulfilled; except where such fulfillment is impossible, in which case the disposition vests, unless the condition was the sole motive thereof, and the impossibility was unknown to the testator, or arose from an unavoidable event subsequent to the execution of the will. **Effect of condition precedent.**

§ 610. A condition precedent in a will is to be deemed performed when the testator's intention has been substantially, though not literally, complied with. **Conditions precedent, when deemed performed.**

Condition subsequent, what.

§ 611. A condition subsequent is where an estate or interest is so given as to vest immediately, subject only to be divested by some subsequent act or event.

Devisees and legatees take as tenants in common.

§ 612. A devise[1] or legacy[2] given to more than one person vests in them as owners in common.

[1] 1 *R. S.*, 727, § 44.

[2] To the contrary, see Putnam *v.* Putnam, 4 *Bradf.*, 308.

Advancements when ademptions.

§ 613. Advancements or gifts are not to be taken as ademptions of general legacies, unless such intention is expressed by the testator in writing.

This provision is new.

CHAPTER III.

GENERAL PROVISIONS.

§ 614. Legacies are distinguished and designated, according to their nature, as follows: Nature and designation of legacies.

1. A legacy of a particular thing, specified, and distinguished from all others of the same kind belonging to the testator, is specific; if such legacy fails, resort cannot be had to the other property of the testator; Specific.

2. A legacy is demonstrative when the particular fund or personal property is pointed out from which it is to be taken or paid; if such fund or property fails, in whole or in part, resort may be had to the general assets, as in case of a general legacy; Demonstrative.

3. An annuity is a bequest of certain specified sums periodically; if the fund or property out of which they are payable fails, resort may be had to the general assets, as in case of a general legacy; Annuities.

4. A residuary legacy embraces only that which remains after all the bequests of the will are discharged; Residuary.

5. All other legacies are general legacies. General.

§ 615. When a decedent dies intestate, the property, except such as is otherwise disposed of under section 640 of this Code, and such as is exempt under the Code of Civil Procedure, is to be resorted to, in the following order, in payment of debts: Order of sale in case of intestacy.

1. Personal property;

2. Real property other than estates of freehold;

3. Estates of freehold.

The reference is to section 83 of Appendix D, in the original draft of this Code.

§ 616. The property of a testator, with the exception specified in the last section, is to be resorted to, in the following order, for the payment of debts and legacies; Order of sale in case of a testator.

1. Personal property, excepting such as is expressly exempted in the will;

2. Real property expressly devised to pay debts or legacies, where the personal property is exempted in

the will, or where the personal property which is not exempted is insufficient;

3. Real property which is not effectually devised;

4. Property, real or personal, charged with debts or legacies; but though real property be charged with the payment of legacies, the personal property is not to be exonerated;

5. The following property, ratably: real property, devised without being charged with debts or legacies, and specific and demonstrative legacies;

6. Personal property expressly exempted in the will.

Legacies, how charged with debts.

§ 617. In the application of the personal property of a decedent to the payment of debts, legacies must be charged in the following order, unless a different intention is expressed in the will:

1. Residuary legacies;

2. General legacies;

3. Legacies given for a valuable consideration, or for the relinquishment of dower, or some right or interest;

4. Specific and demonstrative legacies.

Id.

§ 618. Legacies to husband, widow or kindred of any class, are chargeable only after legacies to persons not related to the testator.

Abatement.

§ 619. Abatement takes place in any class only as between legacies of that class, unless a different intention is expressed in the will.

Specific devises and legacies.

§ 620. In a specific devise or legacy the title passes by the will, but, in case of legacies, possession can only be obtained from the personal representative; and he may be authorized by the surrogate to sell the property devised or bequeathed, in the cases herein provided.

Heir s conveyance good unless

§ 621. The rights of a purchaser or incumbrancer of real property, in good faith, and for value, derived from any person claiming the same by succession, are not impaired by any devise made by the decedent from whom succession is claimed, unless the instrument containing such devise is duly proved as a will, and recorded in the office of the surrogate having jurisdiction thereof, or unless written notice of such devise is filed with the clerk of the county where the real property is situated, within four years after the devisor's death. Will is proved within four years.

The provisions of the Revised Statutes (1 *R. S.*, 748, § 3), from which this section is taken, made the following exceptions to the foregoing rule:

"1. Where the devisee shall have been within the age of twenty-one years, or insane, or imprisoned, or a married woman, or out of the state, at the time of the death of such testator; or,

2. Where it shall appear that the will or codicil containing such devise, shall have been concealed by the heirs of such testator, or some one of them.

In which several cases, the limitation contained in this section shall not commence, until after the expiration of one year from the time when such disability shall have been removed, or such will or codicil shall have been delivered to the devisee, or his representative, or to the proper surrogate."

These disabilities are such as almost to destroy the value of the provision, and the commissioners have therefore omitted them. As, however, the probate is often delayed by litigation, a provision that notice may be filed in the office of the county clerk, with equal effect, has been added.

§ 622. Where specific legacies are for life only, the first legatee must sign and deliver to the second legatee, or, if there is none, to the personal representative, an inventory of the property, expressing that the same is in his custody for life only, and that, on his decease, it is to be delivered and to remain to the use and for the benefit of the second legatee, or to the personal representative, as the case may be. Possession of legatees.

The following sections are new.

§ 623. In case of a bequest of the interest or income of a certain sum or fund, the income accrues from the testator's death. Bequest of interest.

Satisfaction. § 624. A legacy, or a gift in contemplation, fear or peril of death may be satisfied.

Legacies when due. § 625. Legacies are due and deliverable, at the expiration of one year after the testator's decease. Annuities commence at the testator's decease.

Interest. § 626. Legacies bear interest from the time when they are due and payable, except that legacies for maintenance, or to the testator's widow, bear interest from the testator's decease.

Construction of these rules. § 627. The four preceding sections are in all cases to be controlled by a testator's express intention.

Executor according to the tenor. § 628. Where it appears, by the terms of a will, that it was the intention of the testator to commit the execution thereof and the administration of his estate to any person as executor, such person, although not named executor, is entitled to letters testamentary in like manner as if he had been named executor.

Power to appoint void. § 629. An authority to an executor to appoint an executor is void.

Executor not to act till qualified. § 630. No person has any power, as an executor, until he qualifies, except that, before letters have been issued, he may pay funeral charges and take necessary measures for the preservation of the estate.

From 2 *R. S.*, 71, §§ 15, 16.

Executor of an executor. § 631. No executor of an executor, as such, has any power over the estate of the first testator.

2 *R. S.*, 71, § 17; 448, § 11.

Provisions as to revocations. § 632. The provisions of this Title in relation to the revocation of wills, apply to all wills made by any testator living at the expiration of one year from the time this article takes effect.

2 *R. S.*, 68, § 76.

Execution and construction of § 633. The provisions of this Title do not impair the validity of the execution of any will made before this article takes effect, or affect the construction of any such will. Prior wills not affected.

2 *R. S.*, 68, § 87.

§ 634. The term "will," as used in this Code, includes all codicils as well as wills. "Will" includes codicils.

2 *R. S.*, 68, § 77.

§ 635. Except as otherwise provided, the validity and interpretation of wills is governed, when relating to real property within this state, by the law of this state; when relating to personal property, by the law of the testator's domicil. The law of what place applies.

§ 636. Those to whom property is given by will, are liable for the obligations of the testator in the cases and to the extent prescribed by the CODE OF CIVIL PROCEDURE. Liability of beneficiaries for testator's obligations.

See Appendix D, in the original draft of this Code.

TITLE VI.

SUCCESSION.

The object of the very important change proposed by this Title, is to simplify the settlement of estates, and particularly titles to real property, by vesting the whole estate of the decedent in the executors or administrators.

By the existing law the term "real property," as between the heir and the executor, has a very different extent of meaning from the same term in other uses, and doubtless different from that popularly attached to it by testators and others contemplating the provision which their families may require in case of their death.

There seems to be no reason why the property of the landholder should be devolved by law upon one class of persons, while the property of the merchant, who may leave a family situated in the same circumstances, is devolved by law upon another class, or in a different method. For this reason the commissioners recommend one method of distribution for both real and personal property, and for this purpose have followed substantially the method the law now pursues in respect to personal property.

In case it is not thought best to adopt this change, the provisions of another chapter upon this subject contained in Appendix A, in the draft of this Code, will be found to conform to the present distinction between real and personal property as between heir and executor, and the statutes of distribution and descent, with some modifications which those rules seem to require.

Succession defined.

§ 637. Succession is the coming in of another to take the property of one who dies without disposing of it by will.

The term "descent," hitherto chiefly used in this state to denote the devolution of an inheritance, was derived from the ancient principle of the English law, that an inheritance could never ascend or pass from son to father, but must descend or pass to descendants. But as the American law allows property to pass in both ways, there arises an incongruity in continuing this use of the term; an incongruity which causes practical embarrassment, since the word "descendants" must still be confined to its strict meaning, and cannot embrace all those who may take by our statute of descents, so called, and the word "descend" must often be used in the same view and in contradistinction to the devolution of property in the ascending line. The term "succession" is the more appropriate phrase of the civil law, and this, already in common use among us, the commissioners have adopted to denote the transmission of the property of a decedent by operation of law.

Office of personal representatives.

§ 638. The property, both real and personal, of any one who dies without disposing of it by will, passes, in the first instance, to the personal representatives of such person, as trustees:

1. To make the provision for the surviving husband or wife or child, which is directed by section 640;

2. To apply the property to the payment of the debts of the decedent, according to the Title on Wills and the provisions of the CODE OF CIVIL PROCEDURE; and,

3. To distribute any remaining property among those entitled to succeed to the property of the decedent, according to the provisions of this Title.

Who are personal representatives.

§ 639. The personal representatives of a decedent are his executors or administrators, including administrators with will annexed, who have duly qualified according to the provisions of the CODE OF CIVIL PROCEDURE.

See Appendix D, to the original draft of this Code.

Certain property not assets but retained by family.

§ 640. Where a decedent leaves a husband, wife or child, the following property is to be immediately delivered by the personal representative, to such wife or husband, and child or children, and is not to be deemed assets:

1. Any estate or interest, to the value of one thousand dollars, in a lot and buildings thereon, occupied

as a residence by the decedent, and which, by law, is exempt, as a homestead, from sale on execution;

2. All sewing machines, spinning wheels, weaving looms, and stoves, used by the family;

3. The family Bible; one pew, family pictures, and school books used by the family; and books, not exceeding in value one hundred dollars, used as part of the family library;

4. Sheep, to the number of ten, with their fleeces, and the yarn and cloth manufactured from the same; two cows and four swine;

5. All wearing apparel and clothing, and the wife's ornaments, proper for her station; all necessary beds, bedsteads and bedding; necessary cooking utensils; three tables, twelve chairs; knives and forks; plates, teacups and saucers; one sugar-dish, one milkpot, one teapot, one coffeepot, and twelve spoons;

6. All family stores, or provisions, or supplies, for ordinary domestic use;

7. Household furniture, or other personal property, or money, to the value or amount of two hundred and fifty dollars; and,

8. Letters and other private writings.

Who to retain such property.

§ 641. The property mentioned in the last section is to remain in the possession of the husband or wife, if there is one, during the time such husband or wife resides with and provides for the child or children of the marriage. When any child ceases so to reside, he is entitled to receive an equal share, or the value thereof, of such property, except that a wife may retain, as her own, her wearing apparel and ornaments, and one bedstead and bedding.

These two sections are modified from 2 *R. S.*, 83, §§ 9, 10; *Laws of* 1850, 499; *Laws of* 1859, 343; subdivision 8 of § 640, is new.

Order of succession.

§ 642. All property remaining after payment of a decedent's debts, and satisfaction of the dispositions of his will, is to be distributed, together with any damages recovered by the personal representatives for any wrongful act, neglect or default which caused the decedent's death, to the successors of the decedent as follows:

1. If the decedent leaves a husband, the whole surplus goes to him, notwithstanding that it was the separate property of the wife, unless during the marriage she alienated such property, or effectually disposed thereof on her decease, by will or by gift in view of death;[1] Husband.

2. If the decedent leaves a wife and lineal descendants, one-third part goes to the wife, and the other two-thirds to the nearest lineal descendants and the successors of those who are deceased; Widow and children.

3. If the decedent leaves a wife and no descendants, and leaves a father or mother, brother or sister, the whole surplus, if it does not exceed in value at the time of distribution ten thousand dollars, goes to the wife; if it exceeds ten thousand dollars, but does not exceed twenty thousand dollars, then ten thousand dollars go to her; if it exceeds twenty thousand dollars, then one-half goes to her; the remainder, if any, goes to the father and mother or the survivor of them, or, if neither is living, to the brothers and sisters, and the successors of those of them who are deceased; Widow and next of kin.

4. If the decedent leaves a wife, and no descendant, parent, brother, or sister, the whole surplus goes to the wife; Widow alone.

5. If the decedent leaves no husband or wife, the whole surplus goes equally to the nearest lineal descendants, and the successors of those who are deceased.[2] Children alone.

[1] It is held that the Married Woman's Acts of 1848 and 1849, do not affect the husband's succession to property left by a wife on her death (Ransom *v.* Nichols, 22 *N. Y.*, 110). Real property is made subject to the rule governing personal property in this respect. This of course is contrary to the present law.

[2] This and the following section are modified from 2 *R. S.*, 96, § 75, as amended by *Laws of* 1845, 257, *ch.* 236.

Where there is neither widow nor children.

§ 643. If a decedent leaves no husband or wife, and no descendant, the whole surplus of the estate goes to the next of kin, and the successors of those who are deceased, as follows:

1. To the father or mother, or either of them;

2. If there is no parent, to the brothers and sisters, in equal shares, and the successors of those who are deceased;

3. If there is no parent or brother or sister, or successor of a brother or sister, then to the next of kin and the successors of those who are deceased.

Successors of deceased parent.

§ 644. The successors of a deceased parent cannot take by representation in place of the parent.

Relatives in equal degree.

In unequal degrees.

§ 645. Where the successors of a decedent, except parents, are all in equal degree of consanguinity to the decedent, their shares are equal; but if several are of unequal degree, each of the nearest degree succeeds to the share to which he would have been entitled had all those in the same degree, who have died leaving issue, been living; and the issue of those who have died, respectively succeed to the shares which such descendants or next of kin would have received if living.

From 2 *R. S.*, 97, § 75, subs. 9 and 10.

Several heirs, how to hold.

§ 646. Whenever real property, or a share thereof, vests in several persons under the provisions of this Title, they take, as owners in common, in proportion to their respective rights.

1 *R. S.*, 753, § 17.

Abolition of dower and curtesy.

§ 647. Dower and curtesy are abolished.

The commissioners recommend this change in connection with the provisions proposed under the chapter on Husband and Wife, and with those proposed in relation to the wife's succession to the husband's estate, in § 642.

§ 648. This Title does not affect any limitation of an estate or interest by deed or will. Certain estates, &c., not to be affected.

1 *R. S.*, 754, § 20; omitting the reference to Dower and Curtesy.

§ 649. The interest of any person in real property held in trust for him, if not devised by him, vests in his successors, according to the provisions of this chapter. Trusts.

1 *R. S.*, 754, § 21.

§ 650. Upon the death of a sole trustee of an express trust, whether a resident of this state or not,[1] the trust estate does not devolve by succession, but the trust, if then unexecuted, vests in the supreme court, with all the powers and duties of the original trustee, and must be executed by a person appointed for that purpose, under the direction of the court.[2] Trust estates vest in supreme court.

[1] Glen *v.* Gibson, 9 *Barb.*, 634.

[2] 1 *R. S.*, 730, § 68. The original statute applies only to trusts of real property (Banks *v.* Wilkes, 3 *Sandf. Ch.*, 99; compare Hawley *v.* Ross, 7 *Paige*, 103).

§ 651. On the death of one of several owners in common, his title passes in like manner with his other property. Property in common.

§ 652. On the death of one of two or more joint owners, with right of survivorship, his title passes to the surviving joint owners. Joint property.

§ 653. On the death of a partner, the surviving partners succeed to all the partnership property, whether real or personal, in trust for the purposes of liquidation,[1] even though the deceased was appointed by agreement sole liquidator;[2] and the interest of the deceased in the ultimate distribution of the partnership assets passes to those who succeed to his other personal property. Partnership property

[1] Evans *v.* Evans, 9 *Paige*, 178; Case *v.* Abeel, 1 *id.*, 393. This is so, even as to non-mercantile partnerships (Allen *v.* Blanchard, 9 *Cow.*, 631).

[2] Murray *v.* Mumford, 6 *Cow.*, 441.

When advancement to be set off or deducted.

§ 654. When any real or personal property, or both, whether within or without this state, of a person who dies intestate as to all his property, has been advanced by such intestate, directly, or by virtue of a beneficial power, or of a power in trust with a right of selection, to a person entitled to succeed to his property, and with a view to a portion or settlement in life, and so expressed in the instrument establishing the settlement or portion, the value thereof as expressed in the instrument must be reckoned, for the purposes of this section only, as part of the property of such intestate which his successors are to receive; and if such advancement equals or exceeds the share which such relative would be entitled to receive, of the property so reckoned, then such relative and his successors have no share in the property of the intestate. But if the advancement is less than such share, he and his successors are to have so much only of the property as is sufficient to make it equal to such share.

Modified from 1 *R. S.*, 754, §§ 23, 24, 25.

The provisions from which this section is taken, although in terms embracing the case of any intestate, apply only in cases of total intestacy (Thompson *v.* Carmichael, 3 *Sandf. Ch.*, 120). Questions of considerable embarrassment, which frequently arise in determining what is to be deemed an advancement, and what is to be taken as its value, have led the commissioners to insert the provision, that in order to constitute a settlement an advancement, within these provisions, its purpose and value must be expressed in the instrument.

Id.

§ 655. The exclusion from succession, and the adjustment of shares under the provisions of the last section, take effect only upon judgment in a civil action.

There seems to be no sufficient reason why the succession should be interrupted or affected until the fact of the existence of the advancement, and its value, have been finally determined. Under the present statute, so long as the question whether gifts made by the deceased were advancements or not, is undetermined, the question as to who is entitled to succeed, or in what shares they are to take, is also in suspense. The commissioners have thought it better, therefore, for the settling of titles, to provide that the succession shall not be affected until a judgment is had, declaring the existence and extent of the advancement.

§ 656. Unless both the purpose and the value of the settlement or portion, are expressed in the instrument of settlement, there is no legal advancement within the provisions of section 654. Id.

1 *R. S.*, 737, § 127.

§ 657. Relatives of the half blood, on either the paternal or maternal side, and their descendants, and the successors of both, succeed equally with those of the whole blood, except that to real property, which came to the decedent by succession, devise or gift of his relative, none who are not in any wise of the blood of such relative can succeed. Relatives of the half blood.

1 *R. S.*, 753, § 15; 2 *id.*, 97, § 75, sub. 10. The modification of the phraseology of the first part of this section is adopted to embrace, distinctly, the case of relatives of the half blood on the mother's side, and of the whole blood on the father's, in accordance with the decision in the case of Brown *v.* Burlingham, 5 *Sandf.*, 418.

In McCarthy *v.* Marsh, 5 *N. Y.*, 263, it was held that the word "ancestors" as used in section 22 of this chapter of the Revised Statutes, embraced collateral kindred as well as progenitors. Since the word, as used in section 15, should doubtless have the same meaning, the commissioners have substituted for it here, as well as in that section, the word "relatives."

The words "of the blood" in the latter part of section 15, include the half blood as well as the whole (Beebe *v.* Griffing, 14 *N. Y.*, 235).

§ 658. In determining succession, degrees of relationship are reckoned by counting from the decedent up to the common ancestor, and then down to the relative in question; reckoning a degree for each person. In such computation the decedent is excluded, the relative included, and the common ancestor counted but once. Computation of degrees.

Id.

§ 659. Brothers and sisters are in the first degree of relationship, which rule applies for the benefit of their successors.

McGregor *v.* Comstock, 3 *N. Y.*, 408.

Aliens.

§ 660. Aliens may take in all cases, by succession, as well as citizens;[1] and no person, capable of succeeding under the provisions of this chapter, is precluded from such succession, by reason of the alienage of any relative.[2]

[1] This provision is new. See section 170, and note on page 51.

[2] From 1 *R. S.*, 754, § 22, and see M'Carthy *v.* Marsh, 5 *N. Y.*, 263.

Mother, &c., of illegitimate decedent may succeed.

§ 661. The mother of an illegitimate child, and the relatives on the part of the mother, succeed to its property as if the child were legitimate.

Illegitimate child may succeed to mother's property.

§ 662. In case of the death of a mother leaving no lawful issue, and no husband, and leaving illegitimate children or their descendants, such children and descendants succeed in the same manner as if such children were legitimate.

Laws of 1855, *ch.* 547.

Illegitimacy.

§ 663. No person can succeed through an illegitimate relationship, except in the cases hereinbefore provided.

1 *R. S.*, 754, § 19.

Posthumous relatives.

§ 664. Relatives of a decedent, conceived before his death, but born thereafter, succeed, as if born in his lifetime and surviving him.

1 *R. S.*, 754, § 18; 2 *id.*, 97, § 75, *subd.* 13.

Divorce bars succession between the parties.

§ 665. Where a marriage has been dissolved for the misconduct of either party thereto, the guilty party is not entitled to succeed to the property of the other.

This provision already exists as against the wife, in cases of dower and succession to personal property (2 *R. S.*, 146, § 48).

§ 666. Where a person, who would have been entitled, if living at the death of another, to succeed to his property, dies before the latter, the property which he would thus have taken by succession, if living, passes to those who would have been entitled to succeed thereto, if he had so taken it, and had died immediately thereafter. Successors of one who dies before the decedent.

§ 667. If there is no one capable of succeeding under the preceding sections, the property of a decedent devolves to the people of the state. Escheat.

§ 668. Real property passing to the state under the last section, whether held by the state or its grantees, is subject to the same charges and trusts to which it would have been subject if it had passed by succession; and the supreme court has power to direct the attorney-general to convey the same to the parties entitled, or to a new trustee appointed by the court. Title of state subject to charges.

1 *R. S.*, 718, §§ 1, 2.

§ 669. Those who succeed to the property of a decedent are liable for his obligations in the cases, and to the extent, prescribed by the CODE OF CIVIL PROCEDURE. Liability of successors for decedent's obligations.

See Appendix D, chapter III, in the original draft of this Code.

DIVISION THIRD.

OBLIGATIONS.

PART I.

OBLIGATIONS IN GENERAL.

TITLE I.

DEFINITION OF OBLIGATIONS.

§ 670. An obligation is a legal duty, by which a person is bound to do or not to do a certain thing. Obligation, what.

§ 671. An obligation arises either from: How created.

1. The contract of the parties; or,
2. The operation of law.

TITLE II.

INTERPRETATION OF OBLIGATIONS.

CHAPTER I.

GENERAL RULES OF INTERPRETATION.

General rules. § 672. The rules which govern the interpretation of contracts are prescribed by Part II of this Division. Other obligations are interpreted by the same rules by which statutes of a similar nature are interpreted.

Obligations may be divided into three classes, arising respectively out of contract, common law, or statute. Those which are imposed by the common law explain themselves, their interpretation being a part of their essential nature. Contracts are interpreted by rules which differ materially from the rules governing the interpretation of statutes, and the two sets of rules, therefore, cannot well be united in one chapter

CHAPTER II.

JOINT OR SEVERAL OBLIGATIONS.

Obligation, joint or several, &c. § 673. An obligation imposed upon several persons, or a right created in favor of several persons, may be:

1. Joint;

2. Several; or,

3. Joint and several.

This is the admitted rule so far as the *liability* of parties is concerned (Peckham *v.* North Parish, 16 *Pick.*, 283; Ludlow *v.* McCrea, 1 *Wend.*, 228). As to the *rights* of parties in whose favor a contract is made, an arbitrary exception is made by the existing law, according to which their rights cannot be joint and several (Anderson *v.* Martindale, 1 *East*, 497; Hopkinson *v.* Lee, 6 *Q. B.*, 964; see Bradburne *v.* Botfield, 14 *M. & W.*, 573; Keightley *v.* Watson, 3 *Exch.*, 721). This exception is purely arbitrary, and although cases are rare in which parties would desire to avail themselves of their liberty to enter into such a contract, the commissioners are unable to perceive any good reason for denying them that liberty. In other respects, this section follows the ruling of the English Court of Exchequer in Sorsbie *v.* Park, 12 *M. & W.*, 140; Keightley *v.* Watson, 3 *Exch.*, 716.

§ 674. An obligation imposed upon several persons, or a right created in favor of several persons, is presumed to be joint, and not several,[1] except in the special cases mentioned in the Title on the INTERPRETATION OF CONTRACTS. This presumption, in the case of a right, can be overcome only by express words to the contrary.[2] When joint.

[1] Yorks *v.* Peck, 14 *Barb.*, 644; Hill *v.* Tucker, 1 *Taunt.*, 7.
[2] See sections 824 and 825.

§ 675. A party to a joint or joint and several obligation, who satisfies more than his share of the claim against all, may require a proportionate contribution from all the parties joined with him. Contribution between joint parties.

Story Cont., § 33 *g.*; Wood *v.* Merritt, 2 *Bosw.*, 368; Parker *v.* Ellis, 2 *Sandf.*, 223; but see Murray *v.* Bogert, 14 *Johns.*, 318.

The three following sections should be inserted in the CODE OF CIVIL PROCEDURE.

§ *a*. A joint obligation cannot be enforced at any time against any of the parties jointly liable, unless it is at the same time, and by the same proceeding, enforced against all. Enforcement of joint promise.

Robertson *v.* Smith, 18 *Johns.*, 484; King *v.* Hoare, 13 *M. & W.*, 494; Ward *v.* Johnson, 13 *Mass.*, 148; disapproving of Sheehy *v.* Mandeville, 6 *Cranch*, 253.

Enforcement of joint and several promise.

§ *b.* A joint and several obligation cannot be enforced by one proceeding against more than one of the promisers, unless it is by the same proceeding enforced against all.[1] But it may be enforced against each of them successively, until satisfied by one of them.[2]

[1] Bangor Bank *v.* Treat, 6 *Greenl.*, 207; Streatfield *v.* Halliday, 3 *T. R.*, 782; Cabell *v.* Vaughan, 1 *Saund.*, 291 *f.*

[2] Brown *v.* Wootton, *Cro. Jac.*, 74.

Enforcement of joint and several right.

§ *c.* A joint and several right can be enforced only once, and either by one party only, or by all.

This provision follows the principle of section *a.* There is no authority on the subject, because all joint and several rights have been construed as joint merely. See note to section 673.

CHAPTER III.

CONDITIONAL OBLIGATIONS.

Obligation, when conditional.

§ 676. An obligation is conditional, when the rights or duties of any party thereto depend upon the occurrence of an uncertain event.

Whether a contract is conditional or not, is to be determined by the rules of interpretation hereafter given. The intention of the parties, as gathered from the whole contract, is superior to all technical rules (Parmelee *v.* Oswego, &c., R. R. Co., 6 *N. Y.*, 74; Selden *v.* Pringle, 17 *Barb.*, 458; Barruso *v.* Madan, 2 *Johns.*, 145; see Tipton *v.* Feitner, 20 *N. Y.*, 423; Grant *v.* Johnson, 5 *id.*, 247; Glaholm *v.* Hays, 2 *Man. & Gr.*, 266).

Conditions, kinds of.

§ 677. Conditions may be precedent, concurrent or subsequent.

§ 678. A condition precedent is one which is to be performed before some right dependent thereon accrues, or some act dependent thereon is performed. Condition precedent.

See Tipton *v.* Feitner, 20 *N. Y.*, 423; Grant *v.* Johnson, 5 *id.*, 247; Parmelee *v.* Oswego, &c., R. R. Co., 6 *id.*, 74; Oakley *v.* Morton, 11 *id.*, 25; Goodwin *v.* Holbrook, 4 *Wend.*, 377; Weisser *v.* Maitland, 3 *Sandf.*, 318; Ellen *v.* Topp, 6 *Exch.*, 424; Graves *v.* Legg, 9 *Exch.*, 709.

§ 679. Conditions concurrent are those which are mutually dependent, and are to be performed at the same time. Conditions concurrent.

See Beecher *v.* Conradt, 13 *N. Y.*, 108; Dunham *v.* Pettee, 8 *id.*, 508; Lester *v.* Jewett, 11 *id.*, 453; Kelley *v.* Upton, 5 *Duer*, 336; Williams *v.* Healey, 3 *Den.*, 363.

§ 680. A condition subsequent is one referring to a future event, upon the happening of which the obligation becomes no longer binding upon the other party, if he chooses to avail himself of the condition. Condition subsequent.

Nicoll *v.* N. Y. & Erie R. R. Co., 12 *N. Y.*, 121, 130.

§ 681. Before any party to an obligation can require another party to perform any act under it, he must fulfill all conditions precedent thereto imposed upon himself;[1] and must be able, and offer, to fulfill all conditions concurrent, so imposed upon him, on the like fulfillment by the other party:[2] except as provided by the next section. Performance, &c., of conditions when essential.

[1] Oakley *v.* Morton, 11 *N. Y.*, 25; Smith *v.* Brady, 17 *N. Y.*, 173; Cunningham *v.* Jones, 20 *id.*, 486; Grant *v.* Johnson, 5 *id.*, 247; Catlin *v.* Tobias, 26 *id.*, 217; Ellen *v.* Topp, 6 *Exch.*, 424.

[2] Beecher *v.* Conradt, 13 *N. Y.*, 108; Dunham *v.* Pettee, 8 *id.*, 508; Lester *v.* Jewett, 11 *id.*, 453.

§ 682. If a party to an obligation gives notice to another, before the latter is in default, that he will not perform the same upon his part, and does not retract such notice before the time at which performance upon his part is due, such other party is entitled When performance, &c., excused.

to enforce the obligation without previously performing or offering to perform any conditions upon his part, in favor of the former party.

Cornwell *v.* Haight, 21 *N. Y.*, 462; Skinner *v.* Tinker, 34 *Barb.*, 333; Crist *v.* Armour, *id.*, 378; Clark *v.* Crandall, 27 *id.*, 73; North *v.* Pepper, 21 *Wend.*, 636; see Crary *v.* Smith, 2 *N. Y.*, 60.

Impossible or unlawful conditions void.

§ 683. A condition in a contract, the fulfillment of which is impossible or unlawful,[1] within the meaning of the article on the OBJECT OF CONTRACTS, or which is repugnant to the nature of the interest created by the contract,[2] is void.

[1] *Story Cont.*, § 32, *b.*

[2] De Peyster *v.* Michael, 6 *N. Y.*, 496.

Conditions involving forfeiture, how construed.

§ 684. A condition involving a forfeiture must be strictly interpreted against the party for whose benefit it is created.

Hitchcock *v.* Northwestern Ins. Co., 26 *N. Y.*, 68; Doe *d.* Abdy *v.* Stevens, 3 *B. & Ad.*, 299; Catlin *v.* Springfield Ins. Co., 1 *Sumner*, 440.

CHAPTER IV.

ALTERNATIVE OBLIGATIONS.

Who has the right of selection.

§ 685. If an obligation requires the performance of one of two acts, in the alternative, the party required to perform has the right of selection; unless it is otherwise provided by the terms of the obligation.

Smith *v.* Sanborn, 11 *Johns.*, 59; Disbrough *v.* Neilson, 3 *Johns. Cas.*, 81; Small *v.* Quincy, 4 *Greenl.*, 497.

Right of selection, how lost.

§ 686. If the party having the right of selection between alternative acts does not give notice of his selection to the other party within the time, if any, fixed by the obligation for that purpose,[1] or, if none is so fixed, before the time at which the obligation ought to be performed,[2] the right of selection passes to the other party.[3]

[1] Sage *v.* Hazard, 6 *Barb.*, 179; McNitt *v.* Clark, 7 *Johns.*, 465.

[2] *Brooke Abr.*, Dette, 159; Choice *v.* Moseley, 1 *Bailey*, 136; Townsend *v.* Wells, 3 *Day*, 327; see Gilbert *v.* Danforth, 6 *N. Y.*, 585, 592.

[3] McNitt *v.* Clark, 7 *Johns.*, 465.

§ 687. The party having the right of selection between alternative acts, must select one of them in its entirety, and cannot select part of one and part of another, without the consent of the other party. Alternatives indivisible.

Code La., 2064; *Code Napoleon*, 1191.

§ 688. If one of the alternative acts required by an obligation is such as the law will not enforce,[1] or becomes unlawful,[2] or impossible of performance, the obligation is to be interpreted as though the other stood alone. Nullity of one or more of alternative obligations.

[1] *Code La.*, 2065; *Code Napoleon*, 1192; Stevens *v.* Webb, 7 *Carr. & P.*, 60.

[2] Esposito *v.* Bowden, 4 *El. & Bl.*, 963.

TITLE III.

TRANSFER OF OBLIGATIONS.

§ 689. The burden of an obligation may be transferred, with the consent of the party entitled to its benefit, but not otherwise, except as provided by section 697. Burden of obligation not transferable.

This is as true of covenants running with the land, as of any other obligations. The original covenantor remains liable to the covenantee, notwithstanding that the land passes into other hands (House *v.* Burr, 24 *Barb.*, 525; Damb *v.* Hoffman, 3 *E. D. Smith*, 361; Port *v.* Jackson, 17 *Johns.*, 239, 479; Jackson *v.* Brownson, 7 *id.*, 227). So where one has agreed to perform a service, he cannot compel the other party to accept the service from a third person and to release him therefrom (Robson *v.* Drummond, 2 *B. & Ad.*, 303). It is not meant by this section to imply that a third person cannot assume the obligations of a contract between other parties, but only that he cannot relieve a party thereto from his obligations, without the consent of the creditor.

Rights arising out of obligation transferable.

§ 690. A right arising out of an obligation is the property of the person to whom it is due, and may be transferred as such.

See section 367; Short *v.* Spackman, 2 *B. & Ad.*, 962; Hitchcock *v.* Northwestern Ins. Co., 26 *N. Y.*, 68.

Covenants running with land, what.

§ 691. Certain covenants, contained in grants of estates in real property, are appurtenant to such estates, and pass with them, so as to bind the assigns of the covenantor, and to vest in the assigns of the covenantee, in the same manner as if they had personally entered into them. Such covenants are said to run with the land.

What covenants run with the land.

§ 692. The only covenants which run with the land, are those specified in this Title,[1] and those which are incidental thereto.[2]

[1] Parties cannot, by any form of words, attach newly invented covenants to real property (Keppell *v.* Bailey, 2 *Myl. & K.*, 517; but see Tallmadge *v.* East River Bank, 26 *N. Y.*, 105; Tulk *v.* Moxhay, 2 *Phil.*, 774; 11 *Beav.*, 571; Heriot's Hospital *v.* Gibson, 2 *Dow*, 301).

[2] The contract of a surety for the payment of rent is annexed to the obligation for the rent, and therefore passes therewith (Allen *v.* Culver, 3 *Denio*, 284). This, however, is the necessary result of a principle elsewhere declared (see section 481).

Id.

§ 693. Every covenant contained in a grant of an estate in real property, which is made for the direct benefit of the property, or some part of it then in existence, runs with the land.

Denman *v.* Prince, 40 *Barb.*, 213; Verplanck *v.* Wright, 23 *Wend.*, 506; Norman *v.* Wells, 17 *id.*, 136; Myers *v.* Burns, 33 *Barb.*, 401; Jourdain *v.* Wilson, 4 *B. & Ald.*, 266; Vernon *v.* Smith, 5 *id.*, 1; Martyn *v.* Clue, 18 *Q. B.*, 661; Wakefield *v.* Brown, 9 *id.*, 209; Allen *v.* Culver, 3 *Denio*, 284; Demarest *v.* Willard, 8 *Cow.*, 206.

§ 694. The last section includes covenants of warranty,[1] for quiet enjoyment,[2] or for further assurance,[3] on the part of a grantor,[4] and covenants for the payment of rent,[5] or of taxes or assessments upon the land,[6] on the part of a grantee. Id.

[1] Suydam *v.* Jones, 10 *Wend.*, 180; Withy *v.* Mumford, 5 *Cow.*, 137; Blackwell *v.* Atkinson, 14 *Cal.*, 470; Mitchell *v.* Warner, 5 *Conn.*, 497; Wyman *v.* Ballard, 12 *Mass.*, 306.

[2] Lewis *v.* Campbell, 8 *Taunt.*, 715; Markland *v.* Crump, 1 *Dev. & Bat.*, 94; Campbell *v.* Lewis, 3 *B. & Ald.*, 392; Noke *v.* Awder, *Cro. El.*, 436.

[3] Bennett *v.* Waller, 23 *Ill.*, 97; Colby *v.* Osgood, 29 *Barb.*, 339.

[4] The covenants mentioned in this section are all the "usual covenants" that are recognized in this state as running with the land. In Kingdom *v.* Nottle (1 *M. & Selw.*, 355; 4 *id.*, 53), it was held that a covenant of seisin ran with the land, but this decision has been overruled in the courts of this country (See Mitchell *v.* Warner, 5 *Conn.*, 497; Fowler *v.* Poling, 2 *Barb.*, 300; Greenby *v.* Wilcocks, 2 *Johns.*, 1; Ballard *v.* Child, 34 *Me.*, 355; Thayer *v.* Clemence, 22 *Pick.*, 490; Marston *v.* Hobbs, 2 *Mass.*, 439).

[5] Van Rensselaer *v.* Read, 26 *N. Y.*, 558; Van Rensselaer *v.* Hays, 19 *N. Y.*, 68; Astor *v.* Lent, 6 *Bosw.*, 612; Van Rensselaer *v.* Bonesteel, 24 *Barb.*, 655; Close *v.* Wilberforce, 1 *Beav.*, 113; Jenkins *v.* Portman, 1 *Keen*, 435. It is not necessary that the covenant should express an intention to bind the covenantor's assigns (Jacques *v.* Short, 20 *Barb.*, 269).

[6] Post *v.* Kearney, 2 *N. Y.*, 394; 1 *Sandf.*, 105.

§ 695. A covenant for the addition of some new thing to real property, or for the direct benefit of some part of the property not then in existence or annexed thereto, when contained in a grant of an estate in such property, and made by the covenantor expressly for his assigns or to the assigns of the covenantee, runs with the land so far only as the assigns thus mentioned are concerned. What covenants run with land when assigns are named.

Spencer's Case, 5 *Co. Rep.*, 16; Easterby *v.* Sampson, 6 *Bing.*, 664; Sampson *v.* Easterby, 9 *B. & C.*, 505. Such covenants will not run with the land, unless "assigns" are mentioned in the deed (Spencer's Case, 5 *Co.*, 16; Tallman *v.* Coffin, 4 *N. Y.*, 134; Thompson *v.* Rose, 8 *Cow.*, 266; Doughty *v.* Bowman, 11 *Q. B.*, 444).

Who are bound by covenants.

§ 696. A covenant running with the land binds those only who acquire the whole estate of the covenantor in some part of the property.

Davis *v.* Morris, 35 *Barb.*, 227; *Co. Litt.*, 385, *a.*

Who are not.

§ 697. No one, merely by reason of having acquired an estate subject to a covenant running with the land, is liable for a breach of the covenant before he acquired the estate,[1] or after he has parted with it,[2] or ceased to enjoy its benefits.[3]

[1] Day *v.* Swackhamer, 2 *Hilt.*, 4; Tillotson *v.* Boyd, 4 *Sandf.*, 516; see Astor *v.* Hoyt, 5 *Wend.*, 603.

[2] Young *v.* Peyser, 3 *Bosw.*, 308; Armstrong *v.* Wheeler, 9 *Cow.*, 88; Childs *v.* Clark, 3 *Barb. Ch.*, 52; Wolveridge *v.* Steward, 3 *M. & Scott*, 561; rev'g S. C., 9 *Bing.*, 60; Walker *v.* Reeve, 3 *Doug.*, 19.

[3] Astor *v.* L'Amoreux, 4 *Sandf.*, 524; Carter *v.* Hammett, 18 *Barb.*, 608; McIntyre *v.* Scott, 8 *Johns.*, 169; Eaton *v.* Jacques, 1 *Doug.*, 461. Although Eaton *v.* Jacques has been overruled in England (Williams *v.* Bosanquet, 1 *Brod. & B.*, 238), its doctrine is law in this state.

Apportionment of covenants.

§ 698. Where several persons, holding by several titles, are subject to the burden,[1] or entitled to the benefit[2] of a covenant running with the land, it must be apportioned among them according to the value of the property subject to it held by them respectively, if such value can be ascertained, and if not, then according to their respective interests in point of quantity.[3]

[1] Van Rensselaer *v.* Bradley, 3 *Denio*, 135; Van Rensselaer *v.* Gallup, 5 *id.*, 454; Astor *v.* Miller, 2 *Paige*, 68.

[2] Cole *v.* Patterson, 25 *Wend.*, 456.

[3] Van Rensselaer *v.* Jones, 2 *Barb.*, 643.

TITLE IV.

EXTINCTION OF OBLIGATIONS.

CHAPTER I.

PERFORMANCE.

§ 699. Full performance of an obligation, by the party whose duty it is to perform it,[1] or by any other person on his behalf, and with his assent,[2] if accepted by the creditor, extinguishes it. Obligation extinguished by performance.

[1] Performance by a third person, without authority from the debtor, does not extinguish the debt (Muller *v.* Eno, 14 *N. Y.*, 605; Daniels *v.* Hallenbeck, 19 *Wend.*, 408; Bleakley *v.* White, 4 *Paige*, 655).

[2] Kemp *v.* Balls, 10 *Exch.*, 607; Jones *v.* Broadhurst, 9 *C. B.*, 173; Belshaw *v.* Bush, 11 *C. B.*, 191; Simpson *v.* Eggington, 10 *Exch.*, 845; James *v.* Isaacs, 12 *C. B.*, 791; see Phillips *v.* Berger, 8 *Barb.*, 527.

§ 700. Performance of an obligation, by one of several persons who are jointly liable under it, extinguishes the liability of all. Performance by one of several joint debtors.

§ 701. An obligation in favor of several persons is extinguished by performance rendered to any of them,[1] except in the case of a deposit made by Performance to one of joint creditors.

owners in common, or in joint ownership,[2] which is regulated by the Title on DEPOSIT.

[1] Shepard *v.* Ward, 8 *Wend.*, 542; see Carman *v.* Pultz, 21 *N. Y.*, 547.

[2] Husband *v.* Davis, 10 *C. B.*, 650; Innes *v.* Stephenson, 1 *Moo. & R.*, 145. This provision does not of course apply to partnerships, whose title is distinguished from joint ownership by section 175.

Effect of directions by creditor.

§ 702. If a creditor, or any one of two or more joint creditors, at any time directs the debtor to perform his obligation in a particular manner, the obligation is extinguished by performance in that manner, even though the creditor does not receive the benefit of such performance.

Thus, if the creditor directs money to be sent to him by mail, it is at his risk (Graves *v.* Amer. Exch. Bank, 17 *N. Y.*, 207; Eyles *v.* Ellis, 4 *Bing.*, 112).

Partial performance.

§ 703. A partial performance of an indivisible obligation extinguishes a corresponding proportion thereof, if the benefit of such performance is voluntarily retained by the creditor, but not otherwise.[1] If such partial performance is of such a nature that the creditor cannot avoid retaining it, without injuring his own property, his retention thereof is not presumed to be voluntary.[2]

[1] Smith *v.* Brady, 17 *N. Y.*, 187; Cunningham *v.* Jones, 20 *id.*, 486; Pullman *v.* Corning, 9 *id.*, 93.

[2] *Ib.*

Payment, what.

§ 704. Performance of an obligation for the delivery of money only, is called payment.

Application of general performance.

§ 705. Where a debtor, under several obligations to another, does an act, by way of performance,[1] which is equally applicable to two or more of such obligations, such performance is applied as follows:

1. If, at the time of performance,[2] the intention or desire[3] of the debtor that such performance should be applied to the extinction of any particular obligation, is manifested to the creditor,[4] it is so applied;

2. If no such application is then made,[5] the creditor,[6] within a reasonable time after such performance,[7] may apply it toward the extinction of any obligation,[8] performance of which was due[9] to him from the debtor at the time of such performance; except that if similar obligations were due to him both individually and as a trustee, he must, unless otherwise directed by the debtor, apply the performance to the extinction of all such obligations in equal proportion;[10] and an application once made by the creditor cannot be rescinded without the consent of the debtor;[11]

3. If neither party makes such application, within the time prescribed herein, the performance is applied to the extinction of obligations in the following order; and, if there is more than one obligation of a particular class, to the extinction of all in that class, ratably:

(1.) Of an obligation due at the time of performance;[12]

(2.) Of an obligation not voidable at the option of the debtor;[13]

(3.) Of an obligation secured by a lien, or collateral undertaking;[14]

(4.) Of interest;[15]

(5.) Of the obligation earliest in date of maturity;[16]

(6.) Of the obligation which it is most for the interest of the debtor to extinguish.[17]

[1] This subject is usually treated exclusively with reference to payments of money, which have indeed furnished all the cases upon which decisions have been reported. Obviously, however, the same principles are equally applicable to all classes of contracts, as for example, where one has agreed, at various times, to deliver parcels of merchandise of the same species, such as wheat, flour, fruit, &c.

[2] Allen *v.* Culver, 3 *Den.*, 284; Philpott *v.* Jones, 2 *Ad. & El.*, 41.

[3] Stone *v.* Seymour, 15 *Wend.*, 19; Waters *v.* Tompkins, 2 *Cr. M. & R.*, 725; Shaw *v.* Picton, 4 *B. & C.*, 715.

[4] In Stone *v.* Seymour, it was held that no express direction by the debtor was necessary. In Van

Rensselaer *v.* Roberts (5 *Den.*, 470), somewhat different language is used. On the whole, it seems reasonable to lay down the rule as in the text. The slightest act manifesting such desire is sufficient (see Roberts *v.* Garnie, 3 *Cai.*, 14).

[5] Allen *v.* Culver, 3 *Den.*, 284; Philpott *v.* Jones, 2 *Ad. & El.*, 41.

[6] *Ib.*

[7] See Bridenbecker *v.* Lowell, 32 *Barb.*, 9, 22; Allen *v.* Culver, 3 *Den.*, 284, 291. But in many cases out of this state it has been held that the creditor may exercise this right at *any* time (Mayor of Alexandria *v.* Patten, 4 *Cranch*, 317; Haynes *v.* Waite, 14 *Cal.*, 446; Mills *v.* Fowkes, 5 *Bing. N. C.*, 455; see Philpott *v.* Ellis, 2 *Ad. & El.*, 41).

[8] Arnold *v.* Mayor of Poole, 4 *Man. & Gr.*, 860; Trotter *v.* Grant, 2 *Wend.*, 413; Clark *v.* Burdett, 2 *Hall*, 197; Mills *v.* Fowkes, 5 *Bing. N. C.*, 455; Van Rensselaer *v.* Roberts, 5 *Den.*, 470.

[9] Niagara Bank *v.* Rosevelt, 9 *Cow.*, 409; affirming S. C., *Hopk.*, 579; Baker *v.* Stackpoole, 9 *Cow.*, 420, 436.

[10] See Bridenbecker *v.* Lowell, 32 *Barb.*, 9.

[11] Allen *v.* Culver, 3 *Den.*, 284.

[12] Thomas *v.* Kelsey, 30 *Barb.*, 268; Hunter *v.* Osterhoudt, 11 *id.*, 33; Baker *v.* Stackpoole, 9 *Cow.*, 420; Hall *v.* Clement, 41 *N. H.*, 166.

[13] Wright *v.* Laing, 8 *B. & C.*, 165; Crookshank *v.* Rose, 5 *Carr. & P.*, 19.

[14] Pattison *v.* Hull, 9 *Cow.*, 747; Dows *v.* Morewood, 10 *Barb.*, 183; The Antarctic, *Sprague*, 206. To the contrary is Johnson's Appeal, 37 *Penn. St.*, 268.

[15] People *v.* New York Co., 5 *Cow.*, 331; Connecticut *v.* Jackson, 1 *Johns. Ch.*, 13; French *v.* Kennedy, 7 *Barb.*, 452; Williams *v.* Houghtaling, 3 *Cow.*, 86.

[16] Dows *v.* Morewood, 10 *Barb.*, 183; Wheeler *v.* Cropsey, 5 *How. Pr.*, 288; Allen *v.* Culver, 3 *Den.*, 284.

[17] As to this point there is much controversy. The rule here stated, subject to all the preceding qualifications, is that which, as it appears to the commissioners, is supported by the weight of authority in this state (see Dows *v.* Morewood, 10 *Barb.*, 183, 189; Pattison *v.* Hull, 9 *Cow.*, 747). A payment is to be applied so as to stop the running of interest as soon as possible (Jencks *v.* Alexander, 11 *Paige*, 619). In Pennsylvania, the interest of the creditor is consulted by the court (Johnson's Appeal, 37 *Penn. St.*, 268; Pierce *v.* Sweet, 33 *id.* 151).

CHAPTER II.

OFFER OF PERFORMANCE.

§ 706. An obligation is extinguished by an offer of performance, made in conformity to the rules herein prescribed, and with intent to extinguish the obligation. Obligation extinguished by offer of performance.

This is the present law with respect to all obligations other than for the payment of money (Des Arts *v.* Leggett, 16 *N. Y.*, 582; Billings *v.* Vanderbeck, 23 *Barb.*, 546; Slingerland *v.* Morse, 8 *Johns.*, 474). It is not now the law as to pecuniary obligations, the debtor having no power to rid himself of the debt without the consent of the creditor (see Dixon *v.* Clark, 5 *C. B.*, 365, 377; Waistell *v.* Atkinson, 3 *Bing.*, 290; Kortright *v.* Cady, 23 *Barb.*, 490; 21 *N. Y.*, 343).

§ 707. An offer of partial performance is of no effect. Offer of partial performance.

Dixon *v.* Clark, 5 *C. B.*, 365.

§ 708. An offer of performance must be made by the debtor,[1] or by some person on his behalf and with his assent.[2] By whom to be made.

[1] See Muller *v.* Eno, 14 *N. Y.*, 597.

[2] Read *v.* Goldring, 2 *M. & Selw.*, 86; see Belshaw *v* Bush, 11 *C. B.*, 191; Kemp *v.* Balls, 10 *Exch.*, 607; Simpson *v.* Eggington, *id.*, 845.

To whom to be made.

§ 709. An offer of performance must be made to the creditor,[1] or to any one of two or more joint creditors,[2] or to a person authorized by one or more of them to receive[3] or collect[4] what is due under the obligation, if such creditor or authorized person is present at the place where the offer may be made; and if not, then to a notary public.[5]

[1] Haldane *v.* Johnson, 8 *Exch.*, 689.

[2] Carman *v.* Pultz, 21 *N. Y.*, 547; Douglas *v.* Patrick, 3 *T. R.*, 683; Dawson *v.* Ewing, 6 *Serg. & R.*, 371.

[3] Kirton *v.* Braithwaite, 1 *M. & W.*, 310; Goodland *v.* Blewith, 1 *Camp.*, 477. The agent must have authority to receive payment in some shape (Hargous *v.* Lahens, 3 *Sandf.*, 213; Bingham *v.* Allport, 1 *Nev. & M.*, 398; see Offley *v.* Clay, 2 *M. & G.*, 172; Kirton *v.* Braithwaite, 1 *M. & W.*, 310).

[4] Tender may be made to an agent instructed to collect by process of law (Crozer *v.* Pilling, 4 *B. & C.*, 26); even though forbidden to receive payment from the debtor (Hatch *v.* Hale, 15 *Q. B.*, 10).

[5] This provision is new. It is intended to provide a mode of offer, fair alike to the debtor and to the creditor. A creditor might be absent from the state, when the debt became due, and have no agent here. If, under such circumstances, the debtor could stop the running of interest by a formal offer, addressed to no particular person, it is plain that great injustice might be done.

Where offer may be made.

§ 710. In the absence of an express provision to the contrary, an offer of performance may be made, at the option of the debtor:

1. At any place appointed by the creditor;[1] or,

2. Wherever the person, to whom the offer ought to be made, can be found;[2] or,

3. If such person cannot, with reasonable diligence, be found within this state,[3] and within a reasonable distance from his residence or place of business,[4] or if he evades the debtor,[5] then at his residence,[6] or place of business,[7] if the same can, with reasonable diligence, be found within the state; or,

4. If this cannot be done, then at any place within this state.

[1] Franchot *v.* Leach, 5 *Cow.*, 506; Robinson *v.* Bachelder, 4 *N. H.*, 40; Wyman *v.* Winslow, 2 *Fairf.*, 398.

[2] Hunter *v.* Le Conte, 6 *Cow.*, 728.

[3] Smith *v.* Smith, 2 *Hill*, 351; qualifying S. C., 25 *Wend.*, 405.

[4] This provision is perhaps new (see Smith *v.* Smith, 25 *Wend.*, 405; 2 *Hill*, 351).

[5] Judd *v.* Ensign, 6 *Barb.*, 258; see Smith *v.* Smith.

[6] Smith *v.* Smith; Judd *v.* Ensign.

[7] So many persons now do business in this state, who reside out of the state, that it seems but just to provide for their case.

§ 711. Where an obligation fixes a time for its performance, an offer of performance must be made at that time,[1] within reasonable hours,[2] and not before[3] nor afterwards.[4]

When offer must be made.

[1] See Dixon *v.* Clark, 5 *C. B.*, 365, 378.

[2] Startup *v.* Macdonald, 2 *M. & G.*, 395.

[3] Mitchell *v.* Cook, 29 *Barb.*, 343. In Maryland, however, a tender before the day, of all that would be due upon the day, interest included, is valid (McHard *v.* Whetcroft, 3 *Harr. & McH.*, 85).

[4] Livingston *v.* Harrison, 2 *E. D. Smith*, 197; Poole *v.* Tumbridge, 2 *M. & W.*, 223; Hume *v.* Peploe, 8 *East*, 168; see Kortright *v.* Cady, 21 *N. Y.*, 343.

§ 712. Where an obligation does not fix the time for its performance, an offer of performance may be made at any time, before the debtor, upon a reasonable demand, has refused to perform.

Id.

See Jones *v.* Gibbons, 8 *Exch.*, 922.

§ 713. Where delay in performance is capable of exact and entire compensation, and time has not been expressly declared to be of the essence of the obligation,[1] an offer of performance, accompanied with an offer of such compensation, may be made at any time after it is due,[2] but without prejudice to any rights acquired by the creditor or by any other person in the meantime.

Compensation after delay in performance.

[1] This provision, which is new, is intended to obviate the difficulties which constantly arise in determining whether time is of the essence of a contract, or not.

[2] This provision is also new. But as such tender is permitted by statute after an action has been commenced (2 *R. S.*, 554, § 20), it clearly ought to be allowed before any litigation is had, to stop interest and

avoid costs. Undoubtedly it is not allowed by the common law (Poole *v.* Tumbridge, 2 *M. & W.*, 223; Hume *v.* Peploe, 8 *East*, 168); but the judges acknowledged the hardship of the law on this point. In Connecticut, the rule here proposed has become law through usage (Tracy *v.* Strong, 2 *Conn.*, 659).

Offer to be made in good faith.

§ 714. An offer of performance must be made in good faith, and in such manner as is most likely, under the circumstances, to benefit the creditor.

Good faith is manifestly essential.

Conditional offer.

§ 715. An offer of performance must be free from any conditions[1] which the creditor is not bound on his part to perform.[2]

[1] Brooklyn Bank *v.* Degrauw, 23 *Wend.*, 342; Wood *v.* Hitchcock, 20 *id.*, 47; Eddy *v.* O'Hara, 14 *id.*, 221. An offer conditioned upon a receipt in full (Loring *v.* Cooke, 3 *Pick.*, 48; Thayer *v.* Brackett, 12 *Mass.*, 450; Finch *v.* Miller, 5 *C. B.*, 428), or a receipt of any kind (Laing *v.* Meader, 1 *Carr. & P.*, 257; Griffith *v.* Hodges, *id.*, 419; Ryder *v.* Townsend, 7 *Dowl. & Ryl.*, 119; see Wood *v.* Hitchcock, 20 *Wend.*, 47) being given; or upon the amount tendered being accepted in full of all or any demands (Wood *v.* Hitchcock, 20 *Wend.*, 47; Strong *v.* Harvey, 3 *Bing.*, 304) is bad at common law. It is proposed, however, to sanction a demand for a receipt.

[2] Bevans *v.* Rees, 5 *M. & W.*, 306. Thus an offer of more than is due, conditioned upon the creditor taking out of it the amount which he claims to be due, is good (*Ib.;* Dean *v.* James, 4 *B. & Ad.*, 546; see Hubbard *v.* Chenango Bank, 8 *Cow.*, 100), if the creditor is not required to make change, for that he is not bound to do (*Ib.;* Betterbee *v.* Davis, 3 *Camp.*, 71). Where the creditor is bound by law to give a release upon payment, an offer conditioned upon his doing so is good (Saunders *v.* Frost, 5 *Pick.*, 260, 270). So a party to a negotiable instrument may require its surrender upon payment (Wilder *v.* Seelye, 8 *Barb.*, 408), unless the holder has other claims upon it (Hargous *v.* Lahens, 3 *Sandf.*, 213).

Ability and willingness essential.

§ 716. An offer of performance is of no effect, if the person making it is not able and willing to perform according to the offer.

All the precedents assume this to be essential. Ability, however, and not readiness, is the true test. If a debtor knows that his creditor will not accept performance, he should not be required to prepare anything for delivery, at a useless cost of time and trouble.

§ 717. The thing to be delivered, if any, need not in any case be actually produced, upon an offer of performance, unless the offer is accepted. Production of thing to be delivered, not necessary.

This is an innovation upon the common law, as far as obligations for the payment of money (Bakeman *v.* Pooler, 15 *Wend.*, 637; Hornby *v.* Cramer, 12 *How. Pr.*, 491; Finch *v.* Brook, 1 *Bing. N. C.*, 253), or for the delivery of a written instrument (see Brooklyn Bank *v.* Degrauw, 23 *Wend.*, 342), are concerned. But the present rule seems useless. In respect to bulky articles, this section is in conformity with the common law (Slingerland *v.* Morse, 8 *Johns.*, 474; Myers *v.* Davis, 26 *Barb.*, 367; Coit *v.* Houston, 3 *Johns. Cas.*, 243).

§ 718. A thing, when offered by way of performance, must not be mixed with other things from which it cannot be separated immediately and without difficulty. Thing offered to be kept separate.

Hamilton *v.* Ganyard, 34 *Barb.*, 204; Betterbee *v.* Davis, 3 *Camp.*, 71; Bates *v.* Churchill, 32 *Maine*, 31; Leballister *v.* Nash, 24 *id.*, 316; Wyman *v.* Winslow, 2 *Fairf.*, 398; Veazy *v.* Harmony, 7 *Greenl.*, 91; Barney *v.* Bliss, 1 *D. Chipm.*, 399.

§ 719. When a debtor is entitled to the performance of a condition precedent to, or concurrent with, performance on his part, he may make his offer to depend upon the due performance of such condition. Performance of condition precedent.

See § 681, and notes.

§ 720. A debtor has a right to require from his creditor a written receipt for any property delivered in performance of his obligation. Written receipt,

This provision is new (see note to § 715). Its propriety should seem scarcely to admit of doubt.

§ 721. An obligation for the payment of money is extinguished by a due offer of payment, if the amount is immediately deposited in the name of Extinction of pecuniary obligation.

the creditor, with some bank of deposit within this state, of good repute, and notice thereof is given to the creditor.

This is contrary to the present law upon this subject, which makes a tender operative only so far as to stop interest. The same rule has been applied to obligations for the delivery of deeds and other instruments (Brooklyn Bank *v.* De Grauw, 23 *Wend.*, 342). But this has been wisely overruled (Des Arts *v.* Leggett, 16 *N. Y.*, 582). The provisions of this section have long been the law, in substance, of Louisiana and France. It seems to the commissioners to be all that creditors can reasonably ask. The common law compels a debtor to keep the money which he owes, at his own risk. This is often an inconvenience, and sometimes a positive loss to him.

Objections to mode of offer.

§ 722. All objections to the mode of an offer of performance, which the creditor has an opportunity to state at the time to the person making the offer, and which could be then obviated by him,[1] are waived by the creditor, if not then stated.[2]

[1] Insuperable objections are not waived by silence (Friess *v.* Rider, 24 *N. Y.*, 367; Mitchell *v.* Cook, 29 *Barb.*, 353).

[2] Carman *v.* Pultz, 21 *N. Y.*, 547; Kernochan *v.* Bowery Ins. Co., 17 *id.*, 428; Bumstead *v.* Dividend Mut. Ins. Co., 12 *id.*, 81.

Title to thing offered.

§ 723. The title to a thing duly offered in performance of an obligation passes to the creditor, if the debtor at the time signifies his intention to that effect.

Des Arts *v.* Leggett, 16 *N. Y.*, 582; Lamb *v.* Lathrop, 13 *Wend.*, 95; Rix *v.* Strong, 1 *Root*, 55; see Smith *v.* Loomis, 7 *Conn.*, 110. At present this rule does not apply to money, but that is because a tender does not extinguish a pecuniary debt. The change proposed by section 721 removes the ground of this distinction.

Custody of thing offered.

§ 724. The person offering a thing, other than money, by way of performance, must, if he means to treat it as belonging to the creditor, retain it as a depositary for hire,[1] until the creditor accepts it, or until he has given reasonable notice to the creditor that he will retain it no longer, and, if with reason able diligence he can find a suitable depositary therefor, until he has deposited it with such person.[2]

[1] Sheldon *v.* Skinner, 4 *Wend.*, 525.

[2] These rules seem reasonable, though they are not established (or denied) by adjudged cases.

§ 725. An offer of payment or other performance, duly made, though the title to the thing offered be not transferred to the creditor, stops the running of interest on the obligation, and has the same effect upon all its incidents as a performance thereof.

Effect of offer on accessories of obligation.

Kortright *v.* Cady, 21 *N. Y.*, 343; Law *v.* Jackson, 9 *Cow.*, 641; Raymond *v.* Bearnard, 12 *Johns.*, 274; Chilton *v.* Carrington, 15 *C. B.*, 95, 730.

§ 726. If anything is given to a creditor by way of performance, which he refuses to accept as such, he is not bound to return it without demand; but if he retains it, he is a gratuitous depositary thereof.

Credi[t] retent[ion] of thi[ng] which refuse[d] accep[tance]

Kingston Bank *v.* Gay, 19 *Barb.*, 460; Gordon *v.* Strange, 1 *Exch.*, 477.

CHAPTER III.

PREVENTION OF PERFORMANCE OR OFFER.

§ 727. The want of performance of an obligation, or of an offer of performance, in whole or in part, or any delay therein, is excused by the following causes, to the extent to which they operate:[1]

What excuses performance, &c.

1. When such performance or offer is prevented or delayed by the act of the creditor,[2] or by the operation of law,[3] even though there may have been a stipulation that this shall not be an excuse;

2. When it is prevented or delayed by an irresistible superhuman cause, or by the act of public enemies of this state or of the United States, unless the parties have expressly agreed to the contrary;[4] or,

3. When the debtor is induced[5] not to make it, by any act[6] of the creditor intended or naturally tending to have that effect,[7] done at or before the time at which such performance or offer may be made,[8] and not rescinded before that time.[9]

[1] Where performance is simply *delayed*, and not made forever impossible, delay only is excused (Williams *v.* Vanderbilt, 29 *Barb.*, 491; Schilizzi *v.* Derry, 4 *El. & Bl.*, 873; White *v.* Mann, 26 *Maine*, 368), unless the delay is for an indefinite or unreasonable period, as in case of a blockade, which puts an end to an obligation to enter the harbor (Scott *v.* Libby, 2 *Johns.*, 336; The Tutela, 6 *Rob. Adm.*, 177; see The Isabella Jacobina, 4 *Rob. Adm.*, 77).

[2] Masterton *v.* Mayor, &c., of Brooklyn, 7 *Hill*, 61; McConihe *v.* N. Y. & Erie R. R. Co., 20 *N. Y.*, 495; Ellen *v.* Topp, 6 *Exch.*, 424, 440.

[3] Jones *v.* Judd, 4 *N. Y.*, 411; People *v.* Bartlett, 3 *Hill*, 570; Esposito *v.* Bowden, 4 *El. & Bl.*, 963.

[4] The rule laid down in Tompkins *v.* Dudley (25 *N. Y.*, 272), and Harmony *v.* Bingham (12 *id.*, 99), is that not even the act of God excuses the non-performance of a *contract*, though it relieves from an obligation created merely by operation of law. But this doctrine was not absolutely necessary to the decision of those cases, nor to that of those there cited; and the commissioners cannot see how such a principle can be reconciled with the decision in Wolfe *v.* Howes (20 *N. Y.*, 197). The clause here inserted is consistent with all that was actually decided in these cases. and is certainly no more than just. There can be no doubt that parties to contracts do not contemplate such a strict liability; the only doubt is whether they do not assume the existence of even a much more liberal rule. See Williams *v.* Lloyd, *W. Jones*, 179; Taylor *v.* Caldwell, 3 *Best & S.*, 826.

[5] It is not necessary that the debtor should be literally *prevented* by the creditor from performing. If he is induced by the creditor, in any way, to abstain from or to delay performance, that is sufficient excuse (see Young *v.* Hunter, 6 *N. Y.*, 203; Carman *v.* Pultz, 21 *id.*, 547; Fleming *v.* Gilbert, 3 *Johns.*, 531; Farnham *v.* Ross, 2 *Hall*, 167; Higgins *v.* Solomon, *id.*, 482; Southworth *v.* Smith, 7 *Cush.*, 391; Gilmore *v.* Holt, 4 *Pick.*, 258).

[6] Not only a positive request of the creditor (Carman *v.* Pultz, 21 *N. Y.*, 547), but any act on his part which would make performance or an offer thereof useless

(Cornwell *v.* Haight, 21 *N. Y.*, 462), excuses the want of performance.

[7] This is obviously just.

[8] Skinner *v.* Tinker, 34 *Barb.*, 333; Crist *v.* Armour, *id.*, 378.

[9] *Id.*

§ 728. If performance of an obligation is prevented by the creditor, the debtor is entitled to all the benefits which he would have obtained by its performance on both sides. Effect of prevention of performance.

Masterton *v.* Mayor of Brooklyn, 7 *Hill*, 61; see Clark *v.* Mayor, &c., of New York, 4 *N. Y.*, 338.

§ 729. If a debtor is dissuaded by his creditor from performance, but is not actually forbidden to perform, he may, at his option, omit to perform, and retain whatever he has received under the contract, but he is entitled to nothing more. Id.

§ 730. If performance of an obligation is prevented by any cause excusing performance, other than the act of the creditor, the debtor is entitled to a ratable proportion of the consideration to which he would have been entitled upon full performance,[1] according to the benefit which the creditor receives from the actual performance.[2] Id.

[1] In Clark *v.* Gilbert (26 *N. Y.*, 279; reversing S. C., 32 *Barb.*, 576), it was held that the contract price should furnish the measure of damages in such case, and that the party performing was not confined to a mere reasonable compensation.

[2] Where full performance is prevented by the intervention of law, or of a superhuman cause, the party required to perform cannot recover the entire compensation to which he would have been entitled upon full performance, even though he is entirely without fault (Melville *v.* De Wolf, 4 *El. & Bl.*, 843). But he is entitled to a compensation according to the proportion of time or labor expended by him, subject to the rule of the text (Wolfe *v.* Howes, 20 *N. Y.*, 197). Thus, if an author should die, leaving any quantity of undigested manuscript, prepared under a contract with a publisher, nothing could be recovered by his representatives. (*Id.*)

Effect of refusal to accept performance before offer.

§ 731. A refusal by a creditor to accept performance, made before an offer thereof, is equivalent to an offer and refusal,[1] unless, before performance is actually due, he gives notice to the debtor of his willingness to accept it.[2]

[1] Meserole *v.* Archer, 3 *Bosw.*, 376, 382; North *v.* Pepper, 21 *Wend.*, 638.

[2] Traver *v.* Halstead, 23 *Wend.*, 66.

CHAPTER IV.

ACCORD AND SATISFACTION.

Accord, what.

§ 732. An accord is an agreement to accept, in extinction of an obligation, something to which the person agreeing to accept is not otherwise entitled.

Williams *v.* London Com. Exch. Co., 10 *Exch.*, 569; Scott *v.* Hunt, 2 *How. Pr.*, 58; Seymour *v.* Minturn, 17 *Johns.*, 169; Keeler *v.* Neal, 2 *Watts*, 424.

Effect of accord.

§ 733. Though the parties to an accord are bound to execute it,[1] yet it does not extinguish the obligation until it is fully[2] executed.[3]

[1] Billings *v.* Vanderbeck, 23 *Barb.*, 546.

[2] Gabriel *v.* Dresser, 15 *C. B.*, 622.

[3] Day *v.* Roth, 18 *N. Y.*, 456; Russell *v.* Lytle, 6 *Wend.*, 390; Tilton *v.* Alcott, 16 *Barb.*, 598; Mitchell *v.* Hawley, 4 *Denio*, 417.

Satisfaction, what.

§ 734. Acceptance, by the creditor, of the consideration of an accord, extinguishes the obligation, and is called satisfaction.

Hall *v.* Flockton, 16 *Q. B.*, 1039; Jones *v.* Sawkins, 5 *C. B.*, 142. Though an accord and satisfaction is not at common law a defense to a claim founded upon a record or specialty (Mitchell *v.* Hawley, 4 *Den.*, 414), the commissioners do not think it wise to retain this distinction.

§ 735. Payment of an amount less than that of a liquidated[1] debt then payable,[2] is not a satisfaction thereof, though accepted as such.[3] Accord of liquidated debt.

[1] Palmerton *v.* Huxford, 4 *Denio*, 166; Neary *v.* Bostwick, 2 *Hilt.*, 514; see Evans *v.* Powis, 1 *Exch.*, 601; Wilkinson *v.* Byers, 1 *Ad. & El.*, 106.

[2] Brooks *v.* White, 3 *Metc.*, 286; Goodnow *v.* Smith, 18 *Pick.*, 414; Smith *v.* Brown, 3 *Hawks*, 580.

[3] Von Gerhard *v.* Lighte, 13 *Abb. Pr.*, 101; Harrison *v.* Wilcox, 2 *Johns.*, 448; Dederick *v.* Leman, 9 *id.*, 333; Scott *v.* Hunt, 2 *How. Pr.*, 58; Down *v.* Hatcher, 10 *Ad. & El.*, 121; Thomas *v.* Heathorn, 2 *B. & C.*, 477; Fitch *v.* Sutton, 5 *East*, 230; Cumber *v.* Wane, 1 *Str.*, 426. This rule of the common law is not founded upon natural justice, nor can it be supported upon any other than technical grounds. An agreement to accept a barrel of flour in satisfaction of a debt of $1,000 is valid, and if the flour is delivered the debt is satisfied. So a release under seal, without any consideration, extinguishes the debt. But an agreement to accept $999 in satisfaction of the debt is unavailing, and the obligation to pay the other dollar is unimpaired. In Pennsylvania, the rule has been disavowed for over thirty years past (Milliken *v.* Brown, 1 *Rawle*, 391). It has been abolished in Maine, by statute (*Laws* 1851, *ch.* 213). The commissioners recommend the omission of this section, and the insertion of the following substitute:

§ 735. Part performance of an obligation, either before or after a breach thereof, when expressly accepted by the creditor in satisfaction and rendered in pursuance of an agreement for that purpose, though without any new consideration, extinguishes the obligation.

CHAPTER V.

NOVATION.

§ 736. Novation is the substitution of a new obligation for an existing one. Novation, what.

Modes of novation.

§ 737. Novation is made:

1. By the substitution of a new and higher obligation between the same parties, with intent to extinguish the old obligation;[1]

2. By the substitution of a new debtor in place of the old one, with intent to release the latter;[2] or

3. By the substitution of a new creditor in place of the old one, with intent to transfer the rights of the latter to the former.[3]

[1] The acceptance of a debtor's own note does not discharge the debt (see § 739). But the substitution of a contract under seal for one not under seal, extinguishes the latter.

[2] Conkling *v.* King, 10 *N. Y.*, 440; Graves *v.* Friend, 5 *Sandf.*, 568; St. John *v.* Purdy, 1 *id.*, 9; N. Y. State Bank *v.* Fletcher, 5 *Wend.*, 85; Sard *v.* Rhodes, 1 *M. & W.*, 153. But if there is no agreement to accept the new obligation in satisfaction, it is not a satisfaction (Noel *v.* Murray, 13 *N. Y.*, 167; Vail *v.* Foster, 4 *id.*, 312; Monroe *v.* Hoff, 5 *Den.*, 360). The intent is the material question (Jobbitt *v.* Goundry, 29 *Barb.*, 509).

[3] *Code La.*, 2185; *Code Napoleon*, 1271.

Novation, a contract.

§ 738. Novation is made by contract, and is subject to all the rules concerning contracts in general.

Effect of acceptance of new obligation.

§ 739. The acceptance, by a creditor, of a new obligation of the debtor for the payment of money only, in satisfaction of another obligation of as high degree, for the payment of a specific sum of money only, then payable, does not extinguish the latter obligation[1] [unless accepted as a satisfaction under section 735],[2] but extends the time of payment until the new obligation becomes payable.[3]

[1] Spencer *v.* Ballou, 18 *N. Y.*, 331; Hill *v.* Beebe, 13 *id.*, 562; Cole *v.* Sackett, 1 *Hill*, 516.

[2] The clause in brackets depends upon the adoption of the substitute suggested for § 735.

[3] Myers *v.* Welles, 5 *Hill*, 463; Hart *v.* Hudson, 6 *Duer*, 294; Walton *v.* Mascall, 13 *M. & W.*, 452; Kearslake *v.* Morgan, 5 *T. R.*, 513; Okie *v.* Spencer, 2 *Whart.*, 253.

§ 740. When the obligation of a third person, or an order upon such person, is accepted in satisfaction, the creditor may rescind such acceptance, if the debtor prevents such person from complying with the order,[1] or from fulfilling the obligation, or if, before the creditor can with reasonable diligence reach such person, he becomes insolvent.[2] Rescission of novation.

[1] Franklin *v.* Vanderpool, 1 *Hall*, 78; Coyle *v.* Smith, 1 *E. D. Smith*, 400; Purchase *v.* Mattison, 6 *Duer*, 587; Jacks *v.* Darrin, 3 *E. D. Smith*, 557.

[2] Lovett *v.* Cornwell, 6 *Wend.*, 369; aff'g S. C., 1 *Hall*, 56; Timmins *v.* Gibbins, 18 *Q. B.*, 722; Ontario Bank *v.* Lightbody, 13 *Wend.*, 107; see Heubach *v.* Mollman, 2 *Duer*, 227; Benedict *v.* Field, 16 *N. Y.*, 595; but see Des Arts *v.* Leggett, *id.*, 582, 589.

CHAPTER VI.

RELEASE.

SECTION 741. Obligation extinguished by release.
742. Certain claims not affected by general release.
743. Release of several joint debtors.

§ 741. An obligation is extinguished by a release therefrom given to the debtor by the creditor, upon a new consideration, or under seal. Obligation extinguished by release.

A release under seal extinguishes the debt, notwithstanding the provision of the Revised Statutes allowing the want of consideration for a sealed instrument to be shown (Stearns *v.* Tappin, 5 *Duer*, 294). But by the present law, a release, with neither a seal nor a new consideration, is void (Von Gerhard *v.* Lighte, 13 *Abb. Pr.*, 101; Seymour *v.* Minturn, 17 *Johns.*, 169; Dewey *v.* Derby, 20 *id.*, 462; Jackson *v.* Stackhouse, 1 *Cow.*, 122). The justice of its restrictions may well be doubted. The commissioners recommend the substitution of the words "in writing" for "under seal." See notes to section 735.

§ 742. A general release does not extend to claims which the creditor did not know or suspect to exist in his favor, at the time of executing the release. Certain claims not affected by general release.

Lyall *v.* Edwards, 6 *H. & N.*, 337.

Release of several joint debtors.

§ 743. A release of one of two or more joint debtors does not extinguish the obligations of any of the others, unless they are mere guarantors; nor does it affect their right to contribution from him.

This provision is new (see Cornell *v.* Masten, 35 *Barb.*, 157; Bronson *v.* Fitzhugh, 1 *Hill*, 185; Hoffman *v.* Dunlop, 1 *Barb.*, 185; Parsons *v.* Hughes, 9 *Paige*, 591; Catskill Bank *v.* Messenger, 9 *Cow.*, 37; Rowley *v.* Stoddard, 7 *Johns.*, 207). By statute, a release *may* be so drawn as to discharge one only of several joint debtors (3 *R. S.* [*5th ed.*], 65; *Laws* 1838, *ch.* 257): and as the intention of the creditor is evident enough from the form of the release, the justice of this provision can hardly be disputed.

PART II.

CONTRACTS.

TITLE I.

NATURE OF A CONTRACT.

CHAPTER I.

DEFINITION.

§ 744. A contract is an agreement to do or not to do a certain thing. **Contract, what.**

McNulty *v.* Prentice, 25 *Barb.*, 204; Sturges *v.* Crowninshield, 4 *Wheat.*, 197.

§ 745. It is essential to the existence of a contract that there should be: **Essential elements of contract.**

1. Parties capable of contracting;

2. Their consent;

3. A lawful object; and,

4. A sufficient cause or consideration.

Code La., 1772, 1758, 1759; *Code Napoleon*, 1108.

The word "object" has been selected, after much reflection, as a more correct word for the purpose here intended, than "subject" or "subject matter."

CHAPTER II.

PARTIES.

Who may contract. § 746. All persons are capable of contracting, except minors, persons of unsound mind, and persons deprived of civil rights.

The disabilities of married women are entirely removed by section 79.

Minors, &c. § 747. Minors, and persons of unsound mind, have only such capacity as is defined by Part I of the First Division of this Code.

Identification of parties necessary. § 748. It is essential to the validity of a contract, not only that the parties should exist, but that it should be possible to identify them.

Webster *v.* Ela, 5 *N. H.*, 540.

When contract for benefit of third person may be enforced. § 749. A contract, made expressly for the benefit of a third person, may be enforced by him at any time before the parties thereto rescind it.

Burr *v.* Beers, 24 *N. Y.*, 178; Lawrence *v.* Fox, 20 *id.*, 268; Scott *v.* Pilkington, 15 *Abb.*, 280; Steman *v.* Harrison, 42 *Penn. St.*, 49. The rule stated in these cases was limited to promises in which the purpose was expressed, in Hoffman *v.* Schwaebe, 33 *Barb.*, 194.

CHAPTER III.

CONSENT.

§ 750. The consent of the parties to a contract must be: Essentials of consent.

1. Free;

2. Mutual;[1] and,

3. Communicated by each to the other.[2]

[1] Getman *v.* Getman, 1 *Barb. Ch.*, 499; Burnet *v.* Bisco, 4 *Johns.*, 235.

[2] Communication of consent is indispensable (Bentley *v.* Columbian Ins. Co., 17 *N. Y.*, 421; Heubach *v.* Mollman, 2 *Duer*, 256, 257; Fiedler *v.* Tucker, 13 *How. Pr*, 9; Mozley *v.* Tinkler, 1 *Cr. M. & R.*, 692). But it need not be verbally expressed. An understanding between the parties is sufficient (Houghton *v.* Adams, 18 *Barb.* 545).

§ 751. A consent which is not free is nevertheless not absolutely void, but may be rescinded by the Consent, when voidable.

parties, in the manner prescribed by the chapter on RESCISSION.

Murray *v.* Mann, 2 *Exch.*, 538; Gage *v.* Parker, 25 *Barb.*, 141

Apparent consent, when not free.

§ 752. An apparent consent is not real or free when obtained through:

1. Duress;
2. Menace;
3. Fraud;
4. Undue influence; or,
5. Mistake.

Menace has usually been classed with duress, and will be found to be treated under that head in the digests. It is, however, clearly a separate branch of the subject. Accident and surprise are included under the head of Mistake.

When deemed to have been obtained by fraud, &c.

§ 753. Consent is deemed to have been obtained through one of the causes mentioned in the last section, only when it would not have been given had such cause not existed.

Bronson *v.* Wiman, 8 *N. Y.*, 188, 189; Flight *v.* Booth, 1 *Bing. N. C.*, 376; *Code La.*, 1819; Faure *v.* Martin, 7 *N. Y.*, 219. It is not essential that the fraud, &c., should be the *sole* inducement to consent (Shaw *v.* Stine, 8 *Bosw.*, 157; Addington *v.* Allen, 11 *Wend.*, 381; Clarke *v.* Dickson, 6 *C. B.* [*N. S.*], 453).

Duress, what.

§ 754. Duress consists in:

1. Unlawful confinement of the person of the party,[1] or of the husband or wife of such party, or of an ancestor, descendant,[2] or adopted child[3] of such party, husband or wife;[4]

2. Unlawful detention of the property of any such person;[5] or,

3. Confinement of such person, lawful in form, but fraudulently obtained,[6] or fraudulently made unjustly harassing or oppressive.[7]

[1] Foshay *v.* Ferguson, 5 *Hill*, 154; *Bac. Abr.*, Duress, A. If the confinement is lawful there is no duress (Bates *v.* Butler, 46 *Me.*, 387).

[2] *Code La.*, 1847; *Code Napoleon*, 1113; *Bac. Abr.*, Duress, B. See McClintock *v.* Cummins, 3 *McLean*, 158; Eadie *v.* Slimmon, 26 *N. Y.*, 9.

[3] New, but in accordance with the title on ADOPTION.

[4] *Code Napoleon*, 1113.

[5] This is denied (Skeate v. Beale, 11 *Ad. & El.*, 983; Atlee *v.* Backhouse, 3 *M. & W.*, 650). But it was originally so held in privy council (Assize, 5 *Year Book*, fol. 72, pl. 14), and it has been so decided in this country (Collins *v.* Westbury, 2 *Bay*, 211; Sasportas *v.* Jennings, 1 *Bay*, 470; see also Nelson *v.* Suddarth, 1 *Hen. & Munf.*, 350), with the approval of BRONSON, J. (Foshay *v.* Ferguson, 5 *Hill*, 158). It is universally held that *money paid* under such duress may be recovered back (Harmony *v.* Bingham, 12 *N. Y.*, 99; Oates *v.* Hudson, 6 *Exch.*, 346; Atlee *v.* Backhouse, 3 *M. & W.*, 642); and it is very difficult to see why, under precisely similar circumstances, a note given instead of money should be enforced.

[6] Strong *v.* Grannis, 26 *Barb.*, 122; Watkins *v.* Baird, 6 *Mass.*, 511; Richardson *v.* Duncan, 3 *N. H.*, 508.

[7] Severance *v.* Kimball, 8 *N. H.*, 386; Richardson *v.* Duncan, 3 *id.*, 508.

§ 755. Menace consists in a threat: **Menace, what.**

1. Of such duress as is specified in the first and third subdivisions of the last section;[1]

2. Of unlawful and violent injury to the person[2] or property[3] of any such person as is specified in the last section; or,

3. Of injury to the character of any such person.[4]

[1] Eadie *v.* Slimmon, 26 *N. Y.*, 9; Whitefield *v.* Longfellow, 13 *Maine*, 146; compare Biffin *v.* Bignell, 7 *H. & N.*, 877.

[2] *Co. Inst.*, 483; *Bac. Abr.*, Duress, A.

[3] See Foshay *v.* Ferguson, 5 *Hill*, 158; see contra, *Bac. Abr.*, Duress, A. See note below.

[4] This species of threat is not usually included in the definition of duress, and was doubtless not so treated under the old common law, when a libeler could be made to rot in jail until he paid damages, while neither the judgment creditor nor any one else was bound to find him food or drink (Dive *v.* Maningham, 1 *Plowd.*, 68); and when some debtors did actually starve to death. With such a savage remedy for the recovery of pecuniary damages, they might be considered an adequate satisfaction for injuries to property or character, and it was on this

ground that such injuries were not regarded as duress. (*Bac. Abr.*, Duress, A.) The remedy now existing is less effective, even if money were considered equivalent to character. By statute, it is now a criminal offense to send threatening letters for the purpose of extorting money, and that which is thus treated as a crime ought not to be allowed to sustain a contract. These views are further sustained by *Story Cont.*, § 398; 2 *Stark. Ev.*, 482; *Chitt. Cont.*, 208. And see Eadie *v.* Slimmon, 26 *N. Y.*, 9, in which some weight is given to the influence of a threat involving the loss of a husband's character.

Fraud, actual or constructive.

§ 756. Fraud is either actual or constructive.

Conkey *v.* Bond, 34 *Barb.*, 286.

Actual fraud, what.

§ 757. Actual fraud, within the meaning of this chapter,[1] consists in any of the following acts,[2] committed by a party to the contract, or with his connivance,[3] with intent[4] to deceive[5] another party thereto, or to induce him to enter into the contract:[6]

1. The suggestion,[7] as a fact, of that which is not true, by one who does not believe it to be true;[8]

2. The positive assertion, in a manner not warranted by the information of the person making it, of that which is not true, though he believes it to be true;[9]

3. The suppression of that which is true, by one having knowledge or belief of the fact;[10]

4. A promise, made without any intention of performing it;[11] or,

5. Any other act fitted to deceive.

[1] This definition is not to be considered as covering all varieties of fraud, but only such fraud as vitiates the consent of a party to a contract.

[2] Story (*Eq. Jur.*, § 187), defines fraud as a "trick, device or artifice," &c. In Gardner *v.* Heartt (3 *Denio*, 236), it is called "a deceitful practice or willful device." It is at least doubtful whether any peculiar "artifice" is necessary to constitute fraud. In Nichols *v.* Pinner (18 *N. Y.*, 295), and Nichols *v.* Michael (23 *N. Y.*, 264), SELDEN, J., expressed his opinion that there must be something of the kind, in addition to an *intent* to defraud, in order to constitute fraud in a

purchase. But in each of those cases a different opinion was expressed by other judges, and in Hennequin *v.* Naylor, (24 *N. Y.*, 139), the opinion of JAMES, J., which appears to have been concurred in by the whole court, is explicit to the contrary. So is King *v.* Phillips, 8 *Bosw.*, 603. The commissioners incline to the latter view as more sound (see also Brown *v.* Montgomery, 20 *N. Y.*, 287).

[3] A fraudulent representation made by C. to A., with intent to induce A. to enter into a contract with B., would not, it is clear, enable A. to rescind the contract, if B. had no part in or knowledge of the fraud (Holbrook *v.* Wilson, 4 *Bosw.*, 64), at least, on the ground of *fraud.* But if C. was the agent of B., or even if he acted in concert with him, or in short if B. in any way connived at the fraud, A. might rescind (see Cassard *v.* Hinman, 6 *Bosw.*, 8).

[4] For the purpose of avoiding a contract, it is not necessary that the fraud should have been committed with an intent to *injure* the party deceived. Every man has a right to decide for himself whether he will enter into a contract or not, and no one has a right to deceive him even for his own good. The cases in which the question of injury is discussed are direct actions for deceit, in which, of course, if no damage has been suffered, none can be recovered. But a fraudulent intent is nevertheless essential to constitute actual fraud. Even an untrue statement is not *necessarily* a fraud, for it may be made and accepted in jest. Much more is some fraudulent intent necessary to be shown in cases of mere concealment.

[5] An intent to deceive, whenever carried out, constitutes a fraud, even though there may not have been an intent to induce the party deceived to contract. Thus, if A. should, on Monday, out of mere mischief or love of deception, tell B. that Congress had just repealed the duty on paper, and should sustain his assertion by showing public news to the same effect, which he however knows to be erroneous, and should, on Tuesday, purchase paper of B., on terms to which B. was induced to assent, by reason of the falsehood of the day before, B. would clearly have a right to rescind, even though A. did not know or suppose that B. was influenced by his false statements.

The assertion of a certain thing as a matter of fact, when in reality the asserter knows nothing about the matter, may often be a fraud, without any clear intention to deceive. In such cases, it is more satisfactory to fix upon the intent to induce consent as the test of fraud.

[7] The word "suggestion" is used, instead of "assertion," because even a hint, or a true report of what others have untruly said, is a fraud, when conveying an impression which the party knows to be false, and made for that purpose.

[8] Haight *v.* Hayt, 19 *N. Y.*, 464; White *v.* Merritt, 7 *id.*, 352.

[9] Bennett *v.* Judson, 21 *N. Y.*, 238; Craig *v.* Ward, 36 *Barb.*, 377; Evans *v.* Edmonds, 13 *C. B.*, 776.

[10] Nichols *v.* Michael, 23 *N. Y.*, 264; Hennequin *v.* Naylor, 24 *N. Y.*, 139; Hall *v.* Naylor, 18 *id.*, 588; Addington *v.* Allen, 7 *Wend.*, 20; Lee *v.* Jones, 14 *C. B.* [*N. S.*], 386; Bank of Republic *v.* Baxter, 31 *Verm.*, 101; Paddock *v.* Strobridge, 29 *id.*, 470; Martin *v.* Morgan, 1 *Brod. & B.*, 289; Drummond *v.* Tracy, 6 *Jur.* [*N. S.*], 369; see Squire *v.* Whitten, 1 *H. of L. Cas.*, 333; Dolman *v.* Nokes, 22 *Beav.*, 402; Broderick *v.* Broderick, 1 *P. Wms.*, 239.

[11] It has been held that a mere *promise*, though made with an intention not to perform it, and for the purpose of misleading a party to his injury, is not such a fraud as would sustain an action for deceit (Farrington *v.* Bullard, 40 *Barb.*, 512; Gallagher *v.* Brunel, 6 *Cow.*, 346; Fisher *v.* New York C. P., 18 *Wend.*, 608). It is not such a fraud as will sustain an indictment for false pretenses (Ranney *v.* People, 22 *N. Y.*, 413); but it seems to the commissioners to stand upon the same footing with a purchase of goods with intent not to pay, which has been repeatedly held to be a fraud (Hennequin *v.* Naylor, 24 *N. Y.*, 139; Nichols *v.* Michael, 23 *id.*, 264; King *v.* Phillips, 8 *Bosw.*, 603; see especially Bigelow *v.* Heaton, 6 *Hill*, 43). In Seaman *v.* Low (4 *Bosw.*, 337), false representations as to what the seller was *about* to do, were held sufficient to avoid a sale.

Constructive fraud, what.

§ 758. Constructive fraud consists:

1. In any breach of duty which, without an actually fraudulent intent, gains an advantage to the person in fault, or any one claiming under him, by misleading another to his prejudice, or to the prejudice of any one claiming under him;[1] or,

2. In any such act or omission as the law specially declares to be fraudulent, without respect to actual fraud.[2]

[1] Bulkley *v.* Wilford, 2 *Clark & Fin.*, 102, 177, 181.

[2] Conkey *v.* Bond, 34 *Barb.*, 276; People *v.* Kelly, 35 *id.*, 444.

§ 759. Actual[1] fraud is always a question of fact.[2] Actual fraud, a question of fact.

[1] Dunham *v.* Waterman, 17 *N. Y.*, 21; Wilson *v.* Forsyth, 24 *Barb.*, 105.

[2] 2 *R. S.*, 137.

§ 760. Undue influence consists: Undue influence.

1. In the use, by one in whom a confidence is reposed by another,[1] or who holds a real[2] or apparent[3] authority over him, of such confidence or authority for the purpose of obtaining an unfair advantage over him;[4]

2. In taking an unfair advantage of another's weakness of mind;[5] or,

3. In taking a grossly oppressive and unfair advantage of another's necessities or distress.[6]

[1] It may safely be stated as a general rule of equity, that no one can be permitted to make any selfish use of a personal confidence reposed in him. This rule is illustrated in a variety of forms, and sustained by numerous authorities, in the Title on TRUSTS. But it is also proper to be recognized in this place. It is not necessary, in such cases, to show that there was any deception practiced. It is sufficient to show that the confidence reposed was taken advantage of for purposes of gain (see Sears *v.* Shafer, 6 *N. Y.*, 268, 272; Bergen *v.* Udall, 31 *Barb.*, 9; Brock *v.* Barnes, 40 *Barb.*, 521; Baker *v.* Bradley, 7 *De G., M. & G.*, 597; Tyrrell *v.* Bank of London, 10 *H. of L. Cas.*, 26; Dent *v.* Bennett, 4 *Myl. & Cr.*, 269; 7 *Sim.*, 539; Broun *v.* Kennedy, 9 *Jur.* [*N. S.*], 1163; Davies *v.* Davies, *id.*, 1002).

[2] A parent may not acquire anything from his child by the slightest exercise of parental authority (Bury *v.* Oppenheim, 26 *Beav.*, 594; Bergen *v.* Udall, 31 *Barb.*, 9; Taylor *v.* Taylor, 8 *How.* [*U. S.*], 183; Baker *v.* Bradley, 7 *De G., M. & G.*, 597; see Broun *v.* Kennedy, 9 *Jur.* [*N. S.*], 1163; Davies *v.* Davies, *id.*, 1002); and the same rule applies to any one standing in the relation of a parent (Archer *v.* Hudson, 7 *Beav.*, 551), as an uncle with whom his niece lived for a number of years (*id.*), or an elder sister, who had a great ascendancy over the mind of the grantor (Harvey *v.* Mount, 8 *Beav.*, 439). So a deed from a lady to a clergyman whom she believed to be inspired, was set aside (Nottidge *v.* Prince, 2 *Giff.*, 246).

[3] Where agents, appointed by the comptroller to investigate the condition of an insurance company which

had applied to him, pursuant to statute, for leave to do business, after they had made their report, and had in fact no further power, insisted upon the payment of $300 as fees, threatening to revoke their report if the fees were not paid, it was held that the money paid under such a threat might be recovered back (Am. Ex. Fire Ins. Co. *v.* Britton, 8 *Bosw.*, 148; see Steele *v.* Williams, 8 *Exch.*, 625; Dew *v.* Parsons, 2 *B. & Ald.*, 562; Morgan *v.* Palmer, 2 *B. & C.*, 729).

[4] This is all that is necessary. Nothing more than a perverted use of the power of the party need be shown.

[5] Longmate *v.* Ledger, 6 *Jur.* [*N. S.*], 481; Blackford *v.* Christian, 1 *Knapp*, 77; see Tracy *v.* Sacket, 1 *Ohio St.*, 58; Rippy *v.* Grant, 4 *Ired. Eq.*, 443; Whiteburn *v.* Hines, 1 *Munf.*, 557; Dunn *v.* Chambers, 4 *Barb.*, 376.

[6] Breck *v.* Cole, 4 *Sandf.*, 88; Bowes *v.* Heaps, 3 *Ves. & B.*, 119; Wood *v.* Abrey, 3 *Madd.*, 423; Gould *v.* Okeden, 4 *Bro. P. C.*, 198; see Cockshot *v.* Bennet, 2 *T. R.*, 763; Barnardiston *v.* Lingood, 2 *Atk.*, 133; Thornhill *v.* Evans, *id.*, 330; Walmsley *v.* Booth, *id.*, 28, 29; Berney *v.* Pitt, 2 *Vern.*, 14; Nott *v.* Hill, *id.*, 27; Wiseman *v.* Beake, *id.*, 121; Roche *v.* O'Brion, 1 *Ball & B.*, 337, 359; Bromley *v.* Smith, 26 *Beav.*, 664; 5 *Jur.* (*N. S.*), 837; Lamplugh *v.* Cox, *Dick.*, 411; Heron *v.* Heron, 2 *Atk.*, 160. These cases seem to support this view. They are generally classed under the head of fraud (see *Story Eq. Jur.*, §§ 331–337); but the principle on which they depend is not a mere question of fraud.

Mistake, what.

§ 761. Mistake may be either of fact or of law.

As to mistake of fact there is no question. Mistake of law has been often declared to be no ground for relief at law or in equity (see Champlin *v.* Laytin, 18 *Wend.*, 417; Storrs *v.* Parker, 6 *Johns. Ch.*, 166; Lyon *v.* Richmond, 2 *id.*, 61; Kent *v.* Manchester, 29 *Barb.*, 595; *Story Eq. Jur.*, §§ 111–139). But the contrary view has been taken by judges of high authority (see Champlin *v.* Laytin, 18 *Wend.*, 422; Many *v.* Beekman Iron Co., 9 *Paige*, 188; Stone *v.* Godfrey, 5 *De G., M. & G.*, 90; Broughton *v.* Hutt, 3 *De G. & J.*, 501; Evants *v.* Strode, 11 *Ohio*, 480. See also Wheeler *v.* Smith, 9 *How.* [*U. S.*], 55). The commissioners think that the latter cases are better considered. No doubt relief upon this ground must be granted with extreme caution, and in only a limited class of cases; but this by no means proves that such relief should never be granted.

§ 762. Mistake of fact is a mistake, not caused by the neglect of a legal duty[1] on the part of the person making the mistake, and consisting in: **Mistake of fact.**

1. An unconscious[2] ignorance[3] or forgetfulness[4] of a fact past[5] or present,[6] material to the contract; or,

2. Belief in the present existence of a thing material to the contract, which does not exist,[7] or in the past existence of such a thing, which has not existed.[8]

[1] U. S. Bank *v.* Bank of Georgia, 10 *Wheat.*, 343.

[2] McDaniels *v.* Bank of Rutland, 29 *Vt.*, 238; Elwell *v.* Chamberlain, 4 *Bosw.*, 320; Kelly *v.* Solari, 9 *M. & W.*, 54.

[3] Briggs *v.* Vanderbilt, 19 *Barb.*, 222, 239; Bell *v.* Gardiner, 4 *M. & G.*, 11; 4 *Scott N. R.*, 621.

[4] Kelly *v.* Solari, 9 *M. & W.*, 54; Lucas *v.* Worswick, 1 *Moo. & Rob.*, 293. This definition seems to cover all the cases of accident and surprise against which relief can be had.

[5] Willan *v.* Willan, 16 *Ves.*, 72; McCarthy *v.* De Caix, 2 *Russ. & M.*, 614; Durkin *v.* Cranston, 7 *Johns.*, 442.

[6] Huthacher *v.* Harris' Adm'r, 38 *Penn. St.*, 491.

[7] Reel *v.* Hicks, 25 *N. Y.*, 289; Kip *v.* Monroe, 29 *Barb.*, 579; Briggs *v.* Vanderbilt, 19 *id.*, 239; Gardner *v.* Mayor, &c., of Troy, 26 *id.*, 423; Wheadon *v.* Olds, 20 *Wend.*, 174; Mowatt *v.* Wright, 1 *id.*, 360; Allen *v.* Mayor, &c., of N. Y., 4 *E. D. Smith*, 404; Hitchcock *v.* Giddings, 4 *Price*, 135; *Dan.*, 1; Hastie *v.* Couturier, 9 *Exch.*, 102; affirmed 5 *H. of L. Cas.*, 673; Strickland *v.* Turner, 7 *Exch.*, 208. See Belknap *v.* Sealey, 14 *N. Y.*, 143; Martin *v.* M'Cormick, 8 *N. Y.*, 335; Ketchum *v.* Bank of Commerce, 19 *N. Y.*, 502.

[8] See Martin *v.* McCormick, 8 *N. Y.*, 335.

The *dicta* contained in some cases to the effect that a mistake in respect of matters as to which the party had "means of knowledge" does not avoid a contract (see Mutual Life Ins. Co. *v.* Wager, 27 *Barb.*, 354; Clarke *v.* Dutcher, 9 *Cow.*, 674; Milnes *v.* Duncan, 6 *B. & C.*, 716), are not sustained by the decisions (see Allen *v.* Mayor, &c., of N. Y., 4 *E. D. Smith*, 404; Kelly *v.* Solari, 9 *M. & W.*, 54), and have been finally overruled (Townsend *v.* Crowdy, 8 *C. B.* [*N. S.*], 477; Bell *v.* Gardiner, 4 *M. & G.*, 11; Dails *v.* Lloyd, 12 *Q. B.*, 531).

§ 763. Mistake of law constitutes a mistake, within the meaning of this article, only when it arises from: **Mistake of law**

1. A misapprehension of the law by all parties, all supposing that they knew and understood it, and all making substantially the same mistake as to the law;[1] or,

2. A misapprehension of the law by one party, of which the others are aware at the time of contracting, but which they do not rectify.[2]

[1] Many *v.* Beekman Iron Co., 9 *Paige*, 188; Hall *v.* Reed, 2 *Barb. Ch.*, 501; see Pitcher *v.* Turin Plank Road Co., 10 *Barb.*, 436; Wake *v.* Harrop, 6 *H. & N.*, 768.

[2] In Cooke *v.* Nathan (16 *Barb.*, 342), it was held that a misrepresentation of the law by one party, on which the other ignorantly relied, was a fraud. It seems to follow that a transaction such as is described in the text should be relieved against, as a mistake, if not as a fraud.

Mistake of foreign laws.

§ 764. Mistake of foreign laws is a mistake of fact.

Bank of Chilicothe *v.* Dodge, 8 *Barb.*, 233; McCormick *v.* Garnett, 5 *De G., M. & G.*, 278; Haven *v.* Foster, 9 *Pick.*, 113; Leslie *v.* Bailie, 2 *You. & C. Ch.*, 91; see Merchants' Bank *v.* Spalding, 12 *Barb.*, 302.

Mutuality of consent.

§ 765. Consent is not mutual, unless the parties all agree upon the same thing[1] in the same sense.[2] But in certain cases defined by the chapter on INTERPRETATION, they are to be deemed so to agree without regard to the fact.

[1] Scranton *v.* Booth, 29 *Barb.*, 171; Salters *v.* Pruyn, 18 *How. Pr.*, 512.

[2] Hazard *v.* New England Ins. Co., 1 *Sumn.*, 218; Greene *v.* Bateman, 2 *Woodb. & M.*, 359.

Communication of consent.

§ 766. Consent can be communicated with effect, only by some act or omission of the party contracting, by which he intends to communicate it, or which necessarily tends to such communication.

This is intended to exclude the possible case of a declaration of consent made to a person having no interest in the contract, and communicated by him to the other party, without authority.

Id.

§ 767. If a proposal prescribes any conditions concerning the communication of its acceptance, the proposer is not bound unless they are conformed to; but in other cases any reasonable and usual mode may be adopted.

Dunlop *v.* Higgins, 1 *H. of L. Cas.*, 381, 398; Vassar *v.* Camp. 11 *N. Y.*, 451.

§ 768. Consent is deemed to be fully communicated between the parties as soon as the party accepting a proposal has put his acceptance in the course of transmission to the proposer, in conformity to the last section. When communication deemed complete.

This section is intended to recognize the rule that consent is complete as soon as a letter of acceptance is put into the post-office (Mactier *v.* Frith, 6 *Wend.*, 103; Vassar *v.* Camp, 11 *N. Y.*, 441; Dunlop *v.* Higgins, 1 *H. L. Cas.*, 381; Tayloe *v.* Merchants' Fire Ins. Co., 9 *How.* [*U. S.*], 390; Eliason *v.* Henshaw, 4 *Wheat.*, 228; Hamilton *v.* Lycoming Ins. Co., 5 *Penn. St.*, 339; Averill *v.* Hedge, 12 *Conn.*, 436; Beckwith *v.* Cheever, 1 *Fost.* [*N. H.*], 41; Duncan *v.* Topham, 8 *C. B.*, 225. To the contrary is Gillespie *v.* Edmonston, 11 *Humph.* [*Tenn.*], 553).

§ 769. Performance of the conditions of a proposal,[1] or the acceptance of the consideration offered with a proposal,[2] is an acceptance of the proposal. Performance of conditions; acceptance.

[1] Harvey *v.* Johnston, 6 *C. B.*, 304; see Kenyon *v.* People, 26 *N. Y.*, 203.

[2] Decker *v.* Judson, 16 *N. Y.*, 446. So the conditions of a grant are accepted by an acceptance of the grant (Spalding *v.* Hallenbeck, 30 *Barb.*, 292).

§ 770. An acceptance must be absolute and unqualified,[1] or must include in itself an acceptance of that character, which the proposer can separate from the rest, and which will conclude the person accepting.[2] A qualified acceptance is a new proposal. Acceptance must be absolute.

[1] Hough *v.* Brown, 19 *N. Y.*, 114, 115; *Code La.*, 1799; Borland *v.* Guffey, 1 *Grant* (*Pa.*), 394; Duke *v.* Andrews, 2 *Exch.*, 290; Jordon *v.* Norton, 4 *M. & W.*, 155; Wontner *v.* Sharp, 4 *C. B.*, 404, 441; Routledge *v.* Grant, 4 *Bing.*, 653; Cheveley *v.* Fuller, 13 *C. B.*, 122.

[2] *Code La.*, 1801.

Revocation of proposal.

§ 771. A proposal may be revoked at any time before its acceptance is communicated to the proposer,[1] but not afterwards.[2]

[1] Stephens v. Buffalo & N. Y. R. R. Co., 20 *Barb.*, 332; Eskridge v. Glover, 5 *Stew. & Port.*, 264; see Boston & Me. R. R. v. Bartlett, 3 *Cush.*, 224.

[2] Routledge v. Grant, 4 *Bing.*, 653; Head v. Diggon, 3 *Man. & R.*, 97; Cooke v. Oxley, 3 *T. R.*, 653.

Revocation, how made.

§ 772. A proposal is revoked:

1. By the communication of notice of revocation by the proposer to the other party, in the manner prescribed by sections 766 and 768, before his acceptance has been communicated to the former;[1]

2. By the lapse of the time prescribed in such proposal for its acceptance, or if no time is so prescribed, the lapse of a reasonable time without communication of the acceptance;[2]

3. By the failure of the acceptor to fulfill a condition precedent to acceptance; or,

4. By the death or insanity of the proposer.[3]

[1] See last section.

[2] Beckwith v. Cheever, 1 *Fost.* [*N. H.*], 41; Peru v. Turner, 1 *Fairf.*, 185; Moxley v. Moxley, 2 *Metc.* [*Ky.*], 309.

[3] The Palo Alto, *Daveis*, 356.

Ratification of contract void for want of consent.

§ 773. A contract which is voidable solely[1] for want of due consent, may be ratified by a subsequent consent.[2]

[1] Gray v. Hook, 4 *N. Y.*, 449.

[2] Newton v. Bronson, 13 *N. Y.*, 595; Bronson v. Wiman, 8 *id.*, 188; see Sweetman v. Prince, 26 *id.*, 224.

Assumption of obligation by acceptance of benefits.

§ 774. A voluntary acceptance of the benefit of a transaction is equivalent to a consent to all the obligations arising from it, so far as the facts are known, or ought to be known, to the person accepting.

Bennett v. Judson, 21 *N. Y.*, 238.

CHAPTER IV.

OBJECT OF A CONTRACT.

§ 775. The object of a contract is the thing which it is agreed, on the part of the party receiving the consideration, to do or not to do. **Object, what.**

Martin *v.* McCormick, 8 *N. Y.*, 335.

§ 776. The object of a contract must be lawful when the contract is made, and possible[1] and ascertainable[2] by the time the contract is to be performed.[3] **Requisites of object.**

[1] *Code La.*, 1885, 1886. See Tufnell *v.* Constable, 7 *Ad. & El.*, 798; and note 4 to section 727. For a definition of the word "lawful," see Chapter IV of this Title.

[2] *Code La.*, 1880; Richards *v.* Edick, 17 *Barb.*, 260; Abeel *v.* Radcliff, 13 *Johns.*, 300; see Tracy *v.* Albany Exch. Co., 7 *N. Y.*, 474.

[3] Thus, an agreement to pay so much as a barrel of flour may be worth on a particular day, is a common and perfectly valid contract. So an agreement to pay so much as certain persons shall decide, is valid (Brown *v.* Bellows, 4 *Pick.*, 189).

§ 777. Everything is deemed possible, except that which is impossible in the nature of things. **Impossibility, what**

Impossibility is to be determined, not by the means or ability of the party, but by the nature of things (*Code La.*, 1885, 2028; see McNeill *v.* Reed, 9 *Bing.*, 68; Beebe *v.* Johnson, 19 *Wend.*, 500; Harmony *v.* Bingham, 12 *N. Y.*, 99; Warfield *v.* Watkins, 30 *Barb.*, 395; Tufnell *v.* Constable, 7 *Ad. & El.*, 798). Thus a promise to procure the assent of a third person, to any lawful and proper act is valid (Lloyd *v.* Crispe, 5 *Taunt.*, 249; McNeill *v.* Reed, 9 *Bing.*, 68).

§ 778. Where a contract has but a single object, and such object is unlawful,[1] whether in whole or in part,[2] or wholly impossible of performance,[3] or so **When contract wholly void.**

vaguely expressed as to be wholly unascertainable, the entire contract is void.

[1] See Smith *v.* Wilcox, 24 *N. Y.*, 353; Porter *v.* Havens, 37 *Barb.*, 343; Devlin *v.* Brady, 32 *id.*, 518.

[2] Brown *v.* Brown, 34 *Barb.*, 533; Hopkins *v.* Prescott, 4 *C. B.*, 578.

[3] See Faulkner *v.* Lowe, 2 *Exch.*, 595.

When contract partially void.

§ 779. Where a contract has several distinct objects, of which one at least is lawful, and one at least is unlawful in whole or in part, the contract is void as to the latter, and valid as to the rest.

See Bank of Australasia *v.* Bank of Australia, 6 *Moore P. C.*, 152; Leavitt *v.* Palmer, 3 *N. Y.*, 37; Chase's Ex'r *v.* Burkholder, 18 *Penn. St.*, 50; Kerrison *v.* Cole, 8 *East*, 236.

CHAPTER V.

CONSIDERATION.

Good consideration, what.

§ 780. Any benefit conferred,[1] or agreed to be conferred,[2] upon the promiser, by any other person,[3] to which the promiser is not lawfully entitled,[4] or any prejudice suffered,[5] or agreed to be suffered,[6] by such person,[7] other than such as he is at the time of consent lawfully bound to suffer,[8] as an inducement to the promiser, is a good consideration for a promise.

[1] Johnson *v.* Titus, 2 *Hill*, 606; Oakley *v.* Boorman, 27 *Wend.*, 588; see Hamilton College *v.* Stewart, 1 *N. Y.*, 581; Palmer *v.* North, 35 *Barb.*, 282. It is immaterial whether the benefit is small or great (Haigh *v.* Brooks, 10 *Ad. & El.*, 309; Johnston *v.* Nicholls, 1 *C. B.*, 251).

[3] Houghtailing *v.* Randen, 25 *Barb.*, 21; Sage *v.* Hazard, 6 *id.*, 179; Seaman *v.* Hasbrouck, 35 *id.*, 151; Briggs *v.* Tillotson, 8 *Johns.*, 304.

[3] Lawrence *v.* Fox, 20 *N. Y.*, 268; Judson *v.* Gray, 17 *How. Pr.*, 289, 296.

[4] Forbearance of a claim which the claimant knows to be totally unfounded, is no consideration (Wade *v.* Simeon, 2 *C. B.*, 548; Dolcher *v.* Fry, 37 *Barb.*, 152; Morey *v.* Newfane, 8 *id.*, 645). But forbearance of a claim in the least doubtful, made in good faith, even if unfounded, will support a promise (Crans *v.* Hunter, Ct. of Appeals, Jan., 1864; Russell *v.* Cook, 3 *Hill*, 504; Seaman *v.* Seaman, 12 *Wend.*, 381; Longridge *v.* Dorville, 5 *B. & Ald.*, 117). The fulfillment, at the request of A., of a promise previously made to B., has been held a sufficient consideration for a promise by A. (Scotson *v.* Pegg, 6 *H. & N.*, 295).

[5] Waydell *v.* Luer, 3 *Den.*, 410; Livingston *v.* Radcliff, 6 *Barb.*, 201; Miller *v.* Drake, 1 *Caines*, 45; Rutgers *v.* Lucet, 2 *Johns. Cas.*, 92; Parker *v.* Crane, 6 *Wend.*, 647; Stuart *v.* McGuin, 1 *Cow.*, 99; Elting *v.* Vanderlyn, 4 *Johns.*, 237; Smith *v.* Weed, 20 *Wend.*, 184; Heinman *v.* Moulton, 14 *Johns.*, 466; Hilliard *v.* Austin, 17 *Barb.*, 141.

[6] Decker *v.* Judson, 16 *N. Y.*, 449; Smith *v.* Algar, 1 *Barn. & Ad.*, 603; Conover *v.* Brush, 2 *N. Y. Leg. Obs.*, 289.

[7] Decker *v.* Judson, 16 *N. Y.*, 449.

[8] Livingston *v.* Rogers, 1 *Cai.*, 583; Utica & Syracuse R. R. *v.* Brinckerhoff, 21 *Wend.*, 139; Roscorla *v.* Thomas, 3 *Q. B.*, 234.

§ 781. An existing legal[1] obligation resting upon the promiser, or a moral obligation,[2] originating in some benefit conferred upon the promiser, or prejudice suffered by the promisee, is also a good consideration for a promise, to an extent corresponding with the extent of the obligation, but no further or otherwise.[3]

How far legal or moral obligation is a good consideration.

[1] Spencer *v.* Ballou, 18 *N. Y.*, 330.

[2] The common law does not recognize moral obligations, except in a few cases, as sufficient to sustain a promise (Nash *v.* Russell, 5 *Barb.*, 556; Geer *v.* Archer, 2 *Barb.*, 420; Watkins *v.* Halstead, 2 *Sandf.*, 311; Ehle *v.* Judson, 24 *Wend.*, 97; Smith *v.* Ware, 13 *Johns.*, 257; Beaumont *v.* Reeve, 8 *Q. B.*, 483; Eastwood *v.* Kenyon, 11 *Ad. & El.*, 438. But see to the contrary, Doty *v.* Brown, 14 *Johns.*, 381; Lee *v.* Muggeridge, 5 *Taunt.*, 36). The authorities, how-

ever, entirely fail to establish any satisfactory principle upon which to distinguish between the different species of moral obligations. Thus, in Bunn *v.* Winthrop (1 *Johns. Ch.*, 329), past seduction was held a good consideration to support a grant. In Beaumont *v.* Reeve (8 *Q. B.*, 483) the same consideration was held insufficient to support a promise. In Goulding *v.* Davidson (28 *Barb.*, 438), it is said that there must have been at some time an actual *legal* obligation. Yet in Rice *v.* Welling (5 *Wend.*, 595) and Early *v.* Mahon (19 *Johns.*, 147), the original contract was usurious, and therefore void from the beginning. The same may be said of promises to pay debts contracted in infancy, which are held valid. Goulding *v.* Davidson was reversed, 26 *N. Y.*, 604. The rule stated in the text seems to the commissioners to be just, and to be, on the whole, as easily reconcilable with the authorities in this state as any other that can be devised.

[3] Phetteplace *v.* Steere, 2 *Johns.*, 442; Roscorla *v.* Thomas, 3 *Q. B.*, 234; Hopkins *v.* Logan, 5 *M. & W.*, 247; Kaye *v.* Dutton, 8 *Scott N. R.*, 495, 502; S. C., Ray *v.* Dutton, 7 *Man. & G.*, 807; Elderton *v.* Emmens, 6 *C. B.*, 160; 13 *id.*, 495.

Consideration lawful.

§ 782. The consideration of a contract must be lawful, within the meaning of section 827.

Effect of its illegality.

§ 783. If any part of a single consideration for one or more objects, or of several considerations for a single object, is unlawful, the entire contract is void.

This principle is deducible from all the cases taken together, though not to be found thus stated in any one case. Thus there is no doubt that, if the consideration is single, or in other words indivisible, its partial illegality is fatal to the contract (Mills *v.* Mills, 36 *Barb.*, 474; Rose *v.* Truax, 21 *id.*, 361; Pepper *v.* Haight, 20 *id.*, 429; Barton *v.* Port Jackson Plankroad Co., 17 *id.*, 397; Burt *v.* Place, 8 *Cow.*, 431; see Brown *v.* Brown, 34 *Barb.*, 533; Porter *v.* Havens, 37 *id.*, 343). The limitations of the rule are conformable to the principle of sections 778 and 779.

Consideration executed or executory.

§ 784. A consideration may be executed or executory, in whole or in part. In so far as it is executory, it is subject to the provisions of chapter IV of this Title.

§ 785. When a consideration is executory, it is not indispensable that the contract should specify its amount or the means of ascertaining it.[1] It may be left to the decision of a third person,[2] or regulated by any specified standard.[3] Executory consideration.

[1] So held as to sales (Hoadly *v.* McLaine, 10 *Bing.*, 487; Joyce *v.* Swann, 17 *C. B.* [*N. S.*], 84.

[2] So held as to the price of goods sold (Brown *v.* Bellows, 4 *Pick.*, 189).

[3] There is perhaps no precedent for a general provision of this kind under the head of contracts. But finding it necessary to repeat the same section, almost word for word, under the various heads of Sale, Hire, Employment, Deposit, Carriage and Insurance, and perceiving no reason why it could work injustice if applied to other contracts, although in practice it probably is not needed for them, the commissioners have ventured to transfer it to this part of the Code; to which, they think, it properly belongs.

§ 786. When a contract does not determine the amount of the consideration, nor the method by which it is to be ascertained,[1] or when it leaves the amount thereof to the discretion of an interested party,[2] the consideration must be so much money as the object of the contract is reasonably worth. How ascertained.

[1] Hoadly *v.* McLaine, 10 *Bing.*, 487.

[2] Brown *v.* Bellows, 4 *Pick.*, 189.

§ 787. Where a contract provides an exclusive method by which its consideration is to be ascertained, which method is on its face impossible of execution, the entire contract is void. Effect of impossibility of ascertaining consideration.

Pothier on Sale, n. 24.

§ 788. Where a contract provides an exclusive method by which its consideration is to be ascertained, which method appears possible on its face, but in fact is, or becomes, impossible of execution, such provision only is void. Id.

Pothier (*Sale*, n. 24) holds that the contract in such case is voidable, and this view has been adopted by some writers in this country (*Story on Sales*, § 220; 1 *Pars.*

Cont., *5th ed.*, 525), but it seems more probable that the common law would regard the contract as made for a reasonable consideration, to be ascertained in any usual way. Thus, where a covenant to renew a lease provides for an arbitration to determine the rent, and no award is ever made, the court will enforce the renewal at a reasonable rent (Reformed Dutch Church *v.* Parkhurst, 4 *Bosw.*, 491; Dunnell *v.* Keteltas, 16 *Abb. Pr.*, 205)

TITLE II.

MANNER OF CREATING CONTRACTS.

Contracts express or implied.

§ 789. A contract is either express or implied.

Express contract, what.

§ 790. An express contract is one, the terms of which are stated in words.

Implied contract, what.

§ 791. An implied contract is one, the existence and terms of which are manifested by conduct.

The ordinary definition of an implied contract includes obligations imposed by law upon parties, as between each other. These obligations are, however, considered in another part of this Code.

What contracts may be oral.

§ 792. All contracts may be oral, except such as are specially required by statute to be in writing.

See Bank of Rochester *v.* Jones, 4 *N. Y.*, 497; Flory *v.* Denny, 7 *Exch.*, 581.

Contract not in writing through fraud, may be enforced

§ 793. Where a contract, which is required by law to be in writing, is prevented from being put into writing by the fraud of a party thereto, any other party who is by such fraud led to believe that it is in writing, and acts upon such belief to his prejudice, may enforce it against the fraudulent party. against fraudulent party.

Story Eq. Jur., § 768. This principle of equity ought to be recognized in all cases, whether legal or equitable.

§ 794. The following contracts, or some memorandum thereof, expressing[1] the parties,[2] their consent and the object of the contract,[3] must be in writing, subscribed by the party to be charged thereby, or by his agent for the purpose: What contracts must be written.

1. An agreement that, by its terms, cannot[4] be fully[5] performed within one year;[6]

2. An agreement made upon consideration of marriage, other than mutual promises to marry.[7]

[1] The consideration is no longer necessary to be stated (*Laws of* 1863, *ch.* 464). Such at least was the undoubted intention of the legislature, though under the decision in Wain *v.* Warlters (5 *East*, 10), it is difficult to say whether its intention is plainly expressed. The language here proposed is unmistakable in its meaning.

[2] The names of all the parties must be stated in the memorandum (Williams *v.* Lake, 2 *El. & El.*, 349).

[3] The whole object of the contract, and all its terms, must be expressed (Wright *v.* Weeks, 25 *N. Y.*, 153).

[4] The language of the statute is "is not to be," &c. It is construed as applying only to contracts which cannot possibly be executed within a year, under any contingency (Dresser *v.* Dresser, 35 *Barb.*, 573; Artcher *v.* Zeh, 5 *Hill*, 200; Plimpton *v.* Curtiss, 15 *Wend.*, 336; McLees *v.* Hale, 10 *id.*, 426; Moore *v.* Fox, 10 *Johns.*, 244. Compare Day *v.* N. Y. Central R. R., 31 *Barb.* 548; Pitkin *v.* Long Island R. R., 2 *Barb. Ch. R.*, 221; see Talmadge *v.* Rensselaer & Saratoga R. R., 13 *Barb.*, 593).

[5] Day *v.* N. Y. Central R. R., 31 *Barb.*, 548, 556; Amburger *v.* Marvin, 4 *E. D. Smith*, 393; Lockwood *v.* Barnes, 3 *Hill*, 128; Broadwell *v.* Getman, 2 *Den.*, 87; Bracegirdle *v.* Heald, 1 *Barn. & Ald.*, 722.

[6] The words "from the making thereof," are omitted in order to harmonize the rules in relation to contracts affecting both real and personal property, which are now governed by different provisions on this point (Young *v.* Dake, 5 *N. Y.*, 463; overruling Croswell *v.* Crane, 7 *Barb.*, 191.) The commissioners think, moreover, that the strictness of this provision has

worked injustice. Few yearly contracts go into effect instantly.

[7] 2 *R. S.*, 135, § 2.

Effect of writing.

§ 795. The execution of a contract in writing, whether the law requires it to be written or not, supersedes all the oral negotiations or stipulations concerning its matter, which preceded or accompanied the execution of the instrument.

Baker *v.* Higgins, 21 *N. Y.*, 396; Lamatt *v.* Hudson Riv. Ins. Co., 17 *N. Y.*, 199 *n.*; Durgin *v.* Ireland, 14 *N. Y.*, 322; as explained in Blossom *v.* Griffin, 13 *N. Y.*, 573. To same effect, Gridley *v.* Dole, 4 *N. Y.*, 486; Witbeck *v.* Waine, 16 *id.*, 532; Lewis *v.* Jones, 7 *Bosw.*, 366.

Contract in writing takes effect, when.

§ 796. A contract in writing takes effect upon its delivery to the party in whose favor it is made, or to his agent.

Verplank *v.* Sterry, 12 *Johns.*, 536; compare Elsey *v.* Metcalf, 1 *Den.*, 323.

Provisions of chapter on transfers of real property.

§ 797. The provisions of the chapter on TRANSFERS IN GENERAL, concerning the delivery of grants, absolute and conditional, apply to all written contracts.

Seal, what.

§ 798. A corporate[1] or official[2] seal may be affixed to an instrument by a mere impression upon the paper or other material on which such instrument is written. All other seals must be affixed by means of an impression upon a tenacious substance fastened to the instrument.[3]

[1] 3 *R. S.* (*5th ed.*), 687; *Laws* 1848, *ch.* 197.

[2] 2 *R. S.*, 276, 404.

[3] Warren *v.* Lynch, 5 *Johns.*, 239; Andrews *v.* Herriot, 4 *Cow.*, 508; Farmers & Mfrs. Bank *v.* Haight, 3 *Hill*, 493; Bank of Rochester *v.* Gray, 2 *id.*, 227; but see to the contrary Ross *v.* Bedell, 5 *Duer*, 462; Curtis *v.* Leavitt, 17 *Barb.*, 309.

Effect of seal.

§ 799. A seal is presumptive evidence of a consideration.

Whether a seal was, at common law, evidence of a consideration, or whether it was regarded as dispensing with the necessity of any consideration, actual or implied, and as imparting validity to a contract upon entirely different grounds, may be doubtful. It is certain that all the effect which it now has, under our statute (2 *R. S.* 406, § 77), is that which is here stated.

TITLE III.

INTERPRETATION OF CONTRACTS.

§ 800. All contracts, whether public or private, sealed or unsealed, are to be interpreted by the same rules; except as otherwise provided by this Code. Uniformity of interpretation.

Some distinctions are made at common law, which have no substantial foundation in reason. Thus an instrument under seal, signed by an agent in his own name, does not bind his principal (Townsend *v.* Hubbard, 4 *Hill*, 351; Townsend *v.* Corning, 23 *Wend.*, 435; Berkley *v.* Hardy, 5 *B. & C.*, 355), though a contract not under seal, signed in this manner, would bind him (Stanton *v.* Camp, 4 *Barb.*, 274; see Evans *v.* Wells, 22 *Wend.*, 324; Townsend *v.* Hubbard, 4 *Hill*, 351). In Connecticut, this technical distinction does not exist (Magill *v.* Hinsdale, 6 *Conn.*, 464).

Contracts, how to be interpreted.

§ 801. A contract must be so interpreted as to give effect to the mutual[1] intention of the parties,[2] as it existed at the time of contracting,[3] so far as the same is ascertainable and lawful.

[1] The intention of *both* parties must be considered (Briggs *v.* Vanderbilt, 19 *Barb.*, 222, 240).

[2] Belmont *v.* Coman, 22 *N. Y.*, 439; Platt *v.* Lott, 17 *id.*, 478.

[3] *Story Cont.*, § 656; Liddle *v.* Market Fire Ins. Co., 4 *Bosw.*, 179.

Intention of parties, how ascertained.

§ 802. For the purpose of ascertaining the intention of the parties to a contract, if otherwise doubtful, the rules given in this chapter are to be applied.

All rules give way if the intention of the parties is clearly manifested in opposition to them (Platt *v.* Lott, 17 *N. Y.*, 478). The admission of oral evidence is regulated by the CODE OF CIVIL PROCEDURE; and, subject to the rules of evidence, there can be no doubt of the correctness of this proposition. Prof. Parsons (*Contracts*, *5th ed.*, vol. ii., 494) maintains, at some length, that the intention of the parties does not always control the interpretation of a contract, but it will be found that the cases which he cites in support of his views turn upon rules of evidence.

Intention to be ascertained from language.

§ 803. The language of a contract is to govern its interpretation,[1] if the language is clear and explicit, and does not involve an absurdity.[2]

[1] *Code La.*, 1940; see Westcott *v.* Thompson, 18 *N. Y.*, 367; Norton *v.* Woodruff, 2 *id.*, 153.

[2] Buck *v.* Burk, 18 *N. Y.*, 339.

Interpretation of written contract.

§ 804. When a contract is reduced to writing, the intention of the parties is to be ascertained from the writing alone, if possible; subject, however, to the other provisions of this Title.

Westcott *v.* Thompson, 18 *N. Y.*, 367.

Writing, when disregarded.

§ 805. When through fraud,[1] mistake, or accident,[2] a written contract fails to express the real intention of the parties, such intention is to be regarded, and the erroneous parts of the writing disregarded.[3]

[1] De Peyster *v.* Hasbrouck, 11 *N. Y.*, 582.

[2] Wood *v.* Hubbell, 10 *N. Y.*, 479; Gillespie *v.* Moon, 2 *Johns. Ch.*, 585; *Story Eq. Jur.*, § 152.

[3] Under the Code of Procedure, it is not necessary that the contract should be reformed, but it should be construed according to the actual intent of the parties (See Bidwell *v.* Astor Ins. Co., 16 *N. Y.*, 263; N. Y. Ice Co. *v.* N. W. Ins. Co., 12 *Abb. Pr.*, 414; 23 *N. Y.*, 357; see also Burr *v.* Broadway Ins. Co., 16 *N. Y.*, 267). The proof must be clear (Coles *v.* Bowne, 10 *Paige*, 526; Lyman *v.* Mut. Ins. Co., 2 *Johns. Ch.*, 630; affirmed, 17 *Johns.*, 373); but this is a rule of evidence, not necessary to be stated here.

Effect to be given to every part of contract.

§ 806. The whole of a contract is to be taken together, so as to give effect to every part,[1] if reasonably practicable,[2] each clause helping to interpret the others.[3]

[1] *Code La.*, 1950; *Code Napoleon*, 1161; Ward *v.* Whitney, 8 *N. Y.*, 446; Decker *v.* Furniss, 14 *id.*, 615, 622; Hamilton *v.* Taylor, 18 *id.*, 358; Richards *v.* Warring, 39 *Barb.*, 42; James *v.* Tallent, 5 *B. & Ald.*, 889; Barton *v.* Fitzgerald, 15 *East*, 541; see Simonds *v.* Hodgson, 3 *B. & Ad.*, 50. The recitals of a deed may restrict general words in its operative part (Simons *v.* Johnson, 3 *B. & Ad.*, 175; Solly *v.* Forbes, 2 *Brod. & B.*, 38; Payler *v.* Homersham, 4 *M. & Selw.*, 423; Lampon *v.* Corke, 5 *B. & Ald.*, 606; Bell *v.* Bruen, 1 *How.* [*U. S.*], 184; Lawrence *v.* M'Calmont, 2 *id.*, 449).

[2] Westcott *v.* Thompson, 18 *N. Y.*, 363.

[3] Miller *v.* Travers, 8 *Bing.*, 244; *Story Cont.*, § 657; see Aikin *v.* Western R. R. Co., 20 *N. Y.*, 370; Heywood *v.* Perrin, 10 *Pick.*, 228; Gray *v.* Clark, 11 *Verm.*, 583; Merrill *v.* Gore, 29 *Me.*, 346; Sicklemore *v.* Thistleton, 6 *M. & Selw.*, 9.

Several contracts when taken together.

§ 807. Several contracts relating to the same matters, between the same parties, and made as parts of substantially one transaction, are to be taken together.

Hamilton *v.* Taylor, 18 *N. Y.*, 358; Church *v.* Brown, 21 *N. Y.*, 319, 330; Pepper *v.* Haight, 20 *Barb.*, 429. The same rule applies to deeds (Huttemeier *v.* Albro, 18 *N. Y.*, 48; Wright *v.* Douglass, 7 *id.*, 574). Contracts between different parties (Craig *v.* Wells, 11 *N. Y.*, 315), or relating to different matters (Cornell *v.* Todd, 2 *Denio*, 130), or not forming part of one transaction (Mann *v.* Witbeck, 17 *Barb.*, 388), cannot be taken together.

Interpretation in favor of contract.

§ 808. A contract must receive such an interpretation as will make it lawful,[1] operative,[2] definite,[3] reasonable,[4] and capable of being carried into effect, if it can be done without violating the intention of the parties.[5]

[1] *Co. Litt.* 42; 2 *Blacks. Com.*, 380; *Chit. Cont.* (*4th ed.*), 80; Sterry *v.* Clifton, 9 *C. B.*, 110; Harrington *v.* Kloprogge, 4 *Doug.*, 5; see Clark *v.* Pinney, 7 *Cow.*, 681; Shore *v.* Wilson, 9 *Clark & F.*, 397.

[2] Richards *v.* Warring, 39 *Barb.*, 42; Archibald *v.* Thomas, 3 *Cow.*, 284; Boyd *v.* Moyle, 2 *C. B.*, 644; Russell *v.* Phillips, 14 *Q. B.*, 891; Pollock *v.* Stacy, 9 *id.*, 1033; Brown *v.* Slater, 16 *Conn.*, 192; Broom *v.* Batchelor, 1 *Hurlst. & N.*, 255; Mare *v.* Charles, 5 *El. & Bl.*, 978; *Code Napoleon*, 1157.

[3] See Casler *v.* Conn. Mut. Ins. Co., 22 *N. Y.*, 427.

[4] Buck *v.* Burk, 18 *N. Y.*, 337; Braunstein *v.* Accidental Death Ins. Co., 1 *Best & Smith*, 782; Jones *v.* Gibbons, 8 *Exch.*, 922; Dallman *v.* King, 4 *Bing. N. C.*, 105. See Thomas *v.* Fleury, 26 *N. Y.*, 26, in which it was held that a condition requiring a certain architect's certificate, before payment could be demanded, was waived by an *unreasonable* refusal of such certificate.

[5] The language of a contract cannot be perverted, in order to make it lawful (see Porter *v.* Havens, 37 *Barb.*, 343; Mayor of Norwich *v.* Norfolk Railway Co., 4 *El. & Bl.*, 397); nor can an unreasonable stipulation be rejected, if it was clearly the intention of the parties that it should be a part of the contract (Stadhard *v.* Lee, 3 *Best & Sm.*, 364).

Words to be understood in usual sense.

§ 809. The words of a contract are to be understood in their ordinary and popular sense,[1] rather than according to their strict legal meaning;[2] unless used by the parties in a technical sense, or unless a special meaning is given to them by usage,[3] in which case the latter must be followed.

[1] *Story Cont.*, § 647; *Code La.*, 1941; see Casler *v.* Conn. Mut. Ins. Co., 22 *N. Y.*, 427.

[2] See Schenck *v.* Campbell, 11 *Abb. Pr.*, 292; Schuylkill Nav. Co. *v.* Moore, 2 *Whart.*, 491. To the contrary, see Rawlinson *v.* Clarke, 14 *M. & W.*, 187. "Insolvency," even in a state which has an insolvent law, is construed to mean simple inability to pay debts, and not technical insolvency under the statute (Biddlecombe *v.* Bond, 4 *Ad. & El.*, 332; Parker *v.* Gossage, 2 *Cr. M. & R.*, 617).

[3] Smith *v.* Wilson, 3 *B. & Ad.*, 728; see Hinton *v.* Locke, 5 *Hill*, 437; Astor *v.* Union Ins. Co., 7 *Cow.*, 202; Miller *v.* Tetherington, 6 *H. & N.*, 278; Cuth-

bert *v.* Cumming, 11 *Exch.*, 405; affirming 10 *id.*, 809; Coit *v.* Corn Ins. Co., 7 *Johns.*, 385; Clife *v.* Schwabe, 3 *C. B.*, 469.

§ 810. Technical words are to be interpreted as usually understood by persons in the profession or business to which they relate, unless clearly used in a different sense.

Technical words.

Code La., 1942; Dana *v.* Fiedler, 12 *N. Y.*, 40. This is another, and, it is thought, a better form of the maxim, that "technical words are to be taken in their technical sense" (see Worthington *v.* Gimson, 2 *El. & El.*, 618; 6 *Jur.*, [*N. S.*] 1053. A contrary intention will however prevail (Taylor *v.* Caldwell, 3 *Best & Sm.*, 832; James *v.* Plant, 4 *Ad. & El.*, 749; see Doe *d.* Hickman *v.* Haslewood, 6 *id.*, 167).

§ 811. A contract is to be interpreted according to the law and usage of the place where it is to be performed;[1] or, if it does not indicate a place of performance, according to the law and usage of the place where it is made.[2]

Law of place.

[1] *Story Confl. Laws*, §§ 270, 280; Everett *v.* Vendryes, 19 *N. Y.*, 436; Curtis *v.* Leavitt, 15 *id.*, 9; Bowen *v.* Newell, 13 *id.*, 290; Jacks *v.* Nichols, 5 *id.*, 178; Cutler *v.* Wright, 22 *id.*, 480.

[2] *Story Confl. Laws*, § 282; Thompson *v.* Ketcham, 8 *Johns.*, 189; Pomeroy *v.* Ainsworth, 22 *Barb.*, 118, 130; Curtis *v.* Leavitt, 15 *N. Y.*, 9; Gibbs *v.* Fremont, 9 *Exch.*, 25.

§ 812. A contract may be explained by reference to the circumstances under which it was made,[1] and the matter to which it relates.[2]

Contract explained by circumstances.

[1] Westcott *v.* Thompson, 18 *N. Y.*, 363; Blossom *v.* Griffin, 13 *id.*, 569; Moore *v.* Meacham, 10 *id.*, 207; Doolittle *v.* Southworth, 3 *Barb.*, 79; Hasbrook *v.* Paddock, 1 *id.*, 635; Turner *v.* Evans, 2 *El. & Bl.*, 512; see Schenck *v.* Campbell, 11 *Abb. Pr.*, 292.

[2] Peacock *v.* N. Y. Life Ins. Co., 20 *N. Y.*, 293, 296; French *v.* Carhart, 1 *id.*, 96; Rex *v.* Mashiter, 6 *Ad. & El.*, 153; 1 *Nev. & P.*, 326.

§ 813. However broad may be the terms of a contract, it extends only to those things concerning which it appears that the parties intended to contract.

Contract restricted to its evident object.

Code La., 1954; *Code Napoleon*, 1163; see Platt *v.* Lott, 17 *N. Y.*, 478; Lyall *v.* Edwards, 6 *H. & N.*, 337;

Jackson *v.* Stackhouse, 1 *Cow.*, 122; Rich *v.* Lord, 18 *Pick.*, 325; Simons *v.* Johnson, 3 *B. & Ad.*, 175; Payler *v.* Homersham, 4 *M. & Selw.*, 423.

Interpretation in sense in which promiser believed promisee to rely.

§ 814. If the terms of a promise are in any respect ambiguous or uncertain, it must be interpreted in the sense in which the promiser believed, at the time of making it, that the promisee understood it.

Barlow *v.* Scott, 24 *N. Y.*, 40; see Mowatt *v.* Londesborough, 3 *El. & Bl.*, 307; per CAMPBELL, C. J., Wheelton *v.* Hardisty, 8 *id.*, 284.

Particular clause subordinate to general intent.

§ 815. Particular clauses of a contract are subordinate to its general intent.

Decker *v.* Furniss, 14 *N. Y.*, 615; Kelley *v.* Upton, 5 *Duer*, 340; London Gaslight Co. *v.* Chelsea, 8 *C. B.* [*N. S.*], 215; see Ringer *v.* Cann, 3 *M. & W.*, 343.

Contract partly written and partly printed.

§ 816. Where a contract is partly written and partly printed, or where part of it is written or printed under the special directions of the parties, and with a special view to their intention, and the remainder is copied from a form originally prepared without special reference to the particular parties and the particular contract in question, the written parts control the printed parts,[1] and the parts which are purely original control those which are copied from a form.[2] And if the two are absolutely repugnant, the latter must be so far disregarded.

[1] Harper *v.* N. Y. City Ins. Co., 22 *N. Y.*, 444; Harper *v.* Albany Ins. Co., 17 *id.*, 198; Woodruff *v.* Coml. Mut. Ins. Co., 2 *Hilt.*, 122; see People *v.* Saxton, 22 *N. Y.*, 309.

[2] This is the real principle of the foregoing decisions. Printing is only evidence that the contract was partly formal, and partly original.

Repugnancies, how reconciled.

§ 817. Repugnancy in a contract must be reconciled, if possible, by such an interpretation as will give some effect to the repugnant clauses,[1] subordinate to the general intent and purpose of the whole contract.[2]

[1] *Code La.*, 1940; Ward *v.* Whitney, 8 *N. Y.*, 446.

[2] Casler *v.* Conn. Ins. Co., 22 *N. Y.*, 425; see Harper *v.* N. Y. City Ins. Co., *id.*, 441.

§ 818. Words in a contract which are wholly inconsistent with its nature,[1] or with the main intention of the parties,[2] are to be rejected. Inconsistent words rejected.

[1] Mills *v.* Wright, 1 *Freem.*, 247; Simpson *v.* Vaughan, 2 *Atk.*, 32; Vernon *v.* Alsop, *T. Raym.*, 68; *Story Cont.*, §§ 635, 636, 660; Stockton *v.* Turner, 7 *J. J. Marsh.*, 192; see Buck *v.* Burk, 18 *N. Y.*, 337.

[2] Dallman *v.* King, 4 *Bing. N. C.*, 105; see Rex *v.* Erminster, 6 *Ad. & El.*, 598.

§ 819. In cases of uncertainty not removed by the preceding rules,[1] the language of a contract should be interpreted most strongly against the party who caused the uncertainty to exist.[2] The promiser is presumed to be such party;[3] except in a contract between a public officer or body, as such, and a private party, in which it is presumed that all uncertainty was caused by the private party.[4] Words to be taken most strongly against whom.

[1] This rule is to be resorted to only when all others fail (Hargreave *v.* Smee, 6 *Bing.*, 244; *Chit. Cont.* [*4th ed.*], 95; see Browning *v.* Wright, 2 *Bos. & Pul.*, 22; Barton *v.* Fitzgerald, 15 *East*, 546).

[2] *Code La.*, 1952, 1953. See Harper *v.* N. Y. City Ins. Co., 22 *N. Y.*, 441; Marvin *v.* Stone, 2 *Cow.*, 781. For the proper limits to the use of the word "ambiguity," see Ashworth *v.* Mounsey, 9 *Exch.*, 186.

[3] See Rindge *v.* Judson, 24 *N. Y.*, 64; Braunstein *v.* Accidental Death Ins. Co., 1 *Best & Smith*, 782, 799; Richards *v.* Warring, 39 *Barb.*, 42.

[4] Stourbridge Canal Co. *v.* Wheeley, 2 *B. & Ad.*, 792; Priestley *v.* Foulds, 2 *Man. & Gr.*, 194; Jackson *v.* Reeves, 3 *Cai.*, 293, 303; Blakemore *v.* Glamorgan Canal Co., 1 *Myl. & K.*, 154, 162; Hull Dock Co. *v.* La Marche, 8 *B. & C.*, 42, 52; Leeds & Liv. Canal Co. *v.* Hustler, 1 *id.*, 424; Parker *v.* Gt. Western Railw. Co., 7 *M. & G.*, 253, 288; Barrett *v.* Stockton, &c., Railw. Co., 2 *id.*, 134; Gildart *v.* Gladstone, 11 *East*, 675, 685; see Mohawk Bridge Co. *v.* Utica & Schen. R. R. Co., 6 *Paige*, 554.

§ 820. Stipulations which are necessary to make a contract reasonable,[1] or conformable to usage,[2] are implied, in respect to matters concerning which the contract manifests no contrary intention.[3] Reasonable stipulations, when implied.

[1] Jones *v.* Gibbons, 8 *Exch.*, 922; Buck *v.* Burk, 18 *N. Y.*, 337; see Thomas *v.* Fleury, 26 *N. Y.*, 26.

[2] Field *v.* Lelean, 6 *H. & N.*, 617; Pollock *v.* Stables, 12 *Q. B.*, 765; Bayliffe *v.* Butterworth, 1 *Exch.*, 425;

Syers *v.* Jonas, 2 *id.*, 116; Hutton *v.* Warren, 1 *M. & W.*, 475: Humfrey *v.* Dale, 7 *E. & B.*, 266; Dale *v.* Humfrey, *El. B. & El.*, 1004; Brown *v.* Byrne, 3 *E. & B.*, 703.

[3] Mutual Ins. Co. *v.* Hone, 2 *N. Y.*, 241; Vail *v.* Rice, 5 *id.*, 155; Hutton *v.* Warren, 1 *M. & W.*, 475; see Suse *v.* Pompe, 8 *C. B.* [*N. S.*], 538. A stipulation which is clearly in accordance with the intention of the parties must be enforced, though ever so unreasonable (Stadhard *v.* Lee, 3 *Best & Sm.*, 364). A stipulation which cannot be misunderstood, *e. g.*, for the payment of a certain sum of money, cannot be modified by proof of a usage to accept a smaller sum in satisfaction (St. Nicholas Ins. Co. *v.* Mercantile Ins. Co., 5 *Bosw.*, 246).

Necessary incidents implied.

§ 821. All things that in law or usage are considered as incidental to a contract, or as necessary to carry it into effect, are implied therefrom;[1] unless some of them are expressly mentioned therein, when all other things of the same class are deemed to be excluded.[2]

[1] *Code Napoleon*, 1160; Lampman *v.* Milks, 21 *N. Y.*, 505; Huttemeier *v.* Albro, 18 *id.*, 48; Kelsey *v.* Durkee, 33 *Barb.*, 410.

[2] *Co. Litt.*, 210 *a.*; Hare *v.* Horton, 5 *B. & Ad.*, 715; Rex *v.* Sedgley, 2 *id.*, 65; Line *v.* Stephenson, 4 *Bing. N C.*, 678; 5 *id.*, 183; Cook *v.* Jennings, 7 *T. R.*, 381.

Time of performance of contract.

§ 822. If no time is specified for the performance of an act required to be performed, a reasonable time is allowed.[1] If the act is in its nature capable of being done instantly,[2] as for example, if it consists in the payment of money only,[3] it must be performed immediately upon the thing to be done being exactly ascertained.[4]

[1] Atwood *v.* Emery, 1 *C. B.* (*N. S.*), 110; Hoggins *v.* Gordon, 3 *Q. B.*, 466; Sansom *v.* Rhodes, 6 *Bing. N. C.*, 261; 8 *Scott*, 244; Stavart *v.* Eastwood, 11 *M. & W.*, 197; see Thomas *v.* Dickinson, 12 *N. Y.*, 369; Terwilliger *v.* Knapp, 2 *E. D. Smith*, 86. No more than a reasonable time is allowed (see Cross *v.* Beard, 26 *N. Y.*, 85).

[2] Van Boskerck *v.* Mott, Supreme Ct., 1864; see Des Arts *v.* Leggett, 16 *N. Y.*, 588.

[3] Lake Ontario R. R. *v.* Mason, 16 *N. Y.*, 451; Purdy *v.* Philips, 11 *N. Y.*, 406; Wright *v.* Whiting, 40 *Barb.*, 235; Thompson *v.* Ketcham, 8 *Johns.*, 189; Gibbs *v* Southam, 5 *B. & Ad.*, 911.

[4] Penn. Coal Co. *v.* Del. & Hudson Canal Co., 29 *Barb.*, 589; affirmed in Court of Appeals.

§ 823. Time is never considered as of the essence of a contract, unless by its terms expressly so provided. Time, when of essence.

This provision is new. As to the present law upon the subject, see *Story Eq. Jur.*, § 776. It is involved in so much difficulty, that the commissioners deem it wise to adopt this more stringent rule.

§ 824. Where all the parties who unite in a promise receive some benefit from the consideration, whether past or present, their promise is presumed to be joint and several. When contract joint and several.

Yorks *v.* Peck, 14 *Barb.*, 644; Hunt *v.* Rousmanier, 8 *Wheat.*, 174.

§ 825. A promise, made in the singular number, but executed by several persons, is presumed to be joint and several. Id.

Van Alstyne *v.* Van Slyck, 10 *Barb.*, 383; Hemmenway *v.* Stone, 7 *Mass.*, 58.

§ 826. An executed contract is one, the object of which is fully performed. All others are executory. Executed and executory contracts, what.

Fletcher *v.* Peck, 6 *Cranch*, 136.

TITLE IV.

UNLAWFUL CONTRACTS.

§ 827. That is not lawful which is: What is unlawful.

1. Contrary to an express provision of law;[1]

2. Contrary to the policy of express law, though not expressly prohibited;[2] or,

3. Otherwise contrary to good morals.[3]

[1] The law makes no distinction in this respect between *malum prohibitum* and *malum in se* (Pennington *v.* Townsend, 7 *Wend.*, 276; Leavitt *v.* Palmer, 3 *N. Y.*, 19; De Groot *v.* Van Duzer, 20 *Wend.*, 390; Pratt *v.* Adams, 7 *Paige*, 653; Seneca Co. Bk. *v.* Lamb, 26 *Barb.*, 595).

[2] Bell *v.* Leggett, 7 *N. Y.*, 176, 181; Gray *v.* Hook, 4 *N. Y.*, 449.

[3] Lady Cox's Case, 3 *Peere Wms.*, 339; Walker *v.* Perkins, 3 *Burr.*, 1568; Gray *v.* Matthias, 5 *Ves.*, 291; see Trovinger *v.* McBurney, 5 *Cow.*, 253; Wait *v.* Day, 4 *Den.*, 446. The law does not avoid acts merely dishonorable or discreditable (Moore *v.* Remington, 34 *Barb.*, 427).

Certain contracts unlawful.

§ 828. All contracts which have for their object, directly or indirectly, to exempt any one from responsibility for his own fraud, or willful injury to the person or property of another, or violation of law, whether willful or negligent, are against the policy of the law.

See Smith *v.* N. Y. Central R. R., 24 *N. Y.*, 222; Perkins *v.* Same, *id.*, 213.

Penalties void.

§ 829. Penalties imposed by contract for any nonperformance thereof, are void.[1] But this section does not render void such bonds or obligations, penal in form, as have heretofore been commonly used; it merely rejects and avoids the penal clauses.

[1] See Lampman *v.* Cochran, 16 *N. Y.*, 275; Dennis *v.* Cummins, 3 *Johns. Cas.*, 297; Spear *v.* Smith, 1 *Den.* 464; Richards *v.* Edick, 17 *Barb.*, 260; Mills *v.* Fox, 4 *E. D. Smith*, 220; Beale *v.* Hayes, 5 *Sandf.*, 640.

Contract fixing damages, void.

§ 830. Every contract, by which the amount of damage to be paid, or other compensation to be made, for a breach of an obligation, is determined in anticipation thereof, is to that extent void, except as expressly provided by the next section.

Exception.

§ 831. The parties to a contract may agree therein upon an amount which shall be presumed to be the amount of damage sustained by a breach thereof, when, from the nature of the case, it would be impracticable or extremely difficult to fix the actual damage.

The use of the phrase "liquidated damages" leads frequently to an evasion of the law in respect to penalties. The courts, not venturing to declare such contracts void, constantly discourage them. They are oppressive and unconscientious, except in the cases permitted above, and ought not to be allowed. The restrictions imposed by this section are, however, new (see Bagley *v.* Peddie, 16 *N. Y.*, 469; Lampman *v.* Cochran, *id.*, 275).

Restraints upon legal proceedings.

§ 832. Every stipulation or condition in a contract, by which any party thereto is restricted from enforcing his rights under the contract by the usual legal proceedings in the ordinary tribunals, or which limits the time within which he may thus enforce his rights, is void.

The first part of this section is acknowledged law. A covenant in a contract, not to sue for a breach thereof, is void. The latter provision is new. The question involved has been variously decided in different tribunals, with a preponderance of opinion in favor of the right to limit the time of commencing actions, as a matter of law, but with frequent disapprobation of the practice. In support of the right, see Fullam *v.* N. Y. Ins. Co., 7 *Gray*, 6; Brown *v.* Roger Wms. Ins. Co., 5 *R. I.*, 394; North Western Ins. Co. *v.* Phœnix O. & C. Co., 31 *Penn. St.*, 448; Portage Ins. Co. *v.* West, 6 *Ohio St.*, 599; Wilson *v.* Ætna Ins. Co., 27 *Verm.*, 99; also Ames *v.* N. Y. Ins. Co., 14 *N. Y.*, 266. Against it, see Eagle Ins. Co. *v.* Lafayette Ins. Co., 9 *Ind.*, 443; French *v.* Lafayette Ins. Co., 5 *McLean*, 461. The law itself, and the law alone, should regulate the limitations of actions.

Contract in restraint of trade void.

§ 833. Every contract by which any one is restrained from exercising a lawful profession, trade or business of any kind, otherwise than as provided by the next two sections, is to that extent void.

Contracts in restraint of trade have been allowed, by modern decisions, to a very dangerous extent. In Dunlop *v.* Gregory (10 *N. Y.*, 241), a contract not to run a certain steamboat above Saugerties, on the Hudson, was enforced, although there was no sale of a good will, nor any circumstance to justify the contract, except that it was made upon a sale of the vessel by an association of persons who had previously used it to run above Saugerties, and wished to avoid competition. In Whittaker *v.* Howe (3 *Beav.*, 387), a contract not to practice law anywhere in England, was specifically enforced. Such a contract manifestly tends to enforce idleness, and deprives the state of the services of its citizens.

Exception in favor of sale of good will.

§ 834. One who sells the good will of a business may agree with the buyer to refrain from carrying on a similar business within a specified county, so long as the buyer, or any person deriving title to the good will from him, carries on a like business therein.

The district, within which a party may exclude himself from carrying on business, should be accurately defined by law; and no division of the state appears to the commissioners to be more reasonable or convenient, for this purpose, than a county. And no one should be allowed to prevent another from carrying on a business, unless he himself provides the public with the same advantages, in the same county.

Exception in favor of partnership arrangements.

§ 835. Partners may, upon or in anticipation of a dissolution of the partnership, agree that none of them will carry on a similar business within the same city or town where the partnership business has been transacted, or within a specified part thereof.

An agreement of this description, operating equally upon all the partners, gives to all an opportunity to start anew in business upon equal terms. In such cases, an agreement excluding them all from the *county*, would be too broad. It may even be doubted whether "ward" should not be substituted for "city" in the text.

Contract in restraint of marriage void.

§ 836. Every contract in restraint of the marriage of any person, other than a minor, is void.

Contracts in general restraint of marriage are certainly void (Lowe *v.* Peers, 4 *Burr.*, 2225; Hartley *v.* Rice, 10 *East*, 22; Baker *v.* White, 2 *Vern.*, 215; Sterling *v.* Sinnickson, 2 *South.*, 756; see Conrad *v.* Williams, 6 *Hill*, 444). Perhaps a contract, simply in restraint of remarriage of the wife of one of the parties, would be held valid, in analogy to the rule concerning wills; but experience has shown that such stipulations tend to immorality. Restraints upon the marriage of minors are promotive of prudence, without being burdensome.

TITLE V.

EXTINCTION OF CONTRACTS.

CHAPTER I.

CONTRACTS, HOW EXTINGUISHED.

§ 837. A contract may be extinguished in like manner with any other obligation, and also in the manner prescribed by this Title. Contract, how extinguished.

See Title III, of Part I, of this Division.

CHAPTER II.

RESCISSION.

§ 838. A contract is extinguished by its rescission. Rescission extinguishes contract.

§ 839. A party to a contract may rescind the same in the following cases only: When party may rescind.

1. If the consent of the party rescinding, or of any party jointly contracting with him,[1] was given by mistake, or obtained through duress, menace, fraud or undue influence, exercised by or with the connivance of the party as to whom he rescinds, or of any other party to the contract jointly interested with such party;

2. If, through the fault of the party as to whom he rescinds,[2] the consideration for his obligation fails, in whole or in part;[3]

3. If such consideration becomes entirely void[4] from any cause;[5]

4. If such consideration, before it is rendered to him, fails in a material respect, from any cause;[6] or,

5. By consent of all the other parties.[7]

[1] City Bank of Columbus *v.* Bruce, 17 *N. Y.*, 514.

[2] Sherman *v.* White, *How. App. Cas.*, 29; Winter *v.* Livingston, 13 *Johns.*, 54.

[3] Petry *v.* Christy, 19 *Johns.*, 53; see Duncan *v.* Edgerton, 6 *Bosw.*, 36; Morange *v.* Morris, 34 *Barb.*, 311.

[4] Harmon *v.* Bird, 22 *Wend.*, 113.

[5] Head *v.* Stevens, 19 *Wend.*, 411; Cross *v.* Huntley, 13 *id.*, 386; Putnam *v.* Westcott, 19 *Johns.*, 73; Tappen *v.* Van Wagenen, 3 *Johns.*, 465.

[6] Benedict *v.* Field, 16 *N. Y.*, 595. Perhaps this rule is at present confined to executory contracts (see Des Arts *v.* Leggett, 16 *N. Y.*, 582, 589.)

[7] James *v.* Cotton, 7 *Bing.*, 266. Such consent is implied from a refusal or disability on the part of the other party to perform on his part (Withers *v* Reynolds, 2 *B. & Ad.*, 882; see Fletcher *v.* Button, 4 *N. Y.*, 396; Lawrence *v.* Taylor, 5 *Hill*, 107; Van Benthuysen *v.* Crapser, 8 *Johns.*, 257; Prickett *v.* Badger, 1 *C. B.* [*N. S.*], 296; De Bernardy *v.* Harding, 8 *Exch.*, 822).

When stipulations against right to rescind do not defeat it

§ 840. A stipulation that errors of description shall not avoid a contract, or shall be the subject of compensation, or both, does not take away the right of rescission for fraud, nor for mistake, where such mistake is in a matter essential to the inducement of the contract,[1] and is not capable of exact and entire compensation.[2]

[1] Robinson *v.* Musgrave, 8 *Carr. & P.*, 469; Dobell *v.* Hutchinson, 3 *Ad. & El.*, 355.

[2] Sherwood *v.* Robbins, 3 *Carr. & P.*, 339.

Rescission, how effected

§ 841. Rescission, when not effected by consent, can be accomplished only by the use, on the part of the party rescinding, of reasonable diligence[1] to comply with the following rules:

1. He must rescind promptly,[2] upon discovering the facts which entitle him to rescind,[3] if he is free from duress, menace, undue influence,[4] or disability, and is aware of his right to rescind;[5] and,

2. He must restore[6] to the other party everything[7] of value[8] which he has received from him under the contract;[9] or must offer[10] to restore the same, upon condition that such party shall do likewise, unless the latter is unable,[11] or positively refuses, to do so.

[1] Ladd *v.* Moore, 3 *Sandf.*, 589.

[2] Fisher *v.* Fredenhall, 21 *Barb.*, 82; Wheaton *v.* Baker, 14 *id.*, 597; M'Carty *v.* Ely, 4 *E. D. Smith*, 375; Rosenbaum *v.* Gunter, 3 *id.*, 203; Masson *v.* Bovet, 1 *Denio*, 73; Milner *v.* Tucker, 1 *Carr. & P.*, 15; see Sweetman *v.* Prince, 26 *N. Y.*, 224. This is undoubtedly the common law rule. But the rule in equity does not appear to have been so strict. The equitable action for rescission is governed by rules stated in the Fourth Division of this Code.

[3] So long as he is ignorant of any fact material to his right to rescind, the lapse of time is immaterial (Wall *v.* Cockerell, 10 *H. of L. Cas.*, 229; and see cases above).

[4] So long as the influence lasts, the lapse of time is not regarded (Sharp *v.* Leach, 8 *Jur.* [*N. S.*] 1026; 31 *Beav.*, 491; Wood *v.* Downes, 18 *Ves.*, 123; Crowe *v.* Ballard, 3 *Bro. C. C.*, 120; 1 *Ves.*, 214; 2 *Cox*, 253; Gowland *v.* De Faria, 17 *Ves.*, 20; Morse *v.* Royal, 12 *id.*, 374; Roche *v.* O'Brien, 1 *Ball & B.*, 338, 353; Dunbar *v.* Tredennick, 2 *id.*, 316).

[5] *Ib.*

[6] Goelth *v.* White, 35 *Barb.*, 76; Stevens *v.* Hyde, 32 *Barb.*, 171; Fisher *v.* Fredenhall, 21 *Barb.*, 82; Wheaton *v.* Baker, 14 *id.*, 600; Matteawan Co. *v.* Bentley, 13 *id.*, 641; Clarke *v.* Dickson, *El. Bl. & E.*, 148; Beed *v.* Blandford, 2 *You. & J.*, 278; Hunt *v.* Silk, 5 *East*, 449.

[7] Fisher *v.* Conant, 3 *E. D. Smith*, 199; see Nichols *v.* Michael, 23 *N. Y.*, 272.

[8] The note of the adverse party, if not negotiated, is valueless, and need not be restored to him (Nichols *v.* Michael, 23 *N. Y.*, 267, 273; Fraschieris *v.* Henriques, 36 *Barb.*, 276; Nellis *v.* Bradley, 1 *Sandf.*, 560); and so is the note of an insolvent third person (Hawkins *v.* Appleby, 2 *Sandf.*, 421).

[9] Colville *v.* Besly, 2 *Denio*, 139.

[10] Thornton *v.* Wynn, 12 *Wheat.*, 193; Sandford *v.* Travers, 7 *Bosw.*, 498; Baker *v.* Robbins, 2 *Denio*, 136; Hogan *v.* Weyer, 5 *Hill*, 389.

[11] Masson *v.* Bovet, 1 *Denio*, 69; Ladd *v.* Moore, 3 *Sandf.*, 589.

CHAPTER III.

ALTERATION AND CANCELLATION.

Alteration by consent.

§ 842. A contract not under seal may be altered in any respect by consent of the parties, upon a sufficient consideration; and is extinguished thereby to the extent of the alteration.

Alterations generally, but not always, consist in the substitution of a new contract for the one that is superseded. Such an alteration is a novation, and is considered under that head.

A consideration is necessary to make an alteration valid at common law. A novation implies a consideration, but an alteration of any other kind amounts only to a partial release without seal. See the chapter on RELEASE. Even a mere extension of the time for performance requires a consideration to support it (Kellogg *v.* Olmsted, 25 *N. Y.*, 189; aff'g S. C., 28 *Barb.*, 96).

Sealed contracts, how modified.

§ 843. A contract under seal may be altered by an agreement under seal,[1] or by an executed agreement without seal;[2] and not otherwise, except as to the time of performance, which may be extended by any form of agreement.[3]

[1] Allen *v.* Jaquish, 21 *Wend.*, 628; Delacroix *v.* Bulkley, 13 *id.*, 71. The propriety of this restriction is questionable, inasmuch as it is a pure technicality, which is and must be unfamiliar to ordinary business men. An alteration in writing would answer every purpose of justice.

[2] Pierrepont *v.* Barnard, 6 *N. Y.*, 279.

[3] Flynn *v.* McKeon, 6 *Duer*, 203; Clark *v.* Dales, 20 *Barb.*, 42; Stone *v.* Sprague, *id.*, 509; Esmond *v.* Van Benschoten, 12 *Barb.*, 366; Fleming *v.* Gilbert, 3 *Johns.*, 528.

Extinction by cancellation, &c.

§ 844. The destruction or cancellation of a written contract, or of the signature of the parties liable thereon, with intent to extinguish the obligation thereof, extinguishes it as to all the parties consenting to the act.

Gardner *v.* Gardner (Ct. of Errors), 22 *Wend.*, 526.

§ 845. The intentional[1] destruction,[2] cancellation or material alteration[3] of a written contract, by a party entitled to any benefit under it,[4] or with his consent,[5] extinguishes all[6] the executory[7] obligations of the contract[8] in his favor,[9] against parties who do not consent to the act.[10]

Extinction by unauthorized alteration.

[1] An accidental alteration or destruction does not prejudice (See Skip *v.* Huey, 3 *Atk.*, 93; Hornby *v.* Matcham, 16 *Sim.*, 325; Des Arts *v.* Leggett, 16 *N. Y.*, 582). Thus, where a creditor traced ink over the debtor's name, which had become blotted and obscured, and in so doing mispelled it by mistake, this was held immaterial (Dunn *v.* Clements, 7 *Jones Law* [*N. C.*], 58).

[2] Blade *v.* Noland, 12 *Wend.*, 173; see Hinsdale *v.* Bank of Orange, 6 *id.*, 378.

[3] Chappell *v.* Spencer, 23 *Barb.*, 584; Bruce *v.* Westcott, 3 *id.*, 374; Waring *v.* Smyth, 2 *Barb. Ch.*, 119; Nazro *v.* Fuller, 24 *Wend.*, 374; Maybee *v.* Sniffen, 2 *E. D. Smith*, 1; Fay *v.* Smith, 1 *Allen*, 477; Burchfield *v.* Moore, 3 *El. & Bl.*, 683; Warrington *v.* Early, 2 *id.*, 763; Cowie *v.* Halsall, 4 *B. & Ald.*, 197. An alteration which cannot possibly be material, does not vitiate (People *v.* Muzzy, 1 *Denio*, 239; Pequawket Bridge Co. *v.* Mathes, 8 *N. H.*, 139; Nichols *v.* Johnson, 10 *Conn.*, 192; Smith *v.* Crooker, 5 *Mass.*, 540; Langdon *v.* Paul, 20 *Verm.*, 217).

[4] An alteration by a stranger does not affect the contract (Rees *v.* Overbaugh, 6 *Cow.*, 746; see Malin *v.* Malin, 1 *Wend.*, 659). And where an alteration was made in the presence of the creditors, by an agent of the debtor, who believed that he had authority to make it, but in fact had not, it was held that the contract was not avoided thereby (Van Brunt *v.* Eoff, 35 *Barb.*, 501).

[5] Consent is equivalent to an alteration by the party himself (see Martin *v.* Thomas, 24 *How.* [*U. S.*], 315; Waring *v.* Smyth, 2 *Barb. Ch.*, 119).

[6] The *whole* contract is extinguished by a material alteration, however slight. See cases cited under note 3.

[7] An alteration does not divest an interest that has vested under a grant (Smith *v.* McGowan, 3 *Barb.*, 404; Lewis *v.* Payn, 8 *Cow.*, 71; Chessman *v.* Whittemore,

23 *Pick.*, 231; Withers *v.* Atkinson, 1 *Watts*, 236; Barrett *v.* Thorndike, 1 *Greenl.*, 73).

[8] It seems to be doubtful whether the payee of a note, who has lost his rights under it by an alteration, can recover upon the original consideration (Clute *v.* Small, 17 *Wend.*, 237). It has been held that he may (Atkinson *v.* Hawdon, 2 *Ad. & El.*, 628; but compare Alderson *v.* Langdale, 3 *B. & Ad.*, 660). It should seem that he ought not, for the note undoubtedly suspends the time of payment of the original debt until the note becomes due (Hart *v.* Hudson, 6 *Duer*, 294), and under such circumstances the note would never become due. But where a note is altered by consent, and is void for want of a new stamp, the original debt may be recovered (Sutton *v.* Toomer, 7 *B. & Cr.*, 416).

[9] Where there are two creditors having separate interests under a contract, an alteration by one of them does not prejudice the rights of the other.

[10] An alteration does not discharge parties consenting thereto (Sanderson *v.* Symonds, 1 *Brod. & B.*, 426; Coke *v.* Brummell, 8 *Taunt.*, 439), even though other parties jointly and severally liable with them are thereby discharged (Prettyman *v.* Goodrich, 23 *Ill.*, 330; Downes *v.* Richardson, 5 *B. & Ald.*, 674). If their obligations were purely joint, the result might be different.

Alteration of duplicate not to prejudice.

§ 846. Where a contract is executed in duplicate, an alteration or destruction of one copy, while the other exists, is not within the provisions of the last section.

Lewis *v.* Payn, 8 *Cow.*, 71; S. C., 4 *Wend.*, 426.

PART III.

OBLIGATIONS IMPOSED BY LAW.

§ 847. Every person is bound, without contract, to abstain from injuring the person or property of another, or infringing upon any of his rights. **Abstinence from injury.**

See these rights defined in the first and second Divisions of this Code.

§ 848. One who willfully deceives another, with intent[1] to induce him to alter his position to his injury[2] or risk,[3] is liable for any damage which he thereby suffers.[4] **Fraudulent deceit.**

[1] An *intent* to defraud is an essential element of actual fraud (Thomas *v.* Beebe, 25 *N Y.*, 250; Zabriskie *v.* Smith, 13 *id.*, 322; Addington *v.* Allen, 11 *Wend.*, 374; Behn *v.* Kemble, 7 *C. B.* [*N. S.*], 260; Young *v.* Covell, 8 *Johns.*, 23; Cropsey *v.* Robinson, 5 *N. Y. Leg. Obs.*, 20; People *v.* Kelly, 35 *Barb.*, 444).

[2] It is immaterial whether the party committing the fraud receives the benefit of it, or does it for the profit of another (Addington *v.* Allen, 11 *Wend.*, 374; Zabriskie *v.* Smith, 13 *N. Y.*, 322); or whether any person gains an advantage thereby, or not. *Injury*, not *gain*, is the essential element of fraud (White *v.* Merritt, 7 *N. Y.*, 352).

[3] Polhill *v.* Walter, 3 *Barn. & Ad.*, 114; Corbett *v.* Brown, 8 *Bing.*, 33. In these cases the fraud was committed in the belief that no actual injury would ensue.

[4] The law takes no cognizance of a fraud which does not in fact work some injury (People *v.* Cook, 8 *N. Y.*, 67; Eastwood *v.* Bain, 3 *H. & N.*, 738; see Hemingway *v.* Hamilton, 4 *M. & W.*, 115; *Story Eq. Jur.*, § 203).

Deceit, what.

§ 849. A deceit, within the meaning of the last section, is either:

1. The suggestion, as a fact, of that which is not true, by one who does not believe it to be true;[1]

2. The assertion, as a fact, of that which is not true, by one who has no reasonable ground for believing it to be true;[2]

3. The suppression of a fact, by one who is bound to disclose it, or who gives information of other facts which are likely to mislead for want of communication of that fact;[3] or,

4. A promise, made without any intention of performing it.[4]

[1] See § 757, and notes.

[2] See *ib.*

[3] Addington *v.* Allen, 7 *Wend.*, 20. This subdivision is not in the same form as the corresponding subdivision of § 757, as that would be obviously too broad in this case.

[4] See this question discussed in notes to § 757.

Deceit upon the public, &c.

§ 850. One who practices a deceit with intent to defraud the public, or a particular class of persons, is deemed to have intended to defraud every individual in that class, who is actually misled by the deceit.

It is necessary that the party charged with fraud should have intended to defraud *the party* who was in fact misled (Van Kleeck *v.* Le Roy, 37 *Barb.*, 544; Seizer *v.* Mali, 32 *id.*, 76), or to defraud the public (Cross *v.* Sackett, 2 *Bosw.*, 617; 6 *Abb. Pr.*, 247; 16 *How. Pr.*, 62; Cazeaux *v.* Mali, 25 *Barb.*, 578; Newbery *v.* Garland, 31 *id.*, 121; Morse *v.* Swits, 19 *How. Pr.*, 275; Gerhard *v.* Bates, 2 *El. & Bl.*, 476), or a class of persons including the party injured.

Restoration of thing wrongfully acquired.

§ 851. One who obtains a thing without the consent of its owner, or by a consent afterwards rescinded,[1] or by an unlawful exaction which the owner could not at the time prudently refuse,[2] must restore it to the person from whom it was thus obtained, unless he has acquired a title thereto superior to that of such other person,[3] or unless the transaction was corrupt and unlawful on both sides.[4]

[1] This includes duress (Foshay *v.* Ferguson, 5 *Hill*, 154), menace (see Eadie *v.* Slimmon, 26 *N. Y.*, 9), fraud (Chester *v.* Bank of Kingston, 16 *N. Y.*, 336; Hennequin *v.* Naylor, 24 *id.*, 139; Nichols *v.* Michael, 23 *id.*, 264; Abbotts *v.* Barry, 2 *Brod. & B.*, 369), undue influence (Sears *v.* Shafer, 6 *N. Y.*, 272; Nottidge *v.* Prince, 2 *Giff.*, 246), mistake (Bank of Commerce *v.* Union Bank, 3 *N. Y.*, 230; Goddard *v.* Merchants' Bank, 4 *id.*, 147; Martin *v.* McCormick, 8 *id.*, 331; Gardner *v.* Mayor of Troy, 26 *Barb.*, 423; Allen *v.* Mayor of N. Y., 4 *E. D. Smith*, 404; Gompertz *v.* Bartlett, 2 *El. & Bl.*, 849), and cases in which there is a total failure of consideration (Eno *v.* Woodworth, 4 *N. Y.*, 249; see Gillet *v.* Maynard, 5 *Johns.*, 85; Collier *v.* Coates, 17 *Barb.*, 471).

[2] It is by no means easy to reconcile all the authorities on this point with each other, or with natural justice. Justice, rather than the decisions, has been followed in the text. The difficulty seems to be that the courts have established one rule as to the reclamation of money paid, which is simply the rescission of an executed contract, and another as to the rescission of a promise to pay, which is an executory contract. Lord DENMAN, in Skeate *v.* Beale (11 *Ad. & El.*, 983), says "the distinction is obvious," and so it is, but the *principle* of the distinction is not.

There is no doubt that fees, illegally exacted, may be recovered back, although not paid under a mistake of fact (American Exch. Fire Ins. Co. *v.* Britton, 8 *Bosw.*, 148; Britton *v.* Frink [Ct. of Appeals], 3 *How. Pr.*, 102; Dew *v.* Parsons, 2 *B. & Ald.*, 562; Steele *v.* Williams, 8 *Exch.*, 625; Townshend *v.* Dyckman, 2 *E. D. Smith*, 227; Ripley *v.* Gelston, 9 *Johns.*, 201; Frye *v.* Lockwood, 4 *Cow.*, 454). Duress of goods is sufficient to entitle the owner to recover back money paid for their release (Harmony *v.* Bingham, 12 *N. Y.*, 99; Clinton *v.* Strong, 9 *Johns.*, 370; Oates *v.* Hudson, 6 *Exch.*, 346; Atlee *v.* Backhouse, 3 *M. & W.*, 642; Gibbon *v.* Gibbon, 13 *C. B.*, 205; Ashmole *v.* Wainwright, 2 *Q. B.*, 837); and so where a corporation refused to transfer stock upon its books, until the stockholder paid an unjust claim (Bates *v.* N. Y. Ins. Co., 3 *Johns. Cas.*, 238), and where a railway company refused to receive goods until an unlawful charge was paid (Parker *v.* Great Western Railw. Co., 7 *M. & G.*, 253), the money paid was recovered back. And so it has been held where money was obtained by threat of a penal action (Unwin *v.* Leaper, 1 *M. & G.*, 747), or paid in order to prevent a wrongful sale under execution (Wisner *v.* Bulkley, 15 *Wend.*, 321).

On the other hand it has been held that money paid under a claim of right, without compulsion or objection (N. Y. & Harlem R. R. Co. *v.* Marsh, 12 *N. Y.*, 308), or even under protest (Fleetwood *v.* City of N. Y., 2 *Sandf.*, 475; Sprague *v.* Birdsall, 2 *Cow.*, 419), or in mere ignorance of law (Wilson *v.* Ray, 10 *Ad. & El.*, 82), cannot be recovered back.

[3] This is intended to provide for the exceptions created by the Title on NEGOTIABLE INSTRUMENTS, and by section 499.

[4] Daimouth *v.* Bennett, 15 *Barb.*, 541; Best *v.* Strong, 2 *Wend.*, 319; Burt *v.* Place, 6 *Cow.*, 431.

When demand necessary. § 852. The restoration required by the last section must be made without demand;[1] except where a thing is obtained by mutual mistake, in which case the party obtaining the thing is not bound to return it until he has notice of the mistake.[2]

[1] Utica Bank *v.* Van Gieson, 18 *Johns.*, 485; see *Code La.*, 2279, 2280; *Code Napoleon*, 1376, 1377.

[2] See Kelly *v.* Solari, 9 *M. & W.*, 58.

Responsibility for willful acts, negligence, &c. § 853. Every one is responsible, not only for the result of his willful acts, but also for an injury occasioned to another by his want of ordinary care or skill in the management of his property or person;[1] unless the latter has, willfully, or by want of ordinary care, incurred the risk of such injury.[2] The extent of liability in such cases is defined by the Title on COMPENSATORY RELIEF.

[1] *Code La.*, 2295; *Code Napoleon*, 1383; Austin *v.* Hudson River R. R. Co., 25 *N. Y.*, 334; Jones *v.* Bird, 5 *B. & Ald.*, 837; Dodd *v.* Holmes, 1 *Ad. & El.*, 493.

[2] Johnson *v.* Hudson River R. R. Co., 20 *N. Y.*, 69.

Other obligations. § 854. Other obligations are prescribed by the First and Second Divisions of this CODE.

PART IV.

OBLIGATIONS ARISING FROM PARTICULAR TRANSACTIONS.

TITLE I.

SALE.

CHAPTER I.

GENERAL PROVISIONS.

ARTICLE I.

SALE.

Sale, what. § 855. Sale is a contract by which, for a pecuniary consideration, called a price, one transfers to another an interest in property.

Subject of sale. § 856. The subject of sale must be property, the title to which can be immediately transferred from the seller to the buyer.

ARTICLE II.

AGREEMENTS FOR SALE.

Agreement for sale. § 857. An agreement for sale is either:

1. An agreement to sell;

2. An agreement to buy; or,

3. A mutual agreement to sell and buy.

§ 858. An agreement to sell is a contract by which one engages, for a price, to transfer to another the title to a certain thing. Agreement to sell.

§ 859. An agreement to buy is a contract by which one engages to accept from another, and pay a price for the title to a certain thing. Agreement to buy.

§ 860. An agreement to sell and buy is a contract by which one engages to transfer the title to a certain thing to another, who engages to accept the same from him, and to pay a price therefor. Agreement to sell and buy.

§ 861. Any property which, if in existence, might be the subject of sale, may be the subject of an agreement for sale, whether in existence or not. What may be the subject of the contract.

Hale *v.* Rawson, 4 *C. B.* [*N. S.*], 85.

§ 862. An agreement to sell real property binds the seller to execute a grant in the form and manner prescribed by the chapter on TRANSFERS OF REAL PROPERTY. Agreement to sell real property.

This provision, in connection with that to which it refers, is intended to provide a uniform mode of transfer. There can be very little question that no more could, even now, be required from the seller. This section will give the buyer a right to insist upon a simple and well known conveyance, if he desires it.

§ 863. An agreement on the part of a seller of real property to give the usual covenants, binds him to insert in the grant, covenants of seizin, quiet enjoyment, further assurance, general warranty, and against incumbrances. Usual covenants in deeds of grant.

§ 864. The covenants mentioned in the last section must be in substance as follows: Language of usual covenants.

"The party of the first part covenants with the party of the second part, that the former is now seized in fee simple of the property granted; that the latter shall enjoy the same without any lawful disturbance; that the same is free from all incumbrances; that the party of the first part, and all persons acquiring any interest in the same through or for him, will, on demand, execute and deliver to the party of the second part, at the expense of the latter, any further assurance of the same that may be reasonably required; and that the party of the first part will warrant to the party of the second part all the said property against every person lawfully claiming the same."

This provision is new. Its object is the same as that of section 485, namely, to reduce the length of conveyances, and to provide a plain and sufficient form, as is done by the English statute, 8 & 9 *Vict.* c. 119. The commissioners believe that the form here given is sufficient to cover all the intricately worded stipulations usually given in such cases.

ARTICLE III.

FORM OF THE CONTRACT.

Contract for sale of personal property.

§ 865. No sale of personal property, or agreement to buy[1] or sell it, for a price of fifty dollars or more, is valid unless:

1. A memorandum of the contract, showing the parties, their consent, and the subject of sale, is made in writing, and subscribed[2] by the party to be charged; or,

2. The buyer accepts and receives[3] part of the thing sold, or, when it consists of a thing in action, part of the evidences thereof; or,

3. The buyer, at the time of sale,[4] pays a part of the price.[5]

[1] There may possibly be some doubt whether a simple contract binding one to buy, but not binding the other to sell, is now within the statute. It clearly ought to be within it.

[2] This means that the names of the parties must be placed at the foot of the agreement (James *v.* Patten, 6 *N. Y.*, 10; rev'g S. C., 8 *Barb.*, 344; Davis *v.* Shields, 26 *Wend.*, 341).

[3] It is not essential that the delivery of part of the property should take place at the time of sale (Sprague *v.* Blake, 20 *Wend.*, 61; M'Knight *v.* Dunlop, 5 *N. Y.*, 537; overruling Clark *v.* Tucker, 2 *Sandf.*, 157; Seymour *v.* Davis, *id.*, 239). It is essential not only that the buyer should *receive*, but that he should also *accept* the thing sold (Hunt *v.* Hecht, 8 *Exch.*, 814; Outwater *v.* Dodge, 6 *Wend.*, 397; Kent *v.* Hutchinson, 3 *Bos. & Pul.*, 233).

[4] A payment after the sale will not make it binding (Bissell *v.* Balcom, 40 *Barb.*, 98).

[5] 2 *R. S.*, 135, § 3.

§ 866. An agreement to manufacture a thing, from materials furnished by the manufacturer or by another person, is not within the provisions of the last section. Contract to manufacture.

Donovan *v.* Willson, 26 *Barb.*, 138; Parker *v.* Schenck, 28 *Barb.*, 38; Courtwright *v.* Stewart, 19 *Barb.*, 455; Bronson *v.* Wiman, 10 *Barb.*, 406; Robertson *v.* Vaughn, 5 *Sandf.*, 1; Sewall *v.* Fitch, 8 *Cow.*, 215; Crookshank *v.* Burrell, 18 *Johns.*, 58.

§ 867. No agreement for the sale of real property, or of any estate therein, is valid, unless a memorandum thereof, showing the parties, their consent, and the subject of sale[1], is made in writing, and subscribed by the party to be charged,[2] or unless the contract has been partially performed by the party seeking to enforce it, and such part performance has been accepted by the other.[3] Contract for sale of real property.

[1] These particulars are specifically mentioned, in order to avoid the possibility of an interpretation requiring the consideration to be stated.

[2] 2 *R. S.*, 135, § 8; except that "the party to be charged" is substituted for "the vendor," so as to establish a rule uniform with that concerning sales of personal property.

[3] 2 *R. S.*, 135, § 9, retains the equitable doctrines of part performance. This provision is doubtless rather broader than the rules of equity would sustain, as it has always been required that, to take the case out of the statute, the party seeking to enforce an oral

contract must show that he cannot be replaced in his former position (Malins *v.* Brown, 4 *N. Y.*, 403; Bennett *v.* Abrams, 41 *Barb.*, 619; Williston *v.* Williston, *id.*, 635; Lowry *v.* Tew, 3 *Barb. Ch.*, 407; Rhodes *v.* Rhodes, 3 *Sandf. Ch.*, 279; Wolfe *v.* Frost, 4 *id.*, 72; German *v.* Machin, 6 *Paige*, 238; Frame *v.* Dawson, 14 *Ves.*, 386.)

But it is to be remembered that the equitable doctrine of part performance was always in contradiction of the letter of the statute, and that the courts might therefore well hesitate to go so far as their sense of abstract justice would have dictated. In reducing their doctrines to the form of a statute, it seems only proper to adopt the principle which lies at the foundation of those decisions, without the restrictions which were imposed from a regard for the adverse provisions of the statute of frauds.

This provision is inserted in this place, instead of being left to the chapter on SPECIFIC PERFORMANCE, because it is thought that the fusion of law and equity makes this the proper course.

Transfer of real property.

§ 868. The form of a transfer of real property is described by the chapter on such transfers.

See section 485.

CHAPTER II.

RIGHTS AND OBLIGATIONS OF THE SELLER.

ARTICLE I.

RIGHTS AND DUTIES BEFORE DELIVERY.

When seller must act as depositary.

§ 869. After personal property has been sold, and until the delivery is completed, the seller has the rights and obligations of a depositary for hire,[1] except that he must keep the property, without charge, until the buyer has had a reasonable opportunity to remove it.[2]

[1] The seller is bound to keep the thing sold safely, even if the buyer does not come at the proper time to take it (Sheldon *v.* Skinner, 4 *Wend.*, 525). But he is entitled to compensation for his trouble (*id.*) And unquestionably he may discharge himself of the burden upon due notice. See the chapter on DEPOSIT FOR HIRE. He may also deposit the thing with a third person (Bement *v.* Smith, 15 *Wend.*, 493).

[2] This is a matter of course.

§ 870. If a buyer of personal property does not pay for it according to contract, and it remains in the possession of the seller, after payment is due, the seller may rescind the sale,[1] or may enforce his lien for the price in the manner prescribed by the Title on LIENS.[2] When seller may resell.

[1] Fancher *v.* Goodman, 29 *Barb.*, 315; Niel *v.* Cheves, 1 *Bail.* [*S. C.*], 537.

[2] Fancher *v.* Goodman, 29 *Barb.*, 315; Mallory *v.* Lord, *id.*, 454; Sands *v.* Taylor, 5 *Johns.*, 395; Bement *v.* Smith, 15 *Wend.*, 497; Bogart *v.* O'Regan, 1 *E. D.Smith*, 590; Maclean *v.* Dunn, 4 *Bing.*, 722.

ARTICLE II.

DELIVERY.

§ 871. One who sells personal property, whether it was in his possession at the time of sale, or not, must put it into a condition fit for delivery,[1] and deliver it[2] to the buyer within a reasonable time[3] after demand,[4] unless he has a lien thereon. Delivery on demand.

[1] Gerard *v.* Prouty, 34 *Barb.*, 454.

[2] In every sale there is an implied stipulation to deliver (Buddle *v.* Green, 27 *L. J.* [*Ex.*] 33; 3 *H. & N.* [*Am. ed.*] 996), which is broken by the refusal of a third

person in possession, even though unjustifiable on his part (*Ib.*).

[3] Terwilliger *v.* Knapp, 2 *E. D. Smith*, 86; see Kipp *v.* Wiles, 3 *Sandf.*, 585.

[4] See Jones *v.* Gibbons, 8 *Exch.*, 922; Bach *v.* Owen, 5 *T. R.*, 409; Radford *v.* Smith, 3 *M. & W.*, 254.

Delivery, where made

§ 872. Personal property sold is deliverable at the place where it is at the time of the sale or agreement to sell,[1] or, if it is not then in existence, it is deliverable at the place where it is produced.[2]

[1] See Bronson *v.* Gleason, 7 *Barb.*, 472; Barr *v.* Myers, 3 *Watts & S.*, 295.

[2] Rice *v.* Churchill, 2 *Denio*, 145.

Expense of transportation.

§ 873. One who sells personal property must bring it to his own door, or other convenient place, for its acceptance by the buyer, but further transportation is at the risk and expense of the buyer.

Notice of election as to delivery.

§ 874. When either party to a contract of sale has an option as to the time, place, or manner of delivery, he must give the other party reasonable notice of his choice;[1] and if he does not give such notice within a reasonable time, his right of option is waived.[2]

[1] So held as to place (Rogers *v.* Van Hoesen, 12 *Johns.*, 221; Peck *v.* Hubbard, 11 *Verm.*, 612), and the same principle seems to apply to the time and mode of delivery.

[2] The obligation is not extinguished by the failure of either party to give notice of his election as to the mode of its performance (Gilbert *v.* Danforth, 6 *N. Y.*, 585; Livingston *v.* Miller, 11 *id.*, 80).

Buyer's directions as to manner of sending things sold.

§ 875. If a seller agrees to send the thing sold to the buyer, he must follow the directions of the latter as to the manner of sending, or it will be at his own risk during its transportation. If he follows such directions, or if, in the absence of special directions, he uses ordinary care in forwarding the thing, it is at the risk of the buyer.

Bull *v.* Robison, 10 *Exch.*, 342; Orcutt *v.* Nelson, 1 *Gray*, 536; Jones *v.* Sims, 6 *Porter*, 161.

§ 876. The delivery of a thing sold can be offered or demanded only within reasonable hours of the day. Delivery to be within reasonable hours.

Startup *v.* Macdonald, 2 *M. & G.*, 395.

ARTICLE III.

WARRANTY.

§ 877. A warranty is an engagement by which a seller assures to a buyer the existence of some fact affecting the transaction, whether past, present, or future. Warranty what.

See Roberts *v.* Morgan, 2 *Cow.*, 438; Carley *v.* Wilkins, 6 *Barb.*, 557; Cook *v.* Mosely, 13 *Wend.*, 277; Ender *v.* Scott, 11 *Ill.*, 35; Humphreys *v.* Comline, 8 *Blackf.*, 508.

§ 878. Except as prescribed by this article, a mere contract of sale or agreement to sell does not imply a warranty. No implied warranty in mere contract of sale.

As to personal property, *caveat emptor* is the general rule (Beirne *v.* Dord, 5 *N. Y.*, 98).

As to real property, no warranty is implied from a deed (1 *R. S.*, 738; Huntly *v.* Waddell, 12 *Ired. Law* [*N. C.*], 32). And though a warranty of title is nominally implied from an agreement to sell land, it is only nominal, as no substantial damages can be recovered (Conger *v.* Weaver, 20 *N. Y.*, 140; Peters *v.* M'Keon, 4 *Den.*, 546). except in case of fraud (Trull *v.* Granger, 8 *N. Y.*, 115),

Warranty of title to personal property.

§ 879. One who sells or agrees to sell personal property, as his own, thereby warrants that he has a good[1] and unincumbered title thereto.[2]

[1] Defreeze *v.* Trumper, 1 *Johns.*, 274; Reid *v.* Barber, 3 *Cow.*, 272; and see Hoe *v.* Sanborn, 21 *N. Y.*, 555. Whether this warranty is now implied, where the property is not in possession of the vendor, is in dispute. It is held that it is not, in M'Coy *v.* Archer, 3 *Barb.*, 323; Huntington *v.* Hall, 36 *Me.*, 501; that it is, in Smith *v.* Fairbanks, 7 *Foster*, 521; see Strong *v.* Barnes, 11 *Vt.*, 221. It certainly is implied, when the property is in his possession (Burt *v.* Dewey, 31 *Barb.*, 540).

[2] Dresser *v.* Ainsworth, 9 *Barb.*, 619.

Warranty on sale by sample.

§ 880. One who sells or agrees to sell goods by sample, thereby warrants the bulk to be equal to the sample.

Waring *v.* Mason, 18 *Wend.*, 425; Bradford *v.* Manley, 13 *Mass.*, 139; Williams *v.* Spafford, 8 *Pick.*, 250; see Beirne *v.* Dord, 5 *N. Y.*, 95; Hargous *v.* Stone, *id.*, 73.

When seller knows that buyer relies on his judgment, &c.

§ 881. One who sells or agrees to sell personal property, knowing that the buyer relies upon his advice or judgment, thereby warrants to the buyer that neither the seller, nor any agent employed by him in the transaction, knows the existence of any fact concerning the thing sold which would, to his knowledge, destroy the buyer's inducement to buy.

It is utterly impossible to reconcile the cases on this subject. This rule is perhaps as near their result as any that could be stated in as few words (see Hoe *v.* Sanborn, 21 *N. Y.*, 552; Brown *v.* Montgomery, 20 *id.*, 487; 2 *Kent Com.*, 480).

It will be observed that it is only facts *concerning the thing* that are required to be disclosed. This restricts the range of the section to matters which, in morals, ought perhaps to be disclosed in even a broader class of cases.

Merchandise not in existence.

§ 882. One who agrees to sell merchandise not then in existence, thereby warrants that it shall be sound and merchantable[1] at the place of production contemplated by the parties, and as nearly so, at the place of delivery, as can be secured by reasonable care.[2]

[1] This principle, though not directly adjudicated, is clearly at the foundation of the decisions in regard to sales of goods to be manufactured by the seller (see § 883), and is a necessary corollary of the rule which implies a warranty of goods which the buyer has had no opportunity to inspect (see § 885). Hamilton *v.* Ganyard, 34 *Barb.*, 204, supports the rule here stated.

[2] The absolute warranty extends only to the place of production. The inevitable injuries of transportation must be borne by the buyer (Bull *v.* Robison, 10 *Exch.*, 342). But of course this is to be construed in view of the intention of the parties. If an article is purchasable in New York, in perfect condition, and the same kind of thing is imported from London, but is always injured by the voyage, the seller cannot compel the buyer to accept the latter article, unless the parties contemplated London as the place of production.

Manufacturer's warranty against latent defects.

§ 883. One who sells or agrees to sell an article of his own manufacture, thereby warrants it to be free from any latent defect, not disclosed to the buyer, arising from the process of manufacture, and also that neither he nor his agent in such manufacture has knowingly used improper materials therein.

Hoe *v.* Sanborn, 21 *N. Y.*, 552, 566.

Thing bought for particular purpose.

§ 884. One who manufactures an article under an order for a particular purpose, warrants by the sale that it is reasonably fit for that purpose.

Brown *v.* Edgington, 2 *M. & G.*, 279; Shepherd *v.* Pybus, 3 *id.*, 868; Howard *v.* Hoey, 23 *Wend.*, 351; Jones *v.* Bright, 5 *Bing.*, 533; Beals *v.* Olmstead, 24 *Verm.*, 114; see Hoe *v.* Sanborn, 21 *N. Y.*, 552.

When thing can not be examined by buyer.

§ 885. One who sells or agrees to sell merchandise inaccessible to the examination of the buyer, thereby warrants that it is sound and merchantable.

Wieler *v.* Schilizzi, 17 *C. B.*, 619; Cleu *v.* M'Pherson, 1 *Bosw.*, 480; Hamilton *v.* Ganyard, 34 *Barb.*, 204.

Trade marks.

§ 886. One who sells or agrees to sell any article to which there is affixed or attached a trade mark, thereby warrants that mark to be genuine, and lawfully used.

From stat. 25 & 26 *Vict.*, c. 88, § 19. This statute enacts that this warranty can be dispensed with only by a written refusal to warrant.

Other marks.

§ 887. One who sells or agrees to sell any article to which there is affixed or attached a statement or mark to express the quantity or quality thereof, or the place where it was, in whole or in part, produced, manufactured or prepared, thereby warrants the truth thereof.

From the same statute.

Warranty on sale of written instrument.

§ 888. One who sells or agrees to sell an instrument purporting to bind any one to the performance of an act, thereby warrants the instrument to be what it purports to be,[1] and to be binding according to its purport upon all the parties thereto;[2] and also warrants that he has no knowledge of any facts which tend to prove it worthless, such as the insolvency of any of the parties thereto, where that is material,[3] the extinction of its obligations, or its invalidity for any cause.[4]

[1] Gurney *v.* Womersley, 4 *El. & Bl.*, 133; Cabot Bank *v.* Morton, 4 *Gray*, 156; Herrick *v.* Whitney, 15 *Johns.*, 240; Gompertz *v.* Bartlett, 2 *El. & Bl.*, 849; Canal Bank *v.* Bank of Albany, 1 *Hill*, 287.

[2] Delaware Bank *v.* Jarvis, 20 *N. Y.*, 226; Furniss *v.* Ferguson, 15 *id.*, 437; Young *v.* Cole, 2 *Bing. N. C.*, 724; 4 *Scott*, 489.

[3] In some cases the value of an obligation may be entirely independent of the solvency of the party bound thereby, as for example, where he is bound to execute a power.

[4] Brown *v.* Montgomery, 20 *N. Y.*, 287. He does not warrant *the solvency* of the parties (Elwell *v.* Chamberlain, 4 *Bosw.*, 320).

Warranty of provisions for domestic use.

§ 889. One who makes a business[1] of selling provisions for domestic use warrants, by a sale thereof, to one who buys for actual consumption, and not for the purpose of sale,[2] that they are sound and wholesome.[3]

[1] Burnby *v.* Bollett, 16 *M. & W.*, 644.

[2] Moses *v.* Mead, 1 *Denio*, 379; 5 *id.*, 617; Goldrich *v.* Ryan, 3 *E. D. Smith*, 324; Hyland *v.* Sherman, 2 *id.* 234.

[3] Van Bracklin *v.* Fonda, 12 *Johns.*, 468. In a recent English decision (Emmerton *v.* Mathews, 7 *H. & N.*, 586), it was held that no such warranty is implied; that the seller's liability rests solely upon the ground of fraud; and, therefore, that he is not liable unless he knows that the provisions are bad.

§ 890. One who sells the good will of a business, thereby warrants that he will not endeavor to draw off any of the customers. Warranty on sale of goodwill.

§ 891. Upon a judicial sale,[1] the only warranty implied is that the seller does not know that the sale will not pass a good title to the property.[2] Warranty upon judicial sale.

[1] The Monte Allegre, 9 *Wheat.*, 644; Morgan *v.* Fencher, 1 *Blackf.*, 10; Bashore *v.* Whisler, 3 *Watts*, 490.

[2] Peto *v.* Blades, 5 *Taunt.*, 657.

§ 892. A general warranty does not extend to defects inconsistent therewith, of which the buyer was then aware,[1] or which were then easily discernable by him,[2] without the exercise of peculiar skill; but it extends to all other defects.[3] Effect of general warranty.

[1] Schuyler *v.* Russ, 2 *Cai.*, 202; Long *v.* Hicks, 2 *Humph.*, 305; Southern *v.* Howe, 2 *Rolle*, 5; see Bidwell *v.* Northwestern Ins. Co., 24 *N. Y.*, 302.

[2] Horsfall *v.* Thomas, 1 *Hurlst. & Colt.*, 90.

[3] Birdseye, *v.* Frost, 34 *Barb.*, 367.

CHAPTER III.

RIGHTS AND OBLIGATIONS OF THE BUYER.

Price, when to be paid.

§ 893. A buyer must pay the price of the thing sold on its delivery;[1] and must take it away within a reasonable time[2] after the seller offers to deliver it.[3]

[1] Tipton *v.* Feitner, 20 *N. Y.*, 423. Of course this rule, like most of the others, may be varied by agreement.

[2] He is allowed a reasonable time for this purpose, according to circumstances (Buddle *v.* Green, 27 *L. J.* [*Ex.*], 33; 3 *H. & N.* [*Am. ed.*], 996).

[3] The seller must put the buyer in motion, before he can take advantage of this provision (Jones *v.* Gibbons, 8 *Exch.*, 922).

Right to inspect goods.

§ 894. On an agreement for sale, with warranty, the buyer has a right to inspect the thing sold, at a reasonable time, before accepting it; and may rescind the contract if the seller refuses to permit him to do so.

Lorymer *v.* Smith, 1 *B. & C.*, 1; 2 *D. & R.*, 23.

Rights in case of breach of warranty

§ 895. The breach of a warranty entitles the buyer to rescind an agreement for sale,[1] but not an executed sale,[2] unless the warranty was intended by the parties to operate as a condition.[3]

[1] Barker *v.* Palmer, 4 *B. & Ald.*, 387; see Muller *v.* Eno, 14 *N. Y.*, 597, 610.

[2] There has been much doubt upon this point, but it is now settled that a warranty is not presumptively a condition (Kiernan *v.* Rocheleau, 6 *Bosw.*, 148; Voorhees *v.* Earl, 2 *Hill*, 288; Thornton *v.* Wynn, 12 *Wheat.*, 183; Street *v.* Blay, 2 *B. & Ad.*, 456; Gompertz *v.* Denton, 1 *Cr. & M.*, 207; Parsons *v.* Sexton, 4 *C. B.*, 907; see Muller *v.* Eno, 14 *N. Y.*, 597; Behn *v.* Burness, 1 *Best & Sm.*, 877).

[3] Bannerman *v.* White, 10 *C. B.* [*N. S.*], 844.

CHAPTER IV.

SALE BY AUCTION.

§ 896. A sale by auction is a sale by public outcry to the highest bidder on the spot. Sale by auction, what.

§ 897. A sale by auction is complete when the auctioneer publicly announces, by the fall of his hammer, or in any other customary manner, that the thing is sold. Sale, when complete.

§ 898. Until the announcement mentioned in the last section has been made, any bidder may withdraw his bid,[1] if he does so in a manner reasonably sufficient to bring it to the notice of the auctioneer.[2] Withdrawal of bid.

[1] Payne *v.* Cave, 3 *T. R.*, 148.
[2] Jones *v.* Nanney, 11 *Price*, 103; *M'Clel.*, 39.

§ 899. When a sale by auction is made upon written or printed conditions, such conditions cannot be modified by any oral declaration of the auctioneer, except so far as they are for his own benefit. Sale under written conditions.

Shelton *v.* Livius, 2 *Cr. & J.*, 411; Bradshaw *v.* Bennett, 5 *Car. & P.*, 48; Powell *v.* Edmunds, 12 *East*, 6.

§ 900. If, at a sale by auction, the auctioneer, having authority to do so, publicly announces that the sale will be without reserve, or makes any announcement equivalent thereto, the highest bidder in good faith has an absolute right to the completion of the sale to him; and upon such a sale, bids by the seller or any agent for him are void. Rights of buyer upon sale without reserve

Warlow *v.* Harrison, 1 *El. & El.*, 309; 6 *Jur.* [*N. S.*], 66; 29 *L. J.* [*Q. B.*], 14.

The Revised Statutes (i. 529, § 2) prescribe that "goods sold by auction shall in all cases be struck off to the highest bidder." This section does not appear to have been construed as meaning that goods offered at auction cannot be withdrawn.

§ 901. The employment by a seller at a sale by auction, without the knowledge of the buyer, of any person to bid at the sale, without an intention on the part of such bidder to buy, and on the part of the seller to enforce his bid, is a fraud upon the buyer, which entitles him to rescind his purchase. By bidding

Green *v.* Baverstock, 14 *C. B.* [*N. S.*], 204; Crowder *v.* Austin, 3 *Bing.*, 368; Rex *v.* Marsh, 3 *Y. & J.*, 331; Howard *v.* Castle, 6 *T. R.*, 642; Wheeler *v.* Collier, *Moo. & M.*, 126; Baham *v.* Bach, 13 *La.*, 287; Moncrieff *v.* Goldsborough, 4 *Harr. & McH.*, 282; Donaldson *v.* M'Roy, 1 *P. A. Browne*, 346; Thornett *v.* Haines, 15 *M. & W.*, 371. But see Woodward *v.* Miller, 2 *Colly.*, 279; Bramley *v.* Alt, 3 *Ves.*, 619, *n.*; Smith *v.* Clarke, 12 *Ves.*, 477. This rule is sustained in all its stringency, by Chancellor Kent (2 *Kent Com.*, 539).

Auctioneer's memorandum of sale.

§ 902. When property is sold by auction, the auctioneer, or his partner or clerk, may enter in a sale book, at the time of the sale, a memorandum specifying the name of the person for whom he sells, the thing sold, the price, the terms of sale, and the name of the buyer. A memorandum thus made binds both the parties in the same manner as if made by themselves.

2 *R. S.*, 136, modified in form, but not in effect.

TITLE II.

EXCHANGE.

Exchange, what.

§ 903. Exchange is a contract by which the parties mutually give, or agree to give, one thing for another, neither thing, or both things, being money only.

Form of contract.

§ 904. The provisions of section 865 apply to all exchanges in which the value of the thing to be given by either party is fifty dollars or more.

Parties have rights and obligations of sellers and buyers.

§ 905. The provisions of the Title on SALE apply to exchanges. Each party has the rights and obligations of a seller as to the thing which he gives, and of a buyer as to that which he takes.

§ 906. On an exchange of money, each party thereby warrants the genuineness of the money given by him. Warranty of money.

See Timmins *v.* Gibbins, 18 *Q. B.*, 722; Young *v.* Cole, 3 *Bing. N. C.*, 724; 4 *Scott*, 489.

TITLE III.

DEPOSIT.

CHAPTER I.

DEPOSIT IN GENERAL.

ARTICLE I.

NATURE AND CREATION OF DEPOSIT.

§ 907. A deposit may be voluntary or involuntary; and for safe keeping or for exchange. Deposit, kinds of.

§ 908. A voluntary deposit is made by one giving to another, with his consent, the possession of personal property to keep for the benefit of the former, or of a third party. The person giving is called the depositor, and the person receiving the depositary. Voluntary deposit, how made.

Involuntary deposit, how made.

§ 909. An involuntary deposit is made:

1. By the accidental leaving or placing of personal property in the possession of any person, without negligence on the part of its owner; or,

2. In cases of fire, shipwreck, inundation, insurrection, riot, or like extraordinary emergencies, by the owner of personal property committing it, out of necessity, to the care of any person.

Id.

§ 910. The person with whom a thing is deposited, in the manner described in the last section, is bound to take charge of it, if able to do so.

Deposit for keeping, what.

§ 911. A deposit for keeping is one in which the depositary is bound to return the identical thing deposited.

Deposit for exchange, what.

§ 912. A deposit for exchange is one in which the depositary is only bound to return a thing corresponding in kind to that which is deposited.

ARTICLE II.

OBLIGATIONS OF THE DEPOSITARY.

Depositary must deliver on demand.

§ 913. A depositary must deliver the thing to the person for whose benefit it was deposited, on demand, whether the deposit was made for a specified time or not,[1] unless he has a lien upon the thing deposited, or has been forbidden or prevented from doing so by the real owner thereof,[2] or by the act of the law,[3] and has given the notice required by section 916.[4]

[1] Obviously, the depositary has no interest in the prolongation of the deposit, and therefore has no right

to insist upon it. He may be entitled to compensation for the whole period originally agreed upon, but that is another matter.

[2] Bates *v.* Stanton, 1 *Duer*, 79; Hardman *v.* Wilcock, 9 *Bing.*, 372; King *v.* Richards, 6 *Whart.*, 418. In other cases, the depositary cannot dispute his depositor's title (see Marvin *v.* Ellwood, 11 *Paige*, 365, 376; Gosling *v.* Birney, 6 *Bing.*, 339; Hall *v.* Griffin, 10 *id.*, 246; Kiernan *v.* Sanders, 6 *Ad. & El.*, 516).

[3] Bliven *v.* Hudson River R. R. Co., 35 *Barb.*, 188; see Stamford Steamboat Co. *v.* Gibbons, 9 *Wend.*, 327; Edson *v.* Weston, 7 *Cow.*, 278.

[4] Scrantom *v.* Farmers' and Mech. Bk., 24 *N. Y.*, 424, 427, by SUTHERLAND, J.

§ 914. A depositary is not bound to deliver a thing deposited without demand, even where the deposit is made for a specified time.

No obligation to deliver without demand

See Phelps *v.* Bostwick, 22 *Barb.*, 314; Downes *v.* Phœnix Bank, 6 *Hill*, 297; Brown *v.* Cook, 9 *Johns.*, 361.

§ 915. A depositary must deliver the thing deposited at his residence or place of business, as may be most convenient for him.

Place of delivery.

§ 916. A depositary must give prompt notice to the person for whose benefit the deposit was made, of any proceedings taken adversely to his interest in the thing deposited, which may tend to excuse the depositary from delivering the thing to him.

Notice to owner of adverse claim.

See Scrantom *v.* Farmers' & Mech. Bk., 24 *N. Y.*, 424.

§ 917. A depositary, who believes that a thing deposited with him is wrongfully detained from its true owner, may give him notice of the deposit; and if within a reasonable time afterwards he does not claim it, and sufficiently establish his right thereto, and indemnify the depositary against the claim of the depositor, the depositary is exonerated from liability to the person to whom he gave the notice, upon returning the thing to the depositor, or assuming, in good faith, a new obligation changing his position in respect to the thing, to his prejudice.

Notice to owner of thing wrongfully detained.

Modified from *Code La.*, 2931; *Story Bailm.*, §§ 102, 108.

Delivery of thing owned jointly, &c. § 918. If a thing deposited is owned jointly or in common by persons who cannot agree upon the manner of its delivery, the depositary may deliver to each his proper share thereof, if it can be done without injury to the thing.

This provision is new, but is intended to obviate a difficulty which may sometimes arise.

CHAPTER II.

DEPOSIT FOR KEEPING.

ARTICLE I.

GENERAL PROVISIONS.

Depositor must indemnify depositary. § 919. A depositor must indemnify the depositary:

1. For all damage caused to him by the defects or vices of the thing deposited; and,

2. For all expenses necessarily incurred by him about the thing, other than such as are involved in the nature of the undertaking.

Code La., 2931; *Code Napoleon*, 1947.

Obligation of depositary of animals. § 920. A depositary of living animals must provide them with suitable food and shelter, and treat them kindly.

§ 921. A depositary may not use the thing deposited, or permit it to be used, for any purpose, without the consent of the depositor.[1] He may not, if it is purposely fastened by the depositor, open it without the consent of the latter, except in case of necessity.[2]

Obligations as to use of thing deposited.

[1] *Story on Bailm.*, § 89; *Code La.*, 2911.
[2] *Story on Bailm.*, § 92; *Code La.*, 2914.

§ 922. A depositary is liable for any damage happening to the thing deposited during his wrongful use thereof, unless such damage must inevitably have happened though the property had not been thus used.

Liability for damage arising from wrongful use.

Story on Bailm., §§ 413 to 413 *d.*

§ 923. If a thing deposited is in actual danger of perishing before instructions can be obtained from the depositor, the depositary may sell it for the best price obtainable, and retain the proceeds as a deposit, giving immediate notice of his proceedings to the depositor.

Sale of thing in danger of perishing.

Story on Bailm., § 97.

§ 924. If a thing is lost or injured during its deposit, and the depositary refuses to inform the depositor of the circumstances under which the loss or injury occurred, so far as he has information concerning them, or willfully misrepresents the circumstances to him, the depositary is presumed to have willfully or by gross negligence permitted the loss or injury to occur.

Injury to, or loss of thing deposited.

There is no express authority for this provision, but it seems to be reasonable.

§ 925. So far as any service is rendered by a depositary, or required from him, his duties and liabilities are prescribed by the Title on EMPLOYMENT AND SERVICE.

Service rendered by depositary.

§ 926. The liability of a depositary for negligence is limited to the amount which he is informed or has reason to suppose the thing deposited to be worth.

Extent of his liability for negligence.

See *Story on Bailm.*, § 77.

ARTICLE II.

GRATUITOUS DEPOSIT.

Gratuitous deposit, what.

§ 927. Gratuitous deposit is a deposit for which the depositary receives no consideration beyond the mere possession of the thing deposited.

Nature of involuntary deposit.

§ 928. An involuntary deposit is gratuitous, the depositary being entitled to no reward.

Degree of care required of gratuitous depositary.

§ 929. A gratuitous depositary must use at least slight care for the preservation of the thing deposited.

His duties cease, when.

§ 930. The duties of a gratuitous depositary cease:

1. Upon his restoring the thing deposited to its owner; or,

2. Upon his giving reasonable notice to the owner to remove it, and the owner failing to do so within a reasonable time.[1] But an involuntary depositary, under subdivision 2 of section 909, cannot give such notice until the emergency which gave rise to the deposit is past.

[1] Roulston *v.* McClelland, 2 *E. D. Smith*, 60.

ARTICLE III.

STORAGE.

Deposit for hire.

§ 931. A deposit not gratuitous is called storage. The depositary in such case is called a depositary for hire.

§ 932. A depositary for hire must use at least ordinary care for the preservation of the thing deposited. Degree of care required of depositary for hire.

§ 933. In the absence of a different agreement or usage, a depositary for hire is entitled to one week's hire for the sustenance and shelter of living animals during any fraction of a week, and to half a month's hire for the storage of any other property during any fraction of a half month. Rate of compensation for fraction of a week, &c.

This is believed to be the general usage, especially in the city of New York.

§ 934. In the absence of an agreement as to the length of time during which a deposit is to continue, it may be terminated by the depositor at any time. and by the depositary upon reasonable notice. Termination of deposit.

§ 935. Notwithstanding an agreement respecting the length of time during which a deposit is to continue, it may be terminated by the depositor, on paying all that would become due to the depositary in case of the deposit so continuing. Id.

ARTICLE IV.

INNKEEPERS.

§ 936. An innkeeper is liable for all losses[1] of, or injuries[2] to, personal property placed by his guests[3] under his care,[4] unless occasioned by an irresistible superhuman cause, by a public enemy,[5] by the negligence of the owner,[6] or by the act of some one whom he brought into the inn.[7] Inn-keeper's liability.

[1] Gile *v.* Libby, 36 *Barb.*, 70; Clute *v.* Wiggins, 14 *Johns.*, 175.

[2] Washburn *v.* Jones, 14 *Barb.*, 193; Shaw *v.* Berry, 31 *Me.*, 478; see Dawson *v.* Chamney, 5 *Q. B.*, 164.

[3] Ingalsbee *v.* Wood, 36 *Barb.*, 452; Hursh *v.* Byers, 29 *Mo.*, 469; Ewart *v.* Stark, 8 *Rich. L.*, 423; Grinnell *v.* Cook, 3 *Hill*, 485; Wintermute *v.* Clarke, 5 *Sandf.*,

242; Gelley *v.* Clerk, *Cro. Jac.*, 188; see Washburn *v.* Jones, 14 *Barb.*, 193; McDonald *v.* Edgerton, 5 *id.*, 560; Berkshire Woolen Co. *v.* Proctor, 7 *Cush.*, 417.

[4] McDonald *v.* Edgerton, 5 *Barb.*, 560; Piper *v.* Manny, 21 *Wend.*, 282; Clute *v.* Wiggins, 14 *Johns.*, 175; Richmond *v.* Smith, 8 *B. & C.*, 9; Burgess *v.* Clements, 4 *M. & Selw.*, 306. The innkeeper is not responsible for goods which are not, in any proper sense, under his charge (Farnworth *v.* Packwood, 1 *Stark.*, 249; Sneider *v.* Geiss, 1 *Yeates*, 34; Hawley *v.* Smith, 25 *Wend.*, 642; see Burgess *v.* Clements, 4 *M. & Selw.*, 306).

[5] The liability of an innkeeper is regarded as the same as that of a common carrier, according to the weight of American authority (Hulett *v.* Swift, 42 *Barb.*, 230; Piper *v.* Manny, 21 *Wend.*, 282; Clute *v.* Wiggins, 14 *Johns.*, 175; Shaw *v.* Berry, 31 *Me.*, 478; Mateer *v.* Brown, 1 *Cal.*, 221; see McDonald *v.* Edgerton, 5 *Barb.*, 560; Richmond *v.* Smith, 8 *B. & C.*, 9.) To the contrary, see Merritt *v.* Claghorn, 23 *Vt.*, 177; Dawson *v.* Chamney, 5 *Q. B.*, 164.

[6] Purvis *v.* Coleman, 21 *N. Y.*, 111; Armistead *v.* Wilde, 17 *Q. B.*, 261; Burgess *v.* Clements, 4 *M. & Selw.*, 306; Fowler *v.* Dorlon, 24 *Barb.*, 384.

[7] Calye's Case, 8 *Co. Rep.*, 32.

How exempted from liability.

§ 937. If an innkeeper keeps a fireproof safe, and gives notice to a guest, either personally, or by putting up a printed notice in a prominent place in the room occupied by the guest, that he keeps such a safe, and will not be liable for money, jewelry, documents, or other articles of unusual value and small compass, unless placed therein, he is not liable, except so far as his own acts contribute thereto, for any loss of, or injury to, such articles, if not deposited with him, and not required by the guest for present use.

Laws 1855, *ch.* 421; Purvis *v.* Coleman, 21 *N. Y.*, 111

ARTICLE V.

FINDING.

§ 938. One who finds a thing lost, is not bound to take charge of it, but if he does so, he is thenceforward a depositary for the owner,[1] with the rights and obligations of a depositary for hire.[2] Obligation of finder.

[1] Isaac *v.* Clark, 2 *Bulst.*, 306.

[2] This section, and some of the ensuing ones, differ materially from the common law, under which the finder is a gratuitous depositary. Mr. Justice STORY considered the law in this respect to be unsatisfactory, and the commissioners have altered it, giving the finder a reward, and holding him to a corresponding accountability. This is more just to both parties.

§ 939. If the finder of a thing knows or suspects who is the owner, he must, with reasonable diligence, give him notice of the finding; and if he fails to do so, he is liable in damages to the owner, and has no claim to any reward offered by him for the recovery of the thing, or to any compensation for his trouble or expenses. Finder to notify owner.

This provision is manifestly just, and is probably in accordance with the present law.

§ 940. The finder of a thing may, in good faith, before giving it up, require reasonable proof of ownership from any person claiming it. Claimant to prove ownership.

Isaac *v.* Clark, 2 *Bulst.*, 306.

§ 941. The finder of a thing is entitled to compensation for all expenses necessarily incurred by him in its preservation, and for any other service necessarily performed by him about it, and to a reasonable reward for keeping it. Reward, &c., to finder.

See *Story Bailm.*, § 121 *a*; Nicholson *v.* Chapman, 2 *H. Bl.*, 254.

§ 942. The finder of a thing may exonerate himself from liability at any time, by placing it on Finder may put thing found on storage.

storage with any responsible person of good character, at a reasonable expense.

It does not seem just to compel the finder to keep the property in his own charge. On the other hand, he should not be allowed to put the loser to unnecessary expense.

When finder may sell the thing found.

§ 943. The finder of a thing may sell it, if it is a thing which is commonly the subject of sale, when the owner cannot with reasonable diligence be found, or, being found, refuses upon demand to pay the lawful charges of the finder, in the following cases:

1. When the thing is in danger of perishing, or of losing the greater part of its value; or,

2. When the lawful charges of the finder amount to two-thirds of its value.

This provision is new.

How sale is to be made.

§ 944. A sale under the provisions of the last section must be made in the same manner as the sale of a thing pledged.

For the rules governing such a sale, see the chapter on PLEDGE.

Surrender of thing to the finder

§ 945. The owner of a thing found may exonerate himself from the claims of the finder by surrendering it to him in satisfaction thereof.

This provision cannot be supported by the citation of any positive authority, but seems proper, in order to prevent owners from being made responsible for excessive expenses.

Thing abandoned.

§ 946. The provisions of this article have no application to things which have been intentionally abandoned by their owners.

In McGoon *v.* Ankeny, 11 *Ill.*, 558, it was very properly held that the finder of a thing, which the owner had intentionally thrown away, acquired an absolute title thereto.

CHAPTER III.

DEPOSIT FOR EXCHANGE.

§ 947. A deposit for exchange transfers to the depositary the title to the thing deposited, and creates between him and the depositor the relation of debtor and creditor merely. Relations of the parties.

Chapman *v.* White, 6 *N. Y.*, 412; Lund *v.* Seamen's Savings Bank, 37 *Barb.*, 129; Marsh *v.* Oneida Central Bank, 34 *id.*, 598; Commercial Bank *v.* Hughes, 17 *Wend.*, 94; Matter of Franklin Bank, 1 *Paige*, 249.

TITLE IV.

LOAN.

CHAPTER I.

LOAN FOR USE.

§ 948. A loan for use is a contract by which one gives to another the temporary possession and use of personal property, and the latter agrees to return Loan, what.

the same thing to him at a future time, without reward for its use.

Title to property lent.

§ 949. A loan for use does not transfer the title to the thing; and all its increase during the period of the loan belongs to the lender.

Care required of borrower.

§ 950. A borrower for use must use great care for the preservation in safety and in good condition of the thing lent.

Scranton *v.* Baxter, 4 *Sandf.*, 5; Phillips *v.* Condon, 14 *Ill.*, 84; see Howard *v.* Babcock, 21 *id.*, 259.

Id.

§ 951. One who borrows a living animal for use, must treat it with great kindness, and provide everything necessary and suitable for it.

Degree of skill.

§ 952. A borrower for use is bound to have and to exercise such skill in the care of the thing lent, as he causes the lender to believe him to possess.

Story on Bailm., § 237.

Borrowed, when to repair injuries.

§ 953. A borrower for use must repair all deteriorations or injuries to the thing lent, which are occasioned by his negligence, however slight.

Use of thing lent.

§ 954. The borrower of a thing for use may use it for such purposes only as the lender might reasonably anticipate at the time of lending.

Story on Bailm., § 232.

Relending forbidden.

§ 955. The borrower of a thing for use must not part with it to a third person, without the consent of the lender.

Story on Bailm., § 234; Esmay *v.* Fanning, 9 *Barb.*, 176; 5 *How. Pr.*, 228; see Bringloe *v.* Morrice, 1 *Mod.*, 210.

Borrower, when to bear expenses.

§ 956. The borrower of a thing for use must bear all its expenses during the loan, except such as are necessarily incurred by him to preserve it from unexpected and unusual injury. For such expenses he is entitled to compensation from the lender, who may, however, exonerate himself by surrendering the thing to the borrower.

See *Story on Bailm.*, § 273.

§ 957. The lender of a thing for use must indemnify the borrower for damage caused by defects or vices in it, which he knew at the time of lending, and concealed from the borrower. **Lender liable for defects.**

Story on Bailm., § 275; approved, Blakemore *v.* Bristol and Exeter Railway Co., 8 *El. & Bl.*, 1035, 1051; and the rule limited to defects thus known and concealed (M'Carthy *v.* Young, 6 *H. & N.*, 329).

§ 958. The lender of a thing for use may at any time require its return, even though he lent it for a specified time or purpose.[1] But if, on the faith of such an agreement, the borrower has made such arrangements that a return of the thing before the period agreed upon would cause him loss, exceeding the benefit derived by him from the loan, the lender must indemnify him for such loss, if he compels such return, the borrower not having in any manner violated his duty.[2] **Lender may require return of thing lent.**

[1] *Edw. on Bailm.*, 143.
[2] *Story on Bailm.*, § 258.

§ 959. If a thing is lent for use for a specified time or purpose, it must be returned to the lender without demand, as soon as the time has expired, or the purpose has been accomplished. In other cases it need not be returned until demanded. **When returnable without demand.**

Gilbert *v.* Manchester Iron Mfg. Co., 11 *Wend.*, 625.

§ 960. The borrower of a thing for use must return it to the lender, at the place contemplated by the parties at the time of lending; or if no particular place was so contemplated by them, then at the place where it was at that time. **Place of return.**

CHAPTER II.

LOAN FOR EXCHANGE.

Loan for exchange, what.

§ 961. A loan for exchange is a contract by which one delivers personal property to another, and the latter agrees to return to the lender a similar thing at a future time, without reward for its use.

Id.

§ 962. A loan, which the borrower is allowed by the lender to treat as a loan for use, or for exchange, at his option, is subject to all the provisions of this chapter.

This provision is necessary to prevent frauds upon third persons.

Title to property lent.

§ 963. By a loan for exchange the title to the thing lent is transferred to the borrower, and he must bear all its expenses, and is entitled to all its increase.

See Norton *v.* Woodruff, 2 *N. Y.*, 153; Foster *v.* Pettibone, 7 *id.*, 433; Mallory *v.* Willis, 4 *id.*, 76; Hurd *v.* West, 7 *Cow.*, 752; Carpenter *v.* Griffin, 9 *Paige*, 310.

Contract cannot be modified by lender.

§ 964. A lender for exchange cannot require the borrower to fulfill his obligations at a time, or in a manner, different from that which was originally agreed upon.

This follows from the nature of the contract. It is, in fact, simply an executory exchange.

Certain sections applicable.

§ 965. Sections 957, 959, and 960, apply to a loan for exchange.

CHAPTER III.

LOAN OF MONEY.

Originally, no interest was allowed upon a loan of money. But with the progress of business, it became necessary, and the transaction thus entered into, although in strictness a hiring, is universally known as a loan. This use of the word having obtained so long, it would be idle to attempt to change it.

§ 966. A loan of money is a contract by which one delivers a sum of money to another, and the latter agrees to return at a future time a sum equivalent to that which he borrowed. A loan for mere use is governed by the chapter on LOAN FOR USE. *Loan of money.*

§ 967. A borrower of money must pay the amount due in such money as is current at the time when the loan becomes due, whether such money is worth more or less than the actual money lent. *Loan to be repaid in current money.*

Code La., 2884.

§ 968. A loan of money may be made with or without reward, but is presumed to be made for reward. *Loan may be for reward.*

Gillet *v.* Van Rensselaer, 15 *N. Y.*, 397.

§ 969. Reward for the loan, forbearance, or use of money, or its equivalent, is called interest. *Interest, what.*

Annual rate.

§ 970. When a rate of interest is prescribed by a law or contract, without specifying the period of time by which such rate is to be calculated, it is to be deemed an annual rate.

1 *R. S.*, 773.

Legal interest.

§ 971. Under an obligation to pay interest, no rate being specified, interest is payable at the rate of seven one-hundredths of the principal for one year, and in the like proportion for a longer or shorter time;[1] but in the computation of interest for less than a year, three hundred and sixty days are deemed to constitute a year.[2]

[1] 1 *R. S.*, 771.
[2] 1 *R. S.*, 773.

Id.

§ 972. No greater interest than is allowed by the last section may be taken,[1] except from a state or corporation.[2]

[1] 1 *R. S.*, 772.
[2] By *Laws* 1850, 344, ch. 172, corporations are forbidden to interpose the defense of usury. This has been construed as not merely prohibiting them from setting up usury as a *defense*, but also as prohibiting them from maintaining an action to recover back the usury (Butterworth *v.* O'Brien, 23 *N. Y.*, 275; 28 *Barb.*, 187); and, in short, as a repeal of the usury laws so far as they operated in favor of corporations (Curtis *v.* Leavitt, 15 *N. Y.*, 9; Belmont Bank *v.* Hoge, 7 *Bosw.*, 543). It has, however, been held that their sureties can defend on this ground (Hungerford's Bank *v.* Dodge, 30 *Barb.*, 626; 10 *Abb. Pr.*, 24). The provision here introduced would prevent this from being done.

Deduction of amount of interest in advance.

§ 973. The interest which would become due at the end of the term for which a loan is made, not exceeding one year's interest in all, may be deducted from the loan in advance, if the parties thus agree.

Marvine *v.* Hymers, 12 *N. Y.*, 227. Perhaps the term should be less than a year under this decision. The longest term for which there is express authority, is six months, but the decisions have not laid down any precise rule as to time.

§ 983. The hirer of a thing must repair all deteriorations or injuries thereto occasioned by his ordinary negligence.

Must repair injuries, &c.

§ 984. When a thing is let for a particular purpose, the hirer must not use it for any other purpose; and if he does, the letter may hold him responsible for its safety during such use, in all events, or may treat the contract as thereby rescinded.

Thing let for a particular purpose.

This is an established rule as to personal property (Fish *v.* Ferris, 5 *Duer*, 49; *Story Bailm.*, § 43; Columbus *v.* Howard, 6 *Geo.*, 213; Duncan *v.* R. R. Co., 2 *Rich. L.*, 613; see Harrington *v.* Snyder, 3 *Barb.*, 380). It may be doubted whether the same rule is applied to real property.

§ 985. The letter of a thing may terminate the hiring, and reclaim the thing, before the end of the term agreed upon:

When letter may terminate the hiring.

1. When the hirer uses, or permits a use of the thing hired, in a manner contrary to the agreement of the parties; or,

2. When the hirer does not, within a reasonable time after request, make such repairs as he is bound to make.

§ 986. The hirer of a thing may terminate the hiring before the end of the term agreed upon:

When hirer may terminate the hiring.

1. When the letter does not, within a reasonable time after request, fulfill his obligations, if any, as to placing and securing the hirer in the quiet possession of the thing hired, or putting it into good condition, or repairing; or,

2. When the greater part of the thing hired, or that part which was, and which the letter had, at the time of the hiring, reason to believe was, the material inducement to the hirer to enter into the contract, perishes from any other cause than the ordinary negligence of the hirer.

§ 987. The hiring of a thing terminates:

When hiring terminates.

1. At the end of the term agreed upon;

2. By the mutual consent of the parties;

3. By the hirer acquiring a title to the thing hired, superior to that of the letter; or,

4. By the destruction of the thing hired.

As to subdivision 4, see Graves *v.* Berdan, 26 *N. Y.*, 498
The other clauses are matters of course.

When terminated by death, &c., of party.

§ 988. If the hiring of a thing is terminable at the pleasure of one of the parties, it is terminated by notice to the other of his death or incapacity to contract. In other cases, it is not terminated thereby.

Story Bailm., § 419.

Apportionment of hire

§ 989. When the hiring of a thing is terminated before the time originally agreed upon, the hirer must pay the due proportion of the hire for such use as he has actually made of the thing, unless such use is merely nominal, and of no benefit to him.

Modified from *Story on Bailm.*, § 418, 418 *a.*
See Harrington *v.* Snyder, 3 *Barb.*, 380; George *v.* Elliott, 2 *Hen. & Munf.*, 5; Dudgeon *v.* Teass, 9 *Mo.*, 867; Bacot *v.* Parnell, 2 *Bailey*, 424; Williams *v.* Holcombe, 1 *N. C. Law*, 365; Redding *v.* Hall, 1 *Bibb*, 536; Harrison *v.* Murrell, 5 *Monr.*, 359.

CHAPTER II.

HIRING OF REAL PROPERTY.

Lessor to make dwelling house fit for its purpose.

§ 990. The lessor of a building intended for the occupation of human beings must put it into a condition fit for that purpose, and must repair all subsequent dilapidations thereof, except such as are mentioned in section 983.

This section changes the rule upon this subject to conform to that which, notwithstanding steady judicial adherence for hundreds of years to the adverse doctrine, is generally believed by the unprofessional public to be law, and upon which basis they almost always contract. The very fact that there are repeated decisions to the contrary, down to the year 1861, shows that the public do not and cannot understand their justice, or even realize their existence. So familiar a point of law could not rise again and again for adjudication, were it not that the community at large revolt at every application of the rule. A partial reform has been effected by the legislature, in suspending the rent of houses destroyed or injured, in certain cases (*Laws* 1860, *ch.* 345), and it ought to be carried still further.

§ 991. If, within a reasonable time after notice to the lessor of dilapidations which he ought to repair, he neglects to do so, the lessee may repair the same himself, and deduct the expense of such repairs from the rent, or otherwise recover it from the lessor.

When lessee may make repairs, &c.

§ 992. A hiring of real property, other than lodgings, is presumed to extend to the next day upon which it is the usage of the place to make annual hirings of real property. In the cities of New York and Brooklyn, that day is the first of May. In places where there is no usage on the subject, such a hiring is presumed to be for one year from its commencement.

Term of hiring when no limit is fixed.

The most of this section is new. So far as relates to New York, it is from 1 *R. S.*, 744.

§ 993. A hiring of lodgings for an unspecified term is presumed to have been made for such length of time as the parties adopt for the estimation of the rent. Thus a hiring at a weekly rate of rent is presumed to be for one week. In the absence of any agreement respecting the length of time or the rent, the hiring is presumed to be monthly.

Hiring of lodgings for indefinite term.

Code Napoleon, 1758. See Jones *v.* Mills, 10 *C. B.*, [*N. S.*], 788.

§ 994. If a lessee of real property remains in possession thereof, after the expiration of the hiring, and the lessor accepts rent from him, the parties are presumed to have renewed the hiring on the same terms

Renewal of lease by lessee's continued possession.

and for the same time, not exceeding one year, or, in the cities of New York and Brooklyn, not longer than until the next first day of May.

Bishop *v.* Howard, 2 *B. & C.*, 100; see Doe *v.* Amey, 12 *Ad. & El.*, 476; Despard *v.* Walbridge, 15 *N. Y.*, 374.

Notice to quit.

§ 995. Except in the cities of New York and Brooklyn, a hiring of real property, for a term not specified by the parties, is deemed to be renewed as stated in the last section, at the end of the term implied by law, unless one of the parties gives notice to the other of his intention to terminate the same, at least as long before the expiration thereof as the term of the hiring itself, not exceeding one month.

See Jones *v.* Mills, 10 *C. B.* [*N. S.*], 788.

Rent, when payable.

§ 996. The rent of agricultural and wild land is payable yearly at the end of each year. Rents of lodgings are payable monthly at the end of each month. Other rents are payable quarterly at the end of each quarter from the time the hiring takes effect, except in the cities of New York and Brooklyn, where rents are payable quarterly on the first days of August, November, February and May. The rent for a hiring shorter than the periods herein specified, is payable at the termination of the hiring.

The provision concerning the city of New York is from 1 *R. S.*, 744, § 1, extended to Brooklyn, where the same usage exists.

Tenant must deliver notice served on him.

§ 997. Every tenant who receives notice of any proceeding to recover the real property occupied by him, or the possession thereof, must immediately inform his landlord of the same.

1 *R. S.*, 748, § 27.

Letting parts of room forbidden.

§ 998. One who hires part of a room, for a dwelling, is entitled to the whole of the room, notwithstanding any agreement to the contrary; and if a landlord lets a room as a dwelling for more than one family, the person to whom he first lets any part of it is entitled to the possession of the whole room for the term agreed upon, and every tenant in the building, under the same landlord, is relieved from all obligation to pay rent to him.

This provision is intended to prevent one of the chief abuses of tenement houses. Mere penalties, whether civil or criminal, are not likely to be enforced. But the loss of rent would be a punishment that could be enforced by way of defense to an action.

CHAPTER III.

HIRING OF PERSONAL PROPERTY.

§ 999. One who lets personal property must deliver it to the hirer, secure his quiet enjoyment thereof against all lawful claimants, put it into a condition fit for the purpose for which he lets it, and repair all deteriorations thereof not occasioned by the fault of the hirer, and not the natural result of its use. Obligations of letter of personal property.

Story Bailm., § 383.

§ 1000. A hirer of personal property must bear all such expenses concerning it as might naturally be foreseen to attend it during its use by him.[1] All other expenses must be borne by the letter.[2] Ordinary expenses.

[1] See Handford *v.* Palmer, 2 *Brod. & B.*, 359.

[2] *Story Bailm.*, §§ 388, 389; Harrington *v.* Snyder, 3 *Barb.*, 380.

§ 1001. If a letter fails to fulfill his obligations, as prescribed by section 999, the hirer, after giving him notice to do so, if such notice can conveniently be given, may expend any reasonable amount necessary to make good the letter's default, and may recover such amount from him. Extraordinary expenses.

Thus the hirer of an animal may recover the expense of necessary medical attendance and extra accommodations during its sickness (Harrington *v.* Snyder, 3 *Barb.*, 380; Isbell *v.* Norvell, 4 *Gratt.*, 176; see, however, Redding *v.* Hall, 1 *Bibb*, 536).

Return of thing hired. § 1002. At the expiration of the term for which personal property is hired, the hirer must return it to the letter at the place contemplated by the parties at the time of hiring, or if no particular place was so contemplated by them, at the place which it was at that time.

Charter-party, what. § 1003. The contract by which a ship is let is termed a charter-party. By it, the owner may either let the capacity or burden of the ship, continuing the employment of the owner's master, crew and equipments, or may surrender the entire ship to the charterer, who then provides them himself. The master or a part owner may be a charterer.

1 *Pars. Mar. Law*, 229, &c.

TITLE VI.

SERVICE.

CHAPTER I.

SERVICE WITH EMPLOYMENT.

ARTICLE I.

DEFINITION OF EMPLOYMENT.

Employment, what. § 1004. The contract of employment is a contract by which one, who is called the employer, engages another, who is called the employee, to do something for the benefit of the employer or of a third person.

The scope of this chapter is not confined to servants, but includes factors, brokers, carriers, agents, and all similar classes of persons.

ARTICLE II.

OBLIGATIONS OF THE EMPLOYER.

§ 1005. An employer must indemnify his employee, except as prescribed in the next section, for all that he necessarily expends or loses in direct consequence of the discharge of his duties as such,[1] or of his obedience to the directions of the employer,[2] even though unlawful,[3] unless the employee, at the time of obeying such directions, believed them to be unlawful. When employer must indemnify employee.

[1] *Story Agency*, § 335 to § 340; *Code of La.*, 2991, 2993; Castle *v.* Noyes, 14 *N. Y.*, 332; Powell *v.* Newburgh, 19 *Johns.*, 284; Ramsay *v.* Gardner, 11 *id.*, 439; Adamson *v.* Jarvis, 4 *Bing.*, 66; Betts *v.* Gibbins, 2 *Ad. & El.*, 57; Taylor *v.* Stray, 2 *C. B.* (*N. S.*), 196.

[2] Roberts *v.* Smith, 2 *H. & N.*, 213.

[3] Adamson *v.* Jarvis, 4 *Bing.*, 66; see Humphrys *v.* Pratt, 5 *Bligh* (*N. S.*), 154; as explained in Collins *v.* Evans, 5 *Q. B.*, 829, 830.

§ 1006. An employer is not bound to indemnify his employee for losses suffered by the latter in consequence of the ordinary risks of the business in which he is employed, nor in consequence of the negligence of another person employed by the same employer in the same general business,[1] unless he has neglected to use ordinary care in the selection of the culpable employee.[2] When not.

[1] Sherman *v.* Rochester & Syracuse R. R., 17 *N. Y.*, 156; Russell *v.* Hudson River R. R., *id.*, 136; Coon *v.* Syracuse & Utica R. R., 5 *id.*, 492; Boldt *v.* New York Central R. R., 18 *id.*, 432.

[2] See same cases, and Ormond *v.* Holland, *El. B. & E.*, 105.

Employer to indemnify for his own negligence.

§ 1007. An employer must in all cases indemnify his employee for losses caused by his own want of ordinary care.

Ryan *v.* Fowler, 24 *N. Y.*, 410; Roberts *v.* Smith, 2 *H. & N.*, 213; Keegan *v.* Western R. R., 8 *N. Y.*, 175, 180.

ARTICLE III.

OBLIGATIONS OF THE EMPLOYEE.

Duties of gratuitous employee.

§ 1008. One who, without consideration, undertakes to do a service for another, is not bound to perform the same, but if he actually enters upon its performance, he must use at least slight care and diligence therein.

Edson *v.* Watson, 7 *Cow.*, 278; Coggs *v.* Bernard, 2 *Ld. Raym.*, 909; Elsee *v.* Gatward, 5 *T. R.*, 143; Wilson *v.* Brett, 11 *M. & W.*, 113; see Nolton *v.* Western R. R., 15 *N. Y.*, 440.

Id.

§ 1009. One who, by his own special request, induces another to intrust him with the performance of a service, must perform the same fully. In other cases one who undertakes a gratuitous service may relinquish it at any time.

Story Bailm., § 166. This distinction is recognized by the civil law, but it is not clear that it is admitted by the common law. There is good reason for it, since a volunteer of this kind might seriously mislead one who relied upon him, and who would otherwise have employed some one else for a compensation, and thus have been sure of the service he required.

§ 1010. A gratuitous employee, who accepts a written power of attorney, must act under it so long as it remains in force, or until he gives notice to his employer that he will not do so. Id.

Code La., 2971. This provision is new to the common law: but is founded upon justice. By retaining the instrument, the attorney keeps in his hands a power which he may use to the detriment of his principal, and misleads the latter into the belief that he will use it for his benefit.

Duties of employee for reward.

§ 1011. One who, for a good consideration, agrees to serve another, must perform the service, and must use ordinary care and diligence therein, so long as he is thus employed.

Story on Bailm., §§ 398, 399, 429, 442. *Ordinary* care and diligence are all that are required (Johnson *v.* N. Y. Central R. R., 31 *Barb.*, 196; Ackley *v.* Kellogg, 8 *Cow.*, 223; Brown *v.* Denison, 2 *Wend.*, 593; Platt *v.* Hibbard, 7 *Cow.*, 497).

Duties of employee for his own benefit.

§ 1012. One who is employed at his own request to do that which is more for his own advantage than for that of his employer, must use great care and diligence therein to protect the interest of the latter.

Contracts for service limited to two years.

§ 1013. A contract to render personal service, other than a contract of apprenticeship under sections 140, 143, or 149, cannot be enforced against the employee beyond the term of two years from the commencement of service under it, but if the employee voluntarily continues his service under it beyond that time, the contract may be referred to as affording a presumptive measure of the compensation.

This section is new.

Employee must obey employer.

§ 1014. An employee must substantially[1] comply with all the directions of his employer[2] concerning the service on which he is engaged, even though contrary to the provisions of this Title, except where such obedience is impossible[3], or unlawful, or would impose new and unreasonable burdens upon the employee, or in case of an emergency which, according to the best information which the employee can with reasonable diligence obtain, the employer did not contemplate, in which he cannot, with reasonable diligence, be consulted, and in which non-compliance is judged by the employee, in good faith, and in the exercise of reasonable discretion, to be absolutely necessary for the protection of the employer's interests.[4] In all such cases, the employee must conform as nearly to the directions of his employer as may be reasonably practicable, and most for the interest of the latter.[5]

[1] Substantial and not literal obedience, is required (Johnson *v.* N. Y. Central R. R., 31 *Barb.*, 196; Parkhill *v.* Imlay, 15 *Wend.*, 431).

[2] Evans *v.* Root, 7 *N. Y.*, 186; Blot *v.* Boiceau, 3 *id.*, 78; Bruce *v.* Davenport, 36 *Barb.*, 349; Bell *v.* Palmer, 6 *Cow.*, 128; Wilson *v.* Wilson, 26 *Penn. St.*, 394; see Johnson *v.* N. Y. Central R. R., 31 *Barb.*, 196; Ackley *v.* Kellogg, 8 *Cow.*, 223; Turner *v.* Mason, 14 *M. & W.*, 112; Amor *v.* Fearon, 9 *Ad. & El.*, 548.

[3] Johnson *v.* N. Y. Central R. R., 31 *Barb.*, 196; Drummond *v.* Wood, 2 *Cai.*, 310.

[4] *Ib.*; *Story on Agency*, §§ 85, 141, 193; Dusar *v.* Perit, 4 *Binn.*, 361.

[5] Johnson *v.* N. Y. Central R. R., 31 *Barb.*, 196.

Employee to conform to usage

§ 1015. An employee must perform his service in conformity to the usage of the place of performance, unless otherwise directed by his employer, or unless it is impracticable, or manifestly injurious to his employer to do so.

Story on Agency, § 199; Johnson *v.* N. Y. Central R. R., 31 *Barb.*, 196; see Horton *v.* Morgan, 19 *N. Y.*, 170.

Degree of skill required.

§ 1016. An employee is bound to exercise a reasonable degree of skill,[1] unless his employer has notice, before employing him, of his want of skill.[2]

[1] Harmer *v.* Cornelius, 5 *C. B.* (*N. S.*), 236; *Story Bailm.*, §§ 431–435; see Cuckson *v.* Stones, 1 *El. & El.*, 248.

[2] Shiells *v.* Blackburne, 1 *H. Blacks.*, 158; Felt *v.* School Dist., 24 *Vt.*, 297.

§ 1017. An employee is always bound to use such skill as he possesses. **Must use what skill he has.**

Wilson *v.* Brett, 11 *M. & W.*, 113.

§ 1018. Everything which an employee acquires by virtue of his employment, except the compensation, if any, which is due to him from his employer, belongs to the latter, whether acquired lawfully or unlawfully,[1] or during, or after the expiration of,[2] the term of his employment. **What belongs to employer.**

[1] *Code La.*, 2974; see Tenant *v.* Elliott, 1 *Bos. & P.*, 3; Farmer *v.* Russell, *id.*, 296; Bousfield *v.* Wilson, 16 *M. & W.*, 185.

[2] Edmondstone *v.* Hartshorne, 19 *N. Y.*, 9.

§ 1019. An employee must, on demand, render to his employer just accounts of all his transactions in the course of his service, as often as may be reasonable,[1] and must, without demand, give prompt notice to his employer of everything which he receives for his account.[2] **Duty to account.**

[1] *Story on Agency*, § 203; Collyer *v.* Dudley, *Turn. & Russ.*, 421.

[2] By DUER, J., Heubach *v.* Mollmann, 2 *Duer*, 227, 252; see Edmonstone *v.* Hartshorne, 19 *N. Y.*, 9.

§ 1020. An employee, who receives anything on account of his employer, in any capacity other than that of a mere servant, is not bound to deliver it to him until demanded,[1] and is not at liberty to send it to him from a distance without demand,[2] in any mode involving greater risk than its retention by the employee himself.[3] **Employee not bound to deliver without demand.**

[1] This seems to the commissioners to be the true principle upon which the cases holding a demand to be necessary as against a factor (Baird *v.* Walker, 12 *Barb.*, 298; Halden *v.* Crafts, 4 *E. D. Smith*, 490; 2 *Abb. Pr.*, 301; Cooley *v.* Betts, 24 *Wend.*, 203; Ferris *v.* Paris, 10 *Johns.*, 285), an attorney (Stafford *v.* Richardson, 15 *Wend.*, 302; Rathbun *v.* Ingalls, 7 *id.*, 320; Taylor *v.* Bates, 5 *Cow.*, 376; Beardsley *v.* Root, 11 *Johns.*, 464) and other agents (Reina *v.* Cross, 6 *Cal.*, 31), are founded. In Lillie *v.* Hoyt (5 *Hill*, 395), the rule was limited to attorneys and

factors, but without reason. The defendant, in that case, seems to have been a mere servant. In Stacy *v.* Graham (14 *N. Y.*, 492; affirming S. C., 3 *Duer*, 444), the defendant had been *instructed* to remit.

[2] Heubach *v.* Mollmann, 2 *Duer*, 227.

[3] This qualification seems to be only just to the employee.

Preference to be given to employers.

§ 1021. An employee, who has any business to transact on his own account, similar to that intrusted to him by his employer, must always give the latter the preference. If intrusted with similar affairs by different employers, he must give them preference according to their relative urgency, or, other things being equal, according to the order in which they were committed to him.

There is no direct authority for these provisions, but they are required by sound principle.

Responsibility of employee for substitute.

§ 1022. An employee, who is expressly authorized to employ a substitute, is liable to his principal only for want of ordinary care in his selection. The substitute is directly responsible to the principal.

Story on Agency, § 217 *a*.

Responsibility for negligence.

§ 1023. An employee, who is guilty of a culpable degree of negligence, is liable to his employer for the damage thereby caused to the latter; and the employer is liable to him, if the service is not gratuitous, for the value of such services only as are properly rendered.

Surviving employee.

§ 1024. Where service is to be rendered by two or more persons jointly, and one of them dies, the survivor must act alone, if the service to be rendered is such as he can rightly perform without the aid of the deceased person, but not otherwise.

See *Story on Bailm.*, § 202.

Confidential employment.

§ 1025. The obligations peculiar to confidential employments are defined in the Title on Trusts.

ARTICLE IV.

TERMINATION OF EMPLOYMENT.

§ 1026. Every employment, in which the power of the employee is not coupled with an interest in its subject, is terminated by notice to him of: *Termination by death, &c., of employer*

1. The death of the employer; or,
2. His legal incapacity to contract.

This section alters the common law by continuing the power until the agent has notice of the principal's change of condition. Such a rule is advocated by Story (*Agency*, § 495), and is obviously just.

§ 1027. Every employment is terminated: *Employment, how terminated.*

1. By the expiration of its appointed term;
2. By the extinction of its subject;
3. By the death of the employee; or,
4. By his legal incapacity to act as such.

§ 1028. An employee, unless the term of his service has expired, or unless he has a right to discontinue it at any time, without notice, must continue his service after notice of the death or incapacity of his employer, so far as is necessary to protect from serious injury the interests of the employer's successor in interest, until a reasonable time after notice of the facts has been communicated to such successor. The successor must compensate the employee for such service, according to the terms of the contract of employment. *Continuance of service in certain cases.*

Termination at will.

§ 1029. An employment having no specified term may be terminated at the will of either party, on notice to the other, except where otherwise provided by this Title.

Story Ag., §§ 462, 476, 477; Hathaway *v.* Bennett, 10 *N. Y.*, 108; Ward *v.* Ruckman, 34 *Barb.*, 419; see Beeston *v.* Collyer, 4 *Bing.*, 309.

Termination by employer for fault.

§ 1030. An employment, even for a specified term, may be terminated at any time by the employer, in case of any willful breach of duty by the employee, in the course of his employment,[1] or in case of his habitual neglect of his duty,[2] or continued incapacity to perform it.[3]

[1] Mc Donald *v.* Lord, 26 *How. Pr.*, 404; Lilly *v.* Elwin, 11 *Q. B.*, 742; Ridgway *v.* Hungerford Market Co., 3 *Ad. & El.*, 171; Turner *v.* Mason, 14 *M. & W.*, 112.

[2] See Fillieul *v.* Armstrong, 7 *Ad. & El.*, 557; Callo *v.* Brouncker, 4 *Carr. & P.*, 518. A dismissal may be justified on these grounds, whether the employer knew of their existence or not (Spotswood *v.* Barrow, 5 *Exch.*, 110).

[3] Harmer *v.* Cornelius, 5 *C. B.* (*N. S.*), 236; see Cuckson *v.* Stones, 1 *El. & El.*, 248.

Termination by employee for fault.

§ 1031. An employment, even for a specified term, may be terminated by the employee at any time, in case of any willful or permanent breach of the obligations of his employer to him as an employee.

Upon principle, the right of terminating the contract for breach of duty ought to be mutual.

A female servant was held justified in quitting service, on account of indecent assaults by her master's father, although her master had no part in them; his failure to protect her being held sufficient cause for leaving (Patterson *v.* Gage, 23 *Verm.*, 558). A servant who, not being in fault, was required to promise "to do better," as a condition of his remaining, was held to have rightly refused to stay upon those terms (Pritchard *v.* Martin, 27 *Miss.*, 305).

A seaman is justified in quitting the ship if it is unseaworthy (Savary *v.* Clements, 8 *Gray*, 155; Bucker *v.* Klerkgeter, 1 *Abbott Adm.*, 402; Bray *v.* The Atlanta, *Bee Adm.*, 48), or if no provisions are furnished him (The Castalia, 1 *Hagg. Adm.*, 59; Dixon *v.* The Cyrus, 2 *Pet. Adm.*, 407), or if he is cruelly treated (Ward *v.* Ames, 9 *Johns.*, 138; Relf *v.* The Maria, 1 *Pet. Adm.*,

193; The Minerva, 1 *Hagg. Adm.*, 368; Steele *v.* Thatcher, *Ware*, 94), or even threatened with cruelty (Edward *v.* Trevellick, 4 *El. & Bl.*, 59).

The principle upon which these decisions are founded is evidently that stated in the text.

§ 1032. An employee, dismissed by his employer for good cause, is not entitled to any compensation for services rendered since the last day upon which a payment became due to him under the contract. Compensation of employee dismissed for cause.

Thus a clerk, whose salary is payable quarterly, is not entitled to any salary for the fraction of a quarter, in the course of which he is dismissed for cause (Ridgway *v.* Hungerford Market Co., 3 *Ad. & El.*, 171; Turner *v.* Robinson, 5 *B. & Ad.*, 789; 6 *Car. & P.*, 15; Atkin *v.* Acton, 4 *Car. & P.*, 208). But he ought to recover the preceding quarter's salary, if not paid.

§ 1033. An employee, who quits the service of his employer for good cause, is entitled to such proportion of the compensation which would become due in case of full performance, as the services which he has already rendered bear to the services which he was to render as full performance. Compensation of employee leaving for cause.

Patterson *v.* Gage, 23 *Verm.*, 558; Pritchard *v.* Martin, 27 *Miss.*, 305.

CHAPTER II.

PARTICULAR EMPLOYMENTS.

ARTICLE I.

MASTER AND SERVANT.

Servant, what.

§ 1034. A servant is one who is employed to render personal service to his employer, otherwise than in the pursuit of an independent calling, and who in such service remains entirely under the control and direction of the latter, who is called his master.

Term of hiring.

§ 1035. A servant is presumed to have been hired for such length of time as the parties adopt for the estimation of wages. A hiring at a yearly rate is presumed to be for one year; a hiring at a daily rate, for one day; a hiring by piece work, for no specified term.

See Davis *v.* Marshall, 4 *Law Times* [*N. S.*], 216; 6 *H. & N.* [*Am. ed.*], 916.

Id

§ 1036. In the absence of any agreement as to wages, a domestic servant is presumed to be hired by the month; a clerk, or other servant not merely mechanical, or agricultural, by the year; and other servants for no specified term.

See Fawcett *v.* Cash, 5 *B. & Ad.*, 904.

Renewal of hiring.

§ 1037. Where, after the expiration of an agreement respecting the wages and the term of service, the parties continue the relation of master and servant, they are presumed to have renewed the agreement for the same wages and term of service.

Deckert *v.* Camden & Amboy R. R., *Gen. Term, Supreme Court*, 1864.

Time of service.

§ 1038. The entire time of a domestic servant belongs to the master; and the time of other servants to such extent as is usual in the business in which they serve, not exceeding in any case ten hours in the day.

Servant to pay over without demand.

§ 1039. A servant must deliver to his master, as soon as with reasonable diligence he can find him, everything that he receives for his account, without demand; but he is not bound, without orders from his master, to send anything to him through another person.

§ 1040. A master may discharge any servant, other than an apprentice,[1] whether engaged for a fixed term or not: When servant may be discharged.

1. If he is guilty of misconduct in the course of his service,[2] or of gross immorality, though unconnected with the same;[3] or,

2. If, being employed about the person of the master, or in a confidential position, the master discovers that he has been guilty of misconduct, before or after the commencement of his service, of such a nature that, if the master had known or contemplated it, he would not have so employed him.

[1] See Winstone *v.* Linn, 1 *B. & C.*, 460.

[2] Turner *v.* Mason, 14 *M. & W.*, 112; Singer *v.* McCormick, 4 *Watts & S.*, 265; Amor *v.* Fearon, 9 *Ad. & El.*, 548; Callo *v.* Brouncker, 4 *Carr. & P.*, 518.

[3] Atkin *v.* Acton, 4 *Carr. & P.*, 208; Libhart *v.* Wood, 1 *Watts & S.*, 265.

ARTICLE II.

AGENTS.

§ 1041. An agent must not exceed the limits of his actual authority, as defined by the Title on AGENCY. Agent to conform to his authority.

§ 1042. An agent must use ordinary diligence to keep his principal informed of his acts in the course of the agency. Must keep his principal informed.

Story on Agency, § 207. He is not bound to inform the principal of the receipt of instructions, and of his intention to comply therewith (Parkhill *v.* Imlay, 15 *Wend.*, 431).

Collecting agent.

§ 1043. An agent, employed to collect a negotiable instrument, must collect it promptly, and take all measures necessary to charge the parties thereto, in case of its dishonor,[1] and, if it is a bill of exchange, must present it for acceptance with reasonable diligence.[2]

[1] Walker *v.* Bank of State of N. Y., 9 *N. Y.*, 582; Montgomery Co. Bank *v.* Albany City Bank, 7 *id.*, 459.

[2] Allen *v.* Suydam, 20 *Wend.*, 321.

Responsibility of sub-agent.

§ 1044. A mere agent of an agent is not responsible as such to the principal of the latter.

Thus, if A. employs B. to do some act, which B. employs C. to do, C. is not responsible to A. (Montgomery Co. Bank *v.* Albany City Bank, 7 *N. Y.*, 459; Commercial Bank *v.* Union Bank, 11 *id.*, 203). But if B. employs C. as a sub-agent of A., and not merely as his own agent, C. is responsible to his ultimate principal.

ARTICLE III.

FACTORS.

Factor, what.

§ 1045. A factor is an agent who, in the pursuit of an independent calling, is employed by another to sell property for him, and is vested by the latter with the possession or control of the property, or authorized to receive payment therefor from the purchaser.

Obedience required from factor.

§ 1046. A factor must obey the instructions of his principal, to the same extent as any other employee,[1] notwithstanding any advances he may have made to his principal upon the property consigned to him,[2] except that if the principal forbids him to sell[3] at the market price, he may nevertheless sell for his reimbursement, after giving to his principal reasonable notice of his intention to do so, and of the time and place of sale, and proceeding in all respects as a pledgee.[4]

[1] Evans *v.* Root, 7 *N. Y.*, 186.

[2] Blot *v.* Boiceau, 3 *N. Y.*, 78; Marfield *v.* Goodhue, *id.*, 62; Bell *v.* Palmer, 6 *Cow.*, 128.

[3] Marfield *v.* Goodhue, 3 *N. Y.*, 62. The exception does not extend to an *order* to sell, even though for less than advances (Bell *v.* Palmer, 6 *Cow.*, 128).

[4] Marfield *v.* Goodhue, 3 *N. Y.*, 62.

Sales on credit.

§ 1047. A factor may sell property consigned to him on such credit as is usual,[1] but, having once agreed with the purchaser upon the term of credit, may not extend it.[2]

[1] 1 *Story Cont.*, § 150; Van Allen *v.* Vanderpoel, 6 *Johns.*, 69; McKinstry *v.* Pearsall, 3 *id.*, 319; see Robertson *v.* Livingston, 5 *Cow.*, 473.

[2] Douglass *v.* Bernard, *Anth. N. P.*, 278.

Liability of factor under guaranty commission.

§ 1048. A factor, who charges his principal with a guaranty commission upon a sale, thereby assumes absolutely to pay the price when it falls due, as if it were a debt of his own, and not as a mere guarantor for the purchaser;[1] but he does not thereby assume any additional responsibility for the safety of his remittance of the proceeds.[2]

[1] Sherwood *v.* Stone, 14 *N. Y.*, 267; Wolff *v.* Koppel, 5 *Hill*, 358; affirmed 2 *Den.*, 368; Hastie *v.* Couturier, 8 *Exch.*, 40.

[2] Heubach *v.* Mollmann, 2 *Duer*, 227; Leverich *v.* Meigs, 1 *Cow.*, 645.

Factor cannot relieve himself from liability.

§ 1049. A factor who receives property for sale under a general agreement or usage to guaranty the sales, or the remittance of the proceeds, cannot relieve himself from responsibility therefor without the consent of his principal.

Heubach *v.* Mollmann, 2 *Duer*, 227.

ARTICLE IV.

SHIPMASTERS.

Appointment of master.

§ 1050. The master of a ship is appointed by the owner, and holds during his pleasure.

3 *Kent Com.*, 161; Ward *v.* Ruckman, 34. *Barb.*, 419. The French *Code de Commerce*, Art. 219, provides that if a master who is dismissed is one of the owners of the ship, he may renounce his interest to the others and require from them the payment of the value thereof. It would probably be just to establish some such provision in favor of a master dismissed without good cause.

When must be on board.

§ 1051. The master of a ship is bound to be always on board when entering or leaving a port, harbor or river.

Code de Com., art. 227.

Pilotage.

§ 1052. On entering or leaving a port, harbor or river, the master of a ship must take a pilot if one offers himself, and while the pilot is on board, the navigation of the ship devolves on him.

Regulations respecting pilots of this state are contained in the POLITICAL CODE.

Power of master over seamen.

§ 1053. The master of a ship may enforce the obedience of the mate and seamen to his lawful commands by confinement and other reasonable corporal punishment, not prohibited by acts of congress, being responsible for the abuse of his power.

§ 1054. The master of a ship may confine any person on board, during a voyage, for willful disobedience to his lawful commands. Power of master over passengers.

§ 1055. If, during a voyage, the ship's supplies fail, the master, with the advice of the officers, may compel persons who have private supplies on board to surrender them for the common want, on payment of their value or giving security therefor. Impressing private stores.

Code de Com., art. 249.

§ 1056. The master of a ship must not abandon it during the voyage, without the advice of the other officers. When may abandon the ship.

§ 1057. The master of a ship, upon abandoning it, must carry with him, so far as it is in his power, the money and the most valuable of the goods on board, under penalty of being personally responsible. If the articles thus taken are lost from causes beyond his control, he is exonerated from liability. Duties on abandonment.

Code de Com., art. 241.

§ 1058. The master of a ship, who engages for a common profit on the cargo, must not trade on his own account, and if he does, he must account to his employer for all profits thus made by him. When master cannot trade on his own account.

Code de Com., art. 239, 240, modified to conform to the law of partnership.

§ 1059. The master of a ship must use great care and diligence in the performance of his duties, and is responsible for all damage occasioned by his negligence, however slight. Care and diligence.

Code de Com., art. 221.

§ 1060. The authority and liability of the master of a ship, as an agent for the owners of the ship and cargo, are regulated by the Title on AGENCY. Authority of master.

ARTICLE V.

MATES AND SEAMEN.

Mate, what.

§ 1061. The mate of a ship is the officer next in rank to the master, and in case of the master's disability he must take his place. By so doing, he does not lose any of his rights as mate.

2 *Metc.*, 445.

Seamen, what.

§ 1062. All persons employed in the navigation of a ship, or upon a voyage, other than the master and mate, are to be deemed seamen within the provisions of this Code.

See The Prince George, 3 *Hagg. Adm.*, 376; The Jane & Matilda, 1 *id.*, 187; The Highlander, *Sprague*, 588.

Mate and seamen how engaged and discharged.

§ 1063. The mate and seamen of a ship are engaged by the master, and may be discharged by him at any period of the voyage, for willful and persistent disobedience or gross disqualification, but cannot otherwise be discharged before the termination of the voyage.

3 *Kent Com.*, 176.

§ 1064. A mate or seaman is not bound to go to sea in a ship that is not seaworthy; and if there is reasonable doubt of its seaworthiness, he may refuse to proceed until a proper survey has been had. Unseaworthy vessel.

United States *v.* Givings, *Sprague*, 75; The Hibernia, *id.*, 78.

§ 1065. A seaman cannot, by reason of any agreement, be deprived of his lien upon the ship, or of any remedy for the recovery of his wages to which he would otherwise have been entitled. Any stipulation by which he consents to abandon his right to wages in case of the loss of the ship, or to abandon any right he may have or obtain in the nature of salvage, is void. Seamen not to lose wages or lien by agreement.

From 13 & 14 *Vict.*, *c.* 93, § 53.

§ 1066. No special agreement entered into by a seaman can impair any of his rights, or add to any of his obligations, as defined by law, unless he fully understands the effect of the agreement, and receives a fair compensation therefor. Special agreement with seamen.

The Highlander, *Sprague*, 510; Brown *v.* Lull, 2 *Sumn.*, 443; The Juliana, 2 *Dods.*, 504; Mary Paulina, *Sprague*, 45.

§ 1067. Except as hereinafter provided, the wages of seamen are due when, and so far only as, freightage is earned,[1] unless the loss of freightage is owing to the fault of the owner or master.[2] Wages depend on freightage.

[1] Van Beuren *v.* Wilson, 9 *Cow.*, 158; Icard *v.* Goold, 11 *Johns.*, 279; Porter *v.* Andrews, 9 *id.*, 350; Dunnett *v.* Tomhagen, 3 *Johns.*, 154; see Worth *v.* Mumford, 1 *Hilt.*, 1.

[2] Hoyt *v.* Wildfire, 3 *Johns.*, 518; Sullivan *v.* Morgan, 11 *id.*, 66; see Murray *v.* Kellogg, 9 *id.*, 227.

§ 1068. The right of a mate or seaman to wages and provisions begins either from the time he begins work, or from the time specified in the agreement for his beginning work, or from his presence on board, whichever first happens. When wages, &c., begin.

13 & 14 *Vict.*, *c.* 93, § 56.

Wages where voyage is broken up before departure.

§ 1069. Where a voyage is broken up before departure of the ship, the seamen must be paid for the time they have served, and may retain for their indemnity such advances as they have received.

Modified from *Code de Com.*, art. 252.

Wrongful discharge.

§ 1070. When a mate or seaman is wrongfully discharged, or is driven to leave the ship by the cruelty of the master on the voyage, it is then ended with respect to him, and he may thereupon recover his full wages.

2 *Pars. Mar. Law*, 574; Ward *v.* Ames, 9 *Johns.*, 138; The Minerva, 1 *Hagg. Adm.*, 363. Reasonable apprehension of cruelty has been held sufficient excuse for desertion (Edward *v.* Trevellick, 4 *El. & B.*, 59).

Wages when not lost by wreck.

§ 1071. In case of loss or wreck of the ship, a seaman is entitled to his wages up to the time of the loss or wreck, whether freightage has been earned or not, if he exerts himself to the utmost to save the ship, cargo and stores.

This provision is substantially enacted in England (*Stat.* 7 & 8 *Vict.*, *c.* 112, § 17), making the seaman's right, however, absolutely dependent upon the officer's certificate.

Certificate.

§ 1072. A certificate from the master or chief surviving officer of a ship, to the effect that a seaman exerted himself to the utmost to save the ship, cargo, and stores, is presumptive evidence of the fact.

Disabled seamen.

§ 1073. Where a mate or seaman is prevented from rendering service by illness or injury, incurred without his fault,[1] in the discharge of his duty on the voyage, or by being wrongfully discharged, or by a capture of the ship,[2] he is entitled to wages notwithstanding; but in case of capture, a ratable deduction for salvage is to be made.[3]

[1] A seaman cannot recover wages for a period during which he was disabled by his own fault (Johnson *v.* Huckins, *Sprague*, 67; 6 *Law Rep.*, 311).

[2] Wetmore *v.* Henshaw, 12 *Johns.*, 324.

[3] Wetmore *v.* Henshaw, 12 *Johns.*, 324.

§ 1074. If a mate or seaman becomes sick or disabled during the voyage without his fault,[1] the expense of furnishing him with suitable medical advice, medicine, attendance, and other provision for his wants, must be borne by the ship till the close of the voyage.[2] Maintenance of seamen during sickness.

[1] This exception to the rule is recognized in Johnson *v.* Huckins, *Sprague*, 67.

[2] Croucher *v.* Oakman, 3 *Allen*, 185; Harden *v.* Gordon, 2 *Mason*, 541; Freeman *v.* Baker, 1 *Blatchf. & H. Adm.*, 382; Walton *v.* The Neptune, 1 *Pet. Adm.*, 142; The George, 1 *Sumn.*, 151; Reed *v.* Canfield, *id.*, 197; Brown *v.* Overton, *Sprague*, 462; The Forrest, *Ware*, 420; Knight *v.* Parsons, *Sprague*, 279.

§ 1075. If a mate or seaman dies during the voyage, his personal representatives are entitled to his wages to the time of his death, if he would have been entitled to them had he lived to the end of the voyage. Death on the voyage.

§ 1076. Desertion of the ship without cause, or a justifiable discharge by the master during the voyage, for misconduct, or a theft of any part of the cargo or appurtenances of the ship, or a willful injury thereto or to the ship, forfeits all wages due for the voyage to a mate or seaman thus in fault. Theft, &c., forfeits wages.

Spencer *v.* Eustis, 21 *Me.*, 519; Coffin *v.* Jenkins, 3 *Story*, 108; Cloutman *v.* Tunison, 1 *Sumn.*, 373.

§ 1077. A mate or seaman may not, under any pretext, ship goods on his own account, without permission from the master. Seamen cannot ship goods.

Code de Com., art. 251.

§ 1078. If any part of the cargo or appurtenances of a ship is embezzled or injured by the mate or a seaman, the offender, or, if it is not known which is the offender, all those of whom negligence or fault may be presumed, must make good the loss. Embezzlement and injuries.

Lewis *v.* Davis, 3 *Johns.*, 17; Spurr *v.* Pearson, 1 *Mass.*, 104.

§ 1079. The shipment of officers and seamen, and their rights and duties, are further regulated by acts of congress. Law governing seamen.

ARTICLE VI.

SHIPS' MANAGERS.

Manager, what.

§ 1080. The general agent for the owners, in respect to the care of a ship and freight, is called the manager; if he is a part owner he is also called the managing owner.

The commissioners have preferred not to use the phrase "ship's husband."

Duties of manager.

§ 1081. Unless otherwise directed, it is the duty of the manager of a ship to provide for the complete seaworthiness of the ship; to take care of it in port; to see that it is provided with necessary papers, with a proper master, mate and crew, and supplies of provisions and stores.

Compensation.

§ 1082. A managing owner is presumed to have no right to compensation for his own services.

Benson *v.* Heathorn, 1 *Young & C.*, 326; Smith *v.* Lay, 3 *Kay & Johns.*, 105.

CHAPTER III.

SERVICE WITHOUT EMPLOYMENT.

Voluntary interference with property.

§ 1083. One who officiously, and without the consent of the real or apparent owner of a thing, takes it into his possession, for the purpose of rendering a service about it, must complete such service, and use ordinary care, diligence and reasonable skill about the same. He is not entitled to any compensation for his service or expenses, except that he may deduct actual and necessary expenses, incurred by him about such service, from any profits which his service has caused the thing to acquire for its owner, and must account to the owner for the residue.

§ 1084. Any person, other than the master, mate, or a seaman thereof, who rescues a ship, her appurtenances, or cargo, from danger, is entitled to a reasonable compensation therefor, to be paid out of the property saved. He has a lien for such claim, which is regulated by the Title on LIENS. **Salvage.**

Baker *v.* Hoag, 7 *N. Y.*, 557.

TITLE VII.

CARRIAGE.

CHAPTER I.

CARRIAGE IN GENERAL.

§ 1085. The contract of carriage is a contract for the conveyance of property, persons, or messages, from one place to another. **Contract of carriage.**

§ 1086. Carriage is either: **Different kinds of carriers.**

1. Inland; or,

2. Marine.

§ 1087. Carriers upon the ocean, upon arms of the sea, upon the great lakes Ontario, Erie, Huron, **Marine and inland carriers, what**

Michigan and Superior, and upon the rivers and canals connecting those lakes with each other, are marine carriers. All others are inland carriers.

Carriers by railroad and steamboat.

§ 1088. Rights and duties peculiar to carriers by railway and steamers, are defined in the POLITICAL CODE.

Carriers by sea.

§ 1089. Rights and duties peculiar to carriers by sea, are defined by acts of congress.

Obligations of gratuitous carriers.

§ 1090. Carriers without reward are subject to the same rules as employees without reward, except so far as is otherwise provided by this Title.

Obligations of gratuitous carrier who has begun to carry.

§ 1091. A carrier without reward, who has begun to perform his undertaking, must complete it in like manner as if he had received a reward, unless he restores the person or thing[1] carried to as favorable a position as before he commenced the carriage.[2]

[1] This is intended to include messages as well as property.

[2] It would be manifestly unreasonable to allow a railway company to eject a passenger upon a free ticket, when he had made only half his journey. On the other hand, there would be no injustice in a refusal to allow him to start upon the journey.

CHAPTER II.

CARRIAGE OF PERSONS.

ARTICLE I.

GRATUITOUS CARRIAGE OF PERSONS.

Degree of care required.

§ 1092. A carrier of persons without reward must use ordinary care and diligence for their safe carriage.

As *extreme* care is required of carriers for reward (see section 1093) out of regard for human life, it seems to follow that at least ordinary care should be required of gratuitous carriers.

ARTICLE II.

CARRIAGE FOR REWARD.

§ 1093. A carrier of persons for reward must use the utmost care and diligence for their safe carriage, must provide everything necessary for that purpose, and must exercise to that end a reasonable degree of skill. General duties of carrier.

Ang. on Carr., §§ 521–523, 534–539; Edgerton *v.* N. Y. & Harlem R. R., 35 *Barb.*, 193; Bowen *v.* N. Y. Central R. R., 18 *N. Y.*, 408.

§ 1094. A carrier of persons for reward is bound to provide vehicles safe and fit for the purposes to which they are put, and is not excused for default in this respect by any degree of care. Vehicles.

Alden *v.* New York Central R. R. Co., 26 *N. Y.*, 102; see Hegeman *v.* Western R. R., 13 *id.*, 9; Sharp *v.* Grey, 9 *Bing.*, 457; but see Ingalls *v.* Bills, 9 *Metc.*, 1.

§ 1095. A carrier of persons for reward must not overcrowd or overload his vehicle. Not to overload his vehicles.

Angell on Carr., § 528; Derwort *v.* Loomer, 21 *Conn.*, 245.

§ 1096. A carrier of persons for reward must give to passengers all such accommodations as are usual and reasonable,[1] must treat them with civility,[2] and give them a reasonable degree of attention.[3] Treatment of passengers.

[1] *Story on Bailm.*, § 597; *Ang. on Carr.*, § 533.
[2] *Story on Contracts*, § 796 *b.*; Chamberlain *v.* Chandler, 3 *Mason*, 242.
[3] See Hall *v.* Conn. Steamboat Co., 13 *Conn.*, 319.

§ 1097. A carrier of persons for reward must travel at a reasonable rate of speed, and without any unreasonable delay, or deviation from his proper route. Rate of speed and delays.

CHAPTER III.

CARRIAGE OF PROPERTY.

ARTICLE I.

GENERAL DEFINITIONS.

Freight consignor, &c., what.

§ 1098. Property carried is called freight, the reward, if any, to be paid for its carriage is called freightage,[1] the person who delivers the freight to the carrier is called the consignor, and the person to whom it is to be delivered is called the consignee.

[1] See note to section 1449.

ARTICLE II.

OBLIGATIONS OF THE CARRIER.

Care and diligence required of carriers.

§ 1099. A carrier of property for reward must use at least ordinary care and diligence in the performance of all his duties. A carrier without reward must use at least slight care and diligence.

§ 1100. A carrier must comply with the directions of the consignor or consignee, to the same extent that an employee is bound to comply with those of his employer. Carrier to obey directions.

Johnson *v.* Hudson River R. R., 31 *Barb.*, 196; Ackley *v.* Kellogg, 8 *Cow.*, 223.

§ 1101. When the directions of a consignor and consignee are conflicting, the carrier must comply with those of the consignor in respect to all matters except the delivery of the freight, as to which he must comply with the directions of the consignee,[1] unless the consignor has specially forbidden the carrier to receive orders from the consignee inconsistent with his own.[2] Conflict of orders.

[1] Bartlett *v.* London and N. W. Railway Co., 7 *H. & N.*, 400; Sweet *v.* Barney, 23 *N. Y.*, 335.

[2] See Tooker *v.* Gormer, 2 *Hilt.*, 71.

§ 1102. A marine carrier must not stow freight upon deck during the voyage, except where it is usual to do so, nor make any improper deviation from or delay in the voyage, nor do any other unnecessary act which would avoid an insurance in the usual form upon the freight. Stowage, deviation, &c.

Code de Commerce, art. 229.

§ 1103. A carrier of property must deliver it to the consignee, at the place to which it is addressed, in the manner usual at that place. Delivery of freight.

§ 1104. If there is no usage to the contrary at the place of delivery, freight must be delivered as follows: Place of delivery.

1. If carried upon a railway owned or managed by the carrier, it may be delivered at the station nearest the place to which it is addressed;[1]

2. If carried by sea from a foreign country, it may be delivered at the wharf where the ship moors, within a reasonable distance from the place of address; or, if there is no wharf, on board a lighter alongside the ship;[2] or,

3. In other cases, it must be delivered to the consignee or his agent, personally,[3] if either can, with reasonable diligence, be found.

[1] Norway Plains Co. *v.* Boston & Me. R. R. Co., 1 *Gray*, 263; see Smith *v.* Nashua, &c., R. R. Co., 7 *Fost.* [*N. H.*], 86.

[2] See Rowland *v.* Miln, 2 *Hilt.*, 150; Hyde *v.* Trent, &c., Nav. Co., 5 *T. R.*, 389; Dixon *v.* Dunham, 14 *Ill.*, 324; Crawford *v.* Clark, 15 *id.*, 361; Cope *v.* Cordova, 1 *Rawle*, 203. The carrier is not bound to take the goods to the wharf actually nearest the consignee (Chickering *v.* Fowler, 4 *Pick.*, 371).

[3] See Haslam *v.* Adams Express Co., 6 *Bosw.*, 235; Ostrander *v.* Brown, 15 *Johns.*, 39; Hemphill *v.* Chenie, 6 *Watts & S.*, 62.

Obligations of carrier when freight is not delivered to consignee.

§ 1105. If, for any reason, a carrier does not deliver freight to the consignee or his agent personally, he must give notice to the consignee of its arrival, and keep the same in safety, upon his responsibility as a carrier, until the consignee has had a reasonable time to remove it.

Price *v.* Powell, 3 *N. Y.*, 322; Bourne *v.* Gatliffe, 3 *M. & G.*, 643; 7 *id.*, 850; 11 *Cl. & Fin.*, 45; Kohn *v.* Packard, 3 *La.*, 224.

How carrier may terminate his liability.

§ 1106. If a consignee does not accept and remove freight within a reasonable time after the carrier has fulfilled his obligation to deliver, or duly offered to fulfill the same, the carrier may exonerate himself from further liability by placing the freight in a suitable warehouse,[1] on storage, and giving notice thereof to the consignee.[2]

[1] A carrier is not forced to keep goods which the consignee refuses or neglects to take. But he must do some act clearly indicating the termination of his relation as carrier. If he keeps the goods on his vehicle, he cannot claim to do so as a warehouseman (Goold *v.* Chapin, 20 *N. Y.*, 259).

[2] Notice must be given (see Rowland *v.* Miln, 2 *Hilt.*, 150).

When consignee cannot be found.

§ 1107. If a consignee of freight cannot, with reasonable diligence, be found, the carrier may place it in a suitable warehouse for his account, but must give notice thereof to the consignor.

Fisk *v.* Newton, 1 *Denio*, 45; approved, Rowland *v.* Miln, 2 *Hilt.*, 150; see Goold *v.* Chapin, 20 *N. Y.*, 259.

ARTICLE III.

BILL OF LADING.

§ 1108. A bill of lading is an instrument in writing, signed by a carrier or his agent, describing the freight so as to identify it, stating the name of the consignor, the terms of the contract for carriage, and agreeing or directing that the freight be delivered to the order or assigns of a specified person at a specified place. Bill of lading, what.

Holbrook *v.* Vose, 6 *Bosw.*, 76, 109.

§ 1109. All the title to the freight which the first holder of a bill of lading had when he received it, passes to every subsequent indorsee thereof in good faith and for value, in the ordinary course of business, with like effect and in like manner as in the case of a bill of exchange. Bill of lading negotiable.

This provision is conformable to the general intention of merchants, and it is not certain that it is not the law of this state (see Dows *v.* Greene, 24 *N. Y.*, 638; Dows *v.* Rush, 28 *Barb.*, 185: but compare Dows *v.* Perrin, 16 *N. Y.*, 332). A provision, somewhat similar, has been enacted in England (18 & 19 *Vict.*, c. 111; see Foster *v.* Colby, 3 *H. & N.*, 705).

§ 1110. When a bill of lading is made to "bearer," or in equivalent terms, a simple transfer thereof by delivery conveys the same title as an indorsement. Id.

Effect of bill of lading on rights, &c., of carrier.

§ 1111. A bill of lading does not alter the rights or obligations of the carrier, as defined in this chapter, unless it is plainly inconsistent therewith.

Bill of lading to be given to consignor.

§ 1112. A carrier must subscribe and deliver to the consignor, on demand, any reasonable number of bills of lading, of the same tenor, expressing truly the original contract for carriage; and if he refuses to do so, the consignor may take the freight from him, and recover from him besides, all damage thereby occasioned.

Carrier exonerated by delivery according to bill of lading.

§ 1113. A carrier is exonerated from liability for freight, by delivery thereof, in good faith, to any holder of a bill of lading therefor, properly indorsed, or made in favor of the bearer.

This is a necessary result of § 1109.

Carrier may demand surrender of bill of lading before delivery.

§ 1114. When a carrier has given a bill of lading, or other instrument substantially equivalent thereto, he may require its surrender, or a reasonable indemnity against claims thereon, before delivering the freight.

Howard *v.* Shepperd, 9 *C. B.*, 297.

ARTICLE IV.

FREIGHTAGE.

When freightage is to be paid.

§ 1115. A carrier may require his freightage to be paid upon his receiving the freight; but if he does not demand it then, he cannot until he is ready to deliver the freight to the consignee.

See Wyld *v.* Pickford, 8 *M. & W.*, 443, 458.

Consignor, when liable for freightage.

§ 1116. The consignor of freight is presumed to be liable for the freightage, but if the contract between him and the carrier provides that the consignee shall pay it, and the carrier allows the consignee to take the freight, he cannot afterwards recover the freightage from the consignor.

§ 1117. The consignee of freight is liable for the freightage, if he accepts the freight with notice of the intention of the consignor that he should pay it. Consignee, when liable.

Merrick *v.* Gordon, 20 *N. Y.*, 93.

§ 1118. No freightage can be charged upon the natural increase of freight. Natural increase of freight.

1 *Pars. Marit. Law*, 149, 150.

§ 1119. If freightage is apportioned by a bill of lading or other contract made between a consignor and carrier, the carrier is entitled to payment, according to the apportionment, for so much as he delivers. Apportionment by contract.

§ 1120. If a part of the freight is accepted by a consignee, without a specific objection that the rest is not delivered, the freightage must be apportioned and paid as to that part, though not apportioned in the original contract. Id.

1 *Pars. Marit. Law*, 149.

§ 1121. If a consignee voluntarily receives freight at a place short of the one appointed for delivery, the carrier is entitled to a just proportion of the freightage, according to distance.[1] If the carrier, being ready and willing, offers to complete the transit, he is entitled to the full freightage.[2] If he does not thus offer completion, and the consignee receives the freight only from necessity, the carrier is not entitled to any freightage.[3] Apportionment according to distance.

[1] *Ang. on Car.*, § 404; Kinsman *v.* N. Y. Mutual Ins. Co., 5 *Bosw.*, 460.
[2] Violett *v.* Stettinius, 5 *Cranch, C. C.*, 559.
[3] *Ang. on Car.*, § 407.

§ 1122. If freight is carried further, or more expeditiously, than was agreed upon by the parties, the carrier is not entitled to additional compensation, Freight carried further than agreed, &c.

and cannot refuse to deliver it, on the demand of the consignee, at the place and time of its arrival.

Carrier's lien for freightage. § 1123. A carrier has a lien for freightage, which is regulated by the Title on LIENS.

ARTICLE V.

GENERAL AVERAGE.

Jettison and general average, what. § 1124. A carrier by water may, when in case of extreme peril it is necessary for the safety of the ship or cargo, throw overboard, or otherwise sacrifice, any or all of the cargo or appurtenances of the ship. Throwing property overboard for such purpose is called jettison, and the loss incurred thereby is called a general average loss.

Lawrence *v.* Minturn, 17 *How.* [*U. S.*], 100.

Order of jettison. § 1125. A jettison must begin with the most bulky and least valuable articles, so far as possible.

Code de Commerce, art. 411.

By whom made. § 1126. A jettison can be made only by authority of the master of a ship, except in case of his disability, or of an overruling necessity, when it may be made by any other person.

3 *Kent Com.*, 233.

Loss, how borne. § 1127. The loss incurred by a jettison, when lawfully made, must be borne in due proportion by all that part of the ship, appurtenances, freightage and cargo, for the benefit of which the sacrifice is made,[1] as well as by the owner of the thing sacrificed.[2]

[1] Barnard *v.* Adams, 10 *How.* [*U. S.*], 270, 303.
[2] Lee *v.* Grinnell, 5 *Duer*, 431; Simonds *v.* White, 2 *B. & C.*, 805.

§ 1128. The proportions in which a general average loss is to be borne, must be ascertained by an adjustment, in which the owner of each separate interest is to be charged with such proportion of the value of the thing lost, as the value of his part of the property affected bears to the value of the whole.[1] But an adjustment made at the end of the voyage, if valid there, is valid everywhere.[2]

General average loss, how adjusted.

[1] 3 *Kent Com.*, 232.
[2] Simonds *v.* White, 2 *B. & C.*, 805.

§ 1129. In estimating values for the purpose of a general average, the ship and appurtenances must be valued as at the end of the voyage, the freightage at one-half the amount due on delivery, and the cargo as at the time and place of its discharge; adding, in each case, the amount made good by contribution.

Values, how ascertained.

See 3 *Kent Com.*, 242; 5 *Duer*, 429; 1 *Cai.*, 573; 2 *Serg. & R.*, 229.

§ 1130. The owner of things stowed on deck, in case of their jettison, is entitled to the benefit of a general average contribution only in case it is usual to stow such things on deck upon such a voyage.

Things stowed on deck.

Lawrence *v.* Minturn, 17 *How.* [*U. S.*], 100; Sayward *v.* Stevens, 3 *Gray*, 97; Smith *v.* Wright, 1 *Caines*, 43; Lenox *v.* United Ins. Co., 3 *Johns. Cas.*, 178; Harris *v.* Moody, 4 *Bosw.*, 210; Gould *v.* Oliver, 4 *Bing. N. C.*, 134; S. C. again, 2 *M. & G.*, 208; Milward *v.* Hibbert, 3 *Q. B.*, 120.

§ 1131. The rules herein stated concerning jettison are equally applicable to every other voluntary sacrifice of property on a ship, or expense necessarily incurred, for the preservation of the ship and cargo from extraordinary perils.

Application of the foregoing rules.

Birkley *v.* Presgrave, 1 *East*, 228; *Code de Com.*, 440.

CHAPTER IV.

CARRIAGE OF MESSAGES.

Obligations of carrier of messages.

§ 1132. A carrier of messages for reward must deliver them at the place to which they are addressed, or to the persons for whom they are intended.

Degree of care and diligence required.

§ 1133. A carrier of messages for reward must use great care and diligence in the transmission and delivery of messages. A carrier by telegraph must use the utmost diligence therein.

Obviously, messages are sent by telegraph for the express purpose of securing great dispatch. This is an implied condition of the contract, which should be strictly enforced.

CHAPTER V.

COMMON CARRIERS.

ARTICLE I.

COMMON CARRIERS IN GENERAL.

§ 1134. Every one who offers to the public to carry persons, property or messages, is a common carrier of whatever he thus offers to carry. Common carrier, what.

Sweet *v.* Barney, 23 *N. Y.*, 335; Read *v.* Spaulding, 5 *Bosw.*, 395; Place *v.* Union Express Co., 2 *Hilt.*, 19. A telegraph company is a common carrier (Parks *v.* Alta Cal. Tel. Co., 13 *Cal.*, 422).

§ 1135. A common carrier must, if able to do so,[1] accept and carry whatever is offered to him,[2] at a reasonable time and place, of a kind that he undertakes or is accustomed to carry.[3] Obligation to accept freight.

[1] If the carrier's vehicle is full, he is excused (Lovett *v.* Hobbs, 2 *Show.*, 127).

[2] *Story's Bailm.*, § 508; Bennett *v.* Dutton, 10 *N. H.*, 481. So held as to passengers (Bennett *v.* Peninsula Steam Packet Co., 6 *C. B.*, 775), and as to goods (Cranch *v.* London & Northwestern R. R., 14 *C. B.*, 255; Pickford *v.* Grand Junction R. R., 8 *M. & W.*, 372; Jackson *v.* Rogers, 2 *Show.*, 327).

[3] Johnson *v.* Midland R. R., 4 *Exch.*, 367; Sewall *v.* Allen, 6 *Wend.*, 335; Tunnell *v.* Pettijohn, 2 *Harringt.*, 48; Citizens' Bank *v.* Nantucket Steamboat Co., 2 *Story*, 16.

§ 1136. A common carrier must not give preference, in time, price, or otherwise, to one person over another, except where expressly authorized by statute. Obligation not to give preference.

Story's Bailm., § 508; Parker *v.* Great Western Railway Co., 7 *M. & G.*, 253; Pickford *v.* Grand Junc. R. Co., 10 *M. & W.*, 399. It may be that this is not a rule of the common law (see Baxendale *v.* Eastern Cos. R. R. Co., 4 *C. B.* [*N. S.*], 63, 78); but if not, it ought to be incorporated into our law from the English Railway Acts, which generally contain such a provision.

§ 1137. A common carrier must always give a preference in time, and may give a preference in price, to the United States and to this State. What preferences he must give.

§ 1138. A common carrier must start at such time and place as he announces to the public. Starting.

Angell on Carr., § 527, *a.*

Compensation.

§ 1139.. A common carrier is entitled to a reasonable compensation and no more; which he may require to be paid in advance. If payment thereof is refused, he may refuse to carry.

Wyld *v.* Pickford, 8 *M. & W.*, 443, 453.

Obligations of carrier altered only by agreement.

§ 1140. The rights and obligations of a common carrier cannot be altered by notice on his part,[1] or by any other means except a written agreement between him and the person with whom he deals.[2]

[1] Nevins *v.* Bay State Steamboat Co., 4 *Bosw.*, 225; Cole *v.* Goodwin, 19 *Wend.*, 251; approved, Dorr *v.* N. J. Steam Nav. Co., 11 *N. Y.*, 485.

[2] This provision is new, in so far as it requires the agreement to be written; but it seems eminently desirable that such should be the law.

Certain agreements void.

§ 1141. A common carrier cannot be exonerated, by any agreement made in anticipation thereof, from liability for the gross negligence, fraud, or willful wrong, of himself or his servants.

Penn. R. R. *v.* McCloskey, 23 *Penn. St.*, 532; Camden & Amboy R. R. *v.* Baldauff, 16 *id.*, 67; Smith *v.* N. Y. Central R. R., 29 *Barb.*, 132; affirmed, 24 *N. Y.*, 222. The latest cases in this state seem to hold that the carrier may be exempted from such liability for the acts of his servants (Bissell *v.* N. Y. Central R. R., 25 *N. Y.*, 442; reversing S. C., 29 *Barb.*, 502; Perkins *v.* N. Y. Central R. R., 24 *N. Y.*, 196; Wells *v.* Same, *id.*, 181). But these decisions were made by a bare majority of the Court of Appeals, and the commissioners think that the dissenting opinions are entitled to the most weight. It is notorious that the negligence of railroad managers cannot be stopped by criminal prosecutions, and if they are enabled by a reduction of a few cents in the fare, to escape a civil action, they will be practicably irresponsible for the acts of their servants.

Effect of written contract

§ 1142. A passenger, consignor, or consignee, by accepting a ticket, bill of lading or written contract for carriage, with a knowledge of its terms, assents to the rate of hire, the time, place and manner of delivery therein stated. But his assent to any other modification of the carrier's rights or obligations contained in such instrument can only be manifested by his signature to the same.

Nevins *v.* Bay State Steamboat Co., 4 *Bosw.*, 225. This appears to the commissioners to be the only sound rule, notwithstanding its apparent repudiation by a bare majority of the Court of Appeals (see Bissell *v.* N. Y. Central R. R., 25 *N. Y.*, 442).

ARTICLE II.

COMMON CARRIERS OF PERSONS.

§ 1143. A common carrier of persons, unless his vehicle is fitted for the reception of passengers exclusively, must receive and carry a reasonable amount of luggage for each passenger, without any charge except for an excess of weight over one hundred pounds to a passenger. **Obligation to carry luggage.**

§ 1144. Luggage may consist of any articles intended for the use of a passenger while traveling, or for his personal equipment. **Luggage, what.**

Ang. on Carr., § 115; *Story on Cont.*, § 768, *a. b.*; *Redf. on Railw.*, § 144; Nevins *v.* Bay State Steamboat Co., 4 *Bosw.*, 225; Duffy *v.* Thompson, 4 *E. D. Smith*, 178; Davis *v.* Cayuga & Susq. R. R., 10 *How. Pr.*, 330; see Richards *v.* Westcott, 2 *Bosw.*, 589; 7 *id.*, 6; Pardee *v.* Drew, 25 *Wend.*, 459.

§ 1145. The liability of a carrier for luggage received by him with a passenger, is the same as that of a common carrier of property. **Liability for luggage.**

Story on Bailm., §§ 498, 499, 595; *Ang. on Carr.*, § 571; Cary *v.* Cleveland & Toledo R. R., 29 *Barb.*, 35; Cole *v.* Goodwin, 19 *Wend.*, 251; Powell *v.* Myers, 26 *Wend.*, 591.

Luggage, how carried and delivered.

§ 1146. A common carrier must deliver every passenger's luggage, whether within the prescribed weight or not, immediately upon the arrival of the passenger at his destination; and, unless the vehicle would be overcrowded or overloaded thereby, must carry it on the same vehicle by which he carries the passenger to whom it belongs.

Glasco *v.* N. Y. Central R. R. Co., 36 *Barb.*, 557.

Obligation to provide vehicles.

§ 1147. A common carrier of persons, upon a route to which he has an exclusive right, must provide a sufficient number of vehicles to accommodate all the passengers who can be reasonably expected to require carriage at any one time.

Seats for passengers.

§ 1148. A common carrier of persons must provide every passenger with a seat.

Regulations for conduct of business.

§ 1149. A common carrier of persons may make rules for the conduct of his business, and may require passengers to conform to them,[1] if they are lawful, public,[2] uniform in their application, and reasonable.[3]

[1] Vedder *v.* Fellows, 20 *N. Y.*, 126; Barker *v.* Coffin, 31 *Barb.*, 556.

[2] Pollard *v.* N. Y. & N. H. R. R., 7 *Bosw.*, 437.

[3] Vedder *v.* Fellows, 20 *N. Y.*, 126.

Fare, when payable.

§ 1150. A common carrier may demand the fare of passengers, either at starting, or at any subsequent time.

Ejection of passengers.

§ 1151. A passenger, who refuses to pay his fare, or to conform to any lawful regulation of the carrier, may be ejected from the vehicle by the carrier. But this must be done with as little violence as possible, and within a short distance from some dwelling house.

Fare not payable after ejection.

§ 1152. After having ejected a passenger, a carrier has no right to require the payment of any part of his fare.

§ 1153. A common carrier has a lien upon the luggage of a passenger, for the payment of such fare as he is entitled to from him. This lien is regulated by the Title on LIENS. Carrier's lien.

ARTICLE III.

COMMON CARRIERS OF PROPERTY.

§ 1154. Unless the consignor accompanies the freight and retains exclusive control thereof,[1] an inland common carrier of property is liable, from the time that he accepts[2] until he relieves himself from liability pursuant to sections 1103 to 1107,[3] for the loss or injury thereof from any cause whatever, except: Liability of inland carriers for loss.

1. An inherent defect, vice or weakness, or a spontaneous action, of the property itself;[4]

2. The act of a public enemy of the United States, or of this state;[5]

3. The act of the law;[6] or,

4. Any irresistible superhuman cause.[7]

[1] *Sto. Bailm.*, §§ 533, 578; Cohen *v.* Frost, 2 *Duer*, 355; Tower *v.* Utica R. R., 7 *Hill*, 47.

[2] Blossom *v.* Griffin, 13 *N. Y.*, 569; Lakeman *v.* Grinnell, 5 *Bosw.*, 625.

[3] *Story on Bailm.*, §§ 533, 509; Goold *v.* Chapin, 20 *N. Y.*, 259.

[4] *Sto. Bailm.*, § 492, *a.*; *Ang. on Carr.*, § 214, *a.*; Clarke *v.* Rochester R. R., 14 *N. Y.*, 574.

[5] *Sto. Bailm.*, §§ 510, 526.

[6] Van Winkle *v.* U. S. Mail Steamship Co., 37 *Barb.*, 122; Bliven *v.* Hudson River R. R., 35 *id.*, 188.

[7] "Inevitable accident" does not excuse the carrier, if such accident is of human origin (Miller *v.* Steam Navigation Co., 10 *N. Y.*, 431; Goold *v.* Chapin, 20 *id.*, 259; 10 *Barb.*, 612; Merritt *v.* Earle, 31 *id.*, 38; McArthur *v.* Sears, 21 *Wend.*, 190; Hall *v.* Cheney, 36 *N. H.*, 31).

When exemptions do not apply.

§ 1155. A common carrier is liable, even in the cases excepted by the last section, if his ordinary negligence exposes the property to the cause of the loss.

Read *v.* Spaulding, 5 *Bosw.*, 395; Wing *v.* N. Y. & Erie R. R., 1 *Hilt.*, 235.

Liability for delay.

§ 1156. A common carrier is liable for delay, only when it is the effect of his ordinary negligence.

Wibert *v.* N. Y. & Erie R. R., 11 *N. Y.*, 245; Conger *v.* Hudson River R. R., 6 *Duer*, 375.

Liability of marine carriers.

§ 1157. A marine carrier is liable in like manner as an inland carrier, except for loss or injury caused by the perils of the sea or fire.

Id.

§ 1158. The liability of a common carrier by sea is further regulated by acts of congress.

9 *U. S. Stat.*, 635.

Perils of sea, what.

§ 1159. Perils of the sea are from:

1. Storms and waves;
2. Rocks, shoals and rapids;
3. Other obstacles, though of human origin;
4. Changes of climate;
5. The confinement necessary at sea;
6. Animals peculiar to the sea; and,
7. All other dangers peculiar to the sea.

See Aymar *v.* Astor, 6 *Cow.*, 267.

Consignor of valuables to declare their nature.

§ 1160. A common carrier of gold, silver, platina, or precious stones, or of imitations thereof, in a manufactured or unmanufactured state, of timepieces of any description, of negotiable paper or other valuable writings, of pictures, glass or china ware, is not liable for more than fifty dollars upon the loss or injury of any one package of such articles, unless he has notice, upon his receipt thereof, by mark upon the package or otherwise, of the nature of the freight.

Modified from the English Carriers' Act of 1830. The act of congress (March 3, 1851) does not include so many articles.

§ 1161. If a common carrier accepts freight for a place beyond his usual route, he must, unless he stipulates otherwise, deliver it at the end of his route in that direction to some other competent carrier, carrying to the place of address, or connected with those who thus carry, and his liability ceases upon making such delivery. Delivery of freight beyond the usual route.

Van Santvoord *v.* St. John, 6 *Hill*, 157; see Goold *v* Chapin, 20 *N. Y.*, 259.

§ 1162. If freight, addressed to a place beyond the usual route of the common carrier who first received it, is lost or injured, he must, within a reasonable time after demand, give satisfactory proof to the consignor that the loss or injury did not occur while it was in his charge, or he will be himself liable therefor. Proof to be given in case of loss.

This clause is intended to save the consignor from the risk of mistaken actions, by compelling the carrier to give proof that another is liable, the fair presumption being against him.

§ 1163. In respect to any service rendered by a common carrier about freight, other than its carriage and delivery, his rights and obligations are defined by the Titles on DEPOSIT and SERVICE. Carrier's services other than carriage and delivery.

ARTICLE IV.

COMMON CARRIERS OF MESSAGES.

Order of transmission of telegraphic messages.

§ 1164. A carrier of messages by telegraph must, if it is practicable, transmit every such message immediately upon its receipt. But if this is not practicable, and several messages accumulate upon his hands, he must transmit them in the following order:

1. Messages from public agents of the United States or of this State, on public business;

2. Messages intended in good faith for immediate publication in newspapers, and not for any secret use,

3. Messages giving information relating to the sickness or death of any person;

4. Other messages, in the order in which they were received.

Order in other cases.

§ 1165. A common carrier of messages, otherwise than by telegraph, must transmit messages in the order in which he receives them, except messages from agents of the United States or of this State, on public business, to which he must always give priority. But he may fix upon certain times for the simultaneous transmission of messages previously received.

Damages when message is refused or postponed.

§ 1166. Every person whose message is refused or postponed, contrary to the provisions of this chapter, is entitled to recover from the carrier his actual damages, and fifty dollars in addition thereto.

New. Such a provision is needed to protect the rights of parties who are seriously annoyed by delays which nevertheless cannot be shown to have caused them pecuniary damage.

TITLE VIII.

TRUST.

CHAPTER I.

TRUSTS IN GENERAL.

ARTICLE I.

NATURE AND CREATION OF A TRUST.

§ 1167. A trust is either: **Trusts classified.**

1. Voluntary; or
2. Involuntary.

§ 1168. A voluntary trust is an obligation arising out of a personal confidence[1] reposed in, and voluntarily accepted by one, for the benefit of another.[2] **Voluntary trust, what.**

[1] A trust is defined by Story as an equitable title to property (*Eq. Jur.*, § 964). But this is a very narrow definition. So far as his obligations are concerned, a technical trustee stands upon the same footing

with a confidential agent or adviser, a guardian, &c., and there is little difference, so far as business relations are concerned, between his position and that of a husband, wife, parent, or attorney. The *confidence* reposed is the essence of the relation, and it will be found, by reference to the numerous cases cited in the course of this Title, that little or no distinction is made between trustees, strictly so called, and any other persons who accept the personal confidence of another.

[2] No one can be a trustee for himself. But a trust created for the joint benefit of several persons may be held by one of them (see *ex parte* Clutton, 17 *Jur.*, 988). And a trust has been sustained for the benefit of a horse (Pettingall *v.* Pettingall, 11 *L. J.* [*Ch.*], 176).

Involuntary trust, what.

§ 1169. An involuntary trust is one which is created by operation of law.

Parties to the contract.

§ 1170. The person whose confidence creates a trust, is called the trustor;[1] the person in whom the confidence is reposed, is called the trustee; and the person for whose benefit the trust is created, is called the beneficiary.[2]

[1] Lewin, Hill, and other writers, call the creator of the trust the "settlor," a very objectionable word. Trustor is an English word (see Webster's Dictionary, where it is spelled "truster"), and is entirely applicable to the person who creates a trust.

[2] This word is recommended by Story (*Eq. Jur.*, § 321), in place of *cestui que trust*.

What constitutes one a trustee.

§ 1171. Every one who voluntarily assumes a relation of personal confidence with another is deemed a trustee within the meaning of this chapter,[1] not only as to the person who reposes such confidence, but also as to all persons of whose affairs he thus acquires information which was given to such person in the like confidence,[2] or over whose affairs he, by such confidence, obtains any control.[3]

[1] Gardner *v.* Ogden, 22 *N. Y.*, 343; Anderson *v.* Lemon, 8 *N. Y.*, 236; Moore *v.* Moore, 5 *N. Y.*, 256; Blisset *v.* Daniel, 10 *Hare*, 493, 536; Brock *v.* Barnes, 40 *Barb.*, 521.

[2] Gardner *v.* Ogden, 22 *N. Y.*, 350; Whitcomb *v.* Minchin, 5 *Madd.*, 91.

[3] Bulkley *v.* Wilford, 2 *Clark & Fin.*, 102.

§ 1172. A trust may be created for any purpose for which a contract may lawfully be made, except as otherwise prescribed by the Titles on USES AND TRUSTS and on TRANSFERS. For what purpose a trust may be created.

§ 1173. Subject to the provisions of section 280, a voluntary trust is created, as to the trustor and beneficiary, by any words or acts of the trustor, indicating with reasonable certainty: Voluntary trust, how created as to trustor.

1. An intention on the part of the trustor to create a trust; and,

2. The subject, purpose, and beneficiary of the trust.

Fisher *v.* Fields, 10 *Johns.*, 495; Briggs *v.* Penny, 3 *Macn. & G.*, 554; Reeves *v.* Baker, 18 *Beav.*, 372; see Eade *v.* Eade, 5 *Madd.*, 119; Curtis *v.* Rippon, *id.*, 434; Tibbits *v.* Tibbits, 19 *Ves.*, 656; *Jac.*, 317; Morice *v.* Durham, 10 *Ves.*, 536; Moggridge *v.* Thackwell, 7 *id.*, 85; 13 *id.*, 416; Harland *v.* Trigg, 1 *Bro. C. C.*, 142; Wynne *v.* Hawkins, *id.*, 179.

§ 1174. Subject to the provisions of section 280, a voluntary trust is created, as to the trustee, by any words or acts of his, indicating with reasonable certainty: As to trustee.

1. His acceptance of the trust, or his acknowledgment, made upon sufficient consideration, of its existence; and,

2. The subject, purpose and beneficiary of the trust.

Day *v.* Roth, 18 *N. Y.*, 453. These things are necessary to be defined (Cruwys *v.* Coleman, 9 *Ves.*, 323.)

§ 1175. One who wrongfully detains a thing is an involuntary trustee thereof, for the benefit of the owner. Involuntary trustee, who is.

This is a familiar principle of equity in cases of title gained through fraud, mistake, undue influence, or the violation of a trust (Brown *v.* Lynch, 1 *Paige*, 147; Wood *v.* Rowcliffe, 2 *Phil.*, 382; 3 *Hare*, 304; see Anderson *v.* Lemon, 8 *N. Y.*, 236). There seems to be no reason for refusing to extend the rule to all cases of wrongful detention.

§ 1176. One who gains a thing by fraud,[1] accident, mistake, undue influence, the violation of a trust,[2] or Involuntary trust resulting from negligence, &c. other wrongful act,[3] is, unless he has some other and better right thereto, an involuntary trustee of the thing gained, for the benefit of the person who would otherwise have had it.

[1] Mitchell *v.* Cook, 29 *Barb.*, 243; Brown *v.* Lynch, 1 *Paige*, 147.

[2] Anderson *v.* Lemon, 8 *N. Y.*, 236.

[3] Bulkley *v.* Wilford, 2 *Cl. & Fin.*, 102, 177, 181; Howell *v.* Ransom, 11 *Paige*, 538, 541; Segrave *v.* Kirwan, *Beatty*, 157.

ARTICLE II.

OBLIGATIONS OF TRUSTEES.

Trustee's obligation to good faith.

§ 1177. In all matters connected with his trust, a trustee is bound to act in the highest good faith toward his beneficiary, and may not obtain any advantage therein over the latter by the slightest misrepresentation, concealment, threat or adverse pressure of any kind.

Moore *v.* Moore, 5 *N. Y.*, 256; Gardner *v.* Ogden, 22 *N. Y.*, 327, as explained by Dobson *v.* Racey, 8 *N. Y.*, 216. See Abbott *v.* Amer. Hard Rubber Co., 33 *Barb.*, 593; N. Y. Central Ins. Co. *v.* Nat. Pro. Ins. Co., 14 *N. Y.*, 85; Farnam *v.* Brooks, 9 *Pick.*, 212.

Trustee not to use property for his own profit.

§ 1178. A trustee may not use or deal with the trust property for his own profit,[1] or for any other purpose unconnected with the trust,[2] in any manner.

[1] Hoyt *v.* Martense, 16 *N. Y.*, 231; Sweet *v.* Jacocks, 6 *Paige*, 355; Phayre *v.* Peree, 1 *Bligh* [*N. S.*], 594; 3 *Dow*, 128; Holridge *v.* Gillespie, 2 *Johns. Ch.*, 33; Van Horne *v.* Fonda, 5 *id.*, 409; Green *v.* Winter, 1

id., 36; see Anderson *v.* Lemon, 8 *N. Y.*, 236; Burhans *v.* Van Zandt, 7 *id.*, 257.

[2] Thus, a trustee under two separate trusts commits a breach of trust by using the funds of one for the benefit of the other (Att'y Gen. *v.* Newbury, *C. P. C.*, 72.)

§ 1179. Neither a trustee, nor any of his agents,[1] may take part in any transaction concerning the trust, in which he, or any one for whom he acts as agent,[2] has an interest, present or contingent, adverse to that of his beneficiary,[3] except as follows: **Certain transactions forbidden.**

1. When the beneficiary, having capacity to contract,[4] with a full knowledge of the motives of the trustee,[5] and of all other facts concerning the transaction which might affect his own decision,[6] and without the use of any influence on the part of the trustee,[7] permits him to do so;[8]

2. When, the beneficiary not having capacity to contract,[9] the supreme court,[10] upon the like information of the facts, grants the like permission; or,

3. When, some of the beneficiaries having capacity to contract, and some not having it, the former grant permission for themselves, and the supreme court for the latter, in the manner above prescribed.[11]

[1] Gardner *v.* Ogden, 22 *N. Y.*, 327; Whitcomb *v.* Minchin, 5 *Madd.*, 91.

[2] *Ex parte* Bennett, 10 *Ves.*, 399, 400; N. Y. Central Ins. Co. *v.* National Pro. Ins. Co., 14 *N. Y.*, 85; Hawley *v.* Cramer, 4 *Cow.*, 717; Iddings *v.* Bruen, 4 *Sandf. Ch.*, 223; Davoue *v.* Fanning, 2 *Johns. Ch.*, 252.

[3] Gardner *v.* Ogden, 22 *N. Y.*, 327; Moore *v.* Moore, 5 *N. Y.*, 256; Schenck *v.* Dart, 22 *N. Y.*, 423; Jewett *v* Miller, 10 *N. Y.*, 402; Lewis *v.* Hillman, 3 *H. of L. Cas.*, 607, 629; Aberdeen R. R. Co. *v.* Blaikie, 1 *Macq.*, 461; Rothschild *v.* Brookman, 5 *Bligh* (*N. S.*), 190, 197, 202; *Ex parte* James, 8 *Ves.*, 337; Claflin *v.* Farmers' and Cit. Bk., 25 *N. Y.*, 293; Conkey *v.* Bond, 34 *Barb.*, 276.

[4] Campbell *v.* Walker, 5 *Ves.*, 678; 13 *id.*, 601.

[5] Coles *v.* Trecothick, 9 *Ves.*, 247; Murphy *v.* O'Shea, 8 *Irish Eq.*, 329; see Charters *v.* Trevelyan, 11 *Cl. & F.*, 714.

[6] Howell *v.* Ransom, 11 *Paige*, 538; Coles *v.* Trecothick, 9 *Ves.*, 246; Randall *v.* Errington, 10 *Ves.*, 427:

Morse *v.* Royal, 12 *Ves.*, 372; see Bruce *v.* Davenport, 36 *Barb.*, 249.

[7] Gibson *v.* Jeyes, 6 *Ves.*, 276.

[8] Dobson *v.* Racey, 8 *N. Y.*, 216.

[9] See *Ex parte* James, 8 *Ves.*, 352.

[10] Campbell *v.* Walker, 5 *Ves.*, 681, 682.

[11] A distinction has been taken between trustees, strictly so called, and other persons occupying a confidential relation; and it has been said that the former cannot purchase the trust property under any circumstances whatever, without being subject to a rescission of the sale at the discretion of the beneficiary (*Story Eq. Jur.*, § 311). But this distinction, if it exists at all, does not appear to be well founded.

Trustee's influence not to be used for his advantage.

§ 1180. A trustee may not use the influence, which his position gives him, to obtain any advantage from his beneficiary.

Bergen *v.* Udall, 31 *Barb.*, 9; Huguenin *v.* Basely, 14 *Ves.*, 271; Oldham *v.* Hand, 2 *id.*, 259; Walmesley *v.* Booth, 2 *Atk.*, 27; Ayliffe *v.* Murray, 2 *Atk.*, 58; Moore *v.* Frowd, 3 *Myl. & C.*, 48; see Morse *v.* Royal, 12 *Ves.*, 371. Perhaps this rule should be more strongly expressed (see Wright *v.* Proud, 15 *Ves.*, 138; Hatch *v.* Hatch, 9 *Ves.*, 296). But see Hunter *v.* Atkins, 3 *Myl. & K.* 113, in which these cases are limited.

Trustee not to assume a trust adverse to interest of beneficiary.

§ 1181. No trustee, so long as he remains in the trust, may undertake another trust adverse in its nature to the interest of his beneficiary in the subject of the trust, without the consent of the latter.

To disclose adverse interest.

§ 1182. If a trustee acquires any interest, or becomes charged with any duty, adverse to the interest of his beneficiary in the subject of the trust, he must immediately inform the latter thereof, and may be at once removed.

Trustee guilty of fraud, when.

§ 1183. Every violation of the provisions of the preceding sections of this article, is a fraud against the beneficiary of a trust.

Howell *v.* Ransom, 11 *Paige*, 538. A transaction in violation of these provisions is voidable, not absolutely void (Bostwick *v.* Atkins, 3 *N. Y.*, 53).

§ 1184. All transactions between a trustee and his beneficiary, during the existence of the trust, or while the influence acquired by the trustee remains, by which he obtains any advantage from his beneficiary, are presumed to be entered into by the latter without sufficient consideration, and under undue influence. Presumption against trustees.

Ford *v.* Harrington, 16 *N. Y.*, 289; Brock *v.* Barnes, 40 *Barb.*, 521; Gould *v.* Gould, 36 *id.*, 270; Evans *v.* Ellis, 5 *Den.*, 640; Howell *v.* Ransom, 11 *Paige*, 538; Morse *v.* Royal, 12 *Ves.*, 369; Randall *v.* Errington, 10 *id.*, 429.

§ 1185. A trustee who willfully and unnecessarily mingles the trust property with his own, so as to constitute himself in appearance its absolute owner, is liable for its safety in all events. Trustee mingling trust property with his own.

Duffy *v.* Duncan, 32 *Barb.*, 587; Matter of Stafford, 11 *id.*, 353; Mumford *v.* Murray, 6 *Johns. Ch.*, 1; Macdonnell *v.* Harding, 7 *Sim.*, 178; Clarke *v.* Tipping, 9 *Beav.*, 284; Massey *v.* Banner, 4 *Madd.*, 416; Freeman *v.* Fairlie, 3 *Meriv.*, 29. Perhaps the same rule applies to the mixture of one trust fund with another (see Att'y Gen. *v.* Goldsmiths, *C. P. C.*, 292). But this should seem severe.

§ 1186. A trustee who uses or disposes of the trust property, contrary to section 1178, may, at the option of the beneficiary,[1] be required to account for all profits so made,[2] or to pay the value of its use,[3] and, if he has disposed thereof, to replace it, with its fruits, or to account for its proceeds, with interest.[4] Measure of liability for breach of trust.

[1] Heathcote *v.* Hulme, 1 *Jac. & W.*, 128; Pocock *v.* Reddington, 5 *Ves. Jr.*, 794; Forrest *v.* Elwes, 4 *id.*, 497; Harrison *v.* Harrison, 2 *Atk.*, 121.

[2] Docker *v.* Somes, 2 *Myl. & K.*, 665; Crawshay *v.* Collins, 15 *Ves.*, 218; M'Donald *v.* Richardson, 5 *Jur.* [*N. S.*], 9; see Stroud *v.* Gwyer, 6 *id.*, 719.

[3] Duffy *v.* Duncan, 32 *Barb.*, 587; Mumford *v.* Murray, 6 *Johns. Ch.*, 452.

[4] Pocock *v.* Reddington, Forrest *v.* Elwes, Harrison *v.* Harrison, above cited; see Powlett *v.* Herbert, 1 *Atk.*, 297.

§ 1187. A trustee who uses or disposes of the trust property in any manner not authorized by the trust, but in good faith, and with intent to serve the inte- Id.

rest of the beneficiary, is liable only to make good whatever is lost to the beneficiary by his error.

O'Brien *v.* O'Brien, 1 *Molloy*, 533.

Co-trustees, how far liable for each other.

§ 1188. A trustee is responsible for the wrongful acts of a co-trustee, to which he consented,[1] or which by his negligence he enabled the latter to commit;[2] but for no others.[3]

[1] Broadhurst *v.* Balguy, 1 *You. & Coll. C. C.*, 17; French *v.* Hobson, 9 *Ves.*, 103.

[2] Spencer *v.* Spencer, 11 *Paige*, 299; Monell *v.* Monell, 5 *Johns. Ch.*, 283; Brice *v.* Stokes, 11 *Ves.*, 324; Harvey *v.* Blakeman, 4 *id.*, 596; Sadler *v.* Hobbs, 2 *Bro. C. C.*, 114; Joy *v.* Campbell, 1 *Sch. & Lef.*, 341; Boardman *v.* Mosman, 1 *Bro. C. C.*, 68; Hanbury *v.* Kirkland, 3 *Sim.*, 265; Thompson *v.* Finch, 22 *Beav.*, 316.

[3] *Lewin on Trusts*, 302; Kip *v.* Deniston, 4 *Johns.*, 23; Williams *v.* Nixon, 2 *Beav.*, 472; Att'y Gen. *v.* Holland, 2 *Y. & Coll. Ex.*, 683

ARTICLE III.

OBLIGATIONS OF THIRD PERSONS.

Third person, when involuntary trustee.

§ 1189. Every one to whom property is transferred in violation of a trust, holds the same as an involuntary trustee under such trust,[1] unless he purchased it in good faith and for a valuable consideration.[2]

[1] Day *v.* Roth, 18 *N. Y.*, 448; Cumberland Coal Co. *v.* Sherman, 30 *Barb.*, 553; Fisher *v.* Fields, 10 *Johns.*, 495; Shepherd *v.* McEvers, 4 *Johns. Ch.*, 136; Murray *v.* Ballou, 1 *id.*, 566; Adair *v.* Shaw, 1 *Sch. & Lef.*, 262.

[2] See Day *v.* Roth; Cumberland Coal Co. *v.* Sherman, above cited.

When third person must see to application of trust property.

§ 1190. One who actually and in good faith transfers any money or other property to a trustee, as such, is not bound to see to the application thereof;

and his rights can in no way be prejudiced by a misapplication thereof by the trustee.[1] Other persons must, at their peril, see to the proper application of money or other property paid or delivered by them.[2]

[1] 1 *R. S.*, 730, § 66.

[2] Champlin *v.* Haight, 10 *Paige*, 274. The old law applied this rule to all persons.

CHAPTER II.

TRUSTS FOR THE BENEFIT OF THIRD PERSONS.

ARTICLE I.

NATURE AND CREATION OF THE TRUST.

§ 1191. The provisions of this chapter apply only to express trusts, created for the benefit of another than the trustor, and in which the title to the trust property is vested in the trustee; not including, however, those of executors, administrators and guardians, as such.

Who are trustees within scope of this chapter.

§ 1192. The mutual consent of a trustor and trustee creates a trust, of which the beneficiary may take advantage at any time[1] prior to its rescission.[2]

Creation of trust.

[1] Moses *v.* Murgatroyd, 1 *Johns. Ch.*, 119; Shepperd *v.* M'Evers, 4 *id.*, 136; Cumberland *v.* Codrington, 3 *id.*, 261; Weston *v.* Parker, 12 *Johns.*, 276, 281; Neilson *v.* Blight, 1 *Johns. Cas.*, 205.

[2] Acton *v.* Woodgate, 2 *Myl. & K.*, 492.

Trustee appointed by court.

§ 1193. When a trustee is appointed by a court or public officer as such, such court or officer is the trustor, within the meaning of the last section.

Declaration of trust.

§ 1194. The nature, extent and object of a trust are expressed in the declaration of trust.

Id.

§ 1195. All declarations of a trustor to his trustees, in relation to the trust, before its acceptance by the trustees, or any of them, are to be deemed part of the declaration of the trust, except that when a declaration of trust is made in writing, all previous declarations by the same trustor are merged therein.

ARTICLE II.

OBLIGATIONS OF TRUSTEES.

Trustee must obey declaration of trust.

§ 1196. A trustee must fulfill the purpose of the trust, as declared at its creation, and must follow all the directions of the trustor given at that time,[1] except as modified by the consent of all parties interested,[2] in the same manner, and to the same extent, as an employee.[3]

[1] Taylor *v.* Tabrum, 6 *Sim.*, 281.

[2] Wood *v.* Wood, 5 *Paige*, 596.

[3] He has a right to disobey instructions in the same cases in which an employee might do so. Thus, although directed to lend the funds to A. on his bond, he may refuse, if A. becomes insolvent (Boss *v.* Godsall, 1 *Y. & Coll. Ch.*, 617).

Degree of care and diligence in execution of trust.

§ 1197. A trustee, whether he receives any compensation or not, must use at least ordinary care and diligence in the execution of his trust.

So held as to compensated trustees (Litchfield *v.* White, 7 *N. Y.*, 438; aff'g S. C., 3 *Sandf.*, 545); and so as to gratuitous trustees (Caffrey *v.* Darby, 6 *Ves.*, 488). No greater degree of care is required (Higgins *v.* Whitson, 20 *Barb.*, 141; Garrett *v.* Noble, 6 *Sim.*, 504).

§ 1198. If a trustee procures or assents to his discharge from his office, before his trust is fully executed, he must use at least ordinary care and diligence to secure the appointment of a trustworthy successor before accepting his own final discharge. Duty of trustee as to appointment of successor.

This provision is new, and is intended to protect beneficiaries from a hasty resort to the courts in order to shake off the responsibility of a trust; a proceeding by which they have been sometimes irremediably injured; an insolvent and reckless trustee having been appointed in place of an indolent but responsible one.

§ 1199. A trustee must invest money received by him under the trust, as fast as he collects a sufficient amount,[1] in such manner as to afford reasonable security[2] and interest for the same. Investment of money by trustee.

[1] De Peyster *v.* Clarkson, 2 *Wend.*, 77; aff'g S. C., *Hopk.*, 424.

[2] Personal security is not sufficient (Ackerman *v.* Emott, 4 *Barb.*, 626; Smith *v.* Smith, 4 *Johns. Ch.*, 281; Walker *v.* Symonds, 3 *Swanst.*, 2; Ryder *v.* Bickerton, *id.*, 80; Mills *v.* Osborne, 7 *Sim.*, 30; Holmes *v.* Dring, 2 *Cox*, 1; Lowson *v.* Copeland, 2 *Bro. C. C.*, 156), except for a reasonable time, while seeking real security (Emelie *v.* Emelie, 7 *Bro. P. C.*, 259; see France *v.* Woods, *Taml.*, 172).

§ 1200. If a trustee omits to invest the trust moneys according to the last section, he must pay simple interest thereon, if such omission is negligent merely,[1] and compound interest if it is willful.[2] Interest, simple or compound, on omission to invest trust moneys.

[1] Schieffelin *v.* Stewart, 1 *Johns. Ch.*, 620; Dunscomb *v.* Dunscomb, *Id.*, 508.

[2] Schieffelin *v.* Stewart, 1 *Johns. Ch.*, 620; see Spear *v.* Tinkham, 2 *Barb. Ch.*, 211; De Peyster *v.* Clarkson, 2 *Wend.*, 77.

§ 1201. A trustee cannot enforce any claim against the trust property which he purchases after or in contemplation of his appointment as trustee; but he Purchase by trustee of claims against trust fund.

may be allowed, by any competent court, to charge to the trust property what he has in good faith paid for the claim, upon discharging the same.

ARTICLE III.

POWERS OF TRUSTEES.

Trustee's powers as agent.

§ 1202. A trustee is a general agent for the trust property. His authority is such as is conferred upon him by the declaration of trust, and by this chapter, and none other. His acts, within the scope of his authority, bind the trust property to the same extent as the acts of an agent bind his principal.

Coutant *v.* Servoss, 3 *Barb.*, 128; L'Amoureux *v.* Van Rensselaer, 1 *Barb. Ch.*, 34; see Briggs *v.* Davis, 20 *N. Y.*, 15.

All must act.

§ 1203. Where there are several co-trustees, all must unite in any act to bind the trust property, unless the declaration of trust otherwise provides.

Ridgely *v.* Johnson, 11 *Barb.*, 527; see Moir *v.* Brown, 14 *id.*, 39; Van Rensselaer *v.* Akin, 22 *Wend.*, 549.

Discretionary powers.

§ 1204. A discretionary power conferred upon a trustee is presumed not to be left to his arbitrary discretion, but may be controlled by the supreme court if not reasonably exercised,[1] unless an absolute discretion is clearly conferred by the declaration of trust.[2]

[1] Cowley *v.* Hartstonge, 1 *Dow*, 378; Milsington *v.* Mulgrave, 3 *Madd.*, 491; Mortimer *v.* Watts, 14 *Beav.*, 616; Willis *v.* Childe, 13 *id.*, 117. If so exercised, the court will not interfere (Wilkes' Charity, 3 *Macn. & G.*, 440; Contabadie *v.* Contabadie, 6 *Hare*, 410).

[2] Cowley *v.* Hartstonge, 1 *Dow*, 378.

ARTICLE IV.

RIGHTS OF TRUSTEES.

§ 1205. A trustee is entitled to the repayment, out of the trust property, of all expenses actually and properly incurred by him in the performance of his trust.[1] He is entitled to the repayment of even unlawful expenditures, if they were productive of actual benefit to the estate.[2] Indemnification of trustee.

[1] Glover *v.* Holley, 2 *Bradf.*, 291; Worrall *v.* Harford, 8 *Ves.*, 8; Wilkinson *v.* Stuart, 2 *Sim. & Stu.*, 237; Webb *v.* Shaftesbury, 7 *Ves.*, 480; Att'y-Gen. *v.* Norwich, 2 *Myl. & Cr.*, 407; 1 *Keen*, 700.
[2] Duffy *v.* Duncan, 32 *Barb.*, 587.

§ 1206. When a declaration of trust is silent upon the subject of compensation, the trustee is entitled to the same compensation as an executor.[1] If it specifies the amount of his compensation, he is entitled to the amount thus specified, and no more.[2] If it directs that he shall be allowed a compensation, but does not specify the rate or amount, he is entitled to such compensation as may be reasonable under the circumstances.[3] Compensation of trustee.

[1] Meacham *v.* Sternes, 9 *Paige*, 398; Wagstaff *v.* Lowerre, 23 *Barb.*, 209; 3 *Abb. Pr.*, 411; see Litchfield *v.* White, 7 *N. Y.*, 438. Formerly no compensation was allowed (Green *v.* Winter, 1 *Johns. Ch.*, 26; Manning *v.* Manning, *Id.*, 527; Ormsby's case, 1 *Ball & B.*, 189).
[2] Meacham *v.* Sternes, 9 *Paige*, 398.
[3] *Ib.*

§ 1207. An involuntary trustee, who becomes such through his own fault, has none of the rights mentioned in this article. Involuntary trustee.

ARTICLE V.

TERMINATION OF THE TRUST.

Trust, how extinguished.

§ 1208. A trust is extinguished by the entire fulfillment of its object, or by such object becoming impossible or unlawful.

So as to real trusts (1 *R. S.*, 730, § 67; Matter of Craig, 1 *Barb.*, 33; Matter of De Kay, 4 *Paige*, 403), and doubtless as to personal trusts.

Not revocable.

§ 1209. A trust cannot be revoked by the trustor after its acceptance, actual or presumed, by the trustee and beneficiaries, except by the consent of all the beneficiaries, unless the declaration of trust reserves a power of revocation to the trustor, and in that case the power must be strictly pursued.

See Diefendorf *v.* Spraker, 10 *N. Y.*, 246; Petre *v.* Espinasse, 2 *Myl. & K.*, 496.

Trustee's office, how vacated.

§ 1210. The office of a trustee is vacated:

1. By his death; or,

2. By his discharge.

Trustee, how discharged.

§ 1211. A trustee can be discharged from his trust only as follows:

1. By the extinction of the trust;

2. By the completion of his duties under the trust;

3. By such means as may be prescribed by the declaration of trust;

4. By the consent of the beneficiary, if he has capacity to contract;

5. By the judgment of a competent tribunal, in a direct proceeding for that purpose, that he is of unsound mind; or,

6. By the supreme court.

He cannot resign of his own mere will (Diefendorf *v.* Spraker, 10 *N. Y.*, 246; Cruger *v.* Halliday, 11 *Paige*, 314; Shepherd *v.* M'Evers, 4 *Johns. Ch.*, 136; Chalmers *v.* Bradley, 1 *Jac. & W.*, 68).

§ 1212. The supreme court may remove any trustee who has violated or is unfit to execute the trust. Removal by supreme court.

1 *R. S.*, 730, § 70; People *v.* Norton, 9 *N. Y.*, 176. This does not extend to executors and administrators (Emerson *v.* Bowers, 14 *N. Y.*, 449).

ARTICLE VI.

SUCCESSION OR APPOINTMENT OF NEW TRUSTEES.

SECTION 1213. Vacant trusteeship filled by court.
1214. Survivorship between co-trustees.
1215. Supreme court as trustee.

§ 1213. The supreme court may appoint a trustee whenever there is a vacancy, and the declaration of trust does not provide a practicable method of appointment. Vacant trusteeship filled by court.

See 1 *R. S.*, 730, § 71; Leggett *v.* Hunter, 19 *N. Y.*, 459. This provision is broader than the present statute, which applies only to vacancies caused by resignation or removal (Matter of Stevenson, 3 *Paige*, 420; Matter of Van Schoonhoven, 5 *id.*, 559).

§ 1214. On the death,[1] renunciation[2] or discharge[3] of one of several co-trustees, the trust survives to the others. Survivorship between co-trustees.

[1] *Lewin on Trustees*, 299; Belmont *v.* O'Brien, 12 *N. Y.*, 394.

[2] Matter of Van Schoonhoven, 5 *Paige*, 559; De Peyster *v.* Clendining, 8 *id.*, 295.

[3] Matter of Crossman, 20 *How. Pr.*, 350.

§ 1215. When a trust exists without any appointed trustee, or where all the trustees renounce, die or are discharged, the supreme court must execute the trust until another trustee is appointed. Supreme court as trustee.

This is the rule as to real trusts (1 *R. S.*, 730, § 68). Compare, as to personal trusts, Hawley *v.* Ross (7 *Paige*, 103), and Banks *v.* Wilkes (3 *Sandf. Ch.*, 99).

TITLE IX.

AGENCY.

Under this head, the representation of one person by another is the only subject treated. The rights acquired by third persons against both the principal and the agent are here stated. The mutual relations of principal and agent are a branch of SERVICE, and are defined in the Title on that subject. So far as these relations create a mutual trust, they are regulated by the Title on TRUST.

CHAPTER I.

AGENCY IN GENERAL.

ARTICLE I.

DEFINITION OF AGENCY.

Agency, what. § 1216. An agent is one who represents another, called the principal, in dealings with third persons. Such representation is called agency.

§ 1217. Any person, having capacity to contract, may appoint an agent;[1] and any person may be an agent.[2]

Who may appoint and who may be an agent.

[1] *Story on Agency*, § 6. See Bergman *v.* Howell, 3 *Abb. Pr.*, 329; Phillips *v.* Burr, 4 *Duer*, 113.

[2] *Sto. Ag.* § 7; *Bac. Abr.*, Authority, B.; Hopkins *v.* Mollinieux, 4 *Wend.*, 465.

§ 1218. An agent for a particular act or transaction, is called a special agent. All others are general agents.

Agents, general or special.

Story Ag., §§ 17–20.

§ 1219. An agency is either actual or ostensible.

Agency, actual or ostensible.

§ 1220. An agency is actual when the agent is really employed by the principal.

Actual agency.

§ 1221. An agency is ostensible when the principal intentionally, or by want of ordinary care, causes a third person to believe another to be his agent, who is not really employed by him.

Ostensible agency.

ARTICLE II.

AUTHORITY OF AGENTS.

What authority may be conferred.

§ 1222. An agent may be authorized to do any acts which his principal might do, except those to which the latter is bound to give his personal attention.

Agent may perform acts required of principal by Code.

§ 1223. Every act which, according to this Code, may be done by or to any person, may be done by or to the agent of such person for that purpose, unless a contrary intention clearly appears.

Agent cannot have authority to defraud principal.

§ 1224. An agent can never have authority, either actual or ostensible, to do an act which is, and is known or suspected by the person with whom he deals to be, a fraud upon the principal.

Creation of agency.

§ 1225. An agency may be created, and an authority may be conferred, by a precedent authorization, or a subsequent ratification.

Newton *v.* Bronson, 13 *N. Y.*, 594; Moss *v.* Rossie Mining Co., 5 *Hill*, 137; Weed *v.* Carpenter, 4 *Wend.*, 219; Peterson *v.* Mayor of New York, 17 *N. Y.*, 453; Hoyt *v.* Thompson, 19 *id.*, 218.

Consideration, unnecessary.

§ 1226. A consideration is not necessary to make an authority, whether precedent or subsequent, binding upon the principal.

Commercial Bank *v.* Warren, 15 *N. Y.*, 577.

Form of authority.

§ 1227. An oral authorization is sufficient for any purpose,[1] except that:

1. An authority to enter into a contract under seal can only be given by an instrument under seal;[2] and,

2. An authority to enter into a contract for the transfer of real property, or to declare a trust in relation thereto, can only be given in writing.[3]

[1] Bank of N. America *v.* Embury, 33 *Barb.*, 323; 21 *How. Pr.*, 14.

[2] Worrall *v.* Munn, 5 *N. Y.*, 229.

[3] 2 *R. S.*, 135.

§ 1228. A ratification can be made only in the manner that would have been necessary to confer an original authority for the act ratified,[1] or, where an oral authorization would suffice, by accepting or retaining the benefit of the act,[2] with notice thereof.[3]

Ratification of agent's act.

[1] *Story Ag.* § 242; M'Cracken v. San Francisco, 16 *Cal.*, 591, 623; Despatch Line *v.* Bellamy, 12 *N. H.*, 232. See Newton *v.* Bronson, 13 *N. Y.*, 595; Blood *v.* Goodrich, 9 *Wend.*, 68; 12 *id.*, 525; Wells *v.* Evans, 20 *id.*, 251.

[2] Bennett *v.* Judson, 21 *N. Y.*, 238; Clarke *v.* Van Reimsdyck, 9 *Cranch*, 153; Lowenstein *v.* McIntosh, 37 *Barb.*, 251; Decker *v.* Judson, 16 *N. Y.*, 446.

[3] Seymour *v.* Wyckoff, 10 *N. Y.*, 213; Cobb *v.* Dows, *id.*, 341.

§ 1229. Ratification of part of an indivisible transaction is a ratification of the whole.

Ratification of part of a transaction.

Decker *v.* Judson, 16 *N. Y.*, 446; Cobb *v.* Dows, 10 *N. Y.*, 335; Farmers Loan Co. *v.* Walworth, 1 *N. Y.*, 433; Bell *v.* Shibley, 33 *Barb.*, 610; Ferguson *v.* Hamilton, 35 *id.*, 427; *Story Ag.*, § 250. See Bennett *v.* Judson, 21 *N. Y.*, 238; Condit *v.* Baldwin, *id.*, 231.

§ 1230. A ratification is not valid unless, at the time of ratifying the act done, the principal has power to confer authority for such an act.

When ratification void.

M'Cracken *v.* San Francisco, 16 *Cal.*, 591.

§ 1231. No unauthorized act can be made valid, retroactively, to the prejudice of third persons, without their consent.

Ratification not to work injury to third persons.

This is perhaps a broader rule than at present exists. But great difficulty has been felt in attempting to reconcile the cases (See *Story Ag.*, §§ 246, 247; Bliss *v.* Cottle, 32 *Barb.*, 322; Bird *v.* Brown, 4 *Exch.*, 786; Wilson *v.* Tumman, 6 *M. & G.*, 236; Palmer *v.* Stephens, 1 *Denio*, 481; Rossiter *v.* Rossiter, 8 *Wend.*, 499). In Buron *v.* Denman (2 *Exch.*, 167), the defendant had committed a trespass, which the English government expressly ratified. This was held to relieve the defendant from responsibility. In Lucas *v.* Wilkinson (1 *H. & N.*, 420), it was held that an act expressly done on behalf of A., could not be ratified and adopted by B., to the prejudice of C.

Rescission of ratification.

§ 1232. A ratification may be rescinded when made without such consent as is required in a contract, or with an imperfect knowledge of the material facts of the transaction ratified,[1] but not otherwise.[2]

[1] Seymour *v.* Wyckoff, 10 *N. Y.*, 213, 224; Cobb *v.* Dows, *Id.*, 341; Nixon *v.* Palmer, 8 *id.*, 398; Brass *v.* Worth, 40 *Barb.*, 648; Roach *v.* Coe, 1 *E. D. Smith*, 175; M'Cracken *v.* San Francisco, 16 *Cal.*, 591, 625; Freeman *v.* Rosher, 13 *Q. B.*, 780; Owings *v.* Hull, 9 *Peters*, 607.

[2] *Story on Agency*, §§ 242, 250. See Commercial Bank *v.* Warren, 15 *N. Y.*, 577.

Measure of agent's authority.

§ 1233. An agent has such authority as the principal, actually or ostensibly, confers upon him.

Actual authority what.

§ 1234. Actual authority is such as a principal intentionally confers upon the agent, or intentionally, or by want of ordinary care, allows the agent to believe himself to possess.

Ostensible authority, what.

§ 1235. Ostensible authority is such as a principal intentionally, or by want of ordinary care, causes or allows a third person to believe the agent to possess.

Farm. & Mech. B'k *v.* Butch. & Drov. B'k, 16 *N. Y.*, 125; Beaufort *v.* Neeld, 12 *Clark & Fin.*, 290; Sickens *v.* Irving, 7 *C. B.* (*N. S.*), 171, 173; see Smith *v.* McGuire, 3 *H. & N.*, 554.

Agent's authority as to persons having notice of restrictions upon it.

§ 1236. Every agent has actually such authority as is defined by this Title, unless specially deprived thereof by his principal, and has even then such authority ostensibly, except as to persons who have actual or constructive notice of the restriction upon his authority.

Dingle *v.* Hare, 7 *C. B.* (*N. S.*), 159.

Agent's necessary authority.

§ 1237. An agent has authority:

1. To do everything necessary, or proper and usual in the ordinary course of business, for effecting the purpose of his agency; and,

2. To make a representation respecting any matter of fact, not including the terms of his authority, but upon which his right to use his authority depends, and the truth of which cannot be determined by the use of reasonable diligence on the part of the person to whom the representation is made.[2]

[1] *Story on Agency*, §§ 85, 86, 96, 97; Dingle *v.* Hare, 7 *C. B.* (*N. S.*), 159; see Horton *v.* Morgan, 19 *N. Y.*, 170; Waring *v.* Mason, 18 *Wend.*, 434; Graves *v.* Legg, 2 *H. & N.*, 210; Taylor *v.* Stray, 2 *C. B.* (*N. S.*), 191; Pollock *v.* Stables, 12 *Q. B.*, 765; Bayliffe *v.* Butterworth, 1 *Exch.*, 428; Sutton *v.* Tatham, 10 *Ad. & El.*, 27; Bayley *v.* Wilkins, 7 *C. B.*, 886; see, however, Sweeting *v.* Pearce, 7 *C. B.* (*N. S.*), 449; Partridge *v.* Bank of England, 9 *Q. B.*, 396.

[2] Griswold *v.* Haven, 25 *N. Y.*, 595; Farmers' & M. Bank *v.* Butchers' & Drovers' Bank, 16 *id.*, 125; Exchange Bank *v.* Monteath, 26 *id.*, 505; North River Bank *v.* Aymar, 3 *Hill*, 263.

§ 1238. An agent has power to disobey instructions in dealing with the subject of the agency, in cases where it is clearly for the interest of his principal that he should do so, and there is not time to communicate with the principal. **Agent's power to disobey instructions.**

Code La., 2975, 2980; Drummond *v.* Wood, 2 *Caines*, 310.

§ 1239. When an authority is given partly in general, and partly in specific terms, the general authority gives no higher powers than those specifically mentioned. **Authority to be construed by its specific, rather than its general terms.**

Sto. Agency, § 71; *Stair Inst.*, B. 1, t. 12, § 15.

§ 1240. An authority expressed in general terms, however broad, does not authorize an agent: **Exceptions to general authority.**

1. To act in his own name,[1] unless it is the usual course of business to do so;[2]

2. To define the scope of his agency;[3] or,

3. To do any act which a trustee is forbidden to do by article II, of chapter I, of the last Title.[4]

[1] Bank of State of N. Y. *v.* Farmers' Branch Bank, 36 *Barb.*, 332.

[2] Horton *v.* Morgan, 19 *N. Y.*, 170; Whitehouse *v.* Moore, 13 *Abb. Pr.*, 142.

[3] Sup'rs of Rensselaer *v.* Bates, 17 *N. Y.*, 246; Mechanics' Bank *v.* New Haven R. R., 13 *id.*, 599; Gould *v.* Sterling, 23 *id.*, 463; Grant *v.* Norway, 10 *C. B.*, 665; Coleman *v.* Riches, 16 *id.*, 104. But see these cases explained and greatly restricted in Griswold *v.* Haven, 25 *N. Y.*, 295.

[4] Claflin *v.* Farmers', &c., Bank, 25 *N. Y.*, 293; Bentley *v.* Columbian Ins. Co., 17 *id.*, 421; N. Y. Central Ins. Co. *v.* National Prot'n Ins. Co., 14 *id.*, 85; Fellows *v.* Com'rs of Oneida, 36 *Barb.*, 655; Bruce *v.* Davenport, *id.*, 349; Conkey *v.* Bond, 34 *id.*, 276; Cassard *v.* Hinman, 6 *Bosw.*, 8.

What included in authority to sell personal property.

§ 1241. An authority to sell personal property includes authority to warrant the title of the principal, and the quality and quantity of the property.

Waring *v.* Mason, (Ct. of Errors), 18 *Wend.*, 434; see Ferguson *v.* Todd, 35 *Barb.*, 427; Milburn *v.* Belloni, 12 *Abb. Pr.*, 451; *Sto. Agency*, §§ 58, 59; Nelson *v.* Cowing, 6 *Hill*, 336. See, however, Brady *v.* Todd (9 *C. B.* [*N. S.*], 592), which holds these powers to be confined to a *general* agent.

What included in authority to sell real property.

§ 1242. An authority to sell and convey real property includes authority to give the usual covenants of warranty.

Leroy *v.* Beard, 8 *How.* (*U. S.*), 451.

Authority of general agent to receive price of property.

§ 1243. A general agent to sell, who is intrusted by the principal with the possession of the thing sold, has authority to receive the price.

Authority of special agent to receive price.

§ 1244. A special agent to sell has authority to receive the price on delivery of the thing sold, but not afterwards.

Peck *v.* Harriott, 6 *Serg. & R.*, 149.

ARTICLE III.

MUTUAL OBLIGATIONS OF PRINCIPALS AND THIRD PERSONS.

§ 1245. An agent represents his principal for all purposes within the scope of his actual or ostensible[1] authority, and all the rights[2] and liabilities[3] which would accrue to the agent from transactions within such limit,[4] if they had been entered into on his own account, accrue to the principal.

Principal, how affected by acts of agent within the scope of his authority.

[1] Rourke *v.* Story, 4 *E. D. Smith*, 54; Hatch *v.* Taylor, 10 *N. H.*, 538; Farm. & M. B'k *v.* Butch. & Drov. B'k, 16 *N. Y.*, 125, 149.

[2] *Story Agency*, §§ 435, 438.

[3] *Story Agency*, § 127.

[4] See Condit *v.* Baldwin, 21 *N. Y.*, 219; Mechanics' Bank *v.* New Haven R. R., 13 *N. Y.*, 599, 634; Hubbersty *v.* Ward, 8 *Exch.*, 330; Coleman *v.* Riches, 16 *C. B.*, 104.

§ 1246. A principal is bound by an incomplete execution of an authority, when it is consistent with the whole purpose and scope thereof, but not otherwise.

Principal, when bound by incomplete execution of authority

Story Agency, §§ 171, 180.

§ 1247. As against a principal, both principal[1] and agent[2] are deemed to have notice of whatever either has notice of, and ought, in good faith and the exercise of ordinary care and diligence, to communicate to the other.[3]

Notice to agent, when notice to principal.

[1] Fulton Bank *v.* Sharon Canal Co., 4 *Paige*, 137; Bank of U. S. *v.* Davis, 2 *Hill*, 464; Stewart *v.* Stewart, 6 *Clark & Fin.*, 911. See Ingalls *v.* Morgan, 10 *N. Y.*, 184; Weisser *v.* Denison, *id*, 68.

[2] This rule has been declared in a well considered opinion (Fitzsimmons *v.* Joslin, 21 *Vt.*, 129), and seems to be supported by other cases (see Lawrence *v.* Miller, 16 *N. Y.*, 235; Fuller *v.* Wilson, 3 *Q. B.*, 58). To the contrary is the celebrated case of Cornfoot *v.* Fowke (6 *M. & W.*, 386), which has been, however, explained in the house of lords (National Exch. Co. *v.* Drew, 2 *Macq.*, 108, 144) as really turning upon a question of pure fraud.

[3] See Weisser *v.* Denison, 10 *N. Y.*, 68; Hood *v.* Fahnestock, 8 *Watts*, 489; Bracken *v.* Miller, 4 *Watts & S.*, 102. Thus, notice to an agent, before his employment as such, does not affect the principal (Fuller *v.* Bennett, 2 *Hare*, 402; Worsley *v.* Scarborough, 3 *Atk.*, 392; and cases before cited).

Obligation of principal when agent exceeds his authority.

§ 1248. When an agent exceeds his authority, his principal is bound by his authorized acts so far only as they can be plainly separated from those which are unauthorized.

For acts done under a merely ostensible authority.

§ 1249. A principal is bound by acts of his agent, under a merely ostensible authority, to those persons only who have in good faith, and without ordinary negligence, incurred a liability, or parted with value, upon the faith thereof.

See Mechanics' Bank *v.* New Haven R. R., 13 *N. Y.*, 611; Farmers' and Mechanics' Bank *v.* Butchers' and Drovers' Bank, 16 *N. Y.* 127

When exclusive credit is given to agent.

§ 1250. If exclusive credit is given to an agent by the person dealing with him, his principal is exonerated by payment or other satisfaction made by him to his agent in good faith, before receiving notice of the creditor's election to hold him responsible.

Story Agency, § 291; Fish *v.* Wood, 4 *E. D. Smith*, 327; see Heald *v.* Kenworthy, 10 *Exch.*, 739; Hyde *v.* Paige, 9 *Barb.*, 150; Cheever *v.* Smith, 15 *Johns.*, 276; French *v.* Price, 24 *Pick.*, 13; Fitler *v.* Commonwealth, 31 *Penn. St.*, 406. If such credit is not given to the agent, mere delay in calling upon the principal does not exonerate him (Macfarlane *v.* Giannacopulo, 3 *H. & N.*, 860).

Rights of person who deals with agent without knowledge of his agency.

§ 1251. One who deals with an agent, without knowing or having reason to believe that the agent acts as such in the transaction, may set off, against any claim of the principal arising out of the same, all claims which he might have set off against the agent before notice of the agency.

Hogan *v.* Shorb, 24 *Wend.*, 458; George *v.* Clagett, 7 *T. R.*, 359; see Taintor *v.* Prendergast, 3 *Hill*, 72; Ferrand *v.* Bischoffsheim, 4 *C. B.* (*N. S.*), 710; Heald *v.* Kenworthy, 10 *Exch.*, 739; Smethurst *v.* Mitchell, 1 *El. & El.*, 630.

§ 1252. Any instrument within the scope of his authority, whether under seal or not, by which an agent intends to bind his principal, does bind him, if such intent is plainly inferable from the instrument itself.

Effect of a written instrument by which the agent intends to bind the principal.

This section belongs perhaps to the general subject of interpretation of contracts. It is intended to abolish the distinction in this respect between sealed and unsealed instruments. See *Story Ag.*, §§ 147–155.

§ 1253. Unless required by or under the authority of law to employ that particular agent,[1] a principal is responsible to third persons for the negligence of his agent in the transaction of the business of the agency,[2] including wrongful acts committed by such agent in, and as a part of, the transaction of such business;[3] and for his willful omission to fulfill the obligations of the principal.[4]

Principal's responsibility for agent's negligence or omission.

[1] *Story Agency*, § 456.

[2] Drew *v.* Sixth Av. R. R. Co., 26 *N. Y.*, 49; Sadler *v.* Henlock, 4 *E. & B.*, 570; Althorf *v.* Wolfe, 22 *N. Y.*, 355; Blake *v.* Ferris, 5 *N. Y.*, 48.

[3] Chase *v.* N. Y. Central R. R. Co., 26 *N. Y.*, 523; Sanford *v.* Eighth Av. R. R. Co., 23 *N. Y.*, 343; see Griswold *v.* Haven, 25 *N. Y.*, 595.

[4] Weed *v.* Panama R. R., 17 *N. Y.*, 362; *Story Agency*, § 453.

§ 1254. A principal is responsible for no other wrongs committed by his agent, than those mentioned in the last section, unless he has authorized or ratified them,[1] even though they are committed while the agent is engaged in his service.[2]

Principal's responsibility for wrongs willfully committed by the agent.

[1] Steele *v.* Smith, 3 *E. D. Smith*, 321; Eastern C. R. R. *v.* Brown, 6 *Exch.*, 314; Chilton *v.* Croydon R. R., 16 *M. & W.*, 212; Maund *v.* Monmouth Canal Co., 4 *M. & G.*, 452.

[2] *Story Ag.*, § 456; Church *v.* Mansfield, 20 *Conn.*, 284; Condit *v.* Baldwin, 21 *N. Y.*, 219; Richmond Turnpike Co. *v.* Vanderbilt, 2 *N. Y.*, 479; 1 *Hill*, 480; Fellows *v.* Com'rs of Oneida, 36 *Barb.*, 655.

ARTICLE IV.

OBLIGATIONS OF AGENTS TO THIRD PERSONS.

Warranty of authority.

§ 1255. One who assumes to act as an agent thereby warrants, to all who deal with him in that capacity, that he has the authority which he assumes.

White *v.* Madison, 26 *N. Y.*, 117; Collen *v.* Wright, 8 *E. & B.*, 647; 7 *id.*, 301; see Walker *v.* Bank of N. Y., 9 *id.*, 582; Jenkins *v.* Hutchinson, 13 *Q. B.*, 744; Jefts *v.* York, 10 *Cush.*, 395; Polhill *v.* Walter, 3 *B. & Ad.*, 114. The exception established in Smout *v.* Ilbery (10 *M. & W.*, 1), is not necessary to be retained, under the change which is proposed as to the termination of agency.

Agent's responsibility to third persons.

§ 1256. One who assumes to act as an agent is responsible to third persons as a principal for his acts in the course of his agency, in any of the following cases, and in no others:[1]

1. When, with his consent, credit is given to him personally in a transaction;[2]

2. When he enters into a written contract in the name of his principal, without believing, in good faith, that he has authority to do so;[3] or,

3. When his acts are wrongful in their nature.[4]

[1] *Story's Agency*, §§ 261, 310. See Kirkpatrick *v.* Stainer, 22 *Wend.*, 244; Green *v.* Kopke, 18 *C. B.*, 549; Smout *v.* Ilbery, 10 *M. & W.*, 1.

[2] *Sto. Ag.*, § 288. This provision includes the cases in which an agent does not disclose the fact of his agency (Waring *v.* Mason, 18 *Wend.*, 434; *Sto. Ag.*, § 266); those in which the fact of the agency is known, but the principal is unknown (Mills *v.* Hunt, 20 *Wend.*, 431; *Sto. Ag.*, § 267); or where the agent makes himself a party to the contract (Higgins *v.* Senior, 8 *M. & W.*, 834; Tanner *v.* Christian, 4 *E. & B.*, 591; Lennard *v.* Robinson, 5 *E. & B.*, 125; Pentz *v.* Stanton, 10 *Wend.*, 271). In all cases the question is, "to whom was the credit given?" (Green *v.*

Kopke, 18 *C. B.*, 549; Mahony *v.* Kekulé, 14 *id.*, 390. See Kirkpatrick *v.* Stainer, 22 *Wend.*, 244). This is true even concerning public agents who contract in their own names (*Sto. Ag.*, § 302).

[3] This rule seems to be established in this state (Feeter *v.* Heath [Ct. of Errors], 11 *Wend.*, 477; Meech *v.* Smith, 7 *Wend.*, 315; Dusenbery *v.* Ellis, 3 *Johns. Cas.*, 70; Rossiter *v.* Rossiter, 8 *Wend.*, 494; see Palmer *v.* Stephens, 1 *Denio*, 471); though it is confined to the limits here stated (Walker *v.* Bank of N. Y., 9 *N. Y.*, 582); and has been doubted altogether (White *v.* Madison, 26 *N. Y.*, 117). It is not law in England (Collen *v.* Wright, 7 *E. & B.*, 301; Jenkins *v.* Hutchinson, 13 *Q. B.*, 744; Lewis *v.* Nicholson, 18 *id.*, 503), in Massachusetts (Abbey *v.* Chase, 6 *Cush.*, 56; Jefts *v.* York, 4 *id.*, 371; Ballou *v.* Talbot, 16 *Mass.*, 461; Long *v.* Colburn, 11 *id.*, 97), in Connecticut (Ogden *v.* Raymond, 22 *Conn.*, 385), in Maine (Harper *v.* Little, 2 *Greenl.*, 14; Stetson *v.* Patton, *id.*, 358), in Indiana (McHenry *v.* Duffield, 7 *Blackf.*, 41), or Pennsylvania (Hopkins *v.* Mehaffey, 11 *Serg. & R.*, 126).

[4] *Sto. Ag.*, §§ 311, 312. The maxium *respondeat superior* does not exempt the agent from liability even for mere negligence (Arthy *v.* Coleman, 30 *Law Times*, 101; 8 *E. & B.* [*Am. ed.*], 1092).

Obligation of agent to surrender property to third person.

§ 1257. If an agent receives anything for the benefit of his principal, to the possession of which another person is entitled, he must, on demand, surrender it to such person, or so much of it as he has under his control at the time of demand, on being indemnified for any advance which he has made to his principal, in good faith, on account of the same;[1] and is responsible therefor, if, after notice from the owner, he delivers it to his principal.[2]

[1] *Story's Agency*, § 300.

[2] Hearsey *v.* Pruyn, 7 *Johns.*, 179.

Agent not having capacity to contract.

§ 1258. The provisions of this article are subject to the provisions of Part I of the First Division of this Code.

ARTICLE V.

DELEGATION OF AGENCY.

Agent's delegation of his powers.

§ 1259. An agent, unless specially forbidden by his principal to do so, can delegate his powers to another person in any of the following cases, and in no others:[1]

1. When the act to be done is purely mechanical;[2]

2. When it is such as the agent cannot himself, and the sub-agent can, lawfully perform;[3]

3. When it is the usage of the place to delegate such powers;[4] or,

4. When such delegation is specially authorized by the principal.[5]

[1] Ess *v.* Truscott, 2 *M. & W.*, 385; see Powell *v.* Tuttle, 3 *N. Y.*, 396; Moffatt *v.* Wood, 5 *Seld. Notes*, 14; Newton *v.* Bronson, 13 *N. Y.*, 593.

[2] Commercial Bank *v.* Norton, 1 *Hill*, 501; see Powell *v.* Tuttle, 3 *N. Y.*, 407.

[3] *Story Agency*, § 14.

[4] Laussatt *v.* Lippincott, 6 *Serg. & R.*, 393; see Horton *v.* Morgan, 19 *N. Y.*, 170; Whitehouse *v.* Moore, 13 *Abb. Pr.*, 142; Pollock *v.* Stables, 12 *Q. B.*, 765.

[5] *Sto. Agency*, § 14.

Agent's unauthorized employment of sub-agent.

§ 1260. If an agent employs a sub-agent without authority, the former is a principal, and the latter his agent, and the principal of the former has no connection with the latter.

Story Agency, § 217 *a.*; *Code of La.*, 2976.

Sub-agent rightfully appointed represents principal.

§ 1261. A sub-agent, lawfully appointed, represents the principal in like manner with the original agent; and the original agent is not responsible to third persons for the acts of the sub-agent.

See Althorf *v.* Wolfe, 22 *N. Y.*, 355; Sadler *v.* Henlock, 4 *E. & B.*, 570, 578.

ARTICLE VI.

TERMINATION OF AGENCY.

SECTIONS 1262, 1263. Termination of agency.

§ 1262. An agency is terminated, as to every person having notice thereof, by: Termination of agency.

1. The expiration of its term;
2. The extinction of its subject;
3. The death of the agent;
4. His renunciation of the agency; or,
5. The incapacity of the agent to act as such.

Vail *v.* Judson, 4 *E. D. Smith*, 165.

§ 1263. Unless the power of an agent is coupled with an interest in the subject of the agency,[1] it is terminated as to every person having notice[2] thereof, by: Id.

1. Its revocation by the principal;
2. His death;[3] or,
3. His incapacity to contract.[4]

[1] Knapp *v.* Alvord, 10 *Paige*, 205; see Hunt *v.* Rousmaniere, 8 *Wheat.*, 174.

[2] Cassiday *v.* McKenzie, 4 *Watts & Serg.*, 282; Ish *v.* Crane, 8 *Ohio State*, 521. It may be doubted whether this clause is at present law in this state (see Houghtailing *v.* Marvin, 7 *Barb.*, 412), as it certainly is not in England (Blades *v.* Free, 9 *B. & C.*, 167); but, if not, it ought to be, in order to avoid the injustice of which Smout *v.* Ilbery (10 *M. & W.*, 1), furnishes a striking example.

[3] Champney *v.* Coope, 34 *Barb.*, 539; Megary *v.* Funtis, 5 *Sandf.*, 376; Blades *v.* Free, 9 *B. & C.*, 167.

[4] *Story on Agency*, §§ 485, 486. Insanity, not judicially declared, has been held to be no revocation (Wallis *v.* Manhattan Bank, 2 *Hall*, 495); but this was on the ground that otherwise the authority would be thereby revoked *without* notice, an objection which this section obviates.

CHAPTER II.

PARTICULAR AGENCIES.

ARTICLE I.

AUCTIONEERS.

Auctioneer's authority from the seller.

§ 1264. An auctioneer, in the absence of special authorization or usage to the contrary, has authority from the seller, only as follows:

1. To sell by public auction to the highest bidder;[1]

2. To sell for cash only,[2] except such articles as are usually sold on credit at auction;

3. To warrant, in like manner with other agents to sell, according to section 1241;[3]

4. To prescribe reasonable rules and terms of sale;[4]

5. To deliver the thing sold, upon payment of the price;[5]

6. To collect the price;[6] and,

7. To do whatever else is necessary, or proper and usual, in the ordinary course of business, for effecting these purposes.

[1] *Sto. Agency*, § 108.
[2] *Sto. Agency*, §§ 60, 108.
[3] *Sto. Agency*, § 107.
[4] *Sto. Agency*, § 107.
[5] Brown *v.* Staton, 2 *Chitt.*, 353.
[6] Minturn *v.* Main, 7 *N. Y.*, 227.

Auctioneer's authority from the bidder.

§ 1265. An auctioneer has authority from a bidder at the auction, as well as from the seller, to bind both by a memorandum of the contract as prescribed in the Title on SALE.

ARTICLE II.

FACTORS.

§ 1266. A factor is an agent, who is employed to buy or sell property in his own name, and who is intrusted by his principal with the possession thereof. Factor, what.

§ 1267. In addition to the authority of agents in general, a factor has actual authority from his principal, unless specially restricted: Actual authority of factor.

1. To insure property consigned to him uninsured;[1]

2. To sell, on credit, anything intrusted to him for sale,[2] except such things as it is contrary to usage to sell on credit;[3] but not to pledge,[4] mortgage, or barter[5] the same; and,

3. To delegate his authority to his partner or servant,[6] but not to any person in an independent employment.[7]

[1] Brisban *v.* Boyd, 4 *Paige*, 17.
[2] Van Allen *v.* Vanderpool, 6 *Johns.*, 72; Laussatt *v.* Lippincott, 6 *Serg. & R.*, 386.
[3] See *Sto. Agency*, § 110; Delafield *v.* Illinois, 26 *Wend.*, 192; 2 *Hill*, 159.
[4] Buckley *v.* Packard, 20 *Johns.*, 421; Rodriguez *v.* Heffernan, 5 *Johns. Ch.*, 429.
[5] Guerriero *v.* Peile, 3 *B. & Ald.*, 616.
[6] This seems to be reasonable, and is unquestionably the universal custom.
[7] Moffatt *v.* Wood, 5 *Seld. Notes*, 14.

§ 1268. A factor has ostensible authority, as to persons having no notice that the property with which he deals is not his own, to deal with it in any manner. Ostensible authority.

See the Title on PLEDGE.

ARTICLE III.

SHIPMASTERS AND PILOTS.

Authority of shipmaster on behalf of shipowner.

§ 1269. The master of a ship is a general agent for its owner in all matters concerning the same.

Authority to borrow.

§ 1270. The master of a ship has authority to borrow money on the credit of its owner, if it is necessary to enable him to complete the voyage, and if neither the owner nor his proper agent for such matters can be consulted, without injurious delay.

The Fortitude, 3 *Sumn.*, 228; Weston *v.* Wright, 7 *M. & W.*, 396; Arthur *v.* Barton, 6 *id.*, 138; see Beldon *v.* Campbell, 6 *Exch.*, 886.

Authority on behalf of owners of cargo.

§ 1271. The master of a ship, during a voyage, is a general agent for each of the owners of the cargo, and has authority to do whatever they might do for the preservation of their respective interests, except to sell or hypothecate the same.

Nelson *v.* Belmont, 21 *N. Y.*, 36; 5 *Duer*, 310.

Power to make contracts.

§ 1272. The master of a ship may procure all its necessary repairs and supplies,[1] may engage cargo and passengers for carriage, and in a foreign port, may enter into a charter-party;[2] and his contracts for these purposes bind the owner to the full amount of the value of the ship and freightage.

[1] 3 *Kent Com.*, 161; see Provost *v.* Patchin, 9 *N. Y.*, 235. His authority is not confined to purchasing at the port where the vessel lies (Kenzel *v.* Kirk, 37 *Barb.*, 113; 21 *How. Pr.*, 184).

[2] 3 *Kent Com.*, 162.

§ 1273. The master of a ship may hypothecate the ship, freightage and cargo, in the cases prescribed by the chapters on BOTTOMRY and RESPONDENTIA, and in no others. **Power to hypothecate.**

There seems to be no precedent or usage which would justify any other form of hypothecation by a master.

§ 1274. When a ship, whether foreign or domestic,[1] is seriously injured, or the voyage is otherwise broken up, beyond the possibility of pursuing it, the master, in case of necessity,[2] may sell the ship without instructions from the owners, unless by the earliest use of ordinary means of communication, he can inform the owners, and await their instructions.[3] **Master's power to sell ship.**

[1] Scull *v.* Briddle, 2 *Wash. C. C.*, 150; Brig Sarah Ann, 13 *Pet.*, 387, affirming S. C., 2 *Sumn.*, 206.

[2] Chambers *v.* Grantzon, 7 *Bosw.*, 414; Peirce *v.* Ocean Ins. Co., 18 *Pick.*, 83; Patapsco Ins. Co. *v.* Southgate, 5 *Peters*, 604; Brig Sarah Ann, 13 *id.*, 387; Pope *v.* Nickerson, 3 *Story*, 465; Cannan *v.* Meaburn, 1 *Bing.*, 243; Idle *v.* Royal Exch. Ass. Co., 8 *Taunt.*, 755; Somes *v.* Sugrue, 4 *C. & P.*, 276.

[3] Brig Sarah Ann, 2 *Sumn.*; 206; 13 *Peters*, 387; Pike *v.* Balch, 38 *Me.*, 302; Peirce *v.* Ocean Ins. Co., 18 *Pick.*, 83; Hall *v.* Franklin Ins. Co., 9 *id.*, 466.

§ 1275. The master of a ship may sell the cargo, if the voyage is broken up beyond the possibility of pursuing it, and no other ship can be obtained to carry it to its destination,[1] and the sale is otherwise absolutely necessary.[2] **Master's power to sell cargo.**

[1] Searle *v.* Scovell, 4 *Johns. Ch.*, 218.

[2] Freeman *v.* East India Co., 5 *B. & Ald.*, 617; Ewbank *v.* Nutting, 7 *C. B.*, 797; Morris *v.* Robinson, 3 *B. & C.*, 196; Post *v.* Jones, 19 *How.* [*U. S.*], 150; Peters *v.* Ballistier, 3 *Pick.*, 495; Dodge *v.* Union Ins. Co., 17 *Mass.*, 478; Arthur *v.* The Cassius, 2 *Story*, 81.

§ 1276. The master of a ship, in case of its capture, may engage to pay a ransom for it, in money or in **Authority to ransom ship** part of the cargo, and his engagement will bind the ship, freightage and cargo.

3 *Kent Com.*, 172, 173; see The Gratitudine, 3 *Rob. Adm.*, 263.

Abandonment terminates master's power.

§ 1277. The power of the master of a ship to bind its owner, or the owners of the cargo, ceases upon the abandonment of the ship and freightage to insurers.

3 *Kent Com.*, 331.

Personal liability for contracts concerning the ship.

§ 1278. Unless otherwise expressly agreed,[1] or unless the contracting parties give exclusive credit to the owner,[2] the master of a ship is personally liable upon his contracts relative thereto, even when the owner is also liable.

[1] *Story Ag.*, § 294.
[2] *Id.*, § 296.

Liability for acts of persons employed upon the ship.

§ 1279. The master of a ship is liable to third persons for the acts or negligence of persons employed in its navigation, whether appointed by him or not, to the same extent as the owner of the ship.

Denison *v.* Seymour, 9 *Wend.*, 8.

Responsibility for negligence of pilot.

§ 1280. The owner or master of a ship is not responsible for the negligence of a pilot whom he is bound by law to employ; but if he is allowed an option between pilots, some of whom are competent, or is required only to pay compensation to a pilot, whether he employs him or not, he is so responsible to third persons.

Story Ag., § 456, *note.*

ARTICLE IV.

SHIPS' MANAGERS.

What powers manager has.

§ 1281. A ship's manager has power to make contracts requisite for the performance of his duties as such; to enter into charter-parties, or make contracts for carriage; and to settle for freightage and adjust averages.

§ 1282. Without special authority, a ship's manager cannot borrow money, or give up the lien for freightage, or purchase a cargo, or bind the owners of the ship to an insurance. What power he has not.

Turner *v.* Burrows, 8 *Wend.*, 144; affirming 5 *id.*, 541; 1 *Bell's Com.*, 4 *ed.*, 410, 411.

TITLE X.

PARTNERSHIP.

CHAPTER I.

PARTNERSHIP IN GENERAL.

ARTICLE I.

WHAT CONSTITUTES A PARTNERSHIP.

§ 1283. Partnership is the association of two or more persons, for the purpose of carrying on business together, and dividing its profits between them. Partnership, what.

An agreement to divide the gross income of a business does not, it is generally agreed, create a partnership (*Lindley on Partn.*, 40; see Pattison *v.* Blanchard, 5 *N. Y.*, 186; Heyhoe *v.* Burge, 9 *C. B.*, 431). A more difficult question is, whether an agreement by which the net profits, if any, are to be divided between two, while the net loss, if any, is to be borne by one, is a partnership. In Pattison *v.* Blanchard (5 *N. Y.*, 186), GRAY, J., held that it was not. But, although the court seems to have adopted his opinion, the cause was finally decided upon a different point. The same opinion has been expressed in other cases (Heimstreet *v.* Howland, 5 *Den.*, 68; Sage *v.* Sherman, 2 *N. Y.*, 414; see Pott *v.* Eyton, 3 *C. B.*, 32, 39; Hickman *v.* Cox, 3 *C. B.* [*N. S.*], 523, 562). But some English decisions upon the question are well considered, and directly adverse to this view (Bond *v.* Pittard, 3 *M. & W.*, 357; Gilpin *v.* Enderbey, 5 *B. & Ald.*, 954); and these decisions seem to be founded upon a correct principle.

There must be some joint adventure to constitute a partnership (Reynolds *v.* Cleveland, 4 *Cow.*, 282; Porter *v.* McClure, 15 *Wend.*, 187). It may be in real as well as personal property (Sage *v.* Sherman, 2 *N. Y.*, 414; Clagett *v.* Kilbourne, 1 *Black* [*U. S.*], 346; Fall River Wharf Co. *v.* Borden, 10 *Cush.*, 458; Campbell *v.* Colhoun, 1 *Penn.*, 140). A mere joint ownership does not constitute a partnership (Post *v.* Kimberly [*Ct. of Errors*], 9 *Johns.*, 470; Putnam *v.* Wise, 1 *Hill*, 234; Holmes *v.* United Ins. Co., 2 *Johns. Cas.*, 329; Hawes *v.* Tillinghast, 1 *Gray*, 289). And it is not necessary that the capital should be jointly owned (Vassar *v.* Camp, 14 *Barb.*, 341; affirmed, 11 *N. Y.*, 441; Champion *v.* Bostwick, 18 *Wend.*, 175; 11 *id.*, 571. But see Chase *v.* Barrett, 4 *Paige*, 148).

Ship owners.

§ 1284. Part owners of a ship do not, by simply using it in a joint enterprise, become partners as to the ship.

Hopkins *v.* Forsyth, 14 *Penn. St.*, 34.

Formation of partnership.

§ 1285. A partnership can be formed only by the consent of all the parties thereto, and therefore no new partner can be admitted into a partnership, without the consent of every existing member thereof.

Story on Partn., § 5; Putnam *v.* Wise, 1 *Hill*, 234; Murray *v.* Kneeland, 14 *Johns.*, 318; Kingman *v.* Spurr, 7 *Pick.*, 235; see Mathewson *v.* Clarke, 6 *How.* [*U. S.*], 122. No one can be made a partner by inheritance or otherwise against his will (Jacquin *v.* Buisson, 11 *How. Pr.*, 385; Marquand *v.* N. Y. M'fg. Co., 17 *Johns.*, 525).

ARTICLE II.

PARTNERSHIP PROPERTY.

§ 1286. The property of a partnership consists of all that is contributed to the common stock at the formation of the partnership, and of all that is subsequently acquired thereby. Partnership property, what.

Code Napoleon, art. 1839.

§ 1287. The interest of each member of a partnership extends to every portion of its property. Partner's interest in partnership property.

Mabbett *v.* White, 12 *N. Y.*, 442; *Sto. on Part.*, § 16; 2 *Blacks. Com.*, 182.

§ 1288. In the absence of any agreement on the subject, the shares of partners in the profit or loss of the business are equal,[1] and the share of each in the partnership property is the value of his original contribution, increased or diminished by his share of profit or loss.[2] Partner's share in profits and losses.

[1] Hasbrouck *v.* Childs, 3 *Bosw.*, 105; Gould *v.* Gould, 6 *Wend.*, 263; Robinson *v.* Anderson, 7 *De G., M. & G.*, 239; 20 *Beav.*, 98; Webster *v.* Bray, 7 *Hare*, 159; Roach *v.* Perry, 16 *Ill.*, 37; Donelson *v.* Posey, 13 *Ala.*, 752; Lyman *v.* Lyman, 2 *Paine C. C.*, 11.

[2] The cases upon this point are not clear, but the rule here stated appears to be just.

§ 1289. An agreement to divide the profits of a business implies an agreement for a corresponding division of its losses, unless it is otherwise expressly stipulated. When division of losses implied.

To the contrary, as far as the proportion of loss is concerned, is Hasbrouck *v.* Childs, 3 *Bosw.*, 105. BOSWORTH and WOODRUFF, JJ., dissented. Otherwise, this section is doubtless in accordance with existing law.

Partner may require application of partnership property to payment of debts.

§ 1290. Each member of a partnership may require its property to be applied to the discharge of its debts, and has a lien upon the shares of the other partners for this purpose,[1] and for the payment of the general balance, if any, due to him.[2]

[1] Skip *v.* Harwood, 2 *Swanst.*, 586; West *v.* Skip, 1 *Ves., Sr.*, 239; Doddington *v.* Hallett, *id.*, 498; *Ex parte* Ruffin, 6 *Ves.*, 119; *Ex parte* Williams, 11 *id.*, 3; Holderness *v.* Shackels, 8 *B. & C.*, 612.

[2] Wade *v.* Rusher, 4 *Bosw.*, 537.

What property is partnership property.

§ 1291. Property, whether real or personal, acquired with partnership funds, is presumed to be partnership property.

Collumb *v.* Read, 24 *N. Y.*, 505; Buchan *v.* Sumner, 2 *Barb. Ch.*, 165. In Cox *v.* McBurney (2 *Sandf.*, 561), it was held, in conformity with the English authorities, that real property must have been used for partnership purposes; but this doctrine is overruled in Collumb *v.* Read.

ARTICLE III.

MUTUAL OBLIGATIONS OF PARTNERS.

Partners, trustees for each other.

§ 1292. The relations of partners are confidential. They are trustees for each other, within the meaning of Chapter I of the Title on TRUSTS. Their obligations, as such trustees, are defined by that chapter.

Good faith to be observed between partners.

§ 1293. In all proceedings connected with the formation,[1] conduct,[2] dissolution, and liquidation[3] of a partnership, every partner is bound to act in the highest good faith[2] toward his copartners. He may not obtain any advantage over them in the partnership affairs by the slightest misrepresentation, concealment, threat, or adverse pressure of any kind.[3]

[1] Hichens *v.* Congreve, 1 *Russ. & Myl.*, 150; Fawcett *v.* Whitehouse, *id.*, 132; Beck *v.* Kantorowicz, 3 *Kay & J.*, 230.

[2] *Code Justin.*, IV., 37, 3; Burton *v.* Wookey, 6 *Madd.*, 367.

[3] Blisset *v.* Daniel, 10 *Hare*, 493, 522, 536; Perens *v.* Johnson, 3 *Sma. & G.*, 419; Maddeford *v.* Austwick, 1 *Sim.*, 89; affirmed, 2 *Myl. & K.*, 279; Chandler *v.* Dorsett, *Finch*, 431; Featherstonhaugh *v.* Fenwick, 17 *Ves.*, 298; Anderson *v.* Lemon, 8 *N. Y.*, 236.

§ 1294. Each member of a partnership must account to it for everything that he receives on account thereof, and is entitled to reimbursement therefrom for everything that he properly expends for the benefit thereof, and to be indemnified thereby for all losses and risks which he necessarily incurs on its behalf.

Mutual liability of partners to account.

Pothier on Partnership, 127–130; Croxton's case, 5 *De G. & Sm.*, 432; Sedgwick's case, 2 *Jur.* (*N. S.*), 949; Chippendale's case, 4 *De G., M. & G.*, 19.

§ 1295. A partner is not entitled to any compensation for services rendered by him to the partnership.

No compensation for services to firm.

Coursen *v.* Hamlin, 2 *Duer*, 513; Caldwell *v.* Lieber, 7 *Paige*, 483; Bradford *v.* Kimberly, 3 *Johns. Ch.*, 434; Franklin *v.* Robinson, 1 *id.*, 165. An agreement for compensation may however be made (Paine *v.* Thacher, 25 *Wend.*, 450).

ARTICLE IV.

RENUNCIATION OF PARTNERSHIP.

§ 1296. A partner may exonerate himself from all future liability to a third person on account of the partnership, by renouncing, in good faith, all participation in its future profits, and giving notice to such third person, and to his own copartners, that he has made such renunciation, and that, so far as may be in his power, he dissolves the partnership, and does not intend to be liable on account thereof for the future.

Renunciation of future profits exonerates from liability.

The provisions of this and the following section are intended to enable a partner, who is unable to procure an immediate dissolution of the firm, to escape from further entanglement. They are certainly new, in so far as they relate to special partnerships, but may not be, as regards general partnerships (see Skinner *v.* Dayton, 19 *Johns.*, 513, 538).

Effect of renunciation.

§ 1297. After a partner has given notice of his renunciation of the partnership, he cannot claim any of its subsequent profits, and his copartners may proceed to dissolve the partnership.

CHAPTER II.

GENERAL PARTNERSHIP.

ARTICLE I.

WHAT IS A GENERAL PARTNERSHIP.

General partnership, what.

§ 1298. Every partnership that is not formed in accordance with the law concerning special partnership, and every special partnership, so far only as the general partners are concerned, is a general partnership.

ARTICLE II.

POWERS AND AUTHORITY OF PARTNERS.

§ 1299. Unless otherwise expressly stipulated, the decision of the majority of the members of a general partnership binds it in the conduct of its business. Power of majority of partners.

Such decision is binding in the due course of the business (Kirk *v.* Hodgson, 3 *Johns. Ch.*, 400; Kent *v.* Jackson, 2 *De G., M. & G.*, 49; 14 *Beav.* 367; Byron *v.* Met. Sal. Omn. Co., 3 *De G. & J.*, 123), and in nothing else (Natusch *v.* Irving, *Gow on Partn.*, 398; Bagshaw *v.* Eastern Union Railw. Co., 7 *Hare*, 114; 2 *Macn. & G.*, 389; Simpson *v.* Denison, 10 *Hare*, 51; Const *v.* Harris, *Turn. & R.*, 496; York & N. Mid. Railw. Co. *v.* Hudson, 16 *Beav.*, 485; Hodgkinson *v.* National Live Stock Ins. Co., 5 *Jur.* [*N. S.*], 478, 969).

§ 1300. Every general partner is agent for the partnership in the transaction of its business, and has authority to do whatever is necessary to carry on such business in the ordinary manner,[1] and for this purpose may bind his copartners by an agreement under seal.[2] Authority of individual partner.

[1] This authority extends no further (Wilkins *v.* Pearce, 5 *Denio*, 541; Sandilands *v.* Marsh, 2 *B. & Ald.*, 673; see Brettel *v.* Williams, 4 *Exch.*, 630; Dickinson *v.* Valpy, 10 *B. & C.*, 128; Ricketts *v.* Bennett, 4 *C. B.*, 686; *Ex parte* Chippendale, 4 *De G., M. & G.*, 19; Harman *v.* Johnson, 2 *El. & Bl.*, 61; Brown *v.* Kidger, 3 *H. & N.*, 853). Thus he cannot submit a partnership claim to arbitration (Harrington v. Higham, 13 *Barb.*, 660; Stead *v.* Solb, 3 *Bing.*, 101; Karthous *v.* Ferrer, 1 *Peters*, 222).

[2] The common law rule to the contrary is so far broken down, that its further retention in any degree seems useless (see Smith *v.* Kerr, 3 *N. Y.*, 144; Everit *v.* Strong, 5 *Hill*, 163; 7 *id.*, 585; Wells *v.* Evans, 20 *Wend.*, 251).

§ 1301. A partner, as such, has not authority to do any of the following acts, unless his copartners have wholly abandoned the business to him,[1] or are incapable of acting: What authority partner has not.

1. To make an assignment of the partnership property, or any portion thereof, to a creditor,[2] or to a third person,[3] in trust for the benefit of a creditor[2] or of all creditors;[3]

2. To dispose of the good will of the business;[4]

3. To dispose of the whole of the partnership property at once, unless it consists entirely of merchandise;[5]

4. To do any act which would make it impossible to carry on the ordinary business of the partnership;[6] or,

5. To do any other act not within the scope of section 1300.[7]

[1] Kemp *v.* Carnley, 3 *Duer*, 1.

[2] To the contrary is McClelland *v.* Remsen (36 *Barb.*, 622; 14 *Abb. Pr.*, 331), founded upon the decision in Mabbett *v.* White (12 *N. Y.*, 442), which it is proposed to supersede (Compare Pettee *v.* Orser, 6 *Bosw.*, 123).

[3] This rule is usually stated with a reservation in favor of an assignment made by "all who can be consulted," or ratified after its execution, by absent partners. Otherwise it is supported by numerous cases (Pettee *v.* Orser, 6 *Bosw.*, 123; Wetter *v.* Schlieper, 4 *E. D. Smith*, 707; Deming *v.* Colt, 3 *Sandf.*, 284; Havens *v.* Hussey, 5 *Paige*, 30; Hayes *v.* Heyer, 3 *Sandf.*, 293; Fisher *v.* Murray, 1 *E. D. Smith*, 341; Ormsbee *v.* Davis, 5 *R. I.*, 442. See Mabbett *v.* White, 12 *N. Y.*, 442). Neither reservation need be made in this place. A ratification cannot justly take effect retroactively to the disadvantage of third persons; and with that exception is allowable as a matter of course. And there is nothing in the *mere* absence of a partner, which can increase the authority of his copartners.

[4] It is clearly beyond the scope of a partner's authority to prevent the business from being carried on, which a sale of the good will obviously does.

[5] To the contrary is Mabbett *v.* White (12 *N. Y.*, 442); an unfortunate decision, from which DENIO and JOHNSON, JJ., dissented, and which is opposed to the whole current of the best cases, especially the late English decisions. It is eminently desirable that the legislature should interfere to remedy the anomaly thus introduced into the law, by which an authority is conclusively presumed to have been given, which no man of common sense can imagine that a partner really intends to give. See, nevertheless, Arnold *v.* Brown, 24 *Pick.*, 89; Mills *v.* Barber, 4 *Day*, 430; Anderson *v.* Tompkins, 1 *Brock.*, 456.

[6] See dissenting opinion of DENIO, J., in Mabbett *v.* White (12 *N. Y.*, 442). This rule was emphatically asserted

as to corporations in Abbot *v.* American Hard Rubber Co. (33 *Barb.*, 578); and has quite as much application to partnerships.

[7] See cases cited in note to last section.

§ 1302. A partner is not bound by any act of a copartner in bad faith toward him, though within the scope of a partner's powers, except in favor of persons who have in good faith parted with value in reliance upon such act. **Partner's acts in bad faith, when ineffectual.**

It is not certain that this is now the law, but if not, it ought to be. Partners occupy a position of mutual trust, and should be governed by all the rules governing trustees, unless plainly inapplicable (see Croughton *v.* Forrest, 17 *Mo.*, 131; Dob *v.* Halsey, 16 *Johns.*, 34).

ARTICLE III.

MUTUAL OBLIGATIONS OF PARTNERS.

§ 1303. All profits made by a general partner, in the course of any business usually carried on by the partnership, belong to the firm. **Profits of individual partner.**

See Russell *v.* Austwick, 1 *Sim.*, 52.

§ 1304. A general partner, who agrees to give his personal attention to the business of the partnership, may not engage in any business which gives him an interest adverse to that of the partnership, or which prevents him from giving to such business all the attention which would be advantageous to it. **In what business partner may not engage.**

See Lock *v.* Lynam, 4 *Ir. Eq.*, 188; Glassington *v.* Thwaites, 1 *Sim. & Stu.*, 124; England *v.* Curling, 8 *Beav.*, 129; Russell *v.* Austwick, 1 *Sim.*, 52. The rule does not seem to be justly applicable to partners who contribute property only to the firm, unless in peculiar cases, which are sufficiently provided for in the general rule.

In what he may engage.

§ 1305. A partner may engage in any separate business, except as otherwise provided by the last two sections.

Caldwell *v.* Lieber, 7 *Paige*, 483.

Must account to the firm for profits.

§ 1306. A general partner, transacting business contrary to the provisions of this article, may be required by any copartner to account to the partnership for the profits of such business.

Russell *v.* Austwick, 1 *Sim.*, 52.

ARTICLE IV.

LIABILITY OF PARTNERS.

Liability of partners to third persons.

§ 1307. Every general partner is liable to third persons for all the obligations of the partnership, jointly with his copartners

Id.

§ 1308. The liability of general partners for each other's acts is defined by the Title on AGENCY.

The law regulating the liability of partners is a mere branch of the law of agency (Ernest *v.* Nicholls, 6 *H. of L. Cas.*, 417; Cox *v.* Hickman, 9 *C. B.* [*N. S.*], 47, 98).

Liability of one held out as partner.

§ 1309. Any one permitting himself to be represented as a partner, general or special, is liable as such to third persons[1] to whom such representation is communicated, and who on the faith thereof give credit to the partnership.[2]

[1] *Story on Partn.*, §§ 64, 65; Griswold *v.* Waddington, 15 *Johns.*, 57; Stearns *v.* Haven, 14 *Verm.*, 540; Whitman *v.* Leonard, 3 *Pick.*, 177.

[2] This is a necessary element of liability (Irvin *v.* Conklin, 36 *Barb.*, 64).

No one liable as partner, unless held out as such.

§ 1310. No one is liable as a partner, who is not such in fact, except as provided by the last section.

A peculiar rule has long been established at common law, by which any one receiving, or voluntarily acquiring a right to receive, a share of the net profits of a partnership business, is liable to third persons as a partner, whether they were aware of the fact or not (Smith *v.* Wright [Ct. of Appeals], 1 *Abb. Pr.*, 243; Fitch *v.* Hall, 16 *How. Pr.*, 175; Wood *v.* Vallette, 7 *Ohio St.*, 172; Grace *v.* Smith, 2 *W. Blacks.*, 998; Waugh *v.* Carver, 2 *H. Blacks.*, 235; Cheap *v.* Cramond, 4 *B. & Ald.*, 663). But this rule is most earnestly condemned by the best writers on the subject (*Story on Partn.*, § 36; *Lindley on Partn.*, 40, and note); and has been declared to be a bad rule by eminent judges (see French *v.* Styring, 2 *C. B.* [*N. S.*], 362; Cox *v.* Hickman, 9 *id.*, 63; 3 *id.*, 544). A mere agreement for a share in the gross recipts of a business (*Story on Cont.*, § 207; *Lindl. on Partn.*, 38; Pattison *v.* Blanchard, 5 *N. Y.*, 186; see Heyhoe *v.* Burge, 9 *C. B.*, 431); or for a compensation for services (Vanderburgh *v.* Hall, 20 *Wend.*, 70; Rawlinson *v.* Clarke, 15 *M. & W.*, 292; Pott *v.* Eyton, 3 *C. B.*, 32 Loomis *v.* Marshall, 12 *Conn.*, 69; Burckle *v.* Eckhart, 3 *N. Y.*, 132; 1 *Den.*, 337; Brockway *v.* Burnap, 16 *Barb.*, 309), or the use of property (Heimstreet *v.* Howland, 5 *Denio*, 68), to be equal to a specified proportion of the profits (Denny *v.* Cabot, 6 *Metc.*, 82; *Ex parte* Hamper, 17 *Ves.*, 404), does not create a partnership liability. The commissioners therefore recommend the abolition of the rule.

ARTICLE V.

TERMINATION OF PARTNERSHIP.

§ 1311. If no term is prescribed by agreement for its duration, a general partnership continues until dissolved by a partner or by operation of law. Duration of partnership.

§ 1312. A general partnership is dissolved, as to all the partners: Total dissolution of partnership.

1. By lapse of the time prescribed by agreement for its duration;

2. By the expressed will of any partner, if there is no such agreement;

3. By the death of a partner;

4. By the transfer, to a person not a partner, of the interest of any partner in the partnership property;[1]

5. By war, or the prohibition of commercial intercourse, between the country in which one partner resides, and that in which another resides;[2] or,

6. By a judgment of dissolution.

[1] Heath *v.* Sansom, 4 *B. & Ad.*, 175; Johnson *v.* Evans, 7 *M. & G.*, 240; Habershon *v.* Blurton, 1 *De G. & Sm.*, 121; Nerot *v.* Burnand, 4 *Russ.*, 247; Marquand *v.* N. Y. Manufacturing Co., 17 *Johns.*, 525 Mumford *v.* McKay, 8 *Wend.*, 442.

[2] Griswold *v.* Waddington, 16 *Johns.*, 490; 15 *id.*, 57.

Partial dissolution.

§ 1313. A general partnership may be dissolved, as to himself only, by the expressed will of any partner, notwithstanding his agreement for its continuance,[1] subject, however, to liability to his copartners for any damage caused to them thereby,[2] unless the circumstances are such as entitle him to a judgment of dissolution.[3]

[1] PLATT, J., Skinner *v.* Dayton, 19 *Johns.*, 513, 538; see Marquand *v.* N. Y. Mfg. Co., 17 *id.*, 525.

[2] Bagley *v.* Smith, 10 *N. Y.*, 489.

[3] Essell *v.* Hayward, 6 *Jur.* [*N. S.*], 690.

Partner entitled to dissolution.

§ 1314. A general partner is entitled to a judgment of dissolution:

1. When he, or another partner, becomes legally incapable of contracting;[1]

2. When another partner fails to perform his duties under the agreement of partnership, or is guilty of serious misconduct;[2] or,

3. When the business of the partnership can be carried on only at a permanent loss.[3]

[1] Jones *v.* Noy, 2 *Myl. & K.*, 125; Leaf *v.* Coles, 1 *De G., M. & G.*, 171. But in Anon. (2 *Kay & J.*, 441), it was held that insanity was not a sufficient ground

for dissolution, unless it was shown to be probably permanent.

[2] It has been held that slight cause is sufficient to warrant a dissolution (Bishop *v.* Breckles, *Hoffm.*, 534); but the contrary has been ruled in several cases (Anderson *v.* Anderson, 25 *Beav.*, 190; Goodman *v.* Whitcomb, 1 *Jac. & W.*, 569, 592; see Eagle Fire Ins. Co. *v.* Cammet, 2 *Edw. Ch.*, 127).

[3] Jennings *v.* Baddelay, 3 *Kay & J.*, 78; see Harrison *v.* Tennant, 21 *Beav.*, 482; Reeve *v.* Parkins, 2 *Jac. & W.*, 390; Beaumont *v.* Meredith, 3 *Ves. & B.*, 180; Buckley *v.* Cater, 17 *Ves.*, 15; Pierce *v.* Piper, *id.*, 1.

§ 1315. The liability of a general partner for the acts of his copartners continues, even after a dissolution of the partnership, in favor of persons who have had dealings[1] with, and given credit[2] to, the partnership, during its existence, until they have had personal notice of the dissolution; and in favor of other persons, until such dissolution has been advertised in a newspaper[3] published in every county where the partnership, at the time of its dissolution, had a place of business;[4] to the extent, in either case, to which such persons part with value, in good faith, and in the belief that such partner is still a member of the firm.[5]

Notice of termination.

[1] Mechanics' Bk. *v.* Livingston, 33 *Barb.*, 458.

[2] Vernon *v.* Manhattan Co., 22 *Wend.*, 183; approved, Clapp *v.* Rogers, 12 *N. Y.*, 283; 1 *E. D. Smith*, 549.

[3] City Bank *v.* M'Chesney, 20 *N. Y.*, 240; overruling probably Holdane *v.* Butterworth, 5 *Bosw.*, 1.

[4] This clause is new. Perhaps a more stringent regulation would be judicious.

[5] Davis *v.* Allen, 3 *N. Y.*, 168.

§ 1316. A change of the partnership name, which plainly indicates the withdrawal of a partner, is sufficient notice of the fact of such withdrawal to all persons to whom it is communicated. But a change in the name which does not contain such an indication, is not notice of the withdrawal of any partner.

Notice by change of name.

Am. Linen Thread Co. *v.* Wortendyke, 24 *N. Y.*, 550.

ARTICLE VI.

LIQUIDATION.

Powers of partners after dissolution.

§ 1317. After the dissolution of a partnership, the powers and authority of the partners are such only as are prescribed by this article.

Who may act in liquidation.

§ 1318. Any member of a general partnership may act in liquidation of its affairs, except as provided by the next section.

Who may not act in liquidation.

§ 1319. If the liquidation of a partnership is committed, by consent of all the partners, to one or more of them, the others have no right to act therein; but their acts are valid in favor of persons parting with value, in good faith, upon the credit thereof.

Powers of partners in liquidation.

§ 1320. A partner authorized to act in liquidation may collect, compromise or release any debts due to the partnership, pay or compromise any claims against it, and dispose of the partnership property.

See Ward *v.* Barber, 1 *E. D. Smith*, 423.

Id.

§ 1321. A partner authorized to act in liquidation, may enter, in the name of the firm, into any obligation by way of satisfaction of a partnership debt, or as a collateral security therefor,[1] but he cannot make,[2] draw or indorse,[3] any other obligation in its name, nor revive a debt against the firm, by any acknowledgment or part payment, within the provisions of the CODE OF CIVIL PROCEDURE concerning the times of commencing actions.[4]

[1] McPherson *v.* Rathbone, 11 *Wend.*, 96.

[2] Lusk *v.* Smith, 8 *Barb.*, 570; Mitchell *v.* Ostrom, 2 *Hill*, 520; National Bank *v.* Norton, 1 *id.*, 572; Lansing *v.* Gaine, 2 *Johns.*, 300.

[3] Sanford *v.* Mickles, 4 *Johns.*, 224.

[4] Van Keuren *v.* Parmelee, 2 *N. Y.*, 523; see Bloodgood *v.* Bruen, 8 *id.* 362; Shoemaker *v.* Benedict. 11 *id.*, 176.

ARTICLE VII.

OF THE USE OF FICTITIOUS NAMES.

§ 1322. No partnership or person may transact business by a fictitious name, or in the name of a person not interested in such business, except as prescribed in this article. *Fictitious name.*

Enlarged from 3 *R. S.* (*5th ed.*), 978; *Laws* 1833, *ch.* 281.

§ 1323. A commercial partnership, established and transacting business in a place without the United States, may use in this state the partnership name used by it there, although fictitious. *Style of foreign partnership.*

3 *R. S.* (*5th ed.*), 978; *Laws* 1849, *ch.* 347; modified so as to express more clearly the intention of the statute.

§ 1324. The name of a partnership, which has had business relations with places without the United States, may be continued in use by the persons succeeding to its business, and by their successors, upon compliance with the provisions of this article,[1] and with the consent of the persons, if living, whose names are used.[2] *Continuation of style of firm having foreign business relations.*

[1] 3 *R. S.* (*5th ed.*), 66; *Laws* 1854, *ch.* 400. The words "foreign countries" are made more explicit.

[2] New, perhaps implied before.

§ 1325. On every change of the persons continuing the use of a partnership name, under the last section, *Certificates stating names, &c.,*

of persons using such firm name to be filed and published.

the person acquiring the right to use it must sign and acknowledge, before a proper officer for that purpose, a certificate, stating the name of each person dealing under such name, and his place of residence, and must file the same with the clerk of the county in which their principal place of business is situated, and must publish such certificate, or a statement containing the substance thereof, once in each week, for four successive weeks, beginning within one week after his first using such name, in the state paper, and in a newspaper printed in the town in which such principal place of business is situated, or, if no newspaper is printed in such town, in one printed in or nearest to the county town of the county.

3 *R. S.* (*5th ed.*), 67; *Laws* 1854, *ch.* 400.

Register of such firms to be kept by county clerk.

§ 1326. Every county clerk must keep a register of the names of firms and persons mentioned in certificates filed with him, pursuant to the last section, entering in alphabetical order the name of every such partnership, and of each partner therein.

Certified copies from register and affidavit of publication to be evidence.

§ 1327. Copies of the entries of a county clerk as herein directed, when certified by him, and affidavits of publication as herein directed, made by the printer, publisher or chief clerk of a newspaper, are presumptive evidence of the facts therein stated.

3 *R. S.*, (*5th ed.*), 67; *Laws* 1854, *ch.* 400.

CHAPTER III.

SPECIAL PARTNERSHIP.

ARTICLE I.

FORMATION OF THE PARTNERSHIP.

§ 1328. A special partnership may be formed by two or more persons, in the manner and with the effect prescribed in this chapter, for the transaction of any[1] business,[2] except banking or insurance.[3] *Special partnership, how formed.*

[1] The words "mercantile. mechanical or manufacturing," omitted.

[2] The words "within this state" omitted.

[3] 1 *R. S.*, 764, § 1.

§ 1329. A special partnership may consist of one or more persons, called general partners, and one or more persons called special partners. *Constitution of.*

1 *R. S.*, 764, § 2.

§ 1330. Persons desirous of forming a special partnership must severally sign a certificate, stating: *Certificate of special partnership*

1. The name under which such partnership is to be conducted;

2. The general nature of the business intended to be transacted;

3. The names of all the partners, and their residences, specifying which are general and which are special partners;

4. The amount of capital which each special partner has contributed to the common stock; and,

5. The periods at which such partnership will begin and end.

1 *R. S.*, 764, § 4.

Proof of certificate.

§ 1331. A certificate under the last section must be acknowledged or proved, as to the several persons signing the same, in the manner prescribed by sections 516 to 529.

1 *R. S.*, 764; *Laws* 1837, *ch.* 129.

Certificate to be filed and recorded.

§ 1332. The certificate of a special partnership, when duly acknowledged and certified, must be filed with the clerk of the county in which the partnership is to have its principal place of business, and must be recorded by him at large, in a book kept for that purpose, open to public inspection.

1 *R. S.*, 764.

Id.

§ 1333. A transcript of the record made pursuant to the last section, duly certified by the clerk under his official seal, must be filed and recorded in like manner in the office of the clerk of every county in which the partnership has a place of business.

1 *R. S.*, 764.

Affidavit of actual payment of capital by special partner to be filed.

§ 1334. An affidavit of one or more of the general or special partners in a special partnership, stating that the sums specified in the certificate of the partnership as having been contributed by each of the special partners, have been actually and in good faith paid in cash, must be filed in the same office with the original certificate.

1 *R. S.*, 765, § 7, omitting the words "At the time of filing the original certificate," which appear to be un-

necessary and embarrassing, it being sufficient to provide that the partnership is not formed until the affidavit is filed. The words "or special" are new.

§ 1335. No special partnership is formed, until the provisions of the last five sections are complied with. Special partnership, when formed.

1 *R. S.*, 765, § 8.

§ 1336. The certificate mentioned in section 1330, or a statement of its substance, must be published in two or more newspapers, designated by the clerk with whom the original certificate is filed, and published in his judicial district. Such publication must be made once a week for six weeks, beginning within one week from the time of filing the certificate. Publication of certificate.

1 *R. S.*, 765, § 9, as construed, Bowen *v.* Argall, 24 *Wend.*, 501; and modified by inserting "judicial" in place of "senate" district, according to the spirit of the statute as originally framed.

§ 1337. An affidavit of publication pursuant to this chapter, made by the printer, publisher or chief clerk of a newspaper, may be filed with the county clerk with whom the original certificate was filed, and is presumptive evidence of the facts therein stated. Affidavit of publication.

1 *R. S.* 765, § 10, amended.

§ 1338. If the publication directed by section 1336 is not made, the partnership is general from its beginning. But if, from any cause beyond the control of the partners, the publication is not made in exact conformity with that section, it is sufficient if made as nearly in conformity therewith as may be in their power. Effect of omission or informality of publication.

This provision relaxes the strict rule of the present law (see Argall *v.* Smith, 3 *Den.*, 435.)

§ 1339. Every renewal or continuance of a special partnership must be certified, recorded, verified and published in the same manner as upon its original formation. Renewal of special partnership to be certified and published.

1 *R. S.*, 765, § 11.

ARTICLE II.

POWERS, RIGHTS AND DUTIES OF THE PARTNERS.

Firm name, how composed.

§ 1340. The business of a special partnership must be conducted under a name, consisting of the names of one or more of the general partners only, with or without the addition of the words "and company."

1 *R. S.*, 765, § 13; as amended, *Laws* 1862, *ch.* 476.

Authority of special partner.

§ 1341. The general partners only have authority to transact the business of a special partnership. The special partners may negotiate business for it, subject to the subsequent approval of a general partner, but must not act on its behalf in any other manner.

3 *R. S.* (*5th ed.*), 64; *Laws* 1857, *ch.* 414.

His relation to his copartners.

§ 1342. A special partner may at all times investigate the partnership affairs, and advise his partners or their agents as to their management.

1 *R. S.*, 766, § 17.

Loans of special partner to firm.

§ 1343. A special partner may lend money to the partnership, or advance money for it, and take from it security therefor, and as to such loans or advances has the same rights as any other creditor;[1] but, in case of the insolvency of the partnership, all other claims which he may have against it must be postponed until all other creditors are satisfied.[2]

[1] 3 *R. S.* (*5th ed.*), 64, § 17; *Laws* 1857, *ch.* 414.
[2] 1 *R. S.*, 767, § 23.

§ 1344. In all matters relating to a special partnership, its general partners may sue and be sued alone, in the same manner as if there were no special partners. Special partner need not be joined in suit with general partners.

1 *R. S.*, 766, § 14.

§ 1345. No special partner, under any pretense, may withdraw any part of the capital invested by him in the partnership during its continuance. May not withdraw his capital.

1 *R. S.*, 766, § 15.

§ 1346. A special partner may receive such lawful interest, and such proportion of profits, as may be agreed upon, if not paid out of the capital invested in the partnership by him,[1] or by some other special partner,[2] and is not bound to refund the same to meet subsequent losses.[3] May draw profits, &c.

[1] 1 *R. S.*, 766, § 15.

[2] This addition is manifestly just. Perhaps the special partner should also be prohibited from drawing interest when no profits have been earned.

[3] *Code of La.*, 2814.

§ 1347. If a special partner withdraws capital from the firm, contrary to the provisions of section 1345, he must restore the same with interest. Capital withdrawn to be restored.

1 *R. S.*, 766, § 16.

§ 1348. Every transfer of the property of a special partnership, or of a partner therein, made after or in contemplation of the insolvency of such partnership or partner, with intent to give a preference to any creditor of such partnership or partner, over any other creditor of such partnership, is void against the creditors thereof; and every judgment confessed, lien created, or security given, in like manner and with the like intent, is in like manner void. Certain transfers of property, void.

1 *R. S.*, 766, §§ 20, 21.

ARTICLE III.

LIABILITY OF PARTNERS.

Liability of general partner in special partnership.

§ 1349. The general partners in a special partnership are liable to the same extent as partners in a general partnership.

Liability of special partner; what acts render him a general partner.

§ 1350. The contribution of a special partner to the capital of the firm, and the increase thereof, is liable for its debts, but he is not otherwise liable therefor,[1] except as follows:

1. If he has willfully made or permitted a false or materially defective statement in the certificate of the partnership, the affidavit filed therewith, or the published announcement thereof, he is liable as a general partner to all creditors of the firm;[2]

2. If he has willfully interfered with the business of the firm, except as permitted by sections 1341 and 1342, he is liable in like manner;[3] or,

3. If he has willfully joined in, or assented to an act contrary to any of the provisions of sections 1340, 1345 and 1348, he is liable in like manner.[4]

[1] 1 *R. S.*, 764, § 2.
[2] 1 *R. S.*, 765, § 8.
[3] 1 *R. S.*, 766, § 17.
[4] 1 *R. S.*, 767, § 22.

Id.

§ 1351. When a special partner has unintentionally done any of the acts mentioned in the last section, he is liable as a general partner to any creditor of the firm who has been actually misled thereby to his prejudice.

See Bowen *v.* Argall, 24 *Wend.*, 501; Madison County Bank *v.* Gould, 5 *Hill*, 309. But see Smith *v.* Argall, 6 *Hill*, 479; 3 *Denio*, 435.

§ 1352. One who, upon making a contract with a partnership, accepts from or gives to it a written memorandum of the contract, stating that the partnership is special, and giving the names of the special partners, cannot afterwards charge the persons thus named as general partners upon that contract, by reason of any error or defect in the proceedings for the creation of the special partnership, prior to the acceptance of the memorandum, if an effort has been made by the partners, in good faith, to form a special partnership in the manner required by law. Who may not question existence of special partnership.

This provision is new. It is intended to put special partnerships, in this respect, upon the same footing with corporations. The language of the section is carefully worded, so as to exclude cases of fraud, &c., and not to deprive the creditor of the benefit of any irregularity subsequent to his contract.

ARTICLE IV.

ALTERATION AND DISSOLUTION.

§ 1353. A special partnership becomes general, if, within ten days after any partner withdraws from it, or any new partner is received into it, or a change is made in the nature of its business, or in its name, a certificate of such fact, signed by one or more of the partners, is not filed with the clerk with whom the original certificate of the partnership was filed. Partnership made general, by omission to notify changes

3 *R. S.* (*5th ed.*), 63, § 12, modified by omitting the clause concerning "alterations in the names of the general partners" and "in the capital or shares of the special partners." The capital of the special partners cannot be diminished, and it is not easy to see why any other changes need be made public.

§ 1354. New special partners may be admitted into a special partnership, upon a certificate, stating the Admission of new special partners to be notified.

names, residences and contributions to the common stock of each of such partners, signed by each of them, and by the general partners, verified according to section 1334, acknowledged or proved, and filed, according to sections 1331 and 1332, with the clerk with whom the original certificate of the partnership was filed.

3 *R. S.* (*5th ed.*), 63, slightly modified.

Purchaser of interest of special partner, &c. may become special partner.

§ 1355. A special partner, or his legal representatives, may sell his interest in the partnership, and the purchaser thereof may, with the consent of the other partners, become a special partner, without changing the nature of the partnership, upon filing a notice of sale within ten days thereafter with the clerk with whom the original certificate of such partnership was filed.

3 *R. S.*, (*5th ed.*), 63.

Dissolution of special partnership.

§ 1356. A special partnership is subject to dissolution in the same manner as a general partnership,[1] except that no dissolution by the act of the partners is complete, until a notice thereof has been filed and recorded in the office of the clerk with whom the original certificate was recorded, and published once in each week for four weeks, in the state paper and in a newspaper printed in each county where the partnership has a place of business.[2]

[1] Ames *v.* Downing, 1 *Bradf.*, 321.
[2] 1 *R. S.*, 767, § 24.

TITLE XI.

INSURANCE.

CHAPTER I.

INSURANCE IN GENERAL.

In this chapter are inserted some rules which have been judicially determined only in their application to particular species of insurance, but which are deemed applicable to all classes.

ARTICLE I.

DEFINITION OF INSURANCE.

SECTION 1357. Insurance, what.

§ 1357. Insurance is a contract whereby one undertakes to indemnify[1] another against loss, damage or liability, arising from an unknown or contingent event.[2] Insurance, what.

[1] In England, it is held that life insurance is not a contract of indemnity (Dalby *v.* India Life Assurance So., 15 *C. B.*, 365). But a late decision in this state

(Ruse *v.* Mut. Benefit Ins. Co., 23 *N. Y.*, 516), sustains the text.

[2] The contract of insurance (other than of life and health) does not cover injuries which must inevitably occur, even though the parties do not know that they are inevitable (Paterson *v.* Harris, 1 *Best & Sm.*, 336).

ARTICLE II.

WHAT MAY BE INSURED.

What events may be insured against.

§ 1358. Any contingent or unknown event, whether past or future, which may damnify a person having an insurable interest, or create a liability against him, may be insured against, subject to the provisions of this chapter.

See Coggeshall *v.* American Ins. Co., 3 *Wend.*, 283.

Usual kinds of insurance.

§ 1359. The most usual kinds of insurance are:

1. Marine insurance;
2. Fire insurance;
3. Life insurance; and,
4. Health insurance.

All subject to this chapter.

§ 1360. All kinds of insurance are subject to the provisions of this chapter.

ARTICLE III.

PARTIES TO THE CONTRACT.

Designation of parties.

§ 1361. The person who undertakes to indemnify another, by a contract of insurance, is called the insurer, and the person indemnified is called the insured.

As underwriting is not practiced in this state, the term "underwriter" is not used in this Code.

§ 1362. Any one who is capable of making a contract may be an insurer, subject to the restrictions imposed by special statutes upon foreign corporations, non-residents and others. Who may insure.

§ 1363. Any one except a public enemy may be insured. Who may be insured.

§ 1364. Where a mortgagor of property effects insurance in his own name, providing that the loss shall be payable to the mortgagee, or assigns a policy of insurance to the mortgagee, the insurance is deemed to be upon the interest of the mortgagor, who does not cease to be a party to the original contract, and any act of his which would otherwise avoid the insurance will have the same effect, although the property is in the hands of the mortgagee. Assignment to mortgagee of thing insured.

Grosvenor *v.* Atlantic Fire Ins. Co., 17 *N. Y.*, 391; Buffalo Steam Engine Works *v.* Sun Mutual Ins. Co., *id.*, 401; Bidwell *v.* Northwestern Ins. Co., 19 *id.*, 179.

§ 1365. If an insurer assents to the transfer of an insurance from a mortgagor to a mortgagee, and, at the time of his assent, imposes further obligations on the assignee, making a new contract with him, the acts of the mortgagor cannot affect his rights. Id.

ARTICLE IV.

INSURABLE INTEREST.

Insurable interest, what.

§ 1366. Every interest in property, or any relation thereto, or liability in respect thereof, of such a nature that a contemplated peril might directly damnify the insured, is an insurable interest.

27 *N. Y.*, 163, 173.

In what may consist.

§ 1367. An insurable interest in property may consist in:

1. An existing interest;

2. An inchoate interest founded on an existing interest; or,

3. An expectancy, coupled with an existing interest in that out of which the expectancy arises.

Interest of carrier or depositary.

§ 1368. A carrier[1] or depositary[2] of any kind has an insurable interest in a thing held by him as such, to the extent of its value.[3]

[1] Chase *v.* Washington Mut. Insurance Co., 12 *Barb.*, 595; Savage *v.* Corn Exchange Ins. Co., 4 *Bosw.*, 1; Van Natta *v.* Mutual Security Ins. Co., 2 *Sandf.*, 490; Crowley *v.* Cohen, 3 *B. & Ad.*, 478.

[2] Waters *v.* Monarch Assurance Co., 5 *El. & Bl.*, 870; White *v.* Madison, 26 *N. Y.*, 117.

[3] Stilwell *v.* Staples, 19 *N. Y.*, 401.

Mere expectancies.

§ 1369. A mere contingent or expectant interest in anything, not founded on an actual right to the thing, nor upon any valid contract for it, is not insurable.

Stockdale *v.* Dunlop, 6 *M. & W.*, 224; Devaux *v.* Steele, 6 *Bing. N. C.*, 358; Lucena *v.* Crawford, 3 *B. & P.*, 94.

Measure of interest in property.

§ 1370. The measure of an insurable interest in property is the extent to which the insured might be damnified by loss or injury thereof.

Insurance without interest, illegal.

§ 1371. The sole object of insurance is the indemnity of the insured, and if he has no insurable interest the contract is void.

1 *R. S.*, 662, §§ 8–10; 1 *Duer Ins.*, 94; Ruse *v.* Mut Ben. Ins. Co., 23 *N. Y.*, 516.

§ 1372. An interest insured must exist when the insurance takes effect,[1] and when the loss occurs,[2] but need not exist in the meantime.[3] When interest must exist.

[1] Howard *v.* Albany Ins. Co., 3 *Den.*, 301. See Ruse *v.* Mutual Benefit Ins. Co., 23 *N. Y.*, 516. To the contrary, see Rhind *v.* Wilkinson, 2 *Taunt.*, 237.

[2] Shotwell *v.* Jefferson Ins. Co., 5 *Bosw.*, 247, 261; Fowler *v.* N. Y. Indemnity Ins. Co., 26 *N. Y.*, 383; Murdock *v.* Chenango Ins. Co., 2 *N. Y.*, 210.

[3] Hooper *v.* Hudson River Ins. Co., 17 *N. Y.*, 424.

§ 1373. Except in the cases specified in the next four sections, and in the cases of life and health insurance, a change of interest in any part of a thing insured, unaccompanied by a corresponding change of interest in the insurance, suspends the insurance to an equivalent extent, until the interest in the thing and the interest in the insurance are vested in the same person. Effect of transfer.

Hooper *v.* Hudson River Fire Ins. Co., 17 *N. Y.*, 424; 15 *Barb.*, 413.

§ 1374. A change of interest in a thing insured, after the occurrence of an injury which results in a loss,[1] does not affect the right of the insured to indemnity for the loss.[2] Transfer after loss.

[1] Crosby *v.* N. Y. Mutual Ins. Co., 5 *Bosw.*, 369; 19 *How. Pr.*, 312.

[2] Mellen *v.* Hamilton Fire Ins. Co., 17 *N. Y.*, 609.

§ 1375. A change of interest in one or more of several distinct things, separately insured by one policy, does not avoid the insurance as to the others. Exception in the case of several subjects in one policy.

§ 1376. A change of interest, by will or succession, on the death of the insured, does not avoid an insurance; and his interest in the insurance passes to the person taking his interest in the thing insured. In the case of the death of the insured.

This provision is new.

§ 1377. A transfer of interest by one of several partners, joint owners or owners in common, who are jointly insured, to the others, does not avoid an insurance, even though it has been agreed that the In the case of transfer between co-tenants.

insurance shall cease upon an alienation of the thing insured.

Tillou *v.* Kingston Mutual Ins. Co., 7 *Barb.*, 570; approved, Buffalo Steam Works *v.* Sun Mut. Ins. Co., 17 *N. Y.*, 401, 412.

ARTICLE V.

CONCEALMENT AND REPRESENTATIONS.

Concealment, what.

§ 1378. A neglect to communicate that which a party knows, and ought to communicate, is called a concealment.

Effect of concealment.

§ 1379. A concealment, whether intentional or unintentional, entitles the injured party to rescind a contract of insurance.

What must be disclosed

§ 1380. Each party to a contract of insurance must communicate to the other, in good faith, all facts within his knowledge, which are, or which he believes to be material to the contract,[1] and which the other has not the means of ascertaining,[2] and as to which he makes no warranty.[3]

[1] This appears to be the rule in regard to fire insurance (Gates *v.* Madison Co. Ins. Co., 5 *N. Y.*, 469, 476). Though a fuller disclosure is required in marine insurance (see the chapter thereon), it depends not on a difference of principle, but of the extent to which the insurer may be deemed cognizant of the fact (*Ang. Ins.*, 1*st ed.*, § 174).

[2] Le Roy *v.* United Ins. Co., 7 *Johns.*, 343; Seton *v.* Low, 1 *Johns. Cas.*, 1.

[3] N. Y. Firemen's Ins. Co. *v.* De Wolf, 2 *Cow.*, 56; aff'g S. C., 20 *Johns.*, 214. See this case criticised, 2 *Duer Ins.*, 576.

§ 1381. Neither party to a contract of insurance is bound to communicate information of the matters following, except in answer to the inquiries of the other: Matters which need not be communicated without inquiry.

1. Those which the other knows;[1]

2. Those which, in the exercise of ordinary care, the other ought to know, and of which the former has no reason to suppose him ignorant;[2]

3. Those of which the other waives communication;[3]

4. Those which prove or tend to prove the existence of a risk excluded by a warranty, and which are not otherwise material;[4] and,

5. Those which relate to a risk excepted from the policy,[5] and which are not otherwise material.[6]

[1] 2 *Duer Ins.*, 552. This rule is usually stated with the addition that facts which the insurer may be presumed to know need not be communicated; but the true rule seems to be that though the insured trusts to his presumption that the insurer knows facts which he is not bound to know, he does so at his peril. In other words, the presumption is a mere rule of evidence; one method of showing that he had actual knowledge.

[2] 2 *Duer Ins.*, 557–566; Seton *v.* Low, 1 *Johns. Cas.*, 1; Leroy *v.* United Ins. Co., 7 *Johns.*, 343.

[3] 2 *Duer Ins.*, 566–572.

[4] 2 *Duer Ins.*, 572–577; N. Y. Firemen's Ins. Co. *v.* De Wolf, 2 *Cow.*, 56; 20 *Johns.*, 214.

[5] 2 *Duer Ins.*, 577, § 15.

[6] 2 *Duer Ins.*, 579, § 16; Carter *v.* Boehm, 3 *Burr.*, 1905; Chase *v.* Washington Mut. Ins. Co., 12 *Barb.*, 595.

Test of materiality.

§ 1382. Materiality is to be determined not by the event, but solely by the probable and reasonable influence of the facts upon the party to whom the communication is due, in forming his estimate of the disadvantages of the proposed contract, or in making his inquiries.

2 *Duer Ins.*, 382–403; Ely *v.* Hallett, 2 *Cai.*, 57.

Matters which each is bound to know.

§ 1383. Each party to a contract of insurance is bound to know all the general causes which are open to his inquiry, equally with that of the other, and which may affect either the political or material perils contemplated; and all general usages of trade.

2 *Duer Ins.*, 560; see Pacific Ins. Co. *v.* Catlett, 4 *Wend.*, 33.

Waiver of communication.

§ 1384. The right to information of material facts may be waived, either by the terms of insurance, or by neglect to make inquiries as to such facts, where they are distinctly implied in other facts of which information is communicated.

Id.

Interest of insured.

§ 1385. Information of the nature or amount of the interest of one insured need not be communicated unless in answer to inquiry, except as prescribed by section 1401.

Tyler *v.* Ætna Fire Ins. Co., 12 *Wend.*, 507; 16 *id.*, 385; 2 *Am. Lead. Cas.*, 457; Niblo *v.* North Amer. Ins. Co., 1 *Sandf.*, 551.

Fraudulent warranty.

§ 1386. An intentional and fraudulent omission, on the part of one insured, to communicate information of matters proving or tending to prove the falsity of a warranty, entitles the insurer to rescind.

2 *Duer Ins.*, 435, 573.

Matters of opinion.

§ 1387. Neither party to a contract of insurance is bound to communicate, even upon inquiry, information of his own judgment upon the matters in question.

2 *Duer Ins.*, 583.

Representation, what.

§ 1388. A representation may be oral or written.

§ 1389. A representation may be made at the same time with the policy, or before it. When made.

§ 1390. The language of a representation is to be interpreted by the same rules as the language of contracts in general. How interpreted.

§ 1391. A representation as to the future is to be deemed a promise, unless it appears that it was merely a statement of belief or expectation. Representation as to future.

2 *Duer Ins.*, 664.

§ 1392. A representation cannot be allowed to qualify an express provision in a contract of insurance; but it may qualify an implied warranty. How may affect policy.

2 *Duer Ins.*, 671. See Burges *v.* Wickham, 3 *Best & Sm.*, 669.

§ 1393. A representation may be altered or withdrawn before the insurance is effected, but not afterwards. When may be withdrawn.

2 *Duer Ins.*, 679.

§ 1394. The completion of the contract of insurance is the time to which a representation must be presumed to refer. Time intended by representation.

2 *Duer Ins.*, 679; Sillem *v.* Thornton, 3 *E. & B.*, 868.

§ 1395. When a person insured has no personal knowledge of a fact, he may nevertheless repeat information which he has upon the subject, and which he believes to be true, with the explanation that he does so on the information of others, or he may submit the information, in its whole extent, to the insurer; and in neither case is he responsible for its truth,[1] unless it proceeds from an agent of the insured whose duty it is to give the intelligence.[2] Representing information.

[1] 2 *Duer Ins.*, 703; Tidmarsh *v.* Washington Ins. Co., 4 *Mason*, 439; Williams *v.* Delafield, 2 *Cai.*, 329.

[2] 2 *Duer Ins.*, 705; Dennistoun *v.* Lillie, 3 *Bligh*, 202.

§ 1396. A representation is to be deemed false when the facts fail to correspond with its assertions or stipulations. Falsity.

When the representation, whether affirmative or promissory, is made with an intent to deceive, the fraud, in all cases, vitiates the contract. When the falsity of the representation is accidental, if the representation is wholly false, or if it was partially false at the time when made, or at the commencement of the risk, the insurer is exonerated; but when the policy has attached, and the representation is falsified by a subsequent event, such accidental falsity does not render the policy void in its origin.

Effect of falsity.

§ 1397. If a representation is false in a material[1] point, whether affirmative[2] or promissory,[3] the injured party is entitled to rescind the contract from the time when the representation becomes false.

[1] A certain class of representations in marine insurances — *e. g.*, as to the inception of the risk — are held to be in effect warranties, and binding as much as if expressed in the policy (2 *Duer Ins.*, 686, 716). There is, however, no apparent objection to requiring them to be inserted in the policy, if the insurer desires to avail himself of a breach of such stipulation, notwithstanding that it may prove immaterial. This section states the law as it now exists in regard to fire insurance (Farmers' Ins. Co. *v.* Snyder, 16 *Wend.*, 481; Wall *v.* Howard Ins. Co., 14 *Barb.*, 383).

[2] 2 *Duer Ins.*, 680.

[3] Bilbrough *v.* Metropolis Ins. Co., 5 *Duer*, 587. See the review of cases on this point, 2 *Duer Ins.*, 749–769.

Materiality.

§ 1398. The materiality of a representation is determined by the same rule as the materiality of a concealment.

Application of provisions of this article.

§ 1399. The provisions of this article apply as well to a modification of a contract of insurance as to its original formation.

ARTICLE VI.

THE POLICY.

§ 1400. The written instrument, in which a contract of insurance is set forth, is called a policy of insurance. Policy, what.

§ 1401. A policy of insurance must specify: What must be specified in a policy.

1. The parties between whom the contract is made;

2. The rate of premium;

3. The property or life insured;[1]

4. The interest of the insured in property insured, if he is not the absolute owner thereof;[2]

5. The risks insured against; and,

6. The period during which the insurance is to continue.

[1] *Phillips on Ins.*, § 415; Cheriot *v.* Barker, 2 *Johns.*, 346, 351.

[2] This provision is contrary to the common law (White *v.* Hudson River Ins. Co., 7 *How. Pr.*, 341; Crowley *v.* Cohen, 3 *B. & Ad.*, 478; 2 *Pars. Mar. L.* 202). Mr. Duer recommends its introduction from the French law into ours, and the commissioners think the recommendation a good one (see 2 *Duer Ins.*, 463).

§ 1402. When the name of the person intended to be insured is specified in a policy, it can be applied only to his own proper interest. Whose interest is covered.

Kemble *v.* Rhinelander, 3 *Johns. Cas.*, 134, and see Turner *v.* Burrows, 5 *Wend.*, 541; Holmes *v.* United Ins. Co., 2 *Johns. Cas.*, 329; Lawrence *v.* Sebor, 2 *Cai.*, 203; Murray *v.* Columbian Ins. Co., 11 *Johns.*, 302.

§ 1403. When an insurance is made by an agent or trustee, the fact that his principal or beneficiary is Insurance by agent or trustee.

the person really insured may be indicated by describing him as agent or trustee, or by other general words in the policy.

Insurance by part owner.

§ 1404. To render an insurance, effected by one partner[1] or part owner,[2] applicable to the interest of his copartners, or of other part owners, it is necessary that the terms of the policy should be such as are applicable to the joint or common interest.

[1] Graves *v.* Merchants' Ins. Co., 2 *Cranch*, 440; Pearson *v.* Lord, 6 *Mass.*, 81; Turner *v.* Burrows, 5 *Wend.*, 541; 3 *Kent Com.*, 258.

[2] Toomey *v.* Bedford Ins. Co., 8 *Metc.*, 348; Finney *v.* Warren Ins. Co., 1 *Metc.*, 16. But see Holmes *v.* United Ins. Co., 2 *Johns. Cas.*, 329; and Lawrence *v.* Sebor, 2 *Caines*, 203.

General terms.

§ 1405. When the description of the insured in a policy is so general that it may comprehend any person, or any class of persons, he only can claim the benefit of the policy who can show that it was intended to include him.

Newson *v.* Douglass, 7 *Harr. & Johns.*, 451; Seaman *v.* Loring, 1 *Mason*, 127

Successive owners.

§ 1406. A policy may be so framed that it will inure to the benefit of whomsoever, during the continuance of the risk, may become the owner of the interest insured.

This provision is new.

Transfer of the thing insured.

§ 1407. The mere transfer of a thing insured does not transfer the policy, but suspends it until the same person becomes owner of both the policy and the thing insured.

2 *Pars. Mar. L.*, 42; Hooper *v.* Hudson River Ins. Co., 17 *N. Y.*, 428.

Open and valued policies.

§ 1408. A policy is either open or valued.

Open policy what.

§ 1409. An open policy is one in which the value of the thing insured is not agreed upon, but is left to be ascertained in case of loss.

3 *Kent Com.*, 272.

§ 1410. A valued policy is one which expresses on its face an agreement that the thing insured shall be valued at a specified sum. Valued policy, what.

Harris *v.* Eagle Fire Ins. Co., 5 *Johns.*, 368; Laurent *v.* Chatham Fire Ins. Co., 1 *Hall*, 41.

§ 1411. A running policy is one which contemplates successive insurances, and which provides that the object of the policy may be from time to time defined, especially as to the subjects of insurance, by additional statements or indorsements. Running policy, what.

§ 1412. An acknowledgment in a policy of the receipt of premium is conclusive evidence of its payment, so far as to make the policy binding, notwithstanding any stipulation therein that it shall not be binding until the premium is actually paid. Effect of receipt.

N. Y. Central Ins. Co. *v.* National Pro. Ins. Co., 20 *Barb.*, 468; Goit *v.* The same, 25 *id.*, 189. See, however, the contrary view of Emott, J., in Sheldon *v.* Atlantic Ins. Co., 26 *N. Y.*, 460. Compare 2 *Hill*, 557.

§ 1413. An agreement made before a loss, not to transfer the claim of a person insured against the insurer, after the loss has happened, is void. Agreement not to transfer.

Goit *v.* National Protection Ins. Co., 25 *Barb.*, 189; see Courtney *v.* N. Y. City Ins. Co., 28 *id.*, 116; but see to the contrary, Day *v.* Po'keepsie Mut. Ins. Co., 23 *id.*, 623. Clearly, if this is not now law, it ought to be made such by the legislature. Such a covenant is grossly oppressive.

ARTICLE VII.

WARRANTIES.

Warranty, express or implied.

§ 1414. A warranty is either express or implied.

Form.

§ 1415. No particular form of words is necessary to create a warranty.

Warranty must be in policy.

§ 1416. Every express warranty, made at or before the execution of a policy, must be contained in the policy itself, and another instrument, whether upon the same paper or not, cannot be referred to as making a part of the policy for this purpose, even by agreement of the parties.

By the existing law, warranties may be gathered from other instruments referred to by the policy as forming a part of it (Chaffee *v.* Cattaraugus Co. Ins. Co., 18 *N. Y.*, 376; Murdock *v.* Chenango Co. Ins. Co., 2 *id.*, 210; Jennings *v.* The same, 2 *Den.*, 75). A statement made in a paper referred to by the policy, but not made a part of it, is not a warranty (Wall *v.* Howard Ins. Co., 14 *Barb.*, 383; affirmed, see 17 *N. Y.*, 197). This change is recommended in pursuance of the suggestion in Chaffee *v.* Cattaraugus County Mutual Insurance Company, 18 *N. Y.*, 376.

Past, present and future warranties.

§ 1417. A warranty may relate to the past, the present, the future, or to any or all of these.

See *Ang. on Ins.*, 187–195.

Warranty as to past or present.

§ 1418. A statement in a policy, of a matter relating to the person or thing insured, or to the risk, as a fact, is an express warranty thereof.

Fowler *v.* Ætna Ins. Co., 6 *Cow.*, 673; Barker *v.* Phœnix Ins. Co., 8 *Johns.*, 307; 2 *Pars. Mar. L.*, 106; but see Small *v.* Gibson, 16 *Q. B.*, 141.

Warranty as to the future.

§ 1419. A statement in a policy, which imports that it is intended to do or not to do a thing which materially affects the risk, is a warranty that such act or omission shall take place.

Murdock *v.* Chenango Mutual Ins. Co., 2 *N. Y.*, 210; Bilbrough *v.* Metropolis Ins. Co., 5 *Duer*, 587.

Performance excused.

§ 1420. When, before the time arrives for performance of a warranty relating to the future, a loss insured against happens, or performance is made illegal, the omission to fulfill the warranty for either reason does not avoid the policy.

2 *Arnould Ins.*, 584; 2 *Pars. Mar. L.*, 108, and note.

§ 1421. The violation of a material warranty, or other material provision of a policy, on the part of either party thereto, entitles the other to rescind. What acts avoid the policy.

§ 1422. A policy may declare that a violation of specified provisions thereof shall avoid it; otherwise the breach of an immaterial provision does not avoid the policy. Id.

This and the preceding sections are intended to relax the strictness which now requires performance of immaterial conditions.

§ 1423. A breach of warranty, without fraud, merely exonerates an insurer from the time that it occurs, or, where it is broken in its inception, prevents the policy from attaching to the risk. Breach without fraud.

2 *Duer Ins.*, 435.

ARTICLE VIII.

PREMIUM.

§ 1424. An insurer is entitled to payment of the premium, as soon as the thing insured is exposed to the peril insured against. When premium is earned.

§ 1425. A person insured is entitled to a return of premium paid, or a ratable proportion thereof, if no part of his interest in the thing insured is exposed to any of the perils insured against,[1] or, where the insurance is made for a definite period of time, if it is not exposed to such peril for the whole of that time.[2] Return of premium.

[1] Waters *v.* Allen, 5 *Hill*, 421; 2 *Pars. Mar. L.*, 185. As to return ratably, see 2 *Pars. Mar. L.*, 188, 191; Holmes *v.* United Ins. Co., 2 *Johns. Cas.*, 329.

[2] This is a settled usage as far as fire insurance is concerned. As to marine insurance, the law appears to be now the other way (Tyrie *v.* Fletcher, 2 *Cowp.*, 666; Loraine *v.* Thomlinson, 2 *Doug.*, 585).

Id.

§ 1426. A person insured is entitled to a return of the premium when the contract is voidable, on account of the fraud or misrepresentation of the insurer, or on account of facts, of the existence of which the insured was ignorant without his fault; or when, by any default of the insured other than actual fraud, the insurer never incurred any liability under the policy.

Delavigne *v.* United Ins. Co., 1 *Johns. Cas.*, 310; Elbers *v.* United Ins. Co., 16 *Johns.*, 128. He is not entitled to a return of premium where the policy was ineffective by reason of his own or his agent's fraud (Waters *v.* Allen, 5 *Hill*, 421).

When none allowed.

§ 1427. If a peril insured against has existed, and the insurer has been liable, for any period, however short, the insured is not entitled to a return of premium,[1] so far as that particular risk is concerned,[2] unless the insurance was for a definite period of time, in which case he is entitled to a proportionate return under section 1425.[3]

[1] Waters *v.* Allen, 5 *Hill*, 421; Hendricks *v.* Commercial Ins. Co., 8 *Johns.*, 1.

[2] See Waters *v.* Allen, 5 *Hill*, 421.

[3] The cases above cited refer to marine insurances only, which are usually made for a voyage. Fire insurances, being made for a fixed term, do not fall within the same strict rule.

Over-insurance by several insurers.

§ 1428. In case of an over-insurance by several insurers, the insured is entitled to a ratable return of the premium, proportioned to the amount by which the aggregate sum insured in all the policies exceeds the insurable value of the thing at risk.

Contribution.

§ 1429. When an over-insurance is effected by simultaneous policies, the insurers contribute to the premium to be returned, in proportion to the amount insured by their respective policies.

§ 1430. When an over-insurance is effected by successive policies, those only contribute to a return of the premium, who are exonerated by prior insurances from the liability assumed by them, and in proportion as the sum for which the premium was paid exceeds the amount for which, on account of prior insurance, they could be made liable. Id.

2 *Arnould Ins.*, 1229; 2 *Pars. Mar. Law*, 191; Fisk *v.* Masterman, 8 *M. & W.*, 165.

ARTICLE IX.

LOSS.

§ 1431. An insurer is liable for a loss of which a peril insured against was the proximate cause;[1] although a peril not contemplated by the contract may have been a remote cause of the loss;[2] but he is not liable for a loss of which the peril insured against was only a remote cause.[3] Perils, remote and proximate.

[1] Matthews *v.* Howard, 11 *N. Y.*, 9.

[2] See 2 *Pars. Mar. L.* 221, *note.*

[3] This is doubtless the general principle. The difficulty of the subject arises in its application. Insurance against fire does not cover destruction by a shock of lightning, not setting the place on fire (Babcock *v.* Montgomery Mut. Ins. Co., 4 *N. Y.*, 326, affg. 6 *Barb.*, 637; Kenniston *v.* Merrimac Co. Mut. Ins. Co., 14 *N. H.*, 341); nor explosion of a steam boiler (Millandon *v.* New Orleans Ins. Co., 4 *Rob. La.*, 15); nor injury by overheating (Austin *v.* Drew, 6 *Taunt.*, 436); nor injury by removal of goods under reasonable apprehension that the house would be set on fire by a neighboring conflagration (Hillier *v.* Allegany Mut. Ins. Co., 3 *Penn. St.* 470). But it is held to cover injury to goods by water poured on the goods, or the building containing them, for the purpose of ex-

tinguishing a fire, or occurring in the course of their removal from a burning building (*Angell Ins.*, 164), and destruction of a vessel by explosion of gunpowder; because the explosion is caused by fire (Grim *v.* Phœnix Ins. Co., 13 *Johns.*, 451). So of fire fire produced by friction (*Angell Ins.*, 168). So of destruction by blowing up to prevent the spread of a conflagration (City Fire Ins. Co., *v.* Corlies, 21 *Wend.*, 367).

Loss incurred in rescue from peril.

§ 1432. An insurer is liable where the thing insured is rescued from a peril insured against, that would otherwise have caused a loss, if in the course of such rescue the thing is exposed to a peril, not insured against, which permanently deprives the insured of its possession, in whole or in part;[1] or where a loss is caused by efforts to rescue the thing insured from a peril insured against.[2]

[1] Tilton *v.* Hamilton Fire Ins. Co., 1 *Bosw.*, 367.

[2] *Angell Ins.*, § 115; Case *v.* Hartford Fire Ins. Co., 13 *Ill.*, 676; Firemen's Ins. Co. *v.* May, 20 *Ohio*, 211; see Babcock *v.* Montgomery Co. Ins. Co., 6 *Barb.*, 637.

Excepted perils.

§ 1433. Where a peril is specially excepted in a contract of insurance, a loss, which would not have occurred but for such peril, is thereby excepted; although the immediate cause of the loss was a peril which was not excepted.

St. John *v.* Am. Mut. Ins. Co., 11 *N. Y.*, 516; 1 *Duer*, 371.

Negligence and fraud.

§ 1434. An insurer is not liable for a loss caused by the willful act of the insured; but he is not exonerated by the negligence of the insured, nor by fraud or negligence on the part of his agents or others.

Matthews *v.* Howard Ins. Co., 11 *N. Y.*, 9; Gates *v.* Madison Co. Mut. Ins. Co., 5 *id.*, 469; Redman *v.* Wilson, 14 *M. & W.*, 476; Dixon *v.* Sadler, 5 *id.*, 405–415; 8 *id.*, 895; see Walker *v.* Maitland, 5 *B. & Ald.*, 171; Nelson *v.* Suffolk Ins. Co., 8 *Cush.*, 496; Perrin *v.* Protection Ins. Co., 11 *Ohio*, 147. In Waters *v.* Merchants' Ins. Co., 11 *Peters*, 213, it was held that an insurer was not exonerated by the negligence of the agents of the insured, but was exonerated by their fraud.

ARTICLE X.

NOTICE OF LOSS.

§ 1435. In case of loss, an insurer is exonerated, if notice thereof is not given to him by some person insured, or entitled to the benefit of an insurance,[1] without unnecessary delay.[2] Notice of loss.

[1] Cornell *v.* Le Roy, 9 *Wend.*, 163.
[2] Inman *v.* Western Fire Ins. Co., 12 *Wend.*, 452.

§ 1436. Where preliminary proof of loss is required by a policy, the insured is not bound to give such proof as would be necessary in a court of justice; but it is sufficient for him to give the best evidence which he has in his power at the time. Preliminary proofs.

Barker *v.* Phœnix Ins. Co., 8 *Johns.*, 307; Haff *v.* Marine Ins. Co., 4 *id.*, 132; Talcot *v.* Marine Ins. Co., 2 *id.*, 130. See also Braunstein *v.* Accidental Death Ins. Co., 1 *Best & Sm.*, 782.

§ 1437. All defects in a notice of loss, or in preliminary proof thereof, which the insured might remedy, and which the insurer omits to specify to him, without unnecessary delay, as grounds of objection, are waived. Waiver of defects in notice, &c.

Kernochan *v.* Bowery Ins. Co., 17 *N. Y.*, 428; O'Neil *v.* Buffalo Ins. Co., 3 *N. Y.*, 122.

§ 1438. Delay in the presentation to an insurer of notice or proof of loss is waived, if caused by any act of his, or if he omits to make objection promptly and specifically upon that ground. Waiver of delay.

Bumstead *v.* Dividend Mut. Ins. Co., 12 *N. Y.*, 81.

§ 1439. If a policy requires, by way of preliminary proof of loss, the certificate or testimony of another person than the insured, it is sufficient for the insured Certificate, when dispensed with.

to use reasonable diligence to procure it, and in case of the refusal of such person to give it, then to furnish reasonable evidence to the insurer that such refusal was not induced by any just grounds of disbelief in the facts necessary to be certified.

This provision overrules Worsley *v.* Wood, 6 *T. R.*, 710. Compare Thomas *v.* Fleury, 26 *N. Y.*, 26.

ARTICLE XI.

DOUBLE INSURANCE.

Double insurance. § 1440. A double insurance exists where the same person is insured by several insurers separately in respect to the same subject and interest.

See Mut. Fire Ins. Co. *v.* Hone, 2 *N. Y.*, 235.

Contribution in case of double insurance. § 1441. In case of double insurance, the insured may claim payment of a loss from any one of the insurers, who, on paying it, may require the others to contribute ratably thereto.

Godin *v.* London Assur. Co., 1 *Burr.*, 489; Lucas *v.* Jefferson Ins. Co., 6 *Cow.*, 635; *Ang. Ins.*, 22; 3 *Kent Com.*, 280.

ARTICLE XII.

RE-INSURANCE.

Re-insurance, what. § 1442. A contract of re-insurance is one by which an insurer procures a third person to insure him against loss or liability by reason of such original insurance.

§ 1443. Where an insurer obtains re-insurance, he must communicate all the representations of the original insured, and also all the knowledge and information he possesses, whether previously or subsequently acquired, which is material to the risk. Disclosure required.

2 *Duer Ins.*, 429.

§ 1444. A re-insurance is presumed to be a contract of indemnity against liability, and not merely against damage. Re-insurance presumed to be against liability.

Ang. Ins., 138; Hastie *v.* De Peyster, 3 *Cai.*, 190.

§ 1445. The original insured has no interest in a contract of re-insurance. Original insured has no interest.

Herckenrath *v.* Am. Ins. Co., 3 *Barb. Ch.*, 63; Carrington *v.* Com. Fire Ins. Co., 1 *Bosw.*, 152.

CHAPTER II.

MARINE INSURANCE.

Those rules respecting marine insurance which are but applications of the principles of international law to this subject are not embraced in these provisions, as they are not within the scope of a municipal statute.

ARTICLE I.

DEFINITION OF MARINE INSURANCE.

§ 1446. Marine insurance is an insurance against risks connected with navigation, to which a ship, Marine insurance, what.

cargo, freightage, profits, or other insurable interest in movable property, may be exposed during a certain voyage or a fixed period of time.

3 *Kent Com.*, 203.

ARTICLE II.

INSURABLE INTEREST.

Insurable interest in ship.

§ 1447. The owner of a ship has in all cases an insurable interest in it, even when it has been chartered by one who covenants to pay him its value in case of loss.

Hobbs *v.* Hannam, 3 *Camp.*, 93.

Interest reduced by bottomry.

§ 1448. The insurable interest of the owner of a ship hypothecated by bottomry is only the excess of its value over the amount secured by bottomry.

Read *v.* Mutual Safety Ins. Co., 3 *Sandf.*, 54; Smith *v.* Williams, 2 *Cai. Cas.*, 110.

Freightage, what.

§ 1449. Freightage, in the sense of a policy of marine insurance, signifies all the benefit derived by the owner, either from the chartering of the ship or its employment for the carriage of his own goods or those of others.

The word "freightage" is used throughout this Code, instead of "freight," to signify the hire of a carrier, for the obvious reason that the latter word properly means the thing carried. The word "freightage" is given in Webster's, Worcester's and Bouvier's Dictionaries, in the sense in which it is here used.

Expected freightage.

§ 1450. The owner of a ship has an insurable interest in expected freightage which he would have certainly earned but for the intervention of a peril insured against.

23 *Pick.*, 409; 1 *Metc.*, 141; 3 *B. & P.*, 95.

§ 1451. The interest mentioned in the last section exists, in the case of a charter-party, when the ship has broken ground on the chartered voyage;[1] and, if a price is to be paid for the carriage of goods, when they are actually on board, or there is some contract for putting them on board, and both ship and goods are ready for the specified voyage.[2] Id.

[1] Gordon *v.* Com. Ins. Co., 4 *Denio*, 362; Thompson *v.* Taylor, 6 *T. R.*, 478; Horncastle *v.* Suart, 7 *East*, 400.

[2] Forbes *v.* Aspinall, 13 *East*, 331; Montgomery *v.* Eggington, 3 *T. R.*, 362.

§ 1452. One who has an interest in the thing from which profits are expected to proceed, has an insurable interest in the profits. Insurable interest in profits.

Abbott *v.* Sebor, 3 *Johns. Cas.*, 39.

§ 1453. The charterer of a ship has an insurable interest in it, to the extent that he is liable to be damnified by its loss. Insurable interest of charterer.

Oliver *v.* Greene, 3 *Mass.*, 133; Bartlet *v.* Walker, 13 *Mass.*, 267.

ARTICLE III.

CONCEALMENT.

§ 1454. In marine insurance each party is bound to communicate, in addition to what is required by section 1380, all the information which he possesses, material to the risk, except such as is mentioned in section 1381, and to state the exact and whole truth in relation to all matters that he represents, or upon inquiry assumes to disclose. Information must be communicated.

2 *Duer Ins.*, 381, 388; *Ang. Ins.*, 200; 2 *Pars. Mar. L.*, 165; see Russell *v.* Thornton, 4 *H. & N.*, 788.

Material information.

§ 1455. In marine insurance, information of the belief or expectation of a third person, in reference to a material fact, is material.

2 *Duer Ins.*, 388; Willis *v.* Glover, 1 *B. & Pul. N. R.*, 14.

Presumption of knowledge of loss.

§ 1456. A person insured by a contract of marine insurance is presumed to have had knowledge, at the time of insuring, of a prior loss, if the information might possibly have reached him in the usual mode of transmission, and at the usual rate of communication.

This is the rule which prevails in continental Europe; and its adoption here is recommended by Mr. Duer (2 *Duer Ins.*, 433).

Concealments which only affect the risk in question.

§ 1457. The effect of a concealment in a marine insurance, in respect to any of the following matters, is not to vitiate the entire contract, but merely to exonerate the insurer from a loss resulting from the risk concealed:

1. The national character of the insured;

2. The liability of the thing insured to capture and detention;

3. The liability to seizure from breach of foreign laws of trade;

4. The want of necessary documents; and,

5. The use of false and simulated papers.

ARTICLE IV.

REPRESENTATIONS.

Effect of intentional falsity.

§ 1458. If a representation, by a person insured by a contract of marine insurance, is intentionally false in any respect, whether material or immaterial, the insurer may rescind the entire contract.

Park on Ins., 405; *Skin.*, 327.

§ 1459. The eventual falsity of a representation as to expectation does not, in the absence of fraud, avoid a contract of insurance. Representation of expectation.

ARTICLE V.

IMPLIED WARRANTIES.

§ 1460. In every marine insurance upon ship or freightage, or upon anything belonging to the shipowner[1], unless made for a specified length of time,[2] a warranty is implied that the ship[3] shall be seaworthy. Warranty of seaworthiness.

[1] By the present law this warranty is implied in every case (see Knill *v.* Hooper, 2 *H. & N.*, 277). But this is not founded upon reason. Insurers know the quality of vessels much better than shippers.

[2] Fawcus *v.* Sarsfield, 6 *El. & Bl.*, 192, Thompson *v.* Hopper, *id.*, 172; see Gibson *v.* Small, 4 *H. of L. Cas.*, 353; Jenkins *v.* Heycock, 8 *Moore P. C.*, 351; Biccard *v.* Shepherd, 14 *Moore P. C.*, 493; Hathaway *v.* Sun Mutual Ins. Co., 8 *Bosw.*, 33.

[3] No such warranty is implied as to cargo (Koebel *v.* Saunders, 17 *C. B.* [*N. S.*], 71). And if the insurer knows the ship to be unseaworthy, the warranty does not apply (Burges *v.* Wickham, 3 *Best & Sm.*, 669).

§ 1461. A ship is seaworthy, when reasonably fit to perform the services, and to encounter the ordinary perils of the voyage, contemplated by the parties to the policy. Seaworthiness, what.

See M'Lanahan *v.* Universal Ins. Co., 1 *Pet.*, 179; compare Marcy *v.* Sun Mut. Ins. Co., 11 *La. Ann.*, 748.

§ 1462. An implied warranty of seaworthiness is complied with if the ship is seaworthy at the time of the commencement of the risk. At what time seaworthiness must exist.

Id.; American Ins. Co. *v.* Ogden [Ct. of Errors], 20 *Wend.*, 287; Biccard *v.* Shepherd, 14 *Moore P. C.*, 471; Treadwell *v.* Union Ins. Co., 6 *Cow.*, 270; Hathaway *v.* Sun Mut. Ins. Co., 8 *Bosw.*, 33; and see 2 *Pars. Mar. L.*, 134.

What things are required to constitute seaworthiness.

§ 1463. A warranty of seaworthiness extends not only to the condition of the structure of the ship itself, but requires that it be properly laden,[1] and provided with a competent master,[2] a sufficient number of competent officers and seamen,[3] and the requisite appurtenances and equipments, such as ballast,[4] cables and anchors,[5] cordage and sails,[6] food, water, fuel and lights,[7] and other necessary or proper stores and implements for the voyage.

[1] Weir *v.* Aberdeen, 2 *B. & Ald.*, 320; and see Chase *v.* Eagle Ins. Co., 5 *Pick.*, 51; Walden *v.* N. Y. Firemen's Ins. Co., 12 *Johns.*, 128.

[2] Draper *v.* Com. Ins. Co., 4 *Duer*, 234; reversed on the ground that the real master was competent (21 *N. Y.*, 378).

[3] Silva *v.* Low, 1 *Johns. Cas.*, 184.

[4] Deblois *v.* Ocean Ins. Co., 16 *Pick.*, 303.

[5] Wilkie *v.* Geddes, 3 *Dow*, 57.

[6] Wedderburn *v.* Bell, 1 *Camp.*, 1.

[7] Fontaine *v.* Phœnix Ins. Co., 10 *Johns.*, 58; Moses *v.* Sun Mutual Ins. Co., 1 *Duer*, 159.

Different degrees of seaworthiness at different stages of the voyage.

§ 1464. Where different portions of the voyage, contemplated by a policy, differ in respect to the things requisite to make the ship seaworthy therefor, a warranty of seaworthiness is complied with, if, at the commencement of each portion, the ship is seaworthy with reference to that portion.

Biccard *v.* Shepherd, 14 *Moore P. C.*, 471; Bouillon *v.* Lupton, 15 *C. B.* [*N. S.*], 113; Dixon *v.* Sadler, 5 *M. & W.*, 405, 414.

Unseaworthiness during the voyage.

§ 1465. When a ship becomes unseaworthy during the voyage to which an insurance relates, an unreasonable delay in repairing the defect exonerates the insurer from liability for any loss arising therefrom.

This seems to be the law of this state (American Ins. Co. *v.* Ogden, 20 *Wend.*, 287). As to the law elsewhere, see 2 *Pars. Mar. L.*, 140.

§ 1466. A ship which is seaworthy for the purpose of an insurance upon the ship, may, nevertheless, by reason of being unfitted to receive the cargo, be unseaworthy for the purpose of insurance upon the cargo.

Seaworthiness for purposes of insurance on cargo.

1 *Phil. Ins.*, § 723. See also 2 *Pars. Mar. L.*, 145.

§ 1467. Where the nationality or neutrality of a ship[1] or cargo[2] is expressly warranted, it is implied that the ship will carry the requisite documents to show such nationality or neutrality,[1] and that it will not carry any documents which cast reasonable suspicion thereon.[3]

Neutral papers.

[1] Coolidge *v.* N. Y. Firemen's Ins. Co., 14 *Johns.*, 308; Blagge *v.* N. Y. Ins. Co., 1 *Cai.*, 549, 564.
[2] Barker *v.* Phœnix Ins. Co., 8 *Johns.*, 307, 319.
[3] Blagge *v.* N. Y. Ins. Co., 1 *Cai.*, 549.

ARTICLE VI.

THE VOYAGE AND DEVIATION.

§ 1468. When the voyage contemplated by a policy is described by the places of beginning and ending, the voyage insured is one which conforms to the course of sailing fixed by mercantile usage between those places.

Voyage insured, how determined.

Brazier *v.* Clapp, 5 *Mass.*, 1; Phyn *v.* Royal Ex. Ass. Co., 7 *T. R.*, 505.

§ 1469. If the course of sailing is not fixed by mercantile usage, the voyage insured by a policy is the way between the places specified, which, to a master of ordinary skill and discretion, would seem the most natural, direct and advantageous.

Id.

Martin *v.* Del. Ins. Co., 2 *Wash. C. C.*, 254; Brown *v.* Tayleur, 4 *Ad. & El.*, 241; 2 *Pars. Mar. Law*, 281.

Deviation, what.

§ 1470. Deviation is a departure from the course of the voyage insured, mentioned in the last two sections,[1] or an unreasonable delay in pursuing the voyage[2]; or the commencement of an entirely different voyage.

[1] Brown *v.* Tayleur, 4 *Ad. & El.*, 241.

[2] Hamilton *v.* Sheddon, 3 *M. & W.*, 49.

When proper.

§ 1471. A deviation is proper:

1. When caused by circumstances over which neither the master nor the owner of the ship has any control;[1]

2. When necessary to comply with a warranty,[2] or to avoid a peril, whether insured against or not;[3]

3. When made in good faith, and upon reasonable grounds of belief in its necessity to avoid a peril;[4] or

4. When made in good faith, for the purpose of saving human life, or relieving another vessel in distress.[5]

[1] Such as the winds and waves, pirates, enemies, disabling of the crew, &c.

[2] Bouillon *v.* Lupton, 15 *C. B.* [*N. S.*], 113.

[3] See Robinson *v.* Marine Ins. Co., 2 *Johns.*, 89; Riggin *v.* Patapsco Ins. Co., 7 *Harr. & J.*, 279; Scott *v.* Thompson, 1 *B. & Pul. N. R.*, 181; but compare O'Rielly *v.* Royal Exch. Ass. Co., 4 *Camp.*, 246.

[4] Reade *v.* Commercial Ins. Co., 3 *Johns.*, 352; Graham *v.* The same, 11 *id.*, 352; Patrick *v.* Ludlow, 3 *Johns. Cas.*, 10; see Bouillon *v.* Lupton, 15 *C. B.* [*N. S.*], 113.

[5] 3 *Kent Com.*, 323; Perkins *v.* Augusta Ins. Co., 10 *Gray*, 312; Settle *v.* St. Louis Ins. Co., 7 *Mo.*, 379; The Boston, 1 *Sumn.*, 328; see Lawrence *v.* Lydebotham, 6 *East*, 45.

When improper.

§ 1472. Every deviation, not specified in the last section, is improper.

Deviation exonerates the insurer.

§ 1473. An insurer is not liable for any loss happening to a thing insured subsequently to an improper deviation.

Stevens *v.* Commercial Mut. Ins. Co., 26 *N. Y.*, 397; Elliott *v.* Wilson, 7 *Bro. P. C.*, 459.

ARTICLE VII.

LOSS.

§ 1474. A loss may be either total or partial. **Total and partial loss.**

§ 1475. Every loss which is not total is partial. **Partial loss.**

Bouvier's Law Dict., Loss.

§ 1476. A total loss may be either actual or constructive. **Actual and constructive total loss.**

§ 1477. An actual total loss is caused by: **Total loss, what.**

1. A total destruction of the thing insured;

2. The loss of the thing by sinking, or by being broken up;

3. Any damage to the thing which renders it valueless to the owner for the purposes for which he held it; or,

4. Any other event which entirely deprives the owner of the possession, at the port of destination, of the thing insured.

See De Peyster *v.* Sun Mut. Ins. Co., 19 *N. Y.*, 272; Coit *v.* Smith, 3 *Johns. Cas.*, 16; Roux *v.* Salvador, 3 *Bing. N. C.*, 266; Adams *v.* Mackenzie, 13 *C. B.* [*N. S.*], 442; but compare Knight *v.* Faith, 15 *Q. B.*, 649.

§ 1478. A constructive total loss is one which gives to a person insured a right to abandon under section 1487. **Constructive total loss.**

Presumed actual loss.

§ 1479. An actual loss may be presumed from the continued absence of a ship without being heard of; and the length of time which is sufficient to raise this presumption depends on the circumstances of the case.

Gordon *v.* Bowne, 2 *Johns.*, 150; *Marsh. Ins.*, 417; Brown *v.* Neilson, 1 *Cai.*, 525.

Insurance on cargo, &c., when voyage is broken up.

§ 1480. When a ship is prevented, at an intermediate port, from completing the voyage, the master must make every exertion to procure in the same or a contiguous port, another ship, for the purpose of conveying the cargo to its destination; and the liability of a marine insurer thereon continues after they are thus reshipped.

Code de Com., 391, 392; Saltus *v.* Ocean Ins. Co., 12 *Johns.*, 107; Treadwell *v.* Union Ins. Co., 6 *Cow*, 270; Whitney *v.* N. Y. Firemen's Ins. Co., 18 *Johns.*, 208.

Cost of reshipment, &c.

§ 1481. In addition to the liability mentioned in the last section, a marine insurer is bound for damages, expenses of discharging, storage, reshipment, extra freightage, and all other expenses incurred in saving cargo reshipped pursuant to the last section, up to the amount insured.

Code de Com., 393; Bridges *v.* Niagara Ins. Co., 1 *Hall*, 423.

When insured is entitled to payment.

§ 1482. Upon an actual total loss a person insured is entitled to payment without notice of abandonment.

Gordon *v.* Bowne, 2 *Johns.*, 150; Cambridge *v.* Anderton, 2 *B. & C.*, 691.

Abandonment of goods on insurance of profits.

§ 1483. Where profits are insured, but the goods are not insured, a marine insurer is not liable for a constructive total loss unless the insured offers to abandon the goods.

Tom *v.* Smith, 3 *Cai.*, 245.

Average loss.

§ 1484. Where it has been agreed that an insurance upon a particular thing or class of things shall be free from particular average, a marine insurer is not liable for any loss, not depriving the insured of the possession, at the port of destination,[1] of the whole of such thing,[2] or class of things,[3] even though it becomes entirely worthless.

[1] De Peyster *v.* The Sun Mut. Ins. Co., 19 *N. Y.*, 272; 17 *Barb.*, 306; Roux *v.* Salvador, 3 *Bing. N. C.*, 266; 1 *id.*, 526; Navone *v.* Haddon, 9 *C. B.*, 30; Hugg *v.* Augusta Ins. Co., 7 *How.* [*U. S.*], 595; Williams *v.* Kennebec Ins. Co., 31 *Me.*, 455.

[2] Maggrath *v.* Church, 1 *Cai.*, 196; Neilson *v.* Columbian Ins. Co., 3 *id.*, 108; Le Roy *v.* Gouverneur, 1 *Johns. Cas.*, 226; Saltus *v.* Ocean Ins., 14 *Johns.*, 138; Rosetto *v.* Gurney, 11 *C. B.*, 176. See Bargett *v.* Orient Ins. Co., 3 *Bosw.*, 385.

[3] Wadsworth *v.* Pacific Ins. Co., 4 *Wend.*, 33; Biays *v.* Chesapeake Ins. Co., 7 *Cranch*, 415.

§ 1485. An insurance confined in terms to a total loss, does not cover a constructive total loss,[1] but covers any loss which necessarily results in depriving the insured of the possession, at the port of destination, of the entire thing insured;[2] and also a general average loss. Insurance against total loss.

[1] See 2 *Pars. Mar. Law*, 338–343; and the notes to last section. The contrary has, however, been recently held in Massachusetts (Heebner *v.* Eagle Ins. Co., 10 *Gray*, 131).

[2] Adams *v.* Mackenzie, 13 *C. B.* [*N. S.*], 442.

ARTICLE VIII.

ABANDONMENT.

Abandonment, what.

§ 1486. Abandonment is the act by which, after a constructive total loss, a person insured by a contract of marine insurance declares to the insurer that he relinquishes to him his interest in the thing insured.

Emerigon, c., 27. See Jardine *v.* Leathley, 3 *Best & Sm.*, 700.

When insured may abandon.

§ 1487. A person insured by a contract of marine insurance may abandon the thing insured, or any particular portion thereof, separately valued by the policy,[1] or otherwise separately insured,[2] and recover for a total loss thereof, when the cause of the loss is a peril insured against:

1. If more than half thereof, in value, is actually lost, or would have to be expended to recover it from the peril;[3]

2. If it is injured to such an extent as to reduce its value more than one-half;[4]

3. If, the thing insured being a ship, the contemplated voyage cannot be lawfully performed,[5] without incurring an expense to the insured of more than half the value of the thing abandoned,[6] or without incurring a risk which a prudent man would not take under the circumstances;[7] or,

4. If, the thing insured being cargo or freightage, the voyage cannot be performed, nor another ship procured by the master, within a reasonable time, and with reasonable diligence, to forward the cargo, without incurring the like expense or risk.[8] But freightage cannot in any case be abandoned, unless the ship is also abandoned.

[1] Deiderick *v.* Commercial Ins. Co., 10 *Johns.*, 234.

[2] Vandenheuvel *v.* United Ins. Co., 1 *Johns.*, 406.

[3] American Ins. Co. *v.* Center, 4 *Wend.*, 45; Gardiner *v.* Smith, 1 *Johns. Cas.*, 141.

[4] Saurez *v.* Sun Mut. Ins. Co., 2 *Sandf.*, 482.

[5] Ogden *v.* N. Y. Fire Ins. Co., 10 *Johns.*, 177; aff'd 12 *id.*, 25; McBride *v.* Marine Ins. Co., 5 *id.*, 299; Walden *v.* Phœnix Ins. Co., *id.*, 310.

[6] American Ins. Co. *v.* Center, 4 *Wend.*, 45; 7 *Cow.*, 564.

[7] Schmidt *v.* United Ins. Co., 1 *Johns.*, 249; Post *v.* Phœnix Ins. Co., 10 *Johns.*, 79.

[8] From *Code de Com.*, 393.

§ 1488. An abandonment must be neither partial nor conditional. **Must be unqualified.**

Code de Com., art. 372; 2 *Arnould Ins.*, 1149; Suydam *v.* Marine Ins. Co., 1 *Johns.*, 181.

§ 1489. An abandonment must be made within a reasonable time after information of the loss,[1] and after the commencement of the voyage,[2] and before the party abandoning has information of its completion.[3] **When may be made.**

[1] Smith *v.* Steinbach, 2 *Cai. Cas.*, 158; Tom *v.* Smith, 3 *Cai.*, 245; Read *v.* Bonham, 3 *Brod. & B.*, 147; Aldridge *v.* Bell, 1 *Stark.*, 498; see Dean *v.* Hornby, 3 *E. & B.*, 180.

[2] *Code de Com.*, art. 370.

[3] Parage *v.* Dale, 3 *Johns. Cas.*, 156; Pezant *v.* National Ins. Co., 15 *Wend.*, 453.

§ 1490. Where the information upon which an abandonment has been made proves incorrect, or the thing insured was so far restored when the abandonment was made, that there was then in fact no total loss, the abandonment becomes ineffectual. **Abandonment may be defeated.**

Church *v.* Bedient, 1 *Cai. Cas.*, 21; Hallett *v.* Peyton, *id.*, 28; Penny *v.* N. Y. Ins. Co., 3 *Cai.*, 155; Dickey *v.* Am. Ins. Co. [Ct. of Errors], 3 *Wend.*, 658. But as to the conflict in the cases on this question, see 2 *Pars. Mar. L.*, 402, note.

§ 1491. Abandonment is made by giving notice thereof to the insurer; which may be done orally, or in writing. **How made.**

2 *Levi Com. L.*, 159; 2 *Pars. Mar. L.*, 396; see Read *v.* Bonham, 3 *Brod. & B.*, 147; Patapsco Ins. Co. *v.* Southgate, 5 *Peters*, 622. Whether it ought not to be required to be in writing, see Parmenter *v.* Todhunter, 1 *Camp.*, 541.

§ 1492. A notice of abandonment must be explicit; and must specify the particular cause of the abandonment;[1] but need state only enough to show that there is probable cause therefor,[2] and need not be accompanied with proof of interest or of loss.[3] **Requisites of notice.**

[1] Suydam *v.* Marine Ins. Co., 1 *Johns.*, 181; see Dickey *v* N. Y. Ins. Co., 4 *Cow.*, 222; Craig *v.* United Ins. Co., 6 *Johns.*, 226.

[2] McConochie *v.* Sun Ins. Co., 3 *Bosw.*, 99.

[3] Barker *v.* Phœnix Ins. Co., 8 *Johns.*, 307.

No other cause can be relied on.

§ 1493. An abandonment can be sustained only upon the cause specified in the notice thereof.

Suydam *v.* Marine Ins. Co., 1 *Johns.*, 181; but compare Dean *v.* Hornby, 3 *E. & B.*, 180.

Effect.

§ 1494. An abandonment is equivalent to a transfer, by the insured, of his interest, to the insurer, with all the chances of recovery and indemnity.

Rogers *v.* Hosack, 18 *Wend.*, 319; Radcliff *v.* Coster, *Hoffm.*, 98; Atlantic Ins. Co. *v.* Storrow, 5 *Paige*, 285.

Waiver of formal abandonment.

§ 1495. If a marine insurer pays for a loss as if it were an actual total loss, he is entitled to whatever may remain of the thing insured, or its proceeds or salvage, as if there had been a formal abandonment.

2 *Arn. Ins.*, 1001; 2 *Pars. Mar. L.*, 398.

Agents of the insured become agents of the insurer.

§ 1496. Upon an abandonment, acts done in good faith, by those who were agents of the insured in respect to the thing insured, subsequent to the loss, are at the risk of the insurer, and for his benefit.

Gardner *v.* Smith, 1 *Johns. Cas.*, 141; Walden *v.* Phœnix Ins. Co., 5 *Johns.*, 310; Gardere *v.* Columbian Ins. Co., 7 *id.*, 514; Jumel *v.* Marine Ins. Co., 7 *id.*, 412.

Acceptance not necessary.

§ 1497. An acceptance of an abandonment is not necessary to the rights of the insured, and is not to be presumed from the mere silence of the insurer,[1] upon his receiving notice of abandonment.[2]

[1] 2 *Pars. Mar. L.*, 399; Walden *v.* Phœnix Ins. Co., 5 *Johns.*, 310.

[2] Child *v.* Sun Mutual Ins. Co., 2 *Sandf.*, 76.

Acceptance conclusive.

§ 1498. The acceptance of an abandonment, whether express or implied, is conclusive upon the parties, and admits the loss and the sufficiency of the abandonment.

Smith *v.* Robertson, 2 *Dow*, 474.

§ 1499. An abandonment once made and accepted is irrevocable, unless the ground upon which it was made proves to be unfounded. Accepted abandonment, irrevocable.

2 *Levi Com. L.*, 166; 2 *Pars. Mar. L.*, 413.

§ 1500. On an accepted abandonment of a ship, freightage earned previous to the loss belongs to the insurer thereof; but freightage subsequently earned, belongs to the insurer of the ship. Freightage, how affected by abandonment of ship.

United States Ins. Co. *v.* Lenox, 1 *Johns. Cas.*, 377; see Stewart *v.* Greenock Ins. Co., 2 *H. of L. Cas.*, 159.

§ 1501. If an insurer refuses to accept a valid abandonment, he is liable as upon an actual total loss, deducting from the amount any proceeds of the thing insured which may have come to the hands of the insured. Refusal to accept.

Church *v.* Bedient, 1 *Cai. Cas.*, 21.

§ 1502. If a person insured omits to abandon, he may nevertheless recover his actual loss. Omission to abandon.

Suydam *v.* Marine Ins. Co., 2 *Johns.*, 138; Earl *v.* Shaw, 1 *Johns. Cas.*, 313.

ARTICLE IX.

MEASURE OF INDEMNITY.

§ 1503. A valuation in a policy of marine insurance is conclusive between the parties thereto,[1] in the adjustment of either a partial or total loss,[2] if the insured has some interest at risk, and there is no fraud on his part; except that when a thing has been hypothecated by bottomry or respondentia, before its insurance, and without the knowledge of the person Valuation, when conclusive.

actually procuring the insurance, he may show the real value. But a valuation fraudulent in fact entitles the insurer to rescind the contract.

[1] Irving *v.* Manning, 1 *H. of L. Cas.*, 287; 6 *C. B.*, 391; Whitney *v.* Amer. Ins. Co., 3 *Cow.*, 210; Kane *v.* Commercial Ins. Co., 8 *Johns.*, 229; Davy *v.* Hallett, 3 *Cai.*, 16.

[2] 3 *Kent Com.*, 274; 2 *Pars. Mar. L.*, 68.

Partial loss. § 1504. A marine insurer is liable, upon a partial loss, only for such proportion of the amount insured by him, as the loss bears to the value of the whole interest of the insured in the property insured.

2 *Arnould's Ins.*, § 358; Clark *v.* United M. & F. Ins. Co., 7 *Mass.*, 365.

Profits. § 1505. Where profits are separately insured in a contract of marine insurance, the insured is entitled to recover, in case of loss, a proportion of such profits equivalent to the proportion which the value of the property lost bears to the value of the whole.

Loomis *v.* Shaw, 2 *Johns. Cas.*, 36; see Abbott *v.* Sebor, 3 *id.*, 39.

Valuation apportioned. § 1506. In case of a valued policy of marine insurance on freightage or cargo, if a part only of the subject is exposed to risk, the valuation applies only in proportion to such part.

3 *Kent Com.*, 275.

Valuation applied to profits. § 1507. When profits are valued and insured, by a contract of marine insurance, a loss of them is conclusively presumed from a loss of the property out of which they were expected to arise, and the valuation fixes their amount.

Patapsco Ins. Co. *v.* Coulter, 3 *Peters*, 222; 2 *Pars. Mar. L.*, 70, *n.* 4; Abbott *v.* Sebor, 3 *Johns. Cas.*, 39.

Estimating loss under an open policy. § 1508. In estimating a loss under an open policy of marine insurance, the following rules are to be observed:

1. The value of a ship is its value at the beginning of the risk, including all articles or charges which add to its permanent value, or which are necessary to prepare it for the voyage insured;[1]

2. The value of cargo is its actual cost to the insured,[2] when laden on board, or where that cost cannot be ascertained, its market value[2] at the time and place of lading, adding the charges incurred in purchasing and placing it on board,[3] but without reference to any losses incurred in raising money for its purchase,[4] or to any drawback on its exportation,[5] or to the fluctuations of the market at the port of destination, or to expenses incurred on the way, or on arrival;[6]

3. The value of freightage is the gross freightage, exclusive of primage, without reference to the cost of earning it;[7] and,

4. The cost of insurance is in each case to be added to the value thus estimated.[8]

[1] 2 *Pars. Mar. L.*, 70; Kemble *v.* Bowne, 1 *Cai.*, 75; and see 2 *Arnould's Ins.*, 1339; Stevens *v.* Columbian Ins. Co., 3 *Cai.*, 43.

[2] 3 *Kent Com.*, 335, 336; Gahn *v.* Broome, 1 *Johns. Cas.*, 120; Story *v.* United Ins. Co., 7 *Johns.*, 343. But if this rule had not been so long established, its justice might be questioned (see Coffin *v.* Newburyport Ins. Co., 9 *Mass.*, 436).

[3] See Leroy *v.* United Ins. Co., 7 *Johns.*, 343; Stevens *v.* Columbian Ins. Co., 3 *Cai.*, 43.

[4] Ogden *v.* Columbian Ins. Co., 10 *Johns.*, 273.

[5] Gahn *v.* Broome, 1 *Johns. Cas.*, 120; Suydam *v.* Marine Ins. Co., 1 *Johns.*, 181; Minturn *v.* Columbian Ins. Co., 10 *Johns.*, 75.

[6] Lawrence *v.* N. Y. Ins. Co., 3 *Johns. Cas.*, 217.

[7] Stevens *v.* Columbian Ins. Co., 3 *Cai.*, 43.

[8] Ogden *v.* Columbian Ins. Co., 10 *Johns.*, 273; Minturn *v.* The same, *id.*, 75.

§ 1509. If cargo insured against partial loss arrives at the port of destination in a damaged condition, the loss of the insured is deemed to be the same proportion of the value, which the market price at that port of the thing so damaged, bears to the market price it would have brought if sound. **Arrival of thing damaged.**

3 *Kent's Com.*, 336; Lawrence *v.* N. Y. Ins. Co., 3 *Johns. Cas.*, 217; Johnstone *v.* Sheddon, 2 *East*, 581.

§ 1510. A marine insurer is liable for all the expense attendant upon a loss which forces the ship into port **Labor and expenses.**

to be repaired; and where it is agreed that the insured may labor for the recovery of the property, the insurer is liable for the expense incurred thereby; such expense, in either case, being in addition to a total loss if that afterwards occurs.

3 *Kent's Com.*, 339; Watson *v.* Marine Ins. Co., 7 *Johns.*, 57; Jumel *v.* Marine Ins. Co., *id.*, 412; Bordes *v.* Hallet, 1 *Cai.*, 444; Barker *v.* Phœnix Ins. Co., 8 *Johns.*, 397.

General average.

§ 1511. A marine insurer is liable for a loss falling upon the insured, through a contribution in respect to the thing insured, required to be made by him towards a general average loss called for by a peril insured against.

Contribution.

§ 1512. Where a person insured by a contract of marine insurance has a demand against others for contribution, he may claim the whole loss from the insurer, subrogating him to his own right to contribution.

Jumel *v.* Marine Ins. Co., 7 *Johns.*, 412; Maggrath *v.* Church, 1 *Cai.*, 196.

One-third new for old.

§ 1513. In the case of a partial loss of a ship or its equipments, the old materials are to be applied towards payment for the new,[1] and whether the ship is new or old,[2] a marine insurer is liable for only two-thirds of the remaining cost of the repairs, except that he must pay for anchors and cannon in full, and for sheathing metal at a depreciation of only two and one-half per cent for each month that it has been fastened to the ship.[3]

[1] Byrnes *v.* National Ins. Co., 1 *Cow.*, 265.

[2] *Id.*; Dunham *v.* Commercial Ins. Co., 11 *Johns.*, 315.

[3] This is the usage in New York.

CHAPTER III.

FIRE INSURANCE.

False representation.

§ 1514. An insurance against fire is not affected by concealment, nor by the falsity of a representation not inserted in the policy, though in a material particular, unless made with a fraudulent intent.

See Burritt *v.* Saratoga Mut. Fire Ins. Co., 5 *Hill*, 588

§ 1515. An alteration in the use or condition of a thing insured, from that to which it is limited by the policy, made without the consent of the insurer, by means within the control of the insured, and increasing the risk, entitles an insurer to rescind a contract of fire insurance. Alteration

Ang. Ins., 206.

§ 1516. An alteration in the use or condition of a thing insured, from that to which it is limited by the policy, which does not increase the risk, does not affect a contract of fire insurance. Alteration

Ib.; see Stokes *v.* Cox, 1 *H. & N.*, 533; Barrett *v.* Jermy, 3 *Exch.*, 535; Pim *v.* Reid, 6 *M. & G.*, 1.

§ 1517. A contract of fire insurance is not affected by any act of the insured, subsequent to the execution of the policy, which does not violate its provisions, even though it increases the risk,[1] and is the cause of a loss.[2] Acts of the insured.

[1] Stebbins *v.* Globe Ins. Co., 2 *Hall*, 632; Billings *v.* Tolland Co. Ins. Co., 20 *Conn.*, 139; see O'Neil *v.* Buffalo Ins. Co., 3 *N. Y.*, 122.

[2] Young *v.* Washington Co. Mut. Ins. Co., 14 *Barb.*, 545; see Gates *v.* Madison Co. Ins. Co., 5 *N. Y.*, 469.

§ 1518. If there is no valuation in the policy, the measure of indemnity in an insurance against fire is the expense, at the time that the loss is payable, of replacing the thing lost or injured in the condition in which it was at the time of the injury;[1] but the effect of a valuation in a policy of fire insurance is the same as in a policy of marine insurance.[2] Measure of indemnity.

[1] See Niblo *v.* North Am. Ins. Co., 1 *Sandf.*, 551.

[2] By the present law a valuation in a fire policy, as well as in a marine insurance, is conclusive (Harris *v.* Eagle Ins. Co., 5 *Johns.*, 368; Holmes *v.* Charlestown Ins. Co., 10 *Metc.*, 211). Though this rule has been sometimes disapproved, the commissioners have not thought it best to propose a change.

CHAPTER IV.

LIFE AND HEALTH INSURANCE.

Insurance upon life, when payable.

§ 1519. An insurance upon life may be made payable on the death of the person, or on his surviving a specified period, or periodically so long as he shall live, or otherwise contingently on the continuance or determination of life.

Insurable interest.

§ 1520. Every person has an insurable interest in the life and health:

1. Of himself;

2. Of any person on whom he depends wholly or in part for education or support;

3. Of any person under a legal obligation to him for the payment of money, or respecting property or services, of which death or illness might delay or prevent the performance; and,

4. Of any person upon whose life any estate or interest, vested in him, depends.

A sister has an insurable interest in the life of her brother, who stands in place of a parent to her (Lord *v.* Dall, 12 *Mass.*, 115).

Assignee, &c., of life policy need have no interest.

§ 1521. A policy of insurance upon life or health may pass by transfer, will or succession, to any person, whether he has an insurable interest or not, and such person may recover upon it whatever the insured might have recovered.

St. John *v.* Amer. Mut. Life Ins. Co., 13 *N. Y.*, 31; 2 *Duer*, 419; Valton *v.* National Fund Life Ins. Co., 20 *N. Y.*, 32.

Notice of transfer.

§ 1522. Notice to an insurer of a transfer or bequest thereof is not necessary to preserve the validity of a policy of insurance upon life or health unless thereby expressly required.

Ang. Ins., 413.

§ 1523. Unless the interest of a person insured is susceptible of exact pecuniary measurement, the measure of indemnity under a policy of insurance upon life or health is the sum fixed in the policy. Measure of indemnity.

Compare St. John *v.* Amer. Life Ins. Co., 2 *Duer*, 419; 13 *N. Y.*, 31; Mutual Life Ins. Co. *v.* Wager, 27 *Barb.*, 354; Miller *v.* Eagle Life and Health Ins. Co., 2 *E. D. Smith*, 268.

TITLE XII.

INDEMNITY.

§ 1524. Indemnity is a contract by which one engages to save another from a legal consequence of the conduct of one of the parties, or of some other person. Indemnity, what.

§ 1525. An agreement to indemnify a person against an act thereafter to be done, is void, if the act is known by such person, at the time of doing it, to be wrongful. Indemnity for a future wrongful act, void.

Shackell *v.* Rosier, 2 *Bing. N. C.*, 634. Otherwise it is valid (Stone *v.* Hooker, 9 *Cow.*, 154; Allaire *v.* Ouland, 2 *Johns. Cas.*, 62; Coventry *v.* Barton, 17 *Johns.*, 142.)

Indemnity for a past wrongful act, valid.

§ 1526. An agreement to indemnify a person against an act already done, is valid, even though the act was known to be wrongful, unless it was a felony.

Kneeland *v.* Rogers, 2 *Hall*, 579; Parker *v.* Rochester, 4 *Johns. Cas.*, 329.

Indemnity extends to acts of agent.

§ 1527. An agreement to indemnify against the acts of a certain person, applies not only to his acts, and their consequences, but also to those of his agents.

Stone *v.* Hooker, 9 *Cow.*, 154; Hill *v.* Packard, 5 *Wend.*, 375; affirming S. C., 7 *Cow.*, 434.

Indemnity to several.

§ 1528. An agreement to indemnify several persons applies to each unless a contrary intention appears.

Person indemnifying, liable jointly or severally with person indemnified.

§ 1529. One who indemnifies another against an act to be done by the latter, is liable jointly with the person indemnified, and separately, to every person injured by such act.

Herring *v.* Hoppock, 15 *N. Y.*, 409; affirming S. C., 12 *N. Y. Leg. Obs.*, 167: Fonda *v.* Van Horne, 15 *Wend.*, 631; Davis *v.* Newkirk, 5 *Denio*, 92.

Rules for interpreting agreement of indemnity.

§ 1530. In the interpretation of a contract of indemnity, the following rules are to be applied, unless a contrary intention appears:

1. Upon an indemnity against liability, expressly, or in other equivalent terms, the person indemnified is entitled to recover upon becoming liable;[1]

2. Upon an indemnity against claims, or demands, or damages or costs, expressly, or in other equivalent terms, the person indemnified is not entitled to recover without payment thereof;[2]

3. An indemnity against claims, or demands, or liability, expressly, or in other equivalent terms, embraces the costs of defense against such claims,[3] demands or liability incurred in good faith, and in the exercise of a reasonable discretion;[4]

4. The person indemnifying is bound, on request of the person indemnified, to defend actions or pro-

ceedings brought against the latter in respect to the matters embraced by the indemnity,[5] but the person indemnified has the right to conduct such defenses, if he chooses to do so;[6]

5. If, after request, the person indemnifying neglects to defend the person indemnified, a recovery against the latter suffered by him in good faith, is conclusive in his favor against the former;[7]

6. If the person indemnifying, whether he is a principal or a surety in the agreement, has not reasonable notice of the action or proceeding against the person indemnified, or is not allowed to control its defense, judgment against the latter is only presumptive evidence against the former;

7. A stipulation that a judgment against the person indemnified shall be conclusive upon the person indemnifying, is inapplicable if he had a good defense upon the merits, which by want of ordinary care he failed to establish in the action.[9]

[1] Scott *v.* Tyler, 14 *Barb.*, 202; Chace *v.* Hinman, 8 *Wend.*, 452; Weble *v.* Pond, 19 *id.*, 423; Churchill *v.* Hunt, 3 *Den.*, 321; Gilbert *v.* Wiman, 1 *N. Y.*, 350; and see Westervelt *v.* Smith, 2 *Duer*, 449; S. C., 12 *N. Y. Leg. Obs.*, 78.

[2] Aberdeen *v.* Blackmar, 6 *Hill*, 324; Scott *v.* Tyler, 14 *Barb.*, 202; Campbell *v.* Jones, 4 *Wend.*, 306; Churchill *v.* Hunt, 3 *Den.*, 321; Gilbert *v.* Wiman, 1 *N. Y.*, 550; Collinge *v.* Heywood, 9 *Ad. & El.*, 633; Reynolds *v.* Doyle, 1 *Man. & Gr.*, 753.

[3] Westervelt *v.* Smith, 2 *Duer*, 449; Mott *v.* Hicks, 1 *Cow.*, 513, 539; Smith *v.* Compton, 3 *B. & Ad.*, 407; Warwick *v.* Richardson, 10 *M. & W.*, 284.

[4] Short *v.* Kalloway, 11 *Ad. & El.*, 28.

[5] Trustees of Newburgh *v.* Gallatian, 4 *Cow.*, 340.

[6] See Peck *v.* Acker, 20 *Wend.*, 605, where this principle was applied to the case of sheriffs.

[7] Aberdeen *v.* Blackmar, 6 *Hill*, 324; Beers *v.* Pinney, 12 *Wend.*, 308; Trustees of Newburgh *v.* Gallatian, 4 *Cow.*, 340; Given *v.* Driggs, 1 *Cai.*, 450; Stone *v.* Hooker, 9 *Cow.*, 154; Lee *v.* Clark, 1 *Hill*, 56; Holmes *v.* Weed, 19 *Barb.*, 128.

[8] Aberdeen *v.* Blackmar, 6 *Hill*, 324; Riley *v.* Seymour, 1 *Wend.*, 143; Thomas *v.* Hubbell, 15 *N. Y.*, 405. An indemnity against all actions, or in other equivalent terms, has been held to embrace groundless

actions (Trustees of Newburgh *v.* Gallatian, 4 *Cow.*, 340). An indemnity against all claims or demands, or in other equivalent terms, has been held not to embrace groundless demands (Luddington *v.* Pulver, 16 *Wend.*, 404).

[9] Bridgeport Ins. Co. *v.* Wilson, 7 *Bosw.*, 427.

When person indemnifying is a surety.

§ 1531. Where one, at the request of another, engages to answer in damages, whether liquidated or unliquidated, for any violation of duty on the part of the latter, he is entitled to be reimbursed in the same manner as a surety for whatever he may pay.

Bail, what.

§ 1532. Upon those contracts of indemnity which are taken in legal proceedings, as security for the performance of an obligation imposed or declared by the tribunals, and known as undertakings or recognizances, the sureties are called bail.

How regulated.

§ 1533. The obligations of bail are governed by the statutes specially applicable thereto

TITLE XIII.

GUARANTY.

CHAPTER I.

GUARANTY IN GENERAL.

ARTICLE I.

DEFINITION OF GUARANTY.

§ 1534. A guaranty is a promise to answer for the debt, default or miscarriage of another person. Guaranty, what.

This definition is in the precise language of the statute of frauds (2 *R. S.*, 135, § 2), except that it omits the word "special" before "promise." It of course includes a contract of suretyship, but every guarantor is not necessarily a surety.

§ 1535. A person may become guarantor even without the knowledge or consent of the principal. Knowledge of principal not necessary to creation of guaranty.

Code Napoleon, 2014.

ARTICLE II.

CREATION OF GUARANTY.

Necessity of a consideration.

§ 1536. Where a guaranty is entered into at the same time with the original obligation, or with the acceptance of the latter by the guarantee, and forms, with that obligation, a part of the consideration to him, no other consideration need exist. In all other cases there must be a consideration distinct from that of the original obligation.

See Mallory *v.* Gillett, 21 *N. Y.*, 412. The person to whom a guaranty is made, is here called the *guarantee.* This is the proper legal meaning of the word (see Bouvier's Dictionary, also Webster and Worcester), although it is often used in another sense.

Guaranty to be in writing, &c.

§ 1537. Except as prescribed by the next section, a guaranty must be in writing, and signed by the guarantor; but the writing need not express a consideration.

The familiar provision of the Revised Statutes, made every special promise to answer for the debt, default or miscarriage of another person, void, unless "some note or memorandum thereof *expressing the consideration* be in writing, &c. (2 *Rev. Stat.*, 135, § 2, subd. 2). In the draft of this Code, the Commissioners recommended that the requirement that the consideration be expressed, should be omitted (*Dr. Civ. Code*, § 1380). This change in the law has since been made, by the Legislature, by Laws of 1863, ch. 464; and the section in the text, therefore, corresponds to the existing law.

The Commissioners have inserted in the text an express provision that the writing need not express a consideration, because by the section immediately preceding an actual consideration is necessary to support a guaranty in some cases, while in others none is required. It has been lately held by the Court of Appeals that a contract required by the statute of frauds to be in writing, cannot be partly in writing and partly oral; thus where a writing relating to a contract for the sale of land fixes the price, but refers to "terms as specified," which are not stated in writing, the memorandum is insufficient, and cannot be made good by oral evidence of the time agreed upon for payment (Wright *v.* Weeks, 25 *N. Y.*, 153). If, therefore, the section in the text should simply omit the former provision of the statute requiring the consideration to be stated, it might be exposed to the construction that in all those cases in which the consideration is made, by the previous section, essential to the *contract*, it must be stated in reducing the contract to *writing*.

In England the statute, 19 & 20 *Vict.*, *c.* 97, § 3, enables a party to prove the consideration of a guaranty by parol. So in Maine (*Rev. Stat.*, 631).

§ 1538. A promise to answer for the obligation of another, in any of the following cases, is deemed an original obligation of the promiser,[1] and need not be in writing: **Engagement to answer for obligation of another, when deemed original.**

1. Where the promise is made by one who has received property of another upon an undertaking to apply it pursuant to such promise; or by one who has received a discharge from an obligation in whole or in part, in consideration of such promise;[2]

2. Where the creditor parts with value, or enters into an obligation, in consideration of the obligation in respect to which the promise is made, in terms or under circumstances such as to render the party making the promise the principal debtor, and the person in whose behalf it is made, his surety;[3]

3. Where the promise, being for an antecedent obligation of another, is made upon the consideration that the party receiving it cancels the antecedent obligation, accepting the new promise as a substitute therefor; or upon the consideration that the party receiving it releases the property of another from a levy, or his person from imprisonment under an execution on a judgment obtained upon the antecedent obligation; or upon a consideration beneficial to the promiser, whether moving from either party to the antecedent obligation, or from another person;[4]

4. Where a factor undertakes, for a commission, to sell merchandise and guaranty the sale;[5]

5. Where the holder of an instrument for the payment of money, upon which a third person is or may become liable to him, transfers it in payment of a precedent debt of his own, or for a new consideration, and in connection with such transfer enters into a promise respecting such instrument.[6]

[1] The cases upon the very frequently litigated question whether a promise partaking of the character of an engagement for the debt of another, is to be deemed an original or a collateral undertaking, are very numerous, and far from consistent. It is hardly possible to frame rules having the necessary simplicity and clearness, which shall reconcile all the adjudications. In the subdivisions of this section the commissioners have endeavored to supply rules for distinguishing an original undertaking, which, upon the whole, are sustained by the weight of authority; though some of them express views which have been controverted.

The rule that the undertaking of a surety, who signs together with the principal, although he adds the word "surety," to his name, is an original and not a collateral undertaking (Perkins *v.* Goodman, 21 *Barb.*, 218; and see Clark *v.* Rawson, 2 *Den.*, 135), has relation to the expression of a consideration, and becomes unimportant when that element is dispensed with, in the memorandum. The same remark applies to some cases where a guaranty omitting to specify a consideration has been sustained by aid of the fact that it was indorsed on the principal contract (see Bailey *v.* Freeman, 11 *Johns.*, 221).

The rule laid down in Douglass *v.* Jones, 3 *E. D. Smith*, 551, that an agreement by an employer with his clerk, guarantying that his salary at the rates fixed by the contract of employment, shall not fall below a certain sum, need not express a consideration, is not properly an exception to the general principle that a guaranty must be in writing. Such an engagement is not a guaranty properly speaking, nor within the definition employed in this Code. And the decision is put upon the ground that the engagement was not one to answer for the debt, &c., of *another person*, and therefore need not be in writing.

[2] Subdivision 1 embraces, in its first clause, such cases as Wyman *v.* Smith, 2 *Sandf.*, 331; N. Y. & Erie R. R. Co., 16 *How. Pr.*, 564; Lippincott *v.* Ashfield, 4

Sandf., 611; Olmstead *v.* Greenly, 18 *Johns.*, 12; and compare Westfall *v.* Parsons, 16 *Barb.*, 645; and in its second clause, such cases as Van Epps *v.* McGill, *Hill & D. Supp.*, 109; Phillips *v.* Gray, 3 *E. D. Smith*, 69.

[3] Subdivision 2 embraces the common case of goods sold and delivered, or services rendered for the benefit of one upon the request and promise of another; as to which see Chase *v.* Day, 17 *Johns.*, 114; Graham *v.* O'Neil, 2 *Hall*, 474; Darlington *v.* McCunn, 2 *E. D. Smith*, 411; Chesterman *v.* McCostling, 6 *N. Y. Leg. Obs.*, 212; Hanford *v.* Higgins, 1 *Bosw.*, 441; Flanders *v.* Crolius, 1 *Duer*, 206; Briggs *v.* Evans, 1 *E. D. Smith*, 192; Devlin *v.* Woodgate, 34 *Barb.*, 252; Quintard *v.* De Wolf, 34 *Barb.*, 97; State Bank *v.* Mettler, 2 *Bosw.*, 392; Beach *v.* Hungerford, 19 *Barb.*, 258; also such cases as Harrison *v.* Sawtel, 10 *Johns.*, 242; Chapin *v.* Merrill, 4 *Wend.*, 657; with which compare Kingsley *v.* Balcome, 4 *Barb.*, 131; and Stern *v.* Drinker, 2 *E. D. Smith*, 401; King *v.* Despard, 5 *Wend.*, 277.

It excludes cases where the whole credit is not given to the person who comes in to answer for the party immediately benefited; such as Rogers *v.* Kneeland, 13 *Wend.*, 114; aff'g S. C., 10 *Id.*, 218; Marquand *v.* Hipper, 12 *Wend.*, 520; Brady *v.* Sackrider, 1 *Sandf.*, 514; Dixon *v.* Frazee, 1 *E. D. Smith*, 32; Pennell *v.* Pentz, 4 *Id.*, 639; Allen *v.* Scarff, 1 *Hilt.*, 209; Leonard *v.* Vredenburgh, 8 *Johns.*, 29; Larson *v.* Wyman, 14 *Wend.*, 246; Payne *v.* Baldwin, 14 *Barb.*, 570; Brown *v.* Webber, 24 *How. Pr.*, 306; Wilson *v.* Roberts, 5 *Bosw.*, 100.

[4] Subdivision 3 chiefly rests upon the views expressed in the prevailing opinion in Mallory *v.* Gillett (21 *N. Y.*, 412), where numerous cases upon the distinction between original and collateral undertakings are reviewed. See also Cailleux *v.* Hall, 1 *E. D. Smith*, 5; Stymets *v.* Brooks, 10 *Wend.*, 207; Farley *v.* Cleveland, 4 *Cow.*, 432; Meech *v.* Smith, 7 *Wend.*, 314; Blunt *v.* Boyd, 3 *Barb*, 209; Kingsley *v.* Balcome, 4 *Barb.*, 131; Elwood *v.* March, 5 *Wend.*, 231; Mersereau *v.* Lewis, 25 *Wend.*, 243; Barker *v.* Bucklin, 2 *Den.*, 45; Blunt *v.* Boyd, 3 *Barb.*, 209; Earle *v.* Crane, 6 *Duer*, 564; Blyer *v.* Monholland, 2 *Sandf. Ch.*, 478; Stoddard *v.* Graham, 23 *How. Pr.*, 518; Therasson *v.* McSpedon, 2 *Hilt.*, 1.

It will be observed that the last clause of the subdivision — "upon a consideration beneficial to the party engaging," — embraces not only cases where an absolutely new consideration moves to the promisor, but also those in which property of the principal debtor held by the creditor by virtue of a lien or under legal process, or otherwise for his demand is surrendered *to the promisor* (as in Slingerland *v.* Morse, 7 *Johns.*, 463; Skelton *v.* Brewster, 8 *Johns.*, 376; Gardiner *v.* Hopkins, 5 *Wend.*, 23; Stilwell *v.* Otis, 2 *Hilt.*, 148; 7 *Abb. Pr.*, 431); while it excludes cases in which the property is surrendered to the principal debtor (as in Mallory *v.* Gillett, 23 *Barb.*, 610, aff'd, 21 *N. Y.*, 412; Mercein *v.* Andrus, 10 *Wend.*, 461; Fay *v.* Bell, *Hill & D. Supp.*, 251).

[5] See Wolff *v.* Koppel, 2 *Den.*, 368; aff'g S. C., 5 *Hill*, 458; Sherwood *v.* Stone, 14 *N. Y.*, 267, and cases there cited.

[6] The following authorities hold the cases embraced within subdivision 5, to be exempt from the statute of frauds, on the ground that the engagement is original and not a guaranty.

Brown *v.* Curtiss (2 *N. Y.*, 225). Here the payee and holder of a promissory note transferred it to his creditor in exchange for his own note, held by such creditor, and at the same time executed, on the back of the note transferred, a guaranty of the payment thereof. It was held that the guaranty was not within the statute of frauds, and was therefore valid, although it expressed no consideration. Such an undertaking, although in form a promise to answer for the debt of another, is, in substance, an engagement to pay the guarantor's own debt in a particular way, and would be good without any writing. There is a new and distinct consideration moving between the parties to the new promise.

Durham *v.* Manrow (2 *N. Y.*, 535). Here C. P. Durham, one of the defendants, was holder of a note payable to himself or bearer, made by E. Durham. C. P. Durham made a purchase from the plaintiff and transferred to him the note. He, together with his co-defendant, acting by his request, executed a joint guaranty of payment of the note, which, however, expressed no consideration. The Supreme Court (3 *Hill*, 584), held that the undertaking was not within the statute of frauds, and was valid; and their judgment was affirmed in the Court of Appeals (2 *N. Y.*, 535), by an equally divided vote of the judges. The decision of the Supreme Court was also approved, as to the undertaking of the principal guarantor, in Brown *v.* Curtiss, 2 *N. Y.*, 225.

Cardell *v.* McNeil (21 *N. Y.*, 336). Here a contract for the sale of the plaintiff's horse to the defendant, was concluded between the plaintiff and an agent of the defendant. By the terms of the contract, part payment was to be made in a note of C., whom the defendant's agent said he would warrant to be good. The plaintiff delivered the horse, and the note was sent to him the next day. There was no written guaranty of the note of C., which turned out to be worthless. The plaintiff then sued the defendant on the verbal undertaking. It was held, 1. The plaintiff's acceptance of the note on the second day without exacting a written guaranty, was no waiver of the parol undertaking. 2. The parol guaranty was in effect for payment of the note according to its terms, and not for collection by process of law. It was broken, and defendant became liable upon it, when C. failed to pay. 3. The guaranty was not void by the statute of frauds. Although in form it was a collateral undertaking, yet in substance it was an agreement by defendant to pay so much of the price of the horse unless C. should make the payment for him, and thereby discharge him.

Dauber *v.* Blackney (38 *Barb.*, 432). Here it appeared that the defendant purchased from one W., a wagon, at the price of $80. Of this sum the defendant paid $30 in cash, and $50 in a note of B. for that sum; but W. exacted a guaranty of the note from the defendant before he would accept it towards the price. The defendant wrote and signed a guaranty upon the note, without, however, expressing any consideration. W. afterwards sold the note and guaranty to the plaintiff, who, failing to collect the note, brought suit upon the guaranty against the defendant. It was held that the plaintiff was entitled to recover, on the ground that the undertaking was original, and no consideration need be expressed. Whenever the holder of a note against a third person turns it out in payment of his own debt, or in payment of property purchased, or for money received, by him, from the person to whom he transfers it, and at the same time agrees that the note is good, or will be paid at maturity, or that it will be collected by due process of law against the maker, this is an undertaking, in substance, entirely for his own benefit and advantage, and the contract is not within the statute of frauds.

To substantially the same effect are Fowler *v.* Clearwater, 35 *Barb.*, 143; Westcott *v.* Keeler, 4 *Bosw.*, 564.

§ 1539. A mere offer to guaranty is not binding, until notice of its acceptance is communicated by the guarantee to the guarantor;[1] but an absolute

Acceptance of guaranty.

guaranty is binding upon the guarantor without notice of acceptance.[2]

[1] Mozley *v.* Tinker, 1 *Cr. M. & R.*, 692; M'Iver *v.* Richardson, 1 *M. & Selw.*, 557.

[2] This is the rule in this state (Union Bank *v.* Coster, 3 *N. Y.*, 203; Smith *v.* Dann, 6 *Hill*, 543; Douglass *v.* Howland, 24 *Wend.*, 35); though not generally received in the United States (see Adams *v.* Jones, 12 *Peters*, 207; Lee *v.* Dick, 10 *id.*, 482; Norton *v.* Eastman, 4 *Greenl.*, 521; Kay *v.* Allen, 9 *Penn. St.*, 320; Mussey *v.* Rayner, 22 *Pick.*, 223; Taylor *v.* Wetmore, 10 *Ohio*, 490; Walker *v.* Forbes, 25 *Ala.* [*N. S.*], 139; Bell *v.* Kellar, 13 *B. Monr.*, 381; Howe *v.* Nickels, 22 *Me.*, 175; Hill *v.* Calvin, 4 *How.* [*Miss.*], 231; Craft *v.* Isham, 13 *Conn.*, 28). It cannot be denied that the reasons assigned for the decisions in this state are slight.

ARTICLE III.

INTERPRETATION OF GUARANTY.

Guaranty of incomplete contract.

§ 1540. In a guaranty of a contract, the terms of which are not then settled, it is implied that its terms shall be such as will not expose the guarantor to greater risks than he would incur under those terms which are most common, in similar contracts, at the place where the principal contract is to be performed.

A guaranty of the price of things to be thereafter sold, extends only to a sale upon not more than the ordinary length of credit (Combe *v.* Woolf, 8 *Bing.*, 156).

Guaranty that an obligation is good or collectible.

§ 1541. A guaranty to the effect that an obligation is good, or is collectible, imports that the debtor is solvent, and that the demand is collectible by the usual legal proceedings, if taken with reasonable diligence.

Thus a guaranty in these words, indorsed on a note, "I hereby guaranty the collection of the within note," imports a promise that the note can be collected of the maker, if the holder, within a reasonable time and with due diligence, prosecutes the same to judgment and execution against the maker. This obligation to prosecute within a reasonable time, and with due diligence, is a condition precedent to the liability of the maker. What is a reasonable time depends on the circumstances of each case. Generally, delay which cannot have prejudiced the guarantor, will not discharge him (Gallagher *v.* White, 31 *Barb.*, 92; see also Curtis *v.* Smallman, 14 *Wend.*, 231; Cooke *v.* Nathan, 16 *Barb.*, 342; Van Derveer *v.* Wright, 6 *id.*, 547; Warfield *v.* Watkins, 30 *Barb.*, 395).

§ 1542. A guaranty, such as is mentioned in the last section, is not discharged by an omission to take proceedings upon the principal debt, or upon any collateral security for its payment, if no part of the debt could have been collected thereby. Recovery upon such guaranty.

In Cady *v.* Sheldon (39 *Barb.*, 103) the defendants, upon an assignment of a bond and mortgage, made a guaranty in these words: "In consideration of, &c., we guaranty the collection of said bond." On the trial of an action on this guaranty, before a referee, it appeared that the obligors in the bond were insolvent, and unable to pay any part of the bond, and that the premises covered by the mortgage had been sold under a prior mortgage for less than the amount due upon it. The referee, however, nonsuited the plaintiffs. And upon appeal, one question raised was, whether the omission to sue the obligors, or attempt a foreclosure of the mortgage, precluded the plaintiffs from recovering upon the guaranty. The court, after reviewing numerous cases (Cumpston *v.* McNair, 1 *Wend.*, 457; Moakley *v.* Riggs, 19 *Johns.*, 69; Thomas *v.* Woods, 4 *Cow.*, 173; Loveland *v.* Sheppard, 2 *Hill*, 139; Burt *v.* Horner, 5 *Barb.*, 501; Vanderveer *v.* Wright, 6 *Barb.*, 547; Curtis *v.* Smallman, 14 *Wend.*, 231; White *v.* Case, 13 *Wend.*, 543; Kies *v.* Tifft, 1 *Cow.*, 98; Eddy *v.* Stanton, 21 *Wend.*, 255; People *v.* Jansen, 7 *Johns.*, 332; Hart *v.* Hudson, 6 *Duer*, 303; Taylor *v.* Bullen, 6 *Cow.*, 624; Gallagher *v.* White, 31 *Barb.*, 94; Morris *v.* Wadsworth, 11 *Wend.*, 100; 17 *Id.*, 103; Merritt *v.* Lincoln, 21 *Barb.*, 249; Newell *v.* Fowler, 23 *Barb.*, 632), stated the following principles as supported by the weight of authority:

1. That a guaranty of collection implies that a note or other evidence of debt is good and collectible against the principal debtors; and this means collectible by due course of law;

2. That, ordinarily to test that question, it is necessary that the usual legal proceedings should be resorted

to, to wit, a judgment and execution against the parties primarily liable to pay; and a return of an execution unsatisfied is primarily sufficient evidence that it is not collectible;

3. That it is not indispensable that legal proceedings should be resorted to, to test the collectibility of the paper, if it otherwise satisfactorily appears that a resort to such proceedings would be ineffectual; and proof that the principal debtors, from the period of the maturity of the debt, have been uniformly insolvent and unable to pay any part of the debt, is sufficient evidence for this purpose;

4. That legal proceedings are not a condition precedent to the liability of the guarantor, but equivalent evidence of inability to collect any part of the debt will suffice; and that however desirable it may be to have one uniform rule — *e. g.*, the return of an execution unsatisfied against the principal debtor — as the test of the collectibility of a debt, the weight of authority does not allow that rule to be adopted.

Guarantor's liability upon such guaranty.

§ 1543. In the cases mentioned in section 1541, the removal of the principal from the state, leaving no property therein from which the obligation might be satisfied, is equivalent to the insolvency of the principal, in its effect upon the rights and obligations of the guarantor.

This is the principle adopted in Cooke *v.* Nathan, 16 *Barb.*, 342; but see White *v.* Case, 13 *Wend.*, 543; Burt *v.* Horner, 5 *Barb.*, 501; Newell *v.* Fowler, 23 *Barb.*, 628.

ARTICLE IV.

LIABILITY OF GUARANTORS.

Guaranty, how construed.

§ 1544. A guaranty is to be deemed unconditional unless its terms import some condition precedent to the liability of the guarantor.

Morris *v.* Wadsworth, 11 *Wend.*, 100; 17 *id.*, 103; Smith *v.* Dann, 6 *Hill*, 543.

§ 1545. A guarantor of payment or performance is liable to the guarantee immediately upon the default of the principal,[1] and without demand or notice.[2]

Liability upon guaranty of payment or performance.

[1] Van Rensselaer *v.* Miller, *Hill & D. Supp.*, 237; Bank of N. Y. *v.* Livingston, 2 *Johns. Cas.*, 409; Loveland *v.* Shepard, 2 *Hill*, 139; Moakley *v.* Riggs, 19 *Johns.*, 69; Grant *v.* Hotchkiss, 26 *Barb.*, 63; Thomas *v.* Woods, 4 *Cow.*, 173; Backus *v.* Shipherd, 11 *Wend.*, 629.

[2] Brown *v.* Curtis, 2 *N. Y.*, 225; Allen *v.* Rightmere, 20 *Johns.*, 365; Clark *v.* Burdett, 2 *Hall*, 197; Kemble *v.* Wallis, 10 *Wend.*, 374; Morris *v.* Wadsworth, 11 *id.*, 100; 17 *id.*, 103; Mackensie *v.* Farrell, 4 *Bosw.*, 192; Sterns *v.* Marks, 35 *Barb.*, 565; Walton *v.* Mascall, 13 *M. & W.*, 452.

§ 1546. Where one guaranties a conditional obligation, his liability is commensurate with that of the principal, and he is not entitled to notice of the default of the principal, unless he is unable, by the exercise of reasonable diligence, to acquire information of such default, and the creditor has actual notice thereof.

Liability upon guaranty of a conditional obligation.

Douglass *v.* Howland, 24 *Wend.*, 35.

§ 1547. The obligation of a guarantor must be neither larger in amount nor in other respects more burdensome than that of the principal; and if, in its terms, it exceeds it, it is reducible in proportion to the principal obligation.

Obligation of guarantor cannot exceed that of the principal.

Code Napoleon, 2013.

§ 1548. A guarantor is not liable if the contract of the principal is unlawful; but he is liable notwithstanding any mere personal disability of the principal, though the disability be such as to make the contract void against the principal.

Guarantor not liable on an illegal contract.

Kimball *v.* Newell, 7 *Hill*, 116; Swift *v.* Beers, 3 *Denio*, 70; Ledeliey *v.* Powers, 25 *How. Pr.*, 240.

ARTICLE V.

CONTINUING GUARANTY.

Continuing guaranty, what.

§ 1549. A guaranty relating to a future liability of the principal, under successive transactions, which either continue his liability or from time to time renew it after it has been satisfied, is called a continuing guaranty.

See Agawam Bank *v.* Strever, 18 *N. Y.*, 502; Rindge *v.* Judson, 24 *N. Y.*, 64; Gates *v.* McKee, 13 *N. Y.*, 232.

In general an agreement to be responsible for goods delivered to a third person, will not be deemed a continuing undertaking, unless its language clearly indicates that such was the intention of the parties (Dixon *v.* Frazee, 1 *E. D. Smith*, 32; Fellows *v.* Prentiss, 3 *Den.*, 512; Whitney *v.* Groot, 24 *Wend.*, 82).

Revocation.

§ 1550. A continuing guaranty may be revoked at any time by the guarantor, in respect to future transactions, unless there is a continuing consideration as to such transactions, which he does not renounce.

Offord *v.* Davies, 12 *C. B.* [*N. S.*], 748. There seems no sufficient reason for preserving the exception in the case of guaranties under seal, as to which, see Hassell *v.* Long, 2 *M. & Selw.*, 363, 370; Calvert *v.* Gordon, 7 *B. & Cr.*, 809.

ARTICLE VI.

EXONERATION OF GUARANTORS.

§ 1551. A guarantor is exonerated, except so far as he may be indemnified by the principal,[1] if by any act of the creditor,[2] without the consent of the guarantor,[3] the original obligation of the principal is altered[4] in any respect,[5] or the remedies or rights of the creditor against the principal,[6] in respect thereto, in any way[7] impaired[8] or suspended.[9]

What dealings with debtor exonerate guarantor.

[1] Moore *v.* Paine, 12 *Wend.*, 123.

[2] Bowery Savings Bank *v.* Clinton, 2 *Sandf.*, 113; Storm *v.* Waddell, 2 *Sandf. Ch.*, 494. See § 1557.

[3] Of course the consent of the guarantor, at or before the time of altering the contract, makes the alteration binding upon him (N. H. Savings Bk. *v.* Colcord, 15 *N. H.*, 119; Solomon *v.* Gregory, 4 *Harrison*, 112; Suydam *v.* Vance, 2 *McLean*, 99; La Farge *v.* Herter 11 *Barb.*, 159). And his assent, *after* the alteration, revives his liability (Smith *v.* Winter, 4 *M. & W.*, 454; Mayhew *v.* Crickett, 2 *Swanst.*, 193). An authority to "compound" a debt warrants an extension of time (Cowper *v.* Smith, 4 *M. & W.*, 519).

[4] The general rule is that a material alteration of the contract, made between the creditor and the principal debtor, without the consent of the surety, discharges the latter. Woodworth *v.* Bank of America (19 *Johns.*, 330), is a leading case on the subject. In that case a promissory note was made and indorsed for the accomodation of the maker, dated at Albany, where the parties resided. After indorsing the note in blank, the indorser returned it to the maker, who, without the consent of the indorser, wrote and signed in the margin a memorandum;—"payable at the Bank of America." The note was discounted by the Bank of America, and payment was there demanded, at maturity, and notice of non-payment given to the indorser. It was held that the alteration discharged the indorser. See also upon the same rule, Ludlow *v.* Simond, 2 *Cai. Cas.*, 1; Henderson *v.* Marvin, 33 *Barb.*, 297; S. C., 11 *Abb. Pr.*, 142; Bagley *v.* Clarke, 7 *Bosw.*, 94; Dewey *v.* Reed, 40 *Barb.*, 16. In the last mentioned case a note was drawn payable "with interest;" and in that form was signed by the defendant as surety. After it was executed by him it was altered, by agreement between the holder and principal maker, but without the knowledge or consent of the surety, by adding to it the following words: "interest to be paid semi-annually." It was held that this alteration discharged the surety. The surety is exonerated, even though the princi-

pal becomes liable under the contract as it originally stood (Bonar *v.* Macdonald, 3 *H. of L. Cas.*, 226).

[5] A question has been suggested whether this rule should not be qualified so as to prevent the surety from claiming a discharge through an alteration in the principal contract not assented to by him, if the court or jury were of opinion that it operated to benefit him. This qualification of the surety's right to a discharge, finds some support in the language of the New York Common Pleas in Ogden *v.* Rowe (3 *E. D. Smith*, 312). The defendant in that case was surety for rent due on a lease. By the terms of the original lease the rent was payable quarterly; but the tenant, by his subsequent request, was permitted to pay monthly. The court say: "It is now insisted that accepting the payment of rent monthly was an alteration of the lease of the landlord, which discharged the surety. This claim cannot be sustained, for two reasons: First, the proof did not show any binding agreement to pay and accept monthly; and second, the acceptance of the rent, before it became due, by the terms of the lease, was in ease of the surety, and did not in any wise alter the nature or extent of his obligation; it rather reduced the probability that he would be liable at all, by reducing the amount in arrear. As well might a surety on a bond for the payment of money at the expiration of one year, claim that he is discharged because at the end of six months the obligee consented to receive from the principal debtor one-half the sum secured to be paid."

The result reached was doubtless correct, for the reason that the facts amounted only to part payment, and did not show a case of alteration of the original obligation. But a careful examination of the authorities, and a consideration of the grounds of a surety's liability, have convinced the commissioners that the suggestion that an alteration of the principal contract, though never assented to, may be disregarded if perceived to operate in favor of the surety, is inadmissible. The obligation of a surety is founded in his *contract;* and it is a contract which, upon well recognized principles is to be construed favorably for him. His *assent* is an essential element in this contract, and an essential ground of his obligation. There is no more propriety in permitting his principal and the creditor to modify his contract without his assent, and upon the mere ground of a benefit thereby done him, by modifying the contract between themselves for which he stands sponsor, than there would be in allowing one person to enter into an original engagement for another, without his assent, and in holding the latter as a contracting party, on the ground of anticipated benefit to him. The *presumption of assent* may well be aided by the fact of a benefit to be derived. But it is the assent, and not the benefit, which after all constitutes the contract. The surety has the right to judge for himself, and beforehand, whether the proposed change in his obligation is for his benefit or not; and the opinion of a judicial tribunal, taken after the fact, cannot safely be substituted for the judgment of the party interested.

It is settled that the creditor, after he has altered the obligation of the principal debtor, will not be allowed to hold the surety by showing that the change made was *not prejudicial* to the latter. This negative answer to the surety's objection is clearly insufficient. Thus in Birckhead *v.* Brown (5 *Hill*, 634, 640; affd., 2 *Den.*, 375), the court say: "The doctrine is a familiar one that a surety can only be charged where the case is brought within the very terms of his contract. * * * Courts are not at liberty to speculate upon the question whether the surety has or has not been injured by a departure from the terms." To the same effect, see Newton *v.* Chorlton, 10 *Hare*, 646; 2 *Drewry*, 333: Calvert *v.* London Dock Co., 2 *Keen*, 638. See also a strong intimation that an alteration even to the benefit of the surety would discharge him, in Blest *v.* Brown, 8 *Jur.* [*N. S.*], 602.

In Dobbin *v.* Bradley (17 *Wend.*, 422), the defendant guaranteed the paper of Smith to be made payable at a particular bank. Smith gave his note to the plaintiffs, in the course of the business mentioned in the guaranty, but made it payable generally, or in other words, without specifying any place of payment. And although the note was deposited in the particular bank before it came to maturity, it was held that the defendant was not liable. The court refused to go into the inquiry whether the surety had been injured, saying it was enough that the case did not come within the terms of the contract. In Colemard *v.* Lamb (15 *Wend.*, 329, 332), the court, commenting on an alteration in the original agreement, say: "A new contract was thus made between the principal parties, without the consent of the surety, and one for which he had never agreed to be responsible. The arrangement was one which might not improbably prove prejudicial to the surety. But it is unnecessary to speculate upon the consequences which were likely to result from the new agreement made with the principal. It is enough that a new agreement obligatory upon the parties to it, was actually made; and as this was done without the consent of the surety there can be no doubt that he was discharged from all further liability." See to the same effect Miller *v.* McCan, 7 *Paige*, 451.

In Bonser *v.* Cox (4 *Beavan*, 379; 6 *id.*, 110), A. agreed to become surety for B. for the repayment of an advance to be made in the shape of a draft at three months. The advance was made by an immediate payment; and it was held that the surety was discharged.

The reason for the rule which prohibits a surety to be holden simply because the alteration was not injurious to him — viz.: that his assent to be surety upon the altered agreement is needed to constitute him one — is equally valid to forbid that he should be holden because the modification is thought to tend to his benefit; except indeed that there will be cases in which the fact that it was beneficial may aid other circumstances to satisfy the jury of the fact of assent. This principle is unaffected by the section in the text.

Cases enforcing the general rule that modifications of the principal's contract will discharge the surety, in which the particular question of injury or benefit to the surety from the change did not arise, are Rathbone *v.* Warren, 10 *Johns.*, 587; Bangs *v.* Strong, 7 *Hill*, 250, affirming S. C., 10 *Paige*, 11; Coleman *v.* Wattle, 6 *N. Y.*, 44.

The decisions in Shufeldt *v.* Gustin (2 *E. D. Smith*, 57), and Ogden *v.* Sanderson (3 *id.*, 166), rest upon the ground that the negotiations between the creditor and the principal debtor had never reached the point of a binding agreement changing the original obligation.

[6] Reynolds *v.* Ward, 5 *Wend.*, 501; Hall *v.* Constant, 2 *Hall*, 185; Gahn *v.* Niemcewicz, 11 *Wend.*, 312, aff'g S. C., 3 *Paige*, 614; Newsam *v.* Finch, 25 *Barb.*, 175.

[7] Bangs *v.* Strong, 7 *Hill*, 250, aff'g S. C., 10 *Paige*, 11.

[8] Hall *v.* Constant, 2 *Hall*, 185; Vilas *v.* Jones, 1 *N. Y.* 274, affirming S. C., 10 *Paige*, 76; Bower *v.* Teirmann, 3 *Denio*, 378.

[9] Smith *v.* Townsend, 25 *N. Y.*, 479; Huffman *v.* Hulburt, 13 *Wend.*, 377; Draper *v.* Trescott, 29 *Barb.*, 401; Henderson *v.* Marvin, 31 *Barb.*, 297; Hart *v.* Hudson, 6 *Duer*, 294; Cross *v.* Sprigg, 2 *Macn. & G.*, 113; Bank of Ireland *v.* Beresford, 6 *Dow*, 233; Combe *v.* Woolf, 8 *Bing.*, 156; Manuf. & Mech. Bk.

v. Bank of Penna., 7 *Watts & S.*, 335; McComb *v.* Kittridge, 14 *Ohio*, 348; Brigham *v.* Wentworth, 11 *Cush.*, 123; Greely *v.* Dow, 2 *Metc.*, 176; Fowler *v.* Brooks, 13 *N. H.*, 240; Uhler *v.* Applegate, 26 *Penn. St.*, 140; Lime Rock Bank *v.* Mallett, 34 *Me.*, 547; Dorlon *v.* Christie, 39 *Barb.*, 610; and compare Wright *v.* Storrs, 6 *Bosw.*, 600; Taylor *v.* Allen, 36 *Barb.*, 294.

It has been held that a mere covenant *not to sue* the debtor, reserving the right to sue the sureties, does not discharge them (Price *v.* Barker, 4 *E. & B.*, 760; Kearsley *v.* Cole, 16 *M. & W.*, 128; see Sohier *v.* Loring, 6 *Cush.*, 544). As an original question, however, the propriety of this exception has been doubted. And the contrary was held in Austin *v.* Dorwin, 21 *Verm.*, 38; Dickerson *v.* Commissioners, &c., 6 *Ind.*, 128. See, however, Hubbell *v.* Carpenter, 5 *N. Y.*, 171. An agreement between the creditor and a third person to give time to the debtor, does not discharge the surety (Frazer *v.* Jordan, 8 *El. & Bl.*, 303).

Void promises. § 1552. A promise by a creditor, which for any cause is void, or voidable by him at his option, does not alter the obligation or suspend or impair the remedy, within the meaning of the last section.

Hall *v.* Constant, 2 *Hall*, 185; Bangs *v.* Strong, 10 *Paige*, 11; Vilas *v.* Jones, 1 *N. Y.*, 274; compare Draper *v.* Trescott, 29 *Barb.*, 401; also Kellogg *v.* Olmsted, 25 *N. Y.*, 189. In the last mentioned case it is held that a promise by a debtor that he will not pay a debt, then overdue, until a future day named, and that he will then pay the same with interest, is not a good consideration for a promise by the creditor to extend the time for payment.

Rescission of alteration. § 1553. The rescission of an agreement altering the original obligation of a debtor, or impairing the remedy of a creditor, does not restore the liability of a guarantor who has been exonerated by such agreement.

Dewey *v.* Reed, 40 *Barb.*, 16; see Bonar *v.* Macdonald, 3 *H. of L. Cas.*, 227.

Part performance. § 1554. The acceptance, by a creditor, of any thing in partial satisfaction of an obligation, reduces the obligation of a guarantor thereof, in the same measure as that of the principal, but does not otherwise affect it.

To this extent the doctrine of Ogden *v.* Rowe (see note to section 1551) may be admitted. See also Ellis *v.* McCormick, 1 *Hilt.*, 313.

Delay of creditor does not discharge guarantor.

§ 1555. Mere delay on the part of a creditor to proceed against the principal, or to enforce any other remedy, does not exonerate a guarantor.

Williams *v.* Townsend, 1 *Bosw.*, 411; Albany Dutch Church *v.* Vedder, 14 *Wend.*, 165; Sailly *v.* Elmore, 2 *Paige*, 497; Daniels *v.* Patterson, 3 *N. Y.*, 47; Schroeppell *v.* Shaw, 3 *N. Y.*, 446, aff'g S. C., 5 *Barb.*, 580; Goldsmith *v.* Brown, 35 *Barb.*, 484; Miller *v.* Stem, 2 *Penn. St.*, 286; Shook *v.* State, 6 *Ind.*, 113; Nichols *v.* McDowell, 14 *B. Monr.*, 6; Hoyt *v.* French, 4 *Foster* [*N. H.*], 198; Hunter *v.* Jett, 4 *Rand.*, 104; Sawyer *v.* Patterson, 11 *Ala.* [*N. S.*], 523; Clarke Co. *v.* Covington, 26 *Miss.*, 470; Hunt *v.* Bridgham, 2 *Pick.*, 581.

Guarantor indemnified by the debtor not exonerated.

§ 1556. A guarantor, who has been indemnified by the principal, is liable to the creditor to the extent of the indemnity, notwithstanding that the creditor, without the assent of the guarantor, may have modified the contract or released the principal.

Moore *v.* Paine, 12 *Wend.*, 123; Pratt *v.* Adams, 7 *Paige*, 615; Ten Eyck *v.* Holmes, 3 *Sandf. Ch.*, 428; Smith *v.* Steele, 25 *Verm.*, 427.

Discharge of principal by act of law does not discharge guarantor.

§ 1557. A guarantor is not exonerated by the discharge of his principal by operation of law, without the intervention or omission of the creditor.

Bowery Savings Bank *v.* Clinton, 2 *Sandf.*, 113; Storm *v.* Waddell, 2 *Sandf. Ch.*, 494.

CHAPTER II.

SURETYSHIP.

ARTICLE I.

WHO ARE SURETIES.

§ 1558. A surety is one who, at the request of another, and for the purpose of securing to him a benefit,[1] becomes responsible for the performance by the latter of some act in favor of a third person, or hypothecates property as security therefor.[2] Surety, what.

[1] The common definition of a surety (see Webster's, Wharton's and Burrill's Dictionaries), cannot be distinguished from that of a guarantor, and clearly covers the case of an indorser. But an indorser is not necessarily a surety (Pitts *v.* Congdon, 2 *N. Y.*, 352; Hurd *v.* Little, 12 *Mass.*, 502), nor is a guarantor, although their rights are in some important respects alike.

The distinction between a surety and a mere guarantor is, that the former enters into the contract primarily for the benefit of the debtor, while with the latter the benefit of the principal debtor is no material part of the inducement to him to contract.

[2] Vartie *v.* Underwood, 18 *Barb.*, 561; Gahn *v.* Niemcewicz, 11 *Wend.*, 312; 3 *Paige*, 614.

§ 1559. One who appears to be a principal, whether by the terms of a written instrument, or otherwise, may show that he is in fact a surety, except as against persons who have acted on the faith of his apparent character of principal. Apparent principal may show that he is surety.

So held as between the parties themselves (Rouse *v.* Whited, 25 *N. Y.*, 170; Barry *v.* Ransom, 12 *id.*, 446; Griffiths *v.* Reed, 21 *Wend.*, 502); and so as to third persons in equity (Hollier *v.* Eyre, 9 *Clark & Fin.*, 1; Davies *v.* Stainbank, 6 *De G., M. & G.*, 679). At common law, the rule excluding oral evidence to vary a written contract excluded evidence to show that the apparent principal was a surety (Harrison *v.* Courtauld, 3 *B. & Ad.*, 36; Fentum *v.* Pocock, 5 *Taunt.*, 192; see, however, Artcher *v.* Douglass, 5 *Denio*, 509); and upon the authority of these cases alone — the decisions in equity not being cited by counsel on either side — the same rule has been followed in a recent case in this state (Howard Banking Co. *v.* Welchman, 6 *Bosw.*, 280). The fusion of law and equity in this state has superseded the common law rule. In England, since equitable defenses have been admitted in common law courts, the equitable rule has been followed and defined as in the text, by all the judges (Pooley *v.* Harradine, 7 *El. & Bl.*, 431; Greenough *v.* McClelland, 2 *El. & El.*, 424; 6 *Jur.* [*N. S.*], 772; 30 *L. J.* [*Q. B.*], 15; Taylor *v.* Burgess, 5 *Hurlst. & N.* 1). And see Mohawk and Hudson River R. R. Co. *v.* Costigan, 2 *Sandf. Ch.*, 306; Artcher *v.* Douglass, 5 *Denio*, 509. Compare Casey *v.* Brabason, 10 *Abb. Pr.*, 368; Gahn *v.* Niemcewicz, 11 *Wend.*, 312; Elwood *v.* Diefendorf, 5 *Barb.*, 398; Chester *v.* Bank of Kingston, 16 *N. Y.*, 336. The same rule is established in Massachusetts (Weston *v.* Chamberlain, 7 *Cush.*, 404; Carpenter *v.* King, 9 *Metc.*, 511; Harris *v.* Brooks, 21 *Pick.*, 195.)

ARTICLE II.

LIABILITY OF SURETIES.

Limit of surety's obligation. § 1560. A surety cannot be held beyond the express terms of his contract,[1] and if such contract prescribes a penalty for its breach, he cannot in any case be liable for more than the penalty.[2]

[1] Ludlow *v.* Simond, 2 *Cai. Cas.*, 1; Walsh *v.* Bailie, 10 *Johns.*, 180; Penoyer *v.* Watson, 16 *id.*, 100; see also Manhattan Gas Light Co. *v.* Ely, 39 *Barb.*, 174; 25 *How. Pr.*, 237.

[3] Clark *v.* Bush, 3 *Cow.*, 151; Tunison *v.* Cramer, 2 *South.*, 498; see Fairlie *v.* Lawson, 5 *Cow.*, 424; Rayner *v.* Clark, 7 *Barb.*, 581; Dickerson *v.* Cook, 3 *Duer*, 324.

Rules of interpretation. § 1561. In interpreting the terms of a contract of suretyship, the same rules are to be observed as in the case of other contracts.

Gates *v.* McKee, 13 *N. Y.*, 232. See also Ruggles *v.* Holden, 3 *Wend.*, 216; Rochester City Bank *v.* Elwood, 21 *N. Y.*, 88.

Judgment against surety does not alter the relation. § 1562. Notwithstanding the recovery of judgment by a creditor against a surety, the latter still occupies the relation of surety.

Lafarge *v.* Herter, 11 *Barb.*, 159; and see S. C., 9 *N. Y.*, 241; Hubbell *v.* Carpenter, 5 *Barb.*, 580; and see S. C., 5 *N. Y.*, 171; compare Bangs *v.* Strong, 7 *Hill*, 250; Schroeppell *v.* Shaw, 3 *N. Y.*, 446; aff'g S. C., 5 *Barb.*, 580; Bay *v.* Tallmadge, 5 *Johns. Ch.*, 305; Boughton *v.* Bank of Orleans, 2 *Barb. Ch.*, 458; rev'g S. C., 2 *id.*, 484; Storms *v.* Thorn, 3 *Barb.*, 314. But see, to the contrary, Jenkins *v.* Robertson, 2 *Drewry*, 351.

Surety exonerated by performance or offer of performance. § 1563. Performance of the principal obligation, or an offer of such performance, duly made, whether by the principal[1] or by another person,[2] exonerates a surety.

[1] Elmendorph *v.* Tappen, 5 *Johns.*, 176.

[2] This rule seems just, though not fully supported by any express decision. As between the creditor and the principal debtor, the former is not bound to accept payment from a stranger, but as respects the surety, he ought to do so.

Surety discharged by certain acts of the creditor. § 1564. A surety is exonerated:

1. In like manner with a guarantor;

2. To the extent to which he is prejudiced by any act of the creditor which would naturally prove injurious to the remedies of the surety or inconsistent with his rights,[1] or which lessens his security;[2] or,

3. To the extent to which he is prejudiced by an omission of the creditor to do anything, when required by the surety, which it is his duty to do.[3]

[1] Schroeppell *v.* Shaw, 3 *N. Y.*, 446, aff'g S. C., 5 *Barb.*, 580.

[2] Gen. Steam Nav. Co. *v.* Rolt, 6 *C. B.* [*N. S.*], 550; Pledge *v.* Buss, *H. R. V. Johns.*, 663.

[3] The rule in this state is that if a surety requests the creditor to proceed against the principal at a time when the latter is solvent, and the creditor neglects so to do, and the principal subsequently becomes insolvent, the surety is exonerated (King *v.* Baldwin, 17 *Johns.*, 384; Remsen *v.* Beekman, 25 *N. Y.*, 552). And in the last mentioned case it is held that want of notice to the creditor of facts tending to show that the delay was likely to prove injurious to the surety, makes no difference.

It has been said, in some cases, that a creditor is bound to deal in the highest good faith with a surety, and must, if consulted by one intending to become a surety for any claim of such creditor, actual or possible, make a full disclosure to him of all circumstances which would be likely to affect his determination (Owen *v.* Homan, 3 *Macn. & G.*, 378; see Railton *v.* Mathews, 10 *Clark & F.*, 934; Pidcock *v.* Bishop, 3 *B. & Cr.*, 605; Etting *v.* Bank of U. S., 11 *Wheat.*, 59); but on a review of most of these authorities, this doctrine has been denied (North British Ins. Co. *v.* Lloyd, 10 *Exch.*, 523; Pledge *v.* Buss, *H. R. V. Johns.*, 663; see Hamilton *v.* Watson, 12 *Clark & F.*, 109; Wythes *v.* Labouchere, 5 *Jur.* [*N. S.*], 499).

ARTICLE III.

RIGHTS OF SURETIES.

Surety has rights of guarantor.

§ 1565. A surety has all the rights of a guarantor, whether he becomes personally responsible or not.

Vartie *v.* Underwood, 18 *Barb.*, 561; Gahn *v.* Niemcewicz, 11 *Wend.*, 512.

Surety may require the creditor to

§ 1566. A surety may require his creditor to proceed against the principal, or to pursue any other remedy in his power which the surety cannot himself pursue, and which would lighten his burden; and if in such case the creditor neglects to do so, the surety is exonerated to the extent to which he is thereby prejudiced.

proceed against the principal.

This is the settled rule in this state (Remsen *v.* Beekman, 25 *N. Y.*, 552; Pain *v.* Packard, 13 *Johns.*, 174; King *v.* Baldwin, 17 *Johns.*, 384, reversing S. C., 2 *Johns. Ch.*, 554; see Fulton *v.* Matthews, 15 *Johns.*, 433; Valentine *v.* Farrington, 2 *Edw.*, 53; Warner *v.* Beardsley, 8 *Wend.*, 195; Schroeppell *v.* Shaw, 3 *N. Y.*, 446, affirming S. C., 5 *Barb.*, 580). There is some variance on this question, in the decisions of other states (see to same effect Wetzel *v.* Sponsler, 18 *Penn. St.*, 460; Johnston *v.* Thompson, 4 *Watts*, 446; State *v.* Reynolds, 3 *Mo.*, 95; Hogaboom *v.* Herrick, 4 *Verm.*, 131; and to the contrary, Bellows *v.* Lovell, 5 *Pick.*, 307; Davis *v.* Huggins, 3 *N. H.*, 231).

The well settled rule that mere delay by the creditor to pursue the principal does not discharge the surety, is recognized by section 1555 above.

§ 1567. A surety may compel his principal to perform the obligation when due.

Surety may compel principal to perform obligation when due.

Ranelaugh *v.* Hayes, 1 *Vern.*, 190; see Champion *v.* Brown, 6 *Johns. Ch.*, 398; Antrobus *v.* Davidson, 3 *Meriv.*, 569, 578; Padwick *v.* Stanley, 9 *Hare*, 627.

§ 1568. If a surety satisfies the principal obligation, or any part thereof, whether with or without legal proceedings,[1] the principal is bound to reimburse what he has disbursed,[2] including necessary costs and expenses[3]; but the surety has no claim for reimbursement against other persons, though they may have been benefited by his act, except as prescribed by the next section.[4]

A principal bound to reimburse his surety.

[1] Mauri *v.* Heffernan, 13 *Johns.*, 58; Vechte *v.* Brownell, 8 *Paige*, 212.

[2] Bonney *v.* Seely, 2 *Wend.*, 481; Hunt *v.* Amidon, 4 *Hill*, 345; Jones *v.* Steinburgh, 1 *Barb. Ch.*, 250; Cobb *v.* Titus, 10 *N. Y.*, 198; Hunt *v.* Amidon, 4 *Hill*, 345; Seely *v.* Champlain, 4 *Johns.*, 461.

[3] *Laws of* 1858, 506, *ch.* 314, § 3. The language of that act is somewhat broader than that employed in the text, viz.: "That any indorser or other surety, and any assignee, executor, administrator or other

trustee, shall be entitled to and allowed to recover from his principal or *cestui que trust*, all necessary and reasonable costs and expenses, paid or incurred by him in good faith, as surety or trustee, in the prosecution or defense in good faith of any action by or against any assignee, executor, administrator or other trustee as such." Previous to that act the decisions in this state were to the effect that a surety who had been compelled to pay the debt, might recover from his principal the costs of the suit for the collection of it (Elwood *v.* Diefendorf, 5 *Barb.*, 398; Baher *v.*, Martin, 3 *Barb.*, 694); provided no defense was interposed by the surety, but the costs claimed were the mere ordinary costs of a suit not litigated. But that he could not recover costs when he put the party to a useless expense by defending an action which he ought not to have defended, and should be allowed in such a case only the costs of a judgment by default (Holmes *v.* Weed, 24 *Barb.*, 546; see Hayden *v.* Cabot, 17 *Mass.*, 169).

The surety acquires the right of the creditor

§ 1569. A surety, upon satisfying the obligation of the principal, is entitled to enforce every remedy which the creditor then has against the principal, to the extent of reimbursing what he has expended;[1] and also to require all his co-sureties to contribute thereto, without regard to the order of time in which they became such.[2]

[1] Hayes *v.* Ward, 4 *Johns. Ch.*, 123; Bullock *v.* Boyd, *Hoffm.*, 294; Van Horne *v.* Everson, 13 *Barb.*, 526; Cuyler *v.* Ensworth, 6 *Paige*, 32; N. Y. State Bank *v.* Fletcher, 5 *Wend.*, 85.

[2] Norton *v.* Coons, 3 *Denio*, 130; aff'd, 6 *N. Y.*, 33; compare Harris *v.* Warner, 13 *Wend.*, 400.

Surety entitled to benefit of securities held by creditor.

§ 1570. A surety is entitled to the benefit of every security for the performance of the principal obligation, held by the creditor,[1] or by a co-surety,[2] at the time of entering into the contract of suretyship,[1] or acquired by him afterwards,[3] whether the surety was aware of the security or not.[4]

[1] Stirling *v.* Forrester, 3 *Bligh*, 575, 590; Aldrich *v.* Cooper, 8 *Ves.*, 381.

[2] Ramsey *v.* Lewis, 30 *Barb.*, 403.

[3] Pledge *v.* Buss, *H. R. V. Johns.*, 663.

[4] Pearl *v.* Deacon, 24 *Beav.*, 186.

§ 1571. Whenever property of a surety is hypothecated with property of the principal, the surety is entitled to have the property of the principal first applied to the discharge of the obligation. The property of principal to be taken first.

Vartie *v.* Underwood, 18 *Barb.*, 561. For an explanation of the use of the word "hypothecated," see note to § 1608.

ARTICLE IV.

RIGHTS OF CREDITORS.

§ 1572. A creditor is entitled to the benefit of everything which a surety has received from the debtor by way of security for the performance of the obligation; and may, upon the maturity of the obligation, compel the application of such security to its satisfaction. Creditor entitled to benefit of securities held by surety.

Vail *v.* Foster, 4 *N. Y.*, 312; Martin *v.* Campbell, 29 *Barb.*, 188; Pratt *v.* Adams, 7 *Paige*, 615; Ten Eyck *v.* Holmes, 3 *Sandf. Ch.* 428; Lea *v.* Hinton, 5 *De G, M. & G.*, 823; Wright *v.* Morley, 11 *Ves.*, 12. This is so, whether the creditor has knowledge of the security or not (Kramer's Appeal, 37 *Penn. St.*, 71).

ARTICLE V.

LETTER OF CREDIT.

§ 1573. A letter of credit is a written instrument, addressed by one person to another, requesting the Letter of credit, what.

latter to give credit to the person in whose favor it is drawn.

How addressed.

§ 1574. A letter of credit may be addressed to several persons in succession.

Liability of the writer.

§ 1575. The writer of a letter of credit is, upon the default of the debtor, liable to those who gave credit in compliance with its terms.

Letter of credit either general or special.

§ 1576. A letter of credit is either general or special. When the request[1] for credit, in a letter, is addressed to specified persons by name or description, the letter is special. All other letters of credit are general.[2]

[1] That the mere fact of the *letter* being addressed to a particular person does not make it a special letter, see Benedict *v.* Sherrill (*Hill & D. Supp.*, 219); where a letter guarantying the payment of such debts as the bearer might contract for the purchase of goods, was held a general letter, though addressed to a particular person.

[2] Union Bank *v.* Coster, 3 *N. Y.*, 203; affirming S. C., 1 *Sandf.*, 563.

Nature of general letter of credit.

§ 1577. A general letter of credit gives any person to whom it may be shown, authority to comply with its request, and by his so doing it becomes, as to him, of the same effect as if addressed to him by name.

Extent of general letter of credit.

§ 1578. Several persons may successively give credit upon a general letter.

Union Bank *v.* Coster, 3 *N. Y.*, 203; aff'g S. C., 1 *Sandf.*, 563.

A letter of credit may be a continuing guaranty.

§ 1579. If the parties to a letter of credit appear by its terms to contemplate a course of future dealing between the parties, it is not exhausted by giving a credit, even to the amount limited by the letter, which is subsequently reduced or satisfied by payments made by the debtor; but is to be deemed a continuing guaranty.

Gates *v.* McKee, 13 *N. Y.*, 232; and compare Fellows *v.* Prentiss, 3 *Denio*, 512.

§ 1580. The writer of a letter of credit is liable for credit given upon it without notice to him, unless its terms express or imply the necessity of giving notice.

When notice to the writer necessary.

Whitney *v.* Groot, 24 *Wend.*, 82; Union Bank *v.* Coster, 3 *N. Y.*, 203; aff'g S. C., 1 *Sandf.*, 563; Douglass *v.* Howland, 24 *Wend.*, 35; Smith *v.* Dann, 6 *Hill*, 543.

§ 1581. If a letter of credit prescribes the persons by whom, or the mode in which, the credit is to be given, or the term of credit, or limits the amount thereof, the writer is not bound except for transactions which, in these respects, conform strictly to the terms of the letter.

The credit given must agree with the terms of the letter.

Birckhead *v.* Brown, 5 *Hill*, 634, affirmed, 2 *Denio*, 375.

No other person than the one to whom a special letter of credit is addressed, can, by acting upon it, create any obligation against the writer (Birckhead *v.* Brown, 5 *Hill*, 634; affirmed, 2 *Denio*, 375; Robbins *v.* Bingham, 4 *Johns.*, 476; Walsh *v.* Bailie, 10 *id.*, 180). If a special letter is addressed to several jointly, the credit must be given by all, or the writer is not liable (Penoyer *v.* Watson, 16 *Johns.*, 100). The person to whom a special letter is addressed cannot render the writer liable upon it by procuring strangers to give credit to the holder of it (Robbins *v.* Bingham, 4 *Johns.*, 476; Walsh *v.* Bailie, 10 *id.*, 180). A guaranty for six months' credit does not cover a four months' credit (Leeds *v.* Dunn, 10 *N. Y.*, 475).

TITLE XIV.

LIEN.

Although the arrangement of this subject is novel, the commissioners believe that its propriety and advantages will be perceived at a glance. Mortgages are liens, and, under the provisions of this Code, nothing more. They are subject therefore to all the general rules of liens.

CHAPTER I.

LIENS IN GENERAL.

ARTICLE I.

DEFINITION OF LIENS.

Lien, what. § 1582. A lien is a charge imposed upon specific property, by which it is made security for the performance of an act.

A lien is commonly defined as a right to retain possession of a specific thing, until some charge attached to it is satisfied (*Story Eq. Jur.*, § 506; 3 *Pars. Cont.*, *5th ed.*, 234). This definition is a very narrow one, and applicable only to common law liens, exclusive of mortgages, bottomry and respondentia bonds, &c.

In equity, possession was not essential. There might be an equitable lien upon a fund or subject in the hands of another, which could be maintained and enforced without the lienor's having possession, if the identity of the subject could be distinctly traced (Grinnell *v.* Suydam, 3 *Sandf.*, 132). The commissioners wish to preserve, under one name, both the common law and the equitable liens, and have sought to bring under one head all the general principles which affect liens by possession or mortgage.

Liens, general or special.

§ 1583. Liens are either general or special.

General lien, what.

§ 1584. A general lien is one which the holder thereof is entitled to enforce as a security for the performance of all the obligations, or all of a particular class of obligations, which exist in his favor against the owner of the property.

See McFarland *v.* Wheeler, 26 *Wend.*, 467; Houghton *v.* Matthews, 3 *Bos. & P.*, 485.

Special lien, what.

§ 1585. A special lien is one which the holder thereof can enforce only as security for the performance of a particular act or obligation,[1] and of such obligations as may be incidental thereto.[2]

[1] McFarland *v.* Wheeler, 26 *Wend.*, 467.

[2] Where the holder of a special lien is compelled to satisfy a prior lien for his own protection, he may enforce payment of the amount so paid by him, as a part of the claim for which his own lien exists (Robinson *v.* Ryan, 25 *N. Y.*, 320; Bates *v.* Johnson, *H. R. V. Johns.*, 304.)

Contracts subject to provisions of this chapter.

§ 1586. Contracts of mortgage, pledge, bottomry or respondentia, are subject to all the provisions of this chapter.

ARTICLE II.

CREATION OF LIENS.

Lien, how created.

§ 1587. A lien is created:

1. By contract of the parties; or,

2. By operation of law.

No lien for claim not due.

§ 1588. No lien arises by mere operation of law until the time at which the act to be secured thereby ought to be performed.

Foster *v.* Colby, 3 *H. & N.*, 705, 718.

Lien on future interest.

§ 1589. An agreement may be made to create a lien upon property not yet acquired by the party agreeing to give the lien, or not yet in existence. In such case the lien agreed for attaches from the time when the party agreeing to give it acquires an interest in the thing, to the extent of such interest.

Seymour *v.* Canandaigua & Niagara Falls R. R. Co., 25 *Barb.*, 284: but compare Conderman *v.* Smith, 41 *Barb.*, 404.

Lien may be created by contract.

§ 1590. A lien may be created by contract, to take immediate effect, as security for the performance of obligations not then in existence.

Robinson *v.* Williams, 22 *N. Y.*, 380; Murray *v.* Barney, 34 *Barb.*, 336; Truscott *v.* King, 6 *N. Y.*, 147; see Fassett *v.* Smith, 23 *N. Y.*, 252.

ARTICLE III.

EFFECT OF LIENS.

§ 1591. Notwithstanding an agreement to the contrary, a lien or a contract for a lien transfers no title to the property subject to the lien.

Lien, or contract for lien transfers no title.

This provision is in accordance with the law of this state in respect to mortgages of real property (Kortright *v.* Cady, 21 *N. Y.*, 343, 364; Stoddard *v.* Hart, 23 *id.*, 560; Power *v.* Lester, *id.*, 531; Packer *v.* Roch. & Syr. R. R. Co., 17 *id.*, 295; Runyan *v.* Mersereau, 11 *Johns.*, 534). In respect to mortgages of personal property, it is new. By the present law such a mortgage, in its ordinary form of a grant upon condition, transfers the title to the mortgagee (see Bank of Rochester *v.* Jones, 4 *N. Y.*, 507; Butler *v.* Miller, 1 *N. Y.*, 496; Hitchcock *v.* Northwestern Ins. Co., 26 *id.*, 68; Southworth *v.* Isham, 3 *Sandf.*, 448; Shuart *v.* Taylor, 7 *How. Pr.*, 251; Fox *v.* Burns, 12 *Barb.*, 677). It appears to the commissioners desirable to establish a uniform rule upon this subject, and to make all mortgages mere liens upon property. The propriety of the rule, in respect to other liens, will hardly be questioned.

§ 1592. All contracts for the forfeiture of property subject to a lien, in satisfaction of the obligation secured thereby, and all contracts in restraint of the right of redemption from a lien, are void,[1] except in the case specified in section 945.[2]

Certain contracts void.

[1] This is a well settled rule in relation to a mortgage (see Clark *v.* Henry, 2 *Cow.*, 324; Holdridge *v.* Gillespie, 2 *Johns. Ch.*, 30; Remsen *v.* Hay, 2 *Edw.*, 535; Palmer *v.* Gurnsey, 7 *Wend.*, 248). The general maxim of jurisprudence, applicable to such cases is, "once a mortgage always a mortgage" (Compare Bell *v.* Mayor, &c., of New York, 10 *Paige*, 49, 56; Burns *v.* Nevins, 27 *Barb.*, 493, 503).

The rule also applies to a pledge (*Code Napoleon*, 2078; Lucketts *v.* Townsend, 3 *Texas*, 119). Stoher *v.* Cogswell, 25 *How. Pr.*, 267, is a strong case upon this rule.

This beneficent principle doubtless governs in all cases of liens, and the commissioners have felt no hesitation in giving it in this place as a universal rule. They have omitted the qualifying words of some of the decisions, which imply that an agreement in restraint of redemption may be made subsequently to the execution of a mortgage, inasmuch as such a qualification, if it is a correct statement of the law (which is at least extremely doubtful), is certainly not desirable. Of course a mortgagor may sell his property to the mortgagee, but the transaction must be a genuine sale, and not a forfeiture.

[2] The propriety of this exception will appear by reference to the section specified.

Creation of lien does not imply personal obligation.

§ 1593. The creation of a lien does not of itself imply that any person is bound to perform the act for which the lien is a security.

Culver *v.* Sisson, 3 *N. Y.*, 264; Salisbury *v.* Philips, 10 *Johns.*, 57; Hone *v.* Fisher, 2 *Barb. Ch.*, 569; Scott *v.* Field, 7 *Watts*, 360; Smith *v.* Stewart, 6 *Blackf.*, 162; Drummond *v.* Richards, 2 *Munf.*, 337; Suffield *v.* Baskervil, 2 *Mod.*, 36; Briscoe *v.* King, *Cro. Jac.*, 281.

But an acknowledgment of indebtedness, in any instrument except a mortgage of real property, is sufficient foundation for an action (see Elder *v.* Rouse, 15 *Wend.*, 218; Culver *v.* Sisson, 3 *N. Y.*, 264).

Extent of lien.

§ 1594. The existence of a lien upon property does not of itself entitle the person, in whose favor it exists, to a lien upon the same property for the performance of any other obligation than that which the lien originally secured.

This is the American rule, in regard both to a mortgage and a pledge (Jarvis *v.* Rogers, 15 *Mass.*, 389), and while the rule is said to be otherwise in England, in respect to liens upon personal property (*Story Eq. Jur.*, § 1034), though not as to mortgages of real property (*id.*), yet the principle of the text is the one which seems most accordant with justice. The civil law, however, applied the opposite rule to mortgages and pledges of every kind (*Code Napoleon*, 2082).

Existence of lien does not affect the right of creditor.

§ 1595. The existence of a lien, as security for the performance of an obligation, does not affect the right of the creditor to enforce the obligation without regard to the lien.

See on this point, as to a pledge, *Story on Bailm.*, § 315; Wheeler *v.* Newbould, 16 *N. Y.* 398; as to a mortgage, Elder *v.* Rouse, 15 *Wend.*, 218; Roosevelt *v.* Carpenter, 28 *Barb.*, 426.

Holder of lien not entitled to

§ 1596. One who holds property by virtue of a lien thereon, is not entitled to compensation from the owner thereof for any trouble or expense which he incurs respecting it, except to the same extent as a borrower, under sections 956 and 957. compensation.

Somes *v.* British Empire Shipping Co., 8 *H. of L. Cas.*, 338; *El. Bl. & E.*, 353.

ARTICLE IV.

PRIORITY OF LIENS.

Priority of liens.

§ 1597. Other things being equal, different liens upon the same property have priority according to the time of their creation, except in cases of bottomry and respondentia.

Barry *v.* Mutual Ins. Co., 2 *Johns. Ch.*, 608.

Priority of mortgage for price.

§ 1598. A mortgage given for the price of real property, at the time of its conveyance, has priority over all other liens created against the purchaser.

Modified from 1 *R. S.*, 749, § 5.

Order of resort to different funds.

§ 1599. Where one has a lien upon several things, and other persons have subordinate liens upon, or interests in, some but not all of the same things, the person having the prior lien, if he can do so without risk of loss to himself,[1] or of injustice to other persons,[2] must resort to the property in the following order, on the demand of any party interested:

First. To the things upon which he has an exclusive lien;

Second. To the things which are subject to the fewest subordinate liens;

Third. In like manner inversely to the number of subordinate liens upon the same thing; and,

Fourth. When several things are within one of the foregoing classes, and subject to the same number of liens, resort must be had:

1. To the things which have not been transferred since the prior lien was created;

2. To the things which have been so transferred without a valuable consideration; and,

3. To the things which have been so transferred for a valuable consideration.

See notes to § 1917.

ARTICLE V.

REDEMPTION FROM LIEN.

Right to redeem. § 1600. Every person, having an interest in property subject to a lien, has a right to redeem it from the lien,[1] at any time after the claim is due,[2] and before his right of redemption is foreclosed.[3]

[1] Not only the owner of the fee, but also a doweress (Wheeler *v.* Morris, 2 *Bosw.*, 524; see Kinnoul *v.* Money, 3 *Swanst.*, 202, *note*), and any person having an interest in the property (Downe *v.* Morris, 3 *Hare*, 394), may redeem.

[2] Kortright *v.* Cady, 21 *N. Y.*, 343.

[3] Brown *v.* Frost, 10 *Paige*, 243; North River Ins. Co. *v.* Snedeker, 10 *How. Pr.*, 310.

Rights of inferior lienor. § 1601. One who has a lien, inferior to another upon the same property, has a right:

1. To redeem the property in the same manner as its owner might, from the superior lien;[1] and,

2. To be subrogated to all the benefits of the superior lien, when necessary for the protection of his interests,[2] upon satisfying the claim secured thereby.

[1] Averill *v.* Taylor, 8 *N. Y.*, 44; Pardee *v.* Van Auken, 3 *Barb.*, 535; Burnet *v.* Denniston, 5 *Johns. Ch.*, 35: see Brainard *v.* Cooper, 10 *N. Y.*, 356; Van Buren *v.* Olmstead, 5 *Paige*, 9; Benedict *v.* Gilman, 4 *id.*, 58; McKinstry *v.* Mervin, 3 *Johns. Ch.*, 466; Smith *v.* Green, 1 *Collyer*, 555; Fell *v.* Brown, 2 *Bro. C. C.*, 278.

[2] Averill *v.* Taylor, 8 *N. Y.*, 44; see Robinson *v.* Ryan, 25 *N. Y.*, 320. Such subrogation is not allowed when unnecessary to the junior incumbrancer, especially if prejudical to other parties (Jenkins *v.* Continental Ins. Co., 12 *How. Pr.*, 66). But when necessary, it is allowed. Thus, a mortgagee may redeem from an assessment (Rapelye *v.* Prince, 4 *Hill*, 119; Brevoort *v.* Randolph, 7 *How. Pr.*, 398), or from a tax sale (Burr *v.* Veeder, 3 *Wend.*, 412; Kortright *v.*

Cady, 23 *Barb.*, 490; 5 *Abb. Pr.*, 358), or sale under execution (Silver Lake Bank *v.* North, 4 *Johns. Ch.*, 370), and add the amount so paid to his lien (Robinson *v.* Ryan, 25 *N. Y.*, 320).

§ 1602. Redemption from a lien is made by performing, or offering to perform, the act for the performance of which it is a security, and paying, or offering to pay, the damages, if any, to which the holder of the lien is entitled for delay.

Redemption from lien, how made.

Kortright *v.* Cady, 21 *N. Y.*, 343.

ARTICLE VI.

EXTINCTION OF LIENS.

§ 1603. A lien is to be deemed accessory to the act for the performance of which it is a security, whether any person is bound for such performance or not, and is extinguishable in like manner with any other accessory obligation.

Lien deemed accessory to the act whose performance it secures.

A mortgage may be made to secure payment of a sum of money, which no person assumes to pay. In such case an offer to pay the amount would of course extinguish the lien, and yet, strictly speaking, there is no principal *obligation*, since no one is bound. This section is designed to make the rules concerning accessory contracts applicable to all such liens.

A tender of the money due upon a mortgage, at any time before foreclosure, discharges the lien, although not made till after the day named in the bond for payment. It is not necessary, in order to sustain such tender, to show a continued readiness to pay, nor to bring the money into court. That is not requisite, where the tender is relied upon, not to discharge the debt, but only to defeat a particular remedy (Kortright *v.* Cady, 21 *N. Y.*, 343; reversing S. C., 23 *Barb.*, 490; 5 *Abb.*

Pr., 424; 12 *How. Pr.*, 424). But the changes in the law, proposed by the chapter on OFFER OF PERFORMANCE, make it unnecessary to prescribe any peculiar rule here.

Extinction by sale or conversion.

§ 1604. The sale of any property on which there is a lien, in satisfaction of the claim secured thereby, or, in case of personal property, its wrongful conversion by the person holding the lien, extinguishes the lien thereon.

Cortelyou *v.* Lansing, 2 *Cai. Cas.*, 200; Dykers *v.* Allen, 7 *Hill*, 497; Wilson *v.* Little, 2 *N. Y.*, 443; Lewis *v.* Graham, 4 *Abb. Pr.*, 106.

Lien, not extinguished by lapse of time under statute of limitations.

§ 1605. A lien is not extinguished by the mere lapse of the time within which, under the provisions of the CODE OF CIVIL PROCEDURE, an action can be brought upon the principal obligation.

So held as to a mortgage (Pratt *v.* Huggins, 29 *Barb.*, 277; see Waltermire *v.* Westover, 14 *N. Y.*, 16), and as to a pledge (Taunton *v.* Goforth, 6 *Dowl. & Ryl.*, 384; see *Story on Bailm.*, § 362).

Apportionment of lien.

§ 1606. The partial performance of an act secured by a lien does not extinguish the lien upon any part of the property subject thereto, even if it is divisible.

Code of La., 3130, 3131, 3138; *Code Napoleon*, 2083; see, to same effect, Boqut *v.* Coburn, 27 *Barb.*, 230.

When restoration extinguishes lien.

§ 1607. The voluntary[1] restoration of property to its owner, by the holder[2] of a lien thereon, dependent upon possession, extinguishes the lien,[3] as to such property,[4] unless otherwise agreed by the parties;[5] and extinguishes it, notwithstanding any such agreement, as to creditors[6] of the owner, and persons acquiring a title to the property, or a lien thereon, in good faith, and for a good consideration;[7] unless such restoration is made to the owner as a mere employee of the holder of the lien,[8] or for a merely transient purpose.[9]

[1] Of course a restoration obtained by fraud does not affect the lien (Bigelow *v.* Heaton, 6 *Hill*, 43; 4 *Denio*, 496), except as to intervening purchasers, &c., for *value*.

[2] A forcible taking from the lienor does not affect the lien (Baker *v.* Hoag, 7 *N. Y.*, 557).

[3] So held as to an ordinary lien (Bigelow *v.* Heaton, 4 *Denio*, 496; Perkins *v.* Boardman, 14 *Gray*, 481); and so as to a pledge (*Story Bailm.*, § 229).

[4] A lien upon several articles is not lost as to all of them by the surrender of one.

[5] That the parties may otherwise agree, see Bigelow *v.* Heaton, 4 *Denio*, 496.

[6] McFarland *v.* Wheeler, 26 *Wend.*, 467 (Ct. of Errors).

[7] When a lien is void as to general creditors, it is clear that it must be void against purchasers, even without a strictly valuable consideration.

[8] So held as to a pledge (Macomber *v.* Parker, 14 *Pick.*, 497; Reeves *v.* Capper, 5 *Bing. N. C.*, 136), and the rule is equally applicable to any other lien.

[9] So held as to a pledge (Hays *v.* Riddle, 1 *Sandf.*, 248; White *v.* Platt, 5 *Denio*, 269; Roberts *v.* Wyatt, 2 *Taunt.*, 268). Compare, however, McFarland *v.* Wheeler, 26 *Wend.*, 467, which is in principle applicable to all classes of liens dependent upon possession.

CHAPTER II.

MORTGAGE.

ARTICLE I.

MORTGAGES IN GENERAL.

Mortgage, what.

§ 1608. Mortgage is a contract, by which specific property is hypothecated for the performance of an act, without the necessity of a change of possession.

This definition is new. It is designed to make a clear distinction between a pledge and a mortgage, and at the same time to avoid the idea of a mortgage being in any sense a transfer. "Hypothecation" is the proper word for this purpose, as it has a well recognized meaning in the civil and admiralty law, corresponding precisely to the design of the Code (see Stainbank *v.* Sheppard, 13 *C. B.*, 441).

Under the present law, three classes of cases are to be considered. 1. Where the debtor retains the general title to the property and gives possession only to the creditor. This is a pledge. 2. Where the debtor retains the possession and use, giving the creditor only some right to be satisfied out of the property. This is a mortgage. The distinction is not that one relates to personal property and the other to real, but that one involves change of possession, while the other relates to, or affects the change of title (See Cortelyou *v.* Lansing, 2 *Cai. Cas.*, 199; Barrow *v.* Paxton, 5 *Johns.*, 658; McLean *v.* Walker, 10 *id.*, 471; Brownell *v.* Hawkins, 4 *Barb.*, 491; Bank of Rochester *v.* Jones, 4 *N. Y.*, 497, and 4 *Denio*, 489; Stevens *v.* Marsh, 4 *Denio*, 227; Power *v.* Lester, 23 *N. Y.*, 527, 531). 3. A class of cases presenting greater difficulty arises where the property is of a kind not capable of actual manual delivery, unaccompanied by the transfer of some muniments of title, as in the case of shares of stock in an incorporated company. Here a pledge may be created by a written transfer, or authority to require a transfer on the books of the company; and the transaction may be a pledge and not a mortgage, notwithstanding that the legal title passes to the pledgee. Thus, where there was a transfer of stock, absolute in its terms, but a note for borrowed money, given by the plaintiff to the defendant at the time, stated that the stock was "deposited as collateral security," it was held, that the transaction was a pledge and not a mortgage (Wilson *v.* Little, 2 *N. Y.*, 443; affirming S. C., 1 *Sandf.*, 351; Vaupell *v.* Woodward, 2 *Sandf. Ch.*, 143; compare Huntington *v.* Mather, 2 *Barb.*, 538; S. C., 6 *N. Y. Leg. Obs.*, 206; Hasbrouck *v.* Vandervoort, 4 *Sandf.*, 74; McLean *v.* Walker, 10 *Johns.*, 471; Garlick *v.* James, 12 *id.*, 146; White *v.* Platt, 5 *Den.*, 269; Tompkins *v.* Tysen, 16 *Barb.*, 456; Wheeler *v.* Newbould, 16 *N. Y.*, 392; Lewis *v.* Graham, 4 *Abb. Pr.*, 106; Lewis *v.* Varnum, 12 *Abb. Pr.*, 305).

§ 1609. The lien of a mortgage is special, unless otherwise expressly agreed, and is independent of possession. Lien of a mortgage, when special.

§ 1610. Every transfer of an interest in property, made only as a security for the performance of another act, is to be deemed a mortgage,[1] except when, in the case of personal property, it is accompanied by an actual change of possession, in which case it is to be deemed a pledge.[2] Transfer of interest, when deemed a mortgage.

[1] So it is held with respect to real property (Chase *v.* Peck, 21 *N. Y.*, 581; Clark *v.* Henry, 2 *Cow.*, 324; aff'g S. C., 7 *Johns. Ch.*, 40; Elliott *v.* Pell, 1 *Paige*, 263; Stewart *v.* Hutchins, 13 *Wend.*, 485; aff'd, 6 *Hill*, 143; see Lawrence *v.* Farmers' Trust Co., 13 *N. Y.*, 200, 642).

[2] It is intended by this clause, which in some respects involves a material alteration of the law, to relieve chattel mortgages, accompanied with a genuine change of possession, from the necessity of filing, and to prevent the frauds against which the statute requiring the filing of mortgages was aimed, by subjecting such mortgages to the law of pledge, by which it is clear that they ought to be governed.

§ 1611. Contracts of bottomry or respondentia, although in the nature of mortgages, are not affected by any of the provisions of this chapter. Provisions of this chapter do not affect bottomry or respondentia.

Bottomry and respondentia are simply mortgages of a peculiar character, governed by maritime law. A definition of mortgages, which should in a single section exclude these contracts, would be extremely cumbrous and unscientific in its form.

§ 1612. The fact that a transfer was made subject to defeasance on a condition, may, for the purpose of showing such transfer to be a mortgage, be proved, except as against a subsequent purchaser or incumbrancer, for value and without notice, though the fact does not appear by the terms of the instrument. Transfer made subject to defeasance may be proved.

See Clark *v.* Henry, 2 *Cow.*, 324; affirming Henry *v.* Davis, 7 *Johns. Ch.*, 40; James *v.* Johnson, 6 *Johns. Ch.*, 417; Jackson *v.* Green, 4 *Johns.*, 186; Peterson *v.* Clarke, 15 *Johns.*, 205; Brown *v.* Dean, 3 *Wend.*,

208; Palmer *v.* Gurnsey, 7 *Wend.*, 248; Parsons *v.* Mumford, 3 *Barb. Ch.*, 152; Brown *v.* Dewey, 1 *Sandf. Ch.*, 56; Barton *v.* May, 3 *id.*, 450; Hall *v.* Van Cleve, 11 *N. Y. Leg. Obs.*, 281; Slee *v.* Manhattan Co., 1 *Paige*, 48; Whittick *v.* Kane, *id.*, 202; Van Buren *v.* Olmstead, 5 *id.*, 9; Lane *v.* Shears, 1 *Wend.*, 433; Grimstone *v.* Carter, 3 *Paige*, 421; White *v.* Moore, 1 *id.*, 551; Williams *v.* Thorn, 11 *id.*, 459; Despard *v.* Walbridge, 15 *N. Y.*, 374; Tyler *v.* Strang, 21 *Barb.*, 198; Hodges *v.* Tennessee Marine & Fire Ins. Co., 8 *N. Y.*, 418; Sturtevant *v.* Sturtevant, 20 *N. Y.*, 39. Proof of a parol agreement for a defeasance, was formerly admitted only in courts of equity, but the rule is held to be general under the CODE OF CIVIL PROCEDURE.

See also, in connection with this topic the case of Freeman *v.* Auld, 25 *How. Pr.*, 327.

What interests may be mortgaged.

§ 1613. Any interest in property, which is capable of being transferred, may be mortgaged.

Story Eq. Jur., § 1021; Wilson *v.* Wilson, 32 *Barb.*, 328. There may be a mortgage of personal property not yet in being, if it is the anticipated product of property owned by the mortgagor (as where he mortgages all the produce of his farm during a given season), taking effect upon the property as soon as it comes into existence (Conderman *v.* Smith, 41 *Barb.*, 404). But the mere expectancy of an heir apparent cannot be mortgaged (Carlton *v.* Leighton, 3 *Meriv.*, 667). See sections 460 & 461, for a definition of what may be transferred.

Property adversely held may be mortgaged.

§ 1614. A mortgage may be created upon property held adversely to the mortgagor.

1 *R. S.*, 739, § 148.

Power of sale.

§ 1615. A power of sale may be conferred by a mortgage upon the mortgagee or any other person, to be exercised after a breach of the obligation for which the mortgage is a security.

Wilson *v.* Troup, 7 *Johns. Ch.*, 25.

Power of sale, how executed.

§ 1616. A power of sale under a mortgage is a trust, and can be executed only in the manner prescribed by the CODE OF CIVIL PROCEDURE.

The reference is to the Code as reported complete. In Olcott *v.* Tioga R. R. Co., 40 *Barb.*, 179, it was held that a mortgagee of chattels may purchase under a power of sale to himself. Two judges held that the power was not a trust, and the other that although it was a trust, yet the circumstances justified a purchase by the mortgagee. The decision was affirmed by the Court of Appeals, but no opinion has yet been reported. The decision of the Supreme Court was expressly put upon the ground that a chattel mortgage transferred the title absolutely to the mortgagee, upon breach of the condition, and that the power of sale was executed by him for his own benefit. This feature of chattel mortgages is changed by this Code, and they are placed upon the same footing with mortgages of real property, in which a power of sale is unquestionably a power in trust (Jencks *v.* Alexander, 11 *Paige*, 619, 624).

§ 1617. A mortgage is a lien upon everything that would pass by a grant of the property, and upon nothing more. On what a lien.

For applications of this principle in respect to particular things claimed as incident to the mortgaged premises, see the following cases:

As to *fixtures*, King *v.* Wilcomb, 7 *Barb.*, 263; Robinson *v.* Preswick, 3 *Edw.*, 246; Day *v.* Perkins, 2 *Sandf.*, 359; Buckley *v.* Buckley, 11 *Barb.*, 43; Snedeker *v.* Warring, 12 *N. Y.*, 170; Fryatt *v.* Sullivan Co., 5 *Hill*, 116; aff'd, 7 *id.*, 529; Breese *v.* Bange, 2 *E. D. Smith*, 474; Cresson *v.* Stout, 17 *Johns.*, 116; Gardner *v.* Finley, 19 *Barb.*, 317; Ford *v.* Cobb, 20 *N. Y.*, 344; Laflin *v.* Griffiths, 35 *Barb.*, 58.

As to *crops*, Shuart *v.* Taylor, 7 *How. Pr.*, 251; Shepard *v.* Philbrick, 2 *Den.*, 174; Gillett *v.* Balcom, 6 *Barb.*, 370; Aldrich *v.* Reynolds, 1 *Barb. Ch.*, 613; Lane *v.* King, 8 *Wend.*, 584.

As to *growing timber*, Ensign *v.* Colburn, 11 *Paige*, 503; Peterson *v.* Clark, 15 *Johns.*, 205; Wood *v.* Lester, 29 *Barb.*, 145.

As to *rolling stock* on railroads, Farmers' Loan and Trust Co. *v.* Hendrickson, 25 *Barb.*, 484; Stevens *v.* Buffalo & N. Y. City R. R. Co., 31 *Barb.*, 590; Murdock *v.* Gifford, 18 *N. Y.*, 28; Parish *v.* Wheeler, 22 *N. Y.*, 473; Beardsley *v.* Ontario Bank, 31 *Barb.*, 619; Seymour *v.* Canandaigua & Niagara Falls R. R. Co., 25 *Barb.*, 284.

As to after-acquired interest, Watson *v.* Campbell, 28 *Barb.*, 421; Seymour *v.* Canandaigua & Niagara Falls Railway Co., 25 *Barb.*, 284; 14 *How. Pr.*, 531; Lawrence *v.* Delano, 3 *Sandf.*, 333; Holden *v.* Sackett, 12 *Abb. Pr.*, 473.

§ 1618. A mortgage is a lien upon the property mortgaged, in the hands of every one claiming under Against whom a mortgage is a lien.

the mortgagor subsequently to its execution, except purchasers or incumbrancers in good faith, without notice and for value, and except as otherwise provided by article III of this chapter.

The fact that one offering to assign a bond and mortgage is unable to produce the instruments themselves, is held, in Kellogg *v.* Smith, 26 *N. Y.*, 18, to be enough to put the purchaser upon inquiry as to any defect in the assignor's title, and to affect him with notice of a prior assignment, notwithstanding that a false reason is given for the non-production (Compare Williams *v.* Walker, 2 *Sandf. Ch.*, 325, and 3 *N. Y. Leg. Obs.*, 204).

Mortgage of thing held adversely.

§ 1619. A mortgage of property held adversely to the mortgagor takes effect from the time at which he, or one claiming under him, obtains possession of the property; but has precedence over every lien upon the mortgagor's interest in the property, created subsequently to the recording of the mortgage.

1 *R. S.*, 739, § 148.

Mortgage does not entitle mortgagee to possession.

§ 1620. A mortgage does not entitle the mortgagee to the possession of the property,[1] but after the execution of the mortgage the mortgagor may agree to such change of possession upon a new consideration.[2]

[1] This is in accordance with the present law, in regard to real property (see 2 *R. S.*, 312, § 57). In respect to chattel mortgages, the law is at present to the contrary (Rich *v.* Milks, 20 *Barb.*, 616; Shuart *v.* Taylor, 7 *How. Pr.*, 251; Stewart *v.* Hanson, 35 *Me.*, 506; Holmes *v.* Sprowl, 31 *Me.*, 73; Libby *v.* Cushman, 29 *Me.*, 429. See Van Hassell *v.* Borden, 1 *Hilton*, 128). It appears to the commissioners desirable that the same rules should prevail in respect to both kinds of property.

[2] By the present law, no consideration is necessary to sustain such an agreement (Waring *v.* Smyth, 2 *Barb. Ch.*, 135).

Foreclosure

§ 1621. A mortgagee may foreclose the right of redemption of the mortgagor, in the manner prescribed by the CODE OF CIVIL PROCEDURE.

The reference is to the Code as reported complete.

§ 1622. No person whose interest is subject to the lien of a mortgage may do any act which will substantially impair the mortgagee's security. Waste.

Van Pelt *v.* McGraw, 4 *N. Y.*, 111; Gardner *v.* Heartt, 3 *Denio*, 232; see Manning *v.* Monaghan, 23 *N. Y.*, 539, 548.

ARTICLE II.

MORTGAGE OF REAL PROPERTY.

§ 1623. A mortgage of real property can be created, renewed or extended, only by writing, under seal, with the formalities required in the case of a grant of real property. Mortgage, how created

Stoddard *v.* Hart, 23 *N. Y.*, 556.

This section does not recognize a mere deposit of title deeds, as constituting a mortgage. In England the rule is well established and familiar that an advance of money upon a deposit of title deeds, operates as an equitable mortgage. Strictly, it is evidence of an agreement to give a mortgage, which is treated in a court of equity as a mortgage, and enforced as such. In this state there has never been any such general practice of depositing title deeds as renders it desirable to recognize the fact of deposit as one method of mortgaging the land; indeed, it is difficult to see how, under our system of recording title deeds and treating the record as evidence of the title, such a practice can obtain, to any extent. If it could, it ought not to be encouraged; since it contravenes the policy of the statute of frauds, and of the recording acts. For these reasons no mention is made in the text of a deposit of deeds as a method of making a mortgage. Cases in which such deposit is made under circumstances which evince an agreement to give a mortgage, or create a lien upon the deed, are left to the application of the general rules relative to the specific performance of contracts, and to liens.

As to the present law in this state, upon this question, see Rockwell *v.* Hobby, 2 *Sandf. Ch.*, 9; Stoddard *v.* Hart, 23 *N. Y.*, 561; Mandeville *v.* Welsh, 5 *Wheat.*, 277. In support of the views here expressed, see *Ex parte* Whitbread, 19 *Ves.*, 209.

Mortgage not a personal obligation.

§ 1624. A mortgage of real property does not bind the mortgagor personally to perform the act for the performance of which it is a security, unless there is an express covenant therein to that effect.

1 *R. S.*, 738, § 139; Hone *v.* Fisher, 2 *Barb. Ch. R.*, 569. As to what amounts to such a covenant, see Elder *v.* Rouse, 15 *Wend.*, 218.

Mortgages on lands inherited or devised, by whom to be paid.

§ 1625. When real property, subject to a mortgage, passes by succession or will, the successor or devisee must satisfy the mortgage out of his own property, without resorting to the executor or administrator of the mortgagor, unless there is an express direction in the will of the mortgagor, that the mortgage shall be otherwise paid.

1 *R. S.*, 749, § 4.

Mortgage, how recorded.

§ 1626. Mortgages of real property may be recorded in like manner with grants thereof, except that they must be recorded in books kept for mortgages exclusively.

See section 513.

Effect of record.

§ 1627. The record of a mortgage, duly made, operates as notice to all subsequent purchasers and incumbrancers.

1 *R. S.*, 756, § 1; 761, § 33.

The record does not operate as notice to a prior incumbrancer, even with respect to his future acts (Howard Ins. Co. *v.* Halsey, 8 *N. Y.*, 271; Stuyvesant *v.* Hall, 2 *Barb. Ch.*, 151; 1 *Sandf. Ch.*, 419).

What must be recorded as a mortgage.

§ 1628. Every grant of real property, or of any estate therein, which appears, by any other writing, to be intended as a mortgage within the meaning of chapter I of this Title, must be recorded as a mortgage; and if such grant and other writing explanatory of its true character are not recorded together, at the same time and place, the grantee can derive no benefit from such record.

1 *R. S.*, 756, § 3.

§ 1629. An assignment of a mortgage may be recorded in like manner with a mortgage, but in a separate book, and such record operates as notice to all persons subsequently deriving title to the mortgage from the assignor. Recording assignment.

Vanderkemp *v.* Shelton, 11 *Paige*, 37. This section practically covers the ground of 1 *R. S.*, 763, § 41. See Kellogg *v.* Smith, 26 *N. Y.*, 18.

§ 1630. A recorded mortgage must be discharged upon the record, by the officer having custody thereof, on the presentation to him of a certificate signed by the mortgagee, his personal representatives or assigns, acknowledged, or proved and certified, as prescribed by the chapter on RECORDING TRANSFERS, stating that the mortgage has been paid, or otherwise satisfied and discharged. Discharge of records, &c., of mortgage.

1 *R. S.*, 761, § 28.

§ 1631. A certificate of the discharge of a mortgage, and the proof or acknowledgment thereof, must be recorded at length; and a reference made in the record, to the book and page where the mortgage is recorded, and in the minute of the discharge made upon the record of the mortgage, to the book and page where the discharge is recorded. Certificate, how to be recorded.

1 *R. S.*,, 761, § 29; modified by requiring a reference to the record of the mortgage.

ARTICLE III.

MORTGAGE OF PERSONAL PROPERTY.

To be in writing.

§ 1632. A mortgage of personal property can be created, renewed, or extended, only by a writing subscribed by the mortgagor.

This provision is new. By the present law, a mortgage may be oral (Bank of Rochester *v.* Jones, 4 *N. Y.*, 497; Flory *v.* Denny, 7 *Exch.*, 581). But unless it is in writing, and filed, it is void against creditors and purchasers (*Laws* 1833, *ch.* 279); and as it is proposed by this Code to treat every mortgage of personal property, accompanied by a change of possession, as a pledge, there are obvious reasons for requiring mortgages, unaccompanied with such a change, to be in writing.

Foreclosure.

§ 1633. A mortgagee of personal property, when the debt for which it is given is due, may foreclose the mortgagor's right of redemption by a sale of the property, made in the manner and upon the notice prescribed by the Title on PLEDGE, or by proceedings under the CODE OF CIVIL PROCEDURE.

See Patchin *v.* Pierce, 12 *Wend.*, 63; Hart *v.* Ten Eyck, 2 *Johns. Ch.*, 100, and cases cited. The reference is to the Code reported complete. Until sale or proceedings to foreclose, the mortgagor may redeem, although the law day has passed; as in case of a mortgage of land (Hinman *v.* Judson, 13 *Barb.*, 629; Pratt *v.* Stiles, 17 *How. Pr.*, 211; 9 *Abb. Pr.*, 150). A sale of the property, after forfeiture, by the mortgagee, with the consent of the mortgagor, is equivalent to a formal foreclosure (Talman *v.* Smith, 39 *Barb.*, 390).

Mortgage must be filed.

§ 1634. A mortgage of personal property is void as against creditors of the mortgagor, and subsequent purchasers and incumbrancers of the property in good faith[1] and for value,[2] unless it is filed as hereafter prescribed.

[1] *Laws* 1833, *ch.* 279; 3 *R. S.* (*5th ed.*), 222; Gregory *v.* Thomas, 20 *Wend.*, 17; Meech *v.* Patchin, 14 *N. Y.*, 71.

[2] Van Heusen *v.* Radcliff, 17 *N. Y.*, 580; Thompson *v.* Van Vechten, 27 *id.*, 568, 581.

§ 1635. The filing of a mortgage of personal property, in conformity to the provisions of this article, operates as notice thereof to all subsequent purchasers and incumbrancers. Effect of filing.

§ 1636. Except in the cases mentioned in section 1641, a mortgage of personal property is duly filed by depositing the original, or a copy: How filed.

1. In the office of the county register of deeds, if there is one, and his office is situated in the town wherein the mortgagor resides at the time of executing the mortgage, or, if he does not reside in the state, the town wherein the property mortgaged is at such time situated;

2. If there is no register's office so situated, then in the county clerk's office, if it is so situated; or,

3. If neither office is so situated, then in the office of the clerk of such town.

3 *R. S.* (*5th ed.*), 223; *Laws* 1833, *ch.* 279; as modified by various laws establishing registers' offices in different counties, as, for example, *Laws* 1852, p. 77.

§ 1637. A single mortgage of personal property, embracing several things of such character or so situated that, by the provisions of this article, separate mortgages upon them would be required to be filed in different places, is only valid in respect to the things as to which it is duly filed. Mortgage valid only in respect to things as to which it is filed.

Thus a mortgage upon a canal boat and household furniture if filed in the auditor's office only, will be good as to the boat, but void as to the furniture. A mortgage by a non-resident upon property in different counties, must be filed in each of those counties.

§ 1638. A mortgage of personal property ceases to be valid, as against creditors of the mortgagor, and subsequent purchasers or incumbrancers in good faith, after the expiration of one year from the filing thereof, unless, within thirty days next preceding the expiration of such term, a copy of the mortgage, and a statement of the amount of existing debt for which the mortgagee claims a lien, subscribed by Renewal of filing.

him, are filed anew in the office of the clerk or register, in the town in which the mortgagor then resides, or, if he does not then reside in the state, in the same office in which the mortgage was originally filed,[1] or, in the case of mortgages upon canal boats, in the office of the auditor of the canal department.[2] And, in like manner, the mortgage and statement of debt must be refiled from year to year, or it ceases to be valid,[3] as against the parties above mentioned.

[1] *Laws* 1833, *ch.* 279; 3 *R. S.* (*5th ed.*), 223; slightly modified, so as to make the section more explicit. As to what is a sufficient refiling, see Beers *v.* Waterbury, 3 *Bosw.*, 396. As to when it is necessary, Wiles *v.* Clapp, 41 *Barb.*, 645.

[2] *Laws* of 1864, *ch.* 412, § 3.

[3] Nitchie *v.* Townsend, 2 *Sandf.*, 299.

Duty of officers.

§ 1639. The officers mentioned in the last section must receive and file all such instruments as are offered to them under this article, and must keep the same in their offices for the inspection of the public.

3 *R. S.* (*5th ed.*), 223; *Laws* 1833, *ch.* 279.

Id.

§ 1640. Every officer with whom an instrument is filed, pursuant to this chapter, must indorse a number upon the same in regular order, together with the time of receiving the same, and must enter the name of every party thereto in a book kept for the purpose, alphabetically, placing mortgagors and mortgagees under a separate head, and stating in separate columns, opposite each name, the number indorsed on the instrument, the date thereof and of the filing, the amount secured thereby, and the time at which it is due.

Laws 1849, *ch.* 69.

Where mortgages upon canal vessels must be filed.

§ 1641. A mortgage of a canal boat, steam tug, scow, or other craft, navigating the canals of this state, must be filed in the office of the auditor of the canal department.

Laws of 1864, *ch.* 412, § 1.

In regard to mortgages of canal boats it was enacted by *Laws of* 1858, *ch.* 247, as follows: "Any person having any lien or incumbrance on any canal boat, steam tug, scow or other craft navigating the canals of this state, by a chattel mortgage duly filed, may make a statement in writing setting forth the nature of his claim, the time when the same arose, the manner in which it originated, and the amount of such lien or incumbrance; and may annex thereto an affidavit made by himself or his agent or attorney, that the said statement is correct, and the claim just and true, and file the same in the office of the auditor. It shall be the duty of the said auditor, on the receipt of the said statement, to file the same in his office, and to enter the substance in a book to be provided for that purpose, and the amount if any, claimed to be due, which book shall always during office hours be open for the inspection of all persons desiring to examine the same. All claims and liens by chattel mortgage, a statement of which shall be filed as herein provided, shall from the time of such filing have preference and priority over all other claims and liens, in the same manner and to like extent of claims and liens arising on chattel mortgages filed and entered in towns where the mortgagor resides, but shall not have any priority over existing liens and claims."

This act has been disregarded by the commissioners, for the reason that its construction in respect to the legal effect attributable to filing in the auditor's office, is too uncertain and obscure to render it a reliable guide in the revision of the law (see Sweet *v.* Lawrence, 35 *Barb.*, 337), and because the act of 1864, from which the provisions in the text are taken, though professedly an amendment to that of 1858, in effect supersedes it by new and more distinct provisions, complete in themselves, without reference to the act amended.

Neither the act of 1858, nor that of 1864, contain provisions dispensing with filing in the office of the register of deeds, or county or town clerk. Obvious reasons, however, suggest that if filing in the auditor's office is required, filing elsewhere should be dispensed with. The commissioners have framed the sections in the text accordingly.

Duty of auditor upon filing

§ 1642. The auditor must cause every mortgage filed with him pursuant to the last section, upon receipt thereof, to be respectively numbered, the time of receiving the same to be indorsed thereon, and the substance thereof to be entered in a book provided for that purpose, entering alphabetically the names of all the parties to such instrument, with the number indorsed thereon opposite to each name; which entry shall be repeated in the index alphabetically under the name of every party thereto, also indexing the name of each boat mortgaged, with the number of the mortgage opposite to each.

Laws 1864, *ch.* 412, § 4.

Certain errors to be disregarded.

§ 1643. A mortgage is not to be deemed defectively filed, by reason of any errors in the copy filed, which do not tend to mislead a party interested to his prejudice.

This provision is new.

Negligence of officer.

§ 1644. The negligence of the officer with whom a mortgage is filed cannot prejudice the rights of the mortgagee.

Dodge *v.* Potter, 18 *Barb.*, 193; Bishop *v.* Cook, 13 *id.*, 126.

Copy, &c., when evidence.

§ 1645. A copy of any instrument required to be filed under this article, when certified by the officer with whom it is filed, or his deputy, is presumptive evidence of such filing, in the manner and at the time stated in the official indorsement on such instrument. The original indorsement is also evidence to the same extent only.

3 *R. S.*, (*5th ed.*), 223; *Laws* 1833, *ch.* 279; see also, *Laws of* 1864, *ch.* 412, § 6.

To what mortgages this article does not apply.

§ 1646. Sections 1634 to 1645 inclusive, do not apply to any mortgage of a ship or part of a ship, which is required by act of congress to be filed or recorded in any other manner.

By act of congress of July 29, 1850 (9 *U. S. Stat. at L.*, 440), it was provided "that no bill of sale, mortgage, hypothecation or conveyance of any vessel, or part of any vessel of the United States, shall be valid against any person (other than the grantor or mortgagor, his heirs and devisees, and persons having actual notice thereof), unless such bill of sale, mortgage, hypothecation or conveyance be recorded in the office of the collector of the customs where such vessel is registered or enrolled."

It is held at present, that notwithstanding this statute, the state law requiring filing, applies to mortgages of vessels. The act of congress prescribes, as to all vessels of the United States, a rule as obligatory upon the state tribunals as upon those of the United States; but it does not supersede or abolish statutory regulations of a state upon the same subject, which are not inconsistent with it. Hence, if a mortgage of a vessel is not registered at the custom house as required by the act, it will be invalid as to purchasers or mortgagees without notice, although every state law may have been complied with; and on the other hand, although it is registered at the custom house, yet if a state statutory requisition has been neglected, the mortgage will give place to a subsequent transfer or mortgage also registered, and in respect to which the state law has been fulfilled (Thompson *v.* Van Vechten, 5 *Abb. Pr.*, 458), and is void against creditors (Ætna Ins. Co. *v.* Aldrich, 26 *N. Y.*, 82).

This reasoning is doubtless correct. The two statutes are entirely consistent and compatible; and while both remain in force, both must be complied with. But nc good reason is perceived why a mortgage, which by the controlling law of the United States must be registered at the custom house, should also be required by the state to be filed in a state office. Sufficient notice of the lien is given, and all the important objects of recording are secured by the registry required by the national law; and the class of mortgages embraced by that law may be safely left, in the opinion of the commissioners, to its exclusive operation. Only such vessels should be excepted from the state law as are embraced by the law of the United States.

It is to be observed that the power of Congress to regulate the subject has been doubted (see Ætna Ins. Co. *v.* Aldrich, 26 *N. Y.*, 82). If this doubt should be confirmed, this section should be omitted.

CHAPTER III.

PLEDGE.

Pledge, what.

§ 1647. Pledge is a deposit of personal property by way of security for the performance of another act.

Story on Bailm., § 286.

As to what constitutes a pledge in general, see Cortelyou *v.* Lansing, 2 *Cai. Cas.*, 200; Barrow *v.* Paxton, 5 *Johns.*, 258; McLean *v.* Walker, 10 *id.*, 471; Brownell *v.* Hawkins, 4 *Barb.*, 491; Hasbrouck *v.* Vandervoort, 4 *Sandf.*, 74; Bank of Rochester *v.* Jones, 4 *N. Y.*, 497; Stearns *v.* Marsh, 4 *Den.*, 229; Knapp *v.* Alvord, 10 *Paige*, 205. As to the distinction between pledge and mortgage with reference to things in action, see Garlick *v.* James, 12 *Johns.*, 146; White *v.* Platt, 5 *Den.*, 269; Wheeler *v.* Newbould, 16 *N. Y.*, 392; Atlantic Fire & Marine Ins. Co. *v.* Boies, 6 *Duer*, 583; Lewis *v.* Graham, 4 *Abb. Pr.*, 106; Wilson *v.* Little, 2 *N. Y.*, 443; Vaupell *v.* Woodward, 2 *Sandf. Ch.*, 143; Lewis *v.* Varnum, 12 *Abb. Pr.*, 305.

In Brass *v.* Worth, 40 *Barb.*, 648, the defendants were stock brokers, in the city of New York, and the plaintiff entered into a general arrangement with them that they should purchase such stock as he should direct, and pay for the same with their own money, and hold such stock for him, for resale from time to time as he should direct. For their advances and services they were to receive interest and a commission; and for their security against depreciation the plaintiff was to keep on deposit with them a margin of five per cent upon the par value of all purchases of stock made by them for him, which margin was constantly to be kept good. It was held that though the contract did not prescribe with certainty the rights and duties of the defendants in the event of the value of the deposited collaterals falling below the prescribed amount, the defendants were to be regarded as the pledgees of the plaintiff, both in respect to the stocks purchased, and to those deposited as security for moneys advanced; and the contract being silent, the rights and duties of the parties were governed by the law of pledge.

§ 1648. Every contract by which the possession of personal property is transferred, as a security only, is to be deemed a pledge.

When contract is to be deemed a pledge.

It is intended, by this section, to place every mortgage of personal property, accompanied by a change of possession, upon the same footing with a pledge. This is in accordance with the rule of the civil law, and will greatly simplify the law of this state in respect to pledges and mortgages (see *Story Eq. Jur.*, § 1005; *Code Napoleon*, 2071, 2117).

§ 1649. The lien of a pledge is dependent on possession, and no pledge is valid until the property pledged is delivered to the pledgee, or to a pledge-holder, as hereafter prescribed.

Delivery essential to validity of pledge.

Delivery is essential to a pledge (Brownell *v.* Hawkins, 4 *Barb.*, 491).

§ 1650. The increase of property pledged is pledged with the property.

Increase of thing.

§ 1651. One who has a lien upon property may pledge it to the extent of his lien.

Lienor may pledge property to extent of his lien.

This power is not fully recognized by our existing law; but it is established in England, and seems just.

§ 1652. One who has allowed another to assume the apparent ownership of property for the purpose of making any transfer of it, cannot set up his own title, to defeat a pledge of the property, made by the other, to a pledgee who received the property in good faith, and for value.

Real owner cannot defeat pledge of property transferred to apparent owner for purpose of pledge.

This section is an extension of our present rule allowing a pledge by an agent intrusted with indicia of title to be sustained in favor of one who lends upon it without notice of the true owner's title.

At common law,—prior, in England, to 4 *Geo.* 4, *c.* 83, 6 *id.*, *c.* 94, and 5 & 6 *Vict.*, *c.* 39, and in this state to *Laws of* 1830, *ch.* 179—a factor for sale had no power to pledge; not even to the extent of his lien, nor when the object of the pledge was to secure money raised for the use of his principal. The English statute of 6 *Geo.*, 4, *c.* 94 (known as the "factor's act"), provided that: "any person intrusted with, and in possession of any bill of lading, dock warrant, order for delivery of goods, &c., &c., shall be deemed the true owner of the goods described therein so far as to give validity to any contract, &c., made by such person for the sale or disposition of such goods, or any part thereof, or for the deposit or pledge thereof, or, &c., as security for any money or negotiable instrument advanced or given on the faith of such instrument."

Under this statute it was decided by the English House of Lords (in Hatfield *v.* Phillips, 14 *M. & W.*, 665; 12 *Cl. & Fin.*, 343; 10 *Jur.*, 180; aff'g S. C., 9 *M. & W.*, 647), that to render valid a disposal of goods by a person as intrusted with one of the instruments named in the statute, he must be actually intrusted with the particular instrument on the faith of which the consideration passes, by the owner of the goods; or must hold it under such circumstances that an actual intrusting may be inferred. Where a factor was intrusted with the bill of lading by the owner, and entered the goods in his own name at the custom house, and thus obtained a dock warrant, and pledged the dock warrant, it was held, that the pledgee was not entitled to hold the goods. The fact that the factor was enabled to obtain the dock warrant by means of having been intrusted with the bill of lading, was not enough. He must have been intrusted with the warrant by the owner.

The rule in this respect has since been enlarged by statute 5 & 6 *Vict.*, *c.* 39; which enacts that any agent intrusted with the possession of goods or of the documents of title to goods shall be deemed owner so far as to give validity to any contract by way of pledge, lien, &c., for any original or continuing advance—notwithstanding that the party making the advance may have had notice that the party receiving it was only an agent;—and that any bill of lading, &c., or other document used in the ordinary course of business as proof of the possession or control of goods, or authorizing the possessor of such document to transfer or receive goods thereby represented, shall be deemed a "document of title" within the act.

By our own factors' act (*Laws of* 1830, *ch.* 179, § 3), it is provided that every factor or other agent intrusted with a bill of lading, custom house permit, or warehouse-keeper's receipt; and every such factor or agent not having the documentary evidence of title, who shall be entitled to the possession of merchandise for the purpose of sale, or as security for advances, is to be deemed the true owner, so far as to give validity to his contract for the sale or disposal of such merchandise, for any money advanced or negotiable instrument, or other obligation in writing given upon the faith thereof. But a person who takes merchandise from a factor to secure an antecedent debt, acquires no better right than the factor had at the time.

The principle of this act is somewhat extended by *Laws of* 1858, *ch.* 326, § 6, which enacts that warehouse receipts given for any goods, wares, merchandise, grain, flour, produce, or other commodity, stored or deposited with any warehouseman, wharfinger, or other person, may be transferred by indorsement thereof; and any person to whom the same may be so transferred, shall be deemed and taken to be the owner of the goods, wares and merchandise therein specified, so far as to give validity to any pledge, lien or transfer made or created by such person or persons. This section was somewhat obscurely amended by *Laws of* 1859, *ch.* 353.

Under our act of 1830, it has been held that where a pledge, &c., by a factor, is sought to be sustained on the ground *that he was intrusted with the documentary evidence of title* mentioned, it must appear:

1. That the pledgee had no notice, from the language of the document relied on, or otherwise, that the factor was not the true owner.

2. That the document was transferred and delivered to such pledgee simultaneously with his advance, in such manner as to vest in him either the title or the exclusive right and means of obtaining possession.

3. That the document relied on is one of the three enumerated in the statute. A permit for landing goods on which duties have not been paid, to the end that they may be stored in bond, as authorized by acts of Congress, August 6, 1846, and March 28, 1854 (9 *U. S. Stat. at L.*, 53; 10 *id.*, 270), is not such a "custom house permit;" nor is the receipt of the keeper of a bonded warehouse on receiving goods for storage, given under the acts of Congress, such a "warehouse-keeper's receipt" as is embraced within the act.

4. That the document was "intrusted" to the factor by the owner of the goods; *i. e.*, it must have been delivered or transmitted to the factor by the owner, or have been received by the factor in the proper and ordinary mode of discharging his trust.

Unless these elements exist, the validity of the pledge must be determined by the common law.

On the other hand, where a pledge by a factor is sought to be sustained upon the ground *that he was intrusted with the possession of the goods*, it must appear:

1. That he had actual as distinguished from constructive possession. Goods stored in bonded warehouse before payment of duties, are not in possession of the factor within the meaning of the statute.

2. That the change of possession was made at the time of the advance which the pledge was intended to secure. See on this subject, Bonito *v.* Mosquera, 2 *Bosw.*, 401; Walther *v.* Wetmore, 1 *E. D. Smith*, 7; Covell *v.* Hill, 6 *N. Y.*, 374.

The effect of the act is that one who has such documentary evidence of the title to merchandise as gives him the exclusive control of the possession, is deemed the true owner of the property for certain purposes, if the true owner has intrusted him with such evidence for the purpose of disposing of the property. A factor so situated can sell or pledge the whole or a part of the property; or give a lien upon it for advances. If he misappropriates the property his principal must suffer; not the person who has dealt with the factor on the faith of the position in which the owner has placed him. Thus one who has made advances to a factor upon the faith of a warehouseman's receipt of imported goods, given to the factor in consequence of his being intrusted with an invoice of the goods, is protected, though the invoice showed that the goods belonged to the shipper. To bring a case within the act, it is not necessary that the true owner should have intrusted the factor with the identical evidence of title on the faith of which the factor procures the loan. Intrusting him with primary documents out of which others, in the usual course of trade, grow, is equivalent to intrusting him with the latter. Nor is it strictly necessary that the documentary evidence of title should be delivered at the very time when the loan is made. If good faith is shown, the loan may be made at one time, and the pledge created afterwards (Cartwright *v.* Wilmerding, 24 *N. Y.*, 531).

It will be observed that our present act is limited to disposition by a "factor or other agent." The Commissioners propose to extend it to all persons allowed to assume the apparent ownership. This will not, however, extend the rule to all cases of mere possession. Mere possession of goods is not evidence to the world of an unlimited authority to sell them; so as to preclude the owner from showing, as against a purchaser, that they were intrusted to him, not for sale, but for a different purpose — such as transportation or temporary custody (Cook *v.* Beal, 1 *Bosw.*, 497. Compare Zachrisson *v.* Ahman, 2 *Sandf.*, 68).

It is clear that one who takes from the factor or agent, with notice of the true owner's right, is not protected by the act (Stevens *v.* Wilson, 3 *Den.*, 472; aff'g S. C., 6 *Hill*, 512; Covell *v.* Hill, 6 *N. Y.*, 374; Wilson *v.* Nason, 4 *Bosw.*, 155). This principle is preserved by the provisions in the text.

§ 1653. Property may be pledged as security for the obligation of another person than the owner, and in so doing the owner has all the rights of a pledgor for himself, except as hereinafter stated. **Pledge lender, what.**

Code Napoleon, 2077.

§ 1654. A pledgor and pledgee may agree upon a third person with whom to deposit the property pledged; who, if he accepts the deposit, is called a pledgeholder. **Pledge holder, what.**

Code Napoleon, 2076.

§ 1655. One who pledges property as security for the obligation of another, cannot withdraw the property pledged otherwise than as a pledgor for himself might; and, if he receives from the debtor a consideration for the pledge, he cannot withdraw it without his consent. **When pledge lender may withdraw property pledged.**

§ 1656. A pledgeholder for reward cannot exonerate himself from his undertaking; and a gratuitous pledgeholder can do so only by giving reasonable notice to the pledgor and pledgee to appoint a new pledgeholder, and, in case of their failure to agree, by depositing the property pledged with some impartial person, who will then be entitled to a reasonable compensation for his care of the same. **Obligations of pledgeholder.**

§ 1657. A pledgeholder must enforce all the rights of the pledgee, unless authorized by him to waive them. **Pledgeholder must enforce rights of pledgee.**

§ 1658. A pledgee, or a pledgeholder for reward, assumes the duties and liabilities of a depositary for reward. **Obligation of pledgee and pledgeholder for reward.**

Gratuitous pledge-holder.

§ 1659. A gratuitous pledgeholder assumes the duties and liabilities of a gratuitous depositary.

Debtor's misrepresentation of value of pledge.

§ 1660. Where a debtor has obtained credit, or an extension of time, by a fraudulent misrepresentation of the value of property pledged by or for him, the creditor may demand a further pledge to correspond with the value represented; and in default thereof may recover his debt immediately, though it be not actually due.

Code of La., 3141.

When pledgee may sell.

§ 1661. When performance of the act for which a pledge is given is due, in whole or in part, the pledgee may collect what is due to him by a sale of property pledged, subject to the rules and exceptions hereinafter prescribed.

When pledgee must demand performance.

§ 1662. Before property pledged may be sold, and after performance of the act for which it is security is due, the pledgee must demand performance thereof from the debtor.

Wilson *v.* Little, 2 *N. Y.*, 443; aff'g S. C., 1 *Sandf.*, 351; Lewis *v.* Graham, 4 *Abb. Pr.*, 106; Castello *v.* City Bank, 1 *N. Y. Leg. Obs.*, 25; Brown *v.* Ward, 3 *Duer*, 660.

Notice of sale to the pledgor.

§ 1663. A pledgee must give actual notice to the pledgor of the time and place at which the property pledged will be sold, at such a reasonable time before the sale, as will enable the pledgor to attend.

Notice to the pledgor of the sale is an essential prerequisite (Lewis *v.* Graham, 4 *Abb. Pr.*, 106; Castello *v.* City Bank, 1 *N. Y. Leg. Obs.*, 25; Brass *v.* Worth, 40 *Barb.*, 648; Brown *v.* Ward, 3 *Duer*, 660). And this notice must apprise the pledgor of the *time* and *place* of sale. For the object of the notice is, not merely to enable the pledgor to redeem, but also to enable him to be present at the sale, and see that it is fairly conducted (Wheeler *v.* Newbould, 16 *N. Y.*, 392). And where notice cannot be given to him personally, *e. g.*, where he has absconded, the pledgee cannot dispose of the pledge without notice, but must resort to judicial proceedings (Garlick *v.* James, 12 *Johns.*, 146). An advertisement in the newspapers is not sufficient notice (Stearns *v.* Marsh, 4 *Den.*, 227).

§ 1664. Notice of sale may be waived by a pledgor at any time; but is not waived by a mere waiver of demand of performance. Waiver of notice of sale.

Milliken *v.* Dehon, 27 *N. Y.*, 364; Wilson *v.* Little, 2 *id.*, 443.

§ 1665. A debtor or pledgor waives a demand of performance as a condition precedent to a sale of the property pledged, by a positive refusal to perform, after performance is due, but cannot waive it in any other manner except by contract. Waiver of demand.

See Wilson *v.* Little, 2 *N. Y.*, 443.

§ 1666. The sale, by a pledgee, of property pledged, must be made by public auction, in the manner and upon the notice to the public usual at the place of sale, in respect to auction sales of similar property; and must be for the highest obtainable price. Sale must be by auction.

Wheeler *v.* Newbould, 16 *N. Y.*, 392; Brown *v.* Ward, 3 *Duer*, 660. Even in the case of stock pledged, a sale at the rooms of a board of brokers in the city of New York, whose transactions were, by their regulations, not open to the public, has been held invalid, without the consent of the pledgor (Wood *v.* Hamilton, cited in Castello *v.* City Bank, 1 *N. Y. Leg. Obs.*, 25; Rankin *v.* McCullough, 12 *Barb.*, 103; Willoughby *v.* Comstock, 3 *Hill*, 389; Brass *v.* Worth, 40 *Barb.*, 648).

It is, of course, to be understood that this section may be overruled by agreement of the parties.

§ 1667. A pledgee cannot sell any evidence of debt pledged to him, except the obligations of governments, states, or corporations; but he may collect the same when due. Pledgee's sale of securities.

Wheeler *v.* Newbould, 16 *N. Y.*, 397, limited by the exception, which is not inconsistent with the principle of that case (see also Garlick *v.* James, 12 *Johns.*, 146; Nelson *v.* Wellington, 5 *Bosw.*, 178; Brookman *v.* Metcalf, *id.*, 429, 445; White *v.* Platt, 5 *Den.*, 269; Hays *v.* Riddle, 1 *Sandf.*, 248). Of course a different agreement may be made by the parties.

§ 1668. Whenever property pledged can be sold for a price sufficient to satisfy the claim of the pledgee, the pledgor may require it to be sold, and its proceeds to be applied to such satisfaction, when due. Sale on the demand of the pledgor.

This provision is new, or, at least, it is very doubtful whether such a right now exists. But its justice is very clear (*Story Bailm.*, § 320). It is not proposed to extend the same privilege to mortgages, as they are used as permanent securities. A pledge should be used only as a transient security.

Surplus to be paid to pledgor.

§ 1669. After a pledgee has lawfully sold property pledged, or otherwise collected its proceeds, he may deduct therefrom the amount due under the principal obligation, and the necessary expenses of sale and collection, and must pay the surplus to the pledgor, on demand.

Id.

§ 1670. When property pledged is sold before the claim of the pledgee is due, he may retain out of the proceeds all that can possibly become due under his claim, until it becomes due; with the proper rebate of interest.

Pledgee's purchase of property pledged.

§ 1671. A pledgee, or pledgeholder, cannot purchase the property pledged except by direct dealing with the pledgor.

Story on Bailm., § 319; see also Dykers *v.* Allen, 7 *Hill*, 497, and the Title on Trust. But (prior to *Laws of* 1857, *ch.* 414, somewhat enlarging the powers of a special partner) it was held that a special partner of a firm with whom property is pledged is not incapacitated from purchasing it at a sale made by the firm. As he was prohibited from transacting any business on account of the partnership, and could not be employed as agent, attorney or otherwise, no duty devolved upon him in reference to the bailment. He could not aid or direct in the sale; and, hence, was not within the rule that one shall not be permitted to purchase who has a duty inconsistent with the character of purchaser (Lewis *v.* Graham, 4 *Abb. Pr.*, 106).

Pledgee may foreclose right of redemption.

§ 1672. Instead of selling property pledged, as hereinbefore provided, a pledgee may foreclose the right of redemption by a judicial sale under the direction of a competent court; and in that case may be authorized by the court to purchase at the sale.

See Garlick *v.* James, 12 *Johns.*, 146.

CHAPTER IV.

BOTTOMRY.

§ 1673. Bottomry is a contract by which a ship or its freightage is hypothecated[1] as security for a loan, which is to be repaid only in case the ship survives a particular risk, voyage, or period.[2] Bottomry, what.

[1] Stainbank *v.* Sheppard, 13 *C. B.*, 418, 441.

[2] The brig Draco, 2 *Sumn.*, 157, 191; Thorndike *v.* Stone, 11 *Pick.*, 183; Stainbank *v.* Sheppard, 13 *C. B.*, 418; Cole *v.* White, 26 *Wend.*, 511; The Atlas, 2 *Hagg. Adm.*, 48. The fact that the terms of the bond import a transfer of the ship, rather than a mere pledge, makes no difference in the character or operation of the contract (Robertson *v.* United States Ins. Co., 2 *Johns. Cas.*, 250).

In White *v.* Cole, 24 *Wend.*, 116, 126, it was remarked by Judge COWEN, that contracts of bottomry ought to be confined to vessels navigating the ocean, or its great navigable arms; and that they ought not to be permitted upon vessels employed upon the lakes. But this view was disapproved by Senator VERPLANCK, in delivering his opinion in the Court of Errors, upon the reversal of the decision of the Supreme Court (see Cole *v.* White, 26 *Wend.*, 511, 515). The commissioners have not thought it necessary to propose any distinction between ships employed in inland and in ocean navigation in this respect. The only practical objection to allowing a bottomry contract upon an inland ship, is in the danger that excessive interest may be exacted. Sufficient protection against this is afforded by the provision of section 1678, by which the rate of interest agreed on by the parties may be reduced by the court whenever it appears unjustifiable or exorbitant.

Owner of ship may hypothecate.

§ 1674. The owner of a ship may hypothecate it or its freightage, upon bottomry, for any lawful purpose,[1] and at any time and place.[2]

[1] The brig Draco, 2 *Sumn.*, 157, 186; Greely *v.* Waterhouse, 19 *Maine*, 9; sloop Mary, 1 *Paine, C. C.*, 671, Thorndike *v.* Stone, 11 *Pick.*, 183; see the Duke of Bedford, 2 *Hagg. Adm.*, 294.

[2] The brig Draco, 2 *Sumn.*, 157; sloop Mary, 1 *Paine, C. C.*, 671. In England the admiralty law may be otherwise (see the Royal Arch, 1 *Swab. Adm.*, 269, 276).

When master may hypothecate ship.

§ 1675. The master of a ship may hypothecate it upon bottomry, only for the purpose of procuring repairs or supplies which are necessary for accomplishing the objects of the voyage, or for securing the safety of the ship.

The Virgin, 8 *Pet.*, 538; Ross *v.* Ship Active, 2 *Wash. C. C.*, 227; The Aurora, 1 *Wheat.*, 96; The Edmond, 1 *Lush. Adm.*, 57, 211; The North Star, *id.*, 45; The Prince George, 4 *Moore P. C.*, 21; see also, The Orelia, 3 *Hagg. Adm.*, 75; The Boston, 1 *Blatchf. & H. Adm.*, 309; The Alexander, 1 *Dods. Adm.*, 278; The Tartar, 1 *Hagg. Adm.*, 1; The brig Ann C. Pratt, 1 *Curtis, C. C.*, 340; affirmed, 18 *How.* [*U. S.*], 63.

Id.

§ 1676. The master[1] of a ship can hypothecate it upon bottomry, only when he cannot otherwise relieve the necessities of the ship,[2] and is unable to reach adequate funds of the owner, or to obtain any upon the personal credit of the owner,[3] and when previous communication with him is precluded by the urgent necessity of the case.[4]

[1] The master is the only person beside the owner who can hypothecate the ship (The Orelia, 3 *Hagg. Adm.*, 75; The Kennersley Castle, *id.*, 1; The Tartar, 1 *id.*, 1; The Boston, 1 *Blatchf. & H.*, 309; The Ann C. Pratt, 1 *Curt. C. C.*, 340; aff'd, 18 *How.* [*U. S.*], 63; The Alexander, 1 *Dods. Adm.*, 278; The Jane, *id.*, 461).

[2] The Gratitudine, 3 *Rob. Adm.*, 196, 266; The Nelson, 1 *Hagg. Adm.*, 169; The Gauntlet, 6 *Notes of Cas.*, 370; 3 *W. Rob.*, 82.

[3] Tunno *v.* Sloop Mary, *Bee, Adm.*, 120; Ship Packet, 3 *Mason*, 255; Ross *v.* Ship Active, 2 *Wash. C. C.*, 226; and see Walden *v.* Chamberlain, 3 *Wash. C. C.*, 290; The Medora, *Sprague*, 138; The Virgin, 8 *Peters*, 538; The Saxe Cobourg, 3 *Hagg. Adm.*, 387.

[4] The Olivier, 1 *Lush. Adm.*, 484; La Ysabel, 1 *Dods. Adm.*, 273; Arthur *v.* Barton, 6 *M. & W.*, 138. This is the only test, and it is immaterial whether the ship is in a home port or a foreign one, if the master was really unable to communicate with the owner (The Trident, 1 *W. Rob.*, 29; The Ysabel, 1 *Dods. Adm.*, 273). But it has been held, in the English Privy Council, that the master must not only communicate the fact of his distress, but must also communicate his intention to make a bottomry bond (The Oriental, 7 *Moore P. C.*, 398). And communication must be made by telegraph, if that is possible, and the master cannot wait for an answer to a letter by mail (*Ib*).

When master may hypothecate freight-money.

§ 1677. The master of a ship may hypothecate freightage upon bottomry, under the same circumstances as those which authorize an hypothecation of the ship by him.

The Packet, 3 *Mason*, 255; The Zephyr, *id.*, 341.

Rate of interest.

§ 1678. Upon a contract of bottomry, the parties may lawfully stipulate for a rate of interest higher than that allowed by the law upon other contracts. But a competent court may reduce the rate stipulated when it appears unjustifiable and exorbitant.

The Atlas, 2 *Hagg. Adm.*, 48, 58; The Cognac, *id.*, 377; Sharpley *v.* Hurrel, *Cro. Jac.*, 208; see Simonds *v.* Hodgson, 3 *B. & Ad.*, 57; The Huntley, 1 *Lush. Adm.*, 24; The Zodiac, 1 *Hagg. Adm.*, 320, 326; The Heart of Oak, 1 *W. Rob.*, 204.

Rights of lender when no necessity for bottomry existed.

§ 1679. A lender upon a contract of bottomry, made by the master of a ship, as such, may enforce the contract, though the circumstances necessary to authorize the master to hypothecate the ship did not in fact exist, if, after due diligence and inquiry, the lender had reasonable grounds to believe, and did in good faith believe, in the existence of such circumstances.

Conard *v.* Atlantic Ins. Co., 1 *Peters*, 386; 4 *Wash. C. C.*, 662; see Carrington *v.* Pratt, 18 *How.* [*U. S.*], 63; Thomas *v.* Osborn, 19 *id.*, 22, 31; Soares *v.* Rahn, 3 *Moore, P. C.*, 1; Walden *v.* Chamberlain, 3 *Wash. C. C.*, 290; The Prince of Saxe Coburg, 3 *Hagg. Adm.*, 387; The Orelia, 3 *id.*, 84, 86; The Nelson, 1 *id.*, 169, 176.

Stipulation for personal liability, void.

§ 1680. A stipulation, in a contract of bottomry, imposing any liability for the loan independent of the maritime risks, is void.

Stainbank *v.* Sheppard, 13 *C. B.*, 418, 444; The Nelson, 1 *Hagg. Adm.*, 169; compare The Tartar, *id.*, 1, 13. But a bottomry bond may be given as collateral security for a personal obligation (The Emancipation, 1 *W. Rob.*, 124; The Augusta, 1 *Dods. Adm.*, 283).

When money loaned is to be repaid.

§ 1681. In case of a total loss of the thing hypothecated, from a risk to which the loan was subject, the lender upon bottomry can recover nothing;[1] in case of a partial loss, he can recover only to the extent of the net value to the owner of the part saved.[2]

[1] The brig Draco, 2 *Sumn.*, 157, 191; Thorndike *v.* Stone, 11 *Pick.*, 183; The Atlas, 2 *Hagg. Adm.*, 48; Bray *v.* Bates, 9 *Metc.*, 237.

[2] *Code de Com.*, 327. Such is the usage in New York. The capture and sale of a ship is not a total loss within this section, if its *proceeds* are restored. See Appleton *v.* Crowninshield, 3 *Mass.*, 448.

When bottomry loan becomes due.

§ 1682. Unless it is otherwise expressly agreed, a bottomry loan becomes due immediately upon the termination of the risk, although a term of credit is specified in the contract.

The brig Draco, 2 *Sumn.*, 157, 193.

Bottomry lien, how lost.

§ 1683. A bottomry lien is independent of possession, and is lost by omission to enforce it within a reasonable time.

The Virgin, 8 *Peters*, 538, 554; The Tartar, 1 *Hagg. Adm.*, 1, 13; The Royal Arch, 1 *Swab. Adm.*, 269, 282; Ship Charles Carter, 4 *Cranch*, 328; Leland *v.* The Medora, 2 *Woodb. & M.*, 105.

Preference of bottomry lien over other liens.

§ 1684. A bottomry lien, if created out of a real or apparent necessity,[1] in good faith, is preferred to every other lien or claim upon the same thing, excepting only a lien for seamen's wages,[2] a subsequent lien of materialmen for supplies or repairs, indispensable to the safety of the ship,[3] and a subsequent lien for salvage.[4]

[1] A bottomry lien, created by the owner, without necessity, and without any reason for the lender to believe that the loan was necessary, has not a preference

over any prior lien (The Dunvegan Castle, 3 *Hagg. Adm.*, 331; see The Royal Arch, 1 *Swab. Adm.*, 269).

[2] Madonna D'Idra, 1 *Dods. Adm.*, 37, 40; Sydney Cove, *id.*, 1, 13; The Charles Carter, 4 *Cranch*, 328; The Virgin, 8 *Peters*, 538; see The Mary Ann, 9 *Jur.*, 94; The Louisa Bertha, 1 *Eng. L. & E.*, 665; 14 *Jur.*, 1006. This is true of wages earned before, as well as after the bond is given (The Union, 1 *Lush. Adm.*, 128), and a third person, who at the master's request, has advanced the seamen's wages, has the same right of lien (The W. F. Safford, 1 *Lush. Adm.*, 69), but an owner has not (The Janet Wilson, 1 *Swab. Adm.*, 261).

[3] The Jerusalem, 2 *Gall.*, 345; compare the W. F. Safford, 1 *Lush. Adm.*, 69.

[4] See The W. F. Safford, 1 *Lush. Adm.*, 69.

§ 1685. Of two or more bottomry liens on the same subject, the latter in date has preference,[1] if created out of necessity.[2] Priority of bottomry liens.

[1] The Exeter, 1 *Rob. Adm.*, 146; The Trident, 1 *W. Rob.*, 29; The Betsey, 1 *Dods. Adm.*, 289; Leland *v.* The Medora, 2 *Woodb. & M.*, 113; Furniss *v.* The Magoun, *Olcott Adm.*, 66; The Duke of Bedford, 2 *Hagg. Adm.*, 294; The Priscilla, 1 *Lush. Adm.*, 1.

[2] The Dunvegan Castle, 3 *Hagg. Adm.*, 331.

CHAPTER V.

RESPONDENTIA.

§ 1686. Respondentia is a contract by which a cargo, or some part thereof, is hypothecated as security for a loan, the repayment of which is dependent on maritime risks. Respondentia, what.

In England a separate contract of respondentia is not known (see La Constancia, 4 *Notes of Cas.*, 285; 3 *Kent Com.*, 354). And in this country, it is rarely entered into by a shipmaster as such.

Respondentia by owner.

§ 1687. The owner of cargo may hypothecate it upon respondentia, at any time and place, and for any lawful purpose.

Conard *v.* Atlantic Ins. Co., 1 *Peters*, 386, 436; see Franklin Ins. Co. *v.* Lord, 4 *Mason*, 248.

Respondentia by master.

§ 1688. The master of a ship may hypothecate its cargo upon respondentia, only in a case in which he would be authorized to hypothecate the ship and freightage, but is unable to borrow sufficient money thereon for repairs or supplies which are necessary for the successful accomplishment of the voyage; and he cannot do so, even in such case, if there is no reasonable prospect of benefiting the cargo thereby.

The Gratitudine, 3 *Rob. Adm.*, 196, 263; ship Active, 2 *Wash. C. C.*, 237; see Pope *v.* Nickerson, 3 *Story*, 465; The Osmanli, 3 *W. Rob.*, 214; 7 *Notes of Cas.*, 322; The Lord Cochrane, 2 *W. Rob.*, 312; The Prince Regent, cited, 2 *id.*, 83; The Priscilla, 1 *Lush. Adm.*, 1; La Constancia, 4 *Notes of Cases*, 285.

Rate of interest.

§ 1689. The provisions of sections 1678 to 1685 apply equally to loans on respondentia.

See The Gratitudine, 3 *Rob. Adm.*, 196, 260; The Nostra Senora del Carmine, 29 *Eng. L. & E.*, 572; 18 *Jur.*, 730; The Osmanli, 3 *W. Rob.*, 214; 7 *Notes of Cas.*, 322.

Obligations of ship owner.

§ 1690. The owner of a ship is bound to repay to the owner of its cargo all which the latter is compelled to pay, under a contract of respondentia made by the master, in order to discharge its lien.

Duncan *v.* Benson, 1 *Exch.*, 537.

CHAPTER VI.

OTHER LIENS.

Lien of seller of real property.

§ 1691. One who sells[1] real property has a special lien thereon, independent of possession,[2] for so much[3] of the price[4] as remains unpaid,[5] and unsecured[6] otherwise than by the personal obligation of the buyer.[7]

[1] This lien exists only in favor of the seller, and one who lends the purchase-money to the buyer cannot enforce it (Marquat *v.* Marquat, 7 *How. Pr.*, 417); see McKillip *v.* McKillip, 8 *Barb.*, 552. But persons claiming under the seller may do so (Selby *v.* Selby, 4 *Russ.*, 336).

[2] *Story Eq. Jur.*, § 1218.

[3] The receipt of security for part of the price (Hallock *v.* Smith, 3 *Barb.*, 267) or payment of such part (4 *Kent Com.*, 151; Garson *v.* Green, 1 *Johns. Ch.*, 308), does not affect the lien for the residue. But in Fish *v.* Howland (1 *Paige*, 20), it was held that acceptance of a mortgage on the land sold, for *part* of the price, waived the entire lien.

[4] This lien exists only where land has been sold for *money*, and cannot be used to enforce any other obligation (McKillip *v.* McKillip, 8 *Barb.*, 552). "Price" has been elsewhere defined as a pecuniary consideration.

[5] *Story Eq. Jur.*, § 1217; Garson *v.* Green, 1 *Johns. Ch.*, 308; Bradley *v.* Bosley, 1 *Barb. Ch.*, 125; Stafford *v.* Van Rensselaer, 9 *Cow.*, 316; Mackreth *v.* Symmons, 15 *Ves.*, 329; Nairn *v.* Prouse, 6 *id.*, 752. This lien exists upon the sale of a mere equitable title, as well as in the case of a legal one (Warren *v.* Fenn, 28 *Barb.*, 333).

[6] The acceptance of any security, except as mentioned, waives the lien (Coit *v.* Fougera, 36 *Barb.*, 195; Vail *v.* Foster, 4 *N. Y.*, 312; Fish *v.* Howland, 1 *Paige*, 20; Warner *v.* Van Alstyne, 3 *id.*, 513; Gilman *v.* Brown, 1 *Mason*, 191; aff'd, 4 *Wheat.*, 255).

[7] Taking the buyer's note or bond does not waive this lien (Garson *v.* Green, 1 *Johns. Ch.*, 308; Hallock *v.* Smith, 3 *Barb.*, 267).

When transfer of contract waives lien.

§ 1692. Where a buyer of real property gives to the seller a written contract for payment of all or part of the price, an absolute transfer of such contract, by the seller, waives his lien to the extent of the sum payable under the contract.

Hallock *v.* Smith, 3 *Barb.*, 267. A transfer in trust to pay debts, and return the surplus, does not waive the lien (*Id*).

Extent of seller's lien.

§ 1693. The liens defined in sections 1691 and 1695 are valid against every one claiming under the debtor, except a purchaser or incumbrancer in good faith[1] and for value.[2]

[1] Hallock *v.* Smith, 3 *Barb.*, 267; Champion *v.* Brown, 6 *Johns. Ch.*, 398.

[2] Warren *v.* Fenn, 28 *Barb.*, 333; Burlingame *v.* Robbins, 21 *id.*, 327; Shirley *v.* Congress, &c., Refinery, 2 *Edw.*, 505. But compare Bayley *v.* Greenleaf, 7 *Wheat.*, 46.

Lien of seller of personal property

§ 1694. One who sells personal property has a special lien thereon, dependent on possession, for its price, if it is in his possession when the price becomes payable; and may enforce his lien in like manner as if the property was pledged to him for the price.

Thus, the seller may resell the property for account of the buyer (Sands *v.* Taylor, 5 *Johns.*, 395; Bement *v.* Smith, 15 *Wend.*, 497; Bogart *v.* O'Regan, 1 *E. D. Smith*, 590; Maclean *v.* Dunn, 4 *Bing.*, 722); and he must give notice of the sale (see Mallory *v.* Lord, 29 *Barb.*, 454; Fancher *v.* Goodman, *id.*, 315). These rules are the same as those concerning the sale of a pledge. It has indeed been held that the property may be resold at private sale, in certain cases (Crooks *v.* Moore, 1 *Sandf.*, 297), but upon the whole, the commissioners recommend a different rule.

Purchaser's lien on real property.

§ 1695. One who pays to the owner any part of the price of real property, under an agreement for the sale thereof, has a special lien upon the property, independent of possession, for such part of the amount paid as he may be entitled to recover back, in case of a failure of consideration.

Tompkins *v.* Seely, 29 *Barb.*, 212; Burgess *v.* Wheate, 1 *Wm. Blacks.*, 123; Lacon *v.* Mertins, 3 *Atk.*, 1; Shirley *v.* Shirley, 7 *Blackf.*, 452.

§ 1696. Every person who, while lawfully in possession of an article of personal property, renders any service to the owner thereof by labor or skill employed for the protection, improvement, safe keeping or carriage thereof, has a special lien thereon, dependent on possession, for the compensation, if any, which is due to him from the owner for such service. Lien for services.

It is believed that this section is in accordance with the present law of this state (see Morgan *v.* Congdon, 4 *N. Y.*, 552; Baker *v.* Hoag, 7 *id.*, 557; Steinman *v.* Wilkins, 7 *Watts & S.*, 466; Schmidt *v.* Blood, 9 *Wend.*, 268); though it undoubtedly gives a broader right of lien than is allowed in England (see Scarfe *v.* Morgan, 4 *M. & W.*, 283; Jackson *v.* Cummins, 5 *M. & W.*, 342; Steadman *v.* Hockley, 15 *M. & W.*, 553), or than is allowed by some decisions in this state (Grennell *v.* Cook, 3 *Hill*, 485; Fox *v.* M'Gregor, 11 *Barb.*, 41).

§ 1697. A factor has a general lien, dependent on possession, for all that is due to him as such, upon all articles of commercial value that are intrusted to him by the same principal. Lien of factor.

Coote Mortg., 283; Knapp *v.* Alvord, 10 *Paige*, 205; Bryce *v.* Brooks, 26 *Wend.*, 367; Buckley *v.* Packard, 20 *Johns.*, 421; Reynolds *v.* Davis, 5 *Sandf.*, 267; and see Bank of Rochester *v.* Jones, 4 *N. Y.*, 497; Winter *v.* Coit, 7 *N. Y.*, 288; Enoch *v.* Wehrkamp, 3 *Bosw.*, 398.

§ 1698. A banker has a general lien, dependent on possession, upon all property in his hands belonging to a customer, for the balance due to him from such customer in the course of the business. Banker's lien.

Davis *v.* Bowsher, 5 *T. R.*, 488. See Brandao *v.* Burnett, 3 *C. B.*, 519; rev'g S. C., 6 *M. & G.*, 630; and affirming S. C., 1 *M. & G.*, 908; Bank of Metropolis *v.* New England Bank, 1 *How.* [*U. S.*], 234; 6 *id.*, 212; Van Amee *v.* Bank of Troy, 8 *Barb.*, 312; 5 *How. Pr.*, 161; McBride *v.* Farmers' Bank, 25 *Barb.*, 657; 26 *N. Y.*, 450.

§ 1699. The master of a ship has a general lien,[1] independent of possession, upon the ship[2] and freightage,[3] for advances necessarily made, or liabilities Shipmaster's lien.

necessarily incurred by him for the benefit of the ship, but has no lien for his wages.[4]

[1] In England, this lien was not recognized at common law, as to either ship (Hussey *v.* Christie, 9 *East*, 426; 13 *Ves.*, 594; Wilkins *v.* Carmichael, 1 *Doug.*, 101; The Johannes Christoph, 33 *Eng. L. & E.*, 600) or freightage (Bristow *v.* Whitmore, 4 *De Gex. & J.*, 325; Gibson *v.* Ingo, 6 *Hare*, 112; Atkinson *v.* Cotesworth, 3 *B. & C.*, 647; Smith *v.* Plummer, 1 *B. & Ald.*, 575; The Favorite, 2 *Rob. Adm.*, 232), but it is now established by statute.

[2] In Van Bokkelin *v.* Ingersoll, 5 *Wend.*, 315, 326, Chancellor Walworth said: "I know of no principle which would give an equitable lien upon the freight, except as incidental to a lien on the ship." And although the decision of the point was not absolutely necessary in that case, yet it is clear that this was the ground upon which the actual determination was put, and the remark of the chancellor appears to be just. See also The Packet, 3 *Mason*, 255; Gardner *v.* The New Jersey, 1 *Peters Adm.*, 223.

[3] This is the settled rule in this country (Van Bokkelin *v.* Ingersoll, 5 *Wend.*, 315; 7 *Cow.*, 670; The Packet, 3 *Mason*, 255; Richardson *v.* Whiting, 18 *Pick.*, 530; Sorley *v.* Brewer, 18 *How. Pr.*, 276).

[4] This point is settled in this state by the unanimous decision of the Court of Errors (Van Bokkelin *v.* Ingersoll, 5 *Wend.*, 315), and is generally so held in other states (The Grand Turk, 1 *Paine C. C.*, 73; Fisher *v.* Willing, 8 *Serg. & R.*, 118), except in Massachusetts (Lewis *v.* Hancock, 11 *Mass.*, 72; Drinkwater *v.* The Spartan, *Ware*, 149). In England, the master has, by recent statutes, the same lien as a seaman (17 & 18 *Vict.*, *c.* 104; 24 *Vict.*, *c.* 10. See The Salacia, 1 *Lush. Adm.*, 545).

Seamen's lien.

§ 1700. The mate[1] and seamen[2] of a ship have a general lien, independent of possession, upon the ship and freightage for their wages,[3] which is superior to every other lien.[4]

[1] The May Queen, *Sprague*, 588; Bayly *v.* Grant, 1 *Salk.*, 33; Hook *v.* Moreton, 1 *Ld. Raym.*, 397.

[2] Brown *v.* Lull, 2 *Sumn.*, 443. All classes of persons who render maritime services are included under the name of seamen (The Prince George, 3 *Hagg. Adm.*, 376; Black *v.* The Louisiana, 2 *Peters Adm.*, 268; Turner's case, *Ware*, 83; Wheeler *v.* Thompson, 2 *Str.*, 707; The Jane & Matilda, 1 *Hagg. Adm.*, 187; Sageman *v.* The Brandywine, 1 *Newb. Adm.*, 5;

Wolverton *v.* Lacey, 18 *Bost. Law Rep.*, 672; The Highlander, *Sprague*, 588).

[3] As seamen cannot have authority to make advances for the benefit of the ship, except by order of the master, there is no reason for giving them a peculiar lien for such advances.

[4] See section 1684.

§ 1701. An officer, who levies an attachment or execution upon personal property, acquires a special lien, dependent on possession, upon such property, which authorizes him to hold it until the process is discharged or satisfied, or a judicial sale of the property is had. Officer's lien.

Rhoads *v.* Woods, 41 *Barb.*, 471.

§ 1702. An attorney-at-law has a lien, which is defined and regulated by the CODE OF CIVIL PROCEDURE. Attorney's lien.

See section 520 of the Code, reported complete.

§ 1703. The lien of a judgment is regulated by the CODE OF CIVIL PROCEDURE. Judgment lien.

See Field *v.* Sands, 8 *Bosw.*, 685; Conger *v.* Sands, 19 *How. Pr.*, 8; Smith *v.* Gage, 41 *Barb.*, 60.

§ 1704. The liens of mechanics, for materials and services upon real property, are regulated by special statutes. Mechanics' lien.

§ 1705. Debts amounting to at least fifty dollars, contracted for the benefit of ships, are liens in the cases provided by the CODE OF CIVIL PROCEDURE. Lien on ships.

The reference is to the Code of Civil Procedure as reported complete.

§ 1706. The mode of proceeding by a creditor to enforce a lien within this state, is regulated by the CODE OF CIVIL PROCEDURE. Enforcement of lien.

As reported complete.

CHAPTER VII.

STOPPAGE IN TRANSIT.

When consignor may stop goods.

§ 1707. A seller or consignor[1] of property, whose claim for its price or proceeds has not been extinguished,[2] may, upon the insolvency of the buyer or consignee becoming known to him[3] after parting with the property, stop it while on its transit to the buyer or consignee, and resume possession thereof.

[1] See Feise *v.* Wray, 3 *East*, 93; Kinlock *v.* Craig, 3 *T. R.*, 119; Clark *v.* Manrau, 3 *Paige*, 373. The right is intended to be recognized as held by those who dispose of the thing as owners, only. A mechanic having a lien on goods for work done, but forwarding them to the owner, cannot exercise a right to stop them in transit to enforce his demand for the work. His lien is destroyed by relinquishing possession (Sweet *v.* Pym, 1 *East*, 4). And a mere surety for the price, upon whom there is no primary liability to pay for the goods, cannot stop them upon the insolvency of the vendee, merely to save himself from loss (Siffken *v.* Wray, 6 *East*, 371). But one who remits money upon a particular account or for a particular purpose, other than an antecedent debt, may stop the same on hearing of the insolvency of the consignee (Smith *v.* Bowles, 2 *Esp.*, 578).

[2] Feise *v.* Wray, 3 *East*, 93; Jenkins *v.* Usborne, 7 *M. & G.*, 698.

[3] It was held in Rogers *v.* Thomas (20 *Conn.*, 53), that the right of stoppage in transit can only arise upon an insolvency occurring after the sale. See, however, to the contrary, Reynolds *v.* Railroad, 43 *N. H.*, 580. The commissioners propose to extend the right to cases in which an insolvency of the buyer existing before the sale, but then unknown to the seller, comes to the knowledge of the latter while the goods are yet on their way. It is obvious that where one sells goods with a full knowledge of the facts affecting the buyer's credit, he should abide by his act. But no reason, founded in justice or required by the convenience of merchants, is per-

ceived for distinguishing between the case of an insolvency occurring after the sale, and one occurring before, but unknown to the seller until afterward.

§ 1708. A person is insolvent, within the meaning of the last section, when he ceases to pay his debts in the manner usual with persons of his business, or when he declares his inability or unwillingness to do so.

What is insolvency of consignee.

Rogers *v.* Thomas, 20 *Conn.*, 53; Hays *v.* Mouille, 14 *Penn. St.*, 48; Newsom *v.* Thornton, 6 *East*, 17; Vertue *v.* Jewell, 4 *Campb.*, 31; Thompson *v.* Thompson, 4 *Cush.*, 134; Shone *v.* Lucas, 3 *Dowl. & R.*, 218; Bayly *v.* Schofield, 1 *M. & Selw.*, 338; Secomb *v.* Nutt, 14 *B. Monr.*, 324. Compare the definition of "insolvency," in Herrick *v.* Borst, 4 *Hill*, 650, with that in Curtis *v.* Leavitt, 15 *N. Y.*, 9, 199.

§ 1709. The transit of property is at an end when it comes into the possession of the consignee,[1] or into that of his agent, unless such agent is employed merely to forward the property to the consignee.[2]

Transit, when ended

[1] Mottram *v.* Heyer, 5 *Denio*, 629; 1 *id.*, 483; Cowasjee *v.* Thompson, 5 *Moore P. C.*, 165; Covell *v.* Hitchcock, 23 *Wend.*, 611; Buckley *v.* Furniss, 15 *Wend.*, 137.

[2] Harris *v.* Pratt, 17 *N. Y.*, 249; Holbrook *v.* Vose, 6 *Bosw.*, 76.

§ 1710. Stoppage in transit can be effected only by notice to the carrier or depositary of the property, or by taking actual possession thereof.

Stoppage, how effected.

Mottram *v.* Heyer, 5 *Denio*, 629; Whitehead *v.* Anderson, 9 *M. & W.*, 518.

§ 1711. Stoppage in transit does not of itself rescind a sale, but is a means of enforcing the lien of the seller.

Effect of stoppage.

There has been a good deal of doubt upon this question (see Wentworth *v.* Outhwaite, 10 *M. & W.*, 436; Clay *v.* Harrison, 10 *Barn. & Cr.*, 99; Bloxam *v.* Sanders, 4 *id.*, 941; Martindale *v.* Smith, 1 *Q. B.*, 389); but at the present day, and in this country, the principle may be deemed settled as here stated (Newhall *v.* Vargas, 13 *Maine*, 93; 15 *id.*, 314; Rogers *v.* Thomas, 20 *Conn.*, 53; see Rowley *v.* Bigelow, 12 *Pick.*, 307; Ash *v.* Putnam, 1 *Hill*, 302; *Parsons on Contr.*, *5th ed.*, 598).

66

TITLE XV.

NEGOTIABLE INSTRUMENTS.

The word "negotiable" has been so long used in its application to commercial paper, that the commissioners have not thought themselves at liberty to propose in the text a substitute for it. They would have preferred the word "circulating" as more precise and expressive, and if they had not felt bound by the present usage, they would have designated the instruments mentioned in this Title as "CIRCULATING INSTRUMENTS."

CHAPTER I.

NEGOTIABLE INSTRUMENTS IN GENERAL.

ARTICLE I.

GENERAL DEFINITIONS.

§ 1712. The provisions of this Title apply only to negotiable instruments, as defined in this article. To what instruments this Title is applicable.

§ 1713. A negotiable instrument is a written[1] promise[2] or request[3] for the payment of a certain[4] sum of money,[5] to order[6] or bearer,[7] in conformity to the provisions of this article. Negotiable instrument, what.

[1] 1 *R. S.*, 768. It is not necessary that the maker's name should be subscribed (Taylor *v.* Dobbins, 1 *Strange*, 399; Elliot *v.* Cooper, 2 *Ld. Raym.*, 1376).

It is provided in another part of the Code that the act of the agent is equivalent to the act of the principal; and it is not, therefore, necessary to say anything in this section about signature by an agent.

[2] 1 *R. S.*, 768, § 1.

[3] The direction may be in form a request (Wheatley *v.* Strobe, 12 *Cal.*, 92); though it must be in spirit an order.

[4] The amount to be paid must be fixed by the instrument (*Story on Notes*, § 20; Lent *v.* Hodgman, 15 *Barb.*, 274).

[5] An obligation to pay in anything other than money is not negotiable (Jerome *v.* Whitney, 7 *Johns.*, 21; Saxton *v.* Johnston, 10 *id.*, 418; Clark *v.* King, 2 *Mass.*, 524; Bunker *v.* Athearn, 35 *Me.*, 364; Wingo *v.* McDowell, 8 *Rich. L.*, 446; Rhodes *v.* Lindley, 3 *Hamm.*, 51; Peay *v.* Pickett, 1 *Nott & McC.*, 254). In Iowa such notes are made negotiable by statute (see Riggs *v.* Price, 3 *Greene*, 334). In this state, a note payable in current bank notes has been held to be negotiable (Judah *v.* Harris, 19 *Johns.*, 144; Keith *v.* Jones, 9 *Johns.*, 120). The same rule is followed in some other states (Swetland *v.* Creigh, 15 *Ohio*, 118; Williams *v.* Sims, 22 *Ala.*, 512; Barnes *v.* Gorman, 9 *Rich. L.*, 297) but not universally (see McCormick *v.* Trotter, 10 *Serg. & R.*, 94; London S. F. So. *v.* Hagerstown Bank, 36 *Penn. St.*, 498; Smith *v.* Philadelphia Bank, 14 *id.*, 525; Lowe *v.* Bliss, 24 *Ill.*, 168; Fry *v.* Rousseau, 3 *McLean*, 106; Hasbrook *v.* Palmer, 2 *id.*, 10). A note payable in the currency of another state (Little *v.* Phœnix Bank, 2 *Hill*, 425; 7 *id.*, 359; Lieber *v.* Goodrich, 5 *Cow.*, 186) or country (Thompson *v.* Sloan, 23 *Wend.*, 71), is not negotiable.

[6] An instrument payable "to A. B." simply, without adding "or his order," or equivalent words, is not negotiable (Richards *v.* Warring, 39 *Barb.*, 42; Reed *v.* Murphy, 1 *Geo.*, 236).

[7] 1 *R. S.*, 768, § 1. It is essential that the instrument should be made payable to *somebody* (White *v.* Joy, 13 *N. Y.*, 83; Douglass *v.* Wilkeson, 6 *Wend.*, 637).

Must be for unconditional payment of money.

§ 1714. A negotiable instrument must be made payable in money only,[1] and without any condition not certain of fulfillment.[2]

[1] See note 5 to last section.

[2] An obligation dependent upon an uncertain contingency is not negotiable (Sackett *v.* Palmer, 25 *Barb.*, 179; Cook *v.* Satterlee, 6 *Cow.*, 108; Van Wagner *v.* Terrett, 27 *Barb.*, 181; Seacord *v.* Burling, 5 *Denio*, 444; Robins *v.* May, 11 *Ad. & E.*, 213; Palmer *v.* Pratt, 2 *Bing.*, 185; Kingston *v.* Long, 4 *Doug.*, 9). An obligation payable *only* out of a particular fund is therefore not negotiable, because payment is dependent upon the state of the fund (see Gallery *v.* Prindle, 14 *Barb.*, 186; Worden *v.* Dodge, 4 *Denio*, 159). A bill payable out of a certain fund, if sufficient, but if not, then payable absolutely, is not the less negotiable (Bull *v.* Sims, 23 *N. Y.*, 570). And so of an obligation to pay upon an event which *must* occur at some time, however indefinite that time may be (Prindle *v.* Caruthers, 15 *N. Y.*, 425; see Sackett *v.* Palmer, 25 *Barb.*, 179).

Payee.

§ 1715. The person, to whose order a negotiable instrument is made payable, must be ascertainable at the time the instrument is made.

A note payable to "the order of the secretary of the A. Co., for the time being" at a future day, is not negotiable (Cowie *v.* Stirling, 6 *El. & Bl.*, 333; aff'g Storm *v.* Stirling, 3 *id.*, 832; Yates *v.* Nash, 8 *C. B.* [*N. S.*], 581). But a note payable "to the order of the indorser" is negotiable, because any holder may indorse it (United States *v.* White, 2 *Hill*, 59). And so it has been held, where the name of the payee was left blank (Crutchly *v.* Mann, 5 *Taunt.*, 529).

Instrument may be in alternative.

§ 1716. A negotiable instrument may give to the payee an option between the payment of the sum specified therein, and the performance of another act;[1] but as to the latter, the instrument is not within the provisions of this Title.[2]

[1] Hodges *v.* Shuler, 22 *N. Y.*, 114; Hosstatter *v.* Wilson, 36 *Barb.*, 307.

[2] See Hosstatter *v.* Wilson, 36 *Barb.*, 307.

Date, seal, &c.

§ 1717. A negotiable instrument may be with or without date;[1] with or without seal;[2] and with or without designation of the time[3] or place of payment.[4]

[1] Mechanics' & F. Bank *v.* Schuyler, 7 *Cow.*, 337, *a.*

[2] It has been held that a seal destroyed the negotiability of the instrument (Clark *v.* Farmers' W. Mf'g Co., 15 *Wend.*, 256; Enthoven *v.* Hoyle, 13 *C. B.*, 373). But the contrary is now settled in this state (Brainerd *v.* N. Y. & Harlem R. R., 25 *N. Y.*, 496; Bank of Rome *v.* Rome, 19 *N. Y.*, 20; see People *v.* Mead, 24 *N. Y.*, 125; Delafield *v.* Illinois, 2 *Hill*, 159). And the same rule as that now prevailing here prevails in other states (Bain *v.* Wilson, 10 *Ohio St.*, 14; Porter *v.* McCollum, 15 *Geo.*, 529); and in the Supreme Court of the United States (Gelpcke *v.* Dubuque, 1 *Wallace* [*U. S.*], 175).

[3] Mechanics' & F. Bank *v.* Schuyler, 7 *Cow.*, 337, *a.*

[4] *Story on Notes*, § 49.

§ 1718. A negotiable instrument may contain a pledge of collateral security, with authority to dispose thereof. May contain a pledge, &c.

Arnold *v.* Rock River Co., 5 *Duer*, 207.

§ 1719. A negotiable instrument must not contain any other contract than such as is specified in this article. What it must not contain.

An obligation to pay money and to do anything in addition, is not negotiable (Austin *v.* Burns, 16 *Barb.*, 643; Martin *v.* Chauntry, 2 *Str.*, 1271). It has been said that an instrument cannot be made negotiable by calling it so on its face (Carruth *v.* Walker, 8 *Cal.*, 252). But it may be worthy of consideration whether parties should not be allowed by express words to bring any contract within the rules of negotiable paper.

§ 1720. Any date may be inserted by the maker of a negotiable instrument, whether past, present, or future,[1] and the instrument is not invalidated by his death or incapacity at the time of the nominal date.[2] Date.

[1] Brewster *v.* McCardel, 8 *Wend.*, 478; Pasmore *v.* North, 13 *East*, 516.

[2] *Story on Notes*, § 48.

§ 1721. There are six classes of negotiable instruments, namely: Different classes of negotiable paper.

1. Bills of exchange;
2. Promissory notes;
3. Bank notes;
4. Cheques;

5. Bonds;

6. Certificates of deposit.

Originally, bills of exchange only were negotiable. Promissory notes were of at least doubtful negotiability prior to the statute of 3 & 4 *Anne*, which was re-enacted in this state, while yet a colony. Of course bank notes were included. The negotiability of the other classes mentioned, has been the subject of controversy down to a very recent period, but it is well settled that cheques (Keene *v.* Beard, 8 *C. B.* [*N. S.*], 381; Eyre *v.* Waller, 5 *H. & N.*, 460), bonds (Brainerd *v.* N. Y. & Harlem R. R., 25 *N. Y.*, 496; Bank of Rome *v.* Rome, 19 *N. Y.*, 20; Gelpcke *v.* Dubuque, 1 *Wallace* [*U. S.*], 175), and certificates of deposit (Miller *v.* Austen, 13 *How.* [*U. S.*], 218), are subject to all the rules of negotiable paper.

ARTICLE II.

INTERPRETATION OF NEGOTIABLE INSTRUMENTS.

Time and place of payment.

§ 1722. A negotiable instrument which does not specify the time of payment, is payable immediately.

Lake Ontario R. R. *v.* Mason, 16 *N. Y.*, 451; Cornell *v.* Moulton, 3 *Den.*, 12; Peets *v.* Bratt, 6 *Barb.*, 662; Thompson *v.* Ketcham, 8 *Johns.*, 189; Jones *v.* Brown, 11 *Ohio St.*, 601.

Place of payment not specified.

§ 1723. A negotiable instrument which does not specify a place of payment, is payable wherever it is held at its maturity.

See Haldane *v.* Johnson, 8 *Exch.*, 689.

Instruments payable to a person or his order, how construed.

§ 1724. An instrument, otherwise negotiable in form, payable to a person named, but adding the words, "or to his order," or "or to bearer," or words equivalent thereto, is in the former case payable to the written order of such person, and in the latter case, payable to the bearer.

This section is intended partly to avoid a difficulty in the general definition of negotiable paper, and partly to establish the right of the payer to require the indorsement of the payee — a right which is assumed in practice, but which has not been adjudged.

§ 1725. A negotiable instrument, made payable to the order of the maker, or of a fictitious person, if issued by the maker for a valid consideration, without indorsement, has the same effect against him and all other persons having notice of the facts, as if payable to the bearer. Unindorsed note, when negotiable.

1 *R. S.*, 768; modified by making it more explicit, but not changing the sense.

§ 1726. A negotiable instrument, made payable to the order of a person obviously fictitious, is payable to the bearer. Fictitious payee.

Willets *v.* Phœnix Bank, 2 *Duer*, 121.

§ 1727. The signature of every drawer, acceptor and indorser of a negotiable instrument, is presumed to have been made for a valuable consideration,[1] before the maturity of the instrument,[2] and in the ordinary course of business.[3] Presumption of consideration.

[1] Mechanics' Bank *v.* Livingston, 33 *Barb.*, 458. So held as to the maker of a note (Tibbetts *v.* Blood, 21 *id.*, 650; Hatch *v.* Trayes, 11 *Ad. & El.*, 702; Bristol *v.* Warner, 19 *Conn.*, 7; Clark *v.* Schneider, 17 *Mo.*, 295); as to the acceptor of a bill (Vere *v.* Lewis, 3 *T. R.*, 183; Thurman *v.* Van Brunt, 19 *Barb.*, 409; Atlantic Ins. Co. *v.* Boies, 6 *Duer*, 583); and as to an indorser (Case *v.* Mechanics' B'kg Asso., 4 *N. Y.*, 166; Pratt *v.* Adams, 7 *Paige*, 615; Vallett *v.* Parker, 6 *Wend.*, 615; Mills *v.* Barber, 1 *M. & W.*, 425).

[2] So held as to indorsers (Pratt *v.* Adams, 7 *Paige*, 615; Pinkerton *v.* Bailey, 8 *Wend.*, 600; Lewis *v.* Parker, 4 *Ad. & El.*, 838; Webster *v.* Lee, 5 *Mass.*, 339); and as to an acceptor (Roberts *v.* Bethell, 12 *C. B.*, 778).

[3] So held as to indorsers (Erwin *v.* Downs, 15 *N. Y.*, 575).

ARTICLE III.

INDORSEMENT.

Indorsement, what

§ 1728. One who writes his name upon a negotiable instrument, otherwise than as a maker or acceptor, and delivers it, with his name thereon, to another person, is called an indorser, and his act is called indorsement.

Both the signature and delivery are necessary to constitute an indorsement (Marston *v.* Allen, 8 *M. & W.*, 494; Brind *v.* Hampshire, 1 *id.*, 365; Belcher *v.* Campbell, 8 *Q. B.*, 1; Cox *v.* Troy, 5 *B. & Ald.*, 474), and both must be made or authorized by the same person. Thus a signature by A., and delivery by B., his executor, constitute no indorsement on the part of either A. or B. (Bromage *v.* Lloyd, 1 *Exch.*, 31).

This section will oblige those who wish to guaranty the payment of negotiable paper to write the contract upon another instrument. Holders are likely to be misled by the guaranties now sometimes written on bills and notes.

By the common law, an indorsement was essential to pass title to a bill drawn to order (Cunliffe *v.* Whitehead, 3 *Bing. N. C.*, 828; Prevot *v.* Abbott, 5 *Taunt.*, 786). But that was because of the general rule prohibiting transfers of things in action. An assignment by mere delivery, without indorsement, transferred the equitable title (Franklin Bank *v.* Raymond, 3 *Wend.*, 69); and, under the Code of Civil Procedure, the equitable title is in effect the whole title, so that the holder under such circumstances can sue in his own name (Savage *v.* Bevier, 12 *How. Pr.*, 166; Hastings *v.* McKinley, 1 *E. D. Smith*, 273; aff'd, 4 *Seld. Notes*, 19); Marine Bank *v.* Vail, 6 *Bosw.*, 421).

§ 1729. One who agrees to indorse a negotiable instrument is bound to write his signature upon the back of the instrument, if there is sufficient space thereon for that purpose. Agreement to indorse.

This provision is new. Though an indorsement upon the face of the instrument is valid (Young *v.* Glover, 3 *Jur.* [*N. S.*], 637), it is unusual, and would excite suspicion. A creditor, who agrees to accept an indorsed note in satisfaction, ought not to be required to accept such an indorsement.

§ 1730. When there is not room for a signature upon the back of a negotiable instrument, a signature equivalent to an indorsement thereof may be made upon a paper annexed thereto. When may be made on separate paper.

Story on Notes, § 121; Folger *v.* Chase, 18 *Pick.*, 63.

§ 1731. An indorsement may be general or special. Kinds of indorsement.

§ 1732. A general indorsement is one by which no indorsee is named. General indorsement, what.

§ 1733. A special indorsement specifies the indorsee. Special indorsement, what.

§ 1734. A negotiable instrument bearing a general indorsement cannot be afterwards specially indorsed;[1] but any lawful holder may turn a general indorsement into a special one, by writing above it a direction for payment to a particular person.[2] General indorsement, how made special.

[1] Watervliet Bank *v.* White, 1 *Denio*, 608; see Mitchell *v.* Fuller, 15 *Penn. St.*, 268; Walker *v.* Macdonald, 2 *Exch.*, 527; Smith *v.* Clarke, 1 *Esp. N. P.*, 180.

[2] Crutchley *v.* Mann, 5 *Taunt.*, 529.

§ 1735. A special indorsement may, by express words for that purpose, but not otherwise, be so made as to render the instrument not negotiable. Destruction of negotiability by indorser.

Leavitt *v.* Putnam, 3 *N. Y.*, 494; *Story on Notes*, § 139.

67

Implied warranty of indorser.

§ 1736. Every indorser of a negotiable instrument warrants to every subsequent holder thereof, who is not liable thereon to him:

1. That it is in all respects what it purports to be;[1]

2. That he has a good title to it;[2]

3. That the signatures of all prior parties are binding upon them;[3]

4. That if the instrument is dishonored,[4] the indorser will, upon notice thereof duly given to him,[5] or without notice, where it is excused by law, pay so much of the same[6] as the holder paid therefor, with interest;[7] unless exonerated under the provisions of section 1786, 1824, or 1826.

[1] McGregor *v.* Rhodes, 6 *El. & Bl.*, 266.

[2] *Story on Notes*, § 135.

[3] Erwin *v.* Downs, 15 *N. Y.*, 575; Troy City Bank *v.* Lauman, 19 *id.*, 477.

[4] One who indorses an instrument, even after it is due, is not bound to pay it without a presentment to the principal debtor (St. John *v.* Roberts, 6 *Bosw.*, 593). An indorser is bound to pay at once, after presentment, even where *acceptance* of a bill payable at a certain time after date is refused (Walker *v.* Bank of State of N. Y., 9 *N. Y.*, 582).

[5] It is not a condition of an indorser's engagement that notice shall be given for his benefit to prior indorsers (Baker *v.* Morris, 25 *Barb.*, 138). But he is discharged, if due notice is not given to *him* (Bryden *v.* Bryden, 11 *Johns.*, 187).

[6] Suse *v.* Pompe, 8 *C. B.* [*N. S.*], 538.

[7] Cook *v.* Clark, 4 *E. D. Smith*, 213; Cram *v.* Hendricks, 7 *Wend.*, 569, 642; Braman *v.* Hess, 13 *Johns.*, 52; see Ingalls *v.* Lee, 9 *Barb.*, 651.

Indorser, when liable to payee.

§ 1737. One who indorses a negotiable instrument before it is delivered to the payee, is liable to the payee thereon, as an indorser.

This is the substance of the decision in Moore *v.* Cross, 19 *N. Y.*, 227. But previous cases have so complicated the question that it is necessary to clear up the confusion by a positive rule. It has long been maintained that an indorser, before delivery to the payee, does not mean to be responsible to him, and though this doctrine is now overruled, yet the decision is put upon grounds that are needlessly technical.

§ 1738. An indorser may qualify his indorsement with the words, "without recourse," or equivalent words; and upon such indorsement, he is responsible only to the same extent as in the case of a transfer without indorsement. Indorsement without recourse.

Story on Notes, § 146; Rice *v.* Stearns, 3 *Mass.*, 225; Upham *v.* Prince, 12 *id.*, 14; Waite *v.* Foster, 33 *Me.*, 424.

§ 1739. Except as otherwise prescribed by the last section, an indorsement without recourse has the same effect as any other indorsement. Id.

Epler *v.* Funk, 8 *Penn. St.*, 468.

§ 1740. An indorsee of a negotiable instrument has the same rights against every prior party thereto, that he would have had if the contract had been made directly between them in the first instance. Indorsee privy to contract.

See Griswold *v.* Haven, 25 *N. Y.*, 595; Polhill *v.* Walter, 3 *B. & Ad.*, 114. This principle is one of great importance, particularly with reference to representations contained in commercial paper, which are deemed to be made directly to every indorsee.

§ 1741. An indorser has all the rights of a guarantor, as defined by the chapter on GUARANTY IN GENERAL, and is exonerated from liability in like manner. Indorser has rights of guarantor.

Thus an extension of time granted to the principal debtor, discharges an indorser (Platt *v.* Stark, 2 *Hill.*, 399; Kelty *v.* Jenkins, 1 *id.*, 73; Wood *v.* Jefferson Co. Bank, 9 *Cow.*, 194; Hubbly *v.* Brown, 16 *Johns.*, 70; Myers *v.* Welles, 5 *Hill*, 463; Dundas *v.* Sterling, 5 *Penn. St.*, 73; Sargent *v.* Mason, 6 *Mass.*, 85; Moss *v.* Hall, 5 *Exch.*, 46), and a release of an indorser discharges subsequent indorsers (Newcomb *v.* Raynor, 21 *Wend.*, 108). An indorser in the ordinary course of business has not the rights of a surety (Pitts *v.* Congdon, 2 *N. Y.*, 352; Hurd *v.* Little, 12 *Mass.*, 503; see Pring *v.* Clarkson, 1 *B. & C.*, 14).

§ 1742. One who indorses a negotiable instrument, at the request, and for the accommodation of another party to the instrument, has all the rights of a surety, as defined by the chapter on SURETYSHIP, and Rights of accommodation indorser.

is exonerated in like manner, in respect to every one having notice of the facts,[1] except that he is not entitled to contribution from subsequent indorsers.[2]

[1] Rouse *v.* Whited, 25 *N. Y.*, 170; Barry *v.* Ransom, 12 *id.*, 446; Griffiths *v.* Reed, 21 *Wend.*, 502; Greenough *v.* McClelland, 2 *El. & El.*, 424; Pooley *v.* Harradine, 7 *E. & B.*, 431; Davies *v.* Stainbank, 6 *De G., M. & G.*, 679.

[2] Bradford *v.* Corey, 5 *Barb.*, 461; Ailsen *v.* Barkley, 2 *Speers*, 747.

Effect of want of consideration.

§ 1743. The want of consideration for the undertaking of a maker, acceptor, or indorser of a negotiable instrument, does not exonerate him from liability thereon to an indorsee in good faith for a consideration.

Seneca Co. Bank *v.* Neass, 3 *N. Y.*, 442; 5 *Denio*, 329; Purchase *v.* Mattison, 6 *Duer*, 587; Ross *v.* Bedell, 5 *id.*, 462; Robbins *v.* Richardson, 2 *Bosw.*, 248.

It is not necessary that a *valuable* consideration should be given by the indorsee (*id*).

Indorsee in due course, what.

§ 1744. An indorsee in due course is one who, in good faith,[1] in the ordinary course of business,[2] and for value,[3] before its apparent maturity or presumptive dishonor,[4] and without knowledge of its actual dishonor,[5] acquires a negotiable instrument duly indorsed to him, or indorsed generally, or payable to the bearer.

[1] Although it has been held in some cases that gross negligence deprives an indorsee of the protection otherwise afforded to him (Pringle *v.* Phillips, 5 *Sandf.*, 157; Merriam *v.* Granite Bank, 8 *Gray*, 254; Gill *v.* Cubitt, 3 *B. & C.*, 466; Down *v.* Halling, 4 *id.*, 330; Roth *v.* Colvin, 32 *Vt.*, 125; Smith *v.* Mech. & Farm. Bk., 6 *La. Ann.*, 610); the contrary rule is now firmly settled in England, and *good faith* alone declared to be the test. Negligence may be evidence of bad faith, but it is not conclusive (Raphael *v.* Bank of England, 17 *C. B.*, 161; Goodman *v.* Harvey, 4 *Ad. & El.*, 870; Foster *v.* Pearson, 1 *C., M. & R.*, 849; Crook *v.* Jadis, 5 *B. & Ad.*, 909; Uther *v.* Rich, 10 *Ad. & El.*, 784; Bank of Bengal *v.* Fagan, 7 *Moore P. C.*, 72; Carlon *v.* Ireland, 5 *E. & B.*, 771). This ruling is followed by the latest decisions in this state (Steinhart *v.* Boker, 34 *Barb.*, 436; see Magee *v.* Badger, 30 *id.*, 246).

[2] See Meads *v.* Merchants' Bank, 25 *N. Y.*, 143, 147; Claflin *v.* Farmers' & Citizens' Bank, *id.*, 298.

[3] For a definition of "value," and "good faith," see Part V of the Fourth Division.

[4] This phrase is adopted to avoid much circumlocution. See on the general principle, Niver *v.* Best, 10 *Barb.*, 369; Williams *v.* Mathews, 3 *Cow.*, 252; Havens *v.* Huntington, 1 *id.*, 387; Lansing *v.* Lansing, 8 *Johns.*, 454; Lansing *v.* Gaine, 2 *id.*, 300; Johnson *v.* Bloodgood, 1 *Johns. Cas.*, 51. The meaning of the phrase is defined in the next article.

[5] Anderson *v.* Busteed, 5 *Duer*, 485.

§ 1745. An indorsee of a negotiable instrument, in due course, acquires an absolute title thereto, so that it is valid in his hands, notwithstanding any provision of law making it generally void or voidable,[1] and notwithstanding any defect in the title of the person from whom he acquired it.[2] Rights of indorsee in due course.

[1] This is an old rule as to bills void by the common law (Rockwell *v.* Charles, 2 *Hill*, 499; Norris *v.* Langley, 19 *N. H.*, 423; Johnson *v.* Meeker, 1 *Wis.*, 436; see Bank of Genesee *v.* Patchin Bank, 19 *N. Y.*, 312); but it is otherwise as to bills void by statute (Vallett *v.* Parker, 6 *Wend.*, 615; Rockwell *v.* Charles, 2 *Hill*, 499). The rule is established in England, by statute.

[2] This is too well settled to need a citation of authorities. Moreover, an indorsee in due course can give a perfect title to any person whether the latter acts in good faith or not. Thus, if A. obtains a promissory note by fraud, and indorses it to B. for value, B. acting in good faith, a perfect title to the note may be vested in A., notwithstanding his fraud, by a subsequent transfer from B. (Solomons *v.* Bank of England, 13 *East*, 135; Hascall *v.* Whitmore, 19 *Me.*, 104; Thomas *v.* Newton, 2 *Carr. & P.*, 606). For if an indorsee could not freely dispose of his property, selling it to whom he pleased, its value would be diminished in his hands. But if A. takes up the note as an indorser, upon its dishonor, he does not acquire a better title than he had at first (Devlin *v.* Brady, 32 *Barb.*, 518).

§ 1746. One who makes himself a party to an instrument intended to be negotiable, but which is left wholly or partly in blank, for the purpose of filling afterwards, is liable upon the instrument to an indorsee thereof in due course, in whatever manner Instrument left blank;

and at whatever time it may be filled, so long as it remains negotiable in form.

Van Duzer *v.* Howe, 21 *N. Y.*, 531; Hubbard *v.* Harlem R. R. Co., 36 *Barb.*, 286; 14 *Abb. Pr.*, 275; Schultz *v.* Astley, 2 *Bing. N. C.*, 544; 2 *Scott*, 815; Montague *v.* Perkins, 17 *Jur.*, 557; Griggs *v.* Howe, 31 *Barb.*, 100; Violett *v.* Patton, 5 *Cranch*, 142; Fullerton *v.* Sturges, 4 *Ohio St.*, 529; Wiley *v.* Moore, 17 *Serg. & R.*, 438; Siegfried *v.* Levan, 6 *id.*, 170; Russell *v.* Langstaffe, 1 *Doug.*, 516; see Nelson *v.* Wellington, 5 *Bosw.*, 178; Smith *v.* Hall, *id.*, 319.

ARTICLE IV.

PRESENTMENT FOR PAYMENT.

In the treatises upon bills of exchange, it is generally stated that they need not be presented by any one upon a day kept sacred by persons of his faith, and in like manner, that they ought not to be presented to one, upon a day sacred to him (see *Story on Bills*, § 293, &c). But there are no decisions to this effect, in this state, and our rule is probably otherwise.

Effect of want of demand on principal debtor.

§ 1747. It is not necessary to make a demand of payment upon the principal debtor in a negotiable instrument, in order to charge him; but if the instrument is by its terms payable at a specified place, and he is able and willing to pay it there at maturity, such ability and willingness are equivalent to an offer of payment upon his part.

Fairchild *v.* Ogdensburgh R. R. Co., 15 *N. Y.*, 337; Wolcott *v.* Van Santvoord, 17 *Johns.*, 248.

Presentment, how made.

§ 1748. Presentment of a negotiable instrument for payment, when necessary, must be made as follows, as nearly as by reasonable diligence it is practicable:

1. The instrument must be presented by the holder;[1]

2. The instrument must be presented to the principal debtor, if he can be found at the place where presentment should be made,[2] and if not, then it must be presented to some other person of discretion, if one can be found there, and if not, then it must be presented to a notary public within the state;

3. An instrument which specifies a place for its payment must be presented there,[3] and if the place specified includes more than one house, then at the place of residence or business of the principal debtor, if it can be found therein;[4]

4. An instrument which does not specify a place for its payment, must be presented at the place of residence or business of the principal debtor, or wherever he may be found, at the option of the presentor;[5] and,

5. The instrument must be presented upon the day[6] of its apparent maturity, or, if it is payable on demand, at any time before its apparent maturity,[7] within reasonable hours,[8] and, if it is payable at a banking-house, within the usual banking hours of the vicinity;[9] but, by the consent of the person to whom it should be presented, it may be presented at any hour of the day.[10]

[1] Presentment must certainly be made by the holder, or by his agent (see Cooke *v.* Callaway, 1 *Esp. N. P.*, 115; Bank of Utica *v.* Smith, 18 *Johns.*, 230; Shedd *v.* Brett, 1 *Pick.*, 401). Possession of the instrument is, however, sufficient evidence of agency (Cole *v.* Jessup, 10 *N. Y.*, 96).

[2] Mason *v.* Franklin, 3 *Johns.*, 202. The provision in regard to presentment to a notary is new. It is thought desirable that some record of presentment should be kept, when it is not made to the debtor or his agent.

[3] Ferner *v.* Williams, 14 *Abb. Pr.*, 215; 37 *Barb.*, 9; Stewart *v.* Eden, 2 *Cai.*, 121; Saunderson *v.* Judge, 2 *H. Bl.*, 509; Saul *v.* Jones, 1 *El. & El.*, 59; United States Bank *v.* Smith, 11 *Wheat.*, 171; Gay *v.* Paine, 5 *How. Pr.*, 107; Spellman *v.* Weider, *id.*, 5.

[4] See Mason *v.* Franklin, 3 *Johns.*, 202; Boot *v.* Franklin, *id.*, 207.

[5] See Woodworth *v.* Bank of America, 19 *Johns.*, 391; Anderson *v.* Drake, 14 *Johns.*, 114; Spies *v.* Gilmore, 1 *N. Y.*, 321; Benedict *v.* Caffe, 5 *Duer*, 226.

[6] Where the instrument has a certain time to run, a presentment made before (Griffin *v.* Goff, 12 *Johns.*, 423; Bowen *v.* Newell, 8 *N. Y.*, 190; Salter *v.* Burt, 20 *Wend.*, 205), or after it is due (Montgomery Bank *v.* Albany City Bank, 8 *Barb.*, 396; 7 *N. Y.*, 459), does not bind an indorser.

[7] See Sice *v.* Cunningham, 1 *Cow.*, 397; Van Hoesen *v.* Van Alstyne, 3 *Wend.*, 75.

[8] Wilkins *v.* Jadis, 2 *B. & Ad.*, 188; Cayuga Bank *v.* Hunt, 2 *Hill*, 635; Dana *v.* Sawyer, 22 *Me.*, 244; Lunt *v.* Adams, 17 *id.*, 230; Triggs *v.* Newnham, 1 *Carr. & P.*, 631; Morgan *v.* Davison, 1 *Stark.*, 114.

[9] Newark India Rubber Co. *v.* Bishop, 3 *E. D. Smith*, 48.

[10] See Bank of Syracuse *v.* Hollister, 17 *N. Y.*, 46; Bank of Utica *v.* Smith, 18 *Johns.*, 230; Garnett *v.* Woodcock, 1 *Stark.*, 435.

Apparent maturity, when.

§ 1749. The apparent maturity of a negotiable instrument, payable at a particular time, is the day on which by its terms it becomes due; or, when that is a holiday, the next business day.

Salter *v.* Burt, 20 *Wend.*, 205; see Campbell *v.* International Assurance Company, 4 *Bosw.*, 298. If the recommendation of the commissioners in regard to days of grace is not adopted (see section 1781), it will be necessary to add to this section "The usual days of grace are to be added."

Presumptive dishonor of bill, payable after sight.

§ 1750. A bill of exchange, payable at a specified time after sight, which is not accepted within ten days after its date, in addition to the time which would suffice, with ordinary diligence, to forward it for acceptance, is presumed to have been dishonored.

It is very desirable, that the term, at the end of which a bill may be presumed to be dishonored, should be fixed. The decisions are conflicting and unsatisfactory. The commissioners have simply suggested periods which seem reasonable, but do not attach any importance to the particular terms proposed.

Apparent maturity of bill, payable at sight.

§ 1751. The apparent maturity of a bill of exchange, payable at sight or on demand, is:

1. If it bears interest, one year after its date; or,

2. If it does not bear interest, ten days after its date, in addition to the time which would suffice, with ordinary diligence, to forward it for acceptance.

§ 1752. The apparent maturity of a promissory note, payable at sight or on demand, is: Apparent maturity of note.

1. If it bears interest,[1] one year after its date; or,

2. If it does not bear interest, six months after its date.[2]

[1] It is doubtful whether a demand note bearing interest has any "apparent maturity," unless it is known to be dishonored (see Merritt *v.* Todd, 23 *N. Y.*, 28; Brooks *v.* Mitchell, 9 *M. & W.*, 15; Wethey *v.* Andrews, 3 *Hill*, 582; compare Sice *v.* Cunningham, 1 *Cow.*, 397; Losee *v.* Dunkin, 7 *Johns.*, 70).

[2] Loomis *v.* Pulver, 9 *Johns.*, 244; Furman *v.* Haskin, 2 *Cai.*, 369; Carlton *v.* Bailey, 7 *Foster*, 230.

§ 1753. Where a promissory note is payable at a certain time after sight or demand, such time is to be added to the periods mentioned in the last section. Id.

§ 1754. A party to a negotiable instrument may require, as a condition concurrent to its payment by him: Surrender of instrument, when a condition of payment.

1. That the instrument be surrendered to him,[1] unless it is lost or destroyed, or the holder has other claims upon it;[2] or,

2. If the holder has a right to retain the instrument, and does retain it, then that a receipt for the amount paid, or an exoneration of the party paying, be written thereon;[2] or,

3. If the instrument is lost, then that the holder give to him a bond, executed by himself and two sufficient sureties, to indemnify him against any lawful claim thereon;[3] or,

4. If the instrument is destroyed, then that proof of its destruction be given to him.[4]

[1] Wilder *v.* Seelye, 8 *Barb.*, 408; Ranney *v.* Crowe, 1 *Exch.*, 166; Hansard *v.* Robinson, 7 *B. & Cr.*, 90; Smith *v.* Rockwell, 2 *Hill*, 482.

[2] Hargous *v.* Lahens, 3 *Sandf.*, 213.

[3] 1 *R. S.*, 406; see *Story on Notes*, § 106.

[4] Des Arts *v.* Leggett, 16 *N. Y.*, 582. This case does not expressly decide that such proof must be given *to the debtor*, but this seems only reasonable.

ARTICLE V.

DISHONOR OF NEGOTIABLE INSTRUMENTS.

Dishonor, what.

§ 1755. A negotiable instrument is dishonored, when it is either not paid, or not accepted, according to its tenor, on presentment for the purpose, or without presentment, where that is excused.

Story on Bills, § 228; Walker *v.* Bank of State of N. Y., 9 *N. Y.*, 582.

Notice, by whom given.

§ 1756. Notice of the dishonor of a negotiable instrument may be given:[1]

1. By a holder thereof;[2] or,

2. By any party to the instrument[3] who might be compelled to pay it to the holder, and who would, upon taking it up, have a right to reimbursement from the party to whom the notice is given.[4]

[1] It is, of course, a general principle that notice of a fact cannot be given before the fact has occurred (Griffin *v.* Goff, 12 *Johns.*, 422; Jackson *v.* Richards, 2 *Cai.*, 343); but if the instrument has actually been dishonored, it is immaterial whether the party giving notice knew it or not (Jennings *v.* Roberts, 4 *El. & Bl.*, 615).

[2] Notice by a mere stranger is of no effect (Chanoine *v.* Fowler, 3 *Wend.*, 173; Stanton *v.* Blossom, 14 *Mass.*, 116). But any holder, lawfully in possession, may give the notice (Bank of U. S. *v.* Davis, 2 *Hill*, 451; Howard *v.* Ives, 1 *id.*, 263; Mead *v.* Engs, 5 *Cow.*, 303; Ogden *v.* Dobbin, 2 *Hall*, 112); and so may any agent of the holder (Cole *v.* Jessup, 10 *N. Y.*, 96; Rowe *v.* Tipper, 13 *C. B.*, 249).

[3] Chapman *v.* Keane, 3 *Ad. & El.*, 193.

[4] Harrison *v.* Ruscoe, 15 *M. & W.*, 231; approving *Story on Bills*, § 304. It is not necessary that the party giving the notice should be then actually charged with notice (see *id.;* Jennings *v.* Roberts, 4 *El. & Bl.*, 615; Chapman *v.* Keane, 3 *Ad. & El.*, 193).

§ 1757. A notice of dishonor may be given in any form[1] which describes the instrument with reasonable certainty,[2] and substantially informs the party receiving it that the instrument has been dishonored. Form of notice.

[1] The notice need not be in writing (Butt *v.* Hoge, 2 *Hill.*, 81; Cuyler *v.* Stevens, 4 *Wend.*, 566; Williams *v.* Bank of U. S., 2 *Peters*, 97; Housego *v.* Cowne, 2 *M. & W.*, 348; Crosse *v.* Smith, 1 *M. & Selw.*, 545), and may be quite informal (see Miers *v.* Brown, 11 *M. & W.*, 372; Maxwell *v.* Braine, 10 *Jur.* [*N. S.*], 777).

[2] Although two or more instruments are in existence, exactly corresponding to the description given, this is no objection to the notice (Hodges *v.* Shuler, 22 *N. Y.*, 114; Davenport *v.* Gilbert, 6 *Bosw.*, 179); unless the person to whom the notice is given is thereby misled. No error, which cannot mislead, will vitiate the notice (see Bromage *v.* Vaughan, 9 *Q. B.*, 608; Mellersh *v.* Rippon, 7 *Exch.*, 578; Stockman *v.* Parr, 11 *M. & W.*, 809). But a notice not stating the maker's name is bad (Home Ins. Co. *v.* Green, 19 *N. Y.*, 518).

In Solarte *v.* Palmer, 2 *Clark & Fin.*, 93; 1 *Bing. N. C.*, 194; aff'g S. C., 7 *Bing.*, 530, the House of Lords held a notice insufficient, which merely stated that a bill (describing it) had been put into the hands of the attorney giving the notice "with directions to take legal measures for the recovery thereof, unless immediately paid." The judges in that case declared their opinion that a notice must allege a *presentment* as well as non-payment, and must also state that the party giving the notice looks to the party receiving it for payment. Following this decision, it was held that a notice was insufficient, if it merely stated that the bill was "due and unpaid" (Dole *v.* Gold, 5 *Barb.*, 490; Furze *v.* Sharwood, 2 *Q. B.*, 388; Phillips *v.* Gould, 8 *Carr. & P.*, 355), or "not paid," though accompanied with a demand of payment (Strange *v.* Price, 10 *Ad. & El.*, 125; Messenger v. Southey, 1 *M. & G.*, 76). But the courts soon paused, and began to qualify and limit these decisions, openly expressing regret that they had ever been made (Everard *v.* Watson, 1 *El. & Bl.*, 801; Messenger *v.* Southey, 1 *M. & G.*, 76). And notices that a bill was "dishonored" (Chard *v.* Fox, 14 *Q. B.*, 200; King *v.* Bickley, 2 *Q. B.*, 419; Stocken *v.* Collins, 9 *Carr. & P.*, 653), "returned with charges" (Grugeon *v.* Smith, 6 *Ad. & El.*, 499), or unpaid, "amounting, with expenses, to" so much (Everard *v.* Watson, 1 *El. & Bl.*, 801), were held valid. So in this state, "protested for non-payment," is sufficient in a notice (Youngs *v.* Lee, 12 *N. Y.*, 551; Cayuga Bank *v.* Warden, 1 *id.*, 413; Cook *v.* Litchfield, 9 *id.*, 279). In Bailey *v.* Porter, 14 *M. & W.*, 44, all the expressions of opinion in Solarte *v.* Palmer, not absolutely necessary to the decision, were disregarded, and a notice of non-payment, simply, was held sufficient. And this doctrine has been recently established by the unanimous opinion of the judges in the Exchequer Chamber (Paul *v.* Joel, 4 *Hurlst. & N.*, 355; aff'g S. C., 3 *id.*, 455).

So, in opposition to the view expressed in Solarte *v.* Palmer, it is well settled that it is not necessary to add that the party giving the notice looks to the party receiving it for payment (Bank of U. S. *v.* Carneal, 2 *Peters*, 553; Butt *v.* Hoge, 2 *Hilt.*, 81; King *v.* Bickley, 2 *Q. B.*, 419; Cooke *v.* French, 10 *Ad. & El.*, 131; Cowles *v.* Harts, 3 *Conn.*, 516; Shrieve *v.* Duckham, 1 *Littell*, 194; Bank of Cape Fear *v.* Sewell, 2 *Hawks*, 560; Warren *v.* Gilman, 17 *Me.* [5 *Shepl.*], 360).

Notice, how served.

§ 1758. A notice of dishonor may be given:

1. By delivering it to the party to be charged, personally, at any place;[1] or,

2. By delivering it to some person of discretion at the place of residence or business of such party, apparently acting for him;[2] or,

3. By properly folding the notice, directing it to the party to be charged, at his place of residence, according to the best information that the person giving the notice can obtain, depositing it in the post-office most conveniently accessible from the place where the presentment was made, and paying the postage thereon.[3]

[1] Hyslop *v.* Jones, 3 *McLean*, 96.

[2] *Story on Notes*, § 312; Mechanics Bkg. Asso. *v.* Place, 4 *Duer*, 212; see Hunt *v.* Maybee, 7 *N. Y.*, 266; Housego *v.* Cowne, 2 *M. & W.*, 348.

[3] *Laws* 1857, *ch.* 416, § 3. A notice wrongly addressed, when due diligence has not been used to procure the

correct address, is void (Randall *v.* Smith, 34 *Barb.*, 452; Libby *v.* Adams, 32 *id.*, 542; see Lawrence *v.* Miller, 16 *N. Y.*, 235).

§ 1759. In case of the death of a party to whom notice of dishonor should otherwise be given, the notice must be given to one of his personal representatives;[1] or if there are none, then to any member of his family who resided with him at his death; or if there is none, then it must be mailed to his last place of residence, as prescribed by subdivision 3 of the last section.[2] Notice, how served after indorser's death.

[1] Oriental Bank *v.* Blake, 22 *Pick.*, 206.

[2] Modified from *Story on Notes*, § 310; in which it is said that notice should be left at the domicile of the deceased. This would often fail to reach his representatives, more often than under the rule above given.

§ 1760. A notice of dishonor sent to a party after his death, but in ignorance thereof, and in good faith, is valid. Notice given in ignorance of death, valid.

§ 1761. Notice of dishonor, when given by the holder of an instrument, or his agent, otherwise than by mail, must be given on the day of dishonor,[1] or on the next business day thereafter.[2] Notice, when to be given.

[1] Notice *may* be given immediately upon refusal of payment (Hine *v.* Allely, 4 *B. & Ad.*, 624; Burbridge *v.* Manners, 3 *Camp.*, 193; Bussard *v.* Levering, 6 *Wheat.*, 102).

[2] This will suffice (Farmers' Bank of Bridgeport *v.* Vail, 21 *N. Y.*, 485; Howard *v.* Ives, 1 *Hill*, 263; Cuyler *v.* Stevens, 4 *Wend.*, 566; Williams *v.* Smith, 2 *B. & Ald.*, 496). But a later day will not do (Sewall *v.* Russell, 3 *Wend.*, 276).

§ 1762. When notice of dishonor is given by mail, it must be deposited in the post-office in time for the first mail which closes after noon of the first business day succeeding the dishonor, and which leaves the place where the instrument was dishonored, for the place to which the notice should be sent. Notice of dishonor, when to be mailed.

There is no doubt that the notice may be sent by mail on the day after dishonor (Farmers' Bank of Bridgeport *v.* Vail, 21 *N. Y.*, 485); and it may be deemed to be settled that notice may be sent by any mail leaving on that day (Goodman *v.* Norton, 17 *Me.*, 381; Howard *v.* Ives, 1 *Hill*, 263; Whitwell *v.* Johnson, 17 *Mass.*, 449; see Housatonic Bank *v.* Laflin, 5 *Cush.*, 546). But beyond this point there is great diversity of opinion, Thus it has been held on the one hand that notice must be sent by the second day's mail, though the last mail closes at 10½ A. M. (U. S. *v.* Barker, 12 *Wheat.*, 559), 9 A. M. (Lawson *v.* Farmers' Bank, 1 *Ohio St.*, 206), and even earlier (Beckwith *v.* Smith, 22 *Me.*, 125; see Stephenson *v.* Dickson, 24 *Penn. St.*, 148), while on the other hand 5 A. M. (West *v.* Brown, 6 *Ohio St.*, 542), 6 A. M. (Chick *v.* Pillsbury, 24 *Me.*, 458), and even 9½ A. M. (see Hawkes *v.* Salter, 4 *Bing.*, 715; Burgess *v.* Vreeland, 4 *N. J.*, 71), have been considered earlier hours than the holder was bound to send notice by. It is of more importance to have a definite rule than that it should be, abstractly considered, the most just which could be devised.

Notice, how given by agent.

§ 1763. When the holder of a negotiable instrument, at the time of its dishonor, is a mere agent for the owner, it is sufficient for him to give notice to his principal in the same manner as to an indorser, and his principal may give notice to any other party to be charged, as if he were himself an indorser.[1] And if an agent of the owner employs a sub-agent, it is sufficient for each successive agent or sub-agent to give notice in like manner to his own principal.[2]

[1] *Story on Notes*, § 326; West River Bank *v.* Taylor, 7 *Bosw.*, 466; Howard *v.* Ives, 1 *Hill*, 263; Ogden *v.* Dobbin, 2 *Hall*, 112; Mead *v.* Engs, 5 *Cow.*, 303; Farmers' Bank of Bridgeport *v.* Vail, 21 *N. Y.*, 485; Bray *v.* Hadwen, 5 *M. & Selw.*, 68; Firth *v.* Thrush, 8 *B. & C.*, 387.

[2] Clode *v.* Bayley, 12 *M. & W.*, 51.

Additional time for notice by indorser.

§ 1764. Every party to a negotiable instrument, receiving notice of its dishonor, has the like time thereafter to give similar notice to prior parties, as the original holder had after its dishonor.[1] But this additional time is available only to the particular party entitled thereto.[2]

[1] *Story on Notes*, § 331; Darbyshire *v.* Parker, 6 *East*, 3; Howard *v.* Ives, 1 *Hill*, 263; Farmers' Bank *v.* Vail, 21 *N. Y.*, 485.

[2] Rowe *v.* Tipper, 13 *C. B.*, 249; see Harrison *v.* Ruscoe, 15 *M. & W.*, 231.

§ 1765. A notice of the dishonor of a negotiable instrument, if valid in favor of the party giving it, inures to the benefit of all other parties thereto, whose right to give the like notice has not then been lost.

Effect of notice of dishonor.

Harrison *v.* Ruscoe, 15 *M. & W.*, 231; Mead *v.* Engs, 5 *Cow.*, 303; Stafford *v.* Yates, 18 *Johns.*, 327; Lysaght *v.* Bryant, 9 *C. B.*, 46.

ARTICLE VI.

EXCUSE OF PRESENTMENT AND NOTICE.

If the provision of § 1748, requiring presentment to be made to a notary public in certain cases, is not adopted, it will be necessary to insert here a section as follows:

§ . The presentment of a negotiable instrument for payment is excused:

1. When neither the place of payment, if any, designated in the instrument, nor the place of residence or business of the principal debtor can, with reasonable diligence, be ascertained by the holder; or,

2. When no person to whom presentment may properly be made can, with reasonable diligence, be found by the holder; or,

3. When the instrument designates no place of payment, but purports to be signed by the principal debtor within this state, and he resided therein at the time of signing, but has removed therefrom.

Foster *v.* Julien, 24 *N. Y.*, 28; see Spies *v.* Gilmore, 1 *id.*, 321.

§ 1766. Notice of dishonor is excused:

Notice of dishonor, when excused.

1. When the party by whom it should be given cannot, with reasonable diligence, ascertain either the place of residence or business of the party to be charged; or,

2. When there is no post-office communication between the town of the party by whom the notice should be given, and the town in which the place of

residence or business of the party to be charged is situated; or,

3. When the party to be charged is the same person who dishonors the instrument;[1] or,

4. When the notice is waived by the party entitled thereto.[2]

[1] Caunt *v.* Thompson, 7 *C. B.*, 400. In that case, the indorser was executor of the maker, and the note was presented to him, and payment thereof refused by him (Compare, however, Magruder *v.* Union Bank, 3 *Peters*, 87; 7 *id.*, 287; Juniata Bank *v.* Hale, 16 *Serg. & R.*, 157).

[2] Conkling *v.* King, 10 *N. Y.*, 446.

Presentment and notice, when excused.

§ 1767. Presentment and notice are excused as to any party to a negotiable instrument, who informs the holder, within ten days[1] before its maturity, that it will be dishonored.[2]

[1] No term is at present fixed by the law, but if the rule is to be maintained at all, it should be made certain.

[2] Spencer *v.* Harvey, 17 *Wend.*, 489; Leffingwell *v.* White, 1 *Johns. Cas.*, 99.

Id.

§ 1768. If, before or at the maturity of an instrument, an indorser has received full security for the amount thereof, or the maker has assigned all his estate to him as such security, presentment and notice to him are excused.

Mechanics' Bank *v.* Griswold, 7 *Wend.*, 165; Corney *v.* Da Costa, 1 *Esp.*, 302; limited in Seacord *v.* Miller, 13 *N. Y.*, 55.

This rule is founded upon the same principle as the series of cases that were overthrown in Hall *v.* Newcomb, 7 *Hill*, 416, and perhaps ought to share their fate. If the maker intends that the indorser shall waive notice, he will naturally so stipulate with him, or will give the security to the holder outright. The following is suggested instead of this section:

[§ 1768. No transactions between the maker and indorser of a negotiable instrument waive or excuse notice of dishonor to the latter, unless they so agree.]

This latter rule is established in Connecticut (Holland *v.* Turner, 10 *Conn.*, 308, 317).

Delay, when excused.

§ 1769. Delay in presentment, or in giving notice of dishonor, is excused, when caused by circumstances which the party delaying could not have avoided by the exercise of reasonable care and diligence.

The rule at present is liberal (*Story on Bills*, § 234; *Story on Notes*, § 356; Firth *v.* Thrush, 8 *B. & C.*, 387; Baldwin *v.* Richardson, 1 *id.*, 245; Bateman *v.* Joseph, 12 *East*, 433; 2 *Camp.*, 461). Other excuses are mentioned (*Story on Notes*, § 357), but it is doubtful whether they are allowed in this state. It is to be borne in mind that an excuse for delay will not justify a perpetual omission of notice (Beale *v.* Parrish, 20 *N. Y.*, 407).

§ 1770. A waiver of presentment waives notice of dishonor also, unless the contrary is expressly stipulated; but a waiver of notice does not waive presentment. **Waiver of presentment and notice.**

Buchanan *v.* Marshall, 22 *Vt.*, 561; Burnham *v.* Webster, 17 *Me.*, 50.

§ 1771. A waiver of protest on any negotiable instrument other than a foreign bill of exchange, waives presentment and notice. **Waiver of protest.**

Coddington *v.* Davis, 1 *N. Y.*, 186; 3 *Den.*, 16.

ARTICLE VII.

EXTINCTION OF NEGOTIABLE INSTRUMENTS.

§ 1772. The obligation of a party to a negotiable instrument is extinguished: **Obligation of party, when extinguished.**

1. In like manner with that of parties to contracts in general; or,

2. By payment of the amount due upon the instrument, at or after its maturity, in good faith and in the ordinary course of business, to any person having actual possession thereof, and appearing, by its terms, to be entitled to payment.

See sections 1744 and 1745, and notes.

By the commercial law, as recognized in England, a simple agreement to waive the debt created by a negotiable instrument, although without a new consideration or a seal, discharges the debtor (Foster *v.* Dawber, 6 *Exch.*, 839; *Byles on Bills*, 5*th ed.*, 145). But this rule has been either overlooked or overruled in this state (see Seymour *v.* Minturn, 17 *Johns.*, 169; Crawford *v.* Mills, 13 *id.*, 87; Smith *v.* Bartholomew, 1 *Metc.*, 276; Ruggles *v.* Patten, 8 *Mass.*, 480).

Revival of obligation.

§ 1773. If, after its extinction, a negotiable instrument comes into the possession of an indorsee in due course, the obligation thereof revives in his favor.

See Manhattan Co. *v.* Reynolds, 2 *Hill*, 140.

CHAPTER II.

BILLS OF EXCHANGE.

ARTICLE I.

FORM AND INTERPRETATION OF A BILL.

Bill of exchange, what.

§ 1774. A bill of exchange is an instrument, negotiable in form, by which one, who is called the drawer, requests another, called the drawee, to pay a specified sum of money.

Peto *v.* Reynolds, 9 *Exch.*, 410; Davis *v.* Clarke, 6 *Q. B.*, 16. It is an essential element of a bill of exchange, that the drawee should be a person distinct from the drawer (Fairchild *v.* Ogdensburgh R. R., 15 *N. Y.*, 337; Miller *v.* Thomson, 3 *M. & G.*, 576; overruling, in effect, Wheeler *v.* Webster, 1 *E. D. Smith*, 1, on this point).

§ 1775. A bill of exchange may give the name of any person in addition to the drawee, to be resorted to in case of need. **Drawee in case of need.**

§ 1776. A bill of exchange may be drawn in any number of parts, each part stating the existence of the others, and all forming one set. **Bill in parts of a set.**

§ 1777. An agreement to draw a bill of exchange binds the drawer to execute it in three parts, if the other party to the agreement desires it. **When must be in a set.**

§ 1778. Presentment, acceptance, or payment, of a single part in a set of a bill of exchange, is sufficient for the whole. **Presentment, &c., of part of set.**

Story on Bills, § 66.

§ 1779. A bill of exchange is payable: **Bill, where payable.**

1. At the place where, by its terms, it is made payable; or,

2. If it specifies no place of payment, then at the place to which it is addressed; or,

3. If it is not addressed to any place, then at the place of residence or business of the drawee, or wherever he may be found;[1] or,

4. If this cannot be done, then at the office of any notary public in the state.[2]

[1] See *Story on Bills*, § 48.

[2] This provision is new. Compare § 1783 and 1748, which contain similar provisions.

§ 1780. The rights and obligations of the drawer of a bill of exchange, are the same as those of the first indorser of any other negotiable instrument. **Rights and obligations of drawer.**

ARTICLE II.

DAYS OF GRACE.

Days of grace.

§ 1781. Days of grace are not allowed.

The commissioners recommend that no grace be hereafter allowed upon commercial paper. This is the rule upon the continent of Europe. Should this recommendation not be adopted, the following should be substituted for the text:

[§ 1781. The three days following the day on which a bill of exchange, payable otherwise than at sight or on demand, becomes due by its terms, are allowed as days of grace, unless the last of such days is a holiday, in which case the next preceding business day is the last day of grace allowed.]

ARTICLE III.

PRESENTMENT FOR ACCEPTANCE.

When bill may be presented.

§ 1782. At any time before a bill of exchange is payable, the holder may present it to the drawee for acceptance,[1] and if acceptance is refused, the bill is dishonored.[2]

[1] *Story on Bills*, § 228; see Montgomery Co. Bank *v.* Albany City Bank, 8 *Barb.*, 396. He is not bound to present a bill for acceptance if it is payable at a certain time after date (Philpott *v.* Bryant, 3 *Carr. & P.*, 244).

[2] This is so, even though presentment for acceptance was not necessary, as in case of a bill payable four months after its date (Walker *v.* Bank of State N. Y., 9 *N. Y.*, 582; 13 *Barb.*, 636; O'Keefe *v.* Dunn, 6 *Taunt.*, 305).

Presentment, how made.

§ 1783. Presentment for acceptance must be made in the following manner, as nearly as by reasonable diligence it is practicable:

1. The bill must be presented by the holder;

2. It must be presented on a business day, and within reasonable hours;

3. It must be presented to the drawee, if he can be found within the state, and if not, then at his place of residence or business, if within the state, to any person of discretion therein, and if he has no such place of residence or business, or there is no person of discretion therein, then to any notary public in the state; and,

4. If the drawee requests it, the bill must be left with him, until the same hour of the next day, to which time he may postpone his acceptance or refusal.

See *Story on Bills*, § 237; 1 *R. S.*, 768. The clause providing for presentment to a notary public is new, but is in conformity to §§ 1748 and 1779.

§ 1784. Presentment for acceptance to one of several joint drawees, and refusal by him, dispense with presentment to the others. Presentment to joint drawees.

This question has been considered very doubtful (*Story on Bills*, § 229), but is decided in effect by the case of Carman *v.* Pultz (21 *N. Y.*, 531).

§ 1785. A bill of exchange, which specifies a drawee in case of need, must be presented to him for acceptance or payment, as the case may be, before it can be treated as dishonored. When presentment to be made to drawee in case of need.

§ 1786. When a bill of exchange is payable at a specified time after sight, the drawer and indorsers are exonerated, if it is not presented for acceptance within ten days after the time which would suffice, with ordinary diligence, to forward it for acceptance, unless presentment is excused. Presentment, when must be made.

At present the only rule established is that "due diligence" must be used (Wethey *v.* Andrews, 3 *Hill*, 582; Smith *v.* Janes, 20 *Wend.*, 192; Robinson *v.* Ames, 20 *Johns.*, 146). But this is too indefinite.

ARTICLE IV.

ACCEPTANCE.

Acceptance, how made.

§ 1787. An acceptance of a bill must be made in writing,[1] by the drawee, or by an acceptor for honor;[2] and may be made by the acceptor writing his name across the face of the bill, with or without other words.

[1] 1 *R. S.*, 768, omitting the words "or his agent," &c., that being provided for by the general law of agency.

[2] No one but the drawee, or an acceptor for honor, can accept a bill (Walker *v.* Bank of State of N. Y., 9 *N. Y.*, 582; 13 *Barb.*, 636; Davis *v.* Clark, 1 *Carr. & K.*, 177). An acceptance by any other person, with the assent of the holder, transforms it into a promissory note (Peto *v.* Reynolds, 9 *Exch.*, 410).

Holder entitled to acceptance on face of bill.

§ 1788. The holder of a bill of exchange, if entitled to an acceptance thereof, may treat the bill as dishonored, if the drawee refuses to write across its face an unqualified[1] acceptance.[2]

[1] Gammon *v.* Schmoll, 5 *Taunt.*, 344.

[2] Although, by 1 *R. S.*, 768, a refusal to return a bill is an acceptance thereof, it cannot be meant that the holder should be obliged to submit to such an acceptance, if he prefers to seek a remedy against the drawer. It is not, however, certain that a holder might now refuse to receive an acceptance on the back of the bill, but he ought to have such a right.

What acceptance sufficient, with consent of holder.

§ 1789. The holder of a bill of exchange may, without prejudice to his rights against prior parties, receive and treat as a sufficient acceptance:

1. An acceptance written upon any part of the bill, or upon a separate paper;[1]

2. An acceptance qualified so far only as to make the bill payable at a particular place within the city, or town, in which, if the acceptance was unqualified, it would be payable;[2] or,

3. A refusal by the drawee to return the bill to the holder after presentment;[3] in which case the bill is payable immediately, without regard to its terms.[4]

[1] Such an acceptance is undoubtedly sufficient, if the holder consents thereto.

[2] Troy City Bank *v.* Lauman, 19 *N. Y.*, 477. An acceptance payable in another town, if assented to by the holder, exonerates all prior parties (Niagara Bank *v.* Fairman M'f'g Co., 31 *Barb.*, 403; see Walker *v.* Bank of State of N. Y., 9 *N. Y.*, 582; 13 *Barb.*, 636; Rowe *v.* Young, 2 *Brod. & B.*, 165).

[3] 1 *R. S.*, 768.

[4] This provision is new, but seems to be no more than reasonable, the act amounting to a conversion, for which the owner might recover damages to the value of the bill.

Acceptance by separate instrument.

§ 1790. The acceptance of a bill of exchange, by a separate instrument, binds the acceptor only to one to whom it has been shown, and who, upon the faith thereof, has given value for the bill.

1 *R. S.*, 768, § 7. See Burns *v.* Robbins, 40 *Barb.*, 368. There does not seem to be any strong reason for restricting the benefit of such an acceptance to holders for *value*, as distinguished from other holders for a good consideration.

Promise to accept, when equivalent to acceptance.

§ 1791. An unconditional promise, in writing, to accept a bill of exchange,[1] is a sufficient acceptance thereof, in favor of every person to whom it has been shown, and who, upon the faith thereof, has given value for the bill.[2]

[1] The words "before it is drawn" omitted.

[2] 1 *R. S.*, 768, § 8; modified by inserting the words "to whom it has been shown, and," so as to make it uniform with the preceding section. The clause should be contained in both sections, or in neither. See Burns *v.* Robbins, 40 *Barb.*, 368.

Cancellation of acceptance.

§ 1792. The acceptor of a bill of exchange may cancel his acceptance at any time before delivering the bill to the holder,[1] and before the holder has, with the consent of the acceptor, transferred his title to another person who has given value for it upon the faith of such acceptance.[2]

[1] Cox *v.* Troy, 5 *B. & Ald.*, 474.
[2] *Story on Bills*, § 252.

What is admitted by acceptance. § 1793. The acceptance of a bill of exchange admits the capacity of the drawer to draw and indorse it;[1] and if written upon the bill, it also admits the same to be genuine, and binding upon the drawer;[2] but it does not admit the signature of any indorser to be genuine.[3]

[1] Smith *v.* Marsack, 6 *C. B.*, 486; see Braithwaite *v.* Gardenier, 8 *Q. B.*, 473.
[2] Sanderson *v.* Collmann, 4 *M. & G.*, 209; see Goddard *v.* Merchants' Bank, 4 *N. Y.*, 149. In Bank of Commerce *v.* Union Bank (3 *N. Y.*, 230), it was held that nothing but the bare signature of the drawer was admitted by an acceptance, and that if the body of the bill was forged, the acceptance was not binding. But the commissioners are of opinion that this particular exception is not founded in reason. A drawee is allowed time to satisfy himself of the genuineness of the whole instrument, and his decision ought to be conclusive upon him.
[3] Smith *v.* Chester, 1 *T. R.*, 654; Robinson *v.* Yarrow, 7 *Taunt.*, 457; see Brind *v.* Hampshire, 1 *M. & W.*, 365; Dana *v.* Underwood, 19 *Pick.*, 102; Macfarlane *v.* Moses, 1 *Cheves*, 54.

ARTICLE V.

ACCEPTANCE OR PAYMENT FOR HONOR.

When bill may be accepted or paid for honor. § 1794. On the dishonor of a bill of exchange by the drawee, and, in case of a foreign bill, after it has been duly protested, it may be accepted or paid by any person, for the honor of any party thereto.

Story on Bills, § 121.

§ 1795. The holder of a bill of exchange is not bound to allow it to be accepted for honor, but is bound to accept payment for honor. Holder of bill of exchange, bound to accept payment for honor.

Story on Bills, § 122; Mitford *v.* Walcot, 12 *Mod.*, 410.

§ 1796. An acceptor or payer for honor must write a memorandum upon the bill, stating therein for whose honor he accepts or pays,[1] and must give notice to such parties, with reasonable diligence, of the fact of such acceptance or payment.[2] Having done so, he is entitled to reimbursement from such parties, and from all parties prior to them.[3] Acceptance for honor, how made.

[1] *Story on Bills*, § 256.
[2] *Id.*, § 259.
[3] *Id.*, § 124.

§ 1797. A bill of exchange, which has been accepted for honor, must be presented at its maturity to the drawee for payment, and notice of its dishonor by him must be given to the acceptor for honor in like manner as to an indorser; after which the acceptor for honor must pay the bill. How enforced.

Story on Bills, § 123; Schofield *v.* Bayard, 3 *Wend.*, 488; Williams *v.* Germaine, 7 *B. & C.*, 468.

§ 1798. The acceptance of a bill of exchange for honor does not excuse the holder from giving notice of its dishonor by the drawee. Notice of dishonor, not excused by acceptance for honor.

Story on Bills, § 255.

ARTICLE VI.

PRESENTMENT FOR PAYMENT.

Presentment, when bill not accepted, where made

§ 1799. If a bill of exchange is by its terms payable at a particular place, and is not accepted on presentment, it must be presented at the same place for payment, when presentment for payment is necessary.

Boot *v.* Franklin, 3 *Johns.*, 207. This is also the English law, 2 & 3 *W.* 4, *c.* 98. But see Mitchell *v.* Baring, 10 *B. & C.*, 4.

Presentment of bill payable at particular place.

§ 1800. A bill of exchange, accepted payable at a particular place, must be presented at that place[1] for payment, when presentment for payment is necessary, and need not be presented elsewhere.[2]

[1] Gibb *v.* Mather, 8 *Bing.*, 214; see § 1748 and notes.

[2] Hawkey *v.* Borwick, 4 *Bing.*, 135; De Bergareche *v.* Pillin, 3 *id.*, 476.

Effect of delay in presentment in certain cases.

§ 1801. If a bill of exchange, payable at sight, or on demand, without interest, is not duly presented for payment, within ten days after the time in which it could, with reasonable diligence, be transmitted to the proper place for such presentment, the drawer and indorsers are exonerated, unless such presentment is excused.

See § 1786.

Effect, in other cases.

§ 1802. Mere delay in presenting a bill of exchange payable with interest, at sight or on demand, does not exonerate any party thereto.

Merritt *v.* Todd, 23 *N. Y.*, 28.

ARTICLE VII.

EXCUSE OF PRESENTMENT AND NOTICE.

Presentment, when excused.

§ 1803. The presentment of a bill of exchange for acceptance is excused if the drawee has not capacity to accept it.

If the provision of § 1783, requiring presentment to a notary, is not adopted, this section must be modified by inserting after "excused," "if the holder cannot, with reasonable diligence, find any person authorized to accept it; or."

§ 1804. Delay in the presentment of a bill of exchange for acceptance is excused, when caused by circumstances over which the holder has no control. Delay, when excused.

§ 1805. Presentment of a bill of exchange for acceptance or payment, and notice of its dishonor, are excused as to the drawer, if he forbids the drawee to accept, or the acceptor to pay the bill;[1] or if, at the time of drawing, he had no reason to believe that the drawee would accept or pay the same.[2] Presentment and notice, when excused.

[1] Purchase *v.* Mattison, 6 *Duer*, 587; Jacks *v.* Darrin, 3 *E. D. Smith*, 557.

[2] Mobley *v.* Clark, 28 *Barb.*, 390; Coyle *v.* Smith, 1 *E. D. Smith*, 400; Franklin *v.* Vanderpool, 1 *Hall*, 78; Terry *v.* Parker, 6 *Ad. & El.*, 502.

ARTICLE VIII.

FOREIGN BILLS.

§ 1806. An inland bill of exchange is one drawn and payable within this state. All others are foreign. Definitions.

Halliday *v.* McDougall, 20 *Wend.*, 81; 22 *id.*, 272; Buckner *v.* Finley, 2 *Peters*, 586; Bank of U. S. *v.* Daniel, 12 *id.*, 54; Phœnix Bank *v.* Hussey, 12 *Pick.*, 483; Carter *v.* Burley, 9 *N. H.*, 558; Brown *v.* Ferguson, 4 *Leigh*, 37; Cape Fear Bank *v.* Stinemetz, 1 *Hill* [*S. C.*], 44; Schneider *v.* Cochrane, 1 *La. Ann.*, 235; see Mahoney *v.* Ashlin, 2 *B. & Ad.*, 478.

It has been strongly urged upon the commissioners, by gentlemen whose experience entitles their opinion to great weight, that all bills drawn and payable within the United States, should be deemed inland bills. The adoption of this suggestion would, however, involve so great a change that it is considered advisable to leave the text as it is, and submit the question to the wisdom of the legislature.

Protest necessary.

§ 1807. Notice of the dishonor of a foreign bill of exchange can be given only by notice of its protest.

Townsley *v.* Sumrall, 2 *Peters*, 170; Gale *v.* Walsh, 5 *T. R.*, 239; Bryden *v.* Taylor, 2 *Harr. & J.*, 396; Orr *v.* Maginnis, 7 *East*, 360; Fleming *v.* McClure, 1 *Brevard*, 433. No protest is necessary, in the case of an inland bill (Cole *v.* Jessup, 10 *N. Y.*, 96; Burke *v.* McKay, 2 *How.* [*U. S.*], 71; Young *v.* Bryan, 6 *Wheat.*, 152; Wardle *v.* Andrews, 2 *B. & Ald.*, 696).

Protest, by whom made

§ 1808. Protest must be made by a notary public, if with reasonable diligence one can be obtained;[1] and if not, then by any reputable person in the presence of two witnesses.[2]

[1] *Story on Bills*, § 276.
[2] *Ib.*

Protest, how made.

§ 1809. Protest must be made by an instrument in writing, giving a literal copy of the bill of exchange, with all that is written thereon, or annexing the original; stating the presentment, and the manner in which it was made; the presence or absence of the drawee or acceptor, as the case may be; the refusal to accept, or to pay, or the inability of the drawee to give a binding acceptance; and in case of refusal, the reason assigned, if any; and finally protesting against all the parties to be charged.

Story on Bills, § 276; *Code de Commerce*, arts. 173, 174.

Protest, where made

§ 1810. A protest for non-acceptance must be made in the city or town in which the bill is presented for acceptance; and a protest for non-payment in the city or town in which it is presented for payment.

Story on Bills, § 282.

§ 1811. A protest must be noted on the day of presentment, or on the next business day;[1] but it may be written out at any time thereafter.[2] **Protest, when to be made.**

[1] *Story on Bills*, § 283.

[2] Geralopulo *v.* Wieler, 10 *C. B.*, 690.

§ 1812. The want of protest of a foreign bill of exchange, or delay in making the same, is excused in like cases with the want or delay of presentment. **Protest, when excused.**

Story on Bills, § 280.

§ 1813. Notice of protest must be given in the same manner as notice of dishonor, except that it may be given by the notary who makes the protest. **Notice of protest, how given.**

§ 1814. If a foreign bill of exchange on its face waives protest, notice of dishonor may be given to any party thereto, in like manner as of an inland bill; except that if any indorser of such a bill expressly requires protest to be made, by a direction written on the bill at or before his indorsement, protest must be made, and notice thereof given to him and to all subsequent indorsers. **Waiver of protest.**

§ 1815. One who pays a foreign bill of exchange for honor must declare, before payment, in the presence of a person authorized to make protest, for whose honor he pays the same, in order to entitle him to reimbursement. **Declaration before payment for honor.**

Vandewall *v.* Tyrrell, as cited and explained in Geralopulo *v.* Wieler, 10 *C. B.*, 690.

§ 1816. Damages are allowed as hereinafter prescribed, as a full compensation for interest, re-exchange, expenses, and all other damages, in favor of holders for value only, upon bills of exchange drawn or negotiated within this state, and protested for non-acceptance or non-payment. **Damages allowed on dishonor of foreign bill.**

Rate of damages.

§ 1817. Damages are allowed under the last section upon bills drawn upon any person:

1. In any part of the United States except this state, lying north of Virginia and Kentucky, and east of Illinois and Wisconsin, at the rate of three per centum on the principal sum;

2. In any other part of the United States east of the Rocky Mountains, the two Canadas, and British provinces eastward thereof, at the rate of five per centum thereon;

3. In any other part of the United States, at the rate of seven per centum thereon;

4. In any other part of the continent of America, or Europe, or the islands in the Atlantic ocean, at the rate of ten per centum thereon;[1]

5. In any other place, at the rate of twenty per centum thereon.[2]

[1] This scale of damages is proposed as a substitute for that given in the Revised Statutes (1 *R. S.*, 770). There is no reason for giving Georgia a preference to Indiana, or in putting Russia on the same footing with Montreal or Detroit. The latter is as follows:

§ 1817. Damages are allowed under the last section, on bills drawn upon any person:

1. In Maine, New Hampshire, Vermont, Massachusetts, Rhode Island, Connecticut, New Jersey, Pennsylvania, Ohio, Delaware, Maryland, Virginia, or the District of Columbia, at the rate of three per centum on the principal sum;

2. In North Carolina, South Carolina, Georgia, Kentucky, or Tennessee, at the rate of five per centum thereon;

3. In any other part of North or South America, north of the equator, or the islands in the Atlantic ocean, or Europe, at the rate of ten per centum thereon;[1]

4. In any other place, at the rate of twenty per centum thereon.[2]

[2] This is the custom of merchants (Hendricks *v.* Franklin, 4 *Johns.*, 119).

Damages, how estimated.

§ 1818. If the amount of a protested bill of exchange is expressed in money of the United States, damages are estimated upon such amount without regard to the rate of exchange.

1 *R. S.*, 771, § 20.

§ 1819. If the amount of a protested bill of exchange is expressed in foreign money, damages are estimated upon the value of a similar bill at the time of protest, in the place nearest to the place where the bill was negotiated, and where such bills are currently sold. Id.

1 *R. S.*, 771, § 21, modified in form, so as to make it more explicit.

CHAPTER III.

PROMISSORY NOTES.

§ 1820. A promissory note is an instrument, negotiable in form, whereby the signer promises to pay a specified sum of money. Promissory note, what.

§ 1821. An instrument in the form of a bill of exchange, but drawn upon and accepted by the drawer himself, is to be deemed a promissory note. Certain instruments, promissory notes.

Fairchild *v.* Ogdensburgh &c. R. R., 15 *N. Y.*, 337; Miller *v.* Thomson, 3 *M. & G.*, 576.

§ 1822. A bill of exchange, if accepted, with the consent of the owner, by a person other than the drawee, or an acceptor for honor, becomes in effect the promissory note of such person, and all prior parties thereto are exonerated. Bill of exchange, when converted into a note.

See Peto *v.* Reynolds, 9 *Exch.*, 410.

§ 1823. Chapter I of this Title, and sections 1781 and 1802 of this Code, apply to promissory notes. Certain sections applicable to notes.

Effect of delay in presentment.

§ 1824. If a promissory note, payable on demand, or at sight, without interest, is not duly presented for payment, within six months from its date, the indorsers thereof are exonerated, unless such presentment is excused.

Sice *v.* Cunningham, 1 *Cow.*, 397. But whether this rule ought to be maintained, may be doubted (see Brooks *v.* Mitchell, 9 *M. & W.*, 15; Merritt *v.* Todd, 23 *N. Y.*, 28).

CHAPTER IV.

CHEQUES.

Cheque, what.

§ 1825. A cheque is a bill of exchange drawn upon a bank or banker, or a person described as such upon the face thereof, and payable on demand, without interest.

Rules applicable to cheques.

§ 1826. A cheque is subject to all the provisions of this Code concerning bills of exchange,[1] except that:[2]

1. The drawer and indorsers are exonerated by delay in presentment, only to the extent of the injury which they suffer thereby;[3] and are exonerated to that extent by a delay of more than one day in presentment;[4]

2. An indorsee, after its apparent maturity, but without actual notice of its dishonor, acquires a title equal to that of an indorsee before such period.[5]

[1] A cheque is an inland bill of exchange (Chapman *v.* White, 6 *N. Y.*, 412; Keene *v.* Beard, 8 *C. B.* [*N. S.*], 372; Eyre *v.* Waller, 5 *H. & N.*, 460).

It is *not* essential (as was unnecessarily said in Harker *v.* Anderson, 21 *Wend.*, 372; Woodruff *v.* Merchants' Bank, 25 *Wend.*, 673) that it should be payable to *bearer* (Eyre *v.* Waller, 5 *H. & N.*, 463).

[2] By *Laws* 1857, *ch.* 416, no grace is allowed on cheques.

[3] Robinson *v.* Hawksworth, 9 *Q. B.*, 52; Harbeck *v.* Craft, 4 *Duer*, 122; see Little *v.* Phœnix Bank, 2 *Hill*, 425; Keene *v.* Beard, 8 *C. B.* (*N. S.*). 381.

[4] Alexander *v.* Burchfield, 7 *M. & G.*, 1061. One day is allowed (Boddington *v.* Schlenker, 4 *B. & Ad.*, 752; Moule *v.* Brown, 4 *Bing. N. C.*, 266).

[5] Rothschild *v.* Corney, 9 *B. & C.*, 388. See Anderson *v.* Busteed, 5 *Duer*, 485.

CHAPTER V.

BONDS, BANK NOTES AND CERTIFICATES OF DEPOSIT.

§ 1827. A bank note remains negotiable, even after it has been paid by the maker. Bank note negotiable after payment.

§ 1828. A transferee of a bond, bank note or certificate of deposit, after its apparent maturity or actual dishonor within his knowledge, acquires a title equal to that of a transferee before such event. Title acquired by indorsee.

TITLE XVI.

GENERAL PROVISIONS.

§ 1829. Except where it is otherwise declared, the provisions of the foregoing fifteen Titles of this Part, in respect to the rights and obligations of parties to contracts, are subordinate to the intention of the parties, when ascertained in the manner prescribed by the chapter on the INTERPRETATION OF CONTRACTS; and the benefit thereof may be waived by any party entitled thereto, unless such waiver would be against public policy. Parties may waive provisions of Code.

DIVISION FOURTH.

GENERAL PROVISIONS

APPLICABLE TO PERSONS, PROPERTY, AND OBLIGATIONS, OR TO TWO OF THOSE SUBJECTS.

PART I.

RELIEF.

TITLE I.

RELIEF IN GENERAL.

Species of relief.

§ 1830. As a general rule, compensation is the relief or remedy provided by the law of this state for the violation of private rights, and the means of securing their observance; and specific and preventive relief may be given in no other cases than those specified in this Part of the CIVIL CODE.

Relief in case of forfeiture.

§ 1831. Whenever, by the terms of an obligation, a party thereto incurs a forfeiture, or a loss in the nature of a forfeiture, by reason of his failure to comply with its provisions, he may be relieved therefrom, upon making full compensation to the other party, except in case of a grossly negligent, willful or fraudulent breach of duty.

Spaulding *v.* Hallenbeck, 39 *Barb.*, 78; Clute *v.* Robison, 2 *Johns.*, 595, 614; Davis *v.* West, 12 *Ves.*, 475; Sanders *v.* Pope, *id.*, 282; Northcote *v.* Duke, *Ambler*, 513; 2 *Eden*, 314; Woodman *v.* Blake, 2 *Vern.*, 222; Hayward *v.* Angel, 1 *id.*, 222; Popham *v.* Bampfield, *id.*, 83; Wallis *v.* Crimes, 1 *Ch. Ca.*, 90; see Skinner *v.* White, 17 *Johns.*, 357; De Forest *v.* Bates, 1 *Edw.*, 394.

Though this doctrine, especially as applied to contracts, is one in its origin of purely equitable cognizance, it is now to be applied in all actions, and to be considered in estimating damages, as well as in granting specific relief (see Spaulding *v.* Hallenbeck, 39 *Barb.*, 78).

TITLE II.

COMPENSATORY RELIEF.

CHAPTER I.

DAMAGES IN GENERAL.

ARTICLE I.

GENERAL PRINCIPLES.

§ 1832. Every person who suffers detriment from the unlawful act or omission of another, may recover from the person in fault a compensation therefor in money, which is called damages. *Person suffering detriment, may recover damages.*

§ 1833. Detriment is a loss or harm suffered in person or property. *Detriment, what.*

This word is used in order to avoid the repetition of the words "loss or harm" in the numerous places in which they must otherwise occur. Injury signifies the wrongful act, and not its results, while on the other hand there may be loss without injury. The phrase "*damnum absque injuria,*" is familiar to lawyers. The word "harm" alone would be inadequate to express all the meaning of "loss."

§ 1834. Damages may be awarded, in a judicial proceeding, for detriment resulting after the commencement thereof, or certain to result in the future. *Injuries resulting or probable after suit brought.*

Drew *v.* Sixth Avenue R. R., 26 *N. Y.*, 49.

ARTICLE II.

INTEREST AS DAMAGES.

Person entitled to recover damages, may recover interest thereon.

§ 1835. Every person who is entitled to recover damages certain, or capable of being made certain by calculation, and the right to recover which is vested in him upon a particular day, is entitled also to recover interest thereon from that day,[1] except during such time as the debtor is prevented by law, or by the act of the creditor, from paying the debt.[2]

[1] This seems to be the rule in actions for wrongful injuries (Andrews *v.* Durant, 18 *N. Y.*, 496; Jackson *v.* Wood, 24 *Wend.*, 443), as it clearly is in actions upon contract (Dana *v.* Fiedler, 12 *N. Y.*, 40; Van Rensselaer *v.* Jewett, 2 *N. Y.*, 136; Livingston *v.* Miller, 11 *N. Y.*, 80; Purdy *v.* Phillips, 11 *N. Y.*, 406; 1 *Duer*, 369; see Brinckerhoff *v.* Phelps, 24 *Barb.*, 100; Sherman *v.* Wells, 28 *id.*, 403). The obligation to pay interest rests upon the default of the debtor, and not upon his use of the money (Rensselaer Glass Factory *v.* Reid, 5 *Cow.*, 587; People *v.* County of N. Y., *id.*, 331).

[2] If a debtor is prevented from paying by injunction he is not liable for interest (Stevens *v.* Barringer, 13 *Wend.*, 639; Fitzgerald *v.* Caldwell, 2 *Dallas*, 215; Le Braithwait *v.* Halsey, 4 *Halst.*, 3).

In actions other than on contract.

§ 1836. In an action for the breach of an obligation not arising from contract,[1] and in every case of oppression, fraud, or malice, interest may be given, in the discretion of the jury.[2]

[1] *Sedgw. Dam.*, 385, 386.

[2] Wilson *v.* Conine, 2 *Johns.*, 280; Bissel *v.* Hopkins, 4 *Cow.*, 53; Hyde *v.* Stone, 7 *Wend.*, 354; Baker *v.* Weller, 8 *Wend.*, 504; Dillerback *v.* Jerome, 7 *Cow.*, 294; Beals *v.* Guernsey, 8 *Johns.*, 446.

Limit of rate by contract.

§ 1837. Any legal rate of interest stipulated by a contract remains chargeable after a breach thereof, as before, until the contract is superseded by a verdict or other new obligation.

This rule is established in California, by statute (Kohler *v.* Smith, 2 *Cal.*, 597). The common law rule is otherwise. Compare Lawrence *v.* Leake & Watts Orphan House, 2 *Den.*, 577.

§ 1838. Accepting payment of the whole principal, as such, waives all claim to interest.

Acceptance of principal waives claim to interest.

Jacot *v.* Emmett, 11 *Paige*, 142; Gillespie *v.* Mayor, &c., of New York, 3 *Edw.*, 512; Tillotson *v.* Preston, 3 *Johns.*, 229; Johnston *v.* Brannan, 5 *id.*, 268; Williams *v.* Houghtaling, 3 *Cow.*, 86; Consequa *v.* Fanning, 3 *Johns. Ch.*, 587. But receiving a general payment, though precisely enough (People *v.* County of New York, 5 *Cow.*, 331), or more than enough (Stevens *v.* Barringer, 13 *Wend.*, 639) to pay the principal, does not defeat the right to recover the interest. And if payment of interest is stipulated in the contract, it may be recovered, although the principal has been paid (Fake *v.* Eddy, 15 *Wend.*, 76).

ARTICLE III.

EXEMPLARY DAMAGES.

SECTION 1839. Exemplary damages, in what cases allowed.

§ 1839. In any action for the breach of an obligation not arising from contract, where the defendant has been guilty of oppression, fraud or malice, actual or presumed, the jury, in addition to the actual damages, may give damages[1] for the sake of example, and by way of punishing the defendant.[2]

Exemplary damages, in what cases allowed.

[1] In this the commissioners have taken the rule as now settled in this state by the court of appeals (Hunt *v.* Bennett, 19 *N. Y.*, 173; and see Johnson *v.* Jenkins, 24 *N. Y.*, 252; Fry *v.* Bennett, 1 *Abb. Pr.*, 289; 4 *Duer*, 247; Brown *v.* Chadsey, 39 *Barb.*, 253, 259; Sharon *v.* Mosher, 17 *Barb.*, 518). The propriety of allowing damages by way of punishment has been, however, very earnestly and ably questioned. See the discussion of this subject in *Sedgwick on Dam.*, 3*d edition*, *ch.* 18, and especially p. 477, note 2; and Appendix.

[2] Tillotson *v.* Cheatham, 3 *Johns.*, 56, 64.

CHAPTER II.

MEASURE OF DAMAGES.

ARTICLE I.

DAMAGES FOR BREACH OF CONTRACT.

Measure of damages for breach of contract.

§ 1840. For the breach of an obligation arising from contract, the measure of damages, except where otherwise expressly provided by this Code, is the amount which will compensate the party aggrieved for all the detriment proximately caused thereby, which the party in fault had notice, at the time of entering into the contract,[1] or at any time before the breach,[2] and while it was in his power to perform the contract upon his part,[3] would be likely to result from such breach, or which, in the ordinary course of things, would be likely to result therefrom.[1]

[1] Griffin *v.* Colver, 16 *N. Y.*, 489; Hadley *v.* Baxendale, 9 *Exch.*, 341; Gee *v.* Lanc. & Yorksh. Railw. Co., 6 *H. & N.*, 211; Wilson *v.* L. & Y. Railw. Co., 9 *C. B.* [*N. S.*], 632; Landsberger *v.* Magnetic Telegraph Co., 32 *Barb.*, 530; Smeed *v.* Foord, 1 *El. & El.*, 602; Boyd *v.* Fitt, 14 *Irish Law*, 43.

[2] This provision adopts the suggestion of Baron Bramwell, in Gee *v.* L. & Y. Railw. Co. (6 *H. & N.* 211), though it is conceded that it is not undoubted law. See also, as to extraordinary damages, Dunlop *v.* Higgins, 1 *H. of L. Cas.*, 381.

[3] This clause is plainly a just qualification of the preceding one.

§ 1841. No damages can be recovered for a breach of contract, which are not clearly ascertainable in both their nature and origin. **Damages must be certain.**

Griffin *v.* Colver, 16 *N. Y.*, 489, 495.

§ 1842. The detriment caused by the breach of an obligation to pay money only is deemed to be the amount due by the terms of the obligation, with interest thereon. **Breach of promise to pay liquidated sum.**

Sedgw. Dam., 236; *Code La.*, 1929.

§ 1843. For the dishonor of foreign bills of exchange, the damages are prescribed by sections 1817 to 1819, inclusive. **Dishonor of bills of exchange.**

§ 1844. The detriment caused by the breach of a covenant of seizin, of right to convey, of warranty, or of quiet enjoyment, in a grant of an estate in real property, is deemed to be: **Breach of covenant of seizin, &c.**

1. The price paid to the grantor,[1] or, if the breach is partial only, such proportion of the price as the value of the property affected by the breach bore, at the time of the grant, to the value of the whole property;[2]

2. Interest thereon for the time during which the grantee derived no benefit from the property,[3] not exceeding six years;[4] and,

3. Any expenses properly incurred by the covenantee in defending his possession.[5]

[1] *Sedgw. Dam.*, 159; Staats *v.* Ten Eyck, 3 *Cai.*, 111. The grantee is not concluded by the consideration expressed in the deed (Bingham *v.* Weiderwax, 1 *N. Y.*, 509). But he cannot recover for improvements (Pitcher *v.* Livingston, 4 *Johns.*, 1; Bennet *v.* Jenkins, 13 *id.*, 50; Kinney *v.* Watts, 14 *Wend.*, 38. Compare Dimmick *v.* Lockwood, 10 *Wend.*, 142).

[2] Morris *v.* Phelps, 5 *Johns.*, 49.

[3] *Sedgw. Dam.*, 159. Interest is the legal countervail to the use of the land. The annual value cannot be recovered as such (Baxter *v.* Ryerss, 13 *Barb.*, 267).

[4] Bennet *v.* Jenkins, 13 *Johns.*, 50; Caulkins *v.* Harris, 9 *id.*, 324; Baxter *v.* Ryerss, 13 *Barb.*, 267.

[5] Staats *v.* Ten Eyck, 3 *Cai.*, 111; Rickert *v.* Snyder, 9 *Wend.*, 416; House *v.* House, 10 *Paige*, 158.

Breach of covenant against incumbrances

§ 1845. The detriment caused by the breach of a covenant against incumbrances in a grant of an estate in real property, is deemed to be the amount which has been actually expended by the covenantee in extinguishing either the principal or interest thereof;[1] not exceeding in the former case a proportion of the price paid to the grantor, equivalent to the relative value, at the time of the grant, of the property affected by the breach, as compared with the whole;[2] or, in the latter case, interest on a like amount.[3]

[1] Unless something has been actually paid, only nominal damages can be recovered (Grant *v.* Tallman, 20 *N. Y.*, 191; Delavergne *v.* Norris, 7 *Johns.*, 358; Stanard *v.* Eldridge, 16 *id.*, 254; Prescott *v.* Trueman, 4 *Mass.*, 627; see Hall *v.* Dean, 13 *Johns.*, 105). But the covenantee is at liberty to pay off the incumbrance, and recover the amount paid, as stated in the text (*id.;* Braman *v.* Bingham, 26 *N. Y.*, 483).

[2] Grant *v.* Tallman, 20 *N. Y.*, 191; Dimmick *v.* Lockwood, 10 *Wend.*, 142.

[3] Rickert *v.* Snyder, 9 *Wend.*, 423.

Breach of agreement to convey real property.

§ 1846. The detriment caused by the breach of an agreement to convey an estate in real property, is deemed to be the price paid,[1] and the expenses properly incurred in examining the title and preparing the necessary papers,[2] with interest thereon;[3] but adding thereto, in case of bad faith, the difference between the price agreed to be paid, and the value of the estate agreed to be conveyed,[4] at the time of the breach,[5] and the expenses properly incurred in preparing to enter upon the land.[6]

[1] Conger *v.* Weaver, 20 *N. Y.*, 140; Peters *v.* McKeon, 4 *Den.*, 546; Baldwin *v.* Munn, 2 *Wend.*, 399; Flureau *v.* Thornhill, 2 *W. Blacks.*, 1078; Sikes *v.* Wild, 4 *Best & Sm.*, 421; affirming S. C., 1 *id.*, 587.

[2] See Simons *v.* Patchett, 7 *E. & B.*, 572.

[3] Fletcher *v.* Button, 6 *Barb.*, 646; see Peters *v.* M'Keon, 4 *Den.*, 546.

[4] Trull *v.* Granger, 8 *N. Y.*, 115; Driggs *v.* Dwight, 17 *Wend.*, 71; Giles *v.* O'Toole, 4 *Barb.*, 261. Where the seller knew that he had not a good title, but had good reason to expect that he should be able to get it, this was held not to be a case of bad faith (Sikes *v.* Wild, 4 *Best & Sm.*, 421; 1 *id.*, 587).

[5] Brinckerhoff *v* Phelps, 24 *Barb.*, 100; see Peterson *v.* Ayre, 13 *C. B.*, 353; Tempest *v.* Kilner, 3 *id.*, 249.

[6] Driggs *v.* Dwight, 17 *Wend.*, 71; Giles *v.* O'Toole, 4 *Barb.*, 261; see Lawrence *v.* Wardwell, 6 *id.*, 423. Interest is allowed on such damages (Brinckerhoff *v.* Phelps, 24 *Barb.*, 100), but this follows from the general rule prescribed by section 1835.

Breach of agreement to buy real property.

§ 1847. The detriment caused by the breach of an agreement to purchase an estate in real property, is deemed to be the excess, if any, of the amount which would have been due to the seller under the contract, over the value of the property to him.

By the present law of this state, one who has agreed to sell real property may recover the full contract price from the purchaser, without actually transferring the title to him, if he offered to do so before commencing the action (Richards *v.* Edick, 17 *Barb.*, 260; Franchot *v.* Leach, 5 *Cow.*, 506), unless he has actually sold the property to a third person (Wilson *v.* Holden, 16 *Abb. Pr.*, 133). This rule is, however, an unjust one, as was admitted in Richards *v.* Edick (17 *Barb.*, 260), where it was said that if the question was a new one, the rule stated in the text should be adopted, but that the contrary was too well settled in this state to be changed by judicial intervention. This section follows the rule which is settled in England (Laird *v.* Pim, 7 *M. & W.*, 474).

Breach of agreement to sell personal property, not paid for.

§ 1848. The detriment caused by the breach of a seller's agreement to deliver personal property, the price of which has not been fully paid in advance, is deemed to be the excess, if any, of the value of the property to the buyer, over the amount which would have been due to the seller under the contract, if it had been fulfilled.

Dana *v.* Fiedler, 12 *N. Y.*, 40; M'Knight *v.* Dunlop, 5 *N. Y.*, 537; Portman *v.* Middleton, 4 *C. B.* [*N. S.*], 322; Shaw *v.* Holland, 15 *M. & W.*, 136; Shepherd *v.* Hampton, 3 *Wheat.*, 200; see Clark *v.* Pinney, 7 *Cow.*, 681; Pinney *v.* Gleason, 5 *Wend.*, 393.

Breach of agreement to sell personal property, paid for.

§ 1849. The detriment caused by the breach of a seller's agreement to deliver personal property, the price of which has been fully paid to him in advance, is deemed to be the same as in case of a wrongful conversion.

See Clark *v.* Pinney, 7 *Cow.*, 681; Dey *v.* Dox, 9 *Wend.*, 129; Elliott *v.* Hughes, 3 *Fost. & Finl.*, 387.

Breach of agreement to pay for personal property sold.

§ 1850. The detriment caused by the breach of a buyer's agreement to accept and pay for personal property, the title to which is vested in him, is deemed to be the contract price.

Orr *v.* Bigelow, 20 *Barb.*, 21; Bement *v.* Smith, 15 *Wend.*, 493. Of course the seller cannot recover the full price, if he has resold the goods (see Lamond *v.* Davall, 9 *Q. B.*, 1030).

Breach of agreement to buy personal property.

§ 1851. The detriment caused by the breach of a buyer's agreement to accept and pay for personal property, the title to which is not vested in him, is deemed to be:

1. If the property has been resold, pursuant to section 1694, the excess, if any, of the amount due from the buyer, under the contract, over the net proceeds of the resale;[1] or,

2. If the property has not been resold in the manner prescribed by section 1694, the excess, if any, of the amount due from the buyer, under the contract, over the value to the seller[2]; together with the excess, if any, of the expenses properly incurred in carrying the property to market, over those which would have been incurred for the carriage thereof, if the buyer had accepted it.[3]

[1] Sands *v.* Taylor, 5 *Johns.*, 395.

[2] Boorman *v.* Nash, 9 *B. & C.*, 145.

[3] This provision seems to be only reasonable. Some things are marketable only in large cities, yet are manufactured, or owned, in many cases, by persons living in the country. If such things should be bought by a resident of the country, the expense of forwarding them to him might be trifling, compared with the expense of transportation to the nearest market. Justice to the buyer requires that the market price should be allowed to him, but justice to the seller requires that he should be allowed the increased cost of sending the things to market.

§ 1852. The detriment caused by the breach of a warranty of the title of personal property sold, is deemed to be the value thereof to the buyer, when he is deprived of its possession, together with any costs which he has become liable to pay, in an action brought for the property by the true owner. *Breach of warranty of title to personal property.*

A different rule has been laid down in this state, conforming to the rule concerning real property (Armstrong *v.* Percy, 5 *Wend.*, 535); but this section states the law as it appears to be in England (see Simons *v.* Patchett, 7 *E. & B.*, 568), and as appears to be most in accordance with general principles.

§ 1853. The detriment caused by the breach of a warranty of the quality of personal property, is deemed to be the excess, if any, of the value which the property would have had, at the time to which the warranty referred, if it had been complied with, over its actual value at that time. *Breach of warranty of quality of personal property.*

Tallman *v.* Clute, 3 *Barb.*, 424; Cary *v.* Gruman, 4 *Hill*, 625; Comstock *v.* Hutchinson, 10 *Barb.*, 211; Roberts *v.* Carter, 28 *Barb.*, 462; Milburn *v.* Belloni, 34 *Barb.*, 607; 12 *Abb. Pr.*, 451; Voorhees *v.* Earl, 2 *Hill*, 288; Lattin *v.* Davis, *Hill & D. Supp.*, 9; Muller *v.* Eno, 14 *N. Y.*, 597; Prentice *v.* Dike, 6 *Duer*, 220; Fales *v.* McKeon, 2 *Hilt.*, 53.

§ 1854. The detriment caused by the breach of a warranty of the fitness of an article of personal property for a particular purpose, is deemed to be that which is defined by the last section, together *Breach of warranty of quality for special purpose.*

with a fair compensation for the loss incurred by an effort in good faith to use it for such purpose.

Passenger *v.* Thorburn, 35 *Barb.*, 17; see Randall *v.* Raper, *El. B. & E.*, 84.

Breach of carrier's obligation to receive goods, &c.

§ 1855. The detriment caused by the breach of a carrier's obligation to accept freight, messages or passengers, is deemed to be the difference between the amount which he had a right to charge for the carriage, and the amount which it would be necessary to pay for the same service, when it ought to be performed.

Ogden *v.* Marshall, 8 *N. Y.*, 340.

Breach of carrier's obligation to deliver.

§ 1856. The detriment caused by the breach of a carrier's obligation to deliver freight, where he has not converted it to his own use, is deemed to be the value[1] thereof, at the place and on the day at which it should have been delivered,[2] deducting the freightage to which he would have been entitled, if he had completed the delivery.[3]

[1] Smith *v.* Griffith, 3 *Hill*, 333; see Kent *v.* H. R. R. R. Co., 22 *Barb.*, 278.

[2] *Sedgw. Dam.*, 365; Van Winkle *v.* U. S. Steamship Co., 37 *Barb.*, 122; Wheelwright *v.* Beers, 2 *Hall*, 391; As to how the value is to be ascertained, see Harris *v.* Panama R. R. Co., 3 *Bosw.*, 7.

[3] Watkinson *v.* Laughton, 8 *Johns.*, 213; Atkisson *v.* Steamboat Castle Garden, 28 *Miss.*, 124.

Carrier's delay.

§ 1857. The detriment caused by a carrier's delay in the delivery of freight, is deemed to be the depreciation in the intrinsic value of the freight during the delay,[1] and also the depreciation, if any, in the market value thereof, otherwise than by reason of a depreciation in its intrinsic value, at the place where it ought to have been delivered, and between the day at which it ought to have been delivered, and the day of its actual delivery.[2]

[1] Jones *v.* N. Y. & Erie R. R. Co., 29 *Barb.*, 633.

[2] Kent *v.* Hudson River R. R., 22 *Barb.*, 278; Medbury *v.* N. Y. & Erie R. R. Co., 26 *id.*, 564; Collard *v.* Southwestern Railw. Co., 7 *H. & N.*, 79; Wilson *v.*

Lancashire & Yorksh. Railw. Co., 9 *C. B.* [*N. S.*], 632; to the contrary is Jones *v.* N. Y. & Erie R. R., 29 *Barb.*, 633; Wibert *v.* N. Y. & Erie R. R. Co., 19 *id.*, 36; see Conger *v.* Hudson Riv. R. R. Co., 6 *Duer*, 375. The rule here adopted is supported by the weight of authority, and, as the commissioners believe, by the weight of reason. It is to be observed that the latter branch of the rule does not include the former. Goods may advance in the market, and yet be so injured by delay as to diminish their intrinsic value. The carrier ought not to benefit by his own fault.

§ 1858. The detriment caused by the breach of a warranty of an agent's authority, is deemed to be the amount which could have been recovered and collected from his principal if the warranty had been complied with,[1] and the reasonable expenses of legal proceedings taken, in good faith, to enforce the act of the agent against his principal.[2] Breach of warranty of authority.

[1] Simons *v.* Patchett, 7 *E. & B.*, 568.

[2] Collen *v.* Wright, 8 *E. & B.*, 647; aff'g S. C., 7 *id.*, 301; see White *v.* Madison, 26 *N. Y.*, 117.

§ 1859. The damages for the breach of a promise of marriage rest in the sound discretion of the jury. Breach of promise of marriage.

Southard *v.* Rexford, 6 *Cow.*, 254; see Johnson *v.* Jenkins, 24 *N. Y.*, 252.

ARTICLE II.

DAMAGES FOR WRONGS.

§ 1860. For the breach of an obligation not arising from contract, the measure of damages, except where otherwise expressly provided by this Code, is the amount which will compensate for all the detriment Breach of obligation other than contract.

proximately caused thereby, whether it could have been anticipated or not.

See Hart *v.* Ten Eyck, 2 *Johns. Ch.*, 62; Sharon *v.* Mosher, 17 *Barb.*, 518; Lacour *v.* Mayor, &c., of N. Y., 3 *Duer*, 406; St. John *v.* Mayor, &c., of N. Y., 6 *id.*, 315; compare Walrath *v.* Redfield, 11 *Barb.*, 368.

Wrongful occupation of real property.

§ 1861. The detriment caused by the wrongful occupation of real property, in cases not embraced in sections 1862, 1868, 1869, and 1870, is deemed to be the value[1] of the use of the property for the time of such occupation, not exceeding six years next preceding the commencement of the action or proceeding to enforce the right to damages,[2] and the costs, if any, of recovering the possession.[3]

[1] *Sedgw. Dam.*, 125.

[2] 2 *R. S.*, 311, § 50; Jackson *v.* Wood, 24 *Wend.*, 443.

[3] 2 *Burr.*, 665. The abolition of dower in future is proposed in the Second Division of this Code, and therefore no provision is here made in respect to it.

Willful holding over.

§ 1862. For willfully holding over real property, by a person who entered upon the same, as guardian or trustee for an infant, or by right of an estate terminable with any life or lives, after the termination of the trust or particular estate, without the consent of the party immediately entitled after such termination, the measure of damages is the value of the profits received during such holding over.

See 1 *R. S.*, 749, § 7.

Conversion of personal property.

§ 1863. The detriment caused by the wrongful conversion of personal property, is presumed to be:[1]

1. The value of the property at the time of the conversion,[2] with interest from that time,[3] or, where the action has been prosecuted with reasonable diligence, the highest market value of the property at any time between the conversion and the verdict,[4] without interest, at the option of the injured party;[5] and,

2. A fair compensation for the time and money properly expended in pursuit of the property.[6]

[1] In Chinery *v.* Viall (5 *H. & N.*, 288), the plaintiff bought sheep from the defendant, upon credit, and left them with the defendant as bailee. The defendant sold them to another person. It was held that although the plaintiff could sue as for a conversion, yet that his damages could not exceed the amount of his loss by the failure of the bargain. And the court say: "It is not an absolute rule of law that the value of the goods is to be taken as the measure of damage," citing *Mayne on Dam.*, 215; Read *v.* Fairbanks, 13 *C. B.*, 692; Brierly *v.* Kendall, 17 *Q. B.*, 937; Lamond *v.* Davall, 9 *id.*, 1030. So the return of the property, or of any portion thereof, if accepted by the plaintiff, mitigates the damages (Hibbard *v.* Stewart, 1 *Hilt.*, 207; Reynolds *v.* Shuler, 5 *Cow.*, 323; see Hanmer *v.* Wilsey, 17 *Wend.*, 91; Vosburgh *v.* Welsh, 11 *Johns.*, 175; Gibbs *v.* Chase, 10 *Mass.*, 128). So if, after a conversion, the property is seized under an execution in favor of a third person against the lawful owner, the damages are mitigated (Sherry *v.* Schuyler, 2 *Hill*, 204; Higgins *v.* Whitney, 24 *Wend.*, 379), though it is otherwise where the execution is in favor of the wrongdoer (Otis *v.* Jones, 21 *Wend.*, 394; Hanmer *v.* Wilsey, 17 *id.*, 91; Edmonstone *v.* Nuttall, 17 *C. B.* [*N. S.*] 280).

[2] Suydam *v.* Jenkins, 3 *Sandf.*, 614; King *v.* Orser, 4 *Duer*, 431; Smith *v.* Griffith, 3 *Hill*, 333; Kennedy *v.* Strong, 14 *Johns.*, 128.

[3] Andrews *v.* Durant, 18 *N. Y.*, 496.

[4] Romaine *v.* Van Allen, 26 *N. Y.*, 309; Wilson *v.* Mathews, 24 *Barb.*, 295. To the contrary is Suydam *v.* Jenkins (3 *Sandf.*, 614), in which the question is very fully discussed by DUER, J.

[5] There does not seem to be any authority for allowing interest, where the plaintiff elects to take a verdict for the highest price; nor does it seem reasonable to allow it. But there can be little question that he has the option here allowed him.

[6] Bennett *v.* Lockwood, 20 *Wend.*, 223; see Miller *v.* Garling, 12 *How. Pr.*, 203.

§ 1864. The presumption declared by the last section cannot be repelled, in favor of one whose possession was wrongful from the beginning, by his subsequent application of the property to the benefit of the owner, without his consent. Id.

Edmonstone *v.* Nuttall, 17 *C. B.* [*N. S.*], 280; Attack *v.* Bromwell, 3 *Best & Sm.*, 520; Keen *v.* Priest, 4 *H. & N.*, 236; Gillard *v.* Brittan, 8 *M. & W.*, 575; compare Johnson *v.* Stear, 15 *C. B.* [*N. S.*], 330.

Damages of lienor.

§ 1865. One having a mere lien on personal property, cannot recover greater damages for its conversion, from one having a right thereto superior to his, after his lien is discharged, than the amount secured by the lien, and the compensation allowed by section 1863 for loss of time and expenses.

Parish *v.* Wheeler, 22 *N. Y.*, 494; Chadwick *v.* Lamb, 29 *Barb.*, 518; Seaman *v.* Luce, 23 *id.*, 240. Against a mere stranger the lienor recovers the full value (Alt *v.* Weidenberg, 6 *Bosw.*, 176; Dows *v.* Rush, 28 *Barb.*, 157; see Turner *v.* Hardcastle, 11 *C. B.* [*N. S.*], 683).

Seduction.

§ 1866. The damages for seduction rest in the sound discretion of the jury.

Travis *v.* Barger, 24 *Barb.*, 614; Knight *v.* Wilcox, 18 *id.*, 212; Ingersoll *v.* Jones, 5 *id.*, 661; Lee *v.* Hodges, 13 *Gratt.*, 726.

Injuries to animals.

§ 1867. For wrongful injuries to animals, being subjects of property, committed willfully, or by gross negligence, in disregard of humanity, exemplary damages may be given.

Wort *v.* Jenkins, 14 *Johns.*, 352.

ARTICLE III.

PENAL DAMAGES.

Failure to quit, after notice.

§ 1868. For the failure of a tenant to give up the premises held by him, when he has given notice of his intention to do so, the measure of damages is double the rent which he ought otherwise to pay.

See 1 *R. S.*, 745, § 10.

Tenant willfully holding over.

§ 1869. For willfully holding over real property, by a tenant after the end of his term, and after notice to quit has been duly given, and demand of possession made, the measure of damages is double the yearly value of the property, for the time of withholding, in addition to compensation for the detriment occasioned thereby.

See 1 *R. S.*, 745, § 11.

§ 1870. For forcibly ejecting or excluding a person from the possession of real property, the measure of damages is three times such a sum as would compensate for the detriment caused to him by the act complained of. **Forcible exclusion from possession of real property.**

2 *R. S.*, 338, § 4.

§ 1871. For wrongful injuries to timber, trees or underwood upon the land of another, or removal thereof, the measure of damages is three times such a sum as would compensate for the actual detriment, except where the trespass was casual and involuntary, or committed under the belief that the land belonged to the trespasser, or where the wood was taken by the authority of highway officers for the purposes of a highway; in which cases the damages are a sum equal to the actual detriment. **Injuries to trees, &c.**

2 *R. S.*, 338, §§ 1-3.

ARTICLE IV.

GENERAL PROVISIONS.

§ 1872. In estimating damages, the value of property, to a seller thereof, is deemed to be the price[1] which he could have obtained therefor in the market nearest to the place at which it should have been accepted by the buyer,[2] and at such time after the **Value, how estimated in favor of seller.**

breach of the contract as would have sufficed, with reasonable diligence, for the seller to effect a resale.[3]

[1] Obviously, a seller can sustain no injury by reason of any peculiar value of the thing sold.

[2] See Gregory *v.* McDowell, 8 *Wend.*, 435.

[3] Loder *v.* Kekulé, 3 *C. B.* [*N. S.*], 128; see Simons *v.* Patchett, 7 *E. & B.*, 568.

Value, how estimated in favor of buyer.

§ 1873. In estimating damages, except as provided by sections 1874 and 1875, the value of property, to a buyer or owner thereof,[1] deprived of its possession, is deemed to be the price[2] at which he might have bought an equivalent thing,[3] in the market[2] nearest to the place where the property ought to have been put into his possession,[4] and at such time after the breach of duty upon which his right to damages is founded as would suffice, with reasonable diligence, for him to make such a purchase.[5]

[1] It will be found that there is no distinction between the buyer and the owner of goods in respect to the matters to which this section relates.

[2] Havemeyer *v.* Cunningham, 35 *Barb.*, 515; Smith *v.* Griffith, 3 *Hill*, 333; King *v.* Orser, 4 *Duer*, 431; Davis *v.* Shields, 24 *Wend.*, 322; 26 *id.*, 341; see Lawrence *v.* Wardwell, 6 *Barb.*, 423; Comstock *v.* Hutchinson, 10 *id.*, 211; Gerard *v.* Prouty, 34 *id.*, 454; Hamilton *v.* Ganyard, *id.*, 204; Muller *v.* Eno, 14 *N. Y.*, 597; M'Knight *v.* Dunlop, 5 *id.*, 537; Dana *v.* Fiedler, 12 *id.*, 40; Stevens *v.* Low, 2 *Hill*, 132; Cary *v.* Gruman, 4 *id.*, 625.

[3] The price at which a purchase could have been made, is alone to be regarded, even though the purchaser bought for speculation, and could not have sold again at such a price (Dana *v.* Fiedler, 12 *N. Y.*, 40).

[4] Gregory *v.* McDowell, 8 *Wend.*, 435.

[5] Josling *v.* Irvine, 6 *H. & N.*, 512; see Loder *v.* Kekulé, 3 *C. B.* [*N. S.*], 128. The rule usually stated is that the buyer can recover only the price of the day upon which delivery ought to have been made (Dana *v.* Fiedler, 12 *N. Y.*, 40; Clark *v.* Dales, 20 *Barb.*, 42; Belden *v.* Nicolay, 4 *E. D. Smith*, 14; Davis *v.* Shields, 24 *Wend.*, 322; 26 *id.*, 341; Gregory *v.* McDowell, 8 *id.*, 435; Tempest *v.* Kilner, 3 *C. B.*, 249; see Peterson *v.* Ayre, 13 *id.*, 353). But the question discussed in Josling *v.* Irvine was not raised in these cases.

§ 1874. Where certain property has a peculiar value to a person recovering damages for deprivation thereof, or injury thereto, that may be deemed to be its value against one who had notice thereof before incurring a liability to damages in respect thereof, or against a willful wrongdoer. **Property of peculiar value.**

See Suydam *v.* Jenkins, 3 *Sandf.*, 614, 621.

§ 1875. For the purpose of estimating damages, the value of a thing in action is presumed to be equal to that of the property to which it entitles its owner. **Value of thing in action.**

So held as to a note (Decker *v.* Mathews, 12 *N. Y.*, 313; Ingalls *v.* Lord, 1 *Cow.*, 240), or other debt (Thomas v. Dickinson, 12 *N. Y.*, 364; S. C., again, 23 *Barb.*, 431), or an agreement to convey land (Clowes *v.* Hawley, 12 *Johns.*, 484).

This presumption is not conclusive (Allen *v.* Suydam, 20 *Wend.*, 321; Ingalls *v.* Lord, 1 *Cow.*, 240; see Thomas *v.* Dickinson, above cited).

§ 1876. The damages prescribed by this chapter are exclusive of exemplary damages and interest, except where those are expressly mentioned. **Damages allowed in this chapter exclusive of others.**

§ 1877. Notwithstanding the provisions of this chapter, no person can recover a greater amount in damages for the breach of an obligation, than he could have gained by the full performance thereof on both sides, except in the cases specified in the articles on EXEMPLARY DAMAGES and PENAL DAMAGES, and in sections 1859, 1866 and 1867. **Limitation of damages.**

This is an established principle of equity (Skinner *v.* White, 17 *Johns.*, 357; rev'g S. C., 2 *Johns. Ch.*, 526), which, since the union of law and equity, should be recognized as a rule of damages. See a decision upon a similar question in Russell *v.* Roberts, 3 *E. D. Smith*, 318.

§ 1878. Damages must, in all cases, be reasonable, and where an obligation of any kind appears to create a right to unconscionable and grossly oppressive damages, contrary to substantial justice, no more than reasonable damages can be recovered. **Damages to be reasonable.**

James *v.* Morgan, 2 *Levinz*, 111; Thornborow *v.* Whitacre, 2 *Ld. Raym.*, 1164. In the first case, the defendant had agreed to pay, for a horse sold to him, a farthing for his first shoe nail, two farthings for the second, four for the third, and so on, for the thirty-two nails in the horse's shoes. This, of course, amounted to many thousand pounds sterling, for which the plaintiff sued. But the court directed the jury to assess the damages at the actual value of the horse, which was found to be eight pounds. In the latter case, a somewhat similar bargain was entered into, the damages claimed being an enormous sum. The action was sustained on demurrer, and it appears that the court was, at first, about to give judgment for the whole sum demanded; but an *amicus curiæ* mentioning the case of James *v.* Morgan, the action was settled, under an intimation of the court, by the repayment of the consideration received for the contract (2s. 6d.), and costs.

Nominal damages

§ 1879. When a breach of duty has caused no appreciable detriment to the party affected, he may yet recover nominal damages.

Hamlin *v.* Great Northern Railw. Co., 1 *H. & N.*, 408; Marzetti *v.* Williams, 1 *B. & Ad.*, 415.

TITLE III.

SPECIFIC AND PREVENTIVE RELIEF.

CHAPTER I.

GENERAL PRINCIPLES.

§ 1880. Specific or preventive relief may be given in the cases specified in this Title, and in no others. Specific relief, &c., when allowed.

§ 1881. Specific relief is given: Specific relief, how given.

1. By taking possession of a thing, and delivering it to a claimant;[1]

2. By compelling a party himself to do that which ought to be done;[2] or,

3. By declaring and determining the rights of parties, otherwise than by an award of damages.[3]

[1] This includes the ordinary remedies in the common law actions of ejectment and replevin, or, as they may be called under the Code, actions for land, and actions for chattels.

[2] This includes the specific performance of contracts, the delivery of things wrongfully detained, the surrender of instruments to be canceled, &c.

[3] This includes all cases in which a right is determined, without ulterior measures. Thus a contract may be declared void, although the instrument containing it is lost; a judgment may be annulled for fraud; the occupant of land may be declared to have a good title as against a claimant who does not himself sue, &c.

§ 1882. Preventive relief is given by prohibiting a party from doing that which ought not to be done. Preventive relief, how given.

§ 1883. Neither specific nor preventive relief can be granted to enforce a penal law,[1] except in a case of nuisance,[2] nor to enforce a penalty or forfeiture in any case.[3] Not to enforce penalty, &c.

[1] Brandreth *v.* Lance, 8 *Paige*, 24; Mayor &c. of Hudson *v.* Thorne, 7 *id.*, 261.

[2] See Mayor &c. of Hudson *v.* Thorne, 7 *Paige*, 261.

[3] Linden *v.* Hepburn, 3 *Sandf.*, 668; Livingston *v.* Tompkins, 4 *Johns. Ch.*, 415.

CHAPTER II.

SPECIFIC RELIEF.

ARTICLE I.

POSSESSION OF REAL PROPERTY.

Judgment for possession or title.

§ 1884. A person entitled to specific real property, by reason either of a perfected title, or of a claim to title which ought to be perfected, may recover the same in the manner prescribed by the Code of Civil Procedure, either by a judgment for its possession, to be executed by the sheriff, or by a judgment requiring the other party to perfect the title, and to deliver possession of the property.

ARTICLE II.

POSSESSION OF PERSONAL PROPERTY.

Judgment for delivery.

§ 1885. A person entitled to the immediate possession of specific personal property may recover the same in the manner provided by the Code of Civil Procedure.

When holder may be compelled to deliver.

§ 1886. Any person, having the possession or control of a particular article of personal property, of which he is not the owner, may be compelled[1] specifically to deliver it to the person entitled[2] to its immediate possession, in either of the following cases:

1. When the thing claimed is held subject to an express trust in favor of the claimant;[3]

2. When pecuniary compensation would not afford adequate relief for the loss of the thing claimed;[4] or,

3. When it would be extremely difficult to ascertain the actual damage caused by its loss.[5]

[1] This section is intended to provide for the relief granted by courts of equity in the cases specified. The ordinary remedy in an action for chattels may be evaded by any one who has sufficient means to pay their value, by the exercise of a little ingenuity. Accordingly, courts of equity have long intervened to compel a wrongdoer *himself* to deliver up the things detained by him.

[2] It will be observed that this remedy is not confined to cases of *wrongful* possession. It may often happen that one who holds a thing in trust may secretly design to make a wrongful disposition of it, and that the owner may have an intimation or suspicion of this design, but no legal evidence of it. A demand before suit might lead to a sudden disposition of the thing, and result in its total loss. The owner ought therefore to be allowed to sue without a prior demand, subject to the discretion of the court as to costs, if it appears that he has made unnecessary litigation (see Bruce *v.* Tilson, 25 *N. Y.*, 194). But the section is so restricted as not to include the case of a thing agreed to be sold.

[3] Wood *v.* Rowcliffe, 2 *Phillips*, 382; aff'g S. C., 3 *Hare*, 304. In that case, the property consisted of household furniture, the bulk of which did not appear to have any peculiar value. See also Merritt *v.* Thompson, 3 *E. D. Smith*, 283; Cowles *v.* Whitman, 10 *Conn.*, 121; Pooley *v.* Budd, 14 *Beav.*, 34, 44; McGowin *v.* Remington, 12 *Penn. St.*, 56.

[4] The inadequacy of compensation in damages is the true test of a plaintiff's right to this special relief (North *v.* Great Northern Railw. Co., 2 *Giff.*, 69). Thus freight cars for use upon a railway were decreed to be delivered up, on the ground that similar cars could not be bought ready made, and that compensation in damages would not cover the loss which would be caused by delay (*Ib*). It is not therefore deemed advisable to attempt any enumeration, in the text of the Code, of the articles which may be recovered by this process. There would be little danger of injus-

tice being done, if this remedy should be more widely applied. A summary of the principal cases in which a specific delivery has been enforced, may however be useful.

Courts of equity have compelled the delivery of old and rare paintings (Lowther *v.* Lowther, 13 *Ves.*, 95), of family paintings (Hunt *v.* Moultrie, 1 *Bosw.*, 531; aff'd in Ct. of Appeals), of an ancient altar piece in silver, with a Greek inscription (Somerset *v.* Cookson, 3 *P. Wms.*, 389), of a gold snuff box (Fells *v.* Read, 3 *Ves.*, 70), of heir looms (Macclesfield *v.* Davis, 3 *Ves. & B.*, 18; Pusey *v.* Pusey, 1 *Vern.*, 273), of family plate (Geoffry *v.* Davis, *Cary*, 34), of jewels (Saville *v.* Tankred, 1 *Ves. Sr.*, 101; *Bell Supp.*, 70; Young *v.* Eurrel, *Cary*, 54), of farm stock (Nutbrown *v.* Thornton, 10 *Ves.*, 159), of masonic regalia (Lloyd *v.* Loaring, 6 *Ves.*, 773), of mortgage deeds (Jackson *v.* Butler, 2 *Atk.*, 306; Knye *v.* Moore, 1 *Sim. & S.*, 61), of books of account (Evans *v.* Van Hall, *Clarke*, 26; Lingan *v.* Simpson, 1 *Sim. & S.*, 600), and, in slave states, of particular slaves (Hall *v.* Clark, 12 *Sme. & M.*, 189; Butler *v.* Hicks, 11 *id.*, 79; Murphy *v.* Clark, 1 *id.*, 221; Dudley *v.* Mallery, 4 *Geo.*, 52; Sims *v.* Shelton, 2 *Strobh. Eq.*, 221; Ellis *v.* Commander, 1 *id.*, 188; Sarter *v.* Gordon, 2 *Hill's Ch.*, 121; Loften *v.* Espy, 4 *Yerg.*, 84; 10 *id.*, 30; Williams *v.* Howard, 3 *Murph.*, 74; Young *v.* Burton, 1 *McMull. Eq.*, 256). In Dowling *v.* Betjemann (2 *Johns. & Hem.*, 544), the court asserted its right to order the specific delivery of a new painting, upon the application of the artist himself, but the plaintiff in that case having put a valuation on the painting, this was held to show that compensation in damages would be sufficient relief.

[5] See Falcke *v.* Gray, 4 *Drewry*, 651.

ARTICLE III.

SPECIFIC PERFORMANCE OF OBLIGATIONS.

SECTION 1887. In what cases compelled.

In what cases compelled.

§ 1887. Except as otherwise provided in this article, the specific performance of an obligation[1] may be compelled:

1. When the act to be done is in the performance, wholly or partly, of an express trust;[2]

2. When the act to be done is such that pecuniary compensation for its non-performance would not afford adequate relief;[3]

3. When it would be extremely difficult to ascertain the actual damage caused by the non-performance of the act to be done;[4] or,

4. When it has been expressly agreed, in writing, between the parties to the contract, that specific performance thereof may be required by either party, or that damages shall not be considered adequate relief.[5]

[1] The word "obligation" is used, because some obligations created by operation of law may be enforced in this manner. It includes an award, which may be specifically enforced (Bouck *v.* Wilber, 4 *Johns. Ch.*, 405). The obligation must be a subsisting one (Arnoux *v.* Homans, 25 *How. Pr.*, 427).

[2] Thus, a trustee who has wrongfully disposed of stock may be compelled to restore the same amount of stock (Forrest *v.* Elwes, 4 *Ves.*, 497). So the specific delivery of a common article of merchandise will be enforced, when held under a trust (Pooley *v.* Budd, 14 *Beav.*, 34; Mechanics' Bank *v.* Seton, 1 *Peters*, 299; M'Gowin *v.* Remington, 12 *Penn. St.*, 56).

[3] Though in most cases the act which is sought to be specifically enforced is a transfer of property, the jurisdiction is not confined to that class of cases. The courts have thus enforced an agreement to insure (Tayloe *v.* Merchants' Fire Ins. Co., 9 *How.* [*U. S.*], 405; Carpenter *v.* Mutual Ins. Co., 4 *Sandf. Ch.*, 408; Neville *v.* Merchants' Ins. Co., 19 *Ohio*, 452), to indorse a note (see Watkins *v.* Maule, 2 *Jac. & W.*, 242), to form a partnership (Buxton *v.* Lister, 3 *Atk.*, 385; England *v.* Curling, 3 *Beav.*, 129; Birchett *v.* Bolling, 5 *Munf.*, 442; Anon., 2 *Ves. Sr.*, 629), to discharge a judgment (Phillips *v.* Berger, 8 *Barb.*, 527; 2 *id.*, 609), to release a mortgage (Malins *v.* Brown, 4 *N. Y.*, 403), to improve land (Stuyvesant *v.* Mayor, &c., of New York, 11 *Paige*, 414), to build an archway (Stover *v.* Gt. Western Railw. Co., 2 *You. & Coll. Ch.*, 48), &c. The nature of the property affected, whether real or personal, is not decisive of the right to specific performance, which depends entirely upon the inadequacy of damages to compensate the injured party (*Story Eq. Jur.*, § 717; see Cathcart *v.* Robin-

son, 5 *Peters*, 264; Adderley *v.* Dixon, 1 *Sim. & S.*, 607; Harnett *v.* Yielding, 2 *Sch. & Lef.*, 549; Dalzell *v.* Crawford, 1 *Pars. Sel. Eq. Cas.*, 37).

[4] Falcke *v.* Gray, 4 *Drewry*, 651; 5 *Jur.* [*N. S.*], 645. On this ground, contracts for the sale of chattels of singular value (*ib.*), or of stock in a corporation (Cheale *v.* Kenward, 5 *De G. & J.*, 27; Shaw *v.* Fisher, 5 *De G., M. & G.*, 596; Duncuft *v.* Albrecht, 12 *Sim.*, 189), may be specifically enforced.

[5] There is no reported decision upon this proposition, but in these days, when a judgment for damages affords such very unsatisfactory relief in many cases, there seems much reason for allowing parties to enter into such a stipulation.

Remedy mutual.

§ 1888. When either of the parties to an obligation is entitled to a specific performance thereof, according to the provisions of the last section, the other party is also entitled to it, though not within those provisions.

Story Eq. Jur., § 723; Phillips *v.* Berger, 8 *Barb.*, 527; Schroeppel *v.* Hopper, 40 *id.*, 425; Withy *v.* Cottle, 1 *Sim. & S.*, 174; *Turn. & Russ.*, 78; see Crary *v.* Smith, 2 *N. Y.*, 60.

No remedy unless mutual.

§ 1889. Neither party to an obligation can be compelled specifically to perform it, unless the other party thereto has performed, or is compellable specifically to perform, everything to which the former is entitled under the same obligation,[1] either completely, or nearly so, together with full compensation for any want of entire performance.[2]

[1] Flight *v.* Bolland, 4 *Russ.*, 298; Hargrave *v.* Hargrave, 12 *Beav.*, 411; Peto *v.* Brighton, &c., Railw. Co., 1 *Hem. & Mil.*, 468; Pickering *v.* Bp. of Ely, 2 *Y. & Coll. Ch.*, 249.

[2] See Dyer *v.* Hargrave, 10 *Ves.*, 406; Shackleton *v.* Sutcliffe, 1 *De Gex & Sm.*, 609.

Distinction between real and personal property.

§ 1890. It is to be presumed that the breach of an agreement to transfer real property cannot be adequately relieved by pecuniary compensation, and that the breach of an agreement to transfer personal property can be thus relieved.

This rule seems to be the one upon which the courts have generally, if not uniformly, acted. There are so few cases in which a refusal to convey land can be adequately compensated by damages, that it is usually stated in broad terms that specific performance can always be required in respect to contracts for the sale of land, but this is not strictly correct.

§ 1891. A party, who has signed a written contract, may be compelled specifically to perform it, though the other party has not signed it, if the latter has performed, or offers to perform it on his part, and the case is otherwise proper for enforcing specific performance.

Contract signed by one party only, may be enforced by others.

Story Eq. Jur., § 736 *a;* Woodward *v.* Harris, 3 *Sandf.*, 272; Matter of Hunter, 1 *Edw.* 1; Clason *v.* Bailey, 14 *Johns.*, 484; McCrea *v.* Purmort, 16 *Wend.*, 460; Ormond *v.* Anderson, 2 *Ball & B.*, 370; Western *v.* Russell, 3 *Ves. & B.*, 192.

§ 1892. A contract otherwise proper to be specifically enforced, may be thus enforced, though a penalty[1] is imposed, or the damages are liquidated[2] for its breach, and the party in default is willing to pay the same.

Liquidation of damages not a bar to specific performance.

[1] *Story Eq. Jur.*, §§ 715, 751; Logan *v.* Wienholt, 1 *Cl. & F.*, 611; 7 *Bligh* [*N. S.*], 1, 49; Dewey *v.* Watson, 1 *Gray*, 414; Plunkett *v.* Meth. Ch., &c., 3 *Cush.*, 566; Ensign *v.* Kellogg, 4 *Pick.*, 1; Chilliner *v.* Chilliner, 2 *Ves.*, 528; Howard *v.* Hopkyns, 2 *Atk.*, 321; see Fisher *v.* Shaw, 42 *Me.*, 32.

[2] Hull *v.* Sturdivant, 46 *Me.*, 34; Hooker *v.* Pynchon, 8 *Gray*, 550; see Coles *v.* Sims, 5 *De G., M. & G.*, 9; Giles *v.* Hart, 5 *Jur.* [*N. S.*], 1381; Nicholls *v.* Stretton, 7 *Beav.*, 42. This point was involved in Viele *v.* Troy & Boston R. R., 20 *N. Y.*, 184.

§ 1893. The following obligations cannot be specifically enforced:

What cannot be specifically enforced.

1. An obligation to render personal service;[1]

2. An obligation to employ another in personal service;[2]

3. An agreement to submit a controversy to arbitration;[3]

4. An agreement to perform an act, which the party has not power lawfully to perform when required to do so;[4]

5. An agreement to procure the act or consent of the wife of the contracting party, or of any other third person;[5] or,

6. An agreement, the terms of which are not sufficiently certain to make the precise act which is to be done, clearly ascertainable.[6]

[1] Hamblin *v.* Dinneford, 2 *Edw.*, 529; Sanquirico *v.* Benedetti, 1 *Barb.*, 315; Clarke *v.* Price, 2 *Wils. Ch.*, 157; see Lumley *v.* Wagner, 1 *De G., M. & G.*, 604; Fredericks *v.* Mayer, 1 *Bosw.*, 227.

[2] Pickering *v.* Bp. of Ely, 2 *Y. & Coll. Ch.*, 249; compare Ball *v.* Coggs, 1 *Bro. P. C.*, 140.

[3] *Story Eq. Jur.*, § 1457; Greason *v.* Keteltas, 17 *N. Y.*, 491; Toby *v.* Bristol, 3 *Story*, 800; Gourlay *v.* Somerset, 19 *Ves.*, 431; Street *v.* Rigby, 6 *id.*, 815; Mitchell *v.* Harris, 2 *id.*, 131; 4 *Bro. C. C.*, 312; Agar *v.* Macklew, 2 *Sim. & S.*, 418; Crawshay *v.* Collins, 1 *Swanst.*, 40; Kill *v.* Hollister, 1 *Wils. Ch.*, 129; see South Wales Railw. Co. *v.* Wythes, 5 *De G., M. & G.*, 880.

Barlow *v.* Scott, 24 *N. Y.*, 40; Hatch *v.* Cobb, 4 *Johns. Ch.*, 559; Kempshall *v.* Stone, 5 *id.*, 193; Morss *v.* Elmendorf, 11 *Paige*, 277; see Stevenson *v.* Buxton, 15 *Abb. Pr.*, 352; 37 *Barb.*, 9. This want of power is to be carefully distinguished from *impossibility* of performance. Thus a vendor is not to be compelled to convey a thing which he does not own, even though he did own it when he entered into the contract (*Id.*), whereas this is no defense to an action for damages, since money would purchase the thing, and if an exorbitant amount is necessary, that was for the vendor to consider when he made the contract.

And the act required to be done must be lawful for the person required to do it (Harnett *v.* Yeilding, 2 *Sch. & Lef.*, 549, 554; Wood *v.* Griffith, 1 *Swanst.*, 55; Sears *v.* Boston, 16 *Pick.*, 357; Ord *v.* Noel, 5 *Madd.*, 438). A trustee cannot be compelled to commit a breach of trust (White *v.* Cuddon, 8 *Cl. & F.*, 766; Bellringer *v.* Blagrave, 1 *De Gex & Sm.*, 63; Bridger *v.* Rice, 1 *Jac. & W.*, 74; Mortlock *v.* Buller, 10 *Ves.*, 292).

Though the party required to perform had not power to do so when the contract was made, this is immaterial, if he has such power when the judgment is rendered (Allerton *v.* Johnson, 3 *Sandf. Ch.*, 72), or will be able to perform by the time that he is required by the judgment to perform (see Clay *v.* Rufford, 5 *De Gex & S.*, 768).

[5] This section, so far as it relates to the wife of the party, is intended to overrule the contrary decisions in England (Hall *v.* Hardy, 3 *P. Wms.*, 189; see Emery *v.* Wase, 8 *Ves.*, 514; Martin *v.* Mitchell, 2 *Jac. & W.*, 425; Downs *v.* Collins, 6 *Hare*, 437; Morris *v.* Stephenson, 7 *Ves.*, 474), and to adopt the views of Judge Story (*Eq. Jur.*, §§ 731–735), and the intimated views or wishes of the other eminent judges upon this question (see by ELDON, C., Emery *v.* Wase, 8 *Ves.* 514; by ALEXANDER, B., Frederick *v.* Coxwell, 3 *You. & J.*, 514; by MANSFIELD, J., Davis *v.* Jones, 4 *Bos. & Pul.*, 267; Howell *v.* George, 1 *Madd.*, 9). As to any other person than the wife, there is no question (see Thornbury *v.* Devill, 1 *You. & C. Ch.*, 564).

[6] Johnson *v.* Conger, 14 *Abb. Pr.*, 195; Duffield *v.* Whitlock, 26 *Wend.*, 55; Price *v.* Griffith, 1 *De G., M. & G.*, 80; Morgan *v.* Milman, 3 *id.*, 24; Taylor *v.* Portington, 7 *id.*, 328; South Wales Railw. Co. *v.* Wythes, 5 *id.*, 880; Harnett *v.* Yeilding, 2 *Sch. & Lef.*, 549; Colson *v.* Thompson, 2 *Wheat.*, 336; Boston & Me. R. R. *v.* Babcock, 3 *Cush.*, 228; Soles *v.* Hickman, 20 *Penn. St.*, 180; Dodd *v.* Seymour, 21 *Conn.*, 476.

What parties cannot be compelled to perform.

§ 1894. Specific performance cannot be enforced against a party to a contract, in any of the following cases:

1. If he has not received an adequate consideration for the contract;[1]

2. If it is not, as to him, just and reasonable;[2]

3. If his assent was obtained by the misrepresentation,[3] concealment,[4] circumvention,[5] or unfair practices[6] of any party to whom performance would become due under the contract,[7] or by any promise of such party, which has not been substantially fulfilled;[8] or,

4. If his assent was given under the influence of mistake,[9] misapprehension,[10] or surprise,[11] except that where the contract provides for compensation in case of mistake, a mistake within the scope of such provision may be compensated for, and the contract specifically enforced in other respects, if proper to be so enforced.

[1] This rule was expressly adjudged, upon full consideration, by Chancellor KENT, in Seymour *v.* De Lancey (6 *Johns. Ch.*, 222), and sustained by SAVAGE, C. J., and nine senators on appeal (3 *Cow.*, 445) on a point to which such a decision was essential, while it was admitted by the senator who delivered the opinion of the fourteen who voted for reversal. It was also re-affirmed in Slocum *v.* Closson, 1 *How. App. Cas.*, 705, 751, 758; and is expressly adjudged in Falcke *v.* Gray, 4 *Drewry*, 651. To the same effect are Clitherall *v.* Ogilvie, 1 *Dess. Eq.*, 257; Day *v.* Newman, 2 *Cox Ch.*, 77; White *v.* Damon, 7 *Ves.*, 30; Heathcote *v.* Paignon, 2 *Bro. C. C.*, 167. But compare Callaghan *v.* Callaghan, 8 *Cl. & F.*, 374, 401; 4 *Ir. Eq.*, 441; Prebble *v.* Boghurst, 1 *Swanst.*, 329; Coles *v.* Trecothick, 9 *Ves.*, 246; Collier *v.* Brown, 1 *Cox Ch.*, 428.

There is no doubt that the contract must have at least a meritorious consideration (Minturn *v.* Seymour, 4 *Johns. Ch.*, 497; Woodcock *v.* Bennet, 1 *Cow.*, 711; Acker *v.* Phœnix, 4 *Paige*, 305; Hayes *v.* Kershow, 1 *Sandf. Ch.*, 258.)

[2] Seymour *v.* De Lancey, 3 *Cow.*, 445; 6 *Johns. Ch.*, 222; Slocum *v.* Closson, 1 *How. App. Cas.*, 705, 751; Brashier *v.* Gratz, 6 *Wheat.*, 528; Harnett *v.* Yeilding, 2 *Sch. & Lef.*, 549; Lynch *v.* Bischoff, 15 *Abb. Pr.*, 357 *n.;* see Denne *v.* Light, 8 *De G., M. & G.*, 774.

There is no reason for refusing a specific performance *in favor* of the party as to whom the contract is oppressive.

[3] An innocent misrepresentation is good cause for refusing a specific performance (Best *v.* Stow, 2 *Sandf. Ch.*, 298; Clermont *v.* Tasburgh, 1 *Jac. & W.*, 112; Cadman *v.* Horner, 18 *Ves.*, 10; see Drysdale *v.* Mace, 5 *De G., M. & G.*, 103); much more a representation known to be false, though not made with a fraudulent intent (Price *v.* Macaulay, 2 *De G., M. & G.*, 139).

[4] Shirley *v.* Stratton, 1 *Bro. C. C.*, 440.

[5] Phillips *v.* Duke of Bucks, 1 *Vern.*, 227.

[6] O'Rourke *v.* Percival, 2 *Ball & B.*, 62; see Mason *v.* Armitage, 13 *Ves.*, 37.

[7] It is presumed that the use of artifice by a third person would not prevent a specific enforcement of the contract, unless it produced a mistake or misapprehension in the mind of the party required to perform; as to which, see the next section.

[8] Myers *v.* Watson, 1 *Sim.* [*N. S.*], 523.

[9] Coles *v.* Bowne, 10 *Paige*, 526; Schmidt *v.* Livingston, 3 *Edw.*, 213; Malins *v.* Freeman, 2 *Keen*, 25; Web-

ster *v.* Cecil, 30 *Beav.*, 62; compare Swaisland *v.* Dearsley, 29 *Beav.*, 430.

[10] Hamilton *v.* Grant, 1 *Bligh* [*N. S.*], 594; 3 *Dow*, 33; Ricketts *v.* Bell, 1 *De Gex & S.*, 346.

[11] See Seymour *v.* De Lancey, 3 *Cow.*, 445; Mathews *v.* Terwilliger, 3 *Barb.*, 50.

§ 1895. Specific performance cannot be enforced in favor of a party who has not fully and fairly performed all the conditions precedent on his part to the obligation of the other party,[1] except where his failure to perform is only partial, and either entirely immaterial,[2] or capable of being fully compensated;[3] in which case specific performance may be compelled, upon full compensation being made for the default.

What parties cannot have specific performance in their favor.

[1] *Story Eq. Jur.*, § 736, 771; Watt *v.* Rogers, 2 *Abb. Pr.*, 261; Jones *v.* Lynds, 7 *Paige*, 301; Haight *v.* Child, 34 *Barb.*, 186.

[2] Thus the existence of a peppercorn rent on land sold as clear of incumbrance (Winne *v.* Reynolds, 6 *Paige*, 407; see Ten Broeck *v.* Livingston, 1 *Johns. Ch.*, 357), or the liability of an estate to let in future children of a person who could not possibly give birth to a child (Miller *v.* Macomb, 26 *Wend.*, 229; 9 *Paige*, 265), may be disregarded.

[3] Viele *v.* Troy & Boston R. R. Co., 20 *N. Y.*, 184; King *v.* Bardeau, 6 *Johns. Ch.*, 38; Winne *v.* Reynolds, 6 *Paige*, 407; Guynet *v.* Mantel, 4 *Duer*, 86; Clute *v.* Robison, 2 *Johns.*, 595, 614. Failure of title to 209 acres out of 698, was held too great to be compensated (Jackson *v.* Ligon, 3 *Leigh*, 161). And in general, the defect of performance must not be gross (Shackleton *v.* Sutliffe, 1 *De Gex & S.*, 609; Peers *v.* Lambert, 7 *Beav.*, 546), nor can a thing of a different species from that agreed upon, be offered in satisfaction, even if its market value is the same (Madeley *v.* Booth, 2 *De Gex & S.*, 718; Drewe *v.* Corp, 9 *Ves.*, 368; Halsey *v.* Grant, 13 *id.*, 77; Roy *v.* Willink, 4 *Sandf. Ch.*, 525; Collier *v.* Jenkins, *Younge*, 295). Nor can a different parcel of ground be substituted for one agreed upon (Morss *v.* Elmendorf, 11 *Paige*, 277).

§ 1896. Specific performance cannot be compelled, when it would operate more harshly upon the party required to perform, than its refusal would operate upon the party seeking it.

Specific performance not required, when oppressive.

Webb *v.* London & Portsmouth Railw. Co., 3 *De G., M. & G.*, 521; rev'g S. C., 9 *Hare*, 129; Wedgwood *v.* Adams, 6 *Beav.*, 600. Thus, except under special circumstances, a party will not be compelled to do an act subjecting him to a forfeiture (Peacock *v.* Penson, 11 *Beav.*, 355).

Agreement to sell property by one who has no title.

§ 1897. An agreement for the sale of property cannot be specifically enforced in favor of a seller who cannot give to the buyer a title free from reasonable doubt.

Sykes *v.* Sheard, 9 *Jur.* [*N. S.*], 1262; Stapleton *v.* Scott, 16 *Ves.*, 272.

Relief against parties claiming under person bound to perform.

§ 1898. Whenever an obligation in respect to real property would be specifically enforced against a particular person, it may be in like manner enforced against any other person claiming under him by a title created subsequently to the obligation, except a purchaser or incumbrancer in good faith and for value, and except also, that any such person may exonerate himself by conveying all his estate to the person entitled to enforce the obligation.

Story Eq. Jur., § 788; Champion *v.* Brown, 6 *Johns. Ch.*, 398; Daniels *v.* Davison, 16 *Ves.*, 249; 17 *id.*, 433; Taylor *v.* Stibbert, 2 *id.*, 437; Atcherly *v.* Vernon, 10 *Mod.*, 518.

ARTICLE IV.

REVISION OF CONTRACTS.

When contract may be revised.

§ 1899. When through fraud,[1] or a mutual mistake of the parties,[2] or a mistake of one party, which the other at the time knew or suspected,[3] a written contract does not truly express the intention of the parties,[4] it may be revised on the application of a party aggrieved,[5] so as to express that intention,[6] so far as it can be done without prejudice to rights acquired by third persons, in good faith[7] and for value.[8]

[1] De Peyster *v.* Hasbrouck, 11 *N. Y.*, 582; Wiswall *v.* Hall, 3 *Paige*, 313.

[2] Johnson *v.* Taber, 10 *N. Y.*, 319; Bartlett *v.* Judd, 21 *id.*, 200; Haire *v.* Baker, 5 *id.*, 357; Gillespie *v.* Moon, 2 *Johns. Ch.*, 585; Keisselbrack *v.* Livingston, 4 *id.*, 144; Voorhees *v.* De Meyer, 2 *Barb.*, 37; Newcomb *v.* Keteltas, 19 *id.*, 608; Many *v.* Beekman Iron Co., 9 *Paige*, 188; see N. Y. Ice Co. *v.* Northwestern Ins. Co., 23 *N. Y.*, 357; 12 *Abb. Pr.*, 414; Gates *v.* Green, 4 *Paige*, 355; De Riemer *v.* Cantillon, 4 *Johns. Ch.*, 85; Townshend *v.* Stangroom, 6 *Ves.*, 332; Henkle *v.* Royal Assur. Co., 1 *id.*, 317; Bradford *v.* Union Bank, 13 *How.* [*U. S.*], 66; *Story Eq. Jur.*, §§ 155 to 161.

[3] The misapprehension of one party to a contract, if neither known nor suspected by the other, is not sufficient to warrant a revision of the contract (Wright *v.* Goff, 22 *Beav.*, 207; Metropolitan Co. So. *v.* Brown, 26 *id.*, 454; Bradford *v.* Romney, 30 *id.*, 431; Mortimer *v.* Shortall, 2 *Dr. & War.*, 363; 1 *Con. & L.*, 417; Diman *v.* Providence, &c., R. R. Co., 5 *R. I.*, 130.)

[4] If the instrument expresses the intention of the parties, it cannot be altered, even though that intention cannot be carried into effect (Leavitt *v.* Palmer, 3 *N. Y.*, 19). But an instrument which was drawn up under a mistake as to its legal effect, has been revised (Walker *v.* Armstrong, 8 *DeG., M. & G.*, 531).

[5] See notes to section 1903.

[6] This is all that can be taken into consideration. The court cannot add clauses which the parties did not intend to insert, even though they may be necessary to make the contract fair and effective (Thompsonville Scale Mfg. Co. *v.* Osgood, 26 *Conn.*, 16; Hunt *v.* Rousmaniere, 1 *Peters*, 1; 8 *Wheat.*, 174; see Betts *v.* Grener, 31 *Ala.*, 219.)

[7] A purchaser with notice of the mistake is not protected (Gouverneur *v.* Titus, 6 *Paige*, 347; aff'g S. C., 1 *Edw.*, 477).

[8] See Le Roy *v.* Platt, 4 *Paige*, 77; *Story Eq. Jur.*, § 165.

Presumption as to intent of parties.

§ 1900. For the purpose of revising a contract, it must be presumed that all the parties thereto intended to make an equitable and conscientious agreement.

Principles of revision.

§ 1901. In revising a written instrument, the court may inquire what the instrument was intended to mean, and what were intended to be its legal consequences, and is not confined to the inquiry what the language of the instrument was intended to be.

This is contrary to the rule generally acknowledged in the United States (see 3 *N. Y.*, 19; 23 *N. Y.*, 556; 1 *Peters*, 1; 8 *Wheat.*, 174), but is sanctioned by a recent English decision (Walker *v.* Armstrong, 8 *De G., M. & G.*, 531).

Enforcement of revised contract.

§ 1902. A contract may be first revised, and then specifically enforced.

Gillespie *v.* Moon, 2 *Johns. Ch.*, 585; Keisselbrack *v.* Livingston, 4 *id.*, 144; Bouck *v.* Wilber, *id.*, 405.

ARTICLE V.

RESCISSION OF CONTRACTS.

When rescission may be adjudged.

§ 1903. The rescission of a written contract may be adjudged,[1] on the application of a party aggrieved:[2]

1. In any of the cases mentioned in section 839;[3] or,

2. Where the contract is unlawful, for causes not apparent upon its face,[4] and the parties were not equally in fault;[5] or,

3. When the public interest will be prejudiced by permitting it to stand.

[1] It will be observed that this section provides only for a judgment of rescission, without cancellation. Its scope is therefore properly broader than it would be in the latter case. It may be desirable to have a conclusive adjudication upon the validity of a contract, in cases where there is not sufficient ground for further interference. The discretion of the court as to the costs is a sufficient check upon frivolous actions of this nature.

[2] Only the injured party, or those claiming under him, can impeach a contract on account of his want of consent (Jackson *v.* Eaton, 20 *Johns.*, 478). Of course a party committing a fraud cannot have the contract set aside on that ground.

[3] Among a great number of cases in which contracts have been set aside, on grounds mentioned in section 839, the following may be especially referred to. Cases of executory contracts; Belknap *v.* Sealey 14 *N. Y.*, 143; Rosevelt *v.* Fulton, 2 *Cow.*, 129; aff'g S. C., 5 *Johns. Ch.*, 174; Bowes *v.* Heaps, 3 *Ves. & B.*, 117; Broun *v.* Kennedy, 9 *Jur.* [*N. S.*]. 1163; Beasley *v.* Magrath, 2 *Sch. & Lef.*, 31; Martin *v*

Mitchell, 2 *Jac. & W.*, 413; Jones *v.* Thomas, 2 *You. & Coll. Ch.*, 498; Archer *v.* Hudson, 7 *Beav.*, 551; aff'd, 15 *L. J.* [*Ch.*], 211. Cases of executed contracts, such as grants, settlements, deeds, &c.; Sears *v.* Shafer, 6 *N. Y.*, 268; Brock *v.* Barnes, 40 *Barb.*, 521; Bergen *v.* Udall, 31 *id.*, 9; Collins *v.* Hare, 2 *Bligh* [*N. S.*], 106; Nottidge *v.* Prince, 2 *Giff.*, 246; Bury *v.* Oppenheim, 26 *Beav.*, 594.

In cases of mistake, it is not essential that the mistake should be mutual, or that the misapprehension of one party should be known to the other, in order to warrant a judgment of rescission, as in the case of a revision (Scholefield *v.* Templer, *H. R. V. Johns.*, 155; see Mortimer *v.* Shortall, 2 *Dr. & War.*, 363; 1 *Con. & L.*, 417).

[4] Simpson *v.* Howden, 3 *Myl. & Cr.*, 99; Gray *v.* Mathias, 5 *Ves.*, 286; Bromley *v.* Holland, 7 *id.*, 16; see Scott *v.* Onderdonk, 14 *N. Y.*, 9; Ward *v.* Dewey, 16 *id.*, 519; Cox *v.* Clift, 2 *id.*, 118; Piersall *v.* Elliott, 6 *Peters*, 95.

[5] Where the parties are equally in fault, neither can obtain relief (Harrington *v.* Bigelow, 11 *Paige*, 349; Woodworth *v.* Janes, 2 *Johns. Cas.*, 417; Moore *v.* Livingston, 28 *Barb.*, 543; Chamberlain *v.* Barnes, 26 *id.*, 160; Morgan *v.* Chamberlain, *id.*, 163; Gale *v.* Gale, 19 *id.*, 249; Mosely *v.* Mosely, 15 *N. Y.*, 334; Crocker *v.* Crocker, 17 *How. Pr.*, 504; Bolt *v.* Rogers, 3 *Paige*, 154; Manny *v.* Philips, 1 *id.*, 472). But where an attorney induced a client to transfer property to him, for the purpose of defrauding the client's creditors, it was held that, the parties not being *equally* in fault, the client could have the deed set aside (Ford *v.* Harrington, 16 *N. Y.*, 285), and the same rule was applied to the case of a confidential and legal adviser, who was not an admitted lawyer (Freelove *v.* Cole, 41 *Barb.*, 318).

Rescission for mistake.

§ 1904. Rescission cannot be adjudged for mere mistake, unless the party against whom it is adjudged can be restored to substantially the same position as if the contract had not been made.

Court may require party rescinding to do equity

§ 1905. On adjudging the rescission of a contract, for any other cause than usury,[1] the court may require the party to whom such relief is granted to make any compensation to the other which justice may require.[2]

[1] *Laws* 1837, *ch.* 430; and see section 976.

[2] *Story Eq. Jur.*, § 696; Holbrook *v.* Sharpey, 19 *Ves.*, 131; Bromley *v.* Holland, 5 *Ves.*, 618; 7 *id.*, 3, 16; Byne *v.* Vivian, 5 *id.*, 606; Byne *v.* Potter, *id.*, 609; see Harding *v.* Handy, 11 *Wheat.*, 103, 125

ARTICLE VI.

CANCELLATION OF INSTRUMENTS.

When cancellation may be ordered.

§ 1906. A written instrument, in respect to which there is a reasonable apprehension that if left outstanding it may cause serious injury[1] to a person against whom it is void[2] or voidable,[3] may, upon his application,[4] be so adjudged, and ordered to be delivered up or canceled.

[1] This is the principle which seems to govern the numerous and somewhat conflicting decisions upon the cancellation of instruments (see Field *v.* Holbrook, 6 *Duer*, 597; 14 *How. Pr.*, 403; Ward *v.* Dewey, 16 *N. Y.*, 519; Scott *v.* Onderdonk, 14 *id.*, 9; Cox *v.* Clift, 2 *id.*, 118; Williams *v.* Ayrault, 31 *Barb.*, 364; Hamilton *v.* Cummings, 1 *Johns. Ch.*, 517). The difficulty arises in its application. Compare the foregoing cases, and see also Thornton *v.* Knight, 16 *Sim.*, 509; Threlfall *v.* Lunt, 7 *id.*, 627.

[2] Thus a deed of land sold under a void official sale (Craft *v.* Merrill, 14 *N. Y.*, 456; Scott *v.* Onderdonk, *id.*, 9; Lounsbury *v.* Purdy, 18 *N. Y.*, 515; 16 *Barb.*, 376; Tisdale *v.* Jones, 38 *Barb.*, 523; Cook *v.* Newman, 8 *How. Pr.*, 523; Radcliff *v.* Rowley, 2 *Barb. Ch.*, 23), a forged deed (Peake *v.* Highfield, 1 *Russ.*, 559; Seccombe *v.* Fitzgerald, *id.*, 561; see Bp. of Winchester *v.* Tournier, 2 *Ves. Sr.*, 446), or one fraudulently altered (Bushnell *v.* Harford, 4 *Johns. Ch.*, 301), or a lease given immediately after the sale of land by the lessor, and dated of a prior day (Pierce *v.* Webb, 3 *Bro. C. C.*, 16), may be canceled.

[3] A deed may be canceled, or its surrender compelled, on the application of a party whose signature was obtained by fraud (Ogilvie *v.* Jeaffreson, 2 *Giff.*, 353; Vorley *v.* Cooke, 1 *id.*, 230; Brent *v.* Brent, 10 *L. J.* [*Ch.*], 84; Fenn *v.* Craig, 3 *You. & Coll. Ex.*, 216), or by mistake (Willan *v.* Willan, 16 *Ves.*, 72; Underhill *v.* Horwood, 10 *id.*, 200; 14 *id.*, 28), and so in the case of a usurious mortgage (Williams *v.* Ayrault, 31 *Barb.*, 364; Hartson *v.* Davenport, 2 *Barb. Ch.*, 77).

[4] This relief can be granted only upon the application of a party directly interested. Thus, a grantor who has no longer any interest in the land, though he has covenanted with his grantee to procure the discharge

of an apparent lien, cannot sue for its cancellation (Townsend *v.* Goelet, 11 *Abb. Pr.*, 187).

But it is not essential that the applicant's title should be indefeasible (Craft *v.* Merrill, 14 *N. Y.*, 456), nor that he should have the right to immediate possession (Wright *v.* Miller 8 *N. Y.*, 9; rev'g S. C., 4 *Barb.*, 600; and aff'g S. C., 1 *Sandf. Ch.*, 103).

§ 1907. An instrument, the invalidity of which is apparent upon its face,[1] or upon the face of another instrument which is necessary to the use of the former in evidence,[2] is not to be deemed capable of causing injury within the provisions of the last section.

Instrument obviously void.

[1] Hotchkiss *v.* Elting, 36 *Barb.*, 38; Heywood *v.* Buffalo, 14 *N. Y.*, 534.

[2] Ward *v.* Dewey, 16 *N. Y.*, 519; Cox *v.* Clift, 2 *id.*, 118; 3 *Barb.*, 481; Van Doren *v.* Mayor of N. Y., 9 *Paige*, 388; see Mayor of Brooklyn *v.* Meserole, 26 *Wend.*, 132. But compare Bromley *v.* Smith, 7 *Ves.*, 3, 21. This exception does not extend to instruments which require oral evidence only to establish them (see cases cited under last section), and if an instrument is presumptive evidence of the truth of its contents, relief should be granted against it, even though its untruth could be clearly proved (Scott *v.* Onderdonk, 14 *N. Y.*, 9).

§ 1908. Where an instrument is evidence of different rights or obligations, it may be canceled in part, and allowed to stand for the residue.

Cancellation in part.

Thus an indorser of a bill may be entitled to have his indorsement canceled, in a case which would not entitle the drawer to any relief. And an instrument might be partially valid against a party entitled to cancel it in part; although such cases are doubtless rare.

CHAPTER III.

PREVENTIVE RELIEF.

Preventive relief, how granted.

§ 1909. Preventive relief is granted by injunction provisional or final.

Dederick *v.* Hoysradt, 4 *How. Pr.*, 350.

Provisional injunction.

§ 1910. Provisional injunctions are regulated by the CODE OF CIVIL PROCEDURE.

Injunction, when allowed.

§ 1911. Except where otherwise provided by this Title,[1] a final injunction may be granted to prevent the breach of an obligation existing in favor of the applicant:

1. Where pecuniary compensation would not afford adequate relief;[2]

2. Where it would be extremely difficult to ascertain the amount of compensation which would afford adequate relief;[3]

3. Where the restraint is necessary to prevent a multiplicity of judicial proceedings;[4] or,

4. Where the obligation arises from a trust.[5]

[1] For the exceptions referred to, see the next section, and section 1884.

[2] See sections 1887 and 1888, and notes; also Hudson & Del. Canal Co. *v.* N. Y. & Erie R. R. Co., 9 *Paige*, 323.

[3] See sections 1887 and 1888, and notes.

[4] New York & New Haven R. R. Co. *v.* Schuyler, 17 *N. Y.*, 592; 7 *Abb. Pr.*, 41; S. C. again, 8 *Abb. Pr.*, 239; 17 *How. Pr.*, 464; Livingston *v.* Van Ingen, 9 *Johns.*, 507, 570; Mohawk & Hudson R. R. Co. *v.* Artcher, 6 *Paige*, 83; see Baldwin *v.* Buffalo, 29 *Barb.*, 396; Heywood *v.* Buffalo, 14 *N. Y.*, 534; Mayor, &c., of Brooklyn *v.* Meserole, 26 *Wend.*, 132; Croton Turnpike Co. *v.* Ryder, 1 *Johns. Ch.*, 611; Belknap *v.* Belknap, 2 *id.*, 463.

[5] Merritt *v.* Thompson, 3 *E. D. Smith*, 283; see sections 1887 and 1888.

Injunction, when not allowed.

§ 1912. An injunction cannot be granted:

1. To stay a judicial proceeding pending at the commencement of the action in which the injunction is demanded;[1] unless such restraint is necessary to prevent a multiplicity of such proceedings;[2]

2. To stay proceedings in a court of the United States;[3]

3. To stay proceedings, in another state, upon a judgment of a court of that state;[4]

4. To prevent the execution of a public statute, by officers of the law, for the public benefit;[5]

5. To prevent the breach of a contract, the performance of which would not be specifically enforced;[6]

6. To prevent an injury to the person,[7] character,[8] or personal relations[9] of the applicant, not amounting to a nuisance;[10] except that in an action for divorce, an injunction may be granted to prevent interference with a wife or child;

7. To prevent the exercise of a public or private office, in a lawful manner, by the person in possession;[11]

8. To prevent a legislative act by a municipal corporation;[12] or,

9. Where relief, equally efficacious, can be obtained by any other usual mode of proceeding,[13] except in case of breach of trust.[14]

[1] So held, as to actions in the same court (Arndt *v.* Williams, 16 *How. Pr.*, 244; Hunt *v.* Farmers' Loan, &c., Co., 8 *id.*, 416; Dederick *v.* Hoysradt, 4 *id.*, 350; Smith *v.* Am. Life Ins. Co., *Clarke*, 307; Lane *v.* Clarke, *id.*, 309; see Hall *v.* Fisher, 1 *Barb. Ch.*, 53); and so as to actions in any other court of this state (Grant *v.* Quick, 5 *Sandf.*, 612; see Bennett *v.* Leroy, 5 *Abb. Pr.*, 55, 156; 14 *How. Pr.*, 178), or of any other state (Williams *v.* Ayrault, 31 *Barb.*, 364 Burgess *v.* Smith, 2 *Barb. Ch.*, 276; Mead *v.* Merritt, 2 *Paige*, 402).

[2] In an action brought to determine a single question, actions commenced already, as well as others threatened, may be enjoined. This was determined in effect by the Court of Appeals in N. Y. & New Haven R. R. Co. *v.* Schuyler (17 *N. Y.*, 592; 7 *Abb. Pr.*, 41), as will plainly appear by the statement of facts in the report, though not by the opinion; and a provisional injunction for this purpose was afterwards granted (S. C., 17 *How. Pr.*, 464; S. C. again, 8 *Abb. Pr.*, 239). In Minor *v.* Webb (10 *Abb. Pr.*, 284), where a different opinion was expressed, these

last decisions were evidently not brought under the notice of the court.

[3] McKee *v.* Voorhies, 7 *Cranch*, 281; Mead *v.* Merritt, 2 *Paige*, 404; Schuyler *v.* Pelissier, 3 *Edw.*, 193; Phelan *v.* Smith, 8 *Cal.*, 521.

[4] Bicknell *v.* Field, 8 *Paige*, 440.

[5] See Kneedler *v.* Lane, 45 *Penn. St.*, 238, 295; Thompson *v.* Com'rs of Canal Fund, 2 *Abb. Pr.*, 248; compare Hartwell *v.* Armstrong, 19 *Barb.*, 175.

[6] Newbery *v.* James, 2 *Meriv.*, 446; Williams *v.* Williams, 3 *id.*, 160; see Hamblin *v.* Dinneford, 2 *Edw.*, 529; Sanquirico *v.* Benedetti, 1 *Barb.*, 315; compare Lumley *v.* Wagner, 1 *De G., M. & G.*, 604.

[7] Sterman *v.* Kennedy, 15 *Abb. Pr.*, 201. Compare, however, Wood *v.* Brooklyn, 14 *Barb.*, 425.

[8] Thus the publication of a libel will not be restrained (Brandreth *v.* Lance, 8 *Paige*, 24).

[9] As a trespass cannot be restrained, it follows of course that an injury to personal relations cannot be.

[10] See Catlin *v.* Valentine, 9 *Paige*, 575; Brady *v.* Weeks, 3 *Barb.*, 157.

[11] Hartt *v.* Harvey, 32 *Barb.*, 55; 10 *Abb. Pr.*, 321; Mayor, &c., of N. Y. *v.* Conover, 5 *Abb. Pr.*, 171; People *v.* Draper, 24 *Barb.*, 365; 4 *Abb. Pr.*, 333; People *v.* Sampson, 25 *Barb.*, 254; see Youngs *v.* Ransom, 31 *Barb.*, 49; Lewis *v.* Oliver, 4 *Abb. Pr.*, 121.

[12] People *v.* Mayor, &c., of N. Y., 32 *Barb.*, 35; 10 *Abb. Pr.*, 144; People *v.* Lowber, 28 *Barb.*, 65; 7 *Abb. Pr.*, 158. Compare People *v.* Sturtevant, 9 *N. Y.*, 263; Davis *v.* Mayor, &c., of N. Y., 1 *Duer*, 451. As it is not supposable that any court would presume to issue an injunction against any action of the legislature, no provision is made against it.

[13] N. Y. Life Ins. Co. *v.* Supervisors of N. Y., 4 *Duer*, 192. Thus an injunction will not be granted where full relief can be obtained by means of a writ of prohibition (Ward *v.* Kelsey, 14 *Abb. Pr.*, 106), or of certiorari (Marks *v.* Wilson, 11 *Abb. Pr.*, 87; Hyatt *v.* Bates, 35 *Barb.*, 308; Heywood *v.* Buffalo, 14 *N. Y.*, 534; Mayor, &c., of Brooklyn *v.* Meserole, 26 *Wend.*, 132), or by filing a notice of action pending (Mills *v.* Mills, 21 *How. Pr.*, 437; Stevenson *v.* Fayerweather, *id.*, 449; Osborn *v.* Taylor, 5 *Paige*, 515; Waddell *v.* Brune, 4 *Edw.*, 671).

[14] An injunction may be granted to prevent a breach of trust, even where sufficient compensation could be recovered in damages (Merritt *v.* Thompson, 3 *E. D. Smith*, 283; Attorney Gen. *v.* Aspinall, 2 *Myl. & Cr.*, 613; Wood *v.* Rowcliffe, 2 *Phillips*, 382; 3 *Hare*, 304).

PART II.

SPECIAL RELATIONS OF DEBTOR AND CREDITOR.

TITLE I.

GENERAL PRINCIPLES.

§ 1913. A debtor, within the meaning of this Title, is one who, by reason of an existing obligation, is or may become liable to pay money to another, whether such liability is certain or contingent. **Who is debtor.**

Elwood *v.* Diefendorf, 5 *Barb.*, 398.

§ 1914. A creditor, within the meaning of this Title, is one in whose favor an obligation exists, by reason of which he is, or may become, entitled to the payment of money. **Who is a creditor.**

Compare Thompson *v.* Van Vechten, 5 *Abb. Pr.*, 458; Westcott *v.* Gunn, 4 *Duer*, 107; Seward *v.* Jackson, 8 *Cow.*, 406; Morse *v.* Hovey, 1 *Sandf. Ch.*, 187.

§ 1915. In the absence of fraud, every contract of a debtor is valid against all his creditors, existing or subsequent, who have not acquired a lien on the property affected by such contract. **Contracts of debtor are valid.**

Miller *v.* Lewis, 4 *N. Y.*, 554; Candee *v.* Lord, 2 *id.*, 269.

Payments in preference.

§ 1916. A debtor may pay one creditor in preference to another, or may give to one creditor security for the payment of his demand, in preference to another.

Relative rights of different creditors.

§ 1917. Where a creditor is entitled to resort to each[1] of several funds for the satisfaction of his claim, and another person has an interest in, or is entitled as a creditor to resort to, some but not all of them, the latter may require the former to seek satisfaction from those funds to which the latter has no such claim,[2] so far as it can be done without impairing the right of the former to complete satisfaction,[3] and without doing injustice to third persons.[4]

[1] Farmers' Loan & Trust Co. *v.* Walworth, 1 *N. Y.*, 433.

[2] Ingalls *v.* Morgan, 10 *N. Y.*, 178; Besley *v.* Lawrence, 11 *Paige*, 581; Hawley *v.* Mancius, 7 *Johns. Ch.*, 174; Welch *v.* James, 22 *How. Pr.*, 474.

[3] Evertson *v.* Booth, 19 *Johns.*, 486; York & Jersey Steamboat Co. *v.* Jersey Co., *Hopk.*, 460; Herriman *v.* Skillman, 33 *Barb.*, 378.

[4] Reynolds *v.* Tooker, 18 *Wend.*, 591; Dorr *v.* Shaw, 4 *Johns. Ch.*, 17; *Exp.* Kendall, 17 *Ves.*, 20.

TITLE II.

FRAUDULENT INSTRUMENTS AND TRANSFERS.

Transfers, &c., with intent to defraud creditors.

§ 1918. Every transfer of property or charge thereon made, every obligation incurred, and every judicial proceeding taken, with intent to delay or defraud any creditor or other person of his demands, is void[1] against all creditors[2] of the debtor, and their successors in interest,[3] and against any persons upon whom the estate of the debtor devolves in trust for the benefit of others than the debtor.[4]

[1] 2 *R. S.*, 137, § 1.

[2] Such acts are void against *subsequent*, as well as prior creditors (King *v.* Wilcox, 11 *Paige*, 589; Mills *v.* Morris, *Hoffm.*, 419; see Botts *v.* Cozine, *id.*, 79; Sands *v.* Hildreth, 2 *Johns. Ch.*, 35), even though intended to defraud prior creditors only (*id*).

[3] 2 *R. S.*, 137, § 3.

[4] *Laws of* 1858, *ch.* 314.

§ 1919. Every transfer of personal property, other than a thing in action,[1] or a ship or cargo at sea, or in a foreign port, and every lien thereon, other than a contract of bottomry or respondentia, is presumed, if made by a person having at the time the possession or control of the property, and not accompanied by an immediate delivery, and followed by an actual and continued change of possession of the things transferred, to be fraudulent and therefore void,[2] against those who are his creditors while he remains in possession, and the successors in interest of such creditors,[3] and against any persons on whom his estate devolves in trust for the benefit of others than himself,[4] and against purchasers or incumbrancers[5] in good faith subsequent to the transfer.[6] Certain transfers presumed fraudulent.

[1] Browning *v.* Hart, 6 *Barb.*, 91.

[2] 2 *R. S.*, 136, § 7.

[3] 2 *R. S.*, 137, § 3.

[4] *Laws of* 1858, *ch.* 314.

[5] Bennett *v.* Earll, 21 *Wend.*, 117; Baskins *v.* Shannon, 3 *N. Y.*, 310.

[6] Except as otherwise noted, this section is taken from 2 *R. S.*, 136, § 5.

§ 1920. The presumption declared by the last section may be repelled by showing[1] that the transfer was made in good faith and without intent to defraud.[2] Presumption, how repelled.

[1] See Hall *v.* Tuttle, 8 *Wend.*, 375; Brown *v.* Wilmerding, 5 *Duer*, 220; Clute *v.* Fitch, 25 *Barb.*, 428.

[2] 2 *R. S.*, 136, § 5.

§ 1921. The provisions of this Title do not affect the rights of a purchaser or incumbrancer,[1] in good faith and for value.[2] Rights of purchasers and mortgagees.

[1] Hall *v.* Arnold, 15 *Barb.*, 599; and see Baskins *v.* Shannon, 3 *N. Y.*, 310.

[3] The present statute (1 *R. S.*, 137, § 5) instead of the words "good faith," contains this clause — "and without notice of the fraudulent intent of his immediate grantor or mortgagor, or of the fraud rendering void the title of such grantor or mortgagor." *Good faith* includes this, and something more, and is the proper phrase to be used in such cases.

Creditor's right must be judicially ascertained.

§ 1922. A creditor can avoid the act or obligation of his debtor, for fraud, only where the fraud obstructs the enforcement, by legal process, of his right to take the property affected by the transfer or obligation.

Andrews *v.* Durant, 18 *N. Y.*, 496; Reubens *v.* Joel, 13 *id.*, 488; Crippen *v.* Hudson, *id.*, 161; Bishop *v.* Halsey, 3 *Abb. Pr.*, 400; Frisby *v.* Thayer, 25 *Wend.*, 396; Thompson *v.* Van Vechten, 5 *Abb. Pr.*, 458.

Question of fraud, how determined.

§ 1923. In all cases arising under this Title, or under section 535 of this Code, the question of fraudulent intent is one of fact, and not of law; nor can any transfer or charge be adjudged fraudulent solely on the ground that it was not made for a valuable consideration.

2 *R. S.*, 137, § 4. The verdict of a jury on this question is, however, subject to review in like manner as verdicts in other cases; and may be set aside as against evidence (Marston *v.* Vultee, 12 *Abb. Pr.*, 143; 8 *Bosw.*, 129).

TITLE III.

ASSIGNMENTS FOR THE BENEFIT OF CREDITORS.

§ 1924. An insolvent debtor may, in good faith, execute an assignment of property to one or more assignees, in trust for the satisfaction of his creditors, in conformity to the provisions of this chapter;[1] subject, however, to the provisions of this Code relative to trusts and to fraudulent transfers, and to the restrictions imposed by law upon assignments by special partnerships,[2] by corporations[3] or by other specific classes of persons.[4]

When debtor may execute assignment.

[1] The commissioners have already reported, in section 643 of the Penal Code, a provision making it a misdemeanor for an insolvent to make an assignment with preferences, except in the cases in which a preference is expressly allowed to be given by law. And they have stated quite fully, in a note to that section, the reasons which lead them to recommend restricting so closely the right to make preferential assignments. The provisions of the Penal Code upon the subject are, of course, confined to imposing a punishment for attempting to make an illegal assignment. In the present chapter other provisions are presented in respect to the making of preferential assignments and the settlement of assigned estates.

The course of decision in this state upon the right to give preferences, and the various restrictions which have been imposed upon it, will be found reviewed in the *Penal Code*, § 643, note.

[2] 1 *R. S.*, 766, §§ 20, 21, embodied in section 1348 of this Code. See also Mills *v.* Argall, 6 *Paige*, 577; Haggerty *v.* Taylor, 10 *id.*, 261; Robinson *v.* McIntosh, 3 *E. D. Smith*, 221; Innes *v.* Lansing, 7 *Paige*, 583; Whitewright *v.* Stimpson, 2 *Barb.*, 379; Jackson *v.* Sheldon, 9 *Abb. Pr.*, 127; Heyes *v.* Heyer, 3 *Sandf.*,

284; Artisans' Bank *v.* Treadwell, 34 *Barb.*, 553; Fanshawe *v.* Lane, 16 *Abb. Pr.*, 71.

[3] 1 *R. S.*, 591, §§ 7-9; De Ruyter *v.* St. Peter's Church, 3 *N. Y.*, 238; Hurlbut *v.* Carter, 21 *Barb.*, 221; Hill *v.* Reed, 16 *Barb.*, 280; Bowery Bank Case, 5 *Abb. Pr.*, 415; Heroy *v.* Kerr, 21 *How. Pr.*, 409; 8 *Bosw.*, 194; Hoyt *v.* Shelden, 3 *Bosw.*, 267; Robinson *v.* Bank of Attica, 21 *N. Y.*, 406; Loring *v.* U S. Vulcanized Gutta Percha & B. Co., 36 *Barb.*, 329.

[4] As in the case of an assignment by an infant, or by a firm, one of whose members is an infant (Fox *v.* Heath, 16 *Abb. Pr.*, 163; 21 *How. Pr.*, 384); an assignment by a convict under sentence of imprisonment in a state prison (Miller *v.* Finkle, 1 *Park. Cr.*, 374); or a voluntary assignment by a debtor, executed pending proceedings against him to compel an assignment under the non-imprisonment act (Spear *v.* Wardell, 1 *N. Y.*, 144).

Insolvency, what.

§ 1925. A debtor is insolvent, within the meaning of this Title, when he is unable to pay his debts from his own means, as they become due.

See Herrick *v.* Borst, 4 *Hill*, 650; Curtis *v.* Leavitt, 15 *N. Y.*, 9, 199.

Compare also section 1708 of this Code. The definition here given is purposely made more comprehensive than that presented in the section referred to, which relates to stoppage in transit. To bring an assignment within the provisions of this chapter, it is enough that the debtor has become unable to pay. To warrant the exercise of the right of stoppage in transit, he must have "stopped payment." The distinction is warranted by the existing law.

Certain transfers not affected.

§ 1926. The provisions of this Title do not prevent a person residing in another state or country from making there, in good faith, and without intent to evade the laws of this state, a transfer of property situated within it, nor do they affect the power of a person, although insolvent and within this state, to transfer property to a particular creditor for the purpose of paying or securing the whole or a part of a debt, owing to such creditor, whether in his own right or otherwise.

Ackerman *v.* Cross, 40 *Barb.*, 465; Hall *v.* Arnold, 15 *id.*, 599.

§ 1927. An assignment for the benefit of creditors may provide for any subsisting[1] liability of the assignor which he might lawfully pay,[2] whether absolute or contingent.[3]

What debts may be secured.

[1] Barnum *v.* Hempstead, 7 *Paige*, 568; Lansing *v.* Woodworth, 1 *Sandf. Ch.*, 43.

[2] The principal and lawful interest of a usurious debt may be provided for (Murray *v.* Judson, 9 *N. Y.*, 73). A general provision for the payment of debts will not include demands void for usury. But if an intention is clearly expressed that the usurious debt shall be paid, the principal and lawful interest will be payable (Pratt *v.* Adams, 7 *Paige*, 615; Green *v.* Morse, 4 *Barb.*, 352).

[3] Cunningham *v.* Freeborn, 11 *Wend.*, 241; Kellogg *v.* Barber, 14 *Barb.*, 11.

A provision authorizing the payment of debts "due and to grow due," from the assignor to the assignee, cannot be made to cover debts not in existence, and will not therefore invalidate the assignment (Van Dine *v.* Willett, 38 *Barb.*, 319).

§ 1928. Except as otherwise specially provided by statute, an assignment by an insolvent debtor, for the benefit of creditors, may give a preference to one or more creditors or classes of creditors, in the following cases, and in no others:

What preferences may be given.

1. Judgments may be preferred to debts not in judgment;

2. Debts which are liens or charges upon the assigned property, or upon some part of it, may be preferred to debts which are not such liens or charges;

3. Debts for money or other property lent without interest, may be preferred to debts for money lent upon interest, or for property sold, or for services rendered;

4. Debts due from the assignor by virtue of a a trust, may be preferred to debts which are not thus due; and,

5. Debts for personal services performed within six months next before the assignment, may, to an extent not exceeding fifty dollars to any one person, be preferred to other debts not within any of the preceding classes.

This provision is new.

Preference must be absolute.

§ 1929. A preference, in an assignment for the benefit of creditors, can only be given absolutely,[1] and without reserving any power of revocation.[2]

[1] Barnum *v.* Hempstead, 7 *Paige*, 568; Boardman *v.* Halliday, 10 *id.*, 223; Strong *v.* Skinner, 4 *Barb.*, 546; Sheldon *v.* Dodge, 4 *Den.*, 217; Lentilhon *v.* Moffat, 1 *Edw.*, 451; Grover *v.* Wakeman, 11 *Wend.*, 187.

[2] Averill *v.* Loucks, 6 *Barb.*, 470.

Certain rights not affected by preferences in assignment.

§ 1930. No provision in an assignment, giving a preference to a creditor, can affect or impair any right of another creditor to priority of payment, whether created by law, or arising from an obligation or transaction of the parties.

Joint and separate debts.

§ 1931. Joint, or joint and several debtors can prefer their joint creditors only out of joint property; and can prefer the individual creditors of each, only out of the separate property of each.

This provision is partly new. Compare Kirby *v.* Schoonmaker, 3 *Barb. Ch.*, 46; Nicholson *v.* Leavitt, 4 *Sandf.*, 252; Jackson *v.* Cornell, 1 *Sandf. Ch.*, 348; Van Rossum *v.* Walker, 11 *Barb.*, 237; Wilson *v.* Robertson, 21 *N. Y.*, 587; 19 *How. Pr.*, 350; Smith *v.* Howard, 20 *How. Pr.*, 121; Cox *v.* Platt, 32 *Barb.*, 126; 19 *How. Pr.*, 121; Turner *v.* Jaycox, 40 *Barb.*, 164; Scott *v.* Guthrie, 25 *How. Pr.*, 481, 512.

Assignment when void.

§ 1932. An assignment for the benefit of creditors is void against any creditor of the assignor not assenting thereto, in the following cases:

1. If it gives an unlawful preference of one debt or class of debts over another;

2. If it gives a preference dependent upon any condition or contingency, or with any power of revocation reserved;[1]

3. If it tends to coerce any creditor to release or compromise his demand;[2]

4. If it provides for the payment of any claim known to the assignor to be false or fraudulent; or for the payment of more upon any claim than is justly due from the assignor;[3]

5. If it reserves any interest in the assigned property, or in any part thereof, to the assignor or for his benefit, before all his existing debts are paid;[4]

6. If it confers upon the assignee any power which, if exercised, might prevent or delay the immediate conversion of the assigned property to the purposes of the trust;[5]

7. If it exempts him from liability for neglect of duty or misconduct; or,

8. If it violates section 1931 of this Code.

[1] Averill *v.* Loucks, 6 *Barb.*, 470; Sheldon *v.* Dodge, 4 *Den.*, 217.

[2] Grover *v.* Wakeman, 11 *Wend.*, 187; 4 *Paige*, 23; 1 *Am. Lead. Cas.*, 76; Hyslop *v.* Clarke, 14 *Johns.*, 458; Austin *v.* Bell, 20 *id.*, 442; Searing *v.* Brinckerhoff, 5 *Johns. Ch.*, 329; Hone *v.* Henriquez, 13 *Wend.*, 240; Armstrong *v.* Byrne, 1 *Edw.*, 79; Lentilhon *v.* Moffat, 1 *Edw.*, 451; Mills *v.* Leroy, 2 *Edw.*, 183; Berry *v.* Riley, 2 *Barb.*, 307; D'Ivernois *v.* Leavitt, 23 *Barb.*, 63; Gasherie *v.* Apple, 14 *Abb. Pr.*, 64; Spaulding *v.* Strang, 36 *Barb.*, 310. Compare Renard *v.* Graydon, 39 *Barb.*, 548; S. C., sub. nom. Renard *v.* Maydore, 25 *How. Pr.*, 178.

[3] Fiedler *v.* Day, 2 *Sandf.*, 594; compare Griffin *v.* Marquardt, 21 *N. Y.*, 121.

[4] See Goodrich *v.* Downs, 6 *Hill*, 438; Strong *v.* Skinner, 4 *Barb.*, 546; Barney *v.* Griffin, 2 *N. Y.*, 365; Leitch *v.* Hollister, 4 *N. Y.*, 211; Lansing *v.* Woodworth, 1 *Sandf. Ch.*, 43; Hendricks *v.* Robinson, 2 *Johns. Ch.*, 284; Hooper *v.* Tuckerman, 3 *Sandf.*, 311; Wintringham *v.* Lafoy, 7 *Cow.*, 735; Van Rossum *v.* Walker, 11 *Barb.*, 237; Ely *v.* Cook, 18 *id.*, 612; Taylor *v.* Stevens, 7 *How. Pr.*, 415; Mackie *v.* Cairns, 5 *Cow.*, 547; Judson *v.* Gardner, 4 *N. Y. Leg. Obs.*, 424; Sheldon *v.* Dodge, 4 *Den.*, 217; Collumb *v.* Caldwell, 16 *N. Y.*, 484; Dow *v.* Platner, 16 *N. Y.*, 562; Carpenter *v.* Underwood, 19 *N. Y.*, 520.

[5] Smith *v.* Howard, 20 *How. Pr.*, 121; Jessup *v.* Hulse, 21 *N. Y.*, 168; Ogden *v.* Peters, *id.*, 23; Griffin *v.* Marquardt, *id.*, 121. Examples are: a power to name his successor (Planck *v.* Schermerhorn, 3 *Barb. Ch.*, 644); a power to sell within a "convenient time" (Woodburn *v.* Mosher, 9 *Barb.*, 255; compare Bellows *v.* Partridge, 19 *Barb.*, 176); a power to give preferences, or to change those directed by the assignment (Barnum *v.* Hempstead, 7 *Paige*, 568; Boardman *v.* Halliday, 10 *id.*, 223; Strong *v.* Skinner, 4

Barb., 546); a power to nurse the estate (Dunham *v.* Waterman, 17 *N. Y.*, 9; 6 *Abb. Pr.*, 357; Schlussel *v.* Willett, 34 *Barb.*, 615; 12 *Abb. Pr.*, 397; 22 *How. Pr.*, 15); a power to sell on credit (Rogers *v.* De Forest, 7 *Paige*, 272; Barney *v.* Griffin, 2 *N. Y.*, 365; Nicholson *v.* Leavitt, 6 *N. Y.*, 510; and see 10 *id.*, 591; Burdick *v.* Post, 6 *N. Y.*, 522; Porter *v.* Williams, 9 *N. Y.*, 142; Brigham *v.* Tillinghast, 13 *N. Y.*, 215; Lyons *v.* Platner, 11 *N. Y. Leg. Obs.*, 87; Wilson *v.* Robertson, 21 *N. Y.*, 589; 19 *How. Pr.*, 350). A power to employ agents is not within the provision (Mann *v.* Witbeck, 17 *Barb.*, 388; Van Dine *v.* Willett, 38 *Barb.*, 319). Neither is a power to compromise "bad and doubtful" claims (Brigham *v.* Tillinghast, 15 *Barb.*, 618; Dow *v.* Platner, 16 *N. Y.*, 562; Bellows *v.* Partridge, 19 *Barb.*, 176); nor a power "to pay rent and taxes," on real estate, until sold (Van Dine *v.* Willett, 38 *Barb.*, 319; 24 *How. Pr.*, 206); or to pay off mortgages, or to insure (Whitney *v.* Krous, 11 *Barb.*, 198).

The instrument of assignment.

§ 1933. An assignment for the benefit of creditors must be in writing, subscribed by the assignor, or by his agent thereto authorized by writing, and, if it embraces a fee or freehold estate in real property, it must be sealed.[1] It must be acknowledged by the person executing it, or proved by a subscribing witness,[2] in the mode prescribed by the article on Proof and Acknowledgment of Instruments, and the acknowledgment or proof must be certified,[3] before its delivery.[4]

[1] It is proposed to insert the provision for signing and sealing, in accordance with the requirements of the Title on TRANSFER.

[2] It has been held that proof by a subscribing witness is not sufficient under the statute of 1860 (Cook *v.* Kelly, 12 *Abb. Pr.*, 35). It is therefore proposed to insert the words, "or proved by a subscribing witness."

[3] The words of the present statute require the acknowledgment to be indorsed, but this would be satisfied by a certificate annexed (Thurman *v.* Cameron, 24 *Wend.*, 87).

[4] Except where otherwise noted, this section conforms to *Laws* 1860, *ch.* 348, § 1.

Compliance with provisions of last

§ 1934. Unless the provisions of the last section are complied with, an assignment for the benefit of creditors is void against every creditor of the assignor not assenting thereto.

section, necessary to validity of assignment.

Assignee takes subject to rights of third parties.

§ 1935. An assignee for the benefit of creditors is not to be regarded as a purchaser for value, and has no greater rights than his assignor had, in respect to things in action transferred by the assignment.

Curtis *v.* Leavitt, 15 *N. Y.*, 195; Van Heusen *v.* Radcliff, 17 *id.*, 580; Griffin *v.* Marquardt, *id.*, 28; Leger *v.* Bonaffe, 2 *Barb.*, 475; Warren *v.* Fenn, 28 *id.*, 333; Marine & Fire Ins. Bank *v.* Jauncey, 1 *id.*, 486; Matter of Howe, 1 *Paige*, 125; Mead *v.* Phillips, 1 *Sandf. Ch.*, 83; Bliss *v.* Cottle, 32 *Barb.*, 322; Reed *v.* Sands, 37 *id.*, 185; Maas *v.* Goodman, 2 *Hilt.*, 275; Schieffelin *v.* Hawkins, 14 *Abb. Pr.*, 112.

Inventory required.

§ 1936. Within twenty days after an assignment is made for the benefit of creditors, the assignor must make and file, in the manner prescribed by section 1938, a full and true inventory, showing:[1]

1. All the creditors of the assignor;

2. The place of residence of each creditor, if known to the assignor, or if not known, that fact must be stated;

3. The sum owing to each creditor, and the nature of each debt or liability, whether arising on written security, account or otherwise;

4. The true consideration of the liability in each case, and the place where it arose;

5. Every existing judgment, mortgage, or other security for the payment of any debt or liability of the assignor;

6. All property of the assignor at the date of the assignment, which is exempt by law from execution;[2] and,

7. All of the assignor's property at the date of the assignment, both real and personal, of every kind, not so exempt, and the incumbrances existing thereon, and all vouchers and securities relating thereto,

and the value of such property according to the best knowledge of the assignor.

[1] This section is substantially taken from *Laws of* 1860, *ch.* 348, § 2. Much discussion has arisen, under that statute, in determining whether a failure to comply with its various provisions rendered an assignment void, or whether those provisions, or some of them, were not to be considered as merely directory. In Evans *v.* Chapin (12 *Abb. Pr.*, 61; 20 *How. Pr.*, 289), the question arose upon the failure of the assignor to make and deliver the required inventory of his debts and assets. It was held that the provision of the statute requiring that inventory was merely directory; and the assignment was not made invalid by the omission. In Barbour *v.* Everson (16 *Abb. Pr.*, 366), the question arose upon the omission to furnish the required inventory, and the further omission of the assignee to give the bond prescribed by the act. It was held that neither of these departures from the statute affected the assignment. To the same effect is Juliand *v.* Rathbone, 39 *Barb.*, 97. In Fairchild *v.* Gwynne (16 *Abb. Pr.*, 23), the question arose upon the omission of the assignor to acknowledge and record the assignment as required by the act. It was held that in this respect a compliance with the act was essential to the validity of the instrument. To the same effect is Cook *v.* Kelly, 14 *Abb. Pr.*, 466. By the decisions prior to the act of 1860, the omission to annex schedules was held only a badge of fraud, and not conclusive evidence of an intent to defraud the creditors of the assignor (Cunningham *v.* Freeborn, 3 *Paige*, 557; aff'd, 11 *Wend.*, 241; Delaware & Hudson Canal Co. *v.* Elting, 3 *Ch. Sent.*, 29; Van Nest *v.* Yoe, 1 *Sandf. Ch.*, 4; S. C., 2 *N. Y. Leg. Obs.*, 70; Kellogg *v.* Slauson, 15 *Barb.*, 56; aff'd, 11 *N. Y.*, 302. See also the later case of Hotop *v.* Neidig, 17 *Abb. Pr.*, 332). By a subsequent section it is proposed to make both the record of the assignment, and the filing of the inventory, essential. The inventory is therefore required to be filed with the clerk, instead of being delivered to the county judge; as it would be unjust to avoid the assignment on account of the judge's omission to file it.

[2] This provision is new. It is proper that the property which the debtor seeks to exempt should be specified in the inventory, though it need not pass by the assignment.

§ 1937. An affidavit must be made by every person executing an assignment for the benefit of creditors, to be annexed to and filed with the inventory mentioned in the last section, to the effect that the same is in all respects just and true, according to the best of such assignor's knowledge and belief. Verification of inventory.

Laws of 1860, *ch.* 348, § 2.

§ 1938. An assignment for the benefit of creditors must be recorded, and the inventory required by section 1936 filed, with the register, or if there is none, with the clerk, of the county in which the assignor resided at the date of the assignment; or, if he did not then reside in this state, with the like officer of the county in which his principal place of business was then situated; or, if he had not then a residence or place of business in this state, with the like officer of the county in which the principal part of the assigned property was then situated. Recording assignment and filing inventory.

Modified from *Laws of* 1860, *ch.* 348, § 6. See Scott *v.* Guthrie, 25 *How. Pr.*, 481.

§ 1939. If an assignment for the benefit of creditors is executed by more than one assignor, it must be recorded, and a copy of the inventory required by section 1936 must be filed, with the register, or if there is none, with the clerk, of every county in which any of the assignors resided at its date, or in which any of them, not then residing in this state, had then a place of business. Id.

This provision is new.

§ 1940. An assignment for the benefit of creditors is void against creditors of the assignor, and against purchasers from him, if the assignment is not recorded, and the inventory required by section 1936 filed, pursuant to section 1938, within twenty days after the date of the assignment. Effect of omitting to record.

This section is new.

§ 1941. Where an assignment for the benefit of creditors embraces real property, it is subject to the Assignment of real property.

provisions of article IV of the chapter on Recording Transfers, as well as to those of this Title.

Bond of assignees.

§ 1942. Within thirty days after the date of an assignment for the benefit of creditors, the assignee must enter into a bond to the people of this state, in such amount as may be fixed by the county judge of the county in which the original inventory is filed, with sufficient sureties, to be approved by such judge, and conditioned for the faithful discharge of the trust, and the due accounting for all moneys received by the assignee, which bond must be filed in the same office with the original inventory.

Laws of 1860, 595, *ch.* 348, § 3.

Conditions of disposal and conversion.

§ 1943. Until the inventory and affidavit required by sections 1936 and 1937 have been made, and the assignment has been duly recorded, and the inventory filed, and the assignee has given a bond as required by the last section, an assignee for the benefit of creditors has no authority to dispose of the estate or convert it to the purposes of the trust.

Laws of 1860, *ch.* 348, § 3.

Accountings.

§ 1944. After one year from the date of an assignment for the benefit of creditors, the assignee may be required, on the petition of any creditor, to account before the county judge of the county where the accompanying inventory was filed, in the manner prescribed by the CODE OF CIVIL PROCEDURE.

Laws of 1860, *ch.* 348, § 4. The mode of proceeding is left to be regulated by the CODE OF CIVIL PROCEDURE.

Property exempt.

§ 1945. Property exempt from execution, and insurances upon the life of the assignor, do not pass to the assignee by a general assignment for the benefit of creditors, unless the instrument specially mentions them, and declares an intention that they should pass thereby.

This provision is new.

§ 1946. In the absence of any provision in the assignment to the contrary, an assignee for the benefit of creditors is entitled to the same commissions as are allowed by law to executors and guardians,[1] but the assignment cannot grant more, and may restrict the commissions to a less amount, or deny them altogether.[2]

Compensation.

[1] Meacham *v.* Sternes, 9 *Paige*, 398.

[2] Keteltas *v.* Wilson, 36 *Barb.*, 298; 23 *How. Pr.*, 69; Campbell *v.* Woodworth, 24 *N. Y.*, 304. Greater compensation than executors' commissions is not intended to be allowed (see Nichols *v.* McEwen, 17 *N. Y.*, 22; Halsted *v.* Gordon, 34 *Barb.*, 422). A creditor who receives an assignment of property to pay his own debt, and apply the balance to the other debts of the assignor, is not (at least in the absence of a provision in the assignment), entitled to any commissions (see Ireland *v.* Potter, 25 *How. Pr.*, 175).

§ 1947. An assignee for the benefit of creditors is not to be held liable for his acts done in good faith in the execution of the trust, merely for the reason that the assignment is afterward adjudged void.

Assignees protected for acts done in good faith.

Wakeman *v.* Grover, 4 *Paige*, 23; Ames *v.* Blunt, 5 *id.*, 13; Barney *v.* Griffin, 4 *Sandf. Ch.*, 552; Averill *v.* Loucks, 6 *Barb.*, 470; Butler *v.* Stoddard, 7 *Paige*, 163; Bostwick *v.* Beizer, 10 *Abb. Pr.*, 197; Collumb *v.* Read, 24 *N. Y.*, 505.

§ 1948. An assignment for the benefit of creditors, which has been executed and recorded so as to transfer the property to the assignee, cannot afterwards be canceled or modified by the parties thereto, without the consent of every creditor affected thereby.

Assent of creditors necessary to modification of assignment.

Messonier *v.* Kauman, 3 *Johns. Ch.*, 3; Mills *v.* Argall, 6 *Paige*, 577; Porter *v.* Williams, 9 *N. Y.*, 142; Bell *v.* Holford, 1 *Duer*, 58; Sheldon *v.* Smith, 28 *Barb.*, 593.

It seems advisable to insert here the text of the Statute of 1860, from which the foregoing Title is in good part taken; so that the modifications proposed may be more clearly understood.

§ 1. Every conveyance or assignment made by a debtor or debtors, of his, her or their estates, real or personal, or both, in trust, to an assignee or assignees, for the creditors of such debtor or debtors, shall be in

Conveyances to be in writing duly acknowledged.

writing, and shall be duly acknowledged before an officer authorized to take the acknowledgment of deeds, and the certificate of such acknowledgment shall be duly indorsed upon such conveyance or assignment before the delivery thereof to the assignee or assignees therein named.

Inventory to be delivered to county judge.

§ 2. Every debtor or debtors so making an assignment shall at the date thereof, or within twenty days thereafter, make and deliver to the county judge of the county in which such debtor or debtors resided at the date of such assignment, an inventory or schedule containing:

What to contain.

1. A full and true account of all the creditors of such debtor or debtors;

2. The place of residence of each creditor, if known to such debtor or debtors, and if not known, the fact to be so stated;

3. The sum owing to each creditor, and the nature of each debt or demand, whether arising on written security, account or otherwise;

4. The true cause and consideration of such indebtedness in each case, and the place where such indebtedness arose;

5. A statement of any existing judgment, mortgage, collateral or other security for the payment of any such debt;

6. A full and true inventory of all such debtor's estate at the date of such assignment, both real and personal, in law and in equity, and the incumbrances existing thereon, and of all vouchers and securities relating thereto, and the value of such estate according to the best knowledge of such debtor or debtors.

7. An affidavit shall be made by such debtor or debtors, and annexed to, and delivered with such inventory or schedule, that the same is in all respects just and true, according to the best of such debtor or debtors' knowledge and belief.

Assignees to give bond.

§ 3. The assignee or assignees named in any such assignment shall, within thirty days after the date thereof (and before he shall have power or authority to sell, dispose of, or convert to the purposes of the trust, any of the assigned property), enter into a bond to the people of the State of New York, in an amount to be ordered and directed by the county judge of the county where such debtor or debtors resided at the date of such assignment, with sufficient sureties to be approved of by such judge, and conditioned for the faithful discharge of the duties of such assignee or assignees, and for the due accounting for all moneys received by such assignee or assignees, which bond shall be filed in the county clerk's office where the assignment is recorded.

County judge may issue summons.

§ 4. After the lapse of one year from the date of such assignment, the county judge of the county where such inventory is filed, shall, upon the petition of any creditor of such debtor or debtors, have power to issue a citation or summons, compelling such assignee or assignees to appear before him, and show cause why an account of the trust fund created by any such assignment shall not be made, and to decree payment of such creditor's just proportional part of such fund; and such county judge shall also have the same power and jurisdiction to compel such accounting as is now possessed by surrogates in relation to the estates of deceased persons; and also power to examine the parties to such assignment and other persons on oath, in relation to such assignment and accounting, and all matters connected therewith, and to compel their attendance for that purpose; and the parties interested in such accounting shall have the same rights to appeal from any order or decree of such judge in the premises as is now given from the decrees of surrogates in relation to the accounts of executors and administrators.

Duty of county judge in certain cases.

§ 5. Whenever any such assignee or assignees shall omit or refuse to perform any decree or order made against him, her or them by a judge or court having jurisdiction to compel the payment of any debt out of such trust fund, such county judge or court may order the bond of such assignee or assignees to be prosecuted in the name of the people by the district attorney of the county where the said bond is filed, and shall apply the moneys collected thereon in satisfaction of the debts of said debtor or debtors, in the same manner as the same ought to have been applied by such assignee or assignees.

Conveyances, &c., to be recorded in county clerk's office.

§ 6. Every conveyance or assignment made by any debtor or debtors under the provisions of this act, shall be recorded in the clerk's office of the county in which such debtor or debtors resided at the date thereof; and every inventory of the property of such debtor or debtors made under the provisions of this act, shall be filed in the same office where such assignment is recorded.

§ 7. This act shall take effect immediately.

PART III.

NUISANCE.

TITLE I.

GENERAL PRINCIPLES.

§ 1949. A nuisance consists in unlawfully doing an act, or omitting to perform a duty, which act or omission either: Nuisance, what.

1. Annoys, injures or endangers the comfort, repose, health or safety of others; or,

2. Offends decency; or,

3. Unlawfully interferes with, obstructs, or tends to obstruct, or renders dangerous for passage, any lake, or navigable river, bay, stream, canal or basin, or any public park, square, street or highway; or,

4. In any way renders other persons insecure in life, or in the use of property.

This definition corresponds with that given of public nuisance, in the Penal Code, § 430; except that it is modified to embrace private nuisance also. Numerous authorities on the different branches of the definition are collected in a note to the section of the Penal Code referred to. See also People *v.* Vanderbilt, 26 *N. Y.*, 287; 25 *How. Pr.*, 139; 38 *Barb.*, 282; Niagara Falls International Bridge Co. *v.* Great Western R. R. Co., 39 *Barb.*, 212.

Public nuisance.

§ 1950. A public nuisance is one which affects equally the rights of an entire community or neighborhood, although the extent of the damage may be unequal.

Private nuisance.

§ 1951. Every nuisance not included in the definition of the last section is private.

What is not deemed a nuisance.

§ 1952. Nothing which is done or maintained under the express authority of a statute can be deemed a nuisance.

Harris *v.* Thompson, 9 *Barb.*, 350; Plant *v.* Long Island R. R. Co., 10 *id.*, 26; Leigh *v.* Westervelt, 2 *Duer*, 618; Williams *v.* N. Y. Central R. R. Co., 18 *Barb.*, 222; compare Renwick *v.* Morris, 7 *Hill*, 575; Clark *v.* Mayor, &c., of Syracuse, 13 *Barb.*, 32.

Successive owners.

§ 1953. Every successive owner of property who neglects to abate a continuing nuisance upon, or in the use of, such property, created by a former owner, is liable therefor in the same manner as the one who first created it.

Brown *v.* Cayuga & Susquehanna R. R. Co., 12 *N. Y.*, 486; compare Terry *v.* Mayor, &c., of N. Y., 8 *Bosw.*, 504.

Abatement does not preclude action.

§ 1954. The abatement of a nuisance does not prejudice the right of any person to recover damages for its past existence.

Pierce *v.* Dart, 7 *Cow.*, 609.

TITLE II.

PUBLIC NUISANCES.

§ 1955. No lapse of time can legalize a public nuisance, amounting to an actual obstruction of public right. Lapse of time does not legalize.

Mills *v.* Hall, 9 *Wend.*, 315; Renwick *v.* Morris, 7 *Hill*, 375; 3 *id.*, 621; Dygert *v.* Schenck, 23 *Wend.*, 446; People *v.* Cunningham, 1 *Den.*, 524; Peckham *v.* Henderson, 27 *Barb.*, 207.

§ 1956. The remedies against a public nuisance are: Remedies for public nuisance.

1. Indictment;
2. A civil action; or,
3. Abatement.

§ 1957. The remedy by indictment is regulated by the PENAL CODE and the CODE OF CRIMINAL PROCEDURE. Indictment, how regulated.

§ 1958. A private person may maintain an action for a public nuisance if it is specially injurious to himself,[1] but not otherwise.[2] Action.

[1] Pierce *v.* Dart, 7 *Cow.*, 609.

[2] Davis *v.* Mayor, &c., of N. Y., 14 *N. Y.*, 506; Dougherty *v.* Bunting, 1 *Sandf.*, 1; Myers *v.* Malcolm, 6 *Hill*, 292; see Lansing *v.* Smith, 8 *Cow.*, 146; 4 *Wend.*, 9; First Baptist Church *v.* Schenectady & Troy R. R. Co., 5 *Barb.*, 79; Same *v.* Utica & Schenectady R. R. Co., 6 *id.*, 313; Pierce *v.* Dart, 7 *Cow.*, 609.

§ 1959. A public nuisance may be abated by any public body or officer authorized thereto by law. How abated.

Thus a municipal corporation may abate a nuisance within its territorial limits (Hart *v.* Mayor, &c., of Albany, 9 *Wend.*, 571); and boards of health have a similar authority in certain cases (see *Laws of* 1850, *ch.* 324; Reed *v.* People, 1 *Park. Cr.*, 481). The powers of various bodies and officers to act in the abatement of nuisances, are, however, to be sought in the statutes conferring them; they are not properly within the scope of the Civil Code.

§ 1960. Any person may abate a public nuisance[1] which is specially injurious to him,[2] by removing, or, if necessary, destroying the thing, which constitutes Id.

the same, without committing a breach of the peace, or doing unnecessary injury.

[1] 2 *Bouv. Inst.*, 575; Hart *v.* Mayor, &c., of Albany, 9 *Wend.*, 571; 3 *Paige*, 213; Wetmore *v.* Tracy, 14 *Wend.*, 250.

[2] Brown *v.* Perkins, 12 *Law Rep.* (*N. S.*), 98.

TITLE III.

PRIVATE NUISANCES.

Remedies for private nuisance.

§ 1961. The remedies against a private nuisance are:

1. A civil action; or,

2. Abatement.

Abatement, when allowed.

§ 1962. A person injured by a private nuisance may abate it by removing, or, if necessary, destroying the thing which constitutes the nuisance, without committing a breach of the peace, or doing unnecessary injury.

When notice is required.

§ 1963. Where a private nuisance results from a mere omission of the wrongdoer, and cannot be abated without entering upon his land,[1] reasonable notice must be given to him before entering to abate it.[2]

[1] As in the case of overhanging branches (see Aiken *v.* Benedict, 39 *Barb.*, 400).

[2] See 3 *Sharsw. Blackst.*, 5, and note 5.

PART IV.

MAXIMS OF JURISPRUDENCE.

§ 1964. The maxims of jurisprudence hereinafter set forth are intended not to qualify any of the foregoing provisions of this Code, but to aid in their just application.

The maxims given in the text are not meant to be mere translations of the Latin originals mentioned in the notes; but such an explanation of them as is supposed to be most just and consonant with our legal system.

It will be observed that those maxims only are presented which have a general application. Such maxims as "caveat emptor," "qui facit per alium," &c., which apply to sales and agency, more particularly, and others of a like character, are omitted. In respect to such it is thought better to state the proper rules completely in the chapter of the Code relating to the particular topic, than to refer to this Part for any additional principles.

§ 1965. When the reason of a rule ceases, so should the rule itself.

"Cessante ratione legis cessat ipsa lex" (*Co. Litt.* 70 *b.*; *Branch's Maxims*, 68; Richards *v.* Heather, 1 *B. & Ald.*, 33).

The rule of the English law that a legacy from a parent to a child is presumed to be satisfied by a subsequent gift from the parent, says Judge DUER, is one which sprang from and was sustained by the peculiar policy of the English law of real property and succession, and is plainly inconsistent with the spirit of the American law upon those subjects. "The reasons of the doctrine with us have ceased to exist, and if there is any truth or obligatory force in the maxim, *cessante ratione cessat ipsa lex*, the doctrine has perished with them" (Langdon *v.* Astor's Exec'rs, 3 *Duer*, 557).

Again, the rule that the *opinion* of witnesses is not admissible, is "based upon the presumption that the tribunal before which the evidence is given is as capable of forming a judgment on the facts as the witness. When circumstances rebut this presumption, the rule itself naturally ceases. *Cessante ratione*, &c.

Hence it is that on questions of science, skill, trade, or others of the like kind, persons of skill, or experts, are permitted to give their opinions" (Dewitt *v.* Barley, 9 *N. Y.*, 375). The practice of granting injunctions to stay legal proceedings was founded upon the inability of the courts of law to do full justice. The union of law and equity, under the CODE OF CIVIL PROCEDURE, has removed the ground of the rule, and such injunctions are not now to be allowed (Grant *v.* Quick, 5 *Sandf.*, 612). For further illustrations, see Parks *v.* Jackson, 11 *Wend.*, 442, 456; Van Rensselaer *v.* Smith, 27 *Barb.*, 104, 148; Berley *v.* Rampacher, 5 *Duer*, 183, 186; Tate *v.* Jordan, 3 *Abb. Pr.*, 392, 394.

§ 1966. Where the reason is the same, the rule should be the same.

"Ubi eadem ratio ibi idem jus" (*Co. Litt.*, 10 *a.*; *Branch's Max.*, 64). Thus it was long the settled rule respecting a writing under seal that a material alteration of it by the obligee rendered the instrument void (Pigot's Case, 11 *Co. Rep.*, 27; Davidson *v.* Cooper, 11 *M. & W.*, 799). The obvious reason of the rule existed as well in the case of an instrument not sealed, and the rule was therefore applied to bills of exchange and promissory notes (Master *v.* Miller, 4 *T. R.*, 320; 2 *H. Bl.*, 140), and other mercantile contracts, not negotiable (Powell *v.* Divett, 13 *East*, 29; Davidson *v.* Cooper, 11 *M. & W.*, 778). So in Hood *v.* Manhattan Fire Ins. Co. (11 *N. Y.*, 532, 543), the law of fixtures was referred to, upon the strength of this maxim, for the purpose of determining whether certain timber, intended to form part of a vessel, was covered by an insurance upon the vessel. See also Graves *v.* Berdan, 26 *N. Y.*, 498, 500.

§ 1967. One must not change his purpose to the injury of another.

"Nemo potest mutare consilium suum in alterius injuriam" (*Dig.*, 50, 17, 75). The spirit and application of this maxim are examined by Chancellor KENT, in Dash *v.* Van Kleeck, 7 *Johns.*, 54, with special reference to retroactive statutes. In Bonati *v.* Welsch (24 *N. Y.*, 157, 162), it was held, partly upon the authority of this maxim, that a husband's change of domicile did not affect the rights of property which his wife acquired at her marriage by the law of the place where they were married.

§ 1968. Any one may waive the advantage of a law intended solely for his benefit.[1] But a law established for a public reason cannot be contravened by a private agreement.

[1] "Quilibet potest renunciare juri pro se introducto" (*Branch's Max.*, 309). Compare "Modus et conventio vincunt legem." Upon this principle, one may omit to plead his infancy or other disability, or the statute of limitations, or time of prescription, in avoidance of his obligations, or may waive notice of the dishonor by a prior party of a bill or note (Conkling *v.* King, 10 *N. Y.*, 446; and see Buck *v.* Burk, 18 *N. Y.*, 341). One may also, upon the same principle, waive a statutory right (Tombs *v.* Rochester & S. R. R. Co., 5 *Barb.*, 83; Buel *v.* Trustees, &c., 3 *N. Y.*, 197), or a constitutional provision made for his benefit, as, for example, the right of trial by jury (Lee *v.* Tillotson, 24 *Wend.*, 337; People *v.* Murray, 5 *Hill*, 468; Baker *v.* Braman, 6 *id.*, 48; and see People *v.* Van Rensselaer, 9 *N. Y.*, 333; People *v.* Rathbun, 21 *Wend.*, 542; Atkins *v.* Kinman, 20 *Wend.*, 241, 248; United States *v.* Wyngall, 5 *id.*, 16, 20; Stephens *v.* People, 19 *N. Y.*, 549; Wells *v.* N. Y. Central R. R. Co., 24 *N. Y.*, 181, 194; Allen *v.* Jaquish, 21 *Wend.*, 628, 631; Baker *v.* Hoag, 7 *Barb.*, 113, 117; Allen *v.* Merchants' Bank, 22 *Wend.*, 215, 233).

[2] "Privatorum conventio juri publico non derogat" (*Dig.*, 50, 17, 45). "Jus publicum privatorum pactis mutari non potest" (*Papinian*). Though individuals may generally waive provisions which the law prescribes for their advantage or protection, yet their private compacts cannot be permitted either to render that just or sufficient between themselves which the law declares essentially unjust or insufficient, or to injure the legal rights of others, or to impair the integrity of a rule, the strict maintenance of which is necessary to the common welfare. The principle of this maxim has forbidden, in our law, marriage brocage bonds; undue restraint of trade (see § 833), or of marriage (see § 836); a seaman's insurance of his wages; an agreement to waive a claim arising from the fraud of one of two contracting parties (see § 828); a mortgagor's covenant with a mortgagee not to enforce his equitable right of redemption, an agreement to waive the benefit of the exemption laws, &c. (See Kneetle *v.* Newcomb, 22 *N. Y.*, 249; Mann *v.* Herkimer County Ins. Co., 4 *Hill*, 192). So, in a capital case, a prisoner cannot waive trial by a jury of twelve men (Cancemi *v.* People, 18 *N. Y.*, 128; 7 *Abb. Pr.*, 271).

§ 1969. One must so use his own rights as not to infringe upon the rights of another.

"Sic utere tuo ut alienum non lædas" (9 *Co. Rep.*, 59; *Branch's Max.*, 160). See also Platt *v.* Johnson, 15 *Johns.*, 213, 215; Baptist Church of Schenectady *v.* Schenectady & Troy R. R. Co., 5 *Barb.*, 83; Lasala *v.* Holbrook, 4 *Paige*, 71; Van Hoesen *v.* Coventry, 10 *Barb.*, 521; Ellis *v.* Duncan, 21 *Barb.*, 203; Ferrand *v.* Marshall, 21 *Barb.*, 420, 422; Carhart *v.* Auburn Gas-light Co., 22 *Barb.*, 307, 310; Aikin *v.* Western R. R. Co., 20 *N. Y.*, 382; Rogers *v.* Parker, 31 *Barb.*, 454). "The principle of this maxim is a sound and beneficial one. It implies what the law asserts, that all men have equal rights before the law" (Carhart *v.* Auburn Gas Co., 22 *Barb.*, 307). Though the proprietor of land bordering upon a stream may use the water for his own purposes he may not in any way infringe upon the rights of those above him, as for example by checking the flow of the stream; nor the rights of those below him by diminishing the volume or injuring the quality of the water. The maxim is very frequently invoked and applied in cases of nuisance; for though a man may generally use his own land as he pleases, he may not erect upon it a nuisance to the annoyance of his neighbor (Hay *v.* Cohoes Co., 2 *N. Y.*, 161; Brown *v.* Cayuga & S. R. Co., 12 *N. Y.*, 494). "Acts may be harmless in themselves so long as they injure no one, but the consequences of acts often give character to the acts themselves" (Van Pelt *v.* McGraw, 4 *N. Y.*, 43). The rule is not however to be applied without limitation. It extends to all damages for which the law gives redress, but no further. If applied literally, it would deprive us, to a great extent of the legitimate use of our property, and impair, if not destroy its value (Hentz *v.* Long Island R. R. Co., 13 *Barb.*, 658; Pixley *v.* Clarke, 2 *Barb.*, 272). In general a man may use his property as he pleases for all purposes to which such property is usually applied, without being answerable for consequences, if he exercises proper care and skill to prevent any unnecessary injury to others (Fisher *v.* Clark, 41 *Barb.*, 329). No one is liable in damages for the reasonable exercise of a right, when it is accompanied by a cautious regard for the rights of others, if the act is not done maliciously, and when there is no just ground for the charge of negligence, or unskillfulness (Panton *v.* Holland, 17 *Johns.*, 92).

§ 1970. He who consents to an act is not wronged by it.

"Volenti non fit injuria" (*Bracton*, fol. 18; *Branch's Max.*, 127; Hartfield *v.* Roper, 21 *Wend.*, 620; Corwin *v.* N. Y. & Erie R. R. Co., 13 *N. Y.*, 49; Lyon *v.* Tallmadge, 1 *Johns. Ch.*, 187; Palmer *v.* Lord, 6 *Johns. Ch.*, 101; Lemmon *v.* People, 20 *N. Y.*, 628). "Nulla injuria est quæ in volentem fiat" (*Dig.*, 47, 10, 1, 5). A husband who connives at the adultery of his wife has no right to a divorce on the ground of her infidelity (Forster *v.* Forster, 1 *Hagg. Con.*, 144). A father who connives at his daughter's seduction cannot recover damages therefor (Seagar *v.* Sligerland, 2 *Caines*, 219). One who consents to the stowage of his goods upon the deck of a ship, can maintain no action for a wrongful stowage of them (Gould *v.* Oliver, 2 *Scott N. R.*, 257). One who voluntarily pays a just debt contracted during his infancy, or barred by the statute of limitations, has no right to repayment of the money (see Bates *v.* N. Y. Ins. Co., 3 *Johns. Cas.*, 240). This rule is only applied where the party had freedom in exercising his will (Harmony *v.* Bingham, 12 *N. Y.*, 109; see also Moulton *v.* Bennett, 18 *Wend.*, 588).

§ 1971. Acquiescence in error takes away the right of objecting to it.

"*Consensus tollit errorem*, is a maxim of the common law and the dictate of common sense" (Rogers *v.* Cruger, 7 *Johns.*, 611). Upon the principle of this maxim rests an important branch of the doctrine of waiver. An irregularity in the service of a paper in a cause, is generally waived by retaining and acting upon it (Georgia Lumber Co. *v.* Strong, 3 *How. Pr.*, 246). A voluntary and general appearance in an action is a waiver of all defects in the summons or other process (Webb *v.* Mott, 6 *How. Pr.*, 440; and Yates *v.* Russell, 17 *Johns.*, 461). See further illustrations of the rule, in Watkins *v.* Weaver, 10 *Johns.*, 107, 108; Farrington *v.* Hamblin, 12 *Wend.*, 212, 213.

§ 1972. No one can take advantage of his own wrong.

"Nullus commodum capere potest de injuria sua propria." This is a rule of such binding force as to be held obligatory against the wrongdoer, even as between himself and one cognizant or participant of the wrong. If one, for the purpose of defrauding his creditors, conveys his property to another, he cannot set up the fraud to avoid the deed as between himself and his accomplice (Jackson *v* Garnsey, 16 *Johns.*, 189; Safford *v.* Wyckoff, 4 *Hill*, 457. See Moore *v.*

Livingston, 28 *Barb.*, 543; 14 *How. Pr.*, 11; Ford *v.* Harrington, 16 *N. Y.*, 285). So when performance of a condition is rendered impossible by the act of the obligee, the obligor incurs no penalty (*Com. Dig.*, Condition, D. 1; see § 727).

§ 1973. He who has fraudulently dispossessed himself of a thing may be treated as if he still had possession.

"Qui dolo desierit possidere, pro possidente damnatur." On this principle, an action for the possession of specific chattels may be maintained against a defendant who wrongfully parted with their possession before the action was brought (Nichols *v.* Michael, 23 *N. Y.*, 267).

§ 1974. He who can and does not forbid that which is done on his behalf, is deemed to have bidden it.

"Semper qui non prohibet pro se intervenire mandare creditur."

§ 1975. No one should suffer by the act of another.

"Res inter alios acta alteri nocere non debet" (see Gelston *v.* Hoyt, 13 *Johns.*, 361, 381; Sweet *v.* Barney, 23 *N. Y.*, 335, 341; Langdon *v.* Astor, 16 *N. Y.*, 9, 31). The principle of this perhaps most important and useful of the maxims relating to the law of evidence, forbids in general (for necessity has introduced some exceptions to the rule), that any one shall be bound by acts or conduct of others, to which, neither in fact nor in law, he was party or privy. It is illustrated by the rules respecting declarations and private memeranda of third persons; and respecting the effect of judgments, to which one is altogether a stranger (*Broom's Maxims*, 432).

§ 1976. He who takes the benefit must bear the burden.

"Qui sentit commodum, sentire debet et onus" (Paine *v.* Bonney, 6 *Abb. Pr.*, 106; Frost *v.* Saratoga Ins. Co., 5 *Denio*, 158; Bartlett *v.* Crozier, 17 *Johns.*, 453; Hendricks *v.* Judah, 2 *Cai.*, 25, 28; United Ins. Co. *v.* Robinson, *id.*, 280, 288; Matter of Mayor, &c., of New York, 11 *Johns.*, 771). One who takes an estate in land and enjoys the benefits resulting from his title, must bear the burdens of the incumbrances upon the land and of the covenants that run with it (Denman *v.* Prince, 40 *Barb.*, 213; Verplanck *v.* Wright, 23 *Wend.*,

506; Priestly *v.* Foulds, 2 *Scott N. R.*, 225). The right of a partner to share the profits of the partnership business is justly coupled with a corresponding liability for its debts.

§ 1977. One who grants a thing is presumed to grant also whatever is essential to its use.

"Cuicunque aliquis quid concedit, concedere videtur et id sine quo res ipsa esse non potest" (see Sterricker *v.* Dickinson, 9 *Barb.*, 518; Troup *v.* Hurlbut, 10 *id.*, 359; People *v.* Hicks, 15 *id.*, 160; Seymour *v.* Canandaigua, &c., R. R. Co., 25 *id.*, 310). The grant of a piece of land, surrounded by other land of the grantor, grants also by implication the right of a convenient way over such other land. The grant of a corporate franchise implies a grant to make by-laws, and to exercise all other powers which are necessary for effectuating the object of the charter.

§ 1978. For every wrong there is a remedy.

"Ubi jus, ibi remedium" (Johnstone *v.* Sutton, 1 *T. R.*, 312). Every wrongful invasion of a right imports injury and damage, though there be no pecuniary loss, and entitles the person injured to redress (Ashby *v.* White, 2 *Ld. Raym.*, 953; and see Green *v.* Hudson River R. R. Co., 28 *Barb.*, 9, 10). By reference to this principle an action for slander to title of personal property has recently been sustained (Like *v.* McKinstry, 41 *Barb.*, 186).

§ 1979. Between those who are equally in the right, or equally in the wrong, the law does not interpose.

"In æquali jure melior est conditio possidentis" (Ontario Bank *v.* Worthington, 12 *Wend.*, 601; M'Laughlin *v.* Waite, 9 *Cow.*, 674; Graves *v.* Delaplaine, 14 *Johns.*, 159). "In pari delicto potior est conditio defendentis" (see Peck *v.* Burr, 10 *N. Y.*, 294; Tracy *v.* Talmage, 14 *N. Y.*, 162, 181, 216; Candee *v.* Lord, 2 *N. Y.*, 269, 276; Meech *v.* Stoner, 19 *N. Y.*, 28; Bennett *v.* American Art Union, 5 *Sandf.*, 631; Schroeppel *v.* Corning, 5 *Denio*, 241; Nellis *v.* Clark, 20 *Wend.*, 28; 4 *Hill*, 436; Perkins *v.* Savage, 15 *id.*, 415; Westfall *v.* Jones, 23 *Barb.*, 12; Vischer *v.* Yates, 11 *Johns.*, 26). In case of illegal contracts, says STORY, or in those in which one party has placed property in the hands of another for illegal purposes, as for smuggling, if the latter refuses to account for the proceeds, and fraudulently or unjustly withholds them, the former must bear his loss, for *in pari delicto, &c.* (*Eq. Jur.*, §§ 61, 298; *Story on Ag.*, § 198). So when there is equal equity, the defendant has as strong a claim to the protection of a court of equity for his title, as the plaintiff has to its assistance in order to assert his title, and the court will not interpose on either side. But where there is a great preponderance of wrong upon one side, as in cases of usury, or where one party violates a confidence as well as a provision of law, the injured party, although not free from blame, may have redress (Ford *v.* Harrington, 16 *N. Y.*, 285).

§ 1980. Between rights otherwise equal, the earliest is preferred.

"Qui prior est in tempore potior est in jure" (see Muir *v.* Schenck, 3 *Hill*, 228; Poillon *v.* Martin, 1 *Sandf. Ch.*, 578; Watson *v.* Le Row, 6 *Barb.*, 485; Weaver *v.* Toogood, 1 *id.*, 241; Lynch *v.* Utica Ins. Co., 18 *Wend.*, 253, 256; Berry *v.* Mut. Ins. Co., 2 *Johns. Ch.*, 608; Truscott *v.* King, 6 *Barb.*, 351; Seymour *v.* Wilson, 16 *Barb.*, 299; Warner *v.* Blakeman, 36 *Barb.*, 520; Hertell *v.* Bogert, 10 *Paige*, 60; Embree *v.* Hanna, 5 *Johns.*, 103; Wilkes *v.* Harper, 2 *Barb. Ch.*, 354; Cherry *v.* Monroe, *id.*, 618). This principle makes the foundation of all original titles to lands both by private and by public law; the first occupant acquires the first right. The maxim applies also in cases of mortgages, attachments, executions and other liens attaching upon property either by the agreement of parties or by the operation of law.

§ 1981. No man is responsible for that which no man can control.

"Actus Dei facit nemini injuriam." This is a maxim of the common law with regard to obligations created merely by operation of law. But it has not been considered applicable to contracts (Tompkins *v.* Dudley, 25 *N. Y.*, 170; Harmony *v.* Bingham, 12 *N. Y.*, 99; Brown *v.* Royal Ins. Co., 1 *El. & El.*, 853). The commissioners have proposed, however, to extend this principle to contracts (see § 727).

§ 1982. The law helps the vigilant, before those who sleep on their rights.

"Vigilantibus, non dormientibus, leges subveniunt" (Toole *v.* Cook, 16 *How. Pr.*, 144). Thus the law may deny relief to one who has long and negligently delayed to file a bill for specific performance (Milwood *v.* Earl of Thanet, 5 *Ves.*, 720; Alley *v.* Duchamps, 13 *Ves.*, 228). So in the spirit of this maxim the statute of limitations prescribes definite periods, after the expiration of which the law will refuse its aid, however clear may be the right of the party claiming it, or the wrong of his opponent. See, for other illustrations, Smedburg *v.* More, 26 *Wend.*, 238, 247; Hazul *v.* Dunham, 1 *Hall*, 655, 658; Bruen *v.* Hone, 2 *Barb.*, 586, 595; Taylor *v.* Fleet, 4 *id.*, 95, 103; Bench *v.* Sheldon, 14 *id.*, 66, 71; Munn *v.* Worrall, 16 *id.*, 221, 232; Voorhees *v.* Seymour, 26 *id.*, 569, 583; Fanning *v.* Dunham, 5 *Johns. Ch.*, 122, 145; *Story Eq. Jur.*, § 529.

§ 1983. The law respects form less than substance.

Francis' Maxims, No. 13. On this principle the law grants relief to one who has omitted to perform an obligation at a time specified by the contract, when it is evident that punctual performance was not an essential element of the agreement (*Adams' Equity*, 88). So it declares sufficient certain defective executions of powers; and the want of a seal, or of witnesses, or of a signature, or defects in the limitations of the estate or interest, may sometimes be aided. In the same spirit the law upholds in certain cases the defective performance of conditions (*Story Eq. Jur.*, § 97; Spaulding *v.* Hallenbeck, 39 *Barb.*, 78; Clute *v.* Robison, 2 *Johns.*, 595, 614; Popham *v.* Bampfield, 1 *Vern.*, 79; *Francis' Maxims*, 60). So it will mitigate the damages which by a strict interpretation of a contract a party thereto might recover, if it operates oppressively (Skinner *v.* White, 17 *Johns.*, 357). "Qui hæret in litera, hæret in cortice," is a maxim to the same effect, often cited with approval (Wadsworth *v.* Thomas, 7 *Barb.*, 449; Aylesworth *v.* Brown, 10 *id.*, 167; Watervliet Turnpike Co. *v.* M'Kean, 6 *Hill*, 620; Leavitt *v.* Fisher, 4 *Duer*, 23; Langdon *v.* Astor, 3 *id.*, 601; Jackson *v.* Housel, 17 *Johns.*, 284; Pillow *v.* Bushnell, 4 *How. Pr.*, 12).

§ 1984. That which ought to have been done, is to be regarded as done, in favor of him to whom, and against him from whom, performance is due.

Thus an agreement for a valuable consideration will be treated as actually executed from the period when it ought to have been performed in favor of a person entitled to insist on its performance. On this principle money agreed or devised to be laid out in land, will be treated as real estate; and land contracted or devised to be sold will be treated as money (*Story Eq. Jur.*, § 64, *g*; *Adams' Equity*, 74). See, for other illustrations of the maxim, Burch *v.* Newberry, 1 *Barb.*, 648, 664; Hasbrouck *v.* Paddock, 1 *id.*, 635; Craig *v.* Leslie, 3 *Wheat.*, 563; Rosevelt *v.* Bank of Niagara, *Hopk.*, 583.

§ 1985. That which does not appear to exist is to be regarded as if it did not exist.

"De non apparentibus et de non existentibus eadem est ratio" (Johnson *v.* Stagg, 2 *Johns.*, 519). Thus upon a special verdict a court will not assume a fact not stated in it, nor draw inferences of facts necessary for the determination of the case, from other statements therein (Tanerd *v.* Christy, 12 *M. & W.*, 316; Jenks *v.* Hallet, 1 *Caines*, 60). If a notice of dishonor is good upon its face, the court will not entertain an objection founded upon the possible existence of another note, not shown to exist (Youngs *v.* Lee, 12 *N. Y.*, 554; Cook *v.* Litchfield, 5 *Sandf.*, 330, 340).

"Quod non apparet, non est" (Yates *v.* People, 6 *Johns.*, 505).

§ 1986. The law never requires impossibilities.

"Lex non cogit ad impossibilia" (*Co. Litt.*, 231, *b.*; Schroeder *v.* Hudson Riv. R. R. Co., 5 *Duer*, 62). "Impotentia excusat legem" (Jackson *v.* Sellick, 8 *Johns.*, 271; Jackson *v.* Johnson, 5 *Cow.*, 103). If an estate is granted upon a condition subsequent which is essentially impossible, the condition is void, and the estate is absolute (2 *Blacks. Com.*, 186). If performance of the condition of a bond is rendered impossible by the act of the obligee, the obligor is excused (Holmes *v.* Guppy, 3 *M. & W.*, 389). But, except in certain special cases, the law does not excuse the non-performance of impossibilities which one has expressly undertaken to perform.

§ 1987. The law neither does nor requires idle acts.

"Lex non cogit ad vana seu inutilia" (Boot *v.* Franklin, 3 *Johns.*, 210). "Lex nil frustra facit." It is a settled principle, says Chancellor KENT, that a court will not undertake to exercise a power, unless it can exercise it to some purpose (Huntington *v.* Nicoll, 3 *Johns.*, 598). It will, for example, refuse a writ of mandamus, if it is manifest that it must be vain and fruitless, or cannot have a beneficial effect (People *v.* Supervisors of Greene, 12 *Barb.*, 222; People *v.* Tremain, 29 *Barb.*, 96; 17 *How. Pr.*, 142). Nor, on the principle of this maxim, will the law require individuals to bring suits or do other acts which will be fruitless (Loomis *v.* Tift, 16 *Barb.*, 544). A demand is excused, when compliance therewith is impossible (Schroeder *v.* Hudson R. R. R. Co., 5 *Duer*, 62).

§ 1988. The law disregards trifles.

"De minimis non curat lex. Nimia subtiltas in jure reprobatur. Bonæ fidei non convenit de apicibus juris disputare" (*Ulpian, Dig.*, 17, 1, 29; see Shipman *v.* Shafer, 14 *Abb. Pr.*, 456; Matter of Empire City Bank, 18 *N. Y.*, 218). The law will not deprive one of all compensation on account of unintentional and unimportant variations from the terms of his agreement (Smith *v.* Gugerty, 4 *Barb.*, 621). Nor will a court restrain by injunction the publication of a solitary letter, having neither actual value nor literary merit, the publication of which would not be productive of injury nor offend the most delicate sensibility (Woolsey *v.* Judd, 4 *Duer*, 599); nor a trespass of a trifling character (Marshall *v.* Peters, 12 *How. Pr.*, 223). Where a redeeming creditor had paid a few cents too little to the sheriff, the redemption was sustained upon the authority of this maxim (*Ex parte* Becker, 4 *Hill*, 615; Hall *v.* Fisher, 9 *Barb.*, 29). So the Court of Appeals refused to reverse a judgment for the defendant, which should have been in favor of the plaintiff for six cents damages, but with costs to the defendant (M'Conihe *v.* N. Y. & Erie R. R. Co., 20 *N. Y.*, 498). But this maxim never applies to the case of a positive and wrongful invasion of a right (Seneca Road Co. *v.* Auburn, &c., R. R. Co., 5 *Hill*, 170; Ellicottville, &c., Plankroad Co. *v.* Buffalo, &c., R. R. Co., 20 *Barb.*, 651).

§ 1989. Particular expressions qualify those which are general.

"In toto jure generi per speciem derogatur et illud poltissimum habetur quod ad speciem directum est" (see Platt *v.* Lott, 17 *N. Y.*, 478).

§ 1990. Contemporaneous exposition is in general the best.

"Contemporanea expositio est optima et fortissima in lege." In construing a statute, great regard should be paid to the opinion in respect to it, entertained by persons learned in the law, at the time of its passage (*Sedgwick Stat. & Const. Law*, 251; *Dwarris*, 562). "A contemporaneous is generally the best construction of a statute. It gives the sense of a community of the terms made use of by a legislature. If there is ambiguity in the language, the understanding and application of it, when the statute first came into operation, sanctioned by long acquiescence on the part of the legislature and judicial tribunals, is the strongest evidence that it has been rightly explained in practice. A construction under such circumstances becomes established law" (Packard *v.* Richardson, 17 *Mass.*, 143; Curtis *v.* Leavitt, 15 *N. Y.*, 217). "A contemporaneous exposition, even of the Constitution of the United States, practiced and acquiesced in for a period of years, fixes the construction" (4 *Kent Com.*, 465, *note*).

§ 1991. The greater contains the less.

"Omne majus continet in se minus. In eo quod plus est semper inest et minus (*Dig.*, 50, 17, 110). "Non debet cui plus licet. Quod minus est non licere" (*Ulpian Gothofredi, Reg. Juris.* Compare *Dig.*, 50, 17, 26–37). "Omne majus in se minus complectitur" (Kip *v.* Brigham, 6 *Johns.*, 157).

One makes a good tender of a debt due when he tenders in due form more than he is bound to pay (Wade's Case, 5 *Co. Rep.*, 115; Hubbard *v.* Chenango Bank, 8 *Cow.*, 101; Dean *v.* James, 4 *B. & Ad.*, 546); and so acts are valid if, having permission to do several things for his own benefit, a party does some of them (Isherwood *v.* Oldknow, 3 *M. & Selw.*, 392), or if, as the agent of another, he does less than his power authorizes him to do (*Story Agency*, § 172).

A power to sell an estate includes a power to transfer a a limited interest (Williams *v.* Woodard, 2 *Wend.*, 492).

But where a statute, authorizing special proceedings, directs eighteen jurors to be summoned, this maxim does not justify the summoning of twenty (Farrington *v.* Morgan, 20 *Wend.*, 207).

§ 1992. Superfluity does not vitiate.

"Utile per inutile non vitiatur" (Rickets *v.* Livingston, 2 *Johns. Cas.*, 101; Yates' Case, 4 *Johns.*, 367; Ogden *v.* Barker, 18 *id.*, 93; Aylesworth *v.* Brown, 10 *Barb.*, 174). This maxim has long been familiar to the common law. It has had frequent application in the law of conveyancing, of pleading and of evidence. Thus, a deed which grants an estate by language explicit and certain, is not defeated or affected by the presence of words that are repugnant to the general sense. So in pleading, surplusage, or the allegation of purely irrelevant matter, does not affect that which is pertinent and in other respects valid (Edgerton *v.* N. Y. & Harlem R. R. Co., 35 *Barb.*, 389; Fowler *v.* Mott, 19 *id.*, 221; Polly *v.* Saratoga & Wash. R. R. Co., 9 *id.*, 464; People *v.* Adams, 17 *Wend.*, 475; Chapman *v.* Smith, 13 *Johns.*, 80; Mason *v.* Franklin, 3 *id.*, 206; Douglas *v.* Satterlee, 11 *id.*, 19). Nor need any evidence be given of an averment, which is wholly immaterial (Fairchild *v.* Ogdensburgh R. R., 15 *N. Y.*, 337). A verdict which finds the whole issue is not vitiated by finding more (Patterson *v.* United States, 2 *Wheat.*, 225).

§ 1993. That is certain which can be made certain.

"Id certum est quod certum reddi potest" (Olmsted *v.* Loomis, 9 *N. Y.*, 434; Hyland *v.* Stafford, 10 *Barb.*, 565; Ostrander *v.* Walter, 2 *Hill*, 332). Thus when a testator gives his "*back* lands" to certain devisees, the description is rendered definite and certain when it is shown by evidence that particular parcels of land were called and known by that name by the testator and his family (Ryerss *v.* Wheeler, 22 *Wend.*, 148). So where a deed identifies the parties in whose favor it is made, it is sufficient, though it does not name them (Gates *v.* Graham, 12 *Wend.*, 53, 56). So, when a rule for the commitment of a person did not specify the sum for non-payment of which the commitment was ordered, but directed a referee therein named to estimate it, it was declared, on the principle, *id certum est*, &c., that the rule was sufficiently definite in respect to the amount, for the referee's report, when filed and confirmed, became part of the rule and the act of the court (People *v.* Nevins, 1 *Hill*, 158; People *v.* Cavanaugh, 2 *Abb. Pr.*, 88). Upon the authority of this maxim, it has been held that rent, payable in wheat, is to be treated as a liquidated demand (Van Rensselaer *v.* Jones, 2 *Barb.*, 668), and so where rent, though payable in cash, was subject to a deduction for repairs (Smith *v.* Fyler, 2 *Hill*, 648).

§ 1994. Time does not confirm a void act.

"Quod ab initio non valet in tractu temporis non convalescit. Quod initio vitiosum est non potest tractu temporis convalescere."

"The general rule is that whenever any contract or conveyance is void, either by a positive law or upon principles of public policy, it is deemed incapable of confirmation upon the maxim, *quod ab initio*," &c. (*Story Eq. Jur.*, § 306; Vernon's case, 4 *Co. Rep.*, 2 b). "No length of time," said Lord Talbot, "will bar a fraud" (*Cas. temp. Talbot*, 73). "It is certainly true," says Mr. Justice Story, "that length of time is no bar to a trust clearly established; and in a case where fraud is imputed and proved, length of time ought not, upon principles of eternal justice, to be admitted to repel relief. On the contrary, it would seem that the length of time, during which the fraud has been successfully concealed and practiced is an aggravation of the offense, and calls more loudly upon a court of equity to grant ample and decisive relief. But length of time necessarily obscures all human evidence; and as it thus removes from the parties all immediate means to verify the nature of the original transactions, it operates by way of presumption in favor of innocence and against imputation of fraud" (Prevost *v.* Gratz, 6 *Wheat.*, 498).

In certain cases, also, though the original agreement was void, the law presumes a new and valid contract from additional circumstances. Thus in the Roman Law, if a debtor pledged the property of another, and it afterward became his own, his creditor had his action (D. 13, 7, 41). And though if a husband sold his wife's dowry, the sale was invalid; yet if at her death the land became his, the sale was established (D. 41, 3, 42).

§ 1995. The incident follows the principal, not the principal the incident.

Battle *v.* Coit, 26 *N. Y.*, 404. "Accessorium non ducit sed sequitur suum principale." By a general grant of the reversion the rent will pass with it as an incident, though by the grant of the rent generally, the reversion will not pass (Van Wicklen *v.* Paulson, 14 *Barb.*, 654; Demarest *v.* Willard, 8 *Cow.*, 206; Marshall *v.* Moseley, 21 *N. Y.*, 282). So the grantee of land, or the assignee of a lease, assumes the burden of the covenants that run with the land or are reserved by the lease.

So, too, the assignment of a bond or other principal debt, carries with it a mortgage, or other collateral security, given to secure it (Jackson *v.* Blodget, 5 *Cow.*, 202; Langdon *v.* Buel, 9 *Wend.*, 80; Green *v.* Hart, 1 *Johns.*, 580; Rose *v.* Baker, 13 *Barb.*, 230; Parmelee *v.* Dann, 23 *id.*, 461; Jackson *v.* Willard, 4 *Johns.*, 41; Cooper *v.* Newland, 17 *Abb. Pr.*, 342).

§ 1996. An interpretation which gives effect is preferred to one which makes void.

"Ut res magis valeat quam pereat" (Langdon *v.* Astor, 16 *N. Y.*, 47; Nichols *v.* McEwen, 17 *id.*, 25; Laub *v.* Buckmiller, *id.*, 627). This is a general principle which governs the construction of all agreements, oral or written, and of all unilateral instruments, like deeds or wills, which are designed to embody the intention of a party (Fish *v.* Hubbard, 21 *Wend.*, 652; Mason *v.* White, 11 *Barb.*, 173; Aiken *v.* Albany N. & C. R. R. Co., 26 *id.*, 289; Warhus *v.* Bowery Savings Bk., 4 *Duer*, 59; Hall *v.* Newcomb, 3 *Hill*, 233; Jackson *v.* Rowland, 6 *Wend.*, 671; People *v.* Van Rensselaer, 9 *N. Y.*, 333; Schermerhorn *v.* Talman, 14 *id.*, 135; Nichols *v.* McEwen, 17 *id.*, 25; Richards *v.* Edick, 17 *Barb.*, 269; Warhus *v.* Savings Bank, 5 *Duer*, 71; Waterbury *v.* Sinclair, 16 *How. Pr.*, 342, 343; Sherman *v.* Elder, 24 *N. Y.*, 384; Spear *v.* Downing, 34 *Barb.*, 527). It may apply to a judgment (Woodgate *v.* Fleet, 9 *Abb. Pr.*, 239), or a record (Hatcher *v.* Rocheleau, 18 *N. Y.*, 92). Especially is it applied when the effect will be to prevent a forfeiture (Hurd *v.* Hunt, 14 *Barb.*, 575).

§ 1997. Interpretation must be reasonable.

Everything is to have a reasonable construction, and everything necessary to make a rule reasonable is implied (Jones *v.* Gibbons, 8 *Exch.*, 922; see Buck *v.* Burk, 18 *N. Y.*, 339, 341).

§ 1998. Where one of two innocent persons must suffer by the act of a third, he, by whose negligence it happened, must be the sufferer.

In Griswold *v.* Haven (25 *N. Y.*, 595), this maxim is asserted and enforced as a principle upon which, independently of the law of agency, an innocent party may be held responsible for the acts of another. The maxim is also cited and applied in Exchange Bank *v.* Monteath, 26 *N. Y.*, 505, 513; Sandford *v.* Handy, 23 *Wend.*, 268; Root *v.* French, 13 *id.*, 572.

PART V.

DEFINITIONS AND GENERAL PROVISIONS.

§ 1999. Words used in this Code are to be understood in their ordinary sense, except when a contrary intention plainly appears, and except also that the words hereinafter explained are to be understood as thus explained. Words, how used.

§ 2000. Whenever the meaning of a word or phrase is defined in any part of this Code, such definition is Sundry words.

applicable to the same word or phrase wherever it occurs, except where a contrary intention plainly appears.

Degrees of care and diligence. § 2001. There are three degrees of care and of diligence mentioned in this Code, namely, slight, ordinary and great. The latter include the former.

Care and diligence. § 2002. Slight care or diligence is such as persons of ordinary prudence usually exercise about their own affairs of slight importance; ordinary care or diligence is such as they usually exercise about their own affairs of ordinary importance; and great care or diligence is such as they usually exercise about their own affairs of great importance.

Degrees of negligence. § 2003. There are three degrees of negligence mentioned in this Code, namely, slight, ordinary and gross. The latter include the former.

Negligence. § 2004. Slight negligence consists in the want of great care and diligence; ordinary negligence, in the want of ordinary care and diligence; and gross negligence, in the want of slight care and diligence.

Children. § 2005. The term "children," as used in this Code, includes children by birth and by adoption.

Debtor and creditor. § 2006. Except in Part III of this Division, every one who owes to another the performance of an obligation is called a debtor, and the one to whom he owes it is called a creditor.

Good faith. § 2007. Good faith consists in an honest intention to abstain from taking any unconscientious advantage of another, even through the forms or technicalities of law, together with an absence of all information or belief of facts which would render the transaction unconscientious.

See Claflin *v.* Farmers' and Citizens' Bank, 25 *N. Y.*, 293, 298; Starin *v.* Genoa, 23 *id.*, 439; Sanger *v.* Eastwood, 19 *Wend.*, 514; Gregory *v.* Thomas, 20 *id.*, 17; Dunham *v.* Dey, 15 *Johns.*, 569.

§ 2008. Notice is either actual or constructive. Notice.

§ 2009. Actual notice consists in express information of a fact. Actual notice.

§ 2010. Constructive notice is notice imputed by the law to a person not having actual notice. Constructive notice.

§ 2011. Every person who has actual notice of circumstances sufficient to put a prudent man upon inquiry as to a particular fact, and who omits to make such inquiry with reasonable diligence, is deemed to have constructive notice of the fact itself. Certain persons deemed to have constructive notice.

If the party who receives information of circumstances suggesting an inquiry for the principal fact, makes that inquiry with due diligence, the result must be either that he will ascertain the fact, or that he will be prevented from doing so by causes for which he is not to blame, and from which he ought not to suffer. If he ascertains it, he then has actual notice, and the doctrine of constructive notice does not apply. If, notwithstanding due diligence, he fails to ascertain it, notice ought not be imputed to him. The commissioners, therefore, as respects circumstances putting a person upon inquiry, have limited the doctrine of constructive notice to cases in which there is a failure to make diligent inquiry (see Foster *v.* Beals, 21 *N. Y.*, 247; Williamson *v.* Brown, 15 *N. Y.*, 354; Fassett *v.* Smith, 23 *N. Y.*, 252). The decision in Kellogg *v.* Smith, 26 *N. Y.*, 18, is put upon the ground that there was a duty of inquiry, both for the bond, and the mortgage; but the inquiry made was only as to the mortgage.

§ 2012. A notice which is false when given, is not made valid by the subsequent happening of the event. Notice, when impossible.

Griffin *v.* Goff, 12 *Johns.*, 422; Jackson *v.* Richards, 2 *Cai.*, 343. Notice that a party will perform a specified act, is in strictness, notice of an existing intention to perform the act only.

Paper. § 2013. The word "paper," as used in this Code, means any flexible material upon which it is usual to write.

Person. § 2014. The word "person," as used in this Code, except when used by way of contrast, includes not only human beings, but bodies politic or corporate.

Several. § 2015. The word "several," as used in this Code in relation to number, means two or more.

Third persons. § 2016. The words "third persons," as used in this Code, include all who are not parties to the obligation or transaction concerning which the phrase is used.

Holidays. § 2017. Holidays, within the meaning of this Code, are, every Sunday, the first day of January, the twenty-second day of February, the fourth day of July, the twenty-fifth day of December, every day on which an election is held throughout the state, and every day appointed by the president of the United States, or by the governor of this state, for a public fast, thanksgiving, or holiday.

Laws of 1865, *ch.* 146.

Id. § 2018. If the first of January, the twenty-second of February, the fourth of July, or the twenty-fifth of December, falls upon a Sunday, the Monday following is a holiday.

Laws of 1865, *ch.* 146.

Business days. § 2019. All other days than those mentioned in the last two sections are to be deemed business days, for all purposes.

Certain acts not to be done on holidays. § 2020. Whenever any act of a secular nature, other than a work of necessity or mercy, is appointed by law or contract to be performed upon a particular day, which day falls upon a holiday, such act may be performed upon the next business day, with the same effect as if it had been performed upon the day appointed.

§ 2021. Usage, within the meaning of this Code, is a reasonable[1] and lawful[2] public custom concerning transactions of the same nature as those which are to be affected thereby,[3] existing at the place where the obligation is to be performed,[4] and either known to the parties,[5] or so well established,[6] general[7] and uniform,[8] that they must be presumed to have acted with reference thereto.[9] Usage, what.

[1] Bowen *v.* Stoddard, 10 *Metc.*, 30. See Cuthbert *v.* Cumming, 10 *Exch.*, 815; aff'd, 11 *id.*, 405.

[2] Merchants' Bank *v.* Woodruff, 6 *Hill*, 174; Bowen *v.* Newell, 8 *N. Y.*, 190.

[3] Cuthbert *v.* Cumming, 11 *Exch.*, 408; *Code La.*, 1961.

[4] Stewart *v.* Aberdein, 4 *M. & W.*, 211; see Sweeting *v.* Pearce, 7 *C. B.* [*N. S.*], 481; Horton *v.* Morgan, 19 *N. Y.*, 170.

[5] Cuthbert *v.* Cumming, 11 *Exch.*, 405, aff'g S. C., 10 *id.*, 809; Graves *v.* Legg, 2 *H. & N.*, 210, aff'g S. C., 11 *Exch.*, 642; 9 *id.*, 709.

[6] Smith *v.* Wright, 1 *Cai.*, 43; U. S. *v.* Buchanan, 8 *How.* [*U. S.*,] 102.

[7] Sweeting *v.* Pearce, *supra;* Gabay *v.* Lloyd, 3 *B. & C.*, 793; Scott *v.* Irving, 1 *B. & Ad.*, 605; Todd *v.* Reid, 4 *B. & Ald.*, 210; Lewis *v.* Marshall, 7 *M. & G.*, 745; Cope *v.* Dodd, 13 *Penn. St.*, 37.

[8] U. S. *v.* Buchanan, 8 *How.* [*U. S.*], 102; Cope *v.* Dodd, 13 *Penn. St.*, 33, 37; Wood *v.* Wood, 1 *Carr. & P.*, 59; Lewis *v.* Marshall, *supra.*

[9] Hinton *v.* Locke, 5 *Hill*, 439; U. S. *v.* Buchanan, 8 *How.* [*U. S.*], 102. See Wadsworth *v.* Alcott, 6 *N. Y.*, 72.

§ 2022. The words "usual," and "customary," as used in this Code, mean "according to usage." Id.

§ 2023. A valuable consideration, within the meaning of this Code, is a thing of value parted with, or a new obligation assumed, at the time of obtaining a thing, which is a substantial compensation for that which is obtained thereby. It is also called simply "value." Value.

§ 2024. The word "verdict," as used in this Code, includes not only the verdict of a jury, but also the Verdict.

finding upon the facts, of a judge, or of a referee appointed to determine the issues in a cause.

Time. § 2025. The word "year" as used in this Code, means a calendar year, and "month" a calendar month. Fractions of a year are to be computed by the number of months, thus, half a year is six months. Fractions of a day are to be disregarded in computations which include more than one day, and involve no questions of priority.

Genders. § 2026. Words used in this Code in the masculine gender include the feminine, except where a contrary intention plainly appears.

Numbers. § 2027. Words used in this Code in the singular number include the plural, and the plural the singular, except where a contrary intention plainly appears.

Commissioner of deeds. § 2028. Any act required to be done by or before a commissioner of deeds, may be done by or before any officer mentioned in sections 517, 518 and 519 of this Code, subject to the regulations contained in those sections.

Compound interest. § 2029. The words "compound interest," as used in this Code, mean interest computed with semi-annual rests.

Writing. § 2030. The words "writing" and "written," as used in this Code, include "printing" and "printed," except in the case of signatures, and where the words are used by way of contrast to printing. Writing may be made in any manner, except that when a person entitled to require the execution of a writing demands that it be made with ink, it must be so made.

Forms. § 2031. The forms contained in the schedule annexed to this Code are to be deemed sufficient for the purposes designated in the caption of each respectively, and whenever any person is entitled to receive an instrument now commonly known by any such designation, he is entitled to receive it in the form given in the schedule, and cannot require it to be given in any other form, unless it has been otherwise expressly agreed.

§ 2032. The rule that statutes in derogation of the common law are to be strictly construed has no application to this Code. Construction of the Code.

§ 2033. All statutes, laws and rules heretofore in force in this state, inconsistent with the provisions of this Code, are hereby repealed or abrogated; but such repeal or abrogation does not revive any former law heretofore repealed, nor does it affect any right already existing or accrued, or any proceeding already taken, except as in this Code provided. Repeal of former statutes.

§ 2034. This Code shall take effect on the day of , 186 . Time when Code takes effect.

SCHEDULE OF FORMS.

No. 1.

GRANT OF REAL PROPERTY, WITHOUT COVENANTS.

This Grant, made the .... day of ...., in the year ......, between A. B., of ...., of the first part, and C. D., of ...., of the second part, witnesseth:

That the party of the first part hereby grants to the party of the second part, in consideration of .... dollars, now received, all the real property situated in ...., and bounded ....

WITNESS the hand and seal of the party of the first part.

A. B. [*Seal.*]

Sealed and delivered in the presence of
E. F.

No. 2.

GRANT OF REAL PROPERTY, WITH COVENANTS.

This Grant, made the .... day of ...., in the year......, between A. B., of ...., of the first part, and C. D., of ...., of the second part, witnesseth:

I. That the party of the first part hereby grants to the party of the second part, in consideration of .... dollars, now received, all the real property situated in ...., and bounded ....

II. That the party of the first part covenants with the party of the second part, that the former is now seized in fee simple of the property granted; that the latter shall enjoy the same without any lawful disturbance; that the same is free from all incumbrances; that the party of the first part, and all persons acquiring any interest in the same through or for him, will, on demand, execute and deliver to the party of the second part, at the expense of the latter, any further assurance of the same that may be reasonably required; and that the party of the first part will warrant to the party of the second part all the said property against every person lawfully claiming the same.

WITNESS the hand and seal of the party of the first part.

A. B. [*Seal.*]

Sealed and delivered in the presence of }
E. F.

No. 3.
LEASE.

This Lease, made the .... day of ...., in the year......, between A. B., of ...., of the first part, and C. D., of ...., of the second part, witnesseth:

That the party of the first part lets, and the party of the second part hires, the [*describing the property let*], for the term of ...., at the [annual] rent of .... dollars, to be paid by the party of the second part to the party of the first part [in equal quarterly payments].

[*Signatures.*]

No. 4.
MORTGAGE OF REAL PROPERTY.

This Mortgage, made the .... day of ...., in the year ......, between A. B., of ...., of the first part, and C. D., of ...., of the second part, witnesseth:

[I.] That in consideration of .... dollars, now received, the party of the first part hereby mortgages to the party of the second part [*here describe the property*], as security for the payment to him of .... dollars, on [or before] the .... day of ...., 18.., with interest thereon [*or*, as security for the payment of a bond, *describing it, &c.*]

[*If a power of sale is to be given, add,*] II. That in case of the non-payment of the principal sum, or of any part of the interest thereon, when due, the party of the second part may enter upon and sell the property above described, in the manner prescribed by the Civil Code and the Code of Civil Procedure of this State, and apply the proceeds of such sale to the satisfaction of the amount due under this mortgage, and of the expenses of the sale; the residue to be forthwith paid to the party of the first part.

[*If the interest clause is to be inserted, add,*] III. That, if the interest upon the principal sum mentioned herein is not fully paid as it falls due, the entire principal shall become immediately due and payable, at the option of the party of the second part.

[*If the insurance clause is to be inserted, add,*] IV. That the party of the first part shall, at his own expense, keep the [buildings] on the said property insured against fire in a reputable insurance office, for the benefit of the party of the second part, to the extent of .... dollars, until this mortgage is paid or otherwise extinguished.

WITNESS the hand and seal of the party of the first part.

A. B. [*Seal.*]

Sealed and delivered in the presence of }
E. F.

No. 5.

MORTGAGE OF PERSONAL PROPERTY.

This Mortgage, made the .... day of........, in the year......, between A. B., of ...., of the first part, and C. D., of ...., of the second part, witnesseth:

[I.] That in consideration of .... dollars, now received, the party of the first part hereby mortgages to the party of the second part [*here describe the property*], as security for the payment to him of .... dollars, on [or before] the .... day of ...., 18.. with interest thereon [*or, as security for the payment of a bond, describing it, &c.*]

[*If a power of sale is to be given, add,*] II. That in case of the non-payment of the principal sum, or of any part of the interest thereon, when due, the party of the second part may enter upon any place where the said property is situated, and sell the property above described, in the manner prescribed by the Civil Code and the Code of Civil Procedure of this State, and apply the proceeds of such sale to the satisfaction of the amount due under this mortgage, and of the expenses of the sale; the residue to be forthwith paid to the party of the first part.

[*If the interest clause is to be inserted, add,*] III. That, if the interest upon the principal sum mentioned herein is not fully paid as it falls due, the entire principal shall become immediately payable, at the option of the party of the second part.

[*If the insurance clause is to be inserted, add,*] IV. That the party of the first part shall, at his own expense, keep the said property insured against [fire] in a reputable insurance office, for the benefit of the party of the second part, to the extent of .... dollars, until this mortgage is paid or otherwise extinguished.

[*In case the principal obligation is for a term longer than one year, add,*] V. That the party of the first part hereby agrees to execute, upon demand, at any time after eleven months from the date hereof, a new mortgage to the same effect, to secure so much of the obligation for which this mortgage is a security as will remain unsatisfied at the end of one year from this date.

WITNESS the hand and seal of the party of the first part.

A. B. [*Seal.*]

Sealed and delivered in the presence of

E. F.

No. 6.

BOND.

This Bond, made the .... day of ...., in the year ...., between A. B., of ...., of the first part, and C. D., of ...., of the second part, witnesseth:

That the party of the first part, being indebted unto the party of the second part in the sum of .... dollars, hereby binds himself to pay the same to the said party of the second part, or to his order [*or*, to the bearer], [in .... years from the date hereof, with interest at the rate of ..... per cent. a year, payable half-yearly on the .... day of .... and ....]

WITNESS the hand and seal of the party of the first part.

A. B. [*Seal.*]

Sealed and delivered in the presence of

E. F.

No. 7.

BILL OF LADING.

Received, in good order [on board the ship ...., *or*, on the .... railway], from A. B. [*name of consignor*], [one thousand barrels of flour, *or otherwise describing the goods*], to be delivered at ...., to the order of C. D. [*or*, to the bearer], on payment of .... freightage, [and .... primage.]

[*Date.*] [*Signature.*]

No. 8.

CHARTER-PARTY.

This Charter-party, made the .... day of ...., in the year ......, between A. B., of ...., of the first part, and C. D., of ...., of the second part, witnesseth:

I. That the party of the first part lets to the party of the second part, the [ship] ...., now lying at ...., of which E. F. is master, for a voyage to be made from .... to .... [*or*, for the term of .... from the date hereof.]

II. That the party of the first part warrants that the said [ship] shall be [kept] seaworthy, and in every respect fit for the voyage [and shall be provided with a sufficient crew and provisions].

III. That the party of the second part may put on board the said [ship] any goods whatever, except such as are contraband of war.

IV. [*If the vessel is chartered for a voyage only*] That the party of the second part shall be allowed ..... days for loading at the port of ...., and ..... days for discharging [and reloading] at the port of .... [and ..... days for final discharge at the port of ....], exclusive, in each case, of Sundays and legal holidays; and commencing, in each case, from the time that notice is given to the party of the second part, or his proper agent, of the readiness of the vessel to receive or discharge cargo; and that for every day of additional detention of the vessel for these purposes, the party of the second part shall pay to the party of the first part .... dollars.

V. That the party of the second part shall pay to the party of the first part, at ...., within ...... days after the arrival of the said [ship] at that port, ... dollars, in full for the hire of the same [and shall also pay, as they fall due, the expenses of victualing and manning the same, and all port charges and pilotage that may be due thereon].

WITNESS the hands and seals of the parties.

A. B. [*Seal.*]
C. D. [*Seal.*]

Sealed and delivered in the presence of
G. H.

No. 9.
BOTTOMRY BOND.

This Bottomry Bond, made the .... day of ...., in the year ...., between A. B., of ...., the [master] of the [ship] ...., now lying at ...., of the first part, and C. D., of ...., of the second part, witnesseth:

I. That whereas [*stating the circumstances which render the hypothecation proper*], and whereas, the party of the second part has lent to the party of the first part, for the use of the said vessel, the sum of..... dollars; now therefore, the party of the first part binds himself, the said vessel and her freightage, for the repayment to the party of the second part of the said sum, with .... dollars in addition, as maritime interest, within .... days after the arrival of the said vessel uninjured at .... [*or*, on the .... day of ...., 18.., if the said vessel is not previously lost by perils other than its unseaworthiness at setting out, or the barratry of its master].

II. That, in case of the loss or injury of the said vessel [from any of the above mentioned perils], the party of the first part shall pay to the party of the second part so much only of the said sum and interest as may be equivalent to the net value, to the owner, of any portion or proceeds of the said vessel, saved to him.

WITNESS the hand and seal of the party of the first part.

A. B. [*Seal.*]

Sealed and delivered in the presence of
E. F.

No. 10.

RESPONDENTIA BOND.

This Respondentia Bond, made the .... day of ...., in the year ...., between A. B., of ...., the [master] of the [ship] ...., now lying at ...., of the first part, and C. D., of ...., of the second part, witnesseth:

I. That whereas [*stating the circumstances which render the hypothecation proper*], and whereas the party of the second part has lent to the party of the first part, for the use of the said vessel, the sum of..... dollars; now therefore, the party of the first part binds himself, and all the cargo laden and to be laden on board the said vessel, for the repayment to the party of the second part of the said sum, with .... dollars in addition, as maritime interest, within ...... days after the arrival of the said cargo uninjured at .... [*or*, on the .... day of ...., 18.., if the said cargo is not previously lost by perils other than the barratry of the master].

II. That, in case of the loss or injury of the said cargo [from any of the above mentioned perils], the party of the first part shall pay to the party of the second part so much only of the said sum and interest as may be equivalent to the net value, to the owner, of any portion or proceeds of the said cargo, saved to him.

WITNESS the hand and seal of the party of the first part.

A. B. [*Seal.*]

Sealed and delivered in the presence of
E. F.

No. 11.

POLICY OF MARINE INSURANCE ON VESSEL.

This Policy of Marine Insurance, made the .... day of......., in the year ...., between A. B. [*name of insurer*], of........., and C. D. [*name of insured*], of ...., witnesseth:

That in consideration of a premium of......... dollars, being at the rate of.... per cent. upon the amount of insurance, now received from the said C. D., the said A. B. INSURES him to the extent of .... dollars, upon his interest [as mortgagee, *or otherwise, if he is not the absolute owner*] in the [one-fourth part of the ship ....], which interest is hereby valued at .... dollars.

This insurance is made upon the following terms:

I. The period during which this insurance is to continue is from the .... day of ...., 18.., at noon, until the .... day of ...., 18.., at noon [*or*, at and from the port of .... to the port of ...., until the said vessel has been safely moored at the last named port for twenty-four hours].

II. The risks insured against are all perils and losses of every kind, which may happen to the said vessel during the period above specified, except those which are caused by the unseaworthiness of the vessel.

III. In case of any disaster happening to the subject of insurance, the insured must labor for its recovery, and the insurer will contribute to the expense thereof according to the amount insured.

IV. Partial losses, amounting in the aggregate, on a single voyage, to less than [five] per cent. of the value of the subject of insurance, after making the usual deductions, are excepted from this insurance.

V. No act of the insurer or of the insured, in saving or recovering from disaster the property insured, is to be deemed an acceptance or waiver of abandonment.

VI. In adjusting a partial loss, the old materials are to be applied toward payment for the new, and, except in the case of anchors, cannon, and metal sheathing, one-third is to be deducted from the remaining cost of repairs; in the case of metal sheathing, deduction is to be made from the cost of its repair, at the rate of two and a half per cent. for each month during which the old sheathing was on the vessel; in considering a claim for a constructive total loss, similar deductions are to be made from the estimated expense of repairs, and if, after making such deductions, the expense would not exceed one-half the value of the vessel, the loss is to be deemed partial only.

VII. The amount of any note given for premium under this policy, if unpaid, is to be deducted from any payment of loss.

VIII. The amount of a loss insured against is payable to ...., for the benefit of [whom it may concern], within .... days after proof of loss and interest is given to the insurer.

IX. If the insured has effected any prior insurance upon the same subject, the insurer herein is liable only for so much of a loss as is not covered by such prior insurance, and must return the premium upon the rest; but if the insured effects a subsequent insurance, the insurer herein is nevertheless liable to the full amount herein specified, and has no right to contribution from such subsequent insurer.

X. In case the insured is entitled to a return of premium, in whole or in part, the insurer is entitled to retain [one-half of one per cent.] in all events.

[*Signature.*]

No. 12.

POLICY OF MARINE INSURANCE ON CARGO.

This Policy of Marine Insurance, made the .... day of ...., in the year ......, between A. B. [*name of insurer*], of ...., and C. D. [*name of insured*], of ...., witnesseth: That in consideration of a premium of..... ..... dollars, being at the rate of .... per cent. upon the amount of insurance, now received from the said C. D., the said A. B. INSURES him to the extent of .... dollars, upon his interest [as mortgagee, *or otherwise, if he is not the absolute owner*] in [*describing the property*], on board the [ship] ...., of ...., which interest is hereby valued at .... dollars.

This insurance is made upon the following terms:

I. The period during which this insurance is to continue is from the .... day of.........., 18.., at noon, until the .... day of........., 18.., at noon [*or*, from the commencement of loading the cargo insured, at the port of............., until it is safely landed at the port of...........].

II. The risks insured against are all perils and losses of every kind which may happen to the cargo insured, during the period above specified, except those which arise from the inherent nature thereof, without external injury.

III. In case of any disaster happening to the subject of insurance, the insured must labor for its recovery, and the insurer will contribute to the expense thereof according to the amount insured.

IV. Partial losses are excepted from this insurance in the following cases:

1. [*Here specify articles particularly, with the rate of particular average allowed.*]

2. Losses by dampness, change of flavor, mustiness, or mold, unless caused by actual contact of sea water with the articles damaged.

3. Leakage of any liquid, unless caused by stranding or collision with another vessel.

V. No act of the insurer or of the insured, in saving or recovering from disaster the property insured, is to be deemed an acceptance or waiver of abandonment.

VI. The amount of any note given for premium under this policy, if unpaid, is to be deducted from any payment of loss.

VII. The amount of a loss insured against is payable to ...., for the benefit of ...., within ..... days after proof of loss and interest is given to the insurer.

VIII. If the insured has effected any prior insurance upon the same subject, the insurer herein is liable only for so much of a loss as is not covered by such prior insurance, and must return the premium upon the rest; but if the insured effects a subsequent insurance, the insurer herein is nevertheless liable to the full amount herein specified, and has no right to contribution from such subsequent insurer.

IX. In case the insured is entitled to a return of premium, in whole or in part, the insurer herein is entitled to retain [one-half of one per cent.] in all events.

[*Signature.*]

No. 13.

POLICY OF MARINE INSURANCE ON FREIGHTAGE.

This Policy of Marine Insurance, made the .... day of ...., in the year ...., between A. B. [*name of insurer*], of ...., and C. D. [*name of insured*], of ...., witnesseth: That in consideration of a premium of .... dollars, being at the rate of .... per cent. upon the amount of insurance, now received from the said C. D., the said A. B. INSURES him to the extent of .... dollars, upon his interest [*describing it if not absolute*] in the freightage upon all cargo laden or to be laden on board the .... of ...., which interest is hereby valued at .... dollars.

This insurance is made upon the following terms:

I. The period during which this insurance is to continue is from the .... day of ...., 18.., at noon, until the .... day of ...., 18.., at noon [*or*, from the commencement of loading cargo on the said vessel, at the port of ...., until it is safely landed at the port of ....].

II. The risks insured against are all perils and losses of every kind, which may happen during the period above specified, to prevent the said ship from earning the freightage insured; except losses arising from the neglect of the master to save freightage by procuring other vessels to convey the cargo to its destination, when necessary and practicable, or from his neglect to preserve damaged cargo.

III. In case of any disaster happening to the subject of insurance, the insured must labor for its recovery, and the insurer will contribute to the expense thereof according to the amount insured.

IV. Partial losses, amounting in the aggregate, on a single voyage, to less than [five] per cent. of the value of the subject of insurance, after making the usual deductions, are excepted from this insurance.

V. No act of the insurer or of the insured, in saving or recovering from disaster the property insured, is to be deemed an acceptance or waiver of abandonment.

VI. The amount of any note given for premium under this policy, if unpaid, is to be deducted from any payment of loss.

VII. The amount of a loss insured against is payable to .... for the benefit of ...., within ..... days after proof of loss and interest is given to the insurer.

VIII. If the insured has effected any prior insurance upon the same subject, the insurer herein is liable only for so much of a loss as is not covered by such prior insurance, and must return the premium upon the rest; but if the insured effects a subsequent insurance, the insurer herein is nevertheless liable to the full amount herein specified, and has no right to contribution from such subsequent insurer.

IX. In case the insured is entitled to a return of premium, in whole or in part, the insurer is entitled to retain [one-half of one per cent.] in all events.

[*Signature.*]

No. 14.

POLICY OF FIRE INSURANCE.

This Policy of Fire Insurance, made the .... day of ...., in the year ......, between A. B. [*name of insurer*], of ...., and C. D. [*name of insured*], of ...., witnesseth:

That in consideration of a premium of .... dollars, being at the rate of .... per cent. upon the amount of insurance, now received from the said C. D., the said A. B. INSURES him to the extent of .... dollars, upon his interest [as mortgagee, *or otherwise, if he is not the absolute owner*], in [*describing the property*].

This insurance is made upon the following terms:

I. The period during which this insurance is to continue is from the .... day of ...., 18.., at noon, until the .... day of ...., 18.., at noon.

II. The risks insured against are loss or damage by fire.

III. A loss caused by invasion, insurrection, riot, civil commotion, or any military or usurped power, is excepted.

IV. This policy does not cover books of account, written obligations, securities, or evidences of title or of debt, money or bullion, casts, jewelry, medals, musical or scientific instruments (other than a piano-forte in a dwelling house), patterns, pictures, plate, precious stones, printed music, sculptures, statuary, or watches, except so far as the same are specially mentioned herein.

V. If any explosive substance is kept upon the premises herein mentioned, in quantities greater than or in a manner different from that allowed by law, this policy is suspended until the law is obeyed.

VI. This policy is suspended during the use of the premises herein mentioned for any of the following purposes, without the written consent of the insurer [*specifying the purposes*].

VII. In case the property insured is in peril of damage by fire, the insured must use his best efforts to protect it therefrom, the expense of which shall be paid by the insurer to the extent of this insurance.

VIII. The property insured cannot be abandoned to the insurer.

IX. Written notice of loss must be given to the insurer within a reasonable time thereafter, and the insured must deliver to the insurer a statement in writing, verified by his oath or affirmation, showing to the best of his knowledge and belief:

1. The ownership of the thing insured;
2. Its cash value at the time of loss;
3. By whom, and for what purposes, the premises on which the loss occurred were occupied;
4. When and how the fire originated;
5. All other insurances upon the same property, giving a copy of the written portions of each policy.

X. The insurer has a right to enter upon the premises where a loss occurs, and to examine all property insured, after a loss, and all books and papers relating to such property.

XI. The insurer may, at his option, pay for a loss according to the cash value at the time of loss, or replace the thing lost or injured with another thing of the same kind and quality, or repair the injury, if it can be fully repaired; but notice of his election to do so must be given within thirty days after notice of loss, or the right thereof is lost.

XII. In case of any other insurance upon the property hereby insured, the insurer herein is liable only for such proportion of the whole loss, as the amount hereby insured bears to the gross amount of insurance effected; and a floating policy, sufficient in terms to cover the property hereby insured, is to be deemed to cover any excess of the value of such property over the amount specifically insured thereon.

[XIII. This policy shall be void if any other insurance now exists, or is hereafter effected upon the same property, without the written consent of the insurer herein].

XIII. [*or* XIV.] The amount of a loss insured against is payable to the insured in thirty days after proof of loss and interest is given to the insurer.

XIV. [*or* XV.] This insurance may be terminated at any time by the insured, on notice to the insurer; in which case the insurer must refund all premium paid in excess of the customary short rates for the time the policy has been in force. It may also be terminated by the insurer, upon giving notice to the insured, and refunding to him a ratable proportion of the premium paid, according to the time that the policy has been in force.

[*Signature.*]

No. 15.

POLICY OF LIFE INSURANCE.

This Policy of Life Insurance, made the .... day of ...., in the year ......, between A. B. [*name of insurer*], of ...., and C. D. [*name of insured*], of ...., witnesseth:

That in consideration of a premium of .... dollars, being at the rate of ...... per cent. upon the amount of insurance, now received from the said C. D. [and of the annual premium of .... dollars, to be paid on or before the .... day of ...., in every year during the period insured], the said A. B. INSURES him to the extent of .... dollars, upon the life of [*name of person whose life is insured*].

This insurance is made upon the following terms:

I. The period during which this insurance is to continue is the life of .... [*or*, from .... to ....].

II. The amount to be paid in case of the death of the said .... is .... dollars [with participation in profits], which is to be paid to ...., [his executors, administrators or assigns, *or, if the policy is issued to the wife of the person whose life is insured*, for her sole use, or, in case of her death, to her children, or their guardian, for their use, or, if she leaves no child, then to her executors or administrators], at ...., in sixty days after notice and proof of the death of ...., deducting therefrom so much of the premium for the then current year as may be unpaid.

III. If, without the written consent of the insurer, the person whose life is insured passes beyond the boundaries of the United States of America, otherwise than into Canada, Nova Scotia, or New Brunswick; or passes west of the 100th degree of west longitude, or north of the 50th degree of north latitude; or between the 1st of July and the 1st of November passes south of 36 degrees, 30 minutes of north latitude; or enters upon a voyage on the high seas; or becomes personally engaged in blasting, mining, submarine operations, or in the production of highly inflammable or explosive substances, or in working a steam-engine in any capacity, or in service or labor upon any railroad or in any kind of navigation, or in any military or naval service (other than that of the militia when not actually employed in military operations), the insurer shall not be liable to any payment under this policy, in case of his death while so situated or engaged, or in case of his death from any disease contracted or injury suffered while so situated or engaged, and the insurer may in any such case terminate this policy.

IV. If the person whose life is insured commits suicide, or dies from an injury suffered in a duel in which he is in any way engaged, or suffered in consequence of the violation of a penal law, or if the representations made upon the application for this policy are in any material respect untrue, this policy shall be void.

V. Upon the expiration of this policy, or in case it is now or hereafter becomes void, all payments made thereon shall belong to the insurer.

VI. If this policy is transferred or hypothecated, proof of the right of the holder to receive the amount of insurance must be given to the insurer sixty days before payment can be required.

[*Signature.*]

INDEX.

DEFINITIONS—*Continued.*

www.ingramcontent.com/pod-product-compliance
Ingram Content Group UK Ltd.
Pitfield, Milton Keynes, MK11 3LW, UK
UKHW041133071026
15587UKWH00009B/450

9 781886 363380